Kwong Sak Leung   Lai-Wan Chan
Helen Meng (Eds.)

Intelligent Data Engineering and Automated Learning – IDEAL 2000

Data Mining, Financial Engineering, and
Intelligent Agents

Second International Conference
Shatin, N.T., Hong Kong, China, December 13-15, 2000
Proceedings

Springer

Series Editors

Gerhard Goos, Karlsruhe University, Germany
Juris Hartmanis, Cornell University, NY, USA
Jan van Leeuwen, Utrecht University, The Netherlands

Volume Editors

Kwong Sak Leung
Lai-Wan Chan
The Chinese University of Hong Kong
Department of Computer Science and Engineering
Shatin, Hong Kong
E-mail: {ksleung/lwchan}@cse.cuhk.edu.hk

Helen Meng
The Chinese University of Hong Kong
Department of Systems Engineering and Engineering Management
Shatin, Hong Kong
E-mail: hmmeng@cse.cuhk.edu.hk

Cataloging-in-Publication Data applied for

Die Deutsche Bibliothek - CIP-Einheitsaufnahme

Intelligent data engineering and automated learning : data mining,
financial engineering, and intelligent agents ; second international
conference, Shatin, N.T., Hong Kong, December 13 - 15, 2000 ; IDEAL
2000 / Kwong Sak Leung ... (ed.). - Berlin ; Heidelberg ; New York ;
Barcelona ; Hong Kong ; London ; Milan ; Paris ; Singapore ; Tokyo :
Springer, 2000
  (Lecture notes in computer science ; Vol. 1983)
  ISBN 3-540-41450-9

CR Subject Classification (1998): H.3, I.2, H.4, H.5, I.4, J.1

ISSN 0302-9743
ISBN 3-540-41450-9 Springer-Verlag Berlin Heidelberg New York

Springer-Verlag Berlin Heidelberg New York
a member of BertelsmannSpringer Science+Business Media GmbH
© Springer-Verlag Berlin Heidelberg 2000
Printed in Germany

Typesetting: Camera-ready by author
Printed on acid-free paper   SPIN: 10781404   06/3142   5 4 3 2 1 0

Lecture Notes in Computer Science

Edited by G. Goos, J. Hartmanis and J. van

Springer

Berlin
Heidelberg
New York
Barcelona
Hong Kong
London
Milan
Paris
Singapore
Tokyo

Foreword

The goal of establishing an international conference on Intelligent Data Engineering and Automated Learning (IDEAL) is to provide a forum for researchers and engineers from academia and industry to meet and to exchange ideas on the latest developments in an emerging field, that brings theories and techniques from database, data mining and knowledge discovery, statistical and computational learning together for intelligent data processing. The efforts towards this goal have been supported greatly from colleagues both in the Asia Pacific region and all over the world, and further encouraged by the success of IDEAL98. A significant development was achieved in IDEAL 2000 this year, which is evidenced not only by an expansion of the major tracks from two to three, namely, Financial Engineering, Data Mining, and Intelligent Agents, but also by a considerable increase in the number of submissions and a high quality technical program. This achievement comes from the efforts of the program and organizing committee, with a large number of supporters all over the world. It was their hard work, often over sleepless nights, that brought about the successful conference. We would like to take this opportunity to thank them all. Their names and affiliations are shown in the symposium program.

We especially want to express our appreciation to the staff of The Chinese University of Hong Kong for their boundless contributions to this conference, particularly to Prof. Lai-wan Chan and Prof. Kwong Sak Leung as the Program Co-chairs and Prof. Jimmy Lee as the Organizing Chair. We thank the members of the International Program Committee, without whom we could not guarantee the high quality of the papers. Members of the Organizing Committee are instrumental behind the scene. Prof. Irwin King and Prof. Evangeline Young did a superb job in local arrangement, Prof. Wai Lam took care of the registration process, and, last but not least, Prof. Helen Meng ensured the smooth publication of the conference proceedings.

Moreover, we would like to thank Prof. Michael Dempster, Prof. Nick Jennings, Prof. Wei Li, and Heikki Mannila for their support as keynote speakers, bringing us the latest developments and future trends in the emerging fields, and also Prof. Zhenya He and Prof. Weixin Xie for organizing a special panel session, providing an insight into recent advances in the field in China,

Lastly, we hope you enjoyed your stay in Hong Kong and at The Chinese University.

October 2000   Pak-Chung Ching and Lei Xu
                                           General Co-chairs
                                           The Chinese University of Hong Kong

Preface

Data Mining, Financial Engineering, and Intelligent Agents are emerging fields in modern Intelligent Data Engineering. In IDEAL 2000, these fields were selected as the major tracks. IDEAL 2000 was the Second International Conference on Intelligent Data Engineering and Automated Learning, a series of biennial conferences. This year, we received over one hundred regular submissions and each paper was vigorously reviewed by experts in the field. We truly appreciate the work done by the reviewers. Some reviewers wrote lengthy and constructive comments to the authors for improving their papers. The overall program covered various topics in data mining, financial engineering, and agents. We also had a number of papers applying the above techniques to internet and multimedia processing.

We would like to thank our keynote speakers and the organizers of the special sessions and panel session. For Keynote talks,

- Professor M.A.H. Dempster, University of Cambridge, UK, gave a keynote talk on "Wavelet-Based Valuation of Derivative",

- Professor Nick Jennings, University of Southampton, UK, gave a keynote talk on "Automated Haggling: Building Artificial Negotiators",

- Professor Wei Li, Beijing University of Aeronautics and Astronautics, China, gave a keynote talk on "A Computational Framework for Convergent Agents", and

- Professor Heikki Mannila, Helsinki University of Technology, Finland, gave a keynote talk on "Data Mining: Past and Future".

Apart from the regular submissions, we also had two special sessions and a panel session at the conference.

- Professor Shu-Heng Chen of the National Chengchi University and Professor K.Y. Szeto of Hong Kong University of Science and Technology organized the special session on "Genetic Algorithms and Genetic Programming in Agent-Based Computational Finance".

- Dr. Yiu-Ming Cheung of The Chinese University of Hong Kong organized the special session on "Data Analysis and Financial Modeling".

- Professor Zhenya He of the Southeast University and Professor Weixin Xie of the Shenzhou University organized a panel session on "Intelligent Data Engineering Automated Learning : Recent Advances in China".

We would like to express our gratitude to our general chairs, Professors Pak-Chung Ching and Lei Xu for their leadership and support. We appreciate and thank the Organizing and Program Committee members, for their devotion in the organization of the conference, and the reviewing of the papers; in particular, Professor Jimmy Lee, the Organizing Chair of IDEAL 2000, for his great effort in the organization of the conference throughout, and Professors Irwin King, Helen

Meng, Wai Lam, and Evan F. Y. Young for their time, effort, and constructive suggestions. We would also like to thank the supporting staff of the Department of Computer Science and Engineering of the Chinese University of Hong Kong for various help. Last but not the least, we thank Chung Chi College for the sponsorship of the conference.

October 2000
Kwong-Sak Leung and Lai-Wan Chan
Program Co-chairs
The Chinese University of Hong Kong

ORGANIZATION

International Advisory Committee

Yaser Abu-Mostafa
Shun-ichi Amari
Usama M. Fayyad

Nick Jennings
Erkki Oja

General Co-chairs

Pak-Chung Ching

Lei Xu

Organizing Committee

Jimmy H.M. Lee (Chair)
Laiwan Chan
Irwin King
Wai Lam

Kwong Sak Leung
Helen M.L. Meng
Evangeline F.Y. Young

Program Committee

Laiwan Chan (Co-chair)
Kwong Sak Leung (Co-chair)
Amir Atiya
Neil Burgess
Shu-Heng Chen
Sungzoon Cho
Keith Clark
Colin Fyfe
Joydeep Ghosh
Sami Kaski
Irwin King
Wai Lam

Jimmy H.M. Lee
Jiming Liu
Helen M.L. Meng
Ralph Neuneier
Mahesan Niranjan
Takashi Okada
Liz Sonenberg
Ron Sun
Roland Yap
Yiming Ye
Evangeline F.Y. Young
Soe-Tsyr Yuan

List of Reviewers

Esa Alhoniemi
Amir Atiya
Shu-Heng Chen
Sungzoon Cho
Samuel P. M. Choi
Keith Clark
Colin Fyfe
Xiaoying Gao
Joydeep Ghosh
Minghua He
Theodore Hong

Sami Kaski
Irwin King
Markus Koskela
Krista Lagus
Wai Lam
Ho-fung Leung
Bing Liu
Jiming Liu
Hongen Lu
Helen M.L. Meng
Ralph Neuneier

Takashi Okada
Liz Sonenberg
Leon Sterling
Vincent Tam
K.C. Tsui
G. Uchyigit
Juha Vesanto
Roland Yap
Yiming Ye
Evangeline F.Y. Young
Y. Zhang

TABLE OF CONTENTS

A Data Mining and Automated Learning

Clustering

Classification

Association Rules and Fuzzy Rules

Learning Systems

Factor and Correlation Analysis

Temporal Data Mining

B Financial Engineering

C Intelligent Agents

D Internet Applications

E Multimedia Processing

Video Processing

Image Processing

F Special Sessions

Genetic Algorithms and Genetic Programming in Agent-Based Computational Finance

organized by Professors Shu-Heng Chen (National Chengchi University) and K.Y. Szeto (HKUST)

Data Analysis and Financial Modeling
organized by Yiu-Ming Cheung (The Chinese University of Hong Kong)

A.

DATA MINING
AND
AUTOMATED LEARNING

Clustering by Similarity in an Auxiliary Space

Janne Sinkkonen and Samuel Kaski

Neural Networks Research Centre
Helsinki University of Technology
P.O.Box 5400, FIN-02015 HUT, Finland
janne.sinkkonen@hut.fi, samuel.kaski@hut.fi

Abstract. We present a clustering method for continuous data. It defines local clusters into the (primary) data space but derives its similarity measure from the posterior distributions of additional discrete data that occur as pairs with the primary data. As a case study, enterprises are clustered by deriving the similarity measure from bankruptcy sensitivity. In another case study, a content-based clustering for text documents is found by measuring differences between their metadata (keyword distributions). We show that minimizing our Kullback–Leibler divergence-based distortion measure within the categories is equivalent to maximizing the mutual information between the categories and the distributions in the auxiliary space. A simple on-line algorithm for minimizing the distortion is introduced for Gaussian basis functions and their analogs on a hypersphere.

1 Introduction

Clustering by definition produces localized groups of items, which implies that the results depend on the used similarity measure. We study the special case in which additional, stochastic information about a suitable similarity measure for the items $x_k \in \mathbb{R}^n$ exists in the form of discrete auxiliary data c_k. Thus, the data consists of primary-auxiliary pairs (x_k, c_k). In the resulting clusters the data items x are similar by the associated conditional distributions $p(c|x)$. Still, because of their parameterization, the clusters are localized in the primary space in order to retain its (potentially useful) structure. The auxiliary information is only used to learn what distinctions are important in the primary data space.

We have earlier explicitly constructed an estimate $\hat{p}(c|x)$ of the conditional distributions, and a local Riemannian metric based on that estimate [5]. Metrics have additionally been derived from generative models that do not use auxiliary information [3,4]. Both kinds of metrics could be used in standard clustering methods. In this paper we present a simpler method that directly minimizes the within-cluster dissimilarity, measured as distortion in the auxiliary space.

We additionally show that minimizing the within-cluster distortion maximizes the mutual information between the clusters and the auxiliary data. Maximization of mutual information has been used previously for constructing representations of the input data [1].

In another related work, the information bottleneck [7,9], data is also clustered by maximizing mutual information with a relevance variable. Contrary to our work, the bottleneck treats discrete or prepartitioned data only, whereas we create the categories by optimizing a parametrized partitioning of a continuous input space.

2   The Clustering Method

We cluster samples $x \in \mathbb{R}^n$ of a random variable X. The parameterization of the clusters keeps them local, and the similarity of the samples is measured as the similarity of the conditional distributions $p(c|x)$ of the random variable C.

Vector quantization (VQ) is one approach to categorization. In VQ the data space is divided into cells represented by prototypes or codebook vectors m_j, and the average distortion between the data and the prototypes,

$$E = \sum_j \int y_j(x)D(x, m_j)\, p(x)\, dx \, , \tag{1}$$

is minimized. Here $D(x, m_j)$ denotes a dissimilarity between x and m_j, and $y_j(x)$ is the cluster membership function for which $0 \le y_j(x) \le 1$ and $\sum_j y_j(x) = 1$. In the classic "hard" VQ the membership function is binary valued: $y_j(x) = 1$ if $D(x, m_j) \le D(x, m_i)$, $\forall i$, and $y_j(x) = 0$ otherwise. In the "soft" VQ, the $y_j(x)$ attain continuous values and they can be interpreted as conditional densities $p(v_j|x) \equiv y_j(x)$ of a discrete random variable V that indicates the cluster identity. Given x, C and V are conditionally independent: $p(c, v|x) = p(c|x)p(v|x)$. It follows that $p(c, v) = \int p(c|x)p(v|x)p(x)dx$.

Our measure of dissimilarity is the Kullback–Leibler divergence, defined for two multinomial distributions with event probabilities $\{p_i\}$ and $\{q_i\}$ as $D_{\mathrm{KL}}(p_i, q_i) \equiv \sum_i p_i \log(p_i/q_i)$. In our case, the first distribution corresponds to the data x: $p_i \equiv p(c_i|x)$. The second distribution will be the prototype. It can be shown that the optimal prototype, given that the values of the $y_j(x)$ are fixed, is $q_j \equiv p(c_i|v_j) = p(c_i, v_j)/p(v_j)$. By plugging this prototype and the Kullback–Leibler distortion measure into the error function of VQ, equation (1), we get

$$E_{\mathrm{KL}} = \sum_j \int y_j(x)D_{\mathrm{KL}}(p(c|x), p(c|v_j))p(x)dx \, . \tag{2}$$

Instead of computing the distortion between the vectorial samples and vectorial prototypes as in (1), we now have pointwise comparisons between the distributions $p(c|x)$ and the indirectly defined prototypes $p(c|v_j)$. The primary data space has been used to define the domain in the auxiliary space that is used for estimating each prototype.

If the membership functions are parametrized by θ the average distortion becomes

$$E_{\mathrm{KL}} = -\sum_{i,j} \log p(c_i|v_j) \int y_j(x; \theta)p(c_i, x)\, dx + \mathrm{const.}, \tag{3}$$

where the constant is independent of the parameters. Note that minimizing the average distortion E_{KL} is equivalent to maximizing the mutual information between C and V, because $E_{\mathrm{KL}} = -I(C;V) + \mathrm{const}$.

The choice of parameterization of the membership functions depends on the data space. For Euclidean spaces Gaussians have desirable properties. When the data comes from an n-dimensional hypersphere, spherical analogs of Gaussians, the von Mises–Fisher (vMF) basis functions [6] are more approriate. Below we derive the algorithm for vMF's; the derivation for Gaussians is analogous.

Von Mises–Fisher Basis Functions. A normalized n-dimensional vMF basis function is defined for normalized data by

$$y_j(\boldsymbol{x}) = \frac{M(\boldsymbol{x}; \boldsymbol{w}_j)}{\sum_k M(\boldsymbol{x}; \boldsymbol{w}_k)} \;,\quad \text{where}\;\; M(\boldsymbol{x}; \boldsymbol{w}_j) = \frac{\kappa^{\frac{1}{2}n-1}}{(2\pi)^{\frac{1}{2}n} I_{\frac{1}{2}n-1}(\kappa)} \exp \kappa \frac{\boldsymbol{x}^T \boldsymbol{w}_j}{\|\boldsymbol{w}_j\|} \;,$$
(4)

where $I_r(\kappa)$ denotes the modified Bessel function of the first kind and order r. The dispersion parameter κ is selected *a priori*. With the vMF basis functions the gradient of the average distortion (3) becomes

$$\nabla_{\boldsymbol{w}_j} E_{\mathrm{KL}} = \frac{1}{\sigma^2} \sum_i \sum_{l \neq j} \log \frac{p(c_i|v_j)}{p(c_i|v_l)} \int (\boldsymbol{x} - \boldsymbol{w}_j \boldsymbol{w}_j^T \boldsymbol{x}) y_j(\boldsymbol{x}) y_l(\boldsymbol{x}) p(c_i, \boldsymbol{x}) d\boldsymbol{x} \;,$$
(5)

where the $\boldsymbol{w}_j$ are assumed normalized (without loss of generality).

An on-line Algorithm can be derived using $y_j(\boldsymbol{x}) y_l(\boldsymbol{x}) p(c_i, \boldsymbol{x}) = p(v_j, v_l, c_i, \boldsymbol{x})$ as the sampling function for stochastic approximation. The following steps are repeated with $\alpha(t)$ gradually decreasing to zero:

1. At the step t of stochastic approximation, draw a data sample $(\boldsymbol{x}(t), c_i(t))$.
2. Draw independently two basis functions, j and l, according to the probabilities $\{y_k(\boldsymbol{x}(t))\}$.
3. Adapt the parameters $\boldsymbol{w}_j$ according to $\boldsymbol{w}_j(t+1) = \Delta\mathbf{w}_j / \|\Delta\mathbf{w}_j\|$, where

$$\Delta\boldsymbol{w}_j = \boldsymbol{w}_j(t) + \alpha(t) \log \frac{\hat{p}(c_i|v_j)}{\hat{p}(c_i|v_l)} \left(\boldsymbol{x}(t) - \boldsymbol{w}_j(t) \boldsymbol{w}_j(t)^T \boldsymbol{x}(t) \right) \;,$$
(6)

and $\alpha(t)$ is the gradually decreasing step size. The $\hat{p}$ are estimates of the conditional probabilities. The parameters $\boldsymbol{w}_l$ can be adapted at the same step, by exchanging j and l in (6).
4. Adapt the estimates $\hat{p}(c_i|v_j)$ with stochastic approximation, using the expression

$$\hat{p}(c_i|v_j)(t+1) = (1 - \lambda(t))\hat{p}(c_i|v_j)(t) + \lambda(t)$$
$$\hat{p}(c_k|v_j)(t+1) = (1 - \lambda(t))\hat{p}(c_k|v_j)(t) \;, k \neq i$$

where the rate of change $\lambda(t)$ should be larger than $\alpha(t)$. In practice, $2\alpha(t)$ seems to work.

3   Case Studies

We applied our model and two other models to two different data sets. The other models were the familiar mixture model $p(x) = \sum_j p(x|j)P(j)$, and the mixture discriminant model $p(c_i, x) = \sum_j P(c_i|j)p(x|j)P(j)$ (MDA2 [2]). The $P(j)$ are mixing parameters, and the $P(c_i|j)$ are additional parameters that model class distributions.

Clustering of text documents is useful as such, and the groupings can additionally be used to speed-up searches. We demonstrate that grouping based on textual content, with goodness measured by independent *topic* information, can be improved by our method utilizing (manually constructed) metadata (keywords). Thus, in this application our variable C corresponds to the keywords, and the variable X represents the textual content of the documents, encoded into a vector form.

Model performance was measured by the mutual information between the generated (soft) categories and nine *topic classes*, such as nuclear physics and optics, found independently by informaticians.

We carried out two sets of experiments with different preprocessing. The von Mises–Fisher kernels (4) were used both in our model and as the mixture components $p(x|j) = M(x; w_j)$. To encode the textual content, the words in the abstracts and titles were used, converted to base form. The rarest words were discarded. Documents with less than 5 words remaining after the preprocessing were discarded, resulting in about 50,000 data vectors.

The first experiment utilized no prior relevance information of the words: we picked 500 random words and encoded the documents with the "vector space model" [8] with "TF" (term frequency) weighting. In the second experiment more prior information was utilized. Words belonging to a stop-list were removed, and the "TF-IDF" (term frequency times inverse document frequency) weighting was used. In the first experiment with 'random' feature selection, our method performed clearly better than the other models. With the improved feature extraction the margin reduced somewhat (Fig. 1).

Clustering enterprises by bankruptcy sensitivity. We clustered financial statements of small and medium-sized Finnish enterprises by bankruptcy sensitivity, a key issue affecting credit decisions. The data set consisted of 6195 financial statements of which 158 concerned companies later gone bankrupt. Multiple yearly statements from the same enterprise were treated as independent samples.

We compared the MDA2 with our model. The basis functions $M(x; w_j)$ of both models were Gaussians parametrized by their location, with the covariance matrices *a priori* set to $\sigma^2 I$. Measured by the mutual information, our model clearly outperformed MDA2 (Fig. 2. Note that it is not feasible to estimate our model with the straightforward algorithm presented in this paper when σ is very small. The reason is that the gradient (5) becomes very small because of the products $y_j(x)y_l(x)$).

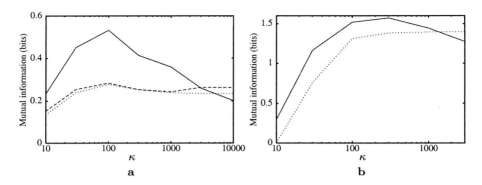

Fig. 1. Mutual information between the nine document clusters and the topics (*not* used in learning). **a** Random feature extraction, dimensionality: 500. **b** Informed feature extraction, dimensionality: 4748. Solid line: our model, dashed line: MDA2, dotted line: mixture model. (Due to slow convergence of MDA2, it was infeasible to compute it for part b. Another comparison with MDA2 is shown in Fig. 2)

4 Conclusions

We have demonstrated that clusters obtained by our method are more informative than clusters formed by a generative mixture model, MDA2 [2], for two kinds of data: textual documents and continuous-valued data derived from financial statements of enterprises. In (unpublished) tests for two additional data sets the results have been favorable to our model, although for one set the margin to MDA2 was narrow compared to the cases presented here.

For the first demonstration with textual documents, it would be interesting to compare the present method with the information bottleneck [7, 9] and metrics derived from generative models [3]. For the continuous data of the second experiment the bottleneck is not (directly) applicable. A generative model could be constructed, and we will compare our approach with such "unsupervised" generative models in subsequent papers.

When the feature extraction was improved using prior knowledge, the margin between our method and the "unsupervised" mixture model reduced. This suggests that our algorithm may be particularly useful when good feature extraction stages are not available but there exists auxiliary information that induces a suitable similarity measure.

Acknowledgments The authors would like to thank Finnvera Ltd., Pentti Bergius and Kimmo Kiviluoto for the bankruptcy data set, and Jaakko Peltonen for helping with the simulations. Academy of Finland provided financial support.

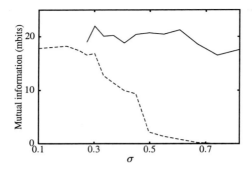

Fig. 2. Mutual information between the posterior probabilities of the ten enterprise clusters and the binary bankruptcy indicator. Solid line: our model, dashed line: MDA2. A set of 25 financial indicators was used as the primary data. The binary variable C indicated whether the statement was followed by a bankruptcy within 3 years

References

1. Becker, S.: Mutual information maximization: models of cortical self-organization. Network: Computation in Neural Systems **7** (1996) 7–31
2. Hastie, T., Tibshirani, R., Buja, A.: Flexible discriminant and mixture models. In: Kay, J., Titterington, D. (eds.): Neural Networks and Statistics. Oxford University Press (1995)
3. Hofmann, T.: Learning the similarity of documents: An information-geometric approach to document retrieval and categorization. In: Solla, S. A., Leen, T. K., Müller, K.-R. (eds.): Advances in Neural Information Processing Systems 12. MIT Press, Cambridge MA (2000) 914–920
4. Jaakkola, T. S., Haussler, D.: Exploiting generative models in discriminative classifiers. In: Kearns, M. S., Solla, S. A., Cohn, D. A. (eds.): Advances in Neural Information Processing Systems 11. Morgan Kauffmann Publishers, San Mateo CA (1999) 487–493
5. Kaski, S., Sinkkonen, J.: Metrics that learn relevance. In: Proc. IJCNN-2000, International Joint Conference on Neural Networks. IEEE (2000) V:547–552
6. Mardia, K. V.: Statistics of directional data. Journal of the Royal Statistical Society, series B **37** (1975) 349–393
7. Pereira, F., Tishby, N., Lee, L.: Distributional clustering of English words. In: Proceedings of the 30th Annual Meeting of the Association for Computational Linguistics (1983) 183–190.
8. Salton, G., McGill, M. J.: Introduction to modern information retrieval. McGraw-Hill, New York (1983)
9. Tishby, N., Pereira, F. C., Bialek, W.: The information bottleneck method. In: 37th Annual Allerton Conference on Communication, Control, and Computing. Illinois (1999)

Analyses on the Generalised Lotto-Type Competitive Learning

Andrew Luk

St B&P Neural Investments Pty Limited, Australia

Abstract. In generalised lotto-type competitive learning algorithm more than one winner exist. The winners are divided into a number of tiers (or divisions), with each tier being rewarded differently. All the losers are penalised (which can be equally or differently). In order to study the various properties of the generalised lotto-type competitive learning, a set of equations, which governs its operations, is formulated. This is then used to analyse the stability and other dynamic properties of the generalised lotto-type competitive learning.

1   Introduction

Recently, there is strong interest in deploying various techniques, such as neural networks, genetic and evolution algorithms, modern statistical methods and fuzzy logics, in financial analysis, modelling, and prediction [1]. Some of these techniques utilise competitive learning to locate features that are essential in financial market modelling and prediciton. The focus of this paper is to analyse a new class of competitive learning paradigm. We begin by introducing the classical view of competitive learning. Each input prototype x_i ($i = 1, 2, ..., M$, and M is the number of prototypes available for training) will activate one member of the output layer (i.e. the winning node or neuron, say node c, such that $c = \arg \min_j \|x_i - \omega_j\|^2$) and its corresponding (long-term) weight vector ω_c (assumed to be of the same dimensionality, say d, as x_i) is being updated by $\eta_c(x_i - \omega_c)$, where η_c is the learning rate of the winning node and $0 \leq \eta_c \leq 1$. The rest of the nodes (i.e. $j \neq c$, $j = 1, 2, ...,$ k, where k is the number of output nodes) in the output layer are not activated and their corresponding weight vectors (ω_j) are not modified. This form of learning is also referred to as winner-take-all (WTA) learning [2-4]. For correct convergence, η_c should reduce with time t. The description given above is the sorting method of implementing the WTA learning.

Alternatively, it can be implemented via a synchronous or an asynchronous network. In both cases, it usually comprises of (a) a competitive network which includes a k by k weight matrix and k competitive nonlinear output nodes, and (b) a matching network which contains a d by k weight matrix. The matching network is for long-term memory (i.e. the weight vectors ω_j in the sorting method) and the competitive network is for short-term memory. In WTA type learning, after an input sample is presented, only one node (the winner) in the competitive network will remain active (or switch on) after a number of iterations (or a single iteration, depending on which type of network is used) and its corresponding long-term memory will be updated. In the past, most of the research efforts have been concentrated in the behaviour of the short-term memory [2-4]. There are many different ways of implementing the short-term memory. Usually, for each of the k nodes, it will be excited by its own weighted output and inhibited by a weighted sum of either its neighbours or other active nodes. The weights for the inhibition signals are usually of the same value (though may be adaptively modified) and usually smaller than the weight of the single excitation signal. These were reviewed in [5, 6].

Currently, there are some efforts in studying the behaviour of the long-term memory. It has been known for a long time [2-4] that some long-term memory of the output nodes simply cannot learn. These nodes are usually refered to as dead units. It is found that a sensitivity or conscience parameter γ [7] (which can be implemented as a winner frequency counter) can be included to prevent such dead units (or nodes) from occurring. The sensitivity parameter counts the number of times that a certain node wins. If that node wins more frequently than other nodes, it will reduce its chances from winning in future iterations. Thereby, giving other less frequently won nodes opportunities to learn. Unfortunately, dead units may still arise if (a) the number of output nodes is more than the number of clusters or (b) the nodes are unfairly initialised. In these cases, the dead units will usually position themselves near the boundaries of the desired clusters or somewhere around their initial locations.

Xu, et al. in [8] proposed to solve this problem by penalising (the long-term weight vector of) the nearest rival node. The update rule for the rival node is similar to the winner, except the de-learning rate η_r is a small negative real number and $|\eta_r| << |\eta_c|$. For correct convergence, it has been shown it is necessary that (a) $8 < |\eta_c/\eta_r| \le 15$ and (b) the number of ouput nodes k cannot exceed twice the number of clusters [9]. This then forms a sort of "push-pull" action on the output nodes and drives the right number of output nodes towards the relevant cluster centres; at the same time, the excess or extra nodes are being pushed away from the area of interest. Variants that are based on either finite mixture or multisets modelling have been proposed [10]. Equally, we proposed that the rival can be rewarded, or it can be randomly rewarded or penalised, and the same "push-pull" action has been observed [11]. (Another variant scheme is proposed in [12] where the weights of the winners for the current and previous iterations are updated if and only if their status have changed. In this case, the current winner is rewarded and the previous winner is penalised.)

More recently, we propose a new class of competitive learning that is based on models of the lottory game. The basic idea of lotto-type competitive learning is that the (long-term weight vector of the) winner is rewarded as in the classical competitive learning and ALL the losers (long-term weight vectors) are penalised (which can either be equally or unequally) [13]. This idea is later extended to include more than one winner – the generalised lotto-type competitve learning [14]. It is shown experimentally that such learning strategies can produce very similar results as that of the rival-penalised competitive learning for both closely and sparsely spaced cluster structures – that is, extra nodes are pushed away from the clusters of interest.

It is also shown in [14] that there are some similarities between the generalized lotto-type competitive learning (LTCL) and the competitively inhibited neural network

(CINN) [15]. Such similarity is exploited to formulate a set of dynamic LTCL equations. This set of equations will be outlined in section 2 and major results on the dynamic behaviour of these equations will be given in section 3. Concluding remarks will be given in section 4.

2   The Lotto-type Competitive Learning Equations

Both the original and generalised lotto-type competitive learnings are first implemented using the sorting method [13-14]. In these cases, only the long-term memory updating rules are of relevance. However, in order to study the other basic properties of the algorithms, it is useful to incooperate some form of short-term memory into the learning paradigm. We have chosen the form proposed in [15] because it is one of the few models that incorporates both the short-term and long-term memory in its analysis. The model is simple, elegant and well studied [15]. However, we would like to modify it so that it reflects the lottory gaming idea not only in the equation that governs the long-term memory but also in those equations that control the short-term memory behaviour.

Formally, the set of lotto-type competitive learning (LTCL) equations is defined as [14]:

$$\dot{y}_j = -y_j + E(x_i, \omega_j) + I_j \tag{1}$$

$$\dot{\omega}_j = f(y_j)\eta_j (x_i - \omega_j) \tag{2}$$

$$f(y_j) = \begin{cases} 1 & \text{if } y_j > 0 \\ -1 & \text{otherwise} \end{cases} \tag{3}$$

$$I_j = \alpha f(y_j) + \beta \sum_{m=1, m \neq j}^{k} f(y_m) \tag{4}$$

Readers may note that (1) and (2) are the short-term memory (STM) and long-term memory (LTM) state equations, respectively. Here, E is defined as a bounded positive decreasing external stimulus function, I is defined as an internal stimulus function, y as the node STM state, with α and β as some positive real constants. (Note that α and β are the two possible values in the STM weight matrix.) The dot above the variable denotes the time derivative of that variable. The function f in (3) is a bipolar switching function. This is a major departure from the set of dynamic equations of the competitively inhibited neural network (CINN). In effect, this equation states that if the node is one of the winners, its neuronal activity (or excitation level) y must be greater than zero. However, if the node belongs to one of the losers, it neuronal activity must be less than or equal to zero. It follows that the inhibitions in (4) are given by the losers, and the excitations are contributed by the winners. The weight vector (of the LTM state) will be updated by (2), which is the difference between the input and the current value (or state) of the weight vector multiplied by its corresponding learning rate. The reward or penalisation of that weight vector (i.e. the sign of the updating rule) is automatically given by the function *f.* (This is the main difference between classical and lotto-type competitive learnings. Here, we also break away from most of the models [2-3] of the neuronal activities, where they are assumed to be self excitation with lateral inhibition. The proposed equations represent a more complicated model of neuronal activities. In our case, the neuronal activity is governed by the neuronal states of a group of k neurons which provide both excitation and inhibition signals.)

In [14] we show that the short-term memory of the proposed LTCL equations will converge stably. We first define the K-orthant for the set of STM states as:

Definition 1 Let K be a finite subset of integers between 1 and k. The K-orthant of the set of STM states is

$$\left\{ y \in \Re^k \middle| \left(y_j > 0 \text{ if } j \in K\right) \text{ and } \left(y_j \le 0 \text{ if } j \notin K\right) \right\} \tag{5}$$

From this definition, a number of lemmas are given and we arrive at the following theorem and corollary:

Theorem 1 There exists a K-orthant of the LTCL's state space which is an attracting invariant set of the network's flow.

Corollary 1 The flow generated by the LTCL equations converges to a fixed point.

These theorem and corollary mean that once an ordered set has been formed among the output nodes, the short-term memory will converge to a point in the sample data space. In this paper, we continue to examine the dynamics of the LTCL equations according to [15].

3　Dynamics of the Lotto-type Competitive Learning Equations

In the competitively inhibited neural network (CINN), it is the sliding threshold ($E > \rho\beta$, where ρ is the number of activated nodes) that determines the number of active neurons. In lotto-type competitive learning, a similar threshold can be derived to determine the number of winners. It is assumed that the same "STM initialization" is valid in LTCL: i.e. (a) the initial LTM states all have unequal external stimuli for a given input x_i, and (b) the initial STM states are all equal and negative. The following theorem can then be derived.

Theorem 2 Assume that (a) the levels of the initial external stimuli are all unequal, (b) the STM initialization condition is valid, and (c) there exists a time after which there are p winners in the network, then the initial stimulus level of the next winning node must exceed the following threshold.

$$E(x_i, \omega_j(0)) > \alpha + (k - 2p - 1)\beta. \tag{6}$$

Thus the first winner must have an initial external stimulus exceeding $\alpha + (k - 3)\beta$. The second one must exceed $\alpha + (k - 5)\beta$ and so on. Finally, the last winner must have an initial external stimulus level which exceeds α. Clearly, the minimum number of nodes in any LTCL algorithms must be three. It is easy to verify that the maximum number of winners is given by the following theorem.

Theorem 3 The number of winners, p, which can be supported by LTCL must satisfy the following inequality,

$$p \leq (k-1)/2 = p_{max}. \tag{7}$$

One interesting consequence of the bipolar function in (3) is that the solution to (2) is given by

$$\omega_j(t) = \omega_j(0) \exp\{\eta_j f(y_j)\} + (1 - \exp\{\eta_j f(y_j)\}) x_i. \tag{8}$$

If the node is a winner, the term inside the exponent will be negative (i.e. $\tau_j = \eta_j f(y_j) < 0$). Thus as $t \rightarrow \infty$ (and, in general, $\eta_j \rightarrow 0$ by definition), the weight vector $\omega_j \rightarrow x_i$. On the other hand, if the node is a loser, the term inside the exponent will be positive. The weight vector will not converge to the input.

The following analysis is adapted from [15]. In that study, Lemmon examines the collective movement of all the output nodes within a finite presentation interval. The objective is to investigate conditions by which such movement will converge to the source density of the input data set. His idea is first to develop equations which govern the movement of the output node, i.e. the neural flux $J(\omega)$ (in his terminology). With these equations, conditions can then be established which guarantee the correct convergence of the output nodes to the source density. Since the analysis is essentially similar to [15], we will only state the results that are useful in our study.

Assume that the neural density $n(\omega)$ is a generalised function in the LTM space. One important result in [15] is that the neural flux follows the conservation law, i.e.

$$\partial n(\omega) / \partial t = -\nabla \cdot J(\omega) \quad . \tag{9}$$

Now we can present a lemma that relates to the presentation interval, external stimulus and neural density.

Lemma 1 Let x be a given input and define the activation interval, $I(x)$, of x as that set of winning nodes due to x. The activation interval of x is the interval, $I(x) = (x-\delta, x+\delta)$, where δ satisfies the following equation,

$$E(x, x+\delta) = [\alpha + (k-1)\beta] - 2k\beta \int_{-\delta}^{\delta} n(x+\upsilon) \, d\upsilon \quad . \tag{10}$$

For convenient, we can define $\zeta = \alpha + (k-1)\beta$ and $\lambda = 2k\beta$. Within this interval, all the nodes will be winners and their corresponding weight vectors will be rewarded. Outside this interval, the nodes will be penalised.

Definition 2 A first order point, ω, of the LTM space as a point where the neural density is constant over the interval $(\omega - 2\delta, \omega + 2\delta)$.

With these definitions, a theorem can be stated concerning the variable δ.

Theorem 4 If ω is a first order point and $E(\omega, \omega + \delta)$ is strictly monotone decreasing in δ, then

$$\delta = \frac{\zeta - E(\omega, \omega + \delta)}{2\,\lambda\,n(\omega)}, \quad \text{and} \tag{11}$$

$$\delta_n = \frac{\partial \delta}{\partial n(\omega)} = \frac{-2\lambda\delta}{E_\delta + 2\,\lambda\,n(\omega)}, \tag{12}$$

where E_δ is the first partial derivative of the external stimulus with respect to δ.

Without going into the details (see [15] for details), a first approximation for the neural flux can be found which is summarised by the following theorem,

Theorem 5   If $n(\omega)$ is continuously differentiable once, then a first order approximation of the neural flux is

$$J(\omega) \approx n(\omega)\,(e^\tau - 1)\,\{\psi_1(\omega) * p_\omega(\omega)\}\,. \tag{13}$$

where $\psi_1(\omega)$ is the first derivative of a box (or rectangular) function $B(\omega)$ (which is unity between minus one and one and which is zero elsewhere, see [15]), $p(\omega)$ is the probability density function of ω, $p_\omega(\omega) = dp(\omega)/d\omega$ and $*$ is the convolution operator.

One of the most important works of Lemmon in CINN is to show how the slope of the characteristics of neural flux can lead to a set of clustering constraints, which restrict the CINN network parameters so that it follows a gradient ascent to a smoothed version of the source density [15]. Thus, the following theorem relates to the slope of the characteristics, i.e.

Theorem 6   If ω is a first order point of the LTM space, then the slope of the characteristic in (ω, t)-space through this point is

$$\omega_t = (e^\tau - 1)\left\{\frac{(\zeta - E)E_\delta}{E_\delta + 2\lambda n}(\psi_1 * p_\omega) - \frac{2(\zeta - E)\delta^2}{E_\delta + 2\lambda n}(\psi_0 * p_\omega)\right\} \tag{14}$$

where $\psi_0(\omega) = B(\omega/\delta)$, and $\psi_1(\omega) = \delta(\delta^2 - \omega^2)\,\psi_0(\omega)$.

Since ψ_1 is approximately equal to $(2/3)\delta^3\psi_0$ [15], we can approximate (14) as

$$\omega_t \approx \frac{2}{3}(e^\tau - 1)\,\delta^3 \left[\frac{(\zeta - E)\left(E_\delta - \dfrac{3}{\delta}\right)}{E_\delta + \dfrac{\zeta - E}{\delta}}\right]\frac{d}{d\omega}(\psi_0 * p) \tag{15}$$

Similar to [15], (15) indicates that the characteristics follow the gradient of a smoothed version of the source density since the probability density function $p(\omega)$ is convolving with a version of the box function ψ_0. It is clear that the bounds for E can be derived from (15), which is

$$\theta\ln(\xi\,\delta) < E < \zeta. \tag{16}$$

where θ and ξ are some positive numbers. Recall that E is a monotone decreasing function between the input x and the weight vector ω, (16) indicates that all those nodes with $E < \zeta$ will converge to the source density.

Furthermore, (15) indicates that there is a region of attraction where E is bounded by (16). Outside this region, it is effectively a repulsive region because the term within the square bracket of (15) is negative. Thus by (15), for unfair initialization (as discussed in section 1), only one node will converge to the source density (see example given in [13]) if the sensitivity parameter γ is not used. The regions attraction and repulsion may therefore account for the push-pull effect observed in the simulation results given in [8-11, 13-14].

These complicated equations indicate that the ensemble of output nodes will converge towards the cluster centres if they satisfy certain constraints and bounds. If these are not satified, the long-term behaviour of those nodes will not follow the source density, which account for the messy vector traces when parameters are not carefully selected in [13].

4   Conclusions

In this paper, the dynamics of lotto-type competitive learning (LTCL) is studied via a set of LTCL equations. The stability of the short-term memory is easily verified. Convergence of the winning nodes follows directly from the differential equation of the update rule. Following the works of Lemmon, the flows of the LTCL equations are carefully analysed. Again, within a presentation interval, it is shown that the slope of the characteristics of the winning nodes will follow a smoothed version of the source density. Comparing (8) and (15), we can clearly see that the winning nodes will converge to the source density. However, the starting point of both equations are different: (8) is a solution to the LTM state equation, and (15) is a consequence of the flow of the nodes in the network as a whole. The bounds on E suggest that it is related to the control parameters α, β and k of the dynamic equations, as well as the presentation interval parameter δ. Finally, the LTCL equations provide an alternative neuronal model for studying more complicated neuronal activities. Future work will concentrate on the capability of the proposed model in handling exceptional situations and cases where the source densities may be unevenly distributed.

Acknowledgements
The authors wish to thanks Profs. W. Dunin-Barkowski, J. Mandziuk, and I. Tetko for reviewing and commenting on an earlier version of the paper.

References

1.   *Proceedings of the IEEE/IAFE 1996-2000 Conference on Computational Intelligence for Financial Engineering (CIFEr)*, New York City, USA, 1996-2000.

2.   S. Grossberg, "On learning and energy-entropy dependence in recurrent and nonrecurrent signed networks," *Journal of Statistical Physics*, vol. 48, pp. 105-132, 1968.

3. S. Grossberg, "Adaptive pattern classification and universal recording: I. Parallel development and coding of neural feature detectors," *Biol. Cybern.*, vol. 23, pp. 121-134, 1976.

4. T. Kohonen, *Self-Organizing Maps*. Second Edition. Berlin: Springer-Verlag, 1997.

5. J.F. Yang and C.M. Chen, "Winner-take-all neural networks using the highest threshold," *IEEE Trans. on Neural Networks*, vol. 11, no. 1, pp.194-199, 2000.

6. R.P. Lippmann, "An introduction to computing with neural nets," *IEEE ASSP Magazine*, vol. 4, no. 2, pp.4-22, 1987.

7. S.C. Ahalt, A.K. Krishnamurty, P. Chen and D.E. Melton, "Competitive learning algorithms for vector quantization," *Neural Networks*, vol. 3, no. 3, pp. 277-291, 1990.

8. L. Xu, A. Krzyzark and E. Oja, "Rival penalized competitive learning for clustering analysis, RBF net and curve detection," *IEEE Trans. on Neural Network*, vol. 4, no. 4, pp. 636-649, 1993.

9. J. Ma and L. Xu, "The correct convergence of the rival penalized competitive learning (RPCL) algorithm," 5th *Intl. Confern. on Neural Information Processing (ICONIP'98)*, Kitakyushu, Japan, Oct. 21-23, 1998, vol. 1, pp. 239-242.

10. L. Xu, "Rival penalized competitive learning, finite mixture, and multisets clustering", *Proceedings of the 1998 International Joint Conference on Neural Networks*, Anchorage, Alasaka, USA, May 4-9, 1998, pp. 2525-2530.

11. A. Luk and S. Lien, "Rival rewarded and randomly rewarded rival competitive learning," *Proceedings of the 1999 International Joint Conference on Neural Networks*, Washington, D.C., USA, July 10-16, 1999.

12. D.C. Park, "Centroid neural network for unsupervised competitive learning," *IEEE Trans. on Neural Networks*, vol. 11, no. 2, pp. 520-528, 2000.

13. A. Luk and S. Lien, "Lotto-type competitive learning," *Progress in Connectionist-Based Information System*, vol. 1, Singapore: Springer-Verlag, 1997, pp. 510-513.

14. A. Luk and S. Lien, "Lotto-type competitive learning and its stability," *Proceedings of the 1999 International Joint Conference on Neural Networks*, Washington, D.C., USA, July 10-16, 1999.

15. M. Lemmon, *Competitively Inhibited Neural Networks for Adaptive Parameter Estimation*, Boston: Kluwer Academic Publishers, 1991.

Extended K-means with an Efficient Estimation of the Number of Clusters

Tsunenori ISHIOKA

National Center for University Entrance Examinations,
2-19-23 Komaba, Meguro-ku, Tokyo 153-8501, JAPAN

Abstract. We present a non-hierarchal clustering algorithm that can determine the optimal number of clusters by using iterations of k-means and a stopping rule based on BIC. The procedure requires twice the computation of k-means. However, with no prior information about the number of clusters, our method is able to get the optimal clusters based on information theory instead of on a heuristic method.

1 Introduction

One of the typical methods for non-hierarchal clustering — k-means — is often used for huge data clustering as well as self-organizing map [8, 9], because it requires only $\mathcal{O}(kN)$ computation for a given number of clusters k and sample size N. In the context of recent research in data mining, several high-performance techniques for k-means have been developed [1, 6].

The different methods for k-means calculations vary in several aspects. In all cases, the problem remains that k-means might not converge to a global optimum, depending on the selection of initial seeds. Nevertheless, from data mining and knowledge discovery perspective, we are convinced that a pre-determinance of the number of clusters is a strict restriction.

Indeed, we can obtain an optimal number of clusters heuristically by performing computations based on different initial settings of cluster numbers. Hardy [2] surveyed seven typical evaluation criteria (two of them can be applied for hierarchal clustering methods) with various datasets. However, varying the number of clusters requires much computation, because we have to use k-means repeatedly.

We propose an algorithm that initially divides data into clusters whose number is sufficiently small, and continues to divide the each cluster into two clusters. We use BIC (Bayesian Information Criterion[7]) as the division criterion. We will show that the division method works well, and present an implementation. The idea was proposed also by [5], but our method differs in the following aspects:

1. Our method can be applied for general or p-dimensional datasets.
2. We consider the magnitude of variance and covariance around the centers of clusters which can be divided progressively.
3. We evaluate the number of clusters by means of computer simulation runs.

Previous research [5] can treat only two-dimensional datasets, and assumes the variance around the cluster centers to be a constant. As a consequence of progressive division, the number of elements which is contained in each cluster becomes fewer, and the variance will become smaller. Therefore, magnitude of variance should be considered.

In section 2, we describe the principle of k-means and show a proposed algorithm in section 3. In section 4, we evaluate the number of final clusters.

2   K-means method

The procedure of k-means proposed by [4] is as follows:

1. Get the initial k-elements in the dataset, and set them as clusters which consist of one element.
2. Allocate the remaining data to the nearest neighborhood cluster centers.
3. Calculate the cluster centers, and regard them as fixed seeds. Repeat once to allocate the all data to the nearest neighbor cluster seeds.

Most k-means procedures, however, require that the data must be allocated repeatedly until the cluster centers will converge.

3   X-means

Pelleg[5] thought of the basic idea for a 2-division procedure and named it x-means, indicating that the number of clusters with k-means is indefinite. The algorithm of x-means is quite simple; we begin to divide data into clusters whose number is sufficiently small, and continue to divide the cluster into two clusters.

The algorithm proposed in this paper is summarized as follows:

step 0: Prepare p-dimensional data whose sample size is n.

step 1: Set an initial number of clusters to be k_0 (the default is 2), which should be sufficiently small.

step 2: Apply k-means to all data with setting $k = k_0$. We name the divided clusters
$$C_1, C_2, \ldots, C_{k_0}.$$

step 3: Repeat the following procedure from step 4 to step 9 by setting $i = 1, 2, \ldots, k_0$.

step 4: For a cluster of C_i, apply k-means by setting $k = 2$. We name the divided clusters
$$C_i^{(1)}, C_i^{(2)}.$$

step 5: We assume the following p-dimensional normal distribution for the data $\mathbf{x}_i$ contained in C_i:

$$f(\theta_i; \mathbf{x}) = (2\pi)^{-p/2} |\mathbf{V}_i|^{-1/2} \exp\left[-\frac{1}{2}(\mathbf{x} - \mu_i)^t \mathbf{V}_i^{-1}(\mathbf{x} - \mu_i)\right], \qquad (1)$$

then calculate the BIC as

$$\mathrm{BIC} = -2\log L(\widehat{\theta}_i; \mathbf{x}_i \in C_i) + q \log n_i, \qquad (2)$$

where $\widehat{\theta}_i = [\widehat{\mu}_i, \widehat{\mathbf{V}_i}]$ is the maximum likelihood estimate of the p-dimensional normal distribution; μ_i is p-dimensional means vector, and $\mathbf{V}_i$ is $p \times p$ dimensional variance-covariance matrix; q is the number of the parameters dimension, and it becomes $2p$ if we ignore the covariance of $\mathbf{V}_i$. $\mathbf{x}_i$ is the p-dimensional data contained in C_i; n_i is the number of elements contained in C_i. L is the likelihood function which indicates $L(\cdot) = \prod f(\cdot)$.
We choose to ignore the covariance of $\mathbf{V}_i$.

step 6: We assume the p-dimensional normal distributions with their parameters $\theta_i^{(1)}, \theta_i^{(2)}$ for $C_i^{(1)}, C_i^{(2)}$ respectively; the probability density function of this 2-division model becomes

$$g(\theta_i^{(1)}, \theta_i^{(2)}; \mathbf{x}) = \alpha_i [f(\theta_i^{(1)}; \mathbf{x})]^{\delta_i} [f(\theta_i^{(2)}; \mathbf{x})]^{1-\delta_i}, \tag{3}$$

where

$$\delta_i = \begin{cases} 1, \text{ if } \mathbf{x} \text{ is included in } C_i^{(1)}, \\ 0, \text{ if } \mathbf{x} \text{ is included in } C_i^{(2)}; \end{cases} \tag{4}$$

$\mathbf{x}_i$ will be included in either $C_i^{(1)}$ or $C_i^{(2)}$; α_i is a constant which lets equation (3) be a probability density function ($1/2 \leq \alpha_i \leq 1$). If obtaining a exact value is wanted, we can use p-dimensional numerical integration. But this requires much computation. Thus, we approximate α_i as follows:

$$\alpha_i = 0.5/K(\beta_i), \tag{5}$$

where β_i is a normalized distance between the two clusters, shown by

$$\beta_i = \sqrt{\frac{\|\mu_1 - \mu_2\|^2}{|\mathbf{V}_1| + |\mathbf{V}_2|}}, \tag{6}$$

$K(\cdot)$ stands for an lower probability of normal distribution.
When we set $\beta_i = 0, 1, 2, 3$, α_i becomes $0.5/0.500 = 1$, $0.5/0.841 = 0.59$, $0.5/0.977 = 0.51$, $0.5/0.998 = 0.50$ respectively.
The BIC for this model is

$$\text{BIC}' = -2 \log L'(\widehat{\theta}_i'; \mathbf{x}_i \in C_i) + q' \log n_i, \tag{7}$$

where $\widehat{\theta}_i' = [\widehat{\theta_i^{(1)}}, \widehat{\theta_i^{(2)}}]$ is a maximum likelihood estimate of two p-dimensional normal distributions; since there are two parameters of mean and variance for each p variable, the number of parameters dimension becomes $q' = 2 \times 2p = 4p$. L' is the likelihood function which indicates $L'(\cdot) = \prod g(\cdot)$.

step 7: If $\text{BIC} > \text{BIC}'$, we prefer the two-divided model, and decide to continue the division; we set

$$C_i \leftarrow C_i^{(1)}.$$

As for $C_i^{(2)}$, we push the p-dimensional data, the cluster centers, the log likelihood and the BIC onto the stack. Return to step 4.

step 8: If BIC $\leq$ BIC$'$, we prefer not to divide clusters any more, and decide to stop.
Extract the stacked data which is stored in step 7, and set

$$C_i \leftarrow C_i^{(2)}.$$

Return to step 4. If the stack is empty, go to step 9.

step 9: The 2-division procedure for C_i is completed. We renumber the cluster identification such that it becomes unique in C_i.

step 10: The 2-division procedure for initial k_0 divided clusters is completed. We renumber all clusters identifications such that they become unique.

step 11: Output the cluster identification number to which each element is allocated, the center of each cluster, the log likelihood of each cluster, and the number of elements in each cluster. [stop]

The reasons why we choose BIC over other common information criteria for model selection are follows:

– BIC considers the selection among from exponential family of distributions.
– BIC is based on prior probability rather than the distance between two distributions.

4 Evaluation of the performance

4.1 An investigation of the number of generated clusters

A simulation procedure is adopted. It generates 250 two-dimensional normal variables; these random variables should be clustered into 5 groups. Each group consists of 50 elements:

$$x_j \sim N(\mu = [0, 0], \ \sigma = [0.2, 0.2]), \ (j = 1, \ldots, 50)$$
$$x_j \sim N(\mu = [-2, 0], \ \sigma = [0.3, 0.3]), \ (j = 51, \ldots, 100)$$
$$x_j \sim N(\mu = [2, 0], \ \sigma = [0.3, 0.3]), \ (j = 101, \ldots, 150)$$
$$x_j \sim N(\mu = [0, 2], \ \sigma = [0.4, 0.4]), \ (j = 151, \ldots, 200)$$
$$x_j \sim N(\mu = [0, -2], \ \sigma = [0.4, 0.4]), \ (j = 201, \ldots, 250)$$

where μ is a mean, and σ^2 is a variance. We set $k_0 = 2$ as an initial division, and performed 1,000 simulation runs of x-means. Two-dimensional normal variables are generated for each simulation run. X-means will call k-means repeatedly; the algorithm of k-means is based on [3], which is provided in R.

Table 1 summarizes the number of clusters generated by x-means (upper row). For 1,000 simulation runs, the most frequent case is when 5 clusters are generated, this occurs 533 times. The second most frequent case is 6 clusters, which occurs 317 times. The middle row shows the results applying AIC (Akeike's Information Criterion) instead of BIC to x-means. We found that x-means by AIC tends to overgenerate clusters. The bottom row in Table 1 shows the number of optimal clusters when the goodness of model for give data is maximum (i.e.,

Table 1. The number of clusters by using 250 random variables of two-dimensional normal distribution

number of clusters	2	3	4	5	6	7	8	9	10	11	12	13	14	total
x-means (BIC)	2	6	9	469	383	99	27	5	0	0	0	0	0	1,000
x-means (AIC)	2	1	1	322	295	162	93	54	36	17	11	2	4	1,000
heuristic method	0	2	37	559	265	90	35	8	4	0	0	0	0	1,000

the AIC for given data is minimum) by varying k applied to k-means. This distribution is very similar to the distribution in upper row.

The cluster centers found by k-means are not always located where the elements cohere; thus x-means often divides a cluster into two clusters until new clusters centers will converge where the elements cohere. Consequently, x-means produces rather more clusters than adequate. Actually in our simulation, when x-means divides all 250 ($= 50 \times 50$)data into two clusters equally (i.e, 125 elements each), both subclusters are often divided into three clusters ($50 + 50 + 25$), resulting in 6 clusters.

4.2 An investigation of the number of cluster elements

After applying x-means to the simulation runs, we can obtain the distributions of the number of cluster elements, as shown in Fig.1. The horizontal axis gives the cluster identification number, which is sorted in increasing order by the number of cluster elements; the vertical axis gives the distribution of number of the cluster elements; box-and-whisker charts are used.

A box-and-whisker chart contains a box surrounding two hinges, two whiskers, and outlier(s) if any; a lower or upper hinge shows 25 or 75 percentile of the distribution; the median(50 percentile) is in between two hinges. The two whiskers stands for tails of the distribution; the whiskers extend to the most extreme data point which is no more than 1.5 times interquartile range from the box; the outlier(s) may be shown if any.

In case (a), i.e, when obtaining 5 clusters, we found that each cluster consists of about 50 elements. In case (b) obtaining 6 clusters, 4 clusters consist of about 50 elements and the remainder is divided into 2 clusters. Case (c), obtaining 7 clusters, is similar to (b); 3 clusters consist of about 50 elements and the remainder is divided into 4 clusters. For cases (b), (c), and (d), the proper division in clusters of 50 was performed, although the generated cluster may be rather small.

4.3 Consideration of the computational amount

X-means requires to find k final clusters, even if it repeats to divide into two clusters. In addition, we need to judge if these k final clusters should not be divided any more. Thus, remembering that k-means requires $\mathcal{O}(kN)$ computation, x-means will take twice as much computation compared to k-means.

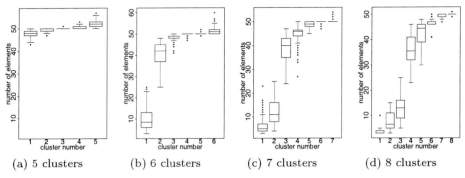

| (a) 5 clusters | (b) 6 clusters | (c) 7 clusters | (d) 8 clusters |

Fig. 1. Distribution of the number of cluster elements contained in final clusters

Indeed the computation of BIC is needed, but we can ignore this because we calculate it only once after fixing the cluster elements. The BIC can be easily obtained from the mean and variance-covariance of a p-dimensional normal distribution. We are convinced that x-means gives us a quite good solution which meets with its computational expense, although the solution may not be an optimum. This program can be obtained via http://www.rd.dnc.ac.jp/~tunenori/src/xmeans.prog.

References

1. Huang, Zhexue: Extension to the k-Means Algorithm for Clustering Large Data Sets with Categorical Values, *Data Mining and Knowledge Discovery*, **2**[3] (1998) 283–304.
2. Hardy, Andre: On the Number of Clusters, *Computational Statistics & Data Analysis*, 1[23] (1996) 83–96.
3. Hartigan, J.A. and Wong, M.A. : A K-means clustering algorithm. *Applied Statistics* 28 (1979) 100–108.
4. MacQueen, J.B.: Some methods for Classification and Analysis of Multivariate Observations," *Proc. Symp. Math. Statist. and Probability, 5th Berkeley*, 1 (1967) 281–297.
5. Pelleg, Dan and Andrew Moore: X-means: Extending K-means with Efficient Estimation of the Number of Clusters, *ICML-2000* (2000).
6. Pelleg, Dan and Andrew Moore: Accelerating Exact *k*-means Algorithms with Geometric Reasoning, *KDD-99* (1999).
7. Schwarz, G.: Estimating the dimension of a model, *Ann. Statist.*, 6–2: (1978) 461-464.
8. Vesanto, Juha and Johan Himberg and Esa Alhoniemi and Juha Parhankangas: Self-Organizing Map in Matlab: the SOM Toolbox, *Proceedings of the Matlab DSP Conference 1999*, Espoo, Finland, November (1999) 35–40.
9. Yang, Ming-Hsuan and Narenda Ahuja: A Data Partition Method for Parallel Self-Organizing Map, *Proceeding of the 1999 IEEE International Joint Conference on Neural Networks (IJCNN 99)*, Washington DC, July (1999).

An Interactive Approach to Building Classification Models by Clustering and Cluster Validation

Zhexue Huang[1], Michael K. Ng[2], Tao Lin[3] and David Cheung[1]

[1] E-Business Technology Institute, The University of Hong Kong.
[2] Department of Mathematics, The University of Hong Kong.
[3] CSIRO Mathematical and Information Science, Canberra, Australia

Abstract. This paper presents the decision clusters classifier (DCC) for database mining. A DCC model consists of a small set of decision clusters extracted from a tree of clusters generated by a clustering algorithm from the training data set. A decision cluster is associated to one of the classes in the data set and used to determine the class of new objects. A DCC model classifies new objects by deciding which decision clusters these objects belong to. In making classification decisions, DCC is similar to the k-nearest neighbor classification scheme but its model building process is different. In this paper, we describe an interactive approach to building DCC models by stepwise clustering the training data set and validating the clusters using data visualization techniques. Our initial results on some public benchmarking data sets have shown that DCC models outperform the some existing popular classification methods.

1 Introduction

We consider a finite set of n objects $\mathcal{X} = \{x_1, x_2, \cdots, x_n\}$ together with m attributes describing the properties of these objects. The data consist of n m-dimensional feature vectors in a sample space $\mathcal{D}$. Most clustering methods formalize the intuitive ideas of a "cluster" of objects, which is typically defined as a subset $\mathcal{C} \subset \mathcal{X}$ such that the objects in $\mathcal{C}$ fulfill certain criteria of homogeneity that are directly verified in the data set. For instance, all pairwise dissimilarities are less than a certain value. To build a classification model from $\mathcal{X}$, it is required that the objects must first be labeled in classes with certain regularities. In spatial context, the basic regularity is that objects close to each other must reflect a "similar" behavior and tend to have the same class. This is the proposition of the k-nearest neighbor classifier (KNN). In relation to clustering, objects in the same cluster tend to have the same class. As such, classification can be viewed as a clustering problem that can be solved with a clustering process. This is also the motivation of our work.

In this paper, we present a decision clusters classifier (DCC) for database mining. A DCC model is defined as a set of p decision clusters generated with a clustering algorithm from the training data set. A decision cluster is labeled of one of the classes in data. The DCC model classifies new objects by deciding to which decision clusters these objects belong. In making classification decisions, DCC is very similar to KNN. However, their model building processes are different. We use the interactive clustering process [5] to build DCC models. Given a training data set, we first interactively partition it into several clusters and build a cluster tree from them. Then, we select a subset of clusters from the tree as a candidate DCC model and use a tuning data set to validate the model. In building the cluster tree, we employ different visualization techniques, including FASTMAP projection [3], to visually validate clusters generated at each step by the k-prototypes clustering algorithm [4] which we have proposed and used. In building a DCC model, we consider an additional measure to validate clusters. We require the objects in a cluster to be dominated by one class as much as possible. In [8], Mui and Fu presented a binary tree classifier for classification of nucleated blood cells. Each terminal node of the tree is a cluster dominated by a particular group of blood cell classes. To partition a nonterminal node, class groupings were first decided by projecting the objects onto a 2-dimensional space using the principal component analysis (PCA) and visually examining how to separate the classes. Then, the decision rule of a quadratic classifier was repeatedly used to test different combinations of features and to select the "best" subset of feature vectors that can be used to partition the objects into the two clusters. Therefore, different feature subsets were used at different non-terminal node of the tree to partition data. This work was later advanced by the use of the k-means algorithm to generate clusters at each non-terminal node and determine the grouping of classes [7].

Mui and Fu's work [8] was an early example of using the interactive approach to building classification models. The main reason was due to the limitation of computing powers available in the early 80s. Although the study of algorithms for building classification models has been focused on automatic approach, the interactive approach has recently been brought to attention again [1] with enhancement of the sophisticated visualization techniques. The great advantage of the interactive approach is that human knowledge can be used to guide the model building process.

The paper is organized as follows. In Section 2, we describe an interactive approach to building DCC models. In Section 3, some experimental results are given to illustrate the effectiveness of DCC models. Finally, some concluding remarks are given in Section 4.

2 Construction of DCC Models

In this section, we describe an interactive approach to building DCC models from training data sets. A cluster tree represents a set of hierarchical clusterings of a data set. Before we discuss our top-down approach to building a cluster tree, we start with the following definitions.

Definition 1. *An m-clustering of $\mathcal{X}$ is a partition of $\mathcal{X}$ into m subsets (clusters), which satisfies:*

$$C_i \neq \emptyset, \quad i = 1, \cdots, m, \ \cup_{i=1}^{m} C_i = \mathcal{X}, \text{ and } C_i \cap C_j = \emptyset, \ i \neq j, \ i,j = 1, \cdots, m.$$

Definition 2. *A clustering S with k clusters is said to be nested in the clustering T, which contains r ($< k$) clusters, if for any cluster C_i in S, there is a cluster C_j in T such that $C_i \subseteq C_j$. And there exists at least one cluster in S, which holds $C_i \subset C_j$ and $C_i \neq C_j$.*

Definition 3. *A cluster tree is a sequence of nested clusterings, so that for any i, j with $i < j$ and for any $C_j \in S_j$, there is $C_i \in S_i$ such that $C_j \subseteq C_i$.*

We remark that a clustering is a DCC model (cf. defined as in Section 1) if clusters in the clustering have dominant classes. Therefore, a cluster tree represents a set of DCC models.

Building a cluster tree from a training data set is to find a sequence of nested clusterings in the data set. We can use a top-down approach to generating a clustering by recursively applying a clustering algorithm. Similar to the process of the construction of a decision tree [8], we start from the whole data set and partition it into k clusters. Then for each cluster, we can further partition it into k' sub-clusters. This process is repeated and a tree of clusters grows until all leaves of the tree are found.

At each node of the tree, we need to decide whether to further partition it into sub-clusters or not and how. This is equivalent to deciding the terminal nodes and the best splitting in decision trees. In fact, our cluster tree is a kind of decision trees although we do not use it to make classification decisions. We determine a cluster as a terminal node based on two conditions: (i) its objects are dominated in one class and (ii) it is a natural cluster in the object space. Condition (i), which is widely used in many decision tree algorithms, is determined based on the frequencies of classes in the cluster. If no clear dominant class exists, the cluster will be further partitioned into sub-clusters.

If a cluster with the dominant class is found, we do not simply determine it as a terminal node. Instead, we investigate whether the cluster is a natural one or not by looking into its compactness and isolation [6]. To do so, we project the objects in the cluster onto a 2-dimensional (2D) space and visually examine the distribution of the objects. If the distribution shows more than one sub-cluster, then we use the clustering algorithm to find these sub-clusters. Otherwise, we identify the cluster as a terminal node with a dominant class.

The Fastmap algorithm [3] is used for projecting objects onto the 2D space because we can deal with categorical data. Given a cluster, the 2D projection allows us to visually identify whether sub-clusters exist in it. If we see any separate clusters in the 2D projection, we can conclude that sub-clusters exist in the original object space. However, if there are no separate clusters on the display, we do not simply conclude that the cluster is a natural cluster. Instead, we visualize the distribution of the distances between objects and the cluster center. This visual information further tells us how compact the cluster is.

In our work, we use the k-prototypes algorithm [4] to cluster data because of its efficiency and capability of processing both numeric and categorical data. To partition a cluster into sub-clusters with k-prototypes, we need to specify k, the number of clusters to be generated. Here, we take advantage of the Fastmap projection to assist the selection of k. By projecting the objects in the cluster onto a 2D space, we visualize objects of different classes in different symbols or colors. We can examine the potential number of clusters and the distribution of object classes in different clusters. Therefore, in determining k, we not only consider the number of potential clusters but also the number and distribution of classes in the cluster.

Let $\mathcal{X}$ denote the training data set, Θ the k-prototypes clustering algorithm and $\mathbf{F}$ the Fastmap algorithm. We summarize the interactive process to building a cluster tree as follows.

1. Begin: Set $\mathcal{X}$ as the root of the cluster tree. Select the root as the current node Sc.
2. Use $\mathbf{F}$ to project Sc onto 2D. Visually examine the projection to decide k, the number of potential clusters.
3. Apply Θ to partition Sc into k clusters.
4. Use $\mathbf{F}$ and other visual methods to validate the partition. (The tuning data set can also be used here to test the increase of classification accuracy of the new clustering.)
5. If the partition is accepted, go to step 6, otherwise, select a new k and go to step 3.
6. Attach the clusters as the children of the partitioned node. Select one as the current node Sc.
7. Validate Sc to determine whether it is a terminal node or not.
8. If it is not a terminal node, go to step 2. If it is a terminal node, but not the last one, select another node as the current node Sc, which has not been validated, and go to step 7. If it is the last terminal node in the tree, stop.

After we build a cluster tree from the training data set using the above process, we have created a sequence of clusterings. In principle, each clustering is a DCC model. Their classification performances are different. Therefore, we use the training data set (or the tuning data set) to identify the best DCC model from a cluster tree. We start from a top level clustering. First, we select all clusters of the top level clustering as decision clusters, use them to classify the training data set and calculate the classification accuracy. Then we identify the decision clusters, which have classified more objects wrongly than other clusters. We replace these clusters with its sub-clusters in the lower level clustering and test the model again. We continue this process until the best DCC model is found.

Each level of clustering in the cluster tree is a partition of the training data set. However, our final DCC model is not necessarily to be a partition. In the final DCC model, we often drop certain clusters from a clustering. These clusters contain few objects in several classes. These are the objects, which are located in the boundaries of other clusters. From our experiment, we found that dropping these clusters from the model can increase the classification accuracy.

3 Experimental Results

We have implemented a prototype system, called VC+, in Java to facilitate the interactive process to build DCC models. VC+ is composed of three major components, a tree mechanism that maintains the tree of clusters gradually growing during the clustering process, a data mining engine based on the k-prototypes algorithm and data projection based on Fastmap. VC+ also contains a number of visual functions, which are used to visualize the characteristics of clusters, cluster compactness and relationships as well as the distribution of classes in clusters. These functions can be applied to any single cluster or group of clusters selected by the user from the tree diagram. VC+ can also be used to solve both clustering and classification problems [5].

In our initial experiments, we tested our DCC models against four public data sets chosen from the UCI machine learning data repository [2] and compared our results with the results of the Quinlan's C5.0 decision tree algorithm, Discrim (a statistical classifier developed by R. Henery), Bayes (a statistical classifier which is a part of IND package from NASA's COSMIC center) and KNN (a statistical classifier, developed by C. Taylor). The characteristics of the four data sets are listed in Table 1. Size, data complexity and classification difficulties were the major considerations in choosing these data sets. The Heart and Credit Card data sets contain both numeric and categorical attributes. The Heart and Diabetes data sets are among those that are difficult to classify (low classification accuracy) [2]. The training and test partitions of these public data sets were taken directly from the data source. In conducting these experiments with VC+, we used training data sets to build cluster trees and used the test sets to select the DCC models. In growing the cluster trees, the training data sets were used as the tuning data to determine the partitions of nodes, together with other visual examinations such as Fastmap projection. We used the Clementine Data Mining System to build the C5.0 and boosted C5.0 models from the same training data sets and tested these models with test data sets. To create better C5.0 models, we used the test data sets to fine-tune the parameters of the algorithm. As such, both our models and C5.0 models were optimistic and comparable.

Table 2 shows the comparison results. The classification results for these four data sets by using Discrim, Bayes and KNN are listed in [9]. For the Heart data, the best test results from VC+ and C5.0 are the same. This is because the Heart data set was very small, it was easy for these models to obtain the best result from the training and test partition. For the Credit Card data, our model was equivalent to the Boosted C5.0 model. For the Diabetes and Satellite Image data, our models produced better results than the C5.0 and Boosted C5.0 models. Particularly, the accuracy increase in the Diabetes data was significant. These results demonstrate that our clustering approach is more suitable for numeric data than the decision tree algorithms like C5.0. The low accuracy of the Boosted C5.0 on the Diabetes data could be caused by the noise in data.

4   Concluding Remarks

We have presented a new classifier, the DCC model, for database mining and a new approach to interactively building DCC models by clustering and cluster validation. Our initial experimental results on four public domain data sets have shown that our models could outperform the popular C5.0 models. Our interactive approach facilitated by a simple visual tool with an efficient clustering algorithm for clustering and a few visual functions for cluster validations can easily achieve a near-optimal solution. Because a DCC model is simply a set of clusters, it is easy to be interpreted and understood. It is also straightforward to deploy a DCC model in the enterprise data warehouse environment, since the only task is to implement the distance function used and the set of cluster center records. The model is also efficient in classifying new data because the number of cluster center records is usually small. Our interactive approach has a special feature. That is, we use the same process and functionality to solve both clustering and classification problems [5]. Such integration will be a great benefit to business users because they do not need to worry about the selection of different algorithms. Instead, they can focus on data and business solutions.

	Name of data sets			
	Heart	Credit Card	Diabetes	Satellite Image
Training records	189	440	537	4435
Test records	81	213	230	2000
Categorical fields	6	9	0	0
Numerical fields	7	6	8	36
Number of classes	2	2	2	6

Table 1: Test data sets

	Name of data sets							
	Heart		Credit Card		Diabetes		Satellite Image	
	train	test	train	test	train	test	train	test
VC+	90.49	87.65	90.23	87.79	83.99	81.74	91.64	91.60
C5.0	96.30	87.65	90.00	84.98	80.26	76.09	98.84	85.90
Boosted C5.0	98.94	87.65	99.09	87.32	96.65	73.91	99.95	90.45
Discrim	68.50	60.70	85.10	85.90	78.00	77.50	85.10	82.90
Bayes	64.90	62.60	86.40	84.90	76.10	73.80	69.20	72.30
KNN	100.00	52.20	100.00	81.90	100.00	67.60	91.10	90.60

Table 2: Classification accuracy (in terms of %) for different methods.

References

1. M. Ankerst, C. Elsen, M. Ester and H.-P. Kriegel: Visual Classification: An Interactive Approach to Decision Tree Construction, in Proc. KDD'99, 5th Intl. Conf. on Knowledge Discovery and Data Mining, San Diego, 1999.
2. C. Blake and C. Merz: UCI Repository of machine learning databases, Department of Information and Computer Science, University of California, Irvine, CA, 1998 [http://www.ics.uci.edu/~mlearn/MLRepository.html].
3. C. Faloulsos and K.I. Lin: FastMap A Fast Algorithm for Indexing, Data- Mining and Visualization of Traditional and Multimedia Datasets, in Proc. ACM SIGMOD Conf., San Jose, CA, 163-174, 1995.
4. Z. Huang: Extensions to the k-means algorithm for clustering large data sets with categorical values, Data Mining and Knowledge Discovery, Vol. 2, No. 3, pp. 283-304, 1998.
5. Z. Huang and T. Lin: A Visual Method of Cluster Validation with Fastmap, PAKDD2000, Japan, 2000.
6. A. Jain and R. Dubes: Algorithms for Clustering Data, Prentice Hall, 1988.
7. Y. Lin and K. Fu: Automatic Classification of Cervical Cells Using a Binary Tree Classifier, Pattern Recognition, Vol. 16, No.1, pp. 68-80, 1983.
8. J. Mui and K. Fu: Automated Classification of Nucleated Blood Cells Using a Binary Tree Classifier, IEEE Transactions on Pattern Analysis and Machine Intelligence, Vol. 2, No. 5, pp. 429-443, 1980.
9. http://www.ncc.up.pt/liacc/ML/statlog/datasets.html.

A New Distributed Algorithm for Large Data Clustering

D K Bhattacharyya[1] and A Das[2]

[1] Dept of Information Technology, Tezpur University, India;
E-mail:dkb@agnigarh.tezu.ernet.in
[2] Dept of Comp. Sc., Anthony's College, Shillong, India

Abstract. This paper presents a new distributed data clustering algorithm, which operates successfully on huge data sets. The algorithm is designed based on a classical clustering algorithm, called PAM [8, 9] and a spanning tree-based clustering algorithm, called Clusterize [3]. It outperforms its counterparts both in clustering quality and execution time. The algorithm also better utilizes the computing resources associated with the clusterization process. The algorithm operates in linear time.

1   Introduction

With the ever-increasing growth in size and number of available databases, mining knowledge, regularities or high-level information from data becomes essential to support decision-making and predict future behavior [2, 4–6]. Data mining techniques can be classified into the following categories: classification, clustering, association rules, sequential patterns, time-series patterns, link analysis and text mining [2, 5, 11]. Due to its undirected nature, clustering is often the best technique to adopt first when a large, complex data set with many variables and many internal structures are encountered. Clustering is a process whereby a set of objects is divided into several clusters in which each of the members is in some way similar and is different from the members of other clusters [8–10, 12]. The most distinct characteristics of clustering analysis is that it often encounters very large data sets, containing millions of objects described by tens or even hundreds of attributes of various types (e.g., interval-scaled, binary, ordinal, categorical, etc.). This requires that a clustering algorithm be scalable and capable of handling different attribute types. However, most classical clustering algorithms either can handle various attribute types but are not efficient when clustering large data sets (e.g., the *PAM* algorithm [8, 9] or can handle large data sets efficiently but are limited to interval-scaled attributes (e.g., the k-means algorithm [1, 2, 7, 10].

In this context, several fast clustering algorithms have been proposed in the literature. Among which, *CLARA* [8] is one, which is designed based on a sampling approach and a classical clustering algorithm, called *PAM* [8, 9]. Instead of finding medoids, each of which is the most centrally located object in a cluster, for the entire data set, *CLARA* draws a sample from the data set and uses the *PAM* algorithm to select an optimal set of medoids from the sample. To alleviate sampling bias, *CLARA* repeats the sampling and clustering process multiple times and, subsequently, selects the best set of medoids as the final clustering.

Since *CLARA* adopts a sampling approach, the quality of its clustering results depends greatly on the size of the sample. When the sample size is small, *CLARA*'s efficiency in clustering large data sets comes at the cost of clustering quality. To overcome it, this paper presents a distributed k-medoid clustering algorithm, designed by utilizing the classical *PAM* and a weighted minimal spanning tree based clustering algorithm. The algorithm aims to offer better clustering quality and execution time, by economic utilization of the computing resources. It is scalable and operates in *linear time*.

Though the search strategies employed by both the clustering algorithms (i.e. *CLARA* and the *proposed* one are fundamentally same, the performances of the proposed algorithm in terms of clustering quality and execution time for clustering large data sets are significant over *CLARA*.

The remainder of the paper is organized as follows. Section 2 reviews the *CLARA* and *Clusterize*. Section 3 details the design of the proposed distributed clustering algorithm. A set of experiments based on synthetic data sets with pre-specified data characteristics was conducted on both the algorithms (i.e. *CLARA* and the proposed one), and the results are summarized in Section 4. Finally, the contributions of the paper is presented in Section 5.

2 Review

This section reviews *CLARA* and *Clusterize* in brief :

2.1 CLARA (Clustering LARge Applications)

It relies on the sampling approach to handle large data sets [8]. Instead of finding medoids for the entire data set, *CLARA* draws a small sample from the data set and applies the *PAM* algorithm to generate an optimal set of medoids for the sample. The quality of resulting medoids is measured by the average dissimilarity between every object in the entire data set D and the medoid of its cluster, defined as the following cost function:

$$Cost(M, D) = \frac{1}{N} \sum_{i=1}^{N} \sum_{v \in C_i} d(v, m_i)$$

where $M = \{m_1, m_2, \ldots, m_k\}$, where k is the cardinality of the set M and $C_i = \{v | d(v, m_i) \leq d(v, m_j) \forall j \neq i\}$. Here, N is the total number of data points and $D = \{v_1, v_2, \ldots, v_n\}$, where n is the cardinality of the set D.

To alleviate sampling bias, *CLARA* repeats the sampling and clustering process a pre-defined number of times and subsequently selects as the final clustering result the set of medoids with the minimal cost. Assume q to be the number of samplings. The *CLARA* algorithm is presented next:

> item Set mincost to a large number;
> Repeat q times
> > Create S by drawing s objects randomly from D;
> > Generate set of medoids M from S by applying PAM;
> > If Cost $(M, D) < mincost$ then
> > > $mincost = \text{Cost}(M, D)$;
> > > $bestset = M$;
> >
> > End-if;
>
> End-repeat;
> Return bestset;

For k number of medoids, the complexity of the above algorithm is $O((s^2 k.R + Nk)q)$, where R is the number of iterations required. As found in [12], for the sample size of $40 + 2k$ and for $q = 5$, the possible order of complexity of CLARA will be $O(Nkq)$ (as k is negligibly smaller than N), which is *linear* in order.

Since *CLARA* adopts a sampling approach, the quality of its clustering results depends greatly on the size of the sample. When the sample size is small, *CLARA*'s efficiency in clustering large data sets comes at the cost of clustering quality.

2.2 Clusterize

This algorithm operates on a m-dimensional space to construct a minimal spanning tree based on the 'weights' i.e. the distances computed for each pair of m-dimensional points. Next, subject to a defined '*distance threshold*' ϵ, it deletes those edges from the tree, which have equal or greater values than ϵ. It will decompose the original tree into k-connected 'subtrees' where each subtree will be a cluster. To represent each of these clusters, *Clusterize* finds the *medoid* for each cluster, by utilizing the 'center' concept for each tree. Next, the algorithm *Clusterize* is presented :

1 : Construct a minimal spanning tree τ for the input m-dim. data points;
2 : Apply '*threshold*', ϵ on τ to decompose it into k-sub-trees i.e. $\tau_1, \tau_2, \cdots, \tau_k$
  (where each τ_j corresponds to a cluster in the m-dim. space;
3 : determine the 'center' c_j $(j = 1, \cdots k)$ for each τ_j, which will be treated as
  a 'medoid' for the corresponding cluster;

The time complexity of the algorithm for finding the spanning tree over 2-D space is $O(elogn)$, where 'e' is the number of edges in the spanning tree and 'n' is the number of vertices. Now, as the algorithm operates over a m-dimensional space for finding k-medoids, the actual complexity will be $O(elogn \times m)$.

3 The Proposed Distributed Algorithm

The proposed algorithm adopts the following symbols and notations:

p, k $\longrightarrow$ no. of machines and medoids respectively;

$d(u, v)$ $\longrightarrow$ Eucledian distance between u and v;

N $\longrightarrow$ total number of points in the database;

m_j^i $\longrightarrow$ j-th medoid in the i-th machine ;

M^i $\longrightarrow$ set of medoids in the i-th machine ;

C_j^i $\longrightarrow$ j-th cluster in the i-th machine ;

$n(x)$ $\longrightarrow$ number of data points represented by a medoid x;

$$n(m_j^i) = |C_j^i|$$

R_i $\longrightarrow$ no. of iterations in the i-th machine and the maximum number of iterations, $R_{max} = \sum_{i=1}^{p} R_i$;

The proposed algorithm operates in six major steps. In step 1, each machine calls *Clusterize* to locally compute a set of k medoids, i.e. for the i-th machine, the set of medoids is $M^i = \{m_1^i, m_2^i, \ldots, m_k^i\}$ and set of clusters is $C^i = \{C_1^i, C_2^i, \ldots, C_k^i\}$. In step 2, a central machine gathers the set of all medoids m_j^i,(where $1 \leq i \leq p$ and $1 \leq j \leq k$). Then in step 3, the central machine computes the k-medoids by calling *PAM*, by using m_j^i's, and call them as $X_1, X_2, \ldots, X_k$, where each X_i represents a cluster Y_i. Here, $X = \{X_1, X_2, \ldots, X_k\} \subseteq M$ and $\cup_{i=1}^{k} Y_i = M$. Afterwards, it computes the 'weighted means' of the elements in Y_i as

$$\frac{1}{\max_{v \in Y_i} n(v)} \cdot \sum_{v \in Y_i} v(n(v)) = D_i$$

and communicates $D_1, D_2, \cdots D_k$ to each of the participating p-machines. In step 4, the i-th machine computes a set of k data points $u_1^i, u_2^i, \cdots u_k^i$ using D_i's, where each u_j^i is a point in the i-th machine closest to D_j. Step 5 involves in gathering the computed $(k \times p)$ points in the central machine and finally, in step 6, it computes the actual set of k-medoids i.e. $v_1, v_2, \cdots v_k$, where each $v_j \in \{u_j^1, u_j^2, \cdots u_j^p\}$ and $d(v_j, D_j) \leq d(u_j^i, D_j)$, for all i. The steps of the algorithm is presented next.

1. i-th machine calls *Clusterize* to compute k medoids $M^i = \{m_1^i, m_2^i, \cdots m_k^i\}$ and corresponding set of k clusters $C^i = \{C_1^i, C_2^i, \cdots C_k^i\}$.
2. Central machine gathers 'p' set of medoids (each of cardinality 'k') $M = \{m_j^i$,where $1 \leq j \leq k$ and $1 \leq i \leq p\}$
3. Central machine -
   3.1. computes k-medoids $\{X_1, X_2, \cdots X_k\} \subseteq M$ and set of the corresponding clusters $\{Y_1, Y_2, \cdots Y_k\}$ using *PAM*, where the cluster Y_i is represented by X_i and $\cup_{i=1}^{k} Y_i = M$.
   3.2. computes k-weighted means $D_1, D_2, \cdots D_k$,
      where $D_i = \frac{1}{\max_{v \in Y_i} (n(v))} \cdot \sum_{v \in Y_i} v(n(v))$;
   3.3. communicates $D_1, D_2, \cdots D_k$ to all the p machines;
4. i-th machine computes k data points $u_1^i, u_2^i, \cdots u_k^i$, where, each u_j^i is a point in the i-th machine closest to D_j;
5. Central machine gathers the p set of computed data points $V = \{u_j^i$, where $1 \leq i \leq p$ and $1 \leq j \leq k\}$;

6. Central machine computes the final set of k-medoids $v_1, v_2, \cdots v_k$, where $v_j \in \{u_j^1, u_j^2, \cdots u_j^p\}$ and $d(v_j, D_j) \leq d(u_j^i, D_j)$ for all i;

3.1 Complexity Analysis

The step-wise complexity analysis of *Disk_k_medoids* is as follows :

Step 1 computes the local medoids, approximately in time $O(\frac{elogn}{p})$. Next, for gathering the data, the time requirement of step 2 is $O(pk)$. Then, the central machine computes the k-medoids in step 3.1, in time $O(p^2k^2)$. In step 3.2, for k-weighted means computation, central machine requires $O(pk)$ and for communicating, similarly as found in step 2, the step 3.3 will require $O(pk)$ time. Step 4, for each i-th machine computation, will require $O(\frac{elogn}{p}.k)$ times and similarly, for gathering the $(p \times k)$ data points, step 5's time requirement will be $O(pk)$ and finally, for the optimum k-medoids computation, step 6 requires $O(pk)$ time;'

However, the complexities due to steps 2, 3.2, 3.3, 5 & 6 are dominated by the complexities offered by steps 1, 3.1 & 4. Among the dominating complexities, it can be seen that- step 1 contributes the major, and which is of *linear* in order.

4 Experimental Results

To justify the efficiency of the algorithm in comparison to *CLARA*, experiments were conducted using 12-dimensional tuple databases of various sizes (where, each tuple represents a document image, characterized with 12 features) on a HP Visualize Workstation (Linux-based) with Intel CPU clock rate 450 MHz and 128 MB RAM. For obtaining unbiased estimates, each experiment was carried out 15 times and an overall performance estimate was calculated by averaging the results of the 15 individual runs. *Table 1* depicts the average experimental results found.

As realised from the *Table*, in terms of the execution time, the proposed algorithm outperforms *CLARA* straightway. However, in terms of clustering quality, *CLARA* slightly outforms it in the initial runs, i.e. when given only a small data size (i.e. fewer than 4000). Later, with the increase of data size, the proposed algorithm can be found to be equally good with *CLARA*.

5 Conclusions

A new, scalable, distributed k-medoids algorithm, capable of dealing large set of data, has been presented in this paper. The algorithm outperforms *CLARA* both in cluster quality and in execution time. A set of experiments based on the 12-dimensional feature data- representing a document image database, was conducted to compare the performances of the proposed algorithm with its counterparts, and the results have been presented. There are futher scopes to improve the performance of the algorithm.

Table 1 : Comparison Results of the *Proposed* algorithm with *CLARA* (Assuming, $p = 5$ machines)

Database Size	No of Medoids k	Average Dissimilarity		Execution Time	
		CLARA	*proposed*	*CLARA*	*proposed*
1000	10	0.01693	0.01932	270	73
2000	10	0.01800	0.01820	540	120
3000	10	0.02120	0.01975	700	150
4000	10	0.02170	0.02085	810	180
5000	10	0.01960	0.02090	900	200
6000	10	0.02035	0.01870	1000	210
7000	10	0.02080	0.01778	1050	220
8000	10	0.01930	0.01740	1080	240

References

1. M. R. Anderberg, *Cluster Analysis for Applications*, Academic Press, Inc., 1973.
2. M. J. A. Berry and G. Linoff, *Data Mining Techniques: For Marketing, Sales, and Customer Support*, John Wiley & Sons, Inc., New York, NY, 1997.
3. D K Bhattacharyya, R K Das and S Nandi, *An Efficient Image Clustering Algorithm*, in Proc of CIT99, pp 244-249, TMH, 1999.
4. P. Cabena, P. Hadjinian, R. Stadler, J. Verhees, and A. Zanasi, *Discovering Data Mining: From Concept to Implementation*, Prentice Hall PTR, Upper Saddle River, NJ, 1998.
5. M. S. Chen, J. Han, and P. S. Yu, "Data Mining: An Overview from a Database Perspective," IEEE Transactions on Knowledge and Data Engineering, Vol. 8, No. 6, 1997.
6. W. Frawley, G. Piatetsky-Shapiro, and C. Matheus, "Knowledge Discovery in Databases: An Overview," AI Magazine, Fall 1992, pp.213-228.
7. A. K. Jain, and R. C. Dubes, *Algorithms for Clustering Data*, Prentice-Hall, Inc., 1988.
8. L. Kaufman and P. J. Rousseeuw, *Finding Groups in Data: An Introduction to Cluster Analysis*, John Wiley & Sons, Inc., New York, NY, 1990.
9. R. Ng and J. Han, "Efficient and Effective Clustering Methods for Spatial Data Mining," Proceedings of International Conference on Very Large Data Bases, Santiago, Chile, Sept. 1994, pp.144-155.
10. H. Spath, *Cluster Analysis Algorithms: For Data Reduction and Classification of Objects*, John Wiley & Sons, Inc., New York, 1980.
11. C. P. Wei, P. Hu, and L. M. Kung, "Multiple-Level Clustering Analysis for Data Mining Applications," Proceedings of the 4th INFORMS Joint Conference on Information Systems and Technology, May 1999.
12. M. Zait and H. Messatfa, "A Comparative Study of Clustering Methods," Future Generation Computer System, Vol. 13, 1997, pp.149-159.

A New Nonhierarchical Clustering Procedure for Symbolic Objects

T.V. Ravi and K. Chidananda Gowda

T.V.Ravi, GE – India Technology Centre, Upper Ground Floor, Unit I and II, Innovator Building, International Technology Park, Bangalore – 560 066. Tel: + 91 (80) 8410702 / 703 Fax : +91 (80) 8410704.
E mail : TV.Ravi@geind.ge.com.
K.Chidananda Gowda, Department of computer science and engineering, S. J. College of engineering, Mysore – 570 006, India. Tel : +91 (80) 512568, Fax: +91 (821) 515770.
E mail: kcgowda@blr.vsnl.net.in.

Abstract: A new nonhierarchical clustering procedure for symbolic objects is presented wherein during the first stage of the algorithm, the initial seed points are selected using the concept of farthest neighbours, and in suceeding stages the seed points are computed iteratively until the seed points get stabilised.

Keywords: Clustering, Symbolic objects, Symbolic similarity, Symbolic dissimilarity, Symbolic Mean.

1. Introduction:

The main objective of cluster analysis is to group a set of objects into clusters such that objects within the same cluster have a high degree of similarity, while objects belonging to different clusters have a high degree of dissimilarity. The clustering of a data set into subsets can be divided into hierarchical and nonhierarchical methods. The general rationale of a nonhierarchical method is to choose some initial partition of the data set and then alter cluster memberships so as to obtain a better partition according to some objective function. On the other hand, in hierarchical clustering methods, the sequence of forming groups proceeds such that whenever two samples belong (or do not belong) to the same cluster at some level, they remain together (or seperated) at all higher levels. Hierarchical clustering procedures can be divided into agglomerative methods, which progressively merge the elements, and divisive methods, which progressively subdivide the data set. A good survey of cluster analysis can be found in literature [1-6].

Symbolic objects are extensions of classical data types. In conventional data sets, the objects are "**individualised**" whereas in symbolic data sets, they are more "**unified**" by means of relationships. Symbolic objects are more complex than conventional data in the following ways[7] ;
1. All objects of a symbolic data set may not be defined on the same variables.
2. Each variable may take one value or an interval of values.
3. In complex symbolic objects, the values that the variables take may include one or more elementary objects.
4. The description of a symbolic object may depend on the relations existing between other objects.
5. The values that the variables take may include typicality values that indicate frequency of occurrence, relative likelihood, level of importance of the values and so on.

A non formal description of various types of symbolic objects can be found in [7]. Ichino [8,9] defines general distance functions for mixed feature variables and also defines generalised Minkowski metrics based on a new mathematical model called as the cartesian space model. Gowda and Diday [7,10] have proposed new similarity and dissimilarity measures and used it for agglomerative clustering of symbolic objects. They form composite symbolic objects using a cartesian join operator whenever mutual pairs of symbolic objects are selected for agglomeration based on minimum dissimilarity [7] or maximum similarity [10]. The combined usage of similarity and dissimilarity measures for agglomerative [11] and divisive clustering [12] of symbolic objects have been presented by Gowda and Ravi [11,12]. A survey of different techniques for handling symbolic data can be found in [13-18]. Most of the algorithms available in literature for clustering symbolic objects, are based on either conventional or conceptual hierarchical techniques using agglomerative or divisive methods as the core of the algorithm. In this paper, we propose a new nonhierarchical clustering scheme for symbolic objects.

The organisation of the paper is as follows: Section 2 discusses the notion of similarity and dissimilarity measures for symbolic objects, along with the concepts of farthest neighbour and composite symbolic object formation. The proposed nonhierarchical clustering scheme is presented in section 3 and section 4 discusses the experimental results. Section 5 concludes the paper.

2. Concepts and definitions:
a.Similarity and dissimilarity between symbolic objects:
Many distance measures are introduced in the literature for symbolic objects[7,8,9,10,11,12]. Here, we follow the similarity and dissimilarity measures introduced by Gowda and Ravi[12] along with a brief explanation of these measures. The similarity and dissimilarity between two symbolic objects A and B is written as, $S(A,B) = S(A_1,B_1) + ...S(A_k,B_k)$, and $D(A,B) = D(A_1,B_1) + ...+ D(A_k,B_k)$. For the k th feature, $S(A_k,B_k)$ and $D(A_k,B_k)$ are defined using the following components namely, $S_p(A_k,B_k)$ and $D_p(A_k,B_k)$ due to position, $S_s(A_k,B_k)$ and $D_s(A_k,B_k)$ due to span and $S_c(A_k,B_k)$ and $D_c(A_k,B_k)$ due to content. The advantages of the proposed similarity and dissimilarity measures are discussed in [11][12].

Quantitative interval type of A_k and B_k:
Let al , au and bl, bu represent lower and upper limit of interval A_k and B_k, inters=length of intersection of A_k and B_k, ls = span length of A_k and B_k = | max(au,bu) - min (al,bl) | where max() and min() represent maximum and minimum values respectively. The similarity and dissimilarity between two samples A_k and B_k is defined on position and span. Similarity due to position is defined as, $S_p(A_k,B_k) = \sin [(1- ((al -bl) / U_k)) * 90]$ and similarity due to span is defined as $S_s(A_k,B_k) = \sin [((la + lb) / (2* ls)) * 90]$, where U_k denotes the length of the maximum interval of the k th feature and la = | au -al| and lb = |bu - bl|. Net similarity between A_k and B_k is $S(A_k,B_k) = S_p(A_k,B_k) + S_s(A_k, B_k)$. Dissimilarity due to position is defined as $D_p(A_k,B_k) = \cos[(1- ((al - bl) / U_k)) * 90]$ and dissimilarity due to span is defined as $D_s(A_k,B_k) = \cos [((la\_lb) /(2*ls)) * 90]$. Net dissimilarity between A_k and B_k is $D(A_k,B_k) = D_p(A_k,B_k) + D_s(A_k,B_k)$.

Qualitative type of A_k and B_k:

For qualitiative type of features the similarity and dissimilarity component due to position are absent. The two components that contribute to similarity and dissimilarity are span and content. Let la and lb represent number of elements in A_k and B_k, inters = number of elements common to A_k and B_k, ls = span length of A_k and B_k combined = la + lb - inters. The similarity component due to span is defined as $S_s(A_k,B_k) = \sin[(la+lb) /(2*ls) *90]$ and the similarity component due to content is defined as, $S_c(A_k,B_k) = \sin[(inters/ls) * 90]$. Net similarity between A_k and B_k is $S(A_k,B_k) = S_s(A_k,B_k) + S_c(A_k,B_k)$. The dissimilarity due to span is defined as $D_s(A_k,B_k) = \cos[((la + lb) / (2*ls)) * 90]$, and the dissimilarity due to content is defined as, $D_c(A_k,B_k) = \cos[(inters/ls) *90]$. Net dissimilarity between A_k and B_k is $D(A_k,B_k) = D_s(A_k,B_k) + D_c(A_k,B_k)$.

b. Composite symbolic object:

Merging is the process of gathering together on the basis of a distance measure, two samples and assigning them the same cluster membership, or label for further clustering. If the two samples that are merged are to be represented by a single sample, one of the frequently used methods is to use the mean of the two as a single representative. In symbolic data analysis, the concept of composite symbolic object is made use of. The method of forming composite symbolic objects when two symbolic objects A_k and B_k are merged is as illustrated below:

Case I: When the K th feature is quantitative interval type: Let n = number of samples, m = mean of the n samples, a = lowest value considering n samples, n_1 = number of samples between a and m, n_2 = number of samples between b and m, n = $n_1 + n_2$, a'm = am * n_1/n, b'm = bm * n_2/n. Here, the length a'b' would represent the composite symbolic object.

Case II: When the K th feature is qualitative nominal: Here, the composite symbolic object is defined as the union of A_k and B_k.

c. Farthest neighbour concept:

Gowda[19] has introduced the concept of **"farthest neighbour"** and successfully used it for classification of multispectral data. In a data set, as the nearest neighbour B can be found for a sample A using a suitable metric, so also the farthest neighbour can be found for sample A. In a sample set, the farthest neighbour of a sample A can be defined as the sample C in the set which is at the greatest distance from A. In the same way, the farthest neighbour of a set of samples S can be defined as the sample which is at the greatest distance from the set S. This of course requires the defintion of distance between a set of samples and another sample outside the set. The distance d between a sample set S and a sample A outside the set is defined as d = a.b where a is the sum of distances from A to the samples in S and b is the distance between A and its nearest neighbour from set S.

3. Algorithm:

The nonhierarchical symbolic clustering algorithm proceeds as follows:

1. Let $\{X_1,X_2,...X_N\}$ be a set of N symbolic objects on k features. Let the initial number of clusters be N with each cluster having a cluster weight of unity.
2. Specify the number of clusters required as C.
3. Compute the dissimilarities between all pairs of symbolic objects in the data set as, $D(X_i,X_j) = D_1(X_i,X_j) + ...+ D_k(X_i,X_j)$, where $D_1(X_i,X_j)$, $D_2(X_i,.X_j)$ ...$D_k(X_i,X_j)$ are determined according to the type of the features.

4. Compute C farthest neighbours of the symbolic data set by making use of the dissimilarity values.
5. Choose the C farthest neighbours selected as the representative samples of C classes.
6. Make i=0;
7. Consider sample X_i of the symbolic data set. Compute the similarity between X_i and the C representative samples. Assign sample X_i to the class having highest similarity.
8. Make $i = i + 1$;
9. If $i ==N$ go to 10 or else go to 7.
10. Recompute the feature values of the C representative samples as the symbolic mean of the samples belonging to each class.
11. If any symbolic mean has changed its value go to 7 or else stop.
12. Merge all the samples of each class to form a composite symbolic object which would give the description of each class.

Symbolic Mean:
1. For quantitative type of data, the symbolic mean is computed as, $al_m = \Sigma_{i=1 \text{ to } n}$ al_i / n, $au_m = \Sigma_{i=1 \text{ to } n} au_i / n$ where al = lower limit of interval, au = upper limit of interval, n = total number of samples in a class.
2. The symbolic mean of qualitative data is computed by taking intoconsideration the number of times an attribute gets repeated.

4. Experimental Results:

In this section, the performance of the proposed algorithm is tested and evaluated using some test data reported in the literature. The data sets used in these experiments are synthetic or real data and their classification is known from other clustering techniques[7,10,11,12]. In order to compare the results of the proposed algorithm, the conventional nonhierarchcial algorithm was applied on the data sets, by randomly selecting the initial seed points of the classes. The clusters obtained using the proposed method were examined for their validity using Hubert's T statistics approach [4] and the level of significance values obtained were recorded. The simulation experiments are explained below:

Experiment 1: The first experiment is such that the input data is of numeric type and the output is symbolic. The objects of numeric type were drawn from a mixture of normal distributions with known number of classes and classification so that the results show the efficacy of the algorithm for clustering the objects and finding the number of classes. The test set is drawn from a mixture of C normal distributions with mean m_i and covariance matrix c_i having individual variances of 0.15 and zero covariances. The different values of the number of classes were 2,3,4,5,6,7,8 and the means chosen were (1,3) (1,3,5) (1,3,5,7) (1,3,5,7,9) (1,3,5,7,9,11) (1,3,5,7,9,11,13) and (1,3,5,7,9,11,13,15). These test samples were independently generated using a Gaussian vector generator. The proposed algorithm was used on this test data set. There was a perfect agreement between the number of classes used for generating Gaussian clusters and the number of classes obtained by the proposed algorithm. In all the seven cases, the classification results were in full agreement with the test samples generated and the classes used.

Experiment 2: The data set for this example is chosen so as to demonstrate the efficacy of the proposed algorithm in clustering data belonging to two classes with lots of overlaps. The data set used is the well known iris data set[4]. The proposed algorithm was applied on the two class iris data(iris setosa and iris versicolor) having 100 samples. The algorithm resulted in two classes which were in perfect agreement with the data set considered. For the two classes of iris data set, the proposed method took two iterations and resulted in a level of significance of 1.00. On the other hand, the conventional algorithm took three iterations and resulted in a level of significance of 1.00. It can be observed that the number of iterations taken by the proposed algorithm is less compared to the conventional algorithm.

Experiment 3: The data set[8] used for this problem consists of data of fats and oils having four quantitative features of interval type and one qualitiative feature. The proposed algorithm was applied on this data set specifying two classes. The samples of the two classes obtained were as follows: {0,1,2,3,4,5} and {6,7}. For the fat oil data set, the proposed algorithm took two iterations and resulted in a level of significance of 0.98. On the other hand, the conventional algorithm took three iterations and resulted in a level of significance of 0.78. It can be observed that the proposed method gives a higher level of significance value and also takes less number of iterations compared to the conventional algorithm.

Experiment 4: The data set of microcomputers[8] is considered for this experiment. The proposed algorithm was tested on this data set by specifying the number of classes as two. The. proposed algorithm took two iterations and resulted in a level of significance of 0.90. On the other hand, the conventional algorithm took three iterations and resulted in a level of significance of 0.82. It can be observed that the proposed method gives a higher level of significance values and takes less number of iterations compared to the conventional algorithm.

Experiment 5: The data set of microprocessors[9] is considered for this experiment. The proposed algorithm was tested on this data set by specifying the number of classes as three. The samples of the three classes obtained were, {0,1,4,5} {3,7,8} and {2,6}. For the microprocessor data set, the proposed algorithm took three iterations and resulted in a level of significance of 0.91. On the other hand, the conventional algorithm took four iterations and resulted in a level of significance of 0.84. It can be observed that the proposed method gives a higher level of significance value and takes less number of iterations compared to the conventional algorithm.

Experiment 6: The data set for this experiment is considered from Botany[8]. It consists of 9 trees belonging to 3 classes. The proposed algorithm for three class case resulted in the following : {0,1,2} {3,4,5} and {6,7,8}. For the botanical data, the proposed algorithm took two iterations and resulted in a level of significance of 1.00. On the other hand, the conventional algorithm took three iterations and resulted in a level of significance of 1.00. It can be observed that the proposed method takes less number of iterations compared to the conventional algorithm.

From the experimental results, it can be seen that the proposed algorithm shows an improvement over the conventional algorithm both in terms of quality of clustering obtained and the number of iterations required.

5. **Conclusion:**

A nonhierarchical clustering procedure for symbolic objects is presented. In the first stage, the initial seed points are selected using the concept of farthest neighbours. During suceeding stages, the seed points are computed iteratively until the seed points get stabilised. The proposed nonhierarchcial clustering procedure works on symbolic data of mixed feature types consisting of quantitaitve (ratio, absolute, interval) and qualitiative (nominal, ordinal, combinational) values. Several artificial and real life data with known number of classes and classification assignments are used to establish the efficacy of the proposed algorithm and the results are presented.

References

1. E.Diday and J.C.Simon, *Clustering Analysis :Communication and Cybernetics, Vol 10, NewYork, Springer Verlag, 1976, pp. 47 - 92.*
2. E.Diday, C.Hayashi, M.Jambu and N.Ohsumi, Eds, *Recent developments in clustering and data analysis,* NewYork: Academic, 1987.
3. H.H.Bock, Ed, *Classification and related methods of data analysis,* Amsterdam: North Hol!and, 1987.
4. A.K.Jain and R.C.Dubes, *Algorithms for clustering data,* Englewood Cliffs, NJ: Prentice Hall, 1988.
5. E.Diday, Ed., *Data analysis, learning symbolic and numeric knowledge,* Antibes, France: Nova Science Publishers, 1989.
6. R.O.Duda and P.E.Hart, *Pattern classification and scene analysis,* NewYork: Wiley Interscience, 1973.
7. K.C.Gowda and E.Diday, "Symbolic clustering using a new dissimilarity measure", *Pattern Recognition, Vol 24,* No. 6, pp. 567 - 578, 1991.
8. M.Ichino, "General metrics for mixed features - The cartesian space theory for pattern recognition", in proc. *IEEE Conf. Systems, Man and Cybernetics,* Atlanta, GA, pp. 14-17, 1988.
9. M.Ichino and H.Yaguchi, "General Minkowsky metric for mixed feature type", *IEEE transactions on Systems, Man and Cybernetics, Vol 24,* pp. 698-708, 1994.
10. K.C.Gowda and E.Diday, "Symbolic clustering using a new similarity measure", *IEEE transactions on Systems, Man and Cybernetics, Vol 22,* No. 2, pp. 368-378, 1992.
11. K.C.Gowda and T.V.Ravi,"Agglomerative clustering of symbolic objects using the concepts of both similarity and dissimilarity", *Pattern Recognition Letters 16 (1995),* pp. 647-652.
12. K.C.Gowda and T.V.Ravi, "Divisive clustering of symbolic objects using the concepts of both similarity and dissimilarity", *Pattern Recognition, Vol 28,* No. 8, pp. 1277-1282, 1995.
13. E.Diday, *The symbolic approach in clustering, classification and related methods of data analysis,* H.H.Bock, Ed. Amsterdam, The Netherlands: Elsevier, 1988.
14. D.H.Fisher and P.Langley, "Approaches to conceptual clustering", in *Proc. 9 th International Joint Conference on Artificial Intelligence,* Los Angeles, CA, 1985, pp. 691 - 697.
15. R.Michalski, R.E.Stepp and E.Diday, " A recent advance in data analysis: clustering objects into classes characterized by conjuctive concepts," *Progress in Pattern Recognition, Vol 1,* L. Kanal and A. Rosenfeld, eds (1981).
16. R.Michalski and R.E.Stepp, "Automated construction of classifications: Conceptual clustering versus numerical taxonomy", *IEEE transactions Pattern Analysis and Machine Intelligence,* PAMI - 5, pp. 396 -410, 1983
17. Y.Cheng and K.S.Fu, "Conceptual clustering in knowledge organisation", *IEEE transactions Pattern Analysis and Machine Intelligence,* PAMI - 7, pp. 592-598, 1985.

18. D.H.Fisher, "Knowledge acquisition via incremental conceputal clustering", *Machine Learning, No. 2,* pp. 103-138, 1987.
19. K.C.Gowda, " A feature reduction and unsupervised classification algorithm for multispectral data", *Pattern Recognition, Vol 17,* No. 6, pp 667 - 676, 1984.

Quantization of Continuous Input Variables for Binary Classification

Michał Skubacz[1] and Jaakko Hollmén[2]

[1] Siemens Corporate Technology, Information and Communications, Neural Computation, 81730 Munich, Germany, Michal.Skubacz@mchp.siemens.de
[2] Helsinki University of Technology, Laboratory of Computer and Information Science, P.O. Box 5400, 02015 HUT, Finland, Jaakko.Hollmen@hut.fi

Abstract Quantization of continuous variables is important in data analysis, especially for some model classes such as Bayesian networks and decision trees, which use discrete variables. Often, the discretization is based on the distribution of the input variables only whereas additional information, for example in form of class membership is frequently present and could be used to improve the quality of the results. In this paper, quantization methods based on equal width interval, maximum entropy, maximum mutual information and the novel approach based on maximum mutual information combined with entropy are considered. The two former approaches do not take the class membership into account whereas the two latter approaches do. The relative merits of each method are compared in an empirical setting, where results are shown for two data sets in a direct marketing problem, and the quality of quantization is measured by mutual information and the performance of Naive Bayes and C5 decision tree classifiers.

1 Introduction

Whereas measurements in many real-world problems are continuous, it may be desirable to represent the data as discrete variables. The discretization simplifies the data representation, improves interpretability of results, and makes data accessible to more data mining methods [6]. In decision trees, quantization as a pre-processing step is preferable to local quantization process as part of the decision tree building algorithm [1,4]. In this paper, quantization of continuous variables is considered in a binary classification problem. Three standard quantization approaches are compared to the novel approach, which attempts to balance the quality of input representation (measured by entropy) and the class separation (measured by mutual information).

The comparison of the four approaches to quantization is performed on two data sets from a direct marketing problem. Mutual information, Naive Bayes classifier, and C5 decision tree [8] are used in measuring the quality of the quantizations.

2 Quantization

Quantization, also called discretization, is the process of converting a continuous variable into a discrete variable. The discretized variable has a finite number of values (J), the number usually being considerably smaller than the number of possible values in the empirical data set. In the binary classification problem, a data sample $(\mathbf{x}_i, y_i)_{i=1}^{N}$ and $y_i \in \{0, 1\}$ is available. Variable $\mathbf{x}_i \in I\!R^k$ is a vector of variables on a continuous scale. In the quantization process, the component k of the x_i later denoted by x_{ik}, is mapped to the discrete counterpart x'_{ik} when the original variable x_{ik} belongs to the interval defined by the lower and upper bounds of the bin. The number of data falling into a bin j is defined as n_{kj} and the probability of a bin as $p_{kj} = \frac{n_{kj}}{N}$.

One could approach the discretization process in many different ways, starting for example from naive testing of random configurations and selecting the best one for a particular problem. More structured approaches may consider discretizing all variables at the same time (global), or each one separately (local). The methods may use all of the available data at every step in the process (global) or to concentrate on a subset of data (local) according to the current level of discretization. Decision trees, for instance, are usually local in both senses. Furthermore, two following search procedures could be employed. The top-down approach [4] starts with a small number of bins, which are iteratively split further. The bottom-up approach [5], on the other hand, starts with a large number of narrow bins which are iteratively merged. In both cases, a particular split or merge operation is based on a defined performance criterion, which can be global (defined for all bins) or local (defined for two adjacent bins only). An example of a local criteria was presented in [5].

In this paper, a globally defined performance criterion is optimized using a greedy algorithm. In each iteration of the one-directional greedy algorithm, a most favorable action at the time is chosen. In the initial configuration one allocates a large number of bins to a variable and starts merging two adjacent bins by choosing the most favorable merge operation. The approaches used in this paper are local in the sense that variables are discretized separately and global in the sense that all the available data are used in every step of the quantization process. Discretizing variables separately assumes independence between them, an assumption which is usually violated in practice. However, this simplifies the algorithms and makes them scalable to large data sets with many variables. In contemporary data mining problems, these attributes become especially important. In a real situations, one particular value on the continuous scale may occur very frequently overwhelming the entire distribution of the variable. For example, the field "total length of the international telephone calls" for a particular private customer is likely to be predominately filled with zeros. This situation corresponds to a peak in the probability density function and can lead to the deterioration of the quantization process. If this is detected, for example by checking if a given value appears in more than 60% of the samples, a dedicated interval should be allocated and these samples removed from the discretization process.

Equal Width Interval By far the simplest and most frequently applied method of discretization is to divide the range of data to a predetermined number of bins [6]. Each bin is by construction equally wide, but the probabilities of the bins may vary according to the data. In classification problems, this approach ignores the information about the class membership of data assigned to each bin.

Maximum Entropy An alternative method is to create bins so that each bin equally contributes to the representation of the input data. In other words, probability of each bin for the data should be approximately equal. In fact, this is achieved by maximizing the entropy of the binned data. The entropy for the binned variables may be defined as $H_k = \sum_{j=1}^{J} p_{kj} \log p_{kj}$, where the sum is over all bins. Entropy has been used in context of discretizing variables in [9].

Maximum Mutual Information In classification problems, it is important to optimize the quantized representation with regard to the distribution of the output variable. In order to measure information about the output preserved in the discretized variable, mutual information may be employed [3]. Mutual information was used in the discretization process of the decision tree construction algorithm (ID3) in [7]. Mutual information is measured in terms of quantized variables as

$$I_k = \sum_{j=1}^{J} P(b_{kj}, y = 1) \log \frac{P(b_{kj}, y = 1)}{P(b_{kj})P(y = 1)} + P(b_{kj}, y = 0) \log \frac{P(b_{kj}, y = 0)}{P(b_{kj})P(y = 0)}$$

Maximum Mutual Information with Entropy By combining the maximum entropy and the mutual information approaches, one hopes to obtain a solution with the merits of both. This should strike a balance between the representation of the input and the knowledge of the output variable at the same time. In other words, one would like to retain balanced bins that turn out to be more reliable (prevent overfitting in this context) but simultaneously to optimize the binning for classification. Our greedy algorithm is based on a criterion function which is the product of the mutual information and the maximum entropy as

$$G_k = H_k I_k.$$

The greedy algorithm approximates the gradient ascent optimization. Writing the gradient of the product of two functions as $\frac{\partial f(x;\theta)g(x;\theta)}{\partial \theta} = f'(x;\theta)g(x;\theta) + g'(x;\theta)f(x;\theta)$, we note that the search direction is driven by the balance of the two factors subject to constraints imposed by data. A similar measure involving mutual information divided by entropy was proposed in the context of discretization in [8]. However, the measure was used for the problem of binary discretization in splitting operation. Our novel approach assumes discretization into several bins and the comparison is done among all merging operations.

3 Experiments

Two data sets were used in the evaluation. Both of them were collected and used in direct marketing campaigns. The input variables represented customer information and the output was the customer's binary response. The data set 1 consisted of 144 input variables and 12496 samples whereas the data set 2 had 75 input variables and 35102 samples. The first data set was artificially balanced to contain an equal number of positive and negative responses, in the second data set only one tenth of the samples belonged to the positive response class as in usually strongly imbalanced direct marketing problems. The evaluation criteria used for measuring the influence of the discretization procedure on the classification problem were mutual information, predicted 50 % response rate based on Naive Bayes, and classification accuracy of C5 classifier. Each experiment was conducted with a randomly selected training set and a testing set of the same size, the results shown are based on the testing set. All the experiments were repeated 25 times. In the case of mutual information, all the variables of each data set were discretized and the mutual information of the discretized variable and the output variable were measured on the test data. From each data set, 10 most relevant variables were chosen and in order to create different subproblems randomly selected subsets of four variables were used for building classifiers. Using response rate together with the Naive Bayes, the possibly imbalanced class priors present in the data do not have any effect. In C5 classifier, a fixed cost matrix was given to flatten out the imbalanced class distribution. All the experiments were repeated with the goal of discretizing the continuous variables to 4, 6, and 8 bins. The results are shown in terms of relative performance in Fig 1.

4 Discussion

Measuring the relative scores by mutual information, the approaches that take into account the class membership of data prove to be superior. Ranking of the methods remains the same in both the balanced and the imbalanced data sets. In general, the addition of bins improves the performance of the discretization methods. Moreover, the mutual information approach is better than the novel method in case of low number of bins, whereas the novel method was superior when the number of bins was bigger, even though mutual information is used as the assessment measure. The importance of the entropy term in the novel method increases along the number of bins. Of the simple methods, which ignore the available output information in the classification problem, the entropy-based method is better than the equal width interval method.

Using 50 % response rate based on Naive Bayes classifier, results are somewhat more difficult to interpret. In this case it is important to note that each variable is treated separately, which is likely to increase the independence of the discretized variables compared with the original ones. It seems that the novel method is superior to all other methods, although the large variance on the estimates makes this subject to a debate. For example, in the case of data set 1 and the experiment with eight intervals, the median of the novel method is the best, 75 % confidence interval is similar to others, and finally the 95 % confidence limits are much worse than in the case of mutual information. On the other hand, the median performance of the novel method proves to be the best in most cases.

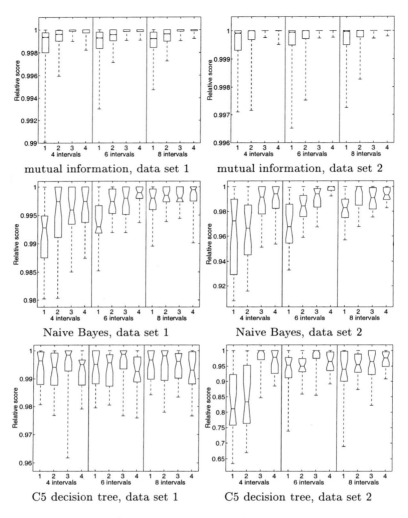

mutual information, data set 1   mutual information, data set 2

Naive Bayes, data set 1   Naive Bayes, data set 2

C5 decision tree, data set 1   C5 decision tree, data set 2

Figure1. Relative scores of the discretization methods measured mutual information are shown for the data set 1 (first row, left panel) and data set 2 (first row, right panel). Relative scores of the discretization methods measured by 50 % response rate of Naive Bayes are shown for the data set 1 (second row, left panel) and data set 2 (second row, right panel). Relative scores of the discretization methods measured by classification performance achieved with C5 classifier are shown for the data set 1 (third row, left panel) and data set 2 (third row, right panel). In all figures, the horizontal axis is divided to three sections for experiments with four, six and eight bins. The order of discretization methods in each section is equal width interval (1), maximum entropy (2), maximum mutual information (3), and maximum mutual information with entropy(4). The performance of repeated experiments are visualized with median, 25 % and 75 % percentiles. In addition, 95 % confidence interval is shown with dashed lines.

In case of a C5 classifier, none of the methods outperforms others, especially on the first data set. The variance of the estimates is also relatively large as to make accurate judgments. In the second data set, however, equal width interval approach is clearly worse than the other presented methods. One possible reason for the questionable performance of the tree classifier could be that our discretization works for each input variable separately, whereas optimal creation of the decision tree would take into account the interdependencies between variables. Using the novel discretization method, these interdependencies are essentially ignored and the solution is likely to weaken the interdependencies between discretized input variables. Taking all the variables into account at the same time may be seen beneficial in this context as proposed in [2].

5 Summary

Methods for quantizing continuous input variables in classification problems were presented. Relative merits of the equal width interval, maximum entropy, maximum mutual entropy and the novel maximum mutual information with entropy approaches were compared with two data sets from direct marketing problems using three criteria. Concluding, none of the tested approaches would be preferred over others whenever the C5 decision tree is to be used for modeling. On the other hand, the novel method proposed in this paper would be recommended for Naive Bayes classifiers where it may lead to performance improvements.

References

1. J. Catlett. On changing continuous attributes into ordered discrete attributes. In *Machine Learning - EWSL-91*, volume 482, pages 164–178. Springer, March 1991.
2. Michał R. Chmielewski and Jerzy W. Grzynala-Busse. Global discretization of continuous attributes as preprocessing for machine learning. *International Journal of Approximate Reasoning*, 15:319–331, 1996.
3. Thomas M. Cover and Joy A. Thomas. *Elements of Information theory*. Wiley Series in telecommunications. John Wiley & Sons, 1991.
4. Usama M. Fayyad and Keki B. Irani. Multi-interval discretization of continuous-valued attributes for classification learning. In *Proceedings of IJCAI-93*, volume 2, pages 1022–1027. Morgan Kaufmann Publishers, August/September 1993.
5. R. Kerber. Chimerge: Discretization of numeric attributes. In *Proceedings of the Tenth National Conference on Artificial Intelligence*, pages 123–128. AAAI Press/MIT Press, 1992.
6. Huan Liu and Hiroshi Motoda. *Feature selection for knowledge discovery and data mining*. Kluwer International Series in Engineering and Computer Science, Secs 454. Kluwer Academic Publishers, 1998.
7. J. Quinlan. Induction of decision trees. *Machine Learning*, 1(1):81–106, 1986.
8. J. Ross Quinlan. *C4.5 : Programs for Machine Learning*. Morgan Kaufmann Series in Machine Learning. Kluwer Academic Publishers, 1993.
9. A.K.C. Wong and D.K.Y. Chiu. Synthesizing statistical knowledge from incomplete mixed-mode data. *IEEE Transactions on Pattern Analysis and Machine Intelligence*, 9(6):796–805, 1987.

Information-Based Classification
by Aggregating Emerging Patterns

Xiuzhen Zhang[1], Guozhu Dong[2], and Kotagiri Ramamohanarao[1]

[1] Department of CSSE, The University of Melbourne, Vic 3010, Australia
[2] Department of CSE, Wright State University, OH 45435, USA

Abstract. Emerging patterns (EPs) are knowledge patterns capturing contrasts between data classes. In this paper, we propose an information-based approach for classification by aggregating emerging patterns. The constraint-based EP mining algorithm enables the system to learn from large-volume and high-dimensional data; the new approach for selecting representative EPs and efficient algorithm for finding the EPs renders the system high predictive accuracy and short classification time. Experiments on many benchmark datasets show that the resulting classifiers have good overall predictive accuracy, and are often also superior to other state-of-the-art classification systems such as C4.5, CBA and LB.

1 Introduction

Classification has long been studied within the machine learning community. Recently, it has also attracted attention from the data mining community, which focused on important issues such as ways to deal with large volume of training data and to achieve higher predictive accuracy [7, 3, 6]. In this paper, we address these issues by proposing a classifier, iCAEP, which performs *i*nformation-based *C*lassification by *A*ggregating *E*merging *P*atterns.

Emerging patterns (EPs) are multi-variate knowledge patterns capturing differences between data classes [2]. For example, e_1 and e_2 are EPs of the Benign and Malignant classes, of the Wisconsin-breast-cancer dataset [1] respectively: e_1=`{(Bare-Nuclei,1),(Bland-Chromatin,3),(Normal-Nucleoli,1),(Mitoses,1)}` e_2=`{Clump-Thickness, 10)}`. Their supports in the whole dataset and in the two classes, and their growth rates (support ratios) are listed below. [2]

EP	support	Malignant_support	Benign_support	growth_rate
e_1	13.45%	0.41%	20.31%	49.54
e_2	28.63%	28.63%	0%	∞

In a classification task, EPs of a class can be seen as the distinguishing features of the class, whose power is indicated by their support and growth rate. In the above example, given a test instance T, if T only contains e_2, we tend to assign T to the Malignant class. However, intricacy arises when T contains EPs of both the Benign and Malignant classes. In iCAEP, rather than relying on a single EP to make decision, we select representative EPs from all the EPs that appear in T for a more reliable decision. Each EP is seen as a message indicating class bias of T. By aggregating the contribution of EPs in an information-based

---

[1] http://www.ics.uci.edu/~mlearn/MLRepository.html
[2] See § 2 for definitions.

approach, we reach a reliable classification decision, taking into consideration the predictive power of EPs and the unbalanced densities of EPs in each class.

We also aim to tackle large-volume and high-dimensional classification tasks. For example, the UCI Connect-4 dataset, consisting of 67,557 instances defined by 42 attributes, is a great challenge to mining algorithms. In iCAEP, at the training stage, the constraint-based mining algorithm ConsEPMiner [12] is adapted to efficiently mine EPs from large high-dimensional datasets; at the classification stage, we propose a new approach to select representative EPs and an algorithm to efficiently find such EPs for classifying a test instance.

Experiments show that, iCAEP is often superior to other state-of-the-art classifiers in classification accuracy, the constraint-based EP mining approach significantly improves training time, the new classification strategy significantly improves classification time. iCAEP can successfully learn from challenging real-world large-volume and high-dimensional training datasets, including Connect-4.

2 Information-based Classification by Aggregating EPs

We assume that datasets are relational tables, where each instance takes a value for each attribute. We preprocess the datasets as follows: Continuous attribute domains are first discretized into disjoint intervals, and each attribute value is mapped to the interval containing it. An (attribute, interval) or (attribute, value) pair is mapped into an item. An instance T defined by n attributes is then mapped to an itemset of n items: $\{a_1, a_2, ..., a_n\}$. The *support* of an itemset X in a dataset D, $supp_D(X)$, is $\frac{|\{t \in D | X \subseteq t\}|}{|D|}$. Given background dataset D' and target dataset D'', the growth rate of an itemset X from D' to D'' is $GR(X) = \frac{supp_{D''}(X)}{supp_{D'}(X)}$ ("define" $\frac{0}{0} = 0$ and $\frac{\geq 0}{0} = \infty$); EPs from D' to D'', or simply EPs of D'', are itemsets whose growth rate is greater than some given threshold ρ ($\rho > 1$). A training dataset D of m classes is partitioned into D_1, ..., D_m, where D_i consists of training instances with class label C_i. The EP set for class C_i, E_i, consists of EPs from $D - D_i$ to D_i.

We employ the minimum encoding inference approach to classify a test instance, using EPs appearing in the instance as messages. According to the Minimum Message Length (MML) [10] or Minimum Description Length (MDL) [9] principle, to assess the quality of a model m_i for a dataset, we construct a description of the model and of the data in terms of the model; a good model is one leading to a concise total description, i.e., its total description length for the theory and data encoded under the theory is minimum. For a training dataset D of m classes, the set of EPs E for all classes, $E = E_1 \cup E_2 \cup ... \cup E_m$, forms a model (theory) for the dataset. For a test instance T, the theory description length is the same, but the encoding length of T under different class assumptions can be different. An EP of E_j, with its contrasting high support in D_j and low support in D_i ($i \neq j$), is a message whose encoding cost is the smallest in C_j among all $C_k (1 \leq k \leq m)$. We select representative EPs from m classes to encode T (see § 3.2):

$$E^T = \bigcup_{j=1}^{m} E_j^T, \ E_j^T = \{X_k \in E_j | k = 1..p_j\} \ is \ a \ partition \ of \ T$$

Note that we consider representative EPs of all classes to decide T's label and this ensures that our decision will not be influenced by the differences in EP sets E_j ($j = 1..m$), such as the number, density of EPs, etc.

Following [11], if a message X_k occurs with probability P_k, we postulate an encoding scheme where the cost of encoding X_k requires $-log_2(P_k)$ bits. The encoding length of T under the assumption of class C_i is defined to be the total cost of encoding EPs in E^T:

$$L(T||C_i) = -\sum_{k=1}^{p} log_2 P(X_k|C_i), \ X_k \in E^T$$

We assign T the class label C_i where $L(T||C_i)$ is the minimum. From a probabilistic point of view, we are "estimating" and ranking $P(T|C_i)$ by aggregating the EPs in a test instance. If T indeed belongs to class C_i, $P(T|C_i)$ should be the maximum; since $P(T|C_i)$ is proportional to $-L(T||C_i)$, $P(T|C_i)$ is the maximum when $L(T||C_i)$ is the minimum.

2.1 Estimating probability

The support (observed frequency) of an itemset can be an unreliable substitution for its probability, especially when the data sets are small or when the training data contains noise. A typical example is a special type of EPs — jumping EPs with a growth rate of $\infty(= \frac{\geq 0}{0})$. To eliminate unreliable estimates and zero-supports, we adopt standard statistical techniques to incorporate a small-sample correction into the observed frequency. In our experiments, given an itemset X, we approximate $P(X|C_i)$ by $\frac{\#(X \wedge C_i)+2\frac{\#X}{\#D}}{\#C_i+2}$, where $\#(X \wedge C_i)$ is the number of training instances belonging to class C_i and containing X, $\#X$ is the total number of training instances containing X, $\#D$ is the total number of training instances, and $\#C_i$ is the number of training instances for class C_i.

3 Algorithms

We describe here the algorithms for efficiently mining EPs at the learning stage and for finding representative EPs for classification at the classification stage.

3.1 Constraint-based approach to mining EPs

On large and high-dimensional datasets, a large number of long EPs appear and this brings challenge to the Apriori [1] mining framework — the number of candidate EPs grow combinatorially. Given target support threshold $minsupp$, growth rate threshold $minrate$, growth-rate improvement threshold $minrateimp$, (for an EP e, the growth-rate improvement of e, $rateimp(e)$ is $min(\forall e' \subset e, GR(e) - GR(e'))$,) ConsEPMiner [12] uses all constraints for effectively controlling the blow-up of candidate EPs and can successfully mine EPs at low support threshold from large high-dimensional datasets; especially, the growth-rate improvement threshold ensures a concise resulting EP set that represents all EPs. In iCAEP, we made the following extensions to ConsEP-Miner for classification purpose: (1) In mining the EPs for class C_i, we compute their support in target D_i, background $D - D_i$, as well as all the other datasets D_j, $j \neq i$. (2) All single-item itemsets are in the EP set of each class, whether they satisfy the given thresholds or not. This ensures that we can always find a partition for an instance.

3.2 Selecting representative EPs for classification

Given a test instance T, a partition of T is a set of itemsets $\{X_1, ..., X_p\}$, where $\cup_{k=1}^{p} X_k = T$ and $X_{k_1} \cap X_{k_2} = \phi(k_1 \neq k_2)$. From E_j, the set of EPs for class C_j, we select disjoint EPs to form the representative EP set E_j^T to encode T. Long itemsets with many items are obviously preferred, as they provide more information about the higher order interactions between attributes. Among the itemsets of equal length, we prefer those of larger growth rate. We organize E_j in a hash tree. EPs are hashed first on their length and then their first item. At each hash node, EPs are organized in decreasing order of their growth rate. We search the hash tree in decreasing order of length and decreasing order of growth rate. This ensures that we always find the most representative EPs of the relevant subtree for the items of T that do not appear in any so-far selected EPs. The search finishes when a partition of T is found.

```
SelectEP(test instance T, the hash tree Tr for E_j)
;; return E_j^T, the set of representative EPs from E_j to encode T
1)   ll ← |T|;  F ← φ;
2)   while T ≠ φ do
3)       for each item t ∈ T do
4)           if ∃X ⊆ T at the node Tr[ll][t] then
5)               found ← 1, F ← F ∪ {X}, T ← T − X, break;
6)       if found=1 then ll ← the smaller of |T| and ll;
7)       else ll ← ll − 1;
8)   retrun F;
```
Fig. 1. Algorithm SelectEP

4 Experiments

We use 24 UCI datasets to evaluate iCAEP. We compare it with CAEP [3], the first EP-based classifier, Naive Bayes(NB), a surprisingly successful classifier compared with more complicated classifiers, C4.5, the widely-known decision tree classifier, and two recent classifiers from the data mining community: LB [8], an extension to NB based on frequent itemsets, and CBA [6], a classifier using association rules [1] for classification. Entropy-based discretization [4] is used to discretize continuous attributes, where the code is taken from the MLC++ machine learning library. [3]

Table 1 describes the datasets and presents the accuracy of different classifiers. The accuracy of iCAEP, CAEP and NB are obtained on exactly the same 10-fold cross validation (CV-10) data. Note that the accuracy of iCAEP and CAEP is obtained without fine tuning any parameters, whereas that of CBA and LB is according to reported CV-10 result in literature. Numbers in bold are the best accuracy for each dataset and '—' indicates that the result is not available in literature. In the CV-10 experiments of CAEP and iCAEP, ConsEPMiner

---
[3] http://www.sgi.com/Technology/mlc/

Table 1. Description of datasets and summary of accuracy

Dataset	Dataset Properties			Accuracy(%)					
	Size	#Cls	#Attr	iCAEP	CAEP	NB	C4.5	CBA	LB
Adult	45,225	2	14	80.88	83.09	83.81	**85.4**	75.21	—
Annealing process	898	6	38	95.06	85.74	96.99	90.4	**98.1**	—
Australian credit approval	690	2	14	**86.09**	78.55	85.51	84.28	85.51	85.65
Breast cancer(Wisc.)	699	2	9	**97.42**	97.00	97.14	95.42	95.28	96.86
Chess(k_rook-k_pawn)	3,169	2	36	94.59	85.45	87.92	**99.5**	98.12	90.24
Connect-4	67,557	3	42	69.90	**72.97**	72.13	—	—	—
German	1,000	2	20	73.10	73.30	74.40	71.7	73.2	**74.8**
Haberman	306	2	3	**71.52**	**71.52**	69.91	—	—	—
Heart diseasse (Cleve.)	303	2	13	80.25	82.52	**82.87**	78.4	81.87	82.22
Hepatitis prognosis	155	2	19	83.33	81.96	**84.62**	81.6	80.2	84.5
Hypothyroid diagnosis	3,163	2	25	96.40	96.49	98.42	**98.8**	98.4	—
Ionosphere	351	2	34	90.60	87.21	89.45	92	**92.1**	—
Iris	150	3	4	93.33	94.00	93.33	**94.7**	92.9	—
Labor	57	2	16	**89.67**	79.33	86.33	79	83	—
Lymphography	148	4	18	79.76	74.38	78.33	78.39	77.33	**84.57**
Mushroom	8124	2	22	**99.81**	93.04	99.68	—	—	—
Nursery	12,961	5	8	84.66	84.37	**90.28**	—	—	—
Pima	768	2	8	72.27	73.30	74.74	72.5	73.1	**75.77**
Solar flare (X class)	1,388	3	10	92.00	89.34	**96.32**	84.4	—	—
Spambase	4,601	2	57	**91.18**	86.42	89.87	—	—	—
Tic-tac-toe	958	2	9	92.06	85.91	70.15	86.3	**100**	—
Vehicle	846	4	18	62.76	55.92	59.57	**69.82**	68.78	68.8
Waveform	5,000	3	21	81.68	**83.92**	80.76	70.4	75.34	79.43
Wine	178	3	13	**98.89**	96.08	89.90	87.9	91.6	—

is employed to mine EPs, with the following settings: $minsupp = 1\%$ or a count of 5, whichever is larger, $minrate = 5$, $minrateimp = 0.01$. We also limit the size of EP set of each class to 100,000 EPs. At the classification stage, the base normalization score for CAEP is set to 85%. We can draw several conclusions from the table: (1) In terms of the best accuracy for each dataset, iCAEP wins on 7 datasets, whereas C4.5, NB, CAEP CBA and LB win on 5, 4, 3, 3 and 3 datasets respectively. (2) In terms of overall performance, the average accuracy of iCAEP, CAEP and NB is 85.72%, 82.99%, and 84.68%; iCAEP is the best. (3) With ConsEPMiner, both iCAEP and CAEP can successfully classify all datasets, including the challenging large-volume high-dimensional datasets like Connect-4 (67,557 instances, 42 attributes, 126 items) and Spambase (4,601 instances, 57 attributes, 152 items). Compared with CAEP, at the training stage, iCAEP saves the time for calculating the base score for normalization; at the classification stage, the new algorithm for selecting representative EPs reduces classification time by 50%.

5   Related Work

The closest related work is CAEP, which is also based on the idea of aggregating EPs for classification. In iCAEP, (1) we aggregate EPs in a different approach, the information-based approach; (2) with the constraint-based EP mining algorithm, we can build classifiers more efficiently and can handle large high-dimensional datasets more effectively; (3) when classifying an instance T, we select a smaller but more representative subset of EPs presented in T. Experiments show that, compared to CAEP, iCAEP has better classification accuracy, and shorter time for training and classification. The current experiments are based on default parameter settings for both algorithms; it would be interesting to further compare their performance after both are fine-tuned.

Jumping EP-based classifiers [5] consider only jumping EPs for classification. Considering finite growth rate EPs and jumping EPs, and treating jumping EPs (§ 2.1) more carefully, iCAEP will behave well in the presence of noise. In large and high-dimensional datasets, a huge number of long jumping EPs are present and this brings difficulty to jumping EP-based classifiers.

Clearly, iCAEP is different from decision tree classifiers, Bayesian family classifiers, or the association classifier CBA. Specifically, CBA and LB, the two classifiers from the data mining community, construct classifiers based on the Apriori framework, which is usually too slow to be useful for real-world large high-dimensional data [12]; CBA and LB use frequent itemsets for classification in a completely sequential way. More generally, the MML or MDL principle has been proved successful in many applications.

6 Conclusions

We have presented a classifier iCAEP, based on Emerging Patterns (EPs). iCAEP classifies an instance T by aggregating the EPs learned from training data that appear in T in an information-based approach. Experiments on many datasets show that, compared to other classifiers, iCAEP achieves better classification accuracy, and it scales well for large-volume high-dimensional datasets. In our future work, we will focus on tuning iCAEP for higher accuracy.

References

1. R Agrawal and R Srikant. Fast algorithm for mining association rules. In *Proc. VLDB'94*, pages 487-499, 1994.
2. G Dong and J Li. Efficient Mining of emerging patterns: Discovering trends and differences. In *Proc. of KDD'99*, 1999.
3. G Dong, X Zhang, L Wong, and J Li. CAEP: Classification by aggregating emerging patterns. In *Proc. of DS'99*, LNCS 1721, Japan, 1999.
4. U M Fayyad and K B Irani. Multi-interval discretization of continuous-valued attributes for classification learning. In *Proc. of IJCAI'93*, 1993.
5. J Li, G Dong, and K Ramamohanarao. Make use of the most expressive jumping emerging patterns for classification. In *Proc. of PAKDD'00*, Japan, 2000.
6. B Liu, W Hsu, and Y Ma. Integrating classification and association rule mining. In *Proc. of KDD'98*, New York, USA, pages 27 – 31, August 1998.
7. M Mehta, R Agrawal, and J Rissanen. SLIQ: A fast scalable classifier for data mining. In *Proc. of EDBT'96*, Avignon, France, March 1996.
8. D Meretakis and B Wüthrich. Extending naive bayes classifiers using long itemsets. In *Proc. of KDD'99*, San Diego, USA, August 1999.
9. J Rissanen. A universal prior for integers and estimation by minimum description length. *Annals of Statistics*, 11:416–431, 1983.
10. C Wallace and D Boulton. An information measure for classification. *Computer Journal*, 11:185-195, 1968.
11. C Wallace and J Patrick. Coding decision trees. *Machine Learning*, 11:7-22, 1993.
12. X Zhang, G Dong, and K Ramamohanarao. Exploring constraints to efficiently mine emerging patterns from large high-dimensional datasets. In *Proc. of KDD'00*, Boston, USA, August 2000.

Boosting the Margin Distribution

Huma Lodhi[1] Grigoris Karakoulas[2] and John Shawe-Taylor[1]

[1] Department of Computer Science, Royal Holloway, University of London, Egham,
TW20 0EX UK
email: huma,jst@dcs.rhbnc.ac.uk
[2] Global Analytics Group, Canadian Imperial Bank of Commerce, 161 Bay St.,
BCE-11, Toronto ON, Canada M5J 2S8
email: grigoris.karakoulas@cibc.ca

Abstract. The paper considers applying a boosting strategy to optimise the generalisation bound obtained recently by Shawe-Taylor and
Cristianini [7] in terms of the two norm of the slack variables. The formulation performs gradient descent over the quadratic loss function which
is insensitive to points with a large margin. A novel feature of this algorithm is a principled adaptation of the size of the target margin. Experiments with text and UCI data shows that the new algorithm improves
the accuracy of boosting. DMarginBoost generally achieves significant
improvements over Adaboost.

1 Introduction

During the last decade new learning methods so called, ensemble methods, have
gained much attention in machine learning community. These methods generally
produce a classifier with a high learning accuracy. It has recently been established
that boosting can be viewed as gradient descent in the function space based on
a criterion derived from the margins of the training examples [2], [3].

The standard boosting algorithm Adaboost optimises a negative exponential function of the margin that corresponds most closely to the hard margin
criterion for Support Vector Machines. This idea generalises well in a low noise
environment but fails to perform well in noisy environments. This opens up the
need for developing new boosting techniques which are robust to noise [3], [6].
For SVM the generalisation results are improved by optimising the 2-norm of
the slack variables in the corresponding optimisation problem [5]. This approach
has recently been placed on firm footing by Shawe-Taylor and Cristianini [7].

Mason et al. [3] give a general formulation of how alternative loss functions
give rise to a general boosting strategy. This paper adopts this approach with one
additional feature: the loss function used depends on the target margin since it
is relative to this margin that the slack variables are calculated. Since fixing the
size of the target margin is difficult a priori, we introduce a method of adapting
its value in response to the progress of the boosting algorithm. This paper adapts
the new generalisation bound for boosting. It propose a new algorithm, develops
a new loss function and shows that the strategy of performing gradient descent
in function space relative to an adapting loss function provides a highly accurate
classifier which is robust to noise.

2 2-norm Soft Margin Bound for boosting

The function classes that we will be considering are of the form $\mathrm{co}(H) = \left\{\sum_{h \in H} a_h h\right\}$, where H is a set of weak learners. We first introduce some notation. If $\mathcal{D}$ is a distribution on inputs and targets, $X \times \{-1, 1\}$, we define the error $\mathrm{err}_{\mathcal{D}}(f)$ of a function $f \in \mathcal{F}$ to be the probability $\mathcal{D}\{(\mathbf{x}, y) : \mathrm{sgn}(f(\mathbf{x})) \neq y\}$, where we have assumed that we obtain a classification function by thresholding at 0, if f is real-valued.

For the background theory required for the derivation of the bound see Definition 2.1, Theorem 2.1, Definition 2.2, Definition 2.3, Theorem 2.2 in [1]. By applying these results to our function class which will be in the form described above, $\mathcal{F} = \mathrm{co}(H) = \left\{\sum_{h \in H} a_h h\right\}$, where we have left open for the time being what the class H of weak learners might contain. The sets $\mathcal{G}$ of Theorem 2.2 in [1] will be chosen as follows $\mathcal{G}_B = \left\{\left(\sum_{h \in H} a_h h, g\right) : \sum_{h \in H} |a_h| + \|g\|_2^2 \leq B\right\}$.

For two classes $\mathcal{G}_1$ and $\mathcal{G}_2$ of real valued functions, we denote by $\mathcal{G}_1 + \mathcal{G}_2$ the class $\mathcal{G}_1 + \mathcal{G}_2 = \{f_1 + f_2 : f_1 \in \mathcal{G}_1, f_2 \in \mathcal{G}_2\}$. Furthermore, by taking the sums of functions from coverings of $\mathcal{G}_1$ and $\mathcal{G}_2$ at scales η and $\gamma - \eta$ respectively, we obtain a covering of $\mathcal{G}_1 + \mathcal{G}_2$ at scale γ.

If we let $\mathcal{F}_B$ be the class $\mathcal{F}_B = \left\{\sum_{h \in H} a_h h : \sum_{h \in H} |a_h| \leq B\right\}$ and the class $\mathcal{H}$ be defined as $\mathcal{H}_B = \left\{g \in L(X) : \|g\|_2^2 \leq B\right\}$, then clearly we have $\mathcal{G}_B \subseteq \mathcal{F}_B + \mathcal{H}_B$. Hence, we can obtain a bound on the covering numbers for $\mathcal{G}_B$ as

$$\mathcal{N}(\mathcal{G}_B, m, \gamma) \leq \mathcal{N}(\mathcal{F}_B, m, \eta)\mathcal{N}(\mathcal{H}_B, m, \gamma - \eta)$$

We can therefore bound the covering numbers of $\mathcal{G}_B$ by bounding those of $\mathcal{F}_B$ and $\mathcal{H}_B$. The techniques presented in [1] can be used to obtain the following bound by [8].

Theorem 1. *For the class $\mathcal{F}_B$ defined above we have that*

$$\log \mathcal{N}(\mathcal{F}_B, m, \gamma) \leq 1 + \frac{144B^2}{\gamma^2}\left(2 + \ln(B_H(m))\right)$$

$$\log\left(2\left\lceil\frac{4B}{\gamma} + 2\right\rceil m + 1\right),$$

where $B_H(m)$ is the maximum number of dichotomies that can be realised by H on m points.

The covering numbers of the second set can be got by applying result in [8].

Theorem 2. *For the class $\mathcal{H}_B$ defined above we have that*

$$\log \mathcal{N}(\mathcal{H}_B, m, \gamma) \leq \frac{36B^2}{\gamma^2}\log\left(2\left\lceil\frac{4B}{\gamma} + 2\right\rceil m + 1\right).$$

Hence, the optimisation of the generalisation bound will be done if we minimise $\log \mathcal{N}(\mathcal{H}_B, m, \gamma)$, which is achieved by minimising $\frac{144B^2}{\eta^2} + \frac{36B^2}{(\gamma-\eta)^2}$. Taking $\eta = 2\gamma/3$ gives $648B^2/\gamma^2 = 648\frac{A^2 + K\mathcal{D}(\gamma)^2}{\gamma^2}$, where $\mathcal{D}(\gamma) = \sqrt{\sum_{i=1}^{m} \xi\left((\mathbf{x}_i, y_i), f, \gamma\right)^2}$, $A = \sum_{h \in H} |a_h|$. Minimisation of this quantity will motivate the DMarginBoost algorithm where we will use the parameter C in place of $\frac{1}{K}$.

3 The DMarginBoost Algorithm

The DMarginBoost algorithm applies the idea of minimising the target margin based loss function. The algorithm takes a set of p labelled examples. It gets a base classifier and assigns weight α to it. The DMarginboost algorithm handles noisy data by assigning quadratic loss to the examples who fail to meet the target margin. The examples with margin greater than the target margin incur no loss. Target margin is updated to minimise the current estimate of the error. **Derivation of target margin γ:** To find target margin γ at each iteration we minimise the error bound derived in previous section. In other words we minimise the quantity $\gamma_t = \arg\min_{\gamma}\left[\dfrac{CA_t^2}{\gamma^2} + \dfrac{\mathcal{D}_t^2(\gamma)}{\gamma^2}\right]$ where $A_t = \sum_i |\alpha_i|$, and $\mathcal{D}_t^2(\gamma) = \sum_i(\gamma - y_i f_{t-1}(x_i))_+^2$ and C is the tradeoff parameter between error and maximising the margin. Optimal C gives best choice of error/margin tradeoff.

$$\frac{CA_t^2}{\gamma^2} + \frac{\sum_i(\gamma - y_i f_{t-1}(x_i))_+^2}{\gamma^2} = \frac{CA_t^2}{\gamma^2} + \sum_i\left(1 - \frac{y_i f_{t-1}(x_i)}{\gamma}\right)_+^2$$

Let $B = \dfrac{1}{\gamma}$ and defining $S_t(B) = \{i : By_i(f_{t-1}(x_i)) < 1\}$, we wish to minimise

$$CA_t^2B^2 + \sum_i\left(1 - By_i f_{t-1}(x_i)\right)_+^2 = CA_t^2B^2 + \sum_{i \in S_t(B)}\left(1 - By_i(f_{t-1}(x_i))\right)^2$$

Taking derivative of the above equation with respect to target margin B

$$2CBA_t^2 + \sum_{i \in S_t(B)} 2\left(1 - By_i(f_{t-1}(x_i))\right)\left(-y_i(f_{t-1}(x_i))\right) = 0$$

$$B = \frac{\sum_{i \in S_t(B)} y_i(f_{t-1}(x_i))}{CA_t^2 + \sum_{i \in S_t(B)}(f_{t-1}(x_i))^2}.$$

We can calculate the value of γ from chosen B. For $t = 1$, $B = \dfrac{2c-p}{p}$ where c is the number of correctly classified examples and p the total number of examples. **Derivation of α:** At each iteration t to calculate the value α of we define $S_t'(\alpha) = \{i : y_i(f_{t-1}(x_i) + \alpha h_t(x_i)) < \gamma_t\}$. We now have

$$F(\alpha) = \sum_{i \in S_t'(\alpha)} \left(\gamma_t - y_i\left(f_{t-1}(x_i) + \alpha h_t(x_i)\right)\right)^2$$

Taking derivative with respect to α and setting equal to zero

$$\frac{\partial F}{\partial \alpha} = -\sum_{i \in S_t'(\alpha)} 2\left(\gamma_t - y_i\left(f_{t-1}(x_i) + \alpha h_t(x_i)\right)\right)y_i h_t(x_i) = 0$$

$$\alpha \sum_{i \in S_t'(\alpha)} \left(h_t(x_i)\right)^2 = \sum_{i \in S_t'(\alpha)} y_i h_t(x_i)\left(\gamma_t - y_i(f_{t-1}(x_i))\right)$$

Algorithm DMarginBoost

Require:

 Training Set: $(x_1, y_1), (x_2, y_2) \ldots \ldots \ldots (x_p, y_p)$ where $x_i \in X$ and $y_i \in \{-1, +1\}$.

 A base learner that takes training set and distribution and generates a base classifier.

Initialize: Let $D_1(i) = \dfrac{1}{p}$, for $i = 1$ to p and $\alpha_1 = 1$

 Call base learner that generates base classifier h_1 and get $f_1 = \alpha_1 h_1(x_i)$

 for $t = 2$ to T **do**

   Calculate desired margin γ_t

   Update Distribution: $D_t(i) = \dfrac{(\gamma_t - y_i f_{t-1}(x_i))_+}{Z_t}$, Z_t is normalisation factor

   Call base learner to get base classifier h_t

   Calculate α_t to minimize $\sum_i (\gamma_t - y_i(f_{t-1}(x_i) + \alpha h_t(x_i)))_+^2$

   Update: $f_t(x_i) = f_{t-1}(x_i) + \alpha_t h_t(x_i)$

 end for

 return $f_T(x)$

In order to solve this we must find the critical values of α for which the set $S'_t(\alpha)$ changes, estimate F for each of these, and then apply the analysis to each interval. If the solution lies in its interval, it becomes a candidate solution. Hence there are at most $2m$ candidates from which the optimal must be chosen.

4 Experiments

To evaluate the performance of DMarginBoost algorithm, we performed a series of experiments on two different domains of data.

Soft Margin Based Text Booster: The first set of experiments evaluates DMarginBoost on a text categorisation task. We used terms (single words or phrases – adjacent words) as base learners following [4]. At each iteration T for each term, the corresponding weak learner classifies a document as relevant if it contains that term. In the next stage, the error of each term is calculated with respect to the distribution D_t. The error is given by $\sum_{h_x(i) \neq y_i} D_t(i)$. The two terms with minimum and maximum error are considered. The negation of the term with maximum error is a candidate since we can also use the negation as a weak learner by taking a negative coefficient α_t. The selected term is the better discriminator of relevance of the two. Finally, all the documents containing the selected term are classified relevant and others irrelevant. Initial experiments showed no significant difference between words and phrases and only words. Therefore experiments have been performed using only words.

Boosting strategy for Reuters: We evaluated the boosting algorithms on the Reuters-21578 Data set compiled by David Lewis. The "ModeApte" split which contains 9603 training and 3299 test documents was used. Punctations and stop words were removed from the documents. For DMarginBoost the optimal values of free parameters were set on a validation set. We selected a subset

Table 1. F1 numberes and Breakeven points for ten largest categories

	Adaboost(F1)	DMarginBoost(F1)	DMarginBoost(B)	SVM(1)	SVM(2)
earn	0.976	0.977	0.977	0.982	0.98
acq	0.906	0.926	0.926	0.926	0.936
money-fx	0.687	0.722	0.725	0.669	0.745
grain	0.898	0.904	0.905	0.913	0.946
crude	0.880	0.879	0.879	0.86	0.889
trade	0.669	0.763	0.763	0.692	0.759
interest	0.570	0.722	0.728	0.698	0.777
ship	0.774	0.838	0.838	0.820	0.856
wheat	0.878	0.909	0.915	0.831	0.918
corn	0.897	0.908	0.911	0.86	0.903

of 6723 documents for the training set and 2880 documents for the validation set. DMarginboost was run for $C = 0.1$, 1.5, 2.5, 4, 8. Optimal C and corresponding T which give minimum error on the validation set were selected. For the chosen values of parameters, DMarginBoost was run using the whole training set of 9603 documents and its performance was evaluated on 3299 test documents. For AdaBoost the number of iterations T was selected as explained in [4].

Results: For evaluation F measures and Breakeven point (see [4]) were used. Figure 1, Figure 2 and Figure 3 demonstrate how the performance of the solution improves with boosting iterations for category 'acq'. Table 1 compares the Breakeven points and F1 numbers of DMarginBoost to AdaBoost, SVM(1) and SVM(2). Results of SVM(1) and SVM(2) have been taken from [9], [10]. The results indicate that in 9 cases the DMarginBoost algorithm gave better results than Adaboost,and in 7 cases it is better than SVM (1) and in 1 case it is equal to SVM(1) and in 2 cases it is also better than SVM(2). The results show the DMarginBoost generally outperforms AdaBoost.

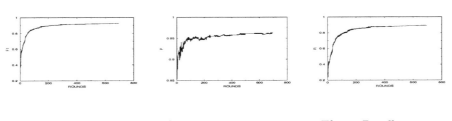

Fig. 1. F1   **Fig. 2.** Precision   **Fig. 3.** Recall

Boosted Decision Trees: We used C4.5 as base learners for our second set of experiments. We selected Ionosphere and Pima-Indiana datasets from the UCI repository. Ten random splits of data were used, taking taking 90% for training and 10% for testing. We fixed the value of $C = 1.0$ and $T = 100$. The perfor

Table 2. Average Test Set Error for Ionosphere and Pima-Indians

	Examples	Features	AdaBoost	DMarginBoost	AdaBoost	DMarginBoost
Ionosphere	768	8	6.9(0)	6.3(0)	13.4(5)	11.9(5)
Pima-Indians	351	34	25.0(0)	24.4(0)	29.8(5)	28.1(5)

mance of DMarginBoost in noisy environments, was investigated by introducing 5% random label noise (in parentheses). DOOM2 on Ionosphere gave errors of 9.7% and AdaBoost 10.1% with decision stumps as base learners (See [3]). Table 2 shows that the performance of DMarginBoost (even with $C = 1$) over Adaboost is better than the performance of DOOM2 over AdaBoost in 3 cases.

5   Conclusion

The paper has developed a novel boosting algorithm. The algorithm optimises the size of the target margin by minimising the error bound. We presented experiments in which the algorithm was compared with Adaboost on a set of categories from the Reuters-21578 data set and data sets form the UCI. The results were very encouraging showing that the new algorithm generally outperforms AdaBoost both in noisy and nonnoisy environments.

References

1. Bennett, K. P., Demiriz, A., Shawe-Taylor, J.: Column generation aproaches to boosting. *In International Conference on Machine Learning (ICML)*, 2000.
2. Friedman, J.: Greedy Function approximation: a gradient boosting machine. Technical report, Stanford University, 1999.
3. Mason, L., Baxter, J., Bartlett, P., Frean, M.: Boosting algorithms as gradient descent in function space. Technical report, RSISE., Australian National University, 1999.
4. Schapire, R., Singer, Y., Singhal, A.: Boosting and rocchio applied to text filtering. *In Proceedings of the 21st Annual International SIGIR conference on Research and Development in Information Retrieval, SIGIR'98*, 1998.
5. Cortes, C., and Vapnik, V.: Support-vector networks. *Machine Learning*, 20:273-297, 1995.
6. Ratsch, G., Onoda, T., and Muller, K.-R.: Regularizing adaboost. *In Advances in Neural Information Processing Systems 11, pp. 564-570.* MIT Press.
7. Shawe-Taylor, J., Cristianini, N.: Further results on the margin distribution. *In Proceedings of the Conference on Computational Learning Theory, COLT 99*, 1999.
8. Zhang, T.: Analysis of regularised linear functions for classification problem. Technical Report RC-21572, IBM, October 1999.
9. Joachima, T.: Text Categorization with support vector machines: Learning with many relevant fetures. *In European Conference on Machine Learning (ECML)*, 1998.
10. Dumais, T. S., Platt, J., Heckerman, D., and Sahami, M.: Inductive learning algorithms and representations for text categorization. *In Proceedings of ACM-CIKM98*.

Detecting a Compact Decision Tree Based on an Appropriate Abstraction

Yoshimitsu Kudoh and Makoto Haraguchi

Division of Electronics and Information Engineering,
Hokkaido University, N 13 W 8 , Sapporo 060-8628 JAPAN
{kudo,makoto}@db-ei.eng.hokudai.ac.jp

Abstract. It is generally convinced that pre-processing for data mining is needed to exclude irrelevant and meaningless aspects of data before applying data mining algorithms. From this viewpoint, we have already proposed a notion of *Information Theoretical Abstraction*, and implemented a system ITA. Given a relational database and a family of possible abstractions for its attribute values, called an *abstraction hierarchy*, ITA selects the best abstraction among the possible ones so that class distributions needed to perform our classification task are preserved as possibly as we can. According to our previous experiment, just one application of abstraction for the whole database has shown its effectiveness in reducing the size of detected rules, without making the classification error worse. However, as C4.5 performs serial *attribute-selection* repeatedly, ITA does not generally guarantee the preservingness of class distributions, given a sequence of attribute-selections. For this reason, in this paper, we propose a new version of ITA, called *iterative ITA*, so that it tries to keep the class distributions in each attribute selection step as possibly as we can.

1 Introduction

Many studies on data mining have concentrated on developing methods for extracting useful knowledge from very large databases effectively. However rules detected by those methods include even meaningless rules as well as meaningful ones. Thus, pre-processings are also important to exclude irrelevant aspects of data. There exist some techniques commonly used in the pre-processing [1, 3, 11]. For instance, feature selection methods focus on a particular subset of attributes relevant to the aim of the mining task. Furthermore, generalization of databases is also a powerful technique not only for preventing the mining task from extracting meaningless rules but also making the detected rules more understandable. The attribute-oriented induction used in DBMiner[5] and a method in INLEN[12] for learning rules with structured attributes are typical instance of the generalization method.

We consider in this paper that such a generalization method is an instance of abstraction strategy [6] shown in Figure 1.1. In general, if it is difficult to find out a solution S from a problem P at concrete level, we transform P into an abstract problem $abs(P)$. Furthermore we find out an abstract solution $abs(S)$ from

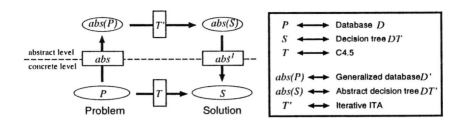

Fig. 1.1. An abstraction strategy in our method

$abs(P)$ and transform $abs(S)$ into S. DBMiner and INLEN are also considered to be based on this abstraction strategy.

We are particularly interested in the problem of determining an appropriate abstraction among possible ones. This is because the abstraction strategy is actually dependent on the choice of abstractions. In the case of an attribute-oriented induction algorithm in DBMiner, given a concept hierarchy with a single inheritance structure, it can decide an adequate abstract level based on a threshold of the number of attribute values. However, for the hierarchy provides only a single inheritance, the abstraction may lose some important aspect of data not covered by the hierarchy. The generalization process in INLEN uses anchor nodes, defined as concepts based on typicality notion, to select the best abstraction. However it is generally hard for user to define such an anchor node before the mining task. Consequently, INLEN also may miss the important aspect of data needed to perform our mining task.

In the previous work[7], we have already proposed a notion of *Information Theoretical Abstraction* (ITA) to overcome these problems particularly on classification tasks. ITA is an extension of the attribute-oriented induction. Compared with the attribute-oriented induction, ITA can automatically select the best abstraction by minimizing the loss of information, where the information needed for our classification is the class distribution. Furthermore assuming that the anchor nodes used in INLEN correspond to our appropriate abstractions, ITA can also automatically decide the anchor nodes.

ITA and iterative ITA, introduced in this paper, generalize databases according to the abstraction strategy in Figure 1.1 in the following sense. Firstly, the original database D is generalized to an abstract database D' by replacing attributes values in D with corresponding abstract values determined by an appropriate abstraction abs. Secondly, it detects a compact decision tree $\mathcal{DT}'$, called *an abstract decision tree*, from D'. Finally, we interpret $\mathcal{DT}'$ and transform $\mathcal{DT}'$ into $\mathcal{DT}$.

In principle, given target classes, ITA automatically selects an appropriate abstraction in abstraction hierarchies with multiple inheritances and generalizes the database based on the selected abstraction. The abstraction is said to be appropriate if for a given target attribute, class distributions in the original database are preserved in the resultant of generalization as possibly as we can,

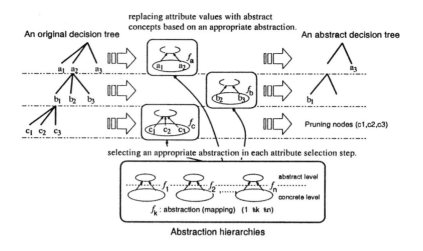

Fig. 1.2. An effect of the abstraction for the decision tree

because such classification systems as C4.5 construct the decision tree based on the class distribution. If the attribute values share the same or a similar class distribution, they can be considered not to have significant differences about the class. So they can be abstracted to a single value at abstract level. On the other hand, when the values have distinguishable class distributions, the difference will be significant to perform classification in terms of attribute values. Hence, the difference should not be disregarded in the abstraction.

We have shown that the same measure, an information gain ratio, as used in C4.5 can be adopted to measure the difference of class distributions[7]. It has already empirically shown that the classification error of the abstract decision tree $\mathcal{DT}'$ is almost the same as the decision tree $\mathcal{DT}$ directly computed by C4.5 from the original database D. Nevertheless, the size of $\mathcal{DT}'$ is drastically reduced, compared with $\mathcal{DT}$.

Thus, just once application of abstraction for whole database has been experimentally shown its effectiveness in reducing the size of detected rules, without making the classification accuracy so worse. However, as C4.5 performs serial attribute selections repeatedly, ITA does not generally guarantee the preservingness of class distributions in each selection step. Hence, when we require that the classification accuracy of $\mathcal{DT}'$ must be almost equal to $\mathcal{DT}$, we can not allow the classification accuracy to go down even slightly. For this reason, in this paper, we propose a new version of ITA, called *iterative ITA* so that it tries to keep the class distribution in each attribute selection step as possibly as we can.

Figure 1.2 illustrates a generalization process in the iterative ITA. Iterative ITA selects an appropriate abstraction in each attribute selection step and constructs a compact decision tree, called *an abstract decision tree*. That is, we propose to perform our generalization process in each *attribute-selection* step in

C4.5, where an attribute based on which a decision tree is expanded. Each node N_i in a tree has the corresponding sub-database D_{N_i} of the original D, where the sub-database is set of instances obtained by selecting tuples. For such a sub-database D_{N_i}, C4.5 selects an another attribute A_i to furthermore expand the tree. We try to find an appropriate abstraction φ for that A_i so that the target class distribution given A_i values can be preserved even after generalizing the A_i values v to more abstract value $\varphi(v)$. The generalized database is also denoted by $D'_{N_i} = \varphi(D_{N_i})$.

At the abstract level, D'_{N_i} is divided according to the abstract A_i values $\varphi(v)$, as similarly to the concrete level division by the concrete A_i values v. It should be noted that the number of new branches of N_i is less than (or equal to) one obtained by dividing D_{N_i}, because the attribute values in D_{N_i} are merged into abstract ones in D'_{N_i}. In addition, since the best abstraction is chosen in each step, the abstract level class distribution is the closest one to the concrete level distribution. In other words, the regression of precision is minimized in each step of attribute selection among the possible abstractions. As the result, the precision of detected rules will become much closer to one of C4.5, while keeping the same property of reducing the size of detected rules as to non-iterative ITA.

This paper is organized as follows. In section 2, we present a brief summary of ITA. Section 3 describes the iterative ITA and its principle. In section 4, we evaluate iterative ITA with some experiments on census database in US Census Bureau. Section 5 concludes this paper.

2　Preliminary

Our system ITA[7] was developed based on the idea that the behavior of the information gain ratio used in C4.5[16] applies to the generalization process in the attribute-oriented induction[5].

2.1　Information gain ratio

Let a data set S be a set of instances of a relational schema $R(A_1, ..., A_m)$, where A_k is an attribute. Furthermore we assume that user specifies an assignment C of a class information to each tuple in S. We regard it as a random variable with the probability $Pr(C = c_i) = freq(c_i, S)/|S|$, where $|S|$ is the cardinality of S, and $freq(c_j, S)$ denotes the number of all tuples in S whose class is c_i. Then the entropy of the class distribution $(\Pr(C = c_1), ..., \Pr(C = c_n))$ over S is given by $H(C) = - \sum_{i=1}^{n} \Pr(C = c_i) \log_2 \Pr(C = c_i)$.

Now, given an attribute value a_j of $A = \{a_1, ..., a_\ell\}$, we obtain a posterior class distribution $(\Pr(C = c_1|A = a_j), ..., \Pr(C = c_n|A = a_j))$ that has the corresponding entropy $H(C|A = a_j) = - \sum_{i=1}^{n} \Pr(C = c_i|A = a_j) \log_2 \Pr(C = c_i|A = a_j)$. The expectation of these entropies of posterior class distributions is called a *conditional entropy* $H(C|A) = \sum_{j=1}^{\ell} \Pr(A = a_j) H(C|A = a_j)$. The subtraction of $H(C|A)$ from $H(C)$ gives an *information gain*, that is also called a *mutual information* $I(C; A)$.

$$gain(A, S) = H(C) - H(C|A) = I(C; A). \qquad (2.1)$$

To normalize the information gain, the entropy of an attribute $A = \{a_1, ..., a_\ell\}$, called a *split information*, is used.

$$split\_info(A, S) = - \sum_{j=1}^{l} \Pr(A = a_j) \log_2 \Pr(A = a_j) = H(A). \qquad (2.2)$$

Finally, the information gain is divided by the split information. The normalized information gain is called an *information gain ratio*

$$gain\_ratio(A, S) = gain(A, S)/split\_info(A, S) = I(C; A)/H(A). \qquad (2.3)$$

2.2 The basic concept of ITA

ITA adopts an information gain ratio to select an appropriate abstraction and controls generalization based on the selected abstraction. In principle, given target classes, a grouping of tuples in a relational database, an abstraction preserving the class distribution of the attribute values is preferred and selected as an appropriate one. If some attribute values $a_1, \ldots, a_m$ of an attribute $A = \{a_1, ..., a_\ell\}(m \leq \ell)$ share an almost same or similar posterior class distribution $(\Pr(C = c_1|A = a_j), ..., \Pr(C = c_n|A = a_j))$, an "abstract class distribution", defined as

$$(\Pr(C = c_1|A \in \{a_1, ..., a_m\}), ..., \Pr(C = c_n|A \in \{a_1, ..., a_m\}))$$
$$= (\Sigma_{j=1}^{m}\lambda_j \Pr(C = c_1|A = a_j), ..., \Sigma_{j=1}^{m}\lambda_j \Pr(C = c_n|A = a_j))$$

also shows an almost same or similar class distribution, where $\lambda_j = \Pr(A = a_j)/\Sigma_{i=1}^{m} \Pr(A = a_i)$. Thus, an abstraction identifying these $a_1, ..., a_m$ preserves the necessary information about classes, so they can be abstracted to a single abstract value. In other words, we consider only an abstraction that preserves class distribution as possibly as we can.

ITA uses the information gain ratio as one of the measure to define a similarity between class distributions. The point is the change of the information gain ratio when the attribute values $a_1, \ldots, a_m$ of A are abstracted to a single value. An abstraction is considered as a mapping $f : A \rightarrow f(A)$, where $f(A)$ is an abstract concept at abstract level.

In general, according to the basic theorem of the entropy and the data-processing theorem described in the literature[2], the following inequalities hold between $H(C|A)$ and $H(C|f(A))$:

$$H(C|A) \leq H(C|f(A)), \quad I(C; A) \geq I(C; f(A))$$

Hence the information gain decreases after the abstraction of attribute values. The difference $e(f) = H(C|f(A)) - H(C|A)$ can show the similarity between the distributions. That is, an abstraction f meets $e(f) \simeq 0$ (i.e. $I(C; A) \simeq I(C; f(A))$) is a preferable mapping.

Furthermore the split information $H(f(A))$ is used to choose one abstraction from two or more preferable abstractions. it can merge most attribute values into the corresponding abstract concept. For example, we assume two abstractions f_1 and f_2 meet $I(C; A) \simeq I(C; f_1(A)) = I(C; f_2(A))$. If f_1 can replace more number of attribute values with the abstract concept as compared with f_2, the split information between f_1 and f_2 holds $H(f_1(A)) < H(f_2(A))$, and then the information gain ratio holds $I(C; f_1(A))/H(f_1(A)) > I(C; f_2(A))/H(f_2(A))$. Thus ITA can select the abstraction f_1. From these observations, our generalization method using the information gain ratio can select an abstraction that preserves the class distribution and replaces more attribute values with the abstract concept.

The generalization process in ITA are summarized as the following algorithm. In the algorithm, the term "change ratio" means the ratio of the information gain ratio after applying generalization to one before applying generalization. An abstraction in abstraction hierarchies is defined as a possible grouping $\{\{a_1^1, \ldots, a_{n_1}^1\}, \ldots, \{a_1^m, \ldots, a_{n_m}^m\}\}$ of attribute values $\{a_1^1, \ldots, a_{n_1}^1, \ldots, a_1^m, \ldots, a_{n_m}^m\}$ in a relational database. An abstraction for attribute values means to replace attribute values in the grouping with the corresponding abstract concept $\{\tilde{a}_1, \ldots, \tilde{a}_m\}$.

Algorithm 2.1 (information theoretical abstraction)
Input : (1) a relational database,
(2) target classes (i.e. target attribute values),
(3) abstraction hierarchies and
(4) a threshold value of the change ratio.
Output : a generalized database.

1. By some relational operations (e.g. projection and selection), extract a data set that are relevant to the target classes.
2. Select an attribute from the database before applying generalization and compute the information gain ratio for the attribute.
3. Compute the information gain ratio for each abstraction in the hierarchies for the attribute and select an abstraction with the maximum information gain ratio.
4. Compute the change ratio. If it is above the threshold value, substitute abstract values in the abstraction for the attribute values in the database.
5. Merge overlapping tuples into one, count the number of merged tuples, and then the special attribute *vote* is added to each tuple in order to record how many tuples in the original database are merged into one abstract tuple as the result.
6. Repeat above four steps for all attributes.

3 Iterative ITA

Since ITA performs just one application of abstraction for whole database, ITA does not generally guarantee the preservingness of class distribution in each attribute selection step in C4.5. That is, in case of requesting that the classification accuracy of the decision tree detected from the generalized database is almost equal to the original one, ITA can not completely respond to this request for the classification accuracy.

For this reason, we propose *iterative ITA* in order to keep the class distribution in each attribute selection step as possibly as we can. The *iterative ITA* in the form of algorithm is shown as follows.

Algorithm 3.1 (Iterative ITA)

   Input : (1) a relational database D,
               (2) target classes c_k $(1 \leq k \leq n)$,
               (3) abstraction hierarchies AHs and
               (4) a threshold value of the change ratio T.
   Output : an abstract decision tree $\mathcal{DT}'$.
   (The following l, m, n, p are constants and x, y, z are any numbers.)

1. Compute the information gain ratios for all attributes in D and select an attribute A_x according to the maximum information gain ratio.
2. Compute the information gain ratios for possible abstractions f_i $(1 \leq i \leq l)$ in AHs for A_x and select an abstraction f_y if its information gain ratio is the highest and its change ratio is higher than T.
3. If f_y is selected at step 2 :
   (i) Select all tuples that contain attribute values correspond to an abstract concept $\tilde{a}_j = f_y(A_x)$ $(1 \leq j \leq m)$.
   (ii) Divide D into sub-databases D_j according to $\tilde{a}_j$.
   Otherwise :
   (i) Select all tuples that contain an attribute value v_j $(1 \leq j \leq p)$.
   (ii) Divide D into sub-databases D_j according to v_j.
4. Compute a classification error rate ER for D and classification error rates ER_j for D_j.
   If any error rate in ER_j is larger than ER :
   (i) Create child nodes correspond to D_j that branch from a current node corresponds to D.
   (ii) For each D_j, regard D_j as D and perform step 1 – 4 for new D repeatedly.
   Otherwise :
   Assign a class label to a current node corresponds to D.

Algorithm 3.1 has the following features.

– The process of constructing the decision tree in C4.5 divides the current node corresponds to D according to all attribute values $\{v_1^1, \ldots, v_{n_1}^1, \ldots, v_1^m, \ldots, v_{n_m}^m\}$ in A_x. The number of the branches in the original decision tree is $n_1 + \cdots + n_m$. On the other hand, iterative ITA divides the current node according to all abstract concepts in the grouping $\{\{v_1^1, \ldots, v_{n_1}^1\}, \ldots, \{v_1^m, \ldots, v_{n_m}^m\}\} = \{\tilde{a}_1, \ldots, \tilde{a}_m\} = f_y(A_x)$ selected in each attribute selection step. The number of the branches in the abstract decision tree is m. An inequality $n_1 + \cdots + n_m \geq m$ holds between $n_1 + \cdots + n_m$ and m. Therefore iterative ITA reduces the branches in the original decision tree constructed by C4.5.

- Roughly speaking, we can say that a condition of terminating the growth of the decision tree in step 4 is concerned with a question of whether the posterior class distributions in the child nodes become to show distinguishable higher probabilities for particular classes or not. Suppose that such a deviation of the class distribution in some child node is larger than the current node. This means that the classification accuracy in D_j is improved. In such a case, our iterative ITA continues a process of constructing the decision tree. Otherwise it terminates the expansion process. Since the class distribution at abstract level is the average of those at concrete level, the deviation at abstract level turns out to be smaller than the deviation at concrete level. In other words, a chance of improving the classification accuracy may be lost by applying abstraction.

  Furthermore, suppose that every posterior class distributions of child nodes at concrete level do not show distinguished deviations. This means that the condition for terminating the expansion process holds. Then, for any abstraction, any posterior class distribution at abstract level does not also show the distinguished deviations. This is again because the abstract distribution is defined as the average of concrete level distributions. As a result, we can say that stopping condition for expansion at abstract level invoke whenever it does at concrete level.

As the result, the precision of the abstract decision tree will be come much closer to one of C4.5, while keeping the same property of reducing the size of the decision tree as to non-iterative ITA.

4 Experiment on Census Database

We have made some experiments using our iterative ITA system that has been improved based on the proposed method and implemented in Visual C++ on PC/AT.

In our experimentation, we try to detect decision trees from *Census Database in US Census Bureau* found in UCI repository[15]. The census database used as training data in our experiment consists of 30162 tuples each of which has values for 11 attributes including *age, workclass, education, occupation, relationship, race, sex, hours-per-week, native-country* and *salary*. Apart from this training data, we prepare a small database (called *test data*) consisting of 15060 tuples in order to check a classification accuracy of a detected decision tree. The abstraction hierarchies for attribute values in the census database are constructed based on a machine readable dictionary WordNet[13, 14] and are given to our system.

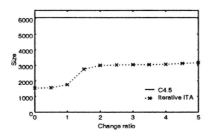

Fig. 4.1. Size of decision trees

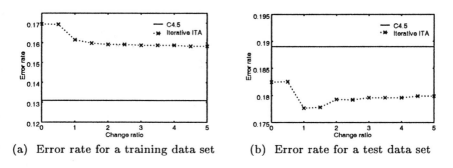

(a) Error rate for a training data set   (b) Error rate for a test data set

Fig. 4.2. Error rate of decision trees

Let us assume that target classes are "$\leq \$50K$" (NOT more than $50000) and "$> \$50K$" (more than $50000) in an attribute *salary*. Iterative ITA generalizes the census database based on the information gain ratio. We adjust a threshold of a change ratio to construct various abstract decision trees using iterative ITA and compare our abstract decision trees constructed by iterative ITA with the original decision tree constructed by C4.5

The sizes and the error rates for their decision trees are shown in Figure 4.1 and Figure 4.2 respectively. The size of each abstract decision tree constructed by iterative ITA is smaller than the original one, because iterative ITA reduces the branches in the original decision tree and its depth, as mentioned in Section3. The form of the graph in Figure 4.1 comes to be nearly flat when the threshold of the change ratio is more than 2.0, because ITA could not select an appropriate abstraction.

Figure 4.2(a) shows that the difference between the error rate of abstract decision tree and the original one is about 0.03 when the change ratio is more than 1.0. The classification ability of C4.5 for the training data has better than iterative ITA. This can be understood in the following manner. Each node in the abstract decision tree keeps the class distribution before generalization as much as possible, However the preservingness of the class distribution in each attribute selection step causes a little error. On the other hand, the error rate of the abstract decision tree for the test data, shown in Figure 4.2(b), is nearly equal to one for the training data. Therefore the original decision tree is too-specific for the training data.

Furthermore when the threshold of the change ratio is about 1.0, the result of constructing the decision tree is shown in Table 4.1. The abstract decision tree constructed by Iterative ITA is the most compact and its error rate for the test data is the best in the three.

Table 4.1. Decision trees

System	Size	Error rate	
		Training data	Test data
C4.5	6048	0.131	0.189
ITA	2562	0.140	0.180
Iterative ITA	1533	0.161	0.177

From these observations, we consider that iterative ITA is useful for constructing a compact decision tree whose error rate is approximately equal to one before generalization, because the size has drastically decreased at the sacrifice of slightly increasing the error rate for the training data.

5 Conclusions and Future Work

In our previous work[7], we have used ITA as the pre-processing for C4.5 which constructs the decision tree. However, assuming that user requests that the classification accuracy of the abstract decision tree is almost equal to the original one, just one application of abstraction for whole database can not meet that request. For this reason, we have proposed iterative ITA which performs our generalization process in each attribute-selection step in C4.5. We can consider that iterative ITA is useful for constructing a compact abstract decision tree, that is more understandable for almost users, whose regression of error rate is minimized among given classes of abstractions. That is, it is important for making the interpretation of the resulting tree easy to apply abstraction to the process of constructing the decision tree. Furthermore if we apply any pruning technique to the abstract decision tree, the tree will be still more compact, and the understandabilty of the tree will be increasingly improving.

Normal ITA generalizes the database in the pre-processing for constructing the decision tree. On the other hand, iterative ITA generalizes a sub-database selected by each node in the decision tree while C4.5 is constructing the decision tree. Ideally, since each node in the abstract decision tree constructed by iterative ITA keeps the class distribution before generalization, we can extract the structure of the original decision tree from the structure of the abstract decision tree. Therefore we consider that iterative ITA can be used as the post-processing for the decision tree (e.g. visualization).

Abstraction hierarchies used in the iterative ITA are manually constructed according to WordNet. It is a hard task for user and system administrators to construct abstraction hierarchies for very large database. Therefore, in future work, we have to develop a method that automatically constructs abstraction hierarchies using a machine readable dictionary, e.g. WordNet. At the moment, we have already developed a first version of the method.

References

1. Adriaans, P. and Zantinge, D.: *Data Mining,* Addison Wesley Longman Ltd., 1996.
2. Arimoto, S: *Probability, Information, Entropy.* Morikita Shuppan, 1980 (in Japanese).
3. Fayyad, U.N., Piatetsky-Shapiro, G., Smyth, P. and Uthurusamy, R.(eds.): *Advances in Knowledge Discovery and Data Mining.* AAAI/MIT Press, 1996.
4. Fayyad, U.N., Piatetsky-Shapiro, G., Smyth, P.: *From Data Mining to Knowledge Discovery: an Overview.* In [3], pp.1-33
5. Han, J. and Fu, Y.: *Attribute-Oriented Induction in Data Mining.* In [3], pp.399-421
6. Holsheimer, M. and Kersten, M: *Architectural Support for Data Mining.* In : CWI Technical Report CS-R9429, Amsterdam, The Netherlands, 1994.
7. Kudoh, Y. and Haraguchi, M.: An Appropriate Abstration for an Attribute-Oriented Induction. Proceeding of The Second International Conference on Discovery Science, LNAI 1721, pp.43 - 55, 1999.
8. Kudoh, Y. and Haraguchi, M.: Data Mining by Generalizing Database Based on an Appropriate Abstraction, In : Journal of Japanese Society for Artificial Intelligence, vol.15, No.4, July, pp.638 – 648, 2000 (in Japanese).
9. Kudoh, Y. and Haraguchi, M.: An Appropriate Abstraction for Constructing a Compact Decision Tree, Proceegin of The Third International Conference on Discovery Science, LNAI, (to appear), 2000.
10. Matsumoto, K., Morita, C. and Tsukimoto, H. *Generalized Rule Discovery in Databases by Finding Similarities* In : SIG-J-9401-15, pp.111-118, Japanese Society for Artificial Intelligence, 1994.
11. Michalski, R.S., Bratko, I. and Kubat, M. (eds.): *Machine Learning and Data Mining: Methods and Applications,* London, John Wiley & Sons, 1997.
12. Michalski, R.S. and Kaufman, K.A.: *Data Mining and Knowledge Discovery: A Reivew of Issues and a Multistrategy Approach* In: [11] pp.71 - 112, 1997.
13. Miller, G.A., Beckwith, R., Fellbaum, C., Gross, D. and Miller, K.: *Intorduction to WordNet : An On-line Lexical Database* In : International Journal of lexicography 3 (4), pp.235 - 244, 1990.
14. Miller, G.A.: *Nouns in WordNet : a lexical inheritance system,* In : International Journal of Lexicography 3 (4), pp. 245 - 264, 1990. ftp://ftp.cogsci.princeton.edu/pub/wordnet/5papers.ps
15. Murphy, P.M. and Aha, D.W.: *UCI Repository of machine learning databases,* http://www.ics.uci.edu/ mlearn/MLRepository.html.
16. Quinlan, J.R.: *C4.5 - Programs for Machine Learning,* Morgan Kaufmann, 1993.

A New Algorithm to Select Learning Examples from Learning Data

B. Chebel-Morello[1], E. Lereno[1], B. P. Baptiste[2]

[1]Laboratoire d'automatique de Besançon
CNRS UMR 6596, ENSMM - UFC
Institut de productique, 25, rue Alain Savary
25000 BESANCON – France
lereno@ens2m.fr

[2] Laboratoire de Productique et Informatique des Systèmes Manufacturiers
I.N.S.A/IF-PRISMA, Bat 502. 20. Avenue Einstein
69621 Villeurbanne - France
baptiste@gprhp.insa-lyon.fr

Abstract. In almost every area of human activity, the formation of huge databases has created a massive request for new tools to transform data into task oriented knowledge. Our work concentrates on real-world problems, where the learner has o handle problems dealing with data sets containing large amounts of irrelevant information. Our objective is to improve the way large data sets are processed. In fact, irrelevant information perturb the knowledge data discovery process. That is why we look for efficient methods to automatically analyze huge data sets and extract relevant features and examples. This paper presents an heuristic algorithm dedicated to example selection. In order to illustrate our algorithm capabilities, we present results of its application to an artificial data set, and the way it has been used to determine the best human resource allocation in a factory scheduling problem. Our experiments have indicated many advantages of the proposed methodology.

1   Introduction

The objective of our research is to allow a better use of large amounts of data, so we have focused our interest in the Knowledge Data Discovery (KDD) process. More precisely, our work attend to the problem of concept learning from examples. In our study, we concentrate on data filtering that is an essential step for the Data Mining phase [1]. Our goal is to draw the underlying structures of the data to be processed trough the KDD successive steps. From input data, *coded* as attribute-value data, we obtain a set of examples (step ❶). During the next step, considering our population, relevant data have to be selected in order to avoid a wrong model representation of the concept to be learned(step ❷). These information are then structured (step ❸) and knowledge is generated in the form of rules, decision trees or *decision structures* [2]. In our experiments, we generate decision trees using the well known J.R. Quinlan's C4.5 algorithm [3].

Data ➔ ❶ Extraction ➔ Examples ➔ ❷ Filtering ➔ ❸ Structuration ➔ Knowledge

Data Filtering

An excess of information can hide useful information. That is why we try to filter noisy data by selecting only data that explain the goal variable (class). The data selection consists in the choice of a data set (variables and examples) as small as possible but necessary and sufficient to describe the target concept. The data dimension can be reduced by selecting reduction variables or selecting relevant examples. Most works emphasize the first approach as in [4], [5], [6], [7], [8], [9], [10], [11], [12], [13]. Still, we decided to stress the example selection problem, just as some attributes are useful than others, so may some examples better aid the learning process than others [14]. Researchers [4], [14], [15] have pointed out three main reasons for selecting relevant examples during the induction process. If we have lots of unlabeled examples, or if they are easy to generate, the cost of labeling is usually high (labels must be obtained from experts). Moreover the learning algorithm can be computationally intensive, in this case for purposes of computational efficiency it's worth learning only from some examples if sufficient training data is available. A third reason for example selection is to increase the rate of learning by focusing attention on informative examples. Liu and Motoda [16] compare different works dealing with data selection and point out four major points, the type of research, the organization of research, the selection criterion and the stopping criterion. Michaut [17] gives a recapitulative table of the filtering algorithms sorting them according these four points and the induction methods used after the selection algorithms. In this paper we propose an heuristic algorithm to reduce the data dimension using a *sequential forward generation* research strategy. In other words, we create a kernel of examples N starting with an empty set. The process is stopped when the obtained kernel N is equivalent to the starting example set Ω. In Section 2 our problem is formalized using Diday's symbolism [18], [19], then Section 3 expose the criterion used in our algorithm that is to say the degree of generality concept, the discriminant power between two objects and the discriminant power between an object and a set of objects. From these definitions we propose Section 4 a new algorithm to select relevant objects. Then, Section 5 describes two examples illustrating the advantages of the proposed methodology.

2. Knowledge Representation

"From the elementary objects characterized by the values taken by several variables, several symbolic objects can be defined" Kodratof, Diday [20].

The Symbolic Objects

A symbolic object is defined as a conjunction of properties on the values taken by the variables. Π is the studied population, Ω the sample of n observed examples (instances) $\Omega = \{\omega_1, \omega_2, \ldots, \omega_n\}$ and Y is the set of r qualitative variables $Y = \{ y_1, \ldots, y_k, \ldots, y_r \}$ defined over Π

$$\text{Let } y_k \text{ be defined as } y_k : \begin{cases} \Omega \rightarrow O_k \\ \omega \rightarrow y_k(\omega) = m_v^k \end{cases} \tag{1}$$

where O_k is the space of modalities containing a finite set of y_k observed values.

$O_k = \{m_1^k, \ldots, m_v^k, \ldots, m_{ms}^k\}$, where m_v^k is the modality v of the variable y_k

with $O = O_1 \times O_2 \times \ldots \times O_k \times \ldots \times O_r$ the set of all possible elementary objects,

and $$\begin{cases} Y : \Omega \rightarrow O \\ \omega \rightarrow Y(\omega) = (y_1(\omega), \ldots, y_r(\omega)) \end{cases} \text{ where } Y(\omega) \text{ is the description of the object } \omega. \tag{2}$$

Elementary Events : An elementary event is denoted $e_i = [y_i = V_i]$ where $V_i \subseteq O_i$ is a predicate expressing that "variable y_i takes its values $y_i(\omega)$ in V_i".

Each ω_i is characterized by a set of r variables (attributes)

$$y_1, \ldots, y_k, \ldots, y_r \begin{cases} \Omega \rightarrow O_k \\ \omega_i \rightarrow y_k(\omega_i) = m_v^k \end{cases} \tag{3}$$

For an *elementary object* ω_i, e_k is restricted to a single value $m_v^k / V_k = m_v^k \qquad \forall k = 1, \ldots, r$
O_k is a set of m_k modalities (values) of the variable y_k.

$O_k = \{m_1^k, \ldots \ldots m_v^k, \ldots, v_{mk}^k\}$ where m_v^k is the modality v of the variable y_k for the elementary object ω_i, $i = 1, \ldots, n$.

Let $O = O_1 \times O_2 \times \ldots \times O_k \times \ldots \times O_r$ the workspace and Y an application : $y : \begin{cases} \Omega \rightarrow O \\ \omega \rightarrow Y(\omega) = (y_1(\omega), \ldots, y_r(\omega)) \end{cases}$

Assertion Objects : We define an assertion object like a logical conjunction of elementary objets. :
$$a = [y_1 = V_1] \wedge \ldots \wedge [y_k = V_k] \wedge \ldots \wedge [y_q = V_q] \text{ with } q \leq r. \tag{4}$$
a is a conjunction of elementary events simultaneously true for a given elementary object ω.

3. Functional Modelisation

The Notion of Relevance

To each variable y_k we associate a function φ_i^k relative to each elementary object e.

$$\varphi_i^k : \begin{cases} \Omega \to \{0,1\} \\ \omega \to \varphi_i^k(\omega_i/m_i^k)=1 \Leftrightarrow y_k(\omega_i)=m_i^k \omega \to \varphi_i^k(\omega_i/m_i^k)=1 \Leftrightarrow y_k(\omega_i)=m_i^k \\ else \varphi_i^k(\omega_i/m_i^k)=0 \end{cases} \tag{5}$$

Let Y be an application, we associate the function Φ_i relative to each assertion object a.

$$\text{We have } Y : \begin{cases} \Omega \to \{0,1\} \\ \omega \to \Phi_i(\omega_i/m_i^1...m_i^k...m_i^r)=1 \Leftrightarrow y_k(\omega_i)=\{y_k(\omega_i)=m_i^1 \wedge...\wedge y_k(\omega_i)=m_i^k \wedge...\wedge y_k(\omega_i)=m_i^r\} \\ else \Phi_i(\omega_i/m_i^1...m_i^k...m_i^r)=0 \end{cases} \tag{6}$$

An assertion object describes a class and we look for the assertion objects corresponding to each class. However, we should give a definition of relevance, Blum and Langley [4], using our own formalism.

Strong relevance : A variable y_k is relevant regarding a goal variable y_{goal} and a population Ω, if two objects belonging to the space Ω having two different values of y_{goal} only differ when considering the value taken by the attribute y_k .

$$For\ \omega_i.and.\omega_j \in \Omega \times \Omega... \forall y_l, l=1..r, \exists k/.y_k(\omega_i) \neq y_k(\omega_j).and\ y_{goal}(\omega_i) \neq y_{goal}(\omega_j) \tag{7}$$

We should stress the fact that this constraint is very strong. Consequently, we give an another definition to make a distinction between a non-pertinent variable and a pertinent but redundant variable. For example, if two variables are redundant, they will not be considerate as relevant, even if they are found pertinent considering them separately. Thus we define a weak relevance.

Weak relevance : A variable y_k is weakly relevant regarding a goal variable y_{goal} and a population Ω, if it is possible to remove a subset of variables so that y_k become strongly relevant. A probabilistic definition also exists but as we do not use it, it is not presented in this paper. We introduce now a Boolean function to measure relevance. Consider the following Boolean functions

$$(\omega_i,\omega_j) \mapsto \varphi_{i,j}^k = \varphi_k(\omega_i,\omega_j)=0 \Leftrightarrow y_k(\omega_i) \neq y_k(\omega_j) \Leftrightarrow \overline{\varphi_{i,j}^k}=1$$

$$(\omega_i,\omega_j) \mapsto \varphi_{i,j}^{goal} = \varphi_{goal}(\omega_i,\omega_j)=0 \Leftrightarrow y_{goal}(\omega_i) \neq y_{goal}(\omega_j) \Leftrightarrow \overline{\varphi_{i,j}^{goal}}=1 \tag{8}$$

We can now define a function relative to **one variable** (attribute) for **a pair of objects**. When a pair of objects is relevant considering the goal variable y_{goal}, then this function takes the value 1.

$$(\omega_i,\omega_j) \mapsto \overline{\varphi_{i,j}^k} \bullet \overline{\varphi_{i,j}^{goal}}=1$$

We define the first variable aggregation measure as the following sum $\quad S=\left[\sum_{k=1}^r \overline{\varphi_{\omega_i\omega_j}^k}\right] \bullet \overline{\varphi_{\omega_i\omega_j}^{goal}} \tag{9}$

If $S=1$ then we only have one relevant attribute. Consequently this measure gives us **the strong relevance** when it takes the value 1.

The following example (Table 1) illustrates the notion of strong relevance :

Table 1. Three objects $\{\omega_1, \omega_2, \omega_3\}$ with y_2 strongly relevant

	y_1	y_2	y_3	y_4	y_{goal}
ω1	2	1	1	3	1
ω2	2	2	1	3	2
ω3	2	4	1	3	2

The variable y_2 is **strongly relevant** regarding the variable y_{goal} because the objects considered only differ when considering the value of attribute y_2.

The degree of generality

The degree of generality g is defined as follows : $\quad g : \begin{cases} \Omega \to R \\ \omega \to g_k(\omega) = \dfrac{Card\ V_k}{O_k} \end{cases} \quad k=1,...,r \tag{10}$

Assertion Objects and Degree of Generality

Let a be an assertion object : $a = [y_1=V_1]\wedge ... \wedge[y_k=V_k]\wedge ... \wedge[y_r=V_r]$

a is composed of a set of elementary objects, like for example $\{\omega_1\ \omega_2\ \omega_3\}$ with :

$$\omega_1 \rightarrow G(a) = \prod_{k=1}^{r}\frac{card(V_k)}{O_k} = g_1(a)\times....\times g_k(a)\times...\times g_r(a) \tag{11}$$

We have :

$$g_k(\omega_i)=\frac{card(V_i)}{card(O_k)} \qquad g_k(s_1)=\frac{card(V_1)}{card(O_k)} \qquad s_2=s_1\cup\omega_i \text{ and } \qquad g_k(s_2)=\frac{card(V_2)}{card(O_k)}=\frac{card(V_1)+\overline{\varphi_{\omega_i s}^{k}}}{card(O_k)}$$

The evaluation of $\varphi_{\omega_i s}^{k}$ is trivial. If $\varphi_{\omega_i s}^{k}=0$ then ω_i is not useful to the intension (set of objects) of the elementary event associated with y_k. In order to take into account all variables we perform an aggregation of the different functions.

$$\text{We obtain : } \Phi(\omega_i,s)=\sum_{k=1}^{r}\overline{\varphi_{\omega_i s}^{k}} \tag{12}$$

If $\Phi(\omega_i,s)=0$ ω_i will not be part of the kernel representing a given class. For each modality of the goal variable we want to define the assertion object. Let Y_{goal} be the goal variable : $Y_{Goal}=[C_1,...,C_{rGoal}]$. C_1 is defined by the assertion object a_1 which intension will be estimated by the aggregation of all elements belonging to Ω. We generalize the function defined for one class to the whole population :

$$\Phi_{goal}(\omega_i,s)=\Phi_{\omega_i,s}^{goal}=\sum_{k=1}^{r}\overline{\varphi_{\omega_i,s}^{k}}\bullet\overline{\varphi_{\omega_i,s}^{goal}} \tag{13}$$

if $\Phi_{goal}(\omega_i,s)=\Phi_{\omega_i,s}^{goal}=0$ ω_i has an intension already described by s so it will not be selected

if $\Phi_{goal}(\omega_i,\omega_l)=\Phi_{\omega_i,\omega_l}^{goal}=1$ ω_i and ω_l are *neighbors* and only differ for a single element.

Let p be the corresponding index with $\overline{\varphi_{\omega_i \omega_j}^{p}}=1$

We can aggregate ω_i and ω_j by creating an assertion object a_m such as :

$$a_m = y_1(\omega_i) \wedge ... \wedge[y_k(\omega_i)]\wedge ... \wedge[y_p(\omega_i)v\ y_p (\omega_l)] \tag{14}$$

In other words , we have to select *the indispensable elementary objects* and use them to build the kernel of objects we look for.

4   Example Selection Algorithm

The algorithm we present is similar to the simple selection greedy algorithms as those proposed by Almuallin and Dietterich [22] or Vignes [23]. It's discribed by the following criteria :

Search Strategy : heuristic, variables are selected in accordance with a criterion which is maximized or minimized

Generation Scheme : sequential forward, the algorithm starts with an empty set

Evaluation Measure : relevance, : discriminant power for the variables and generality degree for the objects

Stopping Criterion : <u>*ODPgoal(S)= ODPgoal(Y)*</u> for the variables and <u>$\Phi(N)=\Phi(\Omega)$</u> for the objects

        Total discriminant power   *Total degree of generality*

Example Selection Algorithm

  ❶ Initialization N = Ø

  ❷ *Extra-class work*

    - Look for the most relevant objects

    - Selection of the strongly relevant pairs

$$\{\omega_i\omega_m\} \text{ such as } \left[\sum_{k=1}^{r}\overline{\varphi_{\omega_i\omega_j}^{k}}\right]\bullet\overline{\varphi_{\omega_i\omega_j}^{goal}}=1 \text{ then } \qquad N=N+\{\omega_i\omega_m\}$$

❸ *Intra-class work*

Stopping Criterion For each class we evaluate the degree of generality of class $\Phi(\Omega_1)$

Repeat Choice of the relevant example

Choice of $\omega_m / \Phi_{\omega_m,s}^{goal} = \max(\Phi_{\omega_{is}}^{goal})$ such as

$$\Phi_{\omega_i,s}^{goal} = \sum_{k=1}^{r} \overline{\varphi_{\omega_{is}}^{k}} \bullet \varphi_{\omega_{is}}^{goal} \qquad \textbf{Until} \qquad \Phi(N_1) = \Phi(\Omega_1)$$

In the next section we present the experimental results our filtering algorithm.

5   Experimental Results

Artificial Data Set

We have used C++ language to implement our algorithm and the pre-processing tasks which prepare the data set to be processed with our method. These pre-processing tasks only perform a sorting by class and write several output data information files to help our algorithm to work faster. We should notice that, this does not interfere in any way with the initial data set content. To facilitate the understanding of our algorithm we consider an artificial data set containing 20 objects (examples) and 4 variables (attributes). The set of objects (see Table 2) does not contain redundant objects because their elimination is trivial. We use J.R. Quinlan's C4.5 algorithm [12],[3], to generate the decision trees. We will now apply our algorithm on the full data set and then generate a new decision tree with the reduced set and compare it with the first one.

Table 2. Data set used to evaluate the object selection algorithm

	y_1	y_2	y_3	y_4	y_{goal}		y_1	y_2	y_3	y_4	y_{goal}
$\omega1$	1	1	1	1	1	$\omega11$	3	3	1	3	4
$\omega2$	1	2	1	2	1	$\omega12$	2	4	1	2	4
$\omega3$	1	1	2	1	1	$\omega13$	3	4	1	3	4
$\omega4$	1	2	2	2	2	$\omega14$	3	4	1	2	4
$\omega5$	2	2	1	2	2	$\omega15$	2	3	1	2	4
$\omega6$	2	2	2	1	2	$\omega16$	1	1	2	3	5
$\omega7$	1	2	3	1	3	$\omega17$	3	1	2	3	5
$\omega8$	2	2	3	2	3	$\omega18$	3	4	2	3	5
$\omega9$	3	2	3	1	3	$\omega19$	1	4	2	3	5
$\omega10$	2	3	1	3	4	$\omega20$	1	4	3	3	5

During step ❶, the algorithm evaluate the strong relevance pairs, and then constructs the kernel of objects to take into consideration. After step ❷ the algorithm gives us the following results :

Strong relevance pairs : $C = \{\omega_2 \, \omega_4\} \, \{\omega_2 \, \omega_5\} \, \{\omega_3 \, \omega_{16}\} \, \{\omega_5 \, \omega_8\} \, \{\omega_5 \, \omega_{12}\} \, \{\omega_5 \, \omega_{15}\} \, \{\omega_{13} \, \omega_{18}\}$

$Kernel = \{\omega_2 \, \omega_3 \, \omega_4 \, \omega_5 \, \omega_8 \, \omega_{12} \, \omega_{13} \, \omega_{15} \, \omega_{16} \, \omega_{18} \omega_{20}\}$

Step ❸ completes the example selection :

Objects to be added to the kernel :

None for class 1 $\{\omega_2 \, \omega_3\}$ None for class 4 $\{\omega_{12} \, \omega_{13} \, \omega_{15}\}$

None for class 2 $\{\omega_4 \, \omega_5\}$ $\{\omega_{20}\}$ for class 5 $\{\omega_{16} \, \omega_{18} \omega_{20}\}$ $\{\omega_7\}$ for class 3 $\{\omega_7 \, \omega_8\}$

At the end of the algorithm we obtain the final set of objects (Table 3). We should stress the fact that the obtained set is **40% smaller.**

Table 3. Reduced set of objects obtained after the algorithm selection : **40% smaller**

	y_1	y_2	y_3	y_4	y_{goal}		y_1	y_2	y_3	y_4	y_{goal}
$\omega2$	1	2	1	2	1	$\omega12$	2	4	1	2	3
$\omega3$	1	1	2	1	1	$\omega13$	3	2	3	1	4
$\omega4$	1	2	2	2	2	$\omega15$	3	3	1	3	4
$\omega5$	2	2	1	2	2	$\omega16$	1	1	2	3	5
$\omega7$	1	2	3	1	3	$\omega18$	3	4	2	3	5
$\omega8$	2	2	3	2	3	$\omega20$	1	4	3	3	5

In order to evaluate our selection of relevant objects we have generated two trees with C4.5. The first decision tree has been generated using the original data set (Table 2) and the second decision tree using the reduced set of objects (Table 3). We observe that the decision trees obtained are exactly the same, which means that there is no *information* loss. As a consequence, if we try to classify the objects eliminated during the filtering phase performed by our algorithm using the decision tree, we obtain a **good classification rate of 100%**. Our algorithm has substantially reduced the number of objects necessary to construct a classifier (set 40% smaller) while maintaining the classification rate unchanged.

A Human Resource Allocation Problem

We have used our algorithm to solve a real-world human resource allocation problem. The case studied is a factory that produces gold chains and chain bracelets. The aim is to obtain a scheduling system capable to learn the human resource allocation and queue heuristics considering the manufacturing orders for a given period. We evaluate the scheduling using the performance metrics given by the scheduling software Preactor : cost, due dates, priority, idle time etc. By repeating the process several times, we obtain a learning base of the best workshop configurations considering the whole set of possible cases. Then, we eliminate all non-pertinent examples in order to construct a learning system able to set up automatically the software parameters when a new set of manufacturing orders arrives. We have implemented our method using Visual C++ and Preactor and the results obtained show a better and faster response of the considered manufacturing system.

Conclusion

This paper described a filtering algorithm to select the significant examples of a learning set. Our example selection algorithm has shown its efficiency to determine a subset of relevant objects from a learning set. As a mater of fact, the classifier obtained using the reduced learning data set offers the same precision that the one induced from the complete learning data set. We also used our algorithm on huge data sets and the results obtained are far more better than those obtained by the *windowing* method used by C4.5 for example. Our methodology allows the reduction of a learning set without information loss and it also gives a smaller data set to perform the induction task. Computational time of algorithms is sometimes important, though the less examples it process the faster it performs induction process. We are improving our algorithm in order to perform an example/attribute selection, this software should be a useful tool to the KDD community.

References

1. Fayyad, U. M., Piatetsky-Shapiro, G., and Smyth, P. "From Data Mining to Knowledge Discovery: An Overview. *Advances in Knowledge Discovery and Data Mining* (pp. 1-34), 1996.
2. Michalski, R. S., Imam, I. F. "On Learning Decision Structures," *Fundamenta Matematicae*, 31(1), Polish Academy of Sciences, (pp. 49-64), 1997.
3. Quinlan, J. R. "Learning Efficient Classification Procedures and Their Application to Chess End Games" In R. S. Michalsky, J. G. Carbonnel, and T. M. Mitchell (Eds.), *Machine Learning: An Artificial Intelligence Approach*. San Francisco: Morgan Kaufmann, 1993.
4. Blum, A. L. "Learning Boolean Functions in a Infinite Attribute Space", *Machine Learning, 9*, (pp. 373-386), 1992.
5. Blum, A. L. and Langley, P. "Selection of Relevant Features and Examples in Machine Learning", *Artificial Intelligence* 97(1-2): (pp.245-271), 1997.
6. Breiman, L.,Friedman, J. H., Olshen, R. A., and Stone, C. J. *Classification and Regression Trees*. Belmont, CA: Wadsworth, 1984.
7. Dhagat, A., and Hellerstein, L. "PAC learning with Irrelevant Attributes" *Proceedings of the IEEE Symposium on Foundations of Computer Science* (pp. 64-74). IEEE, 1994.

8. John, G. H., Kohavi, R., and Pfleger, K. "Irrelevant Features and the Subset Selection Problem" *Proceedings of the Eleventh International Conference on Machine Learning* (pp. 121-129). New Brunswick, NJ: Morgan Kaufmann, 1994.

9. Kira, K., and Rendell, L. "A Practical Approach to Feature Selection" *Proceedings of the Ninth International Conference on Machine Learning* (pp. 249-256). Aberdeen, Scotland: Morgan Kaufmann, 1992.

10. Langley, P., and Sage, S. "Scaling to Domains with Many Irrelevant Features", In R. Greiner (Ed.), *Computational Learning Theory and Natural Learning Systems* Vol. 4. Cambridge, MA: MIT Press, 1997.

11. Mitchell, T. M. "Generalization as Search" *Artificial Intelligence*, 18, 203-226. Reprinted in J. W. Shavlik and T. G. Dietterich (Eds.), *Readings in Machine Learning* San Francisco, CA: Morgan Kaufmann, 1990.

12. Pagallo, G., and Haussler, D. "Boolean Feature Discovery in Empirical Learning." *Machine Learning, 5,* (pp. 71-99), 1990.

13. Quinlan, J. R. *C4.5: Programs for Machine Learning*. San Francisco: Morgan Kaufmann, 1983.

14. Michalsky, R. S. and Larson, J. B. "Selection of Most Representative Training Examples and Incremental Generation of VL_1 Hypotheses : the underlying methodology and the description programs ESEL and AQ11", *Report No 867*, Dept. of Computer Science, University of Illinois, Urbana, 1978.

15. Winston, P. H. "Learning Structural Descriptions From Examples" In P.H. Winston (Ed.), *The Psychology of Computer Vision*. New York : McGraw-Hill, 1975.

16. Liu, H., Motoda, H. *Feature Selection for Knowledge Discovery and Data Mining* Kluwer Acad. Publishers, 1998.

17. Michaut, D. "Filtering and Variable Selection in Learning Processes", *PHD,* University of Franche-Comté, December, 1999.

18. Brito, P., Diday, E., "Pyramidal Representation of Symbolic Objects" in *Knowledge, Data and Computer-Assisted Decisions*, Ed. M Schader and W. Gaul, Springer-Verlag, Berlin Heidelberg, 1990.

19. Diday, E., Brito, P. "Introduction to Symbolic Data Analysis" in *Conceptual and Numerical Analysis of Data*, (pp. 45-84) Ed. O. Opitz, Springer, Berlin Heidelberg New York, 1989.

20. Kodratoff, Y. and Diday, E. "Numeric and Symbolic Induction From Data", In Cepadues-Edition, Cepad, 1991.

21. H. Almuallim, T. G. Dietterich, "Learning with Many Irrelevant Features", *Proc. of the Ninth National Conference on Artificial Intelligence*, (pp. 547-552), 1991

22. R. Vignes, J. Lebbe, "Sélection d'un sous ensemble de descripteurs maximalement discriminant dans une base de connaissances", in : *3èmes journées "Symbolique-Numérique"*, IPMU-92, Paris, (pp. 219-232), 1992

Data Ranking Based on Spatial Partitioning

Gongde Guo, Hui Wang and David Bell

School of information and software Engineering, University of Ulster
Newtownabbey, BT37 0QB, N.Ireland
{G.Guo, H.Wang, DA.Bell}@ulst.ac.uk

Abstract. In applications where preferences are sought it is desirable to order instances of important phenomenon rather than classify them. Here we consider the problem of learning how to order instances based on spatial partitioning. We seek statements to the effect that one instance should be ranked ahead of another.

A two-stage approach to data ranking is proposed in this paper. The first learns to partition the spatial areas using the largest irregular area to represent the same rank data recursively, and gets a series of spatial areas (rules). The second stage learns a binary preference function indicating whether it is advisable to rank one instance before another according to the rules obtained from the first stage. The proposed method is evaluated using real world stock market data set. The results from initial experiments are quite remarkable and the testing accuracy is up to 71.15%.

1 Introduction

Work in inductive learning has mostly concentrated on learning to classify. However, there are many applications in which it is desirable to order instances rather than classify. An example is the personalised stock selecting system that prioritises interesting stocks and states that one stock should be ranked ahead of another. Such preferences are often constructed based on a learned probabilistic classifier or on a regression model.

Ordering and ranking have been investigated in various fields such as decision theory, social sciences, information retrieval and mathematical economics. For instance, it is common practice in information retrieval to rank documents according to their probability of relevance to a query, as estimated by a learned classifier for the concept "relevant document".

Cohen, et al [1] propose a ranking method that builds a preference function from a set of "ranking experts", and the preference function is then used to construct an ordering function that agrees best with the experts. The method used by Bartell, et al [2] adjusts system parameters to maximise the match between the system's document ordering and the user's desired ordering, given by relevance feedback from experts. Bartell [3] proposes a method by which the relevance estimates by different experts can be automatically combined to result in superior retrieval performance. All these methods need a set of "ranking-experts", and can't rank data via analysing the data themselves.

Wang, et al [4] propose a novel method of data reduction to utilise the partial order of data viewed as an algebraic lattice. Data and knowledge are represented uniformly by a logical structure called a *hyper relation*, which is a generalisation of a database relation (2-d table). However, its data reductive operation is based on regular areas in the data space, so its expressive ability is limited.

The method proposed in this paper is an attempt to rank data automatically based on data-spatial partitioning, using the biggest irregular area to represent the same rank data, and to identify the distributed areas of the same rank data via learning from a training data set. The advantage of this method is that it is simple and automatic. It can make judgements automatically via analysing data as it changes to adapt the requests of dynamic scenarios (exemplified here by stock markets), and it doesn't need the intervention of "ranking-experts".

The remainder of the paper is organised as follows. Section 2 introduces the definitions and notation. Section 3 describes the data ranking algorithm based on spatial partitioning, in which the execution process of an example of the algorithm is demonstrated by graphical illustration. The experimental results are described and the evaluation is showed in Section 4. Section 5 ends the paper with a discussion and future work.

2 Definitions and notation

Given two points p_i, p_j and two spatial areas a_i, a_j in multidimensional space, we represent $p_i=(p_{i1}, p_{i2},..., p_{in})$, $p_j=(p_{j1}, p_{j2},..., p_{jn})$, and $a_i=([t_{i11}, t_{i12}], [t_{i21}, t_{i22}],..., [t_{in1}, t_{in2}])$, $a_j =([t_{j11}, t_{j12}], [t_{j21}, t_{j22}],..., [t_{jn1}, t_{jn2}])$, in which, $[t_{il1}, t_{il2}]$ is the projection of a_i to its *l-th* component, and $t_{il2} \geq t_{il1}$, $l=1, 2, ..., n$. In this paper, for simplicity and uniformity, any point p_i is represented as a spatial area in multidimensional space, viz. $p_i =([p_{i1}, p_{i1}], [p_{i2}, p_{i2}],..., [p_{in}, p_{in}])$. This is often a more convenient and uniform representation for analysis.

Definition 1 Given two areas a_i, a_j in multidimensional space, the *merging operation* of two areas denoted by '$\cup$' can be defined as $a_i \cup a_j =([\min(t_{i11}, t_{j11}), \max(t_{i12}, t_{j12})]$, $[\min(t_{i21}, t_{j21}), \max(t_{i22}, t_{j22})], ..., [\min(t_{in1}, t_{jn1}), \max(t_{in2}, t_{jn2})])$.

The *intersection operation* '$\cap$' of two areas in multidimensional space can be defined as $a_i \cap a_j =([\max(t_{i11}, t_{j11}), \min(t_{i12}, t_{j12})], [\max(t_{i21}, t_{j21}), \min(t_{i22}, t_{j22})],...,[\max(t_{in1}, t_{jn1}), \min(t_{in2}, t_{jn2})])$. $a_i \cap a_j$ is empty only if there exists a l such that $\max(t_{il1}, t_{jl1})> \min(t_{il2}, t_{jl2})$, where $l=1,2,..., n$.

A point merging (or intersection) with an area can be regarded as a special case according to above definition.

Definition 2 Given an area a_j in multidimensional space, denoted as $a_j=([t_{j11}, t_{j12}], [t_{j21}, t_{j22}], ..., [t_{jn1}, t_{jn2}])$, the *complementary operation* of a_j is defined as $\overline{a_j} =([\overline{t_{j11},t_{j12}}]$, $[t_{j21}, t_{j22}], ..., [t_{jn1}, t_{jn2}]) \cup ([t_{j11}, t_{j12}], \overline{[t_{j21},t_{j22}]}, ..., [t_{jn1}, t_{jn2}]) \cup ... \cup ([t_{j11}, t_{j12}], [t_{j21}, t_{j22}],$ ..., $\overline{[t_{jn1},t_{jn2}]}) \cup ... \cup ([t_{j11},t_{j12}],\overline{[t_{j21},t_{j22}]}, ..., \overline{[t_{jn1},t_{jn2}]})$, it is the area in the multidimensional space complementary area a_j.

Definition 3 Given a point p_i denoted as $p_i = (p_{i1}, p_{i2},..., p_{in})$ and an area a_j denoted as $a_j=([t_{j11}, t_{j12}], [t_{j21}, t_{j22}],..., [t_{jn1}, t_{jn2}])$ in multidimensional space, the *universal hyper relation* '$\leq$' is defined as $p_i \leq a_j$ (called p_i *falling into area of* a_j), if for all l, $t_{jl1}\leq p_{il}\leq t_{jl2}$, where $l=1, 2, ..., n$.

Definition 4 Let D be a finite set of instances. A *preference function*, *Pref*, is a binary function *Pref*: $D \times D \rightarrow [0,1]$. For u, $v \in D$, *Pref(u,v)*=1 (respectively 0) is interpreted as a strong recommendation that u should be ranked above (respectively, below) v. A special value, denoted $\perp$, is interpreted as an abstention from making a recommendation. The results of data-spatial partitioning will be a series of spatial partition areas (rules) which represent the different rank data, and new instances will be ranked according to their dropping into different spatial areas.

For simplify, all the data attributes used in this paper for data ranking are numerical. Set union operation (respectively intersection operation, complementation operation) can be used to replace the '$\cup$' operation (respectively '$\cap$' operation, '$-$'operation) defined above for categorical data or binary data.

3 Ranking algorithm

Let a training data set be $D = \{d_1, d_2, \ldots, d_m\}$, where $d_i = (d_{i1}, d_{i2}, \cdots, d_{in})$. d_i is a point in multidimensional space which can be represented as $d_i = ([d_{i1}, d_{i1}], [d_{i2}, d_{i2}], \ldots, [d_{in}, d_{in}])$ using spatial area representation, where d_{in} is a continuous valued decision attribute. The data in the training data set D is sorted in decreasing order by decision value at the beginning of spatial partitioning. The sorted result is denoted as $D_0 = \{d_1^0, d_2^0, \cdots, d_m^0\}$. The sorted data set is divided into k equal sets from top to bottom, k is a parameter using for tuning algorithm to optimal dividing. The i-th part has $|q_i|$ data, and $q_i = \{d_j \in D_0 | j = \lfloor((i-1)*n)/k\rfloor+1, \cdots, \lfloor(i*n)/k\rfloor$, $i=1, 2, \ldots, k\}$. Sorting and dividing should be done before the data space is partitioned. The partitions are continuous spaces which might order (see Figure 2.1).

The spatial partitioning algorithm is as follows.

1. $t=0$, set ε be a constant.

2. $n = |D_t|$, $M_i^t = \bigcup_{j=\lfloor((i-1)*n/k\rfloor+1, \cdots \lfloor(i*n)/k\rfloor}\{d_j^t\}$, $d_j^t \in D_t$, $i=1, 2, \ldots, k$.

3. $M_{i,j}^t = M_i^t \cap M_j^t$, $i \neq j$ and $i, j=1, 2, \ldots, k$.

4. $S_i^t = M_i^t \cap \overline{M_{i,1}^t} \cap \ldots \cap \overline{M_{i,j-1}^t} \cap \overline{M_{i,j+1}^t} \cap \ldots \cap \overline{M_{i,k}^t}$, $i=1, 2, \ldots, k$.

5. $D_{t+1} = \{d_i^t \mid d_i^t \in M_{i,j}^t, i \neq j$ and $i, j=1, 2, \ldots, k\}$.

6. If ($|D_{t+1}| \leq \varepsilon$) go to 8

7. $t=t+1$, go to 2

8. $R_i = \{S_i^0, S_i^1, \cdots, S_i^t\}$, $i=1,2,\ldots, k$

Some symbols above are: S_i^t-the biggest irregular area of i part obtained in t-th recurrence. D_t - training data set used in t-th recurrence, and M_i^t - merging area of i-th part data obtained in t-th recurrence, $M_{i,j}^t$-the intersection of M_i^t and M_j^t obtained in t-th recurrence.

It is important to pre-process the training data set. After sorting and dividing the data in the training data set, the decision value of data in the upper parts is greater than that in the lower parts. The partition areas denoted as R_i, in which, $i=1, 2, \ldots, k$ are obtained eventually by running the above algorithm, then the function *Pref(u, v)* of u,

v in the testing data set can be calculated easily based on the definition of preference function.

Given a testing data set D_T and $S_i^l \in R_i$, obtained from the partitioning process, where $i=1, 2, ..., k$. For any testing data u, $v \in D_T$, $Pref(u, v)$ is calculated using the universal hyper relationship $\leq$, by judging which area u, v belong to and ranking accordingly.

The algorithm is as follows.

- If $u \leq S_i^l$, $v \leq S_j^l$, where $j > i$ (respectively $j < i$), $l=1, 2, ..., t$ then $Pref(u, v)$ $=1$, u is preferred to v (respectively $Pref(u, v) =0$, v is preferred to u).
- If $u, v \leq S_i^l$, viz. u and v fall into the same area of S_i^l, then $Pref(u, v)= \bot$, viz. u, v have no preference relationship.
- If $u \leq S_i^l$ and $v \leq S_i^q$ or $u \leq S_i^l$ and $v \leq S_j^q$, in which, $q \neq l$, $i \neq j$ and $l, q = 1, 2, ..., t$ then $Pref(u, v)= \bot$, viz. u, v have no preference relationship.
- If there is not such S_i^l which u or v belongs to, where $i=1, 2, ..., k$ and $l=1, 2, ..., t$ then $Pref(u, v)= \bot$, viz. u, v have no preference relationship.

Consider Figure2-1 for example, the data set D consists of 30 data points. The data points are sorted in decreasing order according to their decision value. The sorted data set is represented as D_0. To simplify, the data in D_0 are divided into three parts and are represented in different colours. Black, grey and white represent the data in the upper part, middle part and lower part respectively. Obviously, Black data in the upper part of D_0 have greater decision value than the grey and the white ones, and grey data in the middle part of D_0 have greater decision value than the white one.

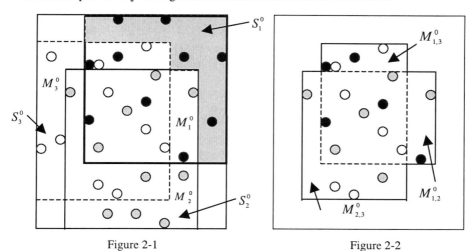

Figure 2-1   Figure 2-2

See Figure 2-1, after merging all the data in the same part, three spatial areas of M_1^0, M_2^0, M_3^0 denoted by bold line, fine line and broken line respectively are obtained.

The intersectional areas of M_1^0, M_2^0, M_3^0 denoted by $M_{1,2}^0, M_{1,3}^0, M_{2,3}^0$, can be seen in Figure2-2, given by: $M_{1,2}^0 = M_1^0 \cap M_2^0$, $M_{1,3}^0 = M_1^0 \cap M_3^0$, $M_{2,3}^0 = M_2^0 \cap M_3^0$

The largest irregular areas of the same rank data at this stage are obtained and denoted as S_1^0, S_2^0, S_3^0, which have the formula as following:

$$S_1^0 = M_1^0 \cap \overline{M_{1,2}^0} \cap \overline{M_{1,3}^0}, \ S_2^0 = M_2^0 \cap \overline{M_{1,2}^0} \cap \overline{M_{2,3}^0}, \ S_3^0 = M_3^0 \cap \overline{M_{1,3}^0} \cap \overline{M_{2,3}^0}$$

Obviously, if a testing data item u falls into S_1^0 and another testing data item v falls into S_2^0 or S_3^0 then $Pref(u, v)=1$; If u falls into S_2^0 and v falls into S_1^0 then $Pref(u, v)=0$; If u falls into S_2^0 and v falls into S_3^0 then $Pref(u, v)=1$; If u falls into S_3^0 and v falls into S_1^0 or S_2^0 then $Pref(u, v)=0$; If u falls into either $M_{1,2}^0$ or $M_{1,3}^0$, or $M_{2,3}^0$, no matter where v falls into, the relationship between u and v can not be estimated, so all the data which belong to one of $M_{1,2}^0$, $M_{1,3}^0$ and $M_{2,3}^0$ are taken out from the D_0 as a new training data set D_1, see Figure2-2. The new training data in D_1 are sorted in decreasing order according to their decision values and are divided into three parts again. Notice that the colour of some data might be changed if they belong to different part after dividing (see Figure2-4 and Figure2-5). This is due to the feature of the algorithm when spatial partitioning are not finished from iteration to iteration. The process of merging and partitioning is repeated until there are no more than ε data in the new training set D_1, see Figure2-3 to Figure2-10.

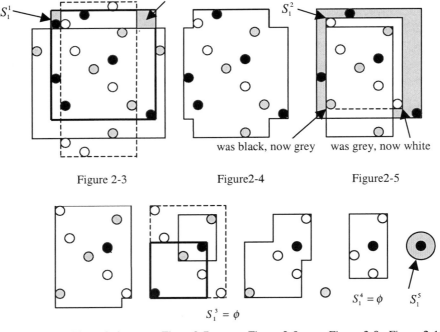

Figure 2-3	Figure2-4	Figure2-5

was black, now grey   was grey, now white

$S_1^3 = \phi$

Figure2-6	Figure2-7	Figure 2-8	Figure 2-9 Figure 2-10

In the end, a series of partition areas of each part are obtained, in which, for example each S_1^q , q=0, 1, ..., t are shown in grey background.

4 Experiment and evaluation

The ultimate goal of data spatial partitioning is to improve prediction accuracy. So we designed an experiment to evaluate the proposed data ranking method to see how well it performs in prediction with a real world database. A ranking system called Rank&Predict using the proposed method above has been developed.

Stocks closing data for the United Kingdom in 45 trading days, beginning on 2 Aug. 1999, and ending on 1 Oct. 1999, were collected from Reuters stock market repository and stored into a file named Dataftse. There were 96 stocks with 17 numerical attributes in one trading day. The parameter k is tuned to 3 for spatial partitioning.

Each continuous ten-day stock data in one month from 2 Aug. 1999 to 2 Sept. 1999 were chosen for training and testing. The prediction efficiency of algorithm was evaluated using 5-fold cross validation, and the testing accuracy used in experiment is defined as:

TA=((*the number of correct ranking*)/(*the total number of ranking*))*100.

The results are shown in Table 1, in which the acronyms are: TA-Testing Accuracy, VP-the Value of Parameter k, and PSD-the Period of Sampling Data.

PSD (1999)	TA:VP(3) (%)	PSD (1999)	TA:VP(3)(%)
2 Aug.-13 Aug.	72.03	3 Aug.-16 Aug.	67.92
4 Aug.-17 Aug.	65.98	5 Aug.-18 Aug.	65.42
6 Aug.-19 Aug.	76.51	9 Aug.-20 Aug.	70.45
10 Aug.-23 Aug.	75.22	11 Aug.-24 Aug.	72.47
12 Aug.-25 Aug.	59.16	13 Aug.-26 Aug.	81.88
16 Aug.-27 Aug.	82.87	17 Aug.-30 Aug.	72.83
18 Aug.-31 Aug.	66.02	19 Aug.-1 Sept.	70.18
20 Aug.-2 Sept.	68.28	Average	71.15

Table 1: The testing accuracy obtained by Rank&Predict.

Stock market data are rich in noise level, filled with random and unpredictable factors, but the results from initial experiments are quite remarkable, and its average testing accuracy is 71.15%. It might be possible to make money from rank&predict.

5 Discussion and Future work

This paper presents a novel approach to data ranking based on spatial partitioning. The spatial partition areas can be regarded as a model of the raw data. The important feature of this ranking method is to find the largest irregular area to represent the same rank data. It executes union, intersection, and complement operations in each dimension using the projection of spatial areas in multidimensional space. It also represents the same rank data using the biggest irregular spatial area to realise the goal of data ranking. A series of spatial partition areas are obtained after learning from a training data set using the spatial partitioning method, and these can be used easily in ranking subsequently.

We have shown that the proposed automatic data ranking method can be regarded as a novel approach to data mining to discover potential rank patterns in databases. A ranking system called Rank&Predict has been developed. Results from initial experiments on stock market data using Rank&Predict system are quite remarkable. Further research is required into how to eliminate noise to improve testing accuracy.

References

1. William W.Cohen, Robert E.Schapire, Yoram Singer. *Learning to order things*. Journal of Artificial Intelligence Research 10(1999) 243-270.
2. Brian T. Bartell, Garrison W.Cottrell, Richard K.Belew. *Learning the optimal parameters in a ranked retrieval system using multi-query relevance feedback*. In Proceedings of the Symposium on Document Analysis and Information Retrieval, Las Vegas, 1994.
3. Brian T. Bartell. *Optimizing Ranking Functions: A Connectionist Approach to Adaptive Information Retrieval*. PhD thesis, Department of Computer Science & Engineering, The University of California, San Diego, 1994.
4. Hui Wang, Ivo Duntsch, David Bell. *Data reduction based on hyper relations*. In Proceedings of KDD98, New York, pages 349-353, 1998.

Logical Decision Rules: Teaching C4.5 to Speak Prolog

Kamran Karimi and Howard J. Hamilton

Department of Computer Science
University of Regina
Regina, Saskatchewan
Canada S4S 0A2
{karimi,hamilton}@cs.uregina.ca

Abstract. It is desirable to automatically learn the effects of actions in an unknown environment. C4.5 has been used to discover associations, and it can also be used to find causal rules. Its output consists of rules that predict the value of a decision attribute using some condition attributes. Integrating C4.5's results in other applications usually requires spending some effort in translating them into a suitable format. Since C4.5's rules are horn clauses and have the same expressive power as Prolog statements, we have modified standard C4.5 so it will optionally generate its rules in Prolog. We have made sure no information is lost in the conversion process. It is also possible for the prolog statements to optionally retain the certainty values that C4.5 computes for its rules. This is achieved by simulating the certainty values as the probability that the statement will fail for no apparent reason. Prolog can move from statement to statement and find a series of rules that have to be fired to get from a set of premises to a desired result. We briefly mention how, when dealing with temporal data, the Prolog statements can be used for recursive searches, thus making C4.5's output more useful.

1   Introduction

C4.5 [4] allows us to extract classification rules from observations of a system. The input to C4.5 consists of a set of records. Each record contains some condition attributes and a single decision attribute. A domain expert should decide on which variable depends on others, and so is to be considered the decision attribute. Though C4.5 has been traditionally used as a classifier, it can even be used to find temporal relations [3].

C4.5 uses a greedy algorithm with one look-ahead step. It computes the information contents of each condition attribute and the results are used to prune the condition attributes and create classification rules that are simpler than the original input records. The output of C4.5 are simple predicates like **if** $\{(a = 1)$ AND $(b = 2)\}$ **then** $\{(c = 4)\}$. There is an error value assigned to each rule, which determines the confidence in that rule. C4.5 creates a decision tree first and then derives decision rules from that tree. After this a program in the C4.5 package called "consult" can be used to actually execute the rules. It prompts for the condition attributes and then outputs the appropriate value of the decision attribute. Any other use of the generated rules, including the integration of C4.5's results in other systems, may require some effort in changing the format of the results in order to make them compatible with the input of the other systems.

C4.5's output can be expressed by horn clauses, so we have modified C4.5 to directly output Prolog statements in addition to its normal output. This enables the results to be readily used in any Prolog-based system, thus making them readily machine-processable. Much of the ground work for this has been presented in detail in [2], where we explain C4.5's usability in deriving association and causal rules in a simple environment. In that paper we also showed the usefulness of having Prolog statements in applications beyond those ordinarily expected from C4.5's output, which are usually meant to be used by people instead of automatic machine processing. In this paper we discuss the improvements and modifications that were needed to make the Prolog statements better represent C4.5's results. This includes preserving more information in the output and also handling the certainty values assigned by C4.5 to its output rules. This is important because Prolog by default considers all its statements to be always reliable. In Section 2 we explain how C4.5's rules are converted into Prolog Statements. Section 3 concludes the paper and gives information as to where the reader can find the patch file needed to modify C4.5.

2   C4.5 Speaks Prolog

The rules created by C4.5 can easily be represented as Prolog statements. The "c4.5rules" program in the C4.5 package generates rules from a decision tree. We have modified this program to optionally output its resulting rules in Prolog [2]. This removes the need of a separate pass for the translation of the rules. When the user gives the command line option of '-p 0' a <file stem>.pl file will be created in addition to the normal output. The generated Prolog statements are in the Edinburgh dialect and can be fed to most Prolog interpreters with no change.

We used the modified c4.5rules program to create Prolog statements from data generated by artificial robots that move around in a two dimensional artificial world called URAL [6]. URAL is a typical Artificial Life simulator. The aim of the robot in this artificial world is to move around and find food. At each time-step the robot randomly chooses to move from its current position to either Up, Down, Left, or Right. The robot does not know the meaning or the results of any of these actions, so for example it does not know that its position may change if it chooses to go to Left. It can not get out of the board, or go through the obstacles that are placed on the board by the simulator. In such cases, a move action will not change the robot's position. The robot can sense which action it takes in each situation. The goal is to learn the effects of its actions after performing a series of random moves. To do this we save the robot's current situation after each action has taken place.

The simulator records the current x and y locations, the move direction, and the next value of x or y. When these data are fed to C4.5, it correctly determines that the next x or y values depend only on the previous location and the movement direction [2]. One example is a rule like: **if** {(X1 = 1) AND (A1 = L)} **then** (X2 = 0) which states that the result of a move to the left is a decrease in the value of *x*. *A1* and *X1* are the previous action and *x* value respectively. *X2* represents the next *x* value. Table 1 shows a few of the Prolog statements generated by the modified c4.5rules as described in [2]. The first statement corresponds to the example C4.5 rule just presented. *A1* and *X1* are as explained in that rule, and the classification is done on the next value of *x*.

class(A1, X1, 0) :- A1 = 2, X1 = 1.
class(A1, X1, 2) :- A1 = 3, X1 = 1.
class(A1, X1, 3) :- A1 = 3, X1 = 2.

Table 1. Three Sample Prolog statements generated by C4.5

In Table 1 a value of 2 and 3 for action *A1* could mean going to the left and right, respectively. Following C4.5's terminology, the results are designated by a predicate called "class." If we had to merge the Prolog statements generated for different decision attributes (because we might need to work with more than one decision attribute) then we could manually rename "class" to something like "classx" and remove any name clashes. In the above case this could happen we want to represent the rules for the moves along the *y* axis too. In the left-hand side of the Prolog statements the condition attributes that are involved in the decision making process come first, and the value of the decision attribute comes last. In the head of the rules, the condition attributes' values are used for the decision making process. All other condition attributes are ignored.

Notice that the automatically generated Prolog statements use Prolog's unification operator (=) instead of the comparison operator (=:=). This allows the user to traverse the rules backward and go from the decision attribute to the condition attributes, or from a set of decision and condition attributes, to the remaining condition attributes. Some example queries are class(A1, 1, 2) (which actions take the creature from *x* = 1 to *x* = 2?) or class(A1, X1, 3) (which action/location pairs immediately lead to *x* = 3?). The ability to interpret the rules in different directions makes C4.5's discovered rules more useful when represented as Prolog statements.

C4.5 can generate rules that rely on threshold testing and set membership testing. If we use the standard Prolog operators of =< and > for threshold testing, and implement a simple member() function for testing set membership, then we would not be able to traverse the rules backward, as they lack the ability to unify variables. So if we had a clause like: class(A, B, C) :- A =< B, member(A, C), then we would be unable to use a query like class(A, 3, [1, 2, 3]), because *A* is not unified, and Prolog can not perform the test =< on variables that are not unified. Adding the unification ability to =<, > and member() will remove this limitation. For example, a unifying *X* > 10 would choose a value above 10 for *X* if it is not already unified, and a unifying member(*X*, [1, 2, 3]) would unify *X* with one of 1, 2, or 3 if it is not already unified. Both cases would always succeed if *X* is not unified, because they make sure that the variable is unified with an appropriate value, but could fail if *X* is already unified because in that case a test will be performed.

In [2] we have provided simple code to do the unification. There we show that this unification ability allows the Prolog statements to be traversed backwards, and so they can be used for automatic planning purposes. This was achieved by first noticing that in Table 1 we are dealing with temporal data, since the decision attribute (the next x position) is actually the same as one of the condition attributes seen at a later time. This can be used to come up with a sequence of moves to change the x or y position one by one and get to a desired destination. Suppose we are at $x = 1$ and the aim is to go from there to $x = 3$. From Table 1 Prolog knows that to go to $x = 3$ one has to be at $x = 2$ and perform a Right move, but to be at $x = 2$, one has to be at $x = 1$ and again go to the right. This complete the planning because we are already at $x = 1$. In other words, $X1 = 1$ in a Prolog statement actually means class(_, _, 1), so the third statement in Table 1 can be converted to this: class(A1, X1, 3) :- A1 = 3, X1 = 2, class(_, _, 2). Intuitively this means that to go to x = 2 with a move to the right one has to be at x = 2 (class(_, _, 2)), and we do not care how we got there. Now prolog will have to satisfy class(_, _, 2) by going to $x = 2$. The changes that have to be done in the statements to allow Prolog to do such recursive searches come in detail in [2].

There is a problem in the way rules were represented in [2]. We use example Prolog statements from the more complex Letter Recognition Database from University of California at Irvine's Machine Learning Repository [1] to clarify our point. This database consists of 20,000 records that use 16 condition attributes to classify the 26 letters of the English alphabet. The implementation in [2] would give us the kind of rules seen in Table 2 below.

class(A10, A13, A14, A15, 8) :- A10 = 7, A13 = 0, A14 = 9, A15 = 4.
class(A10, A11, A13, 8) :- A10 = 13, A11 = 3, A13 = 3.
class(A10, A12, A13, A14, A15, 8) :- A10 = 8, A12 = 5, A13 = 3, A14 = 8, A15 = 5.
class(A7, A13, A14, A16, 8) :- A7 = 9, A13 = 0, A14 = 9, A16 = 7.
class(A6, A10, A11, A13, 8) :- A6 = 9, A10 = 7, A11 = 6, A13 = 0.

Table 2. Some of the Prolog statements from the Letter Recognition Database.

The 16 attributes are named A1 to A16. The decision attribute encodes the index of the letters. Table 2 shows some of the rules created for the letter "I." The problem with this form of rule output is that Prolog's variable names are limited in scope to the statement in which they appear. In the last two statements for example, as far as Prolog is concerned A6 and A7 represent the same thing: Both are place-holders for the first argument of the predicate "class" that has a total of five arguments. This means that the user can not use the name of a variable as he knows it to get its value. A representation like this would allow the user to perform queries such as class(9, 7, A14, 0, 8), and get the answer A14 = 6, which is probably not what he had in mind. This happens because Prolog is using the last statement to derive this result, and that statement actually concerns A11 and not A14.

To prevent this loss of information and the subsequent confusion, the modified c4.5rules program was changed to preserve all the condition attributes in the left-hand side of the Prolog statements. This allows Prolog to distinguish among the condition attributes by using their position, so now there is a way for the user to specify the variables unambiguously. The resulting statements are shown in Table 3.

class(A1, A2, A3, A4, A5, A6, A7, A8, A9, A10, A11, A12, A13, A14, A15, A16, 8) :- A10 = 7, A13 = 0, A14 = 9, A15 = 4.
class(A1, A2, A3, A4, A5, A6, A7, A8, A9, A10, A11, A12, A13, A14, A15, A16, 8) :- A10 = 13, A11 = 3, A13 = 3.
class(A1, A2, A3, A4, A5, A6, A7, A8, A9, A10, A11, A12, A13, A14, A15, A16, 8) :- A10 = 8, A12 = 5, A13 = 3, A14 = 8,
class(A1, A2, A3, A4, A5, A6, A7, A8, A9, A10, A11, A12, A13, A14, A15, A16, 8) :- A7 = 9, A13 = 0, A14 = 9, A16 = 7.
class(A1, A2, A3, A4, A5, A6, A7, A8, A9, A10, A11, A12, A13, A14, A15, A16, 8) :- A6 = 9, A10 = 7, A11 = 6, A13 = 0.

Table 3. Prolog statements with all the condition attributes present.

The statements are longer, but now the users can make sure Prolog understands what a query means. They can issue a query such as class(_, _, _, _, _, _, 9, _, _, _, _, _, 0, A14, _, 7, 8) and get the correct result of A14 = 19.

There is still something missing from the Prolog statements. C4.5 assigns a certainty value to each rule it generates, which shows how reliable that rule is. Standard Prolog does not support the notion of reliability of a statement. To convey this information to the Prolog statements in a way that would be understandable to most Prolog systems, we used a random number generator to fail the rules proportional to their certainty value. A random integer is generated and tested against the certainty value of the rule. A statement can fail if this test fails, no matter what the value of the condition attributes. C4.5 computes the certainty values as a number less than 1 and outputs them with a precision of 0.001. The modified c4.5rules program multiplies this number by 1000 to avoid having to deal with real numbers. The modified c4.5rules program outputs the necessary code to handle the certainty value if the user invokes it with a '-p 1' command line argument. We used a different command line argument for this because the user may not always need to have the certainty values in the output. Statements resulting from this argument are given in Table 4.

class(A1, A2, A3, A4, A5, A6, A7, A8, A9, A10, A11, A12, A13, A14, A15, A16, 8) :- random(1000, N__), N__ < 917, A10 = 7, A13 = 0, A14 = 9, A15 = 4.
class(A1, A2, A3, A4, A5, A6, A7, A8, A9, A10, A11, A12, A13, A14, A15,, A16, 8) :- random(1000, N__), N__ < 870, A10 = 13, A11 = 3, A13 = 3.
class(A1, A2, A3, A4, A5, A6, A7, A8, A9, A10, A11, A12, A13, A14, A15,, A16, 8) :- random(1000, N__), N__ < 793, A10 = 8, A12 = 5, A13 = 3, A14 = 8,
class(A1, A2, A3, A4, A5, A6, A7, A8, A9, A10, A11, A12, A13, A14, A15,, A16, 8) :- random(1000, N__), N__ < 793, A7 = 9, A13 = 0, A14 = 9, A16 = 7.
class(A1, A2, A3, A4, A5, A6, A7, A8, A9, A10, A11, A12, A13, A14, A15,, A16, 8) :- random(1000, N__), N__ < 707, A6 = 9, A10 = 7, A11 = 6, A13 = 0.

Table 4. Prolog statements with the ceratinty values.

We use the first rule in Table 4 to explain the statements. The first rule has a certainty value of 91.7%. The random(1000, N__) function assigns a number between 0 and 999 to N__. This value is then compared to the certainty value of the rule, which is 917. The statement could fail based on the results of the comparison. The random number is named N__ to lessen the chances of an accidental clash with the name of a condition attribute. One could implement the random number generator like this [5]: seed(13).

random(R, N) :- seed(S), N is (S mod R), retract(seed(S)),

NewSeed is (125 * S + 1) mod 4096, asserta(seed(NewSeed)), !.

We have taken an active approach to representing the certainty values, because they can actually cause the statements to fail. In an alternate implementation, we could choose to simply output these values as part of the statements and leave any specific usage to the user. An example, taken from the last statement in Table 4, would be class(A1, A2, A3, A4, A5, A6, A7, A8, A9, A10, A11, A12, A13, A14, A15, A16, N__, 8) :- A6 = 9, A10 = 7, A11 = 6, A13 = 0, N__ = 707.

3   Concluding Remarks

Outputting C4.5's classification rules as Prolog statements allows them to be more useful. They can be traversed in any direction, and can be readily integrated into Prolog-based systems. Prolog's searching abilities can readily be employed to do searches over the rules and go from rule to rule as in a traditional theorem prover. This becomes more useful with the kind of temporal data explained in the paper. The certainty values can be ignored in the output Prolog statements if they are to be used in deterministic environments. The user can also opt to simulate the possible failure of the rules by having the certainty values represented in the rules as thresholds for test against randomly generated numbers.

The modified c4.5rules program retains backward compatibility, and its output is unchanged when the new options are not used. The modifications are available in the form of a patch file that can be applied to standard C4.5 Release 8 source files. It is freely available from http://www.cs.uregina.ca/~karimi or by contacting the authors. C4.5 Release 8's sources are available for download from Ross Quinlan's webpage at http://www.cse.unsw.edu.au/~quinlan/

References

1. Blake, C.L and Merz, C.J., UCI Repository of machine learning databases [http://www.ics.uci.edu/~mlearn/MLRepository.html]. Irvine, CA: University of California, Department of Information and Computer Science, 1998.
2. Karimi, K. and Hamilton, H. J., "Learning With C4.5 in a Situation Calculus Domain," *The Twentieth SGES International Conference on Knowledge Based Systems and Applied Artificial Intelligence (ES2000)*, Cambridge, UK, December 2000.
3. Karimi, K. and Hamilton, H. J., "Finding Temporal Relations: Causal Bayesian Networks vs. C4.5." *The 12th International Symposium on Methodologies for Intelligent Systems (ISMIS'2000)*, Charlotte, NC, USA.
4. Quinlan, J. R., C4.5: Programs for Machine Learning. Morgan Kaufmann, 1993.
5. Clocksin, W.F., Melish, C.S, Programming in Prolog, Springer Verlag, 1984.
6. http://ww.cs.uregina.ca/~karimi/URAL.java

Visualisation of Temporal Interval Association Rules

Chris P. Rainsford[1] and John F. Roddick[2]

[1] Defence Science and Technology Organisation, DSTO C3 Research Centre
Fernhill Park , Canberra, 2600, Australia.
`chris.rainsford@dsto.defence.gov.au`
[2] School of Informatics and Engineering, Flinders University of South Australia
GPO Box 2100, Adelaide 5001, Australia.
`roddick@cs.flinders.edu.au`

Abstract. Temporal intervals and the interaction of interval-based events are fundamental in many domains including medicine, commerce, computer security and various types of normalcy analysis. In order to learn from temporal interval data we have developed a temporal interval association rule algorithm. In this paper, we will provide a definition for temporal interval association rules and present our visualisation techniques for viewing them. Visualisation techniques are particularly important because the complexity and volume of knowledge that is discovered during data mining often makes it difficult to comprehend. We adopt a circular graph for visualising a set of associations that allows underlying patterns in the associations to be identified. To visualize temporal relationships, a parallel coordinate graph for displaying the temporal relationships has been developed.

1 Introduction

In recent years data mining has emerged as a field of investigation concerned with automating the process of finding patterns within large volumes of data [9]. The results of data mining are often complex in their own right and visualisation has been widely employed as a technique for assisting users in seeing the underlying semantics [12]. In addition, mining from temporal data has received increased attention recently as it provides insight into the nature of changes in data [11].

Temporal intervals are inherent in nature and in many business domains that are modelled within information systems. In order to capture these semantics, we have developed an extension to the definition of association rules [1] to accommodate temporal interval data [10]. Association rules have been widely used as a data mining tool for market analysis, inference in medical data and product promotion. By extending these rules to accommodate temporal intervals, we allow users to find patterns that describe the interaction between events and intervals over time. For example, a financial services company may be interested to see the way in which certain products and portfolios are interrelated. Customers may initially purchase an insurance policy and then open an investment portfolio or superannuation fund with the same company. It may then be interesting to see which the customer terminates first. Likewise, a customer history may show that they have held investments in three different investment funds. It may then be interesting to see if all three were held simultaneously, one following the other, or in some overlapping fashion. Looking for underlying trends and patterns in this type of behaviour is likely to be highly useful for analysts who are seeking to market these products, both to new investors and long term clients. In order to increase the comprehensibility of rules that describe such relationships, we have also developed two visualisation tools. The first tool uses a circular graph to display the underlying association rules. This allows the user to see patterns within the underlying associations. The second visualisation uses a parallel coordinate approach to present the temporal relationships that exist within the data in an easily comprehendible format. Importantly, both of these visualisation techniques are capable of displaying large numbers of rules and can be easily represented in a fixed two-dimensional format that can be easily reproduced on paper or other media.

In the next section we will provide a definition for temporal interval association rules. Section 3 discusses our association rule visualisation tool. Section 4 then describes our temporal relationship visualiser. A conclusion is provided in Section 5.

2   Temporal Interval Association Rules

We define a temporal interval association rule to be a conventional association rule that includes a conjunction of one or more temporal relationships between items in the antecedent or consequent. Building upon the original formalism in [1] temporal interval association rules can be defined as follows: Let $I = I_1, I_2,...,I_m$ be a set of binary attributes or items and T be a database of tuples. Association rules were first proposed for use within transaction databases, where each transaction t is recorded with a corresponding tuple. Hence attributes represented items and were limited to a binary domain where $t(k) = 1$ indicated that the item I_k was positive in that case (for example, had been purchased as part of the transaction, observed in that individual, etc.), and $t(k) = 0$ indicated that it had not. Temporal attributes are defined as attributes with associated temporal points or intervals that record the time for which the item or attribute was valid in the modeled domain. Let X be a set of some attributes in I. It can be said that a transaction t satisfies X if, for all attributes I_k in X, $t(k) = 1$. Consider a conjunction of binary temporal predicates $P_1 \wedge P_2...\wedge P_n$ defined on attributes contained in either X or Y where $n \geq 0$. Then by a temporal association rule, we mean an implication of the form $X \Rightarrow Y \wedge P_1 \wedge P_2...\wedge P_n$, where X, the antecedent, is a set of attributes in I and Y, the consequent, is a set of attributes in I that are not present in X. The rule $X \Rightarrow Y \wedge P_1 \wedge P_2...\wedge P_n$ is satisfied in the set of transactions T with the confidence factor $0 \leq c \leq 1$ iff at least c% of transactions in T that satisfy X also satisfy Y. Likewise each predicate P_i is satisfied with a temporal confidence factor of $0 \leq tc_{P_i} \leq 1$ iff at least tc% of transactions in T that satisfy X and Y also satisfy P_i. The notation $X \Rightarrow Y \mid c \wedge P_1 \mid tc \wedge P_2 \mid tc...\wedge P_n \mid tc$ is adopted to specify that the rule $X \Rightarrow Y \wedge P_1 \wedge P_2...\wedge P_n$ has a confidence factor of c and temporal confidence factor of tc. As an illustration consider the following simple example rule:

policyZ $\Rightarrow$ investX,productY $\mid 0.79 \wedge$ *during*(investX,policyZ)$\mid$
$0.75 \wedge$ *before*(productY,investX)$\mid 0.81$

This rule can be read as follows:

The purchase of investment X and product Y are associated with insurance policy Z with a confidence factor of 0.79. The investment in X occurs during the period of policy Z with a temporal confidence factor of 0.75 and the purchase of product Y occurs before investment X with a temporal confidence factor of 0.81

Binary temporal predicates are defined using Allen's thirteen interval-based relationships between two intervals. A thorough description of these relationships can be found in [2]. We also use the neighborhood relationships defined by Freksa that allow generalisation of relationships [5]. A detailed description of our learning algorithm is beyond the scope of this paper and readers are referred to [10].

3 Visualising Associations

Finding patterns within the temporal interval associations may be assisted with the use of visualisation techniques. This is particularly important where the number of association rules is found to be large and the discovery of underlying patterns by inspection is not possible. For this purpose we have devised two separate visualisation techniques. The first can be used to visualise any association rule and the second is specific to temporal associations.

The visualisation of sets of association rules has been addressed in a number of different ways. One approach has been to draw connected graphs [6]. However, if the number of rules is large this approach involves a complex layout process that needs to be optimised in order to avoid cluttering the graph. An elegant three-dimensional model is provided in the *MineSet*™ software tool [4]. We have chosen to develop a visualisation that can handle a large volume of associations and that can be easily reproduced in two-dimensions, e.g. as a paper document, or an overhead projection slide. In addition, it provides an at-a-glance view of the data that does not need to be navigated and explored to be fully understood. This approach complements the approaches of others and is more applicable in some circumstances.

We have adopted a circular graph layout where items involved in rules are mapped around the circumference of a circle, see Figure 1. Associations are then plotted as lines connecting these points, where a gradient in the colour of the line, from blue(dark) to yellow(light) indicates the direction of the association from the antecedent to the consequent. A green line highlights associations that are bi-directional and this allows bi-directional relationships to be immediately identified. Circular graph layouts have been successfully used in several other data mining applications, including *Netmap* [3],[8]. A key characteristic of this type of visualization is its ability to display large volumes of information. The circle graph gives an intuitive feel for patterns within the underlying data. For example, items that have several other items associated with them will have a number of blue lines leaving their node on the circle. These items may be selected for marketing to attract new clients, because it is likely that the clients will also purchase other items or services as part of an overall basket. Note however that no temporal information is provided in this graph. In cases where the number of items is large, concept ascension may be employed to reduce complexity.

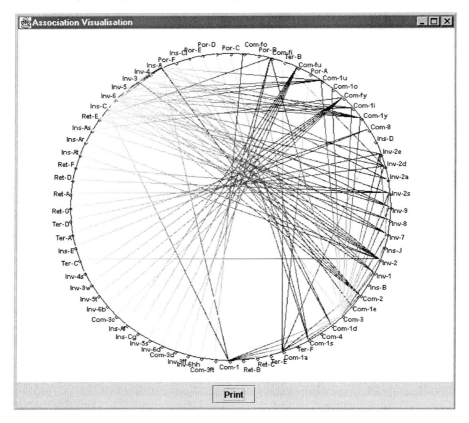

Fig. 1. A screenshot of our association rule visualisation window

4 Visualising Temporal Associations

Our first visualisation does not display the details of discovered temporal relationships between items in the association rules. In order to display this information it has been necessary to develop a new visualization tool. We have developed a simple visualisation technique based upon parallel coordinate visualisation. Parallel coordinate visualization has been used successfully in other data mining tools to display large volumes of data [7]. A screenshot of this visualisation is depicted in Figure 2. We start by plotting all of the items on the right-hand side of temporal predicates along a vertical axis. The items on the left-hand side of the temporal predicate are plotted along an axis on the opposite side of the screen with the labels for the thirty temporal relationships we have adopted lined along a central vertical axis. The temporal relationships can be seen as semi-ordered based upon the location of two intervals with respect to each other along the time axis. Using simple heuristics we have imposed an artificial ordering upon the relationships in order to allow them to be represented meaningfully along a single line. We then draw lines between items that have a temporal relationship and the lines intersect the central axis at the point that corresponds to the nature of that relationship. The lines are coloured to reflect the temporal confidence associated with the underlying relationship.

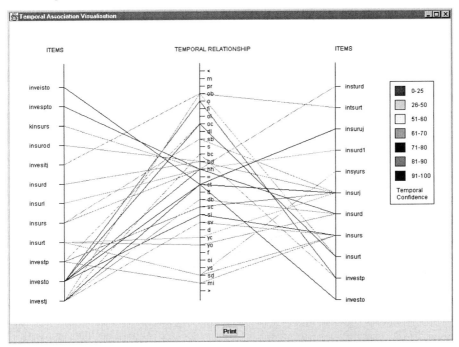

Fig. 2. A screenshot of our temporal interval visualisation window.

Based upon this visualisation it is possible to quickly determine patterns within the data. For example, a financial services company may seek to identify marketing opportunities for items to its current clients. By looking for items on the right-hand side of the graph, that are connected via lines that run predominately through the top half of the temporal relationship line (corresponding to items purchased after the item on the left hand side). The market analyst may then seek to market these services to holders of the connected items on the left-hand side of the graph. The strongest such correlations can be identified based upon the colour of the line which indicates the confidence of the relationship. The colour of these lines can be observed to quickly estimate the strength of relationships.

5 Summary

In this paper we have detailed two visualisation techniques to support the analysis of temporal interval association rules. These techniques are designed to allow a rapid understanding of patterns existing within large sets of rules. The first technique is a circular association rule graph that displays patterns within association rules. The second technique is based upon a parallel coordinate visualisation and it displays the temporal interval relationships between items. Both of these techniques have been successfully used for other data mining applications. Importantly, they are able to handle high volumes of data in a way that still allows users to find underlying patterns. These two techniques are simple and can be represented in two dimensions so that they can be easily reproduced. Research at both DSTO and at Flinders University is continuing and we plan to further refine these techniques and to examine their scalability to larger datasets.

References

1. Agrawal, A., Imielinski, T., Swami, A. Mining Association Rules between Sets of Items in Large Databases. International Conference on Management of Data (SIGMOD'93), May (1993) 207-216.
2. Allen, J. F.: Maintaining knowledge about temporal intervals. Communications of the ACM Vol 26. No.11 (1983).
3. Aumann Y., Feldman R., Yehuda Y.B., Landau D., Liphstat O., Schler Y. Circle Graphs: New Visualization Tools for Text-Mining. in The 3rd European Conference on Principles and Practice of Knowledge Discovery in Databases, (PKDD-99). Prague, Czech Republic, September 15-18 (1999).
4. Brunk, C. K., J. Kohavi, R. MineSet An Integrated System for Data Mining. Third International Conference on Knowledge Discovery and Data Mining (KDD'97), Newport Beach, California, AAAI Press. August 14-17, (1997). 135-138.
5. Freksa, C. Temporal reasoning based on semi-intervals. Artificial Intelligence 54, (1992) 199-227.
6. Klemettinen, M., Mannila H., Ronkainen, P., Toivonen H., Verkamo, A.I. Finding interesting Rules from Large Sets of Discovered Association Rules. Third International Conference on Information and Knowledge Management, Gaithersburg, Maryland, ACM Press. (1994).
7. Lee, H., Ong, H., Sodhi, K.S. Visual Data Exploration. The 3rd International Applied Statistics Conference, Dallas, Texas.(1995).
8. Netmap Technical Manual. The Technical Manual for the Netmap System. Netmap Solutions Pty Ltd, North Sydney NSW, Australia. (1994).
9. Piatetsky-Shapiro, G. and W. Frawley, J., Eds. Knowledge Discovery in Databases. Menlo park, California, AAAI Press, (1991).
10. Rainsford C.P., Roddick J.F. Adding Temporal Semantics to Association Rules. in The 3rd European Conference on Principles and Practice of Knowledge Discovery in Databases, (PKDD-99). Prague, Czech Republic, September 15-18 (1999).
11. Roddick, J. F. and M. Spiliopoulou. "A Survey of Temporal Knowledge Discovery Paradigms and Methods." IEEE Transactions on Knowledge and Data Engineering, to appear. (2000).
12. Tattersall, G. D. and P. R. Limb. Visulisation Techniques for Data Mining., BT Technol Journal 12(4).(1994).

Lithofacies Characteristics Discovery from Well Log Data Using Association Rules

C. C. Fung[1], K. W. Law[1], K. W. Wong[2], and P. Rajagopalan[3]

[1] School of Electrical and Computer Engineering
[3] School of Computing
Curtin University of Technology
Kent St, Bentley
Western Australia 6102
TFUNGCC@cc.curtin.edu.au

[2] School of Information Technology
Murdoch University
South St, Murdoch
Western Australia 6150
K.Wong@murdoch.edu.au

Abstract. This paper reports the use of association rules for the discovery of lithofacies characteristics from well log data. Well log data are used extensively in the exploration and evaluation of petroleum reservoirs. Traditionally, discriminant analysis, statistical and graphical methods have been used for the establishment of well log data interpretation models. Recently, computational intelligence techniques such as artificial neural networks and fuzzy logic have also been employed. In these techniques, prior knowledge of the log analysts is required. This paper investigated the application of association rules to the problem of knowledge discovery. A case study has been used to illustrate the proposed approach. Based on 96 data points for four lithofacies, twenty association rules were established and they were further reduced to six explicit statements. It was found that the execution time is fast and the method can be integrated with other techniques for building intelligent interpretation models.

1   Introduction

Modern societies rely heavily on hydrocarbon products. It is an ongoing quest of the major oil companies to explore new petroleum reservoirs and to determine their viabilities of production. The first phase of characterising a petroleum reservoir is to carry out *well logging* of the region under investigation. Boreholes are first drilled and logging instruments are then lowered by a wireline to obtain the characteristics from the sidewalls. Examples of the measurements include sonic travel time, gamma ray, neutron density, and spontaneous potential. This information is collectively known as *well log* or *wireline log data*. Meanwhile, limited amount of physical rock samples are extracted at the respective depth intervals for core analysis. They are examined intensively in the laboratory to obtain the corresponding petrophysical properties such as porosity, permeability, water saturation, volume of clay, and many other properties. Information determined from such analysis is termed *core data*.

The two approaches of reservoir characterisation are the "genetic" approach of *lithofacies classification* [1] and *petrophysical properties prediction* [2]. The former can also be regarded as the identification of the *litho hydraulic flow units*. *Flow unit* is defined as the representative of physical rock volume in terms of geological and petrophysical properties that influence the fluid flow through it [3]. Since there is a strong correlation between the lithofacies and the corresponding petrophysical properties, an identification of the lithofacies will also provide an estimation of the petrophysical properties. However, accurate estimation of petrophysical properties from wireline logs is difficult to obtain due to the non-linear relationships between the two.

On the other hand, while core data provides the most accurate information about the well, core analysis is expensive and time consuming. It is therefore a challenge for the log analyst to provide an accurate interpretation model of the petrophysical characteristics based on the available wireline log data and the limited core data. Traditionally, discriminant analysis, statistical and graphical methods have been used for the establishment of well log data interpretation models [4,5]. Recently, computational intelligence techniques such as artificial neural networks and fuzzy logic have also been employed [6,7,8]. The objective is to develop a description model to relate the petrophysical properties to the lithofacies. Such a model is based on the available data that embeds the knowledge about the reservoir. In other words, the problem is how to construct an accurate description model according to the properties found in the underlying data.

While the task of establishing the interpretation model is not easy, based on prior knowledge, an experienced log analyst is however capable to identify the lithofacies through the wireline logs data. Such knowledge will be useful for subsequent explorations in the region. Since data mining is particularly suitable for the discovery of interesting and useful knowledge from a large amount of data [9,10,11,12], this approach is therefore appropriate for the problem of well log data analysis. In this paper, the application of association rules to knowledge discovery from well log data and lithofacies is explored. Such knowledge can be used to enhance the understanding of a region under investigation. In the following sections, a brief description of the association rules and the procedure of applying the approach are presented. Results from a test case based on 96 data points are reported and further research directions will also be discussed.

2　Data Mining and Association Rules

In recent years, research areas of Knowledge Discovery in Databases (KDD) and Data Mining (DM) have contributed much understanding to the automatic mining of information and knowledge from large databases. Its continual evolvement has enabled researchers to realise potential applications to many areas including database systems, artificial intelligence, machine learning, expert systems, decision support system, and data visualisation. While a number of new computational intelligence techniques such as Artificial Neural Networks (ANN) and Fuzzy Logic (FL) have been applied to the problems of lithofacies identification and petrophysical prediction, the concepts of applying KDD and DM are new. In the context of this study, the objective is to apply appropriate computational techniques to facilitate understanding large amounts of data by discovering interesting patterns that exist in the data. The technique used in this study is the mining of Association Rules.

The concept of association rules was introduced as a means of mining a large collection of basket data type transactions between sets of items. For example, an association rule is expressed in the form of "63% of transactions that purchase engine oil also purchase oil filter; 13% of all transactions contain both these items". The antecedent of this rule consists of engine oil and the consequent consists of oil filter. The value 63% is the confidence of the rule, and 13%, the support of the rule. In this study, the items will be referred to the well logs such as Gamma Ray (GR), Deep Induction Resistive (ILD), and Sonic Travel Time (DT) and the lithofacies to be associated with are Mudstone, Sandy Mudstone, Muddy Sandstone, and Sandstone.

Once the association rules are generated, knowledge discovery from the wireline log data will be expressed in linguistic rules, and its related lithofacies of interest. By reorganising the rules according to the lithofacies, the items that appears to be dominant or distinct in the rules common to each lithofacie will be selected. The process is illustrated in the following case study.

3   Case Study

A set of 96 data from two typical boreholes within the same region are used to demonstrate the use of association rules in discovering knowledge for the identification of lithofacies. In this study, the data set comprises of a suite of three wireline logs, GR, ILD, DT and their corresponding lithofacies, which are, mudstone (Class 1), sandy mudstone (Class 2), muddy sandstone (Class 3), and sandstone (Class 4). The number of data sets in the four classes are 11, 37, 34 and 14 respectively. The procedure of mining association rules for lithofacies identification follows the one outlined by Agrawal and Srikant in reference [11]:

Step 1: Determine the number of intervals or interval sizes for each wireline log.

Step 2: Map the intervals of those wireline logs to consecutive integers such that the order of the intervals is preserved and the lithofacies to a set of consecutive integers.

Step 3: Using the algorithm *Apriori* in [12], find all combinations of itemsets consisting well log data and lithofacies whose support is greater than the specified minimum support, which is called *frequent itemsets*.

Step 4: If the frequent itemsets satisfies the specified minimum confidence, then generate the association rules.

The study was carried out on a Pentium II 300 MHz PC and the execution time recorded was 50 milli-seconds. A total of 20 association rules were generated. These rules were formatted and presented in the Table 1.

Table 1. Formatted output of the generated association rules.

Rule	GR		ILD		DT		Lith o	Facies
	Min	*Max*	*Min*	*Max*	*Min*	*Max*		

1	429	571	0	200	672	783	1	Mudstone
2	572	714	0	200	560	671	1	Mudstone
3	715	857	0	200	672	783	1	Mudstone
4	572	714	0	200	672	783	2	Sandy Mudstone
5	572	714	201	401	672	783	2	Sandy Mudstone
6	715	857	0	200	672	783	2	Sandy Mudstone
7	715	857	0	200	784	895	2	Sandy Mudstone
8	715	857	201	401	672	783	2	Sandy Mudstone
9	715	857	402	602	672	783	2	Sandy Mudstone
10	858	1000	0	200	672	783	2	Sandy Mudstone
11	572	714	0	200	784	895	3	Muddy Sandstone
12	572	714	201	401	784	895	3	Muddy Sandstone
13	572	714	402	602	784	895	3	Muddy Sandstone
14	715	857	0	200	784	895	3	Muddy Sandstone
15	715	857	201	401	784	895	3	Muddy Sandstone
16	858	1000	0	200	784	895	3	Muddy Sandstone
17	858	1000	201	401	784	895	3	Muddy Sandstone
18	858	1000	0	200	896	1007	4	Sandstone
19	858	1000	201	401	784	895	4	Sandstone
20	858	1000	201	401	896	1007	4	Sandstone

From the Table, it can be observed that GR, ILD, and DT are subdivided into 4, 3, and 4 intervals respectively. In order to make the knowledge to be extracted from these rules more explicit, these intervals are expressed in linguistic terms such as Low (L), Medium (M), High (H). Therefore, the intervals of GR can be regarded as {L, LM, MH, H}, ILD as {L, M, H}, and DT as {L, LM, MH, H}. Table 2 shows the rules indicating the responses from each log in linguistic terms.

Table 2. Expressing the association rules in linguistic terms.

GR				ILD			DT				Facies
L	L M	M H	H	L	M	H	L	L M	M H	H	
	Mudstone
	Mudstone
	Mudstone
	Sandy Mudstone
	Sandy Mudstone
	Sandy Mudstone
	Sandy Mudstone
	Sandy Mudstone
	Sandy Mudstone
	Sandy Mudstone
	Muddy Sandstone
	Muddy Sandstone
	Muddy Sandstone
	Muddy Sandstone
	Muddy Sandstone
	Muddy Sandstone
	Muddy Sandstone
	Sandstone
	Sandstone
	Sandstone

By examining these rules, the presence of distinct wireline logs responses are observed. They are then identified for the implication of the lithofacies of interest. Knowledge from these data sets expressed in explicit statements is listed in Table 3.

Table 3. Implication of distinct wireline log responses from lithofacies.

Litho	Knowledge expressed in linguistic statements
1	For Mudstone, **ILD** is **Low** and **DT** is likely to be **Medium Low**
2	For Sandy Mudstone, **DT** is **Medium Low** and **ILD** is likely to be **Low**
2	For Sandy Mudstone, **DT** is **Medium Low** and **GR** is likely to be **Medium High**
3	For Muddy Sandstone, **DT** is **Medium High** and **ILD** is either **Low or Medium**
4	For Sandstone, **GR** is **High** and **ILD** is likely to be **Medium**
4	For Sandstone, **GR** is **High** and **DT** is likely to be **High**

4   Discussions

Based on the above observations, the following points are deduced:

1. Using the knowledge discovered from Table 2, we can extract some heuristics rules to comment the range of data, which can be used to imply the presence of lithofacies of interest. Such knowledge can be used by the log analysts for cross-examination or referencing with other wells within the region. For example, if the response of ILD is Low, and DT is Medium-Low, then the lithofacies of interest is likely to be Mudstone.

2. We also observed that the lithofacies might not necessarily be associating all three logs. For example, it can be seen from Table 2 that Sandstone associates with a higher value of GR and a high value of DT. Alternatively, it is also associated with a higher value of GR and a medium value of ILD. This fact is also observed from the professional log analysts who tend to work on a limited number of logs at any one time.

3. As some logs are more important and distinctive than the others this knowledge can be used to perform a contribution measure for lithofacies classification under the genetic approach. Such an approach is very important for the prediction model if the available input logs are very large. This also forms the basis of a modular approach to lithofacies identification and petrophysical characteristics prediction.

4. Based on this case study, we can conclude that this proposed approach is fast and user-friendly as compared to other computation intensive methods such as artificial neural networks.

With the discovered knowledge, it paves the way for further investigations. This will include prediction of petrophysical properties and lithofacies classification in petroleum reservoir characterisation. It is anticipated that the proposed technique will be integrated with other methodologies such as ANN, FL and expert systems in order to enhance the intelligence of the well log interpretation model.

5   Conclusion

This paper has reported the use of association rules for mining knowledge from well log data and lithofacies characteristics. Well log data analysis is important as this forms the basis of decision making in any exploration exercise. By using the available log data and lithofacies classes, knowledge in explicit linguistic statements are obtained and presented to the users. This will assist the decision makers in gaining a better understanding of the data and information about the region. In the example case study, the execution time is very fast and the extracted knowledge can be integrated with other prediction techniques in order to build a more intelligent and reliable data interpretation model.

References

1. Jian, F.X., Chork, C.Y., Taggart, I.J., McKay, D.M., and Barlett, R.M.: A Genetic Approach to Prediction of Petrophysical Properties. Journal of Petroleum Geology, Vol. 17, No. 1 (1994) pp. 71-88.
2. Hook, J. R., Nieto, J. A., Kalkomey, C. T. and Ellis, D. "Facies and Permeability Prediction from Wireline Logs and Core – A North Sea Case Study," *SPWLA 35th Annual Logging Symposium*, paper "AAA", June (1994).
3. Ebanks, W.R. Jr.: "Flow Unit Concept – Integrated Approach to Reservoir Description for Engineering Projects." Paper presented at the 1987 AAPG Annual Meeting, Los Angeles (1987).
4. Wong, P. M., Taggart, I. J. and Jian, F. X. "A Critical Comparison of Neural Networks and Discriminant Analysis in Lithofacies, Porosity, and Permeability Predictions," *Journal of Petroleum Geology*, vol. 18(2), April (1995), pp. 191-206.
5. Condert, L., Frappa, M. and Arias, R. "A Statistical Method for Lithofacies Identification", *Journal of Applied Geophysics*, vol 32, (1994), pp. 257-267.
6. Fung, C. C., Wong, K. W. Eren, H. and Charlebois, R. "Lithology Classification using Self-Organising Map," *Proceedings of IEEE International Conference on Neural Networks*, Perth, Western Australia, December (1995), pp. 526-531.
7. Wong, P.M., Gedeon, T.D., and Taggart, I.J.: Fuzzy ARTMAP: A New Tool for Lithofacies Recognition. AI Applications, Vol. 10, No. 2 (1996), pp. 29-39.
8. Rogers, S. J., Fang, J. H., Karr, C. L. and Stanley, D.A. "Determination of Lithology from Well Logs Using a Neural Network," *The AAPG Bulletin*, vol. 76(5), (1992), pp. 731-739.
9. Fayyad, U. M., Piatetsky-Shapiro, G. and Smyth, P.: "From Data Mining to Knowledge Discovery: An Overview," *Advances in Knowledge Discovery and Data Mining*, ed. U. Fayyad, G. Piatetsky-Shapiro, P. Smyth, R. Uthurusamy, The AAAI/MIT Press, Menlo Park, California/Cambridge, Massachusetts, (1996), pp. 1-34.
10. Chen, M. S., Han, J. and Yu, P. S.: "Data Mining: An Overview from a Database Perspective," *IEEE Transactions on Knowledge and Data Engineering*, vol. 8(6), December (1996), pp. 866-883.
11. Agrawal R., and Srikant, R.: Mining Quantitative Association Rules in Large Relational Tables. Proceedings of the 1996 ACM SIGMOD International Conference on Management of Data, Montreal Canada (1996), pp. 1-12.
12. Agrawal, R., Mannila, H., Srikant, R., Toivonen, H., and Verkamo, I.: Fast Discovery of Association Rules. In: Fayyad, U., Piatetsky-Shapiro, G., Smyth, P., and Uthurusamy, R. (eds.): Advances in Knowledge Discovery and Data Mining. AAAI Press/The MIT Press, Menlo Park California/Cambridge Massachusetts (1996), pp. 307-328.

Fuzzy Hydrocyclone Modelling for Particle Separation Using Fuzzy Rule Interpolation

K. W. Wong[1], C. C. Fung[2], and T.D. Gedeon[1]

[1]School of Information Technology
Murdoch University
South St, Murdoch
Western Australia 6150
Email: {k.wong | t.gedeon}@murdoch.edu.au

[2]School of Electrical and Computer Engineering
Curtin University of Technology
Kent St, Bentley
Western Australia 6102
Email: tfungcc@cc.curtin.edu.au

Abstract: This paper reports on the use of a fuzzy rule interpolation technique for the modelling of hydrocyclones. Hydrocyclones are important equipment used for particle separation in mineral processing industry. Fuzzy rule based systems are useful in this application domains where direct control of the hydrocyclone parameters is desired. It has been reported that a rule extracting technique has been used to extract fuzzy rules from the input-output data. However, it is not uncommon that the available input-output data set does not cover the universe of discourse. This results in the generation of sparse fuzzy rule bases. This paper examines the use of an improved multidimensional fuzzy rule interpolation technique to enhance the prediction ability of the sparse fuzzy hydrocyclone model. Fuzzy rule interpolation is normally used to provide interpretations from observations for which there are no overlaps with the supports of existing rules in the rule base.

1. Introduction

Mining and mineral processing are two important industries in Australia. The quality of the products depends heavily on the precise and efficient refinement and separation of the particles according to size and type. One of the most commonly used instruments for this purpose is the Hydrocyclone [1]. Hydrocyclones are used to classify and separate solids suspended in fluids, commonly known as *slurry*. The particles will leave the hydrocyclone through an underflow opening known as the *spigot*. On the other hand, an upward helical flow containing fine and lighter solid particles will exit via the vortex finder on top known as *upperflow*. For a hydrocyclone of fixed geometry, the performance of the system depends on a number of parameters. The separation efficiency of particles of a particular size is determined by an operational parameter known as *d50c*. This value indicates that 50% of particles of a particular size is reported to the upper and underflow streams.

The correct estimation of d50c is important since it is directly related to the efficiency of operations and it will also enable control of the hydrocyclone as illustrated by Gupta and Eren [2]. Computer control of hydrocyclones can be achieved by manipulation of operational parameters such as: diameter of the spigot opening (Du), the vortex finder height (H), the inlet flowrate (Qi), the density (Pi) and the temperature (T) of slurries for a desired d50c. Traditionally, mathematical models based on empirical methods and statistical techniques in describing the performance of the hydrocyclones are used. Although these approaches have long been established in the industry, they have their shortcomings. For example, the experimental conditions may vary, resulting in these empirical models being unreliable. Hence, the conventional approach may not be universally applicable. In recent years, Artificial Neural Network (ANN) [3, 4] and Neural-Fuzzy [5] techniques have been applied. Although ANN techniques have proven to be useful for the prediction of the d50c control parameter, the main disadvantage is their inability to convey the acquired knowledge to the user. As a trained network is represented by a collection of weights, the user will have difficulty in understanding and modifying the model. In many cases, the system may not gain the confidence of the user. The Neural-Fuzzy approach can be shown to be better than the ANN approach as it can generate fuzzy rules for the user to manipulate. However, the fuzzy rules generated to cover the whole sample space are too tedious for the user to examine.

In this paper, a fuzzy hydrocyclone model is proposed. By modifying the on-line control system shown in [2], the proposed fuzzy hydrocyclone model is shown in Figure 1. As in [2], the d50c is set to a desire value. The signals from the instruments are processed to calculate the present value of d50c using the conventional models. To minimise the differences between the set value and the present value, the operating parameters such as diameter of the spigot opening (Du), the vortex finder height (H), and the inlet flowrate (Qi) are changed sequentially until the desired value of d50c is obtained. This is significant as the proposed technique allows users to manipulate the fuzzy rules easily, which also allows the system to perform in situations where no rules are found.

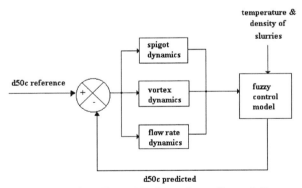

Figure 1: Online Fuzzy Hydrocyclone Control System

2. Fuzzy Hydrocyclone Control Model

Fuzzy control systems have shown to be useful in dealing with many control problems [6]. By far, they are the most important application of the classical fuzzy set theory. However, conventional fuzzy systems do not have any learning algorithms to build the analysis model. Rather, they are based on human or heuristic knowledge, past experience or detailed analysis of the available data in order to build the fuzzy rule base for the control system. Therefore, the major limitation is this difficulty in building the fuzzy rules. Recently, an automatic self-generating fuzzy rules inference system [7] has shown successful results in establishing the well log interpretation model. This method is used in this paper to extract fuzzy rules from the test examples generated by the hydrocyclone model.

The steps involved in the self-generating fuzzy rules inference system are summarised as follows:

(1)   Determine the universe of discourse for each variable depending on its range of value.
(2)   Define the number of fuzzy regions and fuzzy terms for all data. For ease of extraction, only triangular types of membership functions are used.
(3)   The space associated with each fuzzy term over the universe of discourse for each variable is then calculated and divided evenly.
(4)   For each available test case, a fuzzy rule is established by directly mapping the physical value of the variable to the corresponding fuzzy membership function.
(5)   Go through Step (4) with all the available test cases and generate one rule for each input-output data pair.
(6)   Eliminate repeated fuzzy rules.
(7)   The set of remaining fuzzy rules together with the centroid defuzzification algorithm now forms the fuzzy interpretation model.

3. Problems of a Sparse Rule Base

To illustrate the problem of sparse rule base as described in the previous section, a practice case study is presented. Data collected from a Krebs hydrocyclone model D6B-12o-839 have been used. There are a total of 70 training data and 69 testing data used in this study. The input parameters are Qi, Pi, H, Du, and T and the output is $d50c$. The self-generating fuzzy rules technique is used to extract fuzzy rules from the 70 training data. 7-membership function has been selected as it gives the best result. There are a total of 64 fuzzy sparse rules generated from the rule extraction process.

When this set of sparse rules are used to perform control on the testing data, 4 sets of data cannot find any fuzzy rules to fire and are shown in Figure 2. The output plot of the predicted d50c (solid line on the plot) as compared to the observed d50c (dots on the plot) is shown in Figure 3. The four zero output is the case where no rule fires. In this case study, the number of input sets that cannot find any rule to fire is considered minimal. However, in some cases, this may not always be true. If more than half the input instances cannot find any rule to fire, this control system may be considered useless. This is the major drawback for the fuzzy hydrocyclone control model. The problem also exists in most practical cases.

```
Warning: no rule is fired for input [493.0 26.00 85.20 3.750 26.00 ]! 0 is used as default output.
Warning: no rule is fired for input [388.0 24.20 69.50 2.650 33.00 ]! 0 is used as default output.
Warning: no rule is fired for input [462.0 10.20 85.20 3.750 40.00 ]! 0 used as default output.
Warning: no rule is fired for input [267.00 24.50 85.20 3.750 34.00 ]! 0 is used as default output.
```

Figure 2: Warning message for input without firing rules.

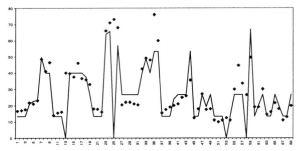

Figure 3: Output plot showing test case results indicating the rules fired.

4. Fuzzy Rule Interpolation

In the case when a rule base contains gaps or is a sparse rule base, classical fuzzy reasoning methods can no longer be used. This is the problem highlighted in the previous section, as an observation finds no rule to fire. Fuzzy rule interpolation techniques provide a tool for specifying an output fuzzy set whenever at least one of the input universes is sparse. Kóczy and Hirota [8] introduced the first interpolation approach known as (linear) KH interpolation.

Two conditions can be applied for the use of linear interpolation. Firstly, there should exist an ordering on the input and output universes. This allows us to introduce a notion of distance between the fuzzy sets. Secondly, the input sets (antecedents, consequents and the observation) should be convex and normal fuzzy (CNF) sets. The method determines the conclusion by its α-cuts in such a way that the ratio of distances between the conclusion and the consequents should be identical with the ones among the observation and the antecedents for all important α-cuts (breakpoint levels).

The KH interpolation possesses several advantageous properties. Firstly, it behaves approximately linearly in between the breakpoint levels. Secondly, its computational complexity is low, as it is sufficient to calculate the conclusion for the breakpoint level set. However, for some input situations, it fails to results in a directly interpretable fuzzy set, because the slopes of the conclusion can collapse [9]. To address this problem, improved fuzzy rule interpolation techniques [9,10] have been developed. While most fuzzy interpolation techniques perform analysis on one-dimensional input space, the improved multidimensional fuzzy interpolation technique [11] proposed in this paper will handle multidimensional input spaces. This has been applied for the development of the fuzzy hydrocyclone control model.

5. Case Study and Discussions

The test case described in this paper incorporates the improved multidimensional fuzzy interpolation method for the development of an accurate hydrocyclone model. As mentioned before, there are a total of four input instances that cannot find any firing rules (refer to Figure 2). From the observation and Euclidean distance measured on each input variable, the nearest fuzzy rules of the four input instances are determined for use by fuzzy interpolation.

Comparison of the results from those generated by the previous fuzzy hydrocyclone control model, and the same fuzzy model with the improved multidimensional fuzzy interpolation technique are shown in Table 1. In order to show the applicability of this proposed fuzzy hydrocyclone model, the results are also used to compare with results generated from the on-line control model as shown in [2]. The graphical plots of the results generated from the model with the improved multidimensional fuzzy interpolation technique are shown in Figure 4.

A few measurements of differences between the predicted d50c (*T*) and observed d50c (*O*) are used. They are: Euclidean Distance $ED = \sqrt{\sum_{i=1}^{P}(T_i - O_i)^2}$; Mean

Character Difference Distance $MCD = \dfrac{\sum_{i=1}^{P}|T_i - O_i|}{P}$; Percent Similarity Coefficient

$PSC = 200\dfrac{\sum_{i=1}^{P}\min(T_i, O_i)}{\sum_{i=1}^{P}(T_i + O_i)}$.

Table 1: Comparisons of results

Model Type	ED	MCD	PSC
Formula from [2]	59.787	5.179	90.096
Fuzzy (no fuzzy interpolation)	101.640	6.409	88.211
Fuzzy (with fuzzy interpolation)	52.97	4.595	91.889

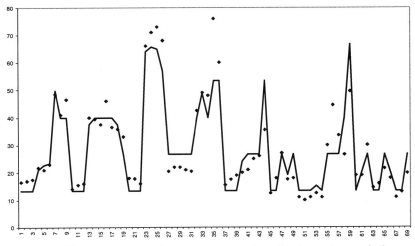

Figure 5: Output plot showing test case results with fuzzy interpolation.

From Table 1, the results show that the fuzzy hydrocyclone model performs unreasonably when no interpolation technique is used. This is mainly due to the four input instances that find no rule to fire and generate a default value of zero With the fuzzy rule interpolation technique, the number of fuzzy rules is not increased, but the prediction ability has improved. This is a desirable characteristic for on-line hydrocyclone control, as an increase in number of fuzzy rules would result in an increase in complexity which would make the examination of the fuzzy rule base more difficult.

6. Conclusion

In this paper, the practical applicability of the self-generating fuzzy rule inference system in hydrocyclone control has been examined. The problem of sparse rule bases and insufficient input data may cause undesirable control actions. This is mainly due to input instances that could not find any rule in the fuzzy rule base. To provide a solution to this problem, the improved multidimensional fuzzy rule interpolation method has been applied. This method can be used to interpolate the gaps between the rules. This ensures that the set of sparse fuzzy rules generated by the self-generating fuzzy rule inference system will be useable in a practical system.

References

[1] D., Bradley, The Hydrocyclone, Pergamon Press, 1965.

[2] A., Gupta and H., Eren, "Mathematical modelling and on-line control of Hydrocyclones," Proceedings Aus. IMM, 295 (2), 1990, pp. 31-41.

[3] H., Eren, C.C., Fung, K.W., Wong and A., Gupta, "Artificial Neural Networks in Estimation of Hydrocyclone Parameter d50c with Unusual Input Vaiables," IEEE Transactions on Instrumentation & Measurement, Vol. 46(4), 1997, pp. 908-912.

[4] H., Eren, C.C., Fung and K.W., Wong, "An Application of Artificial Neural Network for Prediction of Densities and Particle Size Distributions in Mineral Processing Industry," Proceedings of IEEE Instrumentation and Measurement Technology Conference, 1997, pp. 1118-1121.

[5] C.C., Fung, K.W., Wong and H., Eren, "Developing a Generalised Neural-Fuzzy Hydrocyclone Model for Particle Separation," Proceedings of IEEE Instrumentation and Measurement Technology Conference, 1998, pp. 334-337.

[6] B., Kosko, Fuzzy Engineering, Prentice-Hall, 1997.

[7] C.C., Fung, K.W., Wong, H., Eren, "A Self-generating Fuzzy Inference Systems for Petrophysical Properties Prediction," Proceedings of IEEE International Conference on Intelligent Processing Systems, 1997, pp.205-208.

[8] L.T., Kóczy and K., Hirota, "Approximate reasoning by linear rule interpolation and general approximation," Int. J. Approx. Reason, Vol. 9, 1993, pp.197-225.

[9] T.D., Gedeon and L.T., Kóczy, "Conservation of fuzziness in rule interpolation," Intelligent Technologies, Vol. 1. International Symposium on New Trends in Control of Large Scale Systems, 1996, pp. 13-19.

[10] D., Tikk, and P., Baranyi, "Comprehensive Analysis of a New Fuzzy Rule Interpolation Method," IEEE Trans. on Fuzzy Sets, in press.

[11] K.W., Wong, T.D., Gedeon, and T., Tikk, "An Improved Multidimensional α-cut Based Fuzzy Interpolation Technique," Proceedings of International Conference on Artificial Intelligence in Science and Technology AISAT, December 2000 Hobart, in press.

A Data-Driven Fuzzy Approach to Robot Navigation Among Moving Obstacles

Mohannad Al-Khatib and Jean J. Saade

ECE Department, FEA, American University of Beirut, Lebanon
e-mail: jsaade@aub.edu.lb

Abstract: In this paper, a data-driven fuzzy approach is developed for solving the motion planning problem of a mobile robot in the presence of moving obstacles. The approach consists of using a recent data-driven fuzzy controller modeling algorithm, and a devised general method for the derivation of input-output data to construct a fuzzy logic controller off-line. The constructed FLC can then be used on-line by the robot to navigate among moving obstacles. The novelty in the presented approach, as compared to the most recent fuzzy ones, stems from its generality. That is, the devised data-derivation method enables the construction of a single FLC to accommodate a wide range of scenarios. Also, care has been taken to find optimal or near optimal FLC solution in the sense of leading to a sufficiently small robot travel time and collision-free path between the start and target points.

1 Introduction

In dealing with the motion-planning problem of a mobile robot among existing obstacles, different classical approaches have been developed. Within these approaches, we state the path velocity decomposition [1], [2], incremental planning [3], relative velocity paradigm [4], and potential field [5]. Soft-computing techniques, employing various learning methods, have also been used to improve the performance of conventional controllers [6], [7]. Each of the above noted methods is either computationally extensive or capable of solving only a particular type of problems or both.

In order to reduce the computational burden and provide a more natural solution for the dynamic motion-planning (DMP) problem, fuzzy approaches, with emphasis on user-defined rules and collision-free paths, have been suggested [8]-[10]. Recently, a more advanced fuzzy-genetic-algorithm approach has been devised [11]. The emphasis has been not only on obtaining collision-free paths, but also on the optimization (minimization) of travel time (or path) between the start and target points of the robot. Genetic algorithms have, therefore, been used to come up with an optimal or near optimal fuzzy rule-base off-line by employing a number of user-defined scenarios. Although the noted fuzzy-genetic approach provided good testing results on scenarios some of which were used in training and others were not, it had its limitations. A different set of rules needed to be determined for every specific number of moving obstacles.

The approach presented in this study considers the off-line derivation of a general fuzzy rule base; that is a base that can be used on-line by the robot independently of the number of moving obstacles. This is achieved using a recently developed data-driven learning algorithm for the modeling of fuzzy logic controllers (FLC's) [12], and by devising a method for the derivation of the training data based on the general setting of the DMP problem and not on specific scenarios. Furthermore, collision-free paths and reduction of travel time are still within the goals considered in the derivation of the FLC.

2 Problem Definition, Constraints and Data Derivation

In the DMP problem, a robot needs to move from a start point S to a target point G located in some quadrant where the moving obstacles exist. The purpose is to find an obstacle-free path which takes the robot from S to G with minimum time. A fuzzy logic controller represented by a set of inference rules is to be constructed such that when it is used by the robot and supplied with information about the moving obstacles, it provides decisions that enables the achievement of the stated objective. But, what kind of information needs to be supplied to the FLC and what kind of decisions it needs to provide?

Let us first consider the incremental approach related to the motion of the robot and also considered in [11]. The robot, therefore, moves from one point to another in accordance with time steps, each of duration ΔT, and at the end of each step it needs to decide on the movement direction. Due to the problem objective, once the robot is at some point it needs to consider moving in a straight line towards the target point unless the information collected about the moving obstacles tells otherwise due to a possible collision. Hence, the information that needs to be obtained has to relate, in principle, to the position of each obstacle and its velocity relative to the robot position; i.e., the obstacle velocity vector. But, since the robot knows the position of each obstacle at every time step, an alternative to the use of the relative velocity can be the predicted position of each obstacle. This can be computed based on the obstacle present and previous positions. $P_{predicted}$ is assumed the linearly extrapolated position of each obstacle from its present position $P_{present}$ along the line formed by joining $P_{present}$ and $P_{previous}$ (see [11]). Thus,

$$P_{predicted} = P_{present} + (P_{present} - P_{previous})$$

But, to process all this information by the robot controller is difficult. The procedure that can be applied here, and which leads to a simplification of the controller structure, consists of using the collected information to determine the "nearest obstacle forward" (NOF) to the robot [11]. Then, only the information related to this obstacle is used by the FLC to provide decisions. The NOF is the obstacle located in front of the robot and with velocity vector pointing towards the line joining the robot position to the target point. In this way it needs to constitute the most possible collision danger relative to other obstacles whether the robot chooses to move straight to the target (Fig. 1). The NOF can equivalently be identified using the present and predicted positions of each obstacle.

Therefore, what needs to be used are the present and predicted positions of the NOF. The position has two components; angle and distance. The angle is the one between the line joining the target to the robot position and the line between the robot and the NOF. The distance is the one between the robot and the NOF. The FLC output is the deviation angle between the target-point-robot line and the new direction of robot movement (Fig. 1). Based on the noted information the robot will be able to know whether the NOF will get close to or cross the line segment joining the present position of the robot and the point it reaches after ΔT time if it moves straight to the target. This knowledge is in fact necessary for the determination of the angle of deviation.

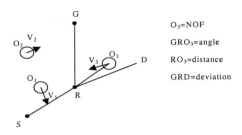

O_3=NOF

GRO_3=angle

RO_3=distance

GRD=deviation

Figure 1. Illustration of NOF and angle, distance and deviation.

But, to include all these variables in the conditions of the FLC will complicate its structure. It will also make the derivation of the input-output data points needed for the construction of the inference rules a difficult task. To make things simpler while maintaining the practicality of the problem, a contraint (constraint #4 below), which is not too restrictive, is considered in addition to other ones implied by the aforementioned problem description and adopted in [11].

1. The robot is considered to be a single point.
2. Each obstacle is represented by its bounding circle.
3. The speed of each obstacle is constant with a fixed direction between its previous, present and predicted positions.
4. The distance traveled by the NOF in ΔT time is comparable to its diameter.

Of course, constraint 3 presupposes that the obstacles do not collide while moving. Also, constraint 4, with the problem configuration as depicted in Figure 2 and its use in the determination of the input-output data (see below), will reduce the number of FLC input variables to 2; predicted angle and distance. The present position of the NOF is still accounted for but not used explicitly in the controller conditions.

Figure 2 considers a quadrant filled by side-to-side obstacles each of which may constitute the predicted position of the NOF. Suppose that the robot is in position R (present position) and the NOF predicted position is in (A_{11}, B_{13}). The robot initial intension is to move straight to G if collision is deemed impossible. Otherwise, an angle of deviation needs to be determined. Due to constraint 4, the present position of the NOF could be any of the neighboring obstacles such that the distance between the center of each of these obstacles and the center of (A_{11}, B_{13}) is approximately equal to the obstacle diameter. The neigboring obstacles are roughly represented by (A_{10}, B_{12}), (A_{11}, B_{12}), (A_{12}, B_{12}), (A_{10}, B_{13}), (A_{12}, B_{13}), (A_{10}, B_{14}), (A_{11}, B_{14}), (A_{12}, B_{14}). Of course, if the segment between the present position of the robot and the point it reaches after ΔT time penetrates the square formed by the outer tangent lines to the noted 8 obstacles, a deviation from the straight line between the robot and target point is required. Otherwise, no deviation is necessary. The amount of deviation is to be specified based on having the robot move in a direction that is just sufficient to avoid hitting not only the predicted obstacle position, but also any of the 8 shown present positions of the obstacles and all obstacles in between. This is because the NOF might be slow compared to the robot speed and thus a collision danger might exist. Among the two directions RR1 and RR2, which lead to the avoidance of the obstacles positions, the one with the smallest deviation angle, i.e.; RR1 is chosen. This serves the travel time reduction objective.

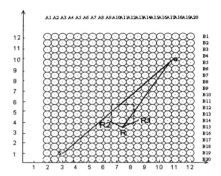

Figure 2. A general configuration of the DMP problem used in the data derivation.

We note also here that the obstacle diameter should not be very large since if a deviation is decided while the actual and predicted obstacle positions are not to demand such deviation (suppose for example that the present position of (A_{11}, B_{13}) is (A_{10}, B_{12})) then the robot would not have moved far away from the direct path and the trajectory length would not increase significantly. This also serves the travel time minimization objective of the DMP problem.

Now, based on the problem configuration in Figure 2 and the described general approach for the determination of the necessary deviation for every possible pair of predicted distance and angle of the NOF, various locations of the NOF within the noted quadrant were considered and accordingly input-output data were derived. The locations of the NOF were selected so that the input pairs cover the input space adequately. This is necessary for the construction of the FLC using the data-driven algorithm in [12].

It needs to be mentioned here that attempts were made to derive the data pairs by considering scenarios each containing a specific number of obstacles [11]. This approach was concluded difficult to use since an adequate coverage of the input space was not within reach. The derived data points are shown in Table 1. These are obtained based on obstacle diameter equal to 0.5 meters and robot traveled distance in ΔT time equal to 2 meters.

3 FLC Construction

The data points in Table 1 were used in the learning algorithm introduced in [12] and a set of inference rules (Table 2) was obtained using the input and output membership functions (MF's) shown in Figure 3. Actually, the algorithm, which relies on the use of a parametrized defuzzification strategy [13], operates based on a consistent modification of the defuzzification parameter and initial rules consequents to reduce the data approximation error and obtain a final fuzzy system. The initial rules consequents are required to be equal to the left-most fuzzy output (i.e., V1 in Figure 3) and the membership functions assigned over the controller variables need to

Table 1. Input-output data pairs obtained using the method described in Section 2.

Distance	Angle	Deviation	Distance	Angle	Deviation	Distance	Angle	Deviation	Distance	Angle	Deviation
0.25	-24	80	0.8	11	-33	1.45	-29	0	2	70	0
0.25	-12	70	0.8	22	-22	1.45	33	0	2.05	-12	7
0.25	30	-65	0.8	75	0	1.5	5	-18	2.05	16	-5
0.25	43	-80	0.8	107	0	1.6	-80	0	2.2	-25	0
0.3	-41	70	1	-43	0	1.6	-15	10	2.25	9	-10
0.35	50	-35	1	4	-30	1.6	22	-3	2.35	-21	0
0.35	139	0	1	90	0	1.6	80	0	2.5	-10	0
0.4	49	0	1.1	-25	10	1.75	-6	15	2.5	3	0
0.45	-90	0	1.1	30	-3	1.75	11	-7	2.55	-30	0
0.5	-90	0	1.1	48	0	1.8	-32	0	2.8	-4	0
0.5	-20	55	1.2	65	0	1.8	37	0	3	-70	0
0.5	-5	70	1.25	-9	18	1.9	-22	0	3	-43	0
0.5	5	-70	1.3	-90	0	1.9	27	0	3	70	0
0.5	20	-55	1.3	15	-10	2	-70	0	3.2	13	0
0.7	-43	12	1.3	80	0	2	3	-16	3.25	16	0
0.8	-17	30	1.4	48	0	2	30	0	5	-43	0

cover the ranges of these variables. The ranges of the distance, angle and deviation as considered are from 0 to 17 meters, −180 to 180 degrees and −90 to 90 degrees respectively. These ranges are considered to account for all possible values. A modification of the number of MF's, their shapes and the density of their coverage of the FLC variables can be done by the designer to lower the data approximation error. The distribution of the input MF's in Fig. 3, which is reasonable since most robot deviations occur at small angles and distances, was verified by the learning tests to serve the error reduction goal.

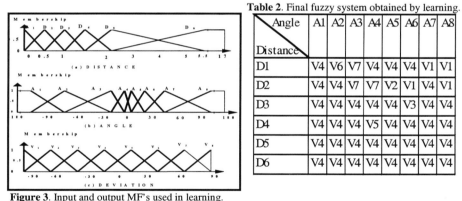

Figure 3. Input and output MF's used in learning.

Table 2. Final fuzzy system obtained by learning.

Angle / Distance	A1	A2	A3	A4	A5	A6	A7	A8
D1	V4	V6	V7	V4	V4	V4	V1	V1
D2	V4	V4	V7	V7	V2	V1	V4	V1
D3	V4	V4	V4	V4	V4	V3	V4	V4
D4	V4	V4	V4	V5	V4	V4	V4	V4
D5	V4	V4	V4	V4	V4	V4	V4	V4
D6	V4	V4	V4	V4	V4	V4	V4	V4

4 Testing Results

In this section, the obtained FLC is tested on various scenarios containing different numbers of obstacles. The cases of 3, 5, and 2 cases of 8 obstacles are considered (Figure 4). In all the cases, the robot travels from point S to point G without hitting any of the obstacles. Also, the traveled paths are optimal in the sense that the deviations which took place at the end of every time step are in most cases just as necessary in order for the robot to remain as close as possible to the robot-destination direct path while not colliding with the obstacles [11]. Moreover, two of these scenarios (Figures 4(a) and 4(d)) were presented in [11] and had obstacles with distinct diameters. Some had diameters close to the one considered in this study, and others with larger diameters. Despite this, the robot path chosen by the constructed FLC does not hit any of the obstacles. This shows that the constructed FLC can work properly for obstacles whose diameter values differ from the one used in the data derivation. Of course, a significant increase in the diameters would make the chances of having the robot hitting the obstacles higher. The clarification of this fact can be obtained by referring back to the described data derivation approach. Also, the case in Figure 4(a) shows the robot passing tangentially by the current position of one of the obtacles. A hit might have occurred had the diameter been larger. Thus, a set of data points different from that in Table 1 needs to be determined for different obstacles diameters. The same applies for the distance traveled by the robot in ΔT time. But the presented data derivation approach is general and can still be used.

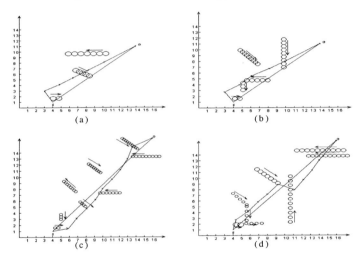

Figure 4. Paths traveled by the robot in 4 scenarios: (a) 3 obstacles, (b) 5 obstacles and (c) and (d) have 8 obstacles each.

Table 3 shows the distance ratio (traveled distance/ direct distance) using the presented data-driven fuzzy approach and the fuzzy-genetic one. The ratio in our approach is a bit higher than that used in [11]. Thus, a slightly higher time duration is required for the robot to reach destination.

Table 3. Traveled distance and ratios for the presented approach and the fuzzy-genetic one.

OBSTACLES	3	5	8	8
DIRECT DISTANCE	14	14	20	20
TRAVELED DISTANCE	15.25	15.35	20.9	21.7
RATIO(OUR APPROACH)	1.089	1.096	1.045	1.085
RATIO(GENETIC)	1.046			1.05

5 Conclusions

A data-driven fuzzy approach has been developed in this study to provide a general framework for solving the DMP problem under some constraints. It consisted of providing a general and well designed method for the derivation of input-output data to construct a single FLC that can be used by the robot to guide its navigation in the presence of moving obstacles and independently of the number of these obstacles. This is the main advantage of the presented approach over the most recent fuzzy-genetic one. In a general robot environment, it is difficult to guess on the number of obstacles that could facing the robot while in navigation. From this perspective, the results in Table 3 are quite acceptable. As compared to other fuzzy approaches [8]-[10], The presented approach is systematic and does not employ user-defined rules, which are mostly derived by trial and error. The devised method has also accounted for collision-free paths and reduction of travel time while lessening the number of FLC variables and hence structure. A recently developed data-driven fuzzy controllers modeling algorithm has been used to construct the FLC.

Acknowledgment

This research has been supported by the Research Board at the American University of Beirut.

References

1. Fujimura, K., Samet, H.: A Hierarchical Strategy for Path Planning Among Moving Obstacles. IEEE Trans. Robotics and Automation, 5(1), (1989) 61-69.
2. Griswold, N.C., .Eem, J.: Conrtol for Mobile Robots in the Presence of Moving Objects. IEEE Trans. Robotics and Automation, 6(2), (1990) 263-268.
3. Lamadrid, J.G. Avoidance of Obstacles with Unknown Trajectories: Locally Optimal Paths and Periodic Sensor Readings. Int.J. Robotics Res., (1994) 496-507.
4. Fiorini, P., Shiller, Z.: Motion Planning in Dynamic Environments Using the Relative Velocity Paradigm. Proc. IEEE Conference on Robotics and Automation, (1993) 560-565.
5 Barraquand, J. Langlois, B. Latombe, J.C.: Numerical Potential Field Techniques for Robot Path Planning. IEEE Trans. Syst., Man and Cybern. 22 (1992) 224-241.
6. Donnart, J.Y., Meyer, J.A.: Learning Reactive and Planning Rules in a Motivationally Autonomous Animat. IEEE Trans. Syst., Man and Cybern. B, 26(3) (1996) 381-395.
7. Floreano, D., Mondada, F.: Evolution of Homing Navigation in a Real Mobile Robot. IEEE Trans. Syst. Man and Cybern. B, 26(3), (1996) 396-407.
8. Matinez, A. et al., Fuzzy Logic Based Collision Avoidance for a Mobile Robot. Robotica, 12, (1994) 521-527.
9. Pin, F.G., Watanabe, Y. Navigation of Mobile Robots Using a Fuzzy Behaviorist Approach and Custom-Designed Fuzzy Inferencing Boards. Robotica, 12, (1994) 491-503.
10. Beaufrere, B., Zeghloul, S.: A Mobile Robot Navigation Method Using a Fuzzy Logic Approach. Robotica, 13, (1995) 437-448.
11. Pratihar, D.K., Deb, K., Ghosh, A.: A Genetic-Fuzzy Approach for Mobile Robot Navigation Among Moving Obstacles. Int. J. Approximate Reasoning, 20, (1999) 145-172.
12. Saade, J.J.: A New Algorithm for the Design of Mamdani-Type Fuzzy Controllers. Proc. EUSFLAT-ESTYLF Joint Conf., Palma de Mallorca, Spain, Sept. 22-25, 1999, 55-58.
13. J.J. Saade, A Unifying Approach to Defuzzification and Comparison of the Outputs of Fuzzy Controllers. IEEE Trans. Fuzzy Systems, 4(3) (1996) 227-237.

Best Harmony Learning

Lei Xu *

Department of Computer Science and Engineering, Chinese University of Hong Kong,
FShatin, NT, Hong Kong, P.R. China, E-mail: lxu@cse.cuhk.edu.hk

Abstract. Bayesian Ying-Yang (BYY) learning is proposed as a unified statistical learning framework firstly in (Xu, 1995) and systematically developed in past years. Its consists of a general BYY system and a fundamental harmony learning principle as a unified guide for developing new parameter learning algorithms, new regularization techniques, new model selection criteria, as well as a new learning approach that implements parameter learning with model selection made automatically during learning (Xu, 1999a&b; 2000a&b). This paper goes further beyond the scope of BYY learning, and provides new results and new understandings on harmony learning from perspectives of conventional parametric models, BYY systems and some general properties of information geometry.

1 Introduction

Specifically, BYY learning with specific structure designs leads to three major paradigms. First, the BYY unsupervised learning provides a number of new results on several existing major unsupervised learning methods [1–5], the details are partly given in [15, 14, 10] and a review is given in [10]. Second, the BYY supervised learning provides not only new understanding on three major supervised learning models, namely three layer forward net with back-propagation learning, Mixture Expert (ME) model [6, 7] and its alternative model as well as normalized radial basis function (RBF) nets and its extensions [13], but also new adaptive learning algorithms and new criteria for deciding the number of hidden units, of experts and of basis functions, with the details referred to [10–13]. Moreover, the temporal BYY learning acts as a general state space approach for modeling data that has temporal relationship among samples, which provides not only a unified point of view on Kalman filter, Hidden Markov model (HMM), ICA and blind source separation (BSS) with extensions, but also several new results such as higher order HMM, independent HMM for binary BSS, temporal ICA and temporal factor analysis for noisy real BSS, with adaptive algorithms for implementation and criteria for selecting the number of states or sources [9].

In this paper, we go beyond the scope of BYY learning and study the harmony learning principle from perspectives of conventional parametric models, BYY systems and information geometry.

* The work described in this paper was fully supported by a grant from the Research Grant Council of the Hong Kong SAR (project No: CUHK4383/99E).

2 Best Harmony Learning Principle

Given two models $p(u) = p(u|\theta_p, k_p), g(u) = q(u|\theta_g, k_g)$, with $\theta = \theta_p, \theta_g$ consisting of all the unknown parameters in each of the models, and $\mathbf{k} = \{k_p, k_g\}$ consisting of integers that indicate structural scales of the models, our fundamental learning principle for estimating the parameter θ and selecting the scale $\mathbf{k}$ is the best harmony in a twofold sense:

– The difference between the obtained $p(u), g(u)$ should be minimized.
– The obtained $p(u), g(u)$ should be in the least in their complexity.

Mathematically, we use a functional to measure the degree of harmony between $p(u)$ and $g(u)$. When both $p(u), g(u)$ are point densities in the form

$$q(u) = \sum_{u_t} q_t \delta(u - u_t), \ \sum_{u_t} q_t = 1, \ u_t \in \mathcal{U}, \tag{1}$$

such a measure is simply given as follows:

$$H(p\|g) = \sum_t p_t \ln g_t, \tag{2}$$

It can be observed that when $p = g$ we have $H(p\|p)$ which is the negative entropy of p. More interestingly, the maximization of $H(p\|g)$ will not only push p, g towards to $p_t = g_t$ but also push $p(u)$ towards the simplest form

$$p(u) = \delta(u - u_\tau), \ with \ \tau = arg \max_t \ g_t, \tag{3}$$

or equivalently $p_\tau = 1$, and $p_t = 0$ for other t, which is of least complexity from the perspective of statistical theory. Thus, the maximization of the functional indeed implements the above harmony purpose mathematically.

When $g(u)$ is a continuous density, we approximate it by either simply its sampling point $g(u_t)$ or its normalized version $g_t = g(u_t)/\sum_t g(u_t)$. Furthermore, when the set $\mathcal{U}$ has a large enough size N with samples uniformly covering the entire space of u such that we can approximately regard that $g(u_t)$ is the value of the corresponding histogram density at u_t within the hyper-cubic bin $v_u = h^{d_u}$, where $h > 0$ is a very small constant and d_u is the dimension of u. Then, we have

$$\sum_t g(u_t) h^{d_u} \approx 1, \ or \ z_g = h^{-d_u}. \tag{4}$$

Including the discrete case, we have a general form

$$g_t = \frac{g(u_t)}{z_g}, \ z_g = \begin{cases} \lim_{d_u \to 0} \frac{1}{\mu(du)}, & \text{(a) } g(u) \text{ is a point density,} \\ 1 & \text{(b) } g(u) \text{ is pointized by its sampling points,} \\ \sum_t g(u_t), & \text{(c) } g(u) \text{ is pointized and normalized,} \\ h^{-d_u}, & \text{(d) } g(u) \text{ is approximated via a histogram,} \end{cases} \tag{5}$$

where $\nu(.)$ is a given measure on u. Particularly, for the Lebesque measure, $\nu(du)$ is the volume of du.

Putting eq.(5) into eq.(2), we have

$$H(p\|g) = \sum_{u_t} p_t \ln g(u_t) - \ln z_g. \tag{6}$$

In other words, given $\mathcal{U}$ we can approximately use eq.(6) in place eq.(2) for implementing the best harmony learning.

We can also approximate a continuous $p(u)$ in the form eq.(5) and get $\sum_{u_t} p(u_t) \ln g(u_t)/z_p$. Then, similar to eq.(4) we have $\sum_{u_t} p(u_t) h^{d_u} \ln g(u_t) \approx \int p(u) \ln g(u) \nu(du)$, which is actually also true when $p(u)$ is a discrete density. Thus, a generalized form of the harmony measure is given as follows:

$$H(p\|g) = \int p(u) \ln g(u) \nu(du) - \ln z_g, \tag{7}$$

with z_g given in eq.(5). Therefore, we implement harmony learning by

$$\max_{\theta, \mathbf{k}} H(\theta, \mathbf{k}), \ \ H(\theta, \mathbf{k}) = H(p\|g). \tag{8}$$

3 Parameter Learning: ML, Posteriori WTA and Two Regularization Methods

Provided that $\mathbf{k}$ is prefixed, we consider typical cases for determining θ or called *parameter learning*, on both the simple parametric model and comprehensive BYY system.

Parameter learning on simple parametric models   Given a data set $\mathcal{U} = \{u_t\}_{t=1}^N$ and a parametric model $g(u|\theta)$, the task now is to specify the value of θ such that $g(u|\theta)$ well fits $\mathcal{U}$.

Learning from the set $\mathcal{U}$ is equivalent to learn from its empirical density:

$$p(u) = p_0(u), \ \ p_0(u) = \frac{1}{N} \sum_{t=1}^N \delta(u - u_t), \ \ \delta(u) = \begin{cases} \lim_{du \to 0} 1/\nu(du), & u = 0, \\ 0, & u \neq 0, \end{cases} \tag{9}$$

where $\nu(.)$ is same as in eq.(5). Putting this $p(u)$ and $g(u|\theta)$ into eq.(7), for the cases (a)&(b) in eq.(5) as well as case (d) at fixed h, d, $\max_\theta H(p\|g)$ becomes equivalent to

$$\max_\theta L(\theta), \ \ L(\theta) = \frac{1}{N} \sum_{u_t} \ln g(u_t|\theta), \tag{10}$$

which is exactly the *Maximum Likelihood (ML)* learning on $g(u|\theta)$.

While for the case (c), we have $\max_\theta H(p\|g)$ becomes

$$\max_\theta L_R(\theta), \ \ L_R(\theta) = L(\theta) - \ln \left[\sum_{u_t} g(u_t|\theta) \right], \tag{11}$$

which consists of ML learning plus a regularization that prevents $g(u|\theta)$ to overfit a finite size data set $\mathcal{U}$. This point can be better observed by comparing the gradients:

$$\nabla_\theta L(\theta) = Gd(\gamma_t)|_{\gamma_t = \frac{1}{N}}, \ \ \nabla_\theta L_R(\theta) = Gd(\gamma_t)|_{\gamma_t = \frac{1}{N} - \tilde{g}(u_t|\theta)},$$
$$Gd(\gamma_t) = \sum_{u_t} \gamma_t \nabla_\theta \ln g(u_t|\theta), \ \ \tilde{g}(u_t|\theta) = g(u_t|\theta)/\sum_\tau g(\tau|\theta). \tag{12}$$

It follows from $\nabla_\theta L_R(\theta)$ that a de-learning is introduced to ML learning for each sample in proportional to the current fitting of the model to the sample. We call this new regularization method *normalized point density*.

Another new regularization method can be obtained from the case (d) in eq.(5) with $p(u)$ not given by eq.(9) but by the Parzen window estimate:

$$p(u) = p_\sigma(u), \quad p_\sigma(u) = \frac{1}{N} \sum_{t=1}^N G(u|u_t, \sigma^2 I_d), \tag{13}$$

where $G(u|m, \Sigma)$ denotes a gaussian of mean m and covariance matrix Σ, I_d is the $d \times d$ identity matrix, and d is the dimension of x. As $\sigma \to 0$, $G(u|u_t, \sigma^2 I_d) \to \delta(u)$, and $p_\sigma(u)$ returns to $p_0(u)$. Generally, $p_\sigma(u)$ is a smoothed modification of $p_0(u)$ by using a kernel $G(u|0, \sigma^2 I_d)$ to blur out each impulse at u_t.

Moreover, similar to eq.(4) we have $\sum_t p_h(u_t) h^{d_u} \approx 1$. It further follows from $p_h(u_t) \approx G(u_t|u_t, \sigma^2 I_d) = (\sqrt{2\pi}\sigma)^{d_u}$ that $h = \sqrt{2\pi}\sigma$. Putting it into eq.(7) with $g(u|\theta)$ and $p(u) = p_h(u)$, we consider the case (d) and get that $\max_\theta H(p\|g)$ becomes equivalent to

$$\max_{\theta,\sigma} L_S(\theta, \sigma^2), \quad L_S(\theta, \sigma^2) = \frac{1}{N} \sum_t \int G(u|u_t, \sigma^2 I_d) \ln g(u|\theta) du + d_u \ln \sigma, \tag{14}$$

which regularizes the ML learning by smoothing each likelihood term $\ln g(u_t|\theta)$ via $G(u|u_t, \sigma^2 I_d)$ in the near-neighbor of u_t. We call this new regularization method *data smoothing*.

We further get $\int G(u|u_t, \sigma^2 I_d) \ln g(u|\theta) du \approx \ln g(u_t|\theta) + 0.5\sigma^2 Tr[H_g(u_t|\theta)]$, where $H_g(u_t|\theta)$ is the Hessian matrix of $\ln g(u|\theta)$ with respect to u. Putting it into eq.(14) we can further get

$$\sigma^2 = N d_u / \sum_\tau Tr[H_g(u_\tau|\theta)]. \tag{15}$$

Thus, $L_S(\theta, \sigma^2)$ consists of the likelihood $L(\theta)$ plus the regularization term $0.5 d_u \ln \sigma^2 + 0.5\sigma^2 \frac{1}{N} \sum_t Tr[H_g(u_t|\theta)]$ under the constraint of eq.(15).

We can simplify the implementation of eq.(14) by alternatively repeating the following two steps:

$$Step\ 1: \text{ fix } \theta, \text{ get } \sigma^2 \text{ by eq.(15)}, \quad Step\ 2: \text{ fix } \sigma^2, \text{ get } \theta^{new} = \theta^{old} + \eta\Delta\theta, \tag{16}$$

where $\eta > 0$ is a small learning stepsize and $\Delta\theta$ is an ascend direction of $\frac{1}{N} \sum_t \int G(u|u_t, \sigma^2 I_d) \ln g(u|\theta) du$, which can be approximately obtained by random sampling, i.e., from $\frac{1}{N'} \sum_t \ln g(u'_t|\theta)$ with a new data set $\{u'_t\}_{t=1}^{N'}$, $u'_t = u_t + \varepsilon_t$ and ε_t being a sample from $G(u|0, \sigma^2 I_d)$.

Parameter learning on BYY learning system   When $u = [x, y]$ consists of $x = [x_1, \cdots, x_d]^T$ which is observable and $y = [y_1, \cdots, y_k]^T$ which is not observable. We can not get $p(u)$ by either eq.(9) or eq.(13) directly. Such cases are widely encountered in intelligent systems. BYY system is proposed for these purposes as a unified statistical learning framework firstly in 1995 [16] and systematically developed in past years [8, 10, 11]. In the BYY system, we describe $p(u), g(u)$ on $x \in X, y \in Y$ in help of two complementary Bayesian representations:

$$p(u) = p_{M_{y|x}}(y|x) p_{M_x}(x), \quad g(u) = p_{M_{x|y}}(x|y) p_{M_y}(y). \tag{17}$$

In this formulation, $p(u)$ is called Yang model, representing the observable or called Yang space by p_{M_x} and the pathway $x \to y$ by $p_{M_{y|x}}$ is called Yang or forward pathway, while $g(u)$ is called the Ying model that represents the invisible state space or Ying space by p_{M_y} and the Ying or backward pathway $y \to x$ by $p_{M_{x|y}}$. Such a pair of Ying-Yang models is called *Bayesian Ying-Yang (BYY) system*. The use of such terms is because the formalization eq.(17) compliments to the famous eastern ancient Ying-Yang philosophy, as discussed in [10].

Now we have four components $p_{M_x}, p_{M_y}, p_{M_{y|x}}$ and $p_{M_{x|y}}$. Given a set of observable samples $\{x_t\}_{t=1}^N$, p_{M_x} is still given by either eq.(9) or eq.(13) with each appearance of u, u_t replaced by x, x_t. p_{M_y} is a parametric model designed according to the representation form of y in different applications, most of which have been summarized into a unified framework called Σ-Π model [8,9]. Each of $p_{M_{y|x}}, p_{M_{x|y}}$ can be two typical types. One is parametric with a set of unknown parameters, i.e., $\theta_{y|x}$ for $p_{M_{y|x}}$ or $\theta_{x|y}$ for $p_{M_{x|y}}$. The other is called *structure-free*, which means no any structural constraints such that p_{M_a} for each $a \in \{x|y, y|x\}$ is free to take any element of $\mathcal{P}_a$, where $\mathcal{P}_{x|y}$ and $\mathcal{P}_{y|x}$ denote the family of all the densities in the form $p(x|y)$ and $p(y|x)$, respectively. As a result, there are three typical architectures, namely *backward, forward, and bi-directional* architectures [10,8,9].

Putting eq.(17) in eq.(7) and eq.(8), with eq.(5) we can obtain the corresponding details for implementing parameter learning on BYY systems. More specifically, when p_{M_x} is given by eq.(9) and $p_{M_{y|x}}$ is either a point density for a discrete y or approximated in help of eq.(5) via a set of sampling point $\{y_t\}_{t=1}^N$. For the choices (a) & (b) of z_g in eq.(5), we have that $H(p\|g)$ takes the following specific form:

$$
\begin{aligned}
&H(p\|g) = L(\theta_{x|y}) + L(\theta_y), \quad L(\theta_{x|y}) = \tfrac{1}{N} \sum_{t=1}^N \ln p_{M_{x|y}}(x_t|y_t), \\
&L(\theta_y) = \tfrac{1}{N} \sum_{t=1}^N \ln p_{M_y}(y_t), \\
&y_t = \begin{cases} \max_y [p_{M_{x|y}}(x_t|y)p_{M_y}(y)], & \text{(a) when } p_{M_{y|x}} \text{ is structure-free,} \\ \max_y p_{M_{y|x}}(y|x_t), & \text{(b) when } p_{M_{y|x}} \text{ is parametric;} \end{cases}
\end{aligned} \qquad (18)
$$

The case (a) is actually in the same form as the case (b) since the maximization of $H(p\|g)$ will lead to

$$
p_{M_{y|x}}(y|x_t) = \frac{p_{M_{x|y}}(x_t|y)p_{M_y}(y)}{p_M(x_t)}, \quad p_M(x_t) = \int p_{M_{x|y}}(x_t|y)p_{M_y}(y)\nu(dx), \qquad (19)
$$

when $p_{M_{y|x}}$ is structure-free. Thus, $\max_y p_{M_{y|x}}(y|x_t) = \max_y [p_{M_{x|y}}(x_t|y)p_{M_y}(y)]$ and y_t is actually obtained via the competition based on the posteriori distribution $p_{M_{y|x}}$ and thus is called *posteriori winner-take-all (WTA)*. Correspondingly, the learning eq.(8) in help of this competition is called *posteriori WTA learning*. Particularly, for the case (a), the competition is made coordinately via the generative model $p_{M_{x|y}}$ and the representation model p_{M_y}, we also call it *coordinated competition learning (CCL)* in [13].

In implementation of eq.(8) with eq.(18) at fixed $\mathbf{k}$, the parameter $\theta_{x|y}, \theta_y$ can be updated via gradient ascending $L(\theta_{x|y}), L(\theta_y)$ respectively. There is no need to update $\theta_{y|x}$ for the case (a), while for the case (b), we consider those models of $p_{M_{y|x}}$ such that

$$
y_t = \max_y p_{M_{y|x}}(y|x_t) = \int_y y p_{M_{y|x}}(y|x_t)\nu(dy) = f(x_t|\theta_{y|x}),
$$

$$thus \quad \nabla_{\theta_{y|x}} H(p\|g) = \Phi(y_t)\nabla_{\theta_{y|x}} f(x_t|\theta_{y|x}), \ \Phi(y) = \frac{\partial H(p\|g)}{\partial y^T}, \tag{20}$$

with which we can make gradient ascend updating on $\theta_{y|x}$ also.

Furthermore, when we consider the choice (c) of z_g in eq.(5) and the choice (d) of z_g in eq.(5) with p_{M_x} given by eq.(13), we can also get the two new regularized learning methods, namely *normalized point density* and *data smoothing*, in various specific forms for the different specific designs of p_{M_y}, $p_{M_{y|x}}$ and $p_{M_{x|y}}$. Readers are referred to [8] for details.

4   Model Selection and Automated Model Selection

The task of selecting the best specific value of **k** is usually called model selection since different values correspond different scale of model architectures. It follows from eq.(8) that searching a best **k** must be made together with parameter learning for searching a best θ. Actually, the task eq.(8) is a typical optimization mixed with θ of continuous parameters and **k** of discrete variables.

We have the following two procedures for its implementation:

• **Parameter learning followed by model selection**   We enumerate **k** from a small scale incrementally, which results in a number of specific settings of **k** by gradually increasing the scales. At each specific **k** we perform parameter learning as in Sec.3 to get the best θ_k^*, and make a selection on a best **k*** by

$$\max_{\mathbf{k}} J(\mathbf{k}), \quad J(\mathbf{k}) = H(\theta_k^*, \mathbf{k}). \tag{21}$$

That is, the entire process consists of the two steps: the step of determining θ^* followed by the step of selecting **k***. Moreover, as further justified in Sec.5, the step of determining θ^* can be replaced by

$$\min_{\theta} KL(\theta), \ KL(\theta) = KL(p\|g) = \int p(u)\ln\frac{p(u)}{g(u)}\nu(du),$$
$$KL(p\|g) = H(p\|p) - H(p\|g), \tag{22}$$

where $H(p\|p)$ is a special case of eq.(7) with $g(u)$ replaced by $p(u)$. We have $KL(p\|g) = 0$ when $p(u) = q(u)$ and $KL(p\|g) > 0$ when $p(u) \neq q(u)$. Thus, the minimization pushes $p(u), g(u)$ to best match, i.e., it realizes the first purpose of harmony learning. However, it has no consideration on the second purpose, i.e., forcing the least complexity, of harmony learning. There may be some discrepancy between the resulted θ^* by the two ways. However, this discrepancy will be further reduced by the same subsequent step of model selection eq.(21).

• **Parameter learning with automated model selection**   Which is another advantage that the harmony learning eq.(8) has but the KL-learning eq.(22) has not. In the cases that setting certain elements in θ to certain specific values (e.g., 0) becomes equivalent to reduce **k** form a higher scale into a lower scale, we can prefix all the integers in **k** to be large enough and then simply implement parameter learning $\max_\theta H(\theta, \mathbf{k})$ as in Sec.3, in which there are forces for both best fitting and the least complexity and thus will effectively reducing the scales of **k**.

For the learning on BYY system given by the case eq.(18), the posteriori WTA may cause many local maximums which will affect the performance. A solution to this problem is

$$\min_{\theta} \ [\lambda H(p\|p) - H(p\|g)], \tag{23}$$

with λ starting at $\lambda = 1$, which is equivalent to eq.(22) and then gradually reducing into zero, which is equivalent to $\max_{\theta} H(\theta, \mathbf{k})$. Such an annealing process can be regarded as a regularization on the harmony learning $\max_{\theta} H(\theta, \mathbf{k})$.

This annealing process becomes unnecessary when $\max_{\theta} H(\theta, \mathbf{k})$ is implemented with regularization via either *normalized point density* or *data smoothing*.

5 Harmony Measure, KL-Divergence and Geometry

We can get further insights on the harmony learning and the KL learning eq.(22) from understanding the geometrical properties of the harmony measure and the KL-Divergence.

We start at reviewing some basic properties in the conventional vector space R^d. We denote $U_c = \{u : u \in R^d \ and \ \|u\|^2 = c, \ \text{for a constant } c > 0\}$. For $u \in U_c, v \in U_{c'}$, the projection of v on u is

$$u^T v = \sum_{j=1}^{d} u_j v_j = \sqrt{cc'} \cos \phi, \quad \phi \text{ is the angle between the direction of } u \text{ and } v (24)$$

with the following properties:

- *The self-projection of u to u is simply the norm $\|u\|^2$.*
- *The projection $u^T v$ is maximized when $\phi = 0$, i.e., v is co-directional with u.*
- *When $c = c'$, $\phi = 0$ implies $u = v$, i.e., the projection is maximized if and only if $u = v$.*
- *$\phi = 0$ maybe achieved by rotating the directions of both u and v or the direction of either u or v.*

Using u to represent v, the error or residual $u - v$ has a projection on u:

$$(u - v)^T u = \|u\|^2 - v^T u = c - v^T u. \tag{25}$$

with the following properties:

- *Its minimization this residual projection is equivalent to maximizing the projection $u^T v$. When $v^T u \geq 0$, i.e., $0 \leq \phi \leq 0.5\pi$, this residual projection $(u-v)^T u$ is actually the difference between the norm of u and the projection $u^T v$.*
- *The residual $u - v$ is said to be orthogonal to u when the residual projection $(u-v)^T u$ becomes zero, where the norm of u and the projection $u^T v$ becomes the same, i.e., $u^T v = \|u\|^2 = c$ or $\sqrt{\frac{c}{c'}} = \cos \phi$.*
- *When $c = c'$, the minimum value of $(u - v)^T u$ is 0 which is reached if and only if $u = v$.*

Therefore, we see that maximizing the projection $u^T v$ and minimizing the residual projection $(u-v)^T u$ are two complementary but equivalent concepts. In general, the minimization of the residual projection $(u - v)^T u$ usually does not result in the orthogonality of $u - v$ to u since the minimum value of $(u - v)^T u$ can be negative. However, when $c = c'$, this minimum is 0 and thus in this case the concepts of maximizing the projection $u^T v$ for the co-directionality of v to u, of minimizing the residual projection $(u - v)^T u$, and of making residual $u - v$ being orthogonal to u are all equivalent.

In an analogy, we consider a functional space

$$\mathcal{G} = \{g(u) : g(u) \geq 0 \text{ and } \int g(u)\mu(du) < \infty\}, \tag{26}$$

where $u \in S_u \subseteq R^d$ and μ is a given measure on the support S_u, and $\mu(du)$ relates to du only but to neither u nor $g(u)$. A useful subspace $\mathcal{P}_c \subset \mathcal{G}$ is

$$\mathcal{P}_c = \{p(u) : p(u) \geq 0 \text{ and } \int p(u)\mu(du) = c, \text{ for a constant } c > 0 \}. \tag{27}$$

Particularly, when $c = 1$, $\mathcal{P}_1$ is the probability density space.

Given $p(u) \in \mathcal{P}_c, g(u) \in \mathcal{P}_{c'}$, we define the projection of $g(u)$ on $p(u)$ by

$$H(p\|g) = \int p(u)\mu(du) \ln (g(u)\mu(du)) = \int p(u) \ln g(u)\mu(du) + \ln \mu(du), \tag{28}$$

where $\mu(du)$ takes the same role as z_g^{-1} in eq.(7) with z_g given in eq.(5). In correspondence to eq.(24), we have the following properties:

- *The self-projection of $p(u)$ to $p(u)$ is $H(p\|p) = \int p(u)\mu(du) \ln [(p(u)\mu(du)]$, which can be regarded a type of norm of p and it becomes the negative entropy of the probability distribution $p(u)\mu(du)$ when $p(u) \in \mathcal{P}_1$ is a density.*
- *$H(p\|g)$ is maximized if and only if $g(u) = \frac{c'}{c}p(u)$, i.e., $g(u)$ has the same shape as $p(u)$, because we always have $\int \hat{p}(u) \ln \hat{g}(u)\mu(du) \leq \int \hat{p}(u) \ln \hat{p}(u)\mu(du)$ with $c\hat{p}(u) = p(u)$, $c'\hat{g}(u) = g(u)$ and $\hat{p}(u), \hat{g}(u) \in \mathcal{P}_1$.*
- *When $c = c'$, $H(p\|g)$ is maximized if and only if $g(u) = p(u)$.*
- *When $p(u)$ is free to be any choice in $\mathcal{P}_c$, the maximization of $H(p\|g)$ will also let $p(u)$ to become $c\delta(u - u_p)$, where $u_p = \arg\max_u g(u)$.*

The last property is quite different from the situation of eq.(24), where when both the directions of u and v are free to change, the maximization of the projection $u^T y$ only ensures u and v being in a same direction but does not impose any specific preference for the direction of u. The maximization of $H(p\|g)$ makes not only that $p(u)$ and $g(u)$ has a same shape in the sense $g(u) = \frac{c'}{c}p(u)$ but also that $p(u)$ prefers to have a simplest shape $c\delta(u - u_p)$. Therefore, when $p(u)$ is free to be any choice in $\mathcal{P}_c$ and $g(u)$ is free to be any choice in $\mathcal{P}_{c'}$, the maximization of $H(p\|g)$ will finally let that both $p(u)$ and $g(u)$ become impulse functions with different scales but located at a same point u_p that can be any point in R^d. When $p(u) \in P, q(u) \in Q$ are constrained to be not able becoming impulse functions, the maximization of $H(p\|g)$ will make that $p(u)$ and $g(u)$ become not only probabilistically simple and but also close in shape.

If we use $p(u) \in \mathcal{P}_c$ to represent $g(u) \in \mathcal{P}_{c'}$ and define the discrepancy or residual [1] by $p(u) \ominus g(u) = p(u)\mu(du)/[g(u)\mu(du)] = p(u)/g(u)$, with $g(u)\mu(du)$ in eq.(28) replaced by the residual in this representation, we can find that the residual projection on $p(u)$ is

$$R(p\|g) = \int p(u) \ln [p(u)/g(u)]\mu(du) = H(p\|p) - H(p\|g). \tag{29}$$

Since $p(u) = c\hat{p}(u)$, $g(u) = c'\hat{g}(u)$ with $\hat{p}(u), \hat{g}(u) \in \mathcal{P}_1$, it follows that

$$R(p\|g) = c[KL(\hat{p}\|\hat{g}) + \ln \frac{c}{c'}], \tag{30}$$

From which we can observe the following properties:

- *Minimizing $R(p\|g)$ is equivalent to minimizing the self-projection of $p(u)$ and maximizing the projection of $g(u)$ on $p(u)$. When the self-projection $H(p\|p)$ is fixed at a constant, minimizing the residual projection is equivalent to maximizing $H(p\|g)$.*
- *Since $H(p\|g) \geq 0$, $R(p\|g)$ is actually the difference between the norm of p and the projection of q on p.*
- *The residual $p(u) \ominus g(u)$ is said to be orthogonal to $p(u)$ when the residual projection $R(p\|g)$ becomes 0 that happens when the norm of p and the projection of q on p become the same, i.e., $H(p\|p) = H(p\|g)$.*
- *When $c = c'$, the minimum value of $R(p\|g)$ is 0 which is reached if and only if $p(u) = g(u)$. Moreover, when $c = c' = 1$, $p(u)$ and $g(u)$ are densities and $R(p\|g) = KL(p\|g)$.*

The concepts of maximizing $H(p\|g)$ for co-directionality and minimizing the residual projection $R(p\|g)$ for orthogonality are complementary and closely related, but not equivalent even when $c = c' = 1$, which is not exactly the same situation as in that for eq.(24) and eq.(25). Specifically, minimizing $R(p\|g)$ only makes $p(u)$ and $g(u)$ become as close as possible in shape but, being different from maximizing $H(p\|g)$, has no force to compress $p(u)$ to become as close as possible to an impulse function. However, it follows from eq.(29) that the two become equivalent under the constraint that $H(p\|p)$ is fixed at a constant H_0, that is, we have

$$\max_{p\in P, q\in Q, \; s.t. \; H(p\|p)=H_0} H(p\|g) \text{ is equivalent to } \min_{p\in P, q\in Q, \; s.t. \; H(p\|p)=H_0} R(p\|g). \tag{31}$$

---

[1] Under this definition, $p(u)\ominus g(u)$ is generally not guaranteed to still remain in $\mathcal{G}$. For a subset $\mathcal{G}_g \subset \mathcal{G}$ with $\mathcal{G}_g = \{g(u) : g(u) \in G, \int_{D_u} g^2(u)\mu(du) < \infty, \int_{D_u} g^{-2}(u)\mu(du) < \infty, \int_{D_u} \mu(du) < \infty\}$, we can define the addition by $r(u) = p(u) \oplus g(u) = p(u)g(u)$ and have $r(u) \in \mathcal{G}_g$. Also, we have the unit $1 = p(u)p^{-1}(u) \in \mathcal{G}_g$ for $u \in S_u$ and the inverse $p^{-1}(u) = 1/p(u) \in \mathcal{G}_g$. In this case, it follows that the induced minus operation $p(u) \ominus g(u) = p(u)/g(u)$ is still in $\mathcal{G}_g$. That is, we get $\mathcal{G}_g$ as an Abel group. Moreover, on an appropriate subset $\mathcal{G}_l$ we can further define the dot product $\alpha \circ p(u) = p(u)^\alpha \in \mathcal{G}_l$ for $\alpha \in R$ and thus get $\mathcal{G}_l$ as a linear functional space. Furthermore, we can introduce the geometrical concepts of the projection eq.(28), the residual projection eq.(29) and the corresponding orthogonality to $\mathcal{G}_g, \mathcal{G}_l$.

Moreover, the minimum value of $R(p\|g)$ again can be negative and thus the minimization of $R(p\|g)$ generally does not result in the orthogonality of the residual $p(u) \ominus g(u)$ to $p(u)$. However, this minimum is 0 when $c = c'$, in which case the concepts of minimizing the residual projection $R(p\|g)$ and making $p(u)\ominus g(u)$ being orthogonal to $p(u)$ are equivalent.

References

1. Amari, S.-I., Cichocki, A., and Yang, H. (1996), "A new learning algorithm for blind separation of sources", in D. S. Touretzky, et al, eds, *Advances in Neural Information Processing 8,* MIT Press: Cambridge, MA, 757-763, 1996.
2. Barlow, H.B. (1989), "Unsupervised learning", *Neural Computation, 1,* 295-311, 1989.
3. Dayan, P., & Zemel, R.S., (1995) "Competition and multiple cause models", *Neural Computation 7,* pp565-579, 1995.
4. Dayan, P. & Hinton, G., E., (1996), "Varieties of Helmholtz machine", *Neural Networks 9,* No.8, 1385-1403.
5. Hinton, G. E., Dayan, P., Frey, B. and Neal, R.M.(1995), "The wake-sleep algorithm for unsupervised learning neural networks", *Science 268,* 1158-1160, 1995.
6. Jacobs, R.A., Jordan, M.I., Nowlan, S., and Hinton, G., E. (1991), "Adaptive mixtures of local experts", *Neural Computation, 3,* 79-87, 1991.
7. Jordan, M.I., and Jacobs, R.A. (1994), "Hierarchical mixtures of experts and the EM algorithm", *Neural Computation 6,* 181-214, 1994.
8. Xu, L. (2000a)," BYY Σ-Π Factor Systems and Harmony Learning : Recent Advances ", *Proc. 7th International Conference on Neural Information Processing (ICONIP-2000),* Nov. 14-18, Taejon, KOREA.
9. Xu, L.(2000b),"Temporal BYY Learning for State Space Approach, Hidden Markov Model and Blind Source Separation", *IEEE Trans on Signal Processing,* Vol. 48, No.7, pp2132-2144, 2000.
10. Xu, L. (1999a), "Bayesian Ying-Yang Unsupervised and Supervised Learning: Theory and Applications", *Proc. 1999 Chinese Conf. on Neural Networks and Signal Processing,* 12-29, Shantou, China, Nov., 1999.
11. Xu, L., (1999b), "BYY Data Smoothing Based Learning on A Small Size of Samples", and "Bayesian Ying-Yang Theory for Empirical Learning, Regularization and Model Selection: General Formulation", *Proc. 1999 Intl. Joint Conf. on Neural Networks,* Vol.1 of 6, pp546-551 and pp552-557, USA, July 10-16,1999.
12. Xu, L.(1999c), "Bayesian Ying-Yang Supervised Learning, Modular Models, and Three Layer Nets", *Proc. 1999 Intl. Joint Conf. on Neural Networks,* Vol.1 of 6, pp540-545, USA, July 10-16, 1999.
13. Xu, L., (1998a), "RBF Nets, Mixture Experts, and Bayesian Ying-Yang Learning", *Neurocomputing,* Vol. 19, No.1-3, 223-257, 1998.
14. Xu, L., (1998b), "Bayesian Kullback Ying-Yang Dependence Reduction Theory ", *Neurocomputing,* Vol.22, No.1-3, 81-112, 1998.
15. Xu, L.(1997), "Bayesian Ying-Yang Machine, Clustering and Number of Clusters", *Pattern Recognition Letters,* Vol.18, No.11-13, 1167-1178, 1997.
16. Xu, L., (1995) "A Unified Learning Scheme: Bayesian-Kullback YING-YANG Machine", *Advances in Neural Information Processing Systems 8,* eds., D. S. Touretzky, et al, MIT Press, 444-450, 1996. A part of its preliminary version on *Proc. ICONIP95, Peking,* Oct 30 - Nov. 3, 977-988, 1995.

Observational Learning with Modular Networks

Hyunjung Shin, Hyoungjoo Lee and Sungzoon Cho

{hjshin72, impatton, zoon}@snu.ac.kr
Department of Industrial Engineering, Seoul National University,
San56-1, ShilimDong, Kwanakgu, Seoul, Korea, 151-742

Abstract. Observational learning algorithm is an ensemble algorithm where each network is initially trained with a bootstrapped data set and virtual data are generated from the ensemble for training. Here we propose a modular OLA approach where the original training set is partitioned into clusters and then each network is instead trained with one of the clusters. Networks are combined with different weighting factors now that are inversely proportional to the distance from the input vector to the cluster centers. Comparison with bagging and boosting shows that the proposed approach reduces generalization error with a smaller number of networks employed.

1 Introduction

Observational Learning Algorithm(OLA) is an ensemble learning algorithm that generates "virtual data" from the original training set and use them for training the networks [1] [2] (see Fig. 1). The virtual data were found to help avoid overfitting, and to drive consensus among the networks. Empirical study showed that

---

[INITIALIZE] *Bootstrap D into L replicates $D_1, \ldots D_L$.*
[TRAIN]
DO FOR $t = 1, \ldots, G$
    [T-STEP] *Train each network :*
        Train j^{th} network f_j^t with D_j^t for each $j \in \{1, \ldots, L\}$.
    [O-STEP] *Generate virtual data set V_j for network j :*
        $V_j^t = \{(\boldsymbol{x}', \boldsymbol{y}') | \boldsymbol{x}' = \boldsymbol{x} + \boldsymbol{\epsilon}, \epsilon \sim N(0, \Sigma), \boldsymbol{x} \in D_j,$
               $\boldsymbol{y}' = \sum_{j=1}^{L} \beta_j f_j^t(\boldsymbol{x}')$ where $\beta_j = 1/L\}$.
    Merge virtual data with original data :
    $D_j^{t+1} = D_j \cup V_j^t$.
END
[FINAL OUTPUT] *Combine networks with weighting factors β's :*
    $f_{com}(\boldsymbol{x}) = \sum_{j=1}^{L} \beta_j f_j^T(\boldsymbol{x})$ where $\beta_j = 1/L$.

Fig. 1. Observational Learning Algorithm (OLA)

the OLA performed better than bagging and boosting [3]. Ensemble achieves the best performance when the member networks' errors are completely uncorrelated [5]. Networks become different when they are trained with different training data sets. In OLA shown Fig. 1, bootstrapped data sets are used. Although they are all different, they are probabilistically identical since they come from the identical original training data set. In order to make them more different, we propose to "specialize" each network by clustering the original training data set and using each cluster to train a network. Clustering assigns each network a cluster center. These centers are used to compute weighting factors when combining network outputs for virtual data generation as well as for recall.

The next section presents the proposed approach in more detail. In Sections 3 and 4, experimental results with artificial and real-world data sets are described. The performance of the proposed approach is compared with that of bagging and boosting. Finally we conclude the paper with a summary of result and future research plan.

2 Modular OLA

The key idea of our approach lies in network specialization and its exploitation in network combining. This is accomplished in two steps. First is to partition the whole training set into clusters and to allocate each data cluster to a network. Second is to use the cluster center locations to compute the weighting factors in combining ensemble networks.

2.1 Data set partitioning with clustering

The original data set D is partitioned into K clusters using K-means clustering or Self Organizing Feature Map (SOFM). Then, a total of K networks are employed for ensemble. Each cluster is used to train each network (see [INITIALIZE] section of Fig. 2). Partitioning the training data set helps to reflect the intrinsic distribution of the data set in ensemble. In addition, exclusive allocation of clustered data sets to networks corresponds to a divide-and-conquer strategy in a sense, thus making a learning task less difficult. Partitioning also solves the problem of choosing the right number of networks for ensemble. The same number of networks is used as the number of clusters. The problem of determining a proper number of ensemble size can be thus efficiently avoided.

2.2 Network combining based on cluster distance

How to combine network outputs is another important issue in ensemble learning. Specialization proposed here helps to provide a natural way to do it. The idea is to measure how confident or familiar each network is for a particular input. Then, the measured confidence is used as a weighting factor for each network in combining networks. The confidence of each network or cluster is considered inversely proportional to the distance from input vector x' to each cluster center.

[INITIALIZE]

  1. *Cluster* D *into* K *clusters, with* K*-means algorithm or SOFM,*
   $D_1, D_2, \ldots, D_K$ *with centers located at* $C_1, C_2, \ldots, C_K$, *respectively.*
  2. *Set the ensemble size* L *equal to the number of clusters* K.

[TRAIN]

DO FOR $t = 1, \ldots, G$

  [T-STEP] *Train each network :*
    Train j^{th} *network* f_j^t *with* D_j^t *for each* $j \in \{1, \ldots, L\}$.

  [O-STEP] *Generate virtual data set for each network* j :
    $V_j^t = \{(\boldsymbol{x'}, \boldsymbol{y'}) | \boldsymbol{x'} = \boldsymbol{x} + \boldsymbol{\epsilon}, \epsilon \sim N(0, \Sigma), \boldsymbol{x} \in D_j,$
      $\boldsymbol{y'} = \sum_{j=1}^{L} \beta_j f_j^t(\boldsymbol{x'})$, where $\beta_j = 1/d_j(\boldsymbol{x'})$
      and $d_j(\boldsymbol{x'}) = \sqrt{(\boldsymbol{x'} - \boldsymbol{C_j})^T \Sigma_j^{-1}(\boldsymbol{x'} - \boldsymbol{C_j})}$ }.

  Merge virtual data with original data :
  $D_j^{t+1} = D_j \cup V_j^t.$

END

[FINAL OUTPUT] *Combine networks with weighting factors* β*'s :*
  $f_{com}(\boldsymbol{x}) = \sum_{j=1}^{L} \beta_j f_j^T(\boldsymbol{x})$ where $\beta_j = 1/d_j(\boldsymbol{x'})$.

Fig. 2. Modular Observational Learning Algorithm (MOLA)

For estimation of the probability density function(PDF) of the training data set, we use a mixture gaussian kernels since we have no prior statistical information [6] [7] [8]. The familiarity of the jth kernel function to input $\boldsymbol{x'}$ is thus defined as

$$\Theta_j(\boldsymbol{x'}) = \frac{1}{(2\pi)^{d/2} |\Sigma_j|^{1/2}} \exp\{-\frac{1}{2}(\boldsymbol{x'} - \boldsymbol{C_j})^T \Sigma_j^{-1}(\boldsymbol{x'} - \boldsymbol{C_j})\}, \quad (j = 1, \ldots, L). \quad (1)$$

Taking natural logarithms of Eq. 1 leads to

$$\log \Theta_j(\boldsymbol{x'}) = -\frac{1}{2} \log |\Sigma_j| - \frac{1}{2}(\boldsymbol{x'} - \boldsymbol{C_j})^T \Sigma_j^{-1}(\boldsymbol{x'} - \boldsymbol{C_j}), \quad (j = 1, \ldots, L). \quad (2)$$

Assuming $\Sigma_j = \Sigma_j'$, for $j \neq j'$, makes a reformulated measure of the degree of familiarity $d_j(\boldsymbol{x'})$,

$$\log \Theta_j(\boldsymbol{x'}) \propto d_j^2(\boldsymbol{x'}) \quad (3)$$

where $d_j(\boldsymbol{x'}) = \sqrt{(\boldsymbol{x'} - \boldsymbol{C_j})^T \Sigma_j^{-1}(\boldsymbol{x'} - \boldsymbol{C_j})}$.

 So, each network's familiarity turns out to be proportional to be negative Mahalanobis distance between an input vector and the center of the corresponding cluster. The network whose cluster center is close to $\boldsymbol{x'}$ is given more weight in combining outputs. The weighting factor β_j is defined as a reciprocal of the distance $d_j(\boldsymbol{x'})$ and $\beta_j = 1/d_j(\boldsymbol{x'})$, both in [O-STEP] and [FINAL OUTPUT] as shown in Fig. 2. Compare it with Fig. 1 where simple averaging was used with β_j of $1/L$.

3   Experimental result I: artificial data

The proposed approach was first applied to an artificial function approximation problem defined by $y = sin(2x_1 + 3x_2^2) + \epsilon$, where ϵ is from a gaussian
distribution $N(0, 0.05^2 I)$. Each input vector x was generated from one of four
gaussian distributions $N(C_j, 0.3^2 I)$, where $\{(x_1, x_2)|(-0.5, -0.5), (0.5, -0.5), (-0.5,
0.5), (0.5, 0.5)\}$. A total of 320 data points were generated, with 80 from each clus-
ter. Some of the data points are shown in Fig. 3. The number of networks was also
set to 4. Note that clustering was not actually performed since the clustered data
sets were used. Four 2-5-1 MLPs were trained with the Levenberg-Marquardt
algorithm for five epochs.

T-step and O-step were iterated for 4 generations. At each generation, 80
virtual data were generated and then merged with the original 80 training data
for training in the next generation. Note that the merged data set size does
not increase at each generation by 80, but instead stays at 160 since the virtual
data are replaced by new virtual data at each generation. For comparison, OLA,
simple-averaging bagging and adaboost.R2 [4] were employed. For bagging, three
different ensemble sizes were tried, 4, 15 and 25. For boosting, the ensemble size
differs in every run. We report an average size which was 36. Experiments were
run 50 times with different original training data sets. Two different test data sets
were employed, a small set for a display purpose and a large set for an accurate
evaluation purpose. The small test set consists of 25 data points with their ID
numbers, shown in Fig. 3 (LEFT). The mesh shown in Fig. 3 (RIGHT) shows
the surface of the underlying function to be approximated while the square dots
represent the output values of the proposed approach MOLA (modular OLA)
for test inputs. MOLA's accuracy is shown again in Fig. 4 where 25 test data
points are arranged by their ID numbers. Note the accuracy of MOLA compared
with other methods, particularly at cluster centers, i.e. 7, 9, 17 and 19. Bagging
used 25 networks here. For those inputs corresponding to the cluster centers, the
familiarity of the corresponding network is highest.

The large test set consists of 400 data points. Table 1 summarizes the result
with average and standard deviation of mean squared error (MSE) of 50 runs.
In terms of average MSE, OLA with 25 networks was best. If we consider MSE
and ensemble size together, however, MOLA is a method of choice with a reasonable accuracy and a small ensemble. Since every network in an ensemble is
trained, the ensemble size is strongly related with the training time. Bagging
achieved the same average MSE with MOLA by employing more than 6 times
more networks. MOLA did better than OLA-4, thus OLA seems to need more
networks than MOLA to achieve a same level of accuracy. Of course, there is an
overhead associated with MOLA, i.e. clustering at initialization. A fair comparison of training time is not straightforward due to difference in implementation
efficiency. Boosting performed most poorly in all aspects. The last row displays
p-value of pair-wise t-tests comparing average MSEs among methods. With a
null hypothesis of "no difference in accuracy" and a one-sided alternative hypothesis "MOLA is more accurate than the other method," a smaller p-value

leads to acceptance of the alternative hypothesis. Statistically speaking, MOLA is more accurate than OLA-4, bagging-4 and boosting, but not others.

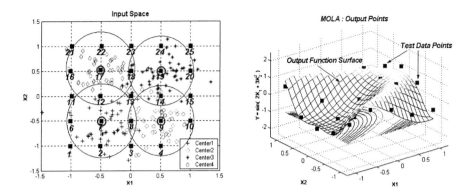

Fig. 3. [LEFT] Artificial data set generated from 4 gaussian distributions with a white noise. Each set is distinguished by graphic symbols. [RIGHT] Simulation results on 25 test data points: the mesh is the surface of the underlying function to be approximated while the square-dots represent the test output values from MOLA.

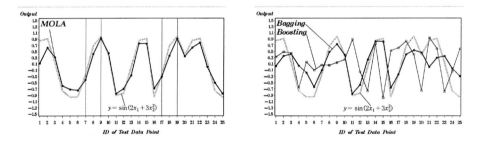

Fig. 4. 25 test data points are arranged by their ID numbers along x-axis. Note the MOLA's accuracy near the cluster centers (7,9,17,19) compared with that of bagging and boosting.

4   Experimental result II: real-world data

The proposed approach was applied to real-world regression problems: Boston Housing [9] and Ozone [10]. Both data sets were partitioned into 10 and 9 clusters with K-means algorithm, respectively. These, 10 13-10-1 MLPs and 9 8-10-1 MLPs were trained with L-M algorithm, respectively. The test results are

Table 1. Experimental Results (Artificial Data)

50 runs	MOLA	OLA			Bagging			Boosting
Ensemble Size	4	4	15	25	4	15	25	Avg(36)
Avg MSE(10^{-2})	5.4	6.5	4.8	4.7	7.3	5.4	5.4	10.5
Std MSE(10^{-2})	4.0	2.0	0.9	0.8	3.0	2.7	1.3	9.2
P-value(T-test)	-	0.04	0.87	0.90	0.01	0.99	1.00	0.00

summarized in Table 2. For Boston housing problem, MOLA outperformed both bagging and boosting (0 p-values). For Ozone problem, MOLA outperformed boosting but not bagging.

Table 2. Experimental Results (RealWorld Data)

Tr/Val/Test 30 runs	Boston Housing 200/106/100			Ozone 200/30/100		
	MOLA	Bagging	Boosting	MOLA	Bagging	Boosting
Ensemble Size	10	25	Avg(48)	9	25	Avg(49)
Avg MSE(10^{-2})	9.3	10.3	10.9	19.2	19.0	21.0
Std MSE(10^{-2})	0.89	0.96	1.39	0.94	0.65	0.82
P-value(T-test)	-	0.00	0.00	-	0.79	0.00

5 Conclusions

In this paper, we proposed a modular OLA where each network is trained with a mutually exclusive subset of the original training data set. Partitioning is performed using K-means clustering algorithm. Then, a same number of networks are trained with the corresponding data clusters. The networks are then combined with weighting factors that are inversely proportional to the distance between the new input vector and the corresponding cluster centers.

The proposed approach was compared with OLA, bagging, and boosting in artificial function approximation problems and real world problems. The MOLA employing a smaller number of networks performed better than OLA and bagging in artificial data. The MOLA did better in one real data and similarly in the other real data. This preliminary result shows that the approach is a good candidate for problems where data sets are clustered well.

Current study has several limitations. First, a more extensive set of data sets have to be tried. Second, in clustering, the number of clusters is hard to find correctly. The experiments done so far produced a relatively small number of clusters, 4 for artificial data and 10 and 9 for real world data. It is worthwhile to investigate the test performance with a larger MOLA ensemble. Third, weighting factors are naively set to the distance between input vector and cluster centers. An alternative would be to use the weighting factors inversely proportional to the training error of the training data close to the input vector.

Acknowledgements

This research was supported by Brain Science and Engineering Research Program sponsored by Korean Ministry of Science and Technology and by the Brain Korea 21 Project to the first author.

References

[1]   Cho, S. and Cha, K., "Evolution of neural network training set through addition of virtual samples," *International Conference on Evolutionary Computations*, 685–688 (1996)

[2]   Cho, S., Jang, M. and Chang, S., "Virtual Sample Generation using a Population of Networks," *Neural Processing Letters*, Vol. 5 No. 2, 83–89 (1997)

[3]   Jang, M. and Cho, S., "Observational Learning Algorithm for an Ensemble of Neural Networks," submitted (1999)

[4]   Drucker, H., "Improving Regressors using Boosting Techniques," *Machine Learning: Proceedings of the Fourteenth International Conference* , 107–115 (1997)

[5]   Perrone, M. P. and Cooper, L. N., "When networks disagree: Ensemble methods for hybrid neural networks," *Artificial Neural Networks for Speech and Vision* , (1993)

[6]   Platt, J., "A Resource-Allocating Network for Function Interpolation," *Neural Computation* , Vol 3, 213–225 (1991)

[7]   Roberts, S. and Tarassenko, L., "A Probabilistic Resource Allocating Network for Novelty Detection," *Neural Computation* , Vol 6, 270–284 (1994)

[8]   Sebestyen, G. S., "Pattern Recognition by an Adaptive Process of Sample Set Construction," *IRE Trans. Info. Theory IT-8* , 82–91 (1962)

[9]   http://www.ics.uci.edu/~ mlearn

[10] http://www.stat.berkeley.edu/users/breiman

Finding Essential Attributes in Binary Data[*]

Endre Boros[1], Takashi Horiyama[2], Toshihide Ibaraki[3], Kazuhisa Makino[4], and
Mutsunori Yagiura[3]

[1] RUTCOR, Rutgers University, 640 Bartholomew Road, Piscataway, NJ
08854-8003, USA; `boros@rutcor.rutgers.edu`
[2] Graduate School of Information Science, Nara Institute of Science and Technology,
Nara 630-0101, Japan; `horiyama@is.aist-nara.ac.jp`
[3] Department of Applied Mathematics and Physics, Graduate School of Informatics,
Kyoto University, Kyoto 606-8501, Japan;
{`ibaraki@i.kyoto-u.ac.jp`; `yagiura@amp.i.kyoto-u.ac.jp`}
[4] Department of Systems and Human Science, Graduate School of Engineering
Science, Osaka University, Toyonaka, Osaka, 560-8531, Japan;
`makino@sys.es.osaka-u.ac.jp`

Abstract. Given a data set, consisting of n-dimensional binary vectors
of positive and negative examples, a subset S of the attributes is called
a support set if the positive and negative examples can be distinguished
by using only the attributes in S. In this paper we consider several selection criteria for evaluating the "separation power" of supports sets, and
formulate combinatorial optimization problems for finding the "best and
smallest" support sets with respect to such criteria. We provide efficient
heuristics, some with a guaranteed performance rate, for the solution of
these problems, analyze the distribution of small support sets in random
examples, and present the results of some computational experiments
with the proposed algorithms.

1 Introduction

We consider the problem of analyzing a data set consisting of positive and negative examples for an unknown phenomenon. We denote by T the set of positive
examples, and by F the set of negative examples, and assume further that each
example is represented as a binary n-dimensional vector[1]. This is a typical problem setting studied in various fields, such as knowledge discovery, data mining,
learning theory and logical analysis of data (see e.g. [2, 3, 8, 15, 16, 22, 24, 25].)

---

[*] This work was partially supported by the Grants in Aid by the Ministry of Education,
Science, Sports and Culture of Japan (Grants 09044160 and 10205211). The visit of
the first author to Kyoto University (January to March, 1999) was also supported
by this grant (Grant 09044160). The research of the first and third authors were
supported in part by the Office of Naval Research (Grant N00014-92-J-1375). The
first author thanks also the National Science Foundation (Grant DMS 98-06389) and
DARPA (Contract N66001-97-C-8537) for partial support.
[1] Even if the input dataset contains non-binary attributes, it can be binarized e.g. by
considering features such as "Age$\leq$ 40", "Color $=$ Blue", etc., see e.g. [7, 21]

Let $\mathbb{B} = \{0,1\}^n$, and let us call a pair (T, F), for $T, F \in \mathbb{B}^n$ a *partially defined Boolean function* (or pdBf, in short). Let us call a Boolean function $f : \mathbb{B} \mapsto \mathbb{B}$ an *extension* of (T, F) if $f(a) = 1$ for all $a \in T$ and $f(b) = 0$ for all $b \in F$. Such an extension (exists iff $T \cap F = \emptyset$) can be interpreted as a logical separator between the sets T and F, or equivalently, as an explanation of the phenomenon represented by the data set (T, F) (see e.g. [10, 11, 15].) It is quite common that the data set contains attributes which are *irrelevant* to the phenomenon under consideration, and also ones which are *dependent* on some other attributes of the data set. It is an interesting problem to recognize these, and to find a (smallest) subset of the *essential attributes*, which still can explain the given data set (T, F). Finding a small subset of the variables, which explains the input data "as much as possible", is in the spirit of Occam's razor [6], and is a frequent subject of studies in computational learning theory (see e.g. "attribute efficient learning" [4, 13, 20]). In some practical applications, such a subset is sought to reduce the cost of data collection.

This problem has been an active research area for many years within statistics and pattern recognition, though most of the papers there dealt with linear regression [5] and used assumptions not valid for most learning algorithms [18]. Many related studies in machine learning considers this problems in conjunction with some specific learning algorithms [1, 14, 19, 17]. In this study we accepted the "small feature set" bias as in [1] and found further supporting evidence by analyzing the distribution of small support sets in random data sets. We also consider feature selection as a stand alone task, independently from the applied learning methods. For this we develop a family of measures, and formulate exact optimization problems for finding the "best" feature subset according to these measures. We propose polynomial time solvable continuous relaxations of these problems providing a "relevance" weight for each attribute (c.f. [12, 19]), standard greedy heuristics, as well as reverse greedy type heuristics with a worst case performance guarantee. We have tested on randomly generated data sets the effects of the presence of both dependent and irrelevant features.[2]

2 Support sets and measures of separation

Let $V = \{1, 2, \ldots, n\}$ denote the set of indices of the attributes in the input data set. For a subset $S \subseteq V$ and a vector $a \in \mathbb{B}^n$, let $a[S]$ denote the projection of a on S, and for a set $X \subseteq \mathbb{B}^n$ let us denote by $X[S] = \{a[S] \mid a \in X\}$ the corresponding family of projections. Let us call a subset $S \subseteq V$ a *support set* of a pdBf (T, F) if $T[S] \cap F[S] = \emptyset$ (c.f. [15].)

First, we estimate the number of support sets of a given size K in randomly generated pdBf-s. Let us suppose that the vectors of T and F are chosen uniformly and independently from $\mathbb{B}^n$, drawing m_T and m_F vectors, respectively.

---

[2] Due to space limitations, we omit proofs, some of the separation measures, and several of the computational results. In the complete version [9] we have also included encouraging results with some real data sets.

(Note that $|T| < m_T$ or $|F| < m_F$ may occur due to duplications.) Let $n(K)$ denote the number of support sets of size K in this random pdBf (T, F).

Theorem 1.

$$\left(\frac{2^K - m_T}{2^K}\right)^{m_F} \leq \frac{\mathbf{E}[n(K)]}{\binom{n}{K}} \leq \min_{\delta > 0} \left(e^{-(m_T(1 - \frac{m_T - 1}{2^{K+1}}) - \delta)\frac{m_F}{2^K}} + e^{-\frac{2\delta^2}{m_T}}\right).$$

These bounds are reasonably close, and imply the following.

Corollary 1. *Suppose $m_T = o(2^{3K/5})$, $m_F = o(2^{3K/5})$, $n \geq ((Ke)^{1/K} + 1)K - 1$ and $\ln\ln n = o(K)$. Then $\mathbf{E}(n(K)) = 1$ implies $K + \log_2 K = \log_2(m_T m_F)(1 + o(1))$, where $o(1) \to 0$ as $K \to \infty$.*

In other words, support sets of size smaller than K, where $K + \log_2 K = \log_2(m_T m_F)$ are rare in random data with $m_T m_F$ sufficiently large. Thus when exists, such a support set is more probable to be related to the real phenomenon, than to random noise.

For two vectors $a, b \in \mathbb{B}^n$, let $d(a, b) = |a \Delta b|$ denote the *Hamming distance* between a and b, where $a \Delta b = \{j | a_j \neq b_j\}$. For a subset $S \subseteq V$ let us consider its *Hamming distance vector* $h(S) = (h_0, h_1, \ldots, h_n)$, where $h_k = h_k(S)$ is the number of pairs (a, b), $a \in T[S]$, $b \in F[S]$ exactly at Hamming distance k. Intuitively, S is *better separating* than S' if $h(S) \leq_L h(S')$, where $\leq_L$ denotes the *lexicographic order*[3]. Defining $\phi_\alpha(S) \stackrel{\text{def}}{=} \sum_{k=0}^n h_k(S)(1 - \alpha^k)$ for some $0 \leq \alpha < 1$, the above inequality is equivalent with $\phi_\alpha(S) \geq \phi_\alpha(S')$, assuming α is small enough. The special case of $\theta(S) \stackrel{\text{def}}{=} \phi_0(S) = |T||F| - h_0(S)$ appears frequently in the literature, similarly to the minimum Hamming distance measure $\rho(S) \stackrel{\text{def}}{=} \min_{a \in T, b \in F} d(a[S], b[S])$. Finally, let us consider the following problem

$$\max\{\psi(S) \mid S \subseteq V, |S| \leq K\} \qquad (\Psi)$$

where ψ can be any of ρ, θ or ϕ_α $(0 \leq \alpha < 1)$, and K is a given threshold. Let us note that for any of the above measures, the smallest parameter K for which (Ψ) has a support set as an optimal solution, is K^*, the size of the smallest possible support set for (T, F). Hence, these optimization problems are NP-hard, in general, since determining K^* is known to be NP-hard (see e.g. [15]).

We propose first a standard *greedy* heuristic to solve problem (Ψ), which is very common in discrete optimization.

ψ-GREEDY: Starting with $S \leftarrow \emptyset$, select iteratively $j \in V \setminus S$ for which $\psi(S \cup \{j\})$ is the largest, and set $S \leftarrow S \cup \{j\}$, **until** $T[S] \cap F[S] = \emptyset$.

We can show that if ψ-GREEDY has a guaranteed worst case performance rate.

---

[3] It is said that $(h_0, ..., h_n) \leq_L (h'_0, ..., h'_n)$ if $h_i < h'_i$, where i is the smallest index j with $h_j \neq h'_j$.

Theorem 2. *Problem (Ψ) is approximable within a factor of $(1 - \frac{1}{e})$ by the (modified) ψ-GREEDY, for $\psi = \phi_\alpha$, $1 > \alpha \geq 0$ (including $\theta = \phi_0$.)*

We can also demonstrate that a similar result is very unlikely for the case of $\psi = \rho$, unless P=NP , see [9].

Let us denote by $\mathbb{U} = [0, 1]$ the unit interval, and for $y \in \mathbb{U}^n$ and $a, b \in \mathbb{B}^n$, let $d_y(a, b) = \sum_{j \in a \Delta b} y_j$. Clearly, d_y can be considered a natural extension of the Hamming distance. Consequently, the measures of separation defined above can also be extended by defining $\rho(y) = \min_{a \in T, b \in F} d_y(a, b)$, $\theta(y) = \sum_{a \in T, b \in F} \min\{d_y(a, b), 1\}$, and $\phi_\alpha(y) = \sum_{a \in T, b \in F}(1 - \alpha^{d_y(a,b)})$ for $0 < \alpha < 1$. Using these notations, the continuous relaxation of (Ψ) for a given pdBf (T, F) can be written as

$$\max \left\{ \psi(y) \mid y \in \mathbb{U}^n, \sum_{j \in V} y_j \leq K \right\} \tag{Ψ^c}$$

It can easily be seen that problem (Ψ^c) becomes a linear programming problem, if $\psi \in \{\rho, \theta\}$, and hence these can be solved efficiently, even for large data sets. If $\psi(y) = \phi_\alpha(y)$ for some $0 < \alpha < 1$, problem (Ψ^c) is a concave maximization over a convex domain, which again is known to be solvable efficiently[4].

Another heuristic to solve problem (Ψ), the *stingy* algorithm is based on (Ψ^c). It can be viewed as a reverse greedy algorithm, as it starts from $S = V$ and then removes elements from S successively until a minimal support set is obtained.

ψ-STINGY: Starting with $K \leftarrow 1$ and $Z \leftarrow \emptyset$, successively solve the optimization problem (Ψ^c) extended with the constraints $\sum_{j \in a \Delta b} y_j \geq 1$ for $a \in T$ and $b \in F$, and $y_j = 0$ for $j \in Z$; if this problem has no feasible solution, then set $K \leftarrow K + 1$, otherwise, let $y^* \in \mathbb{U}^n$ be an optimal solution, set $z^* \leftarrow \min_{a \in T, b \in F} d_{y^*}(a, b)$, and let k be the largest integer for which $\sum_{j=1}^{k} y^*_{i_j} < z^*$, where $y^*_{i_1} \leq y^*_{i_2} \leq \cdots \leq y^*_{i_n}$; if $k \leq |Z|$, then set $K \leftarrow K + 1$, otherwise set $Z \leftarrow \{i_1, i_2, ..., i_k\}$; **until** $K + |Z| < n$.

For the stingy algorithm we can show that

Theorem 3. *Algorithm ψ-STINGY terminates in polynomial time, and returns a binary vector y^* such that the set $S^* = \{j \mid y^*_j = 1\}$ is a minimal support set of pdBf (T, F), assuming that problem (Ψ^c) is solvable in polynomial time.*

3 Computational results

In our experiments, we generate pdBf-s with known support sets, and compare the performance of the above heuristic algorithms on the basis of how much they can recover the original support sets. We partition the variables space $V = H \cup D \cup R$, where H denotes the active variables of the "hidden logic" f, D denotes variables depending on the components in H (via Boolean functions

---

[4] For a concave maximization over a convex domain an $\varepsilon > 0$ approximation can be obtained in polynomial time in the input size and in $1/\varepsilon$, see e.g. [23]

$g_k : \mathbb{B}^H \mapsto \mathbb{B}$, $k \in D$,) and R denotes randomly generated components. Then we draw vectors $x \in \mathbb{B}^V$ randomly, set $x_k = g_k(x[H])$ for $k \in D$, and put x into T or F, according to the value $f(x[H])$.

We have generated three different types of problems: type A with $|H| = 10$, $|D| = |R| = 5$, type B with $|H| = 5$, $|D| = |R| = 10$, and type C with $|H| = 5$, $|D| = 0$ and $|R| = 40$. For each type we have generated 40–40 instances in two different sizes: size 1 with $|T| + |F| = 200$ and size 2 with $|T| + |F| = 400$. Table 1 lists the averages (of 40 runs) for the 3 best performing heuristics for each of the above six categories. We can see that ϕ_α-stingy finds the smallest support sets, and recovers the most of the hidden essential attributes, even if there are many dependent attributes present. In particular, in all C2 instances the hidden support set was recovered perfectly. On the other hand, greedy algorithms perform also reasonably well, and run much faster. In our implementation, greedy runs took only fractions of a second, while the stingy algorithm ran several minutes. We can also see that irrelevant attributes are much easier to filter out than dependent ones (the latter can arguably be expected.)

Types	θ-GREEDY				ϕ_α-GREEDY				ϕ_α-STINGY			
	$|S|$	r_H	r_D	r_R	$|S|$	r_H	r_D	r_R	$|S|$	r_H	r_D	r_R
A1	11.18	0.602	0.131	0.267	11.18	0.615	0.109	0.275	10.75	0.740	0.038	0.222
A2	12.14	0.756	0.076	0.168	12.12	0.771	0.062	0.167	10.78	0.913	0.010	0.078
B1	6.14	0.567	0.400	0.032	6.10	0.595	0.377	0.029	5.80	0.704	0.223	0.073
B2	6.01	0.591	0.392	0.018	6.00	0.596	0.389	0.016	5.70	0.730	0.216	0.053
C1	5.84	0.866	0.000	0.134	5.78	0.885	0.000	0.115	5.67	0.923	0.000	0.077
C2	5.24	0.976	0.000	0.024	5.22	0.976	0.000	0.024	5.00	1.000	0.000	0.000

Table 1. Performance summary for random functions: $\alpha = 0.001$ $r_H = |S \cap H|/|S|$, $r_D = |S \cap D|/|S|$, $r_R = |S \cap R|/|S|$.

References

1. H. Almuallim and T. Dietterich. Learning Boolean concepts in the presence of many irrelevant features. *Artificial Intelligence* **69** (1994) 279-305.
2. R. Agrawal, T. Imielinski and A. Swami. Mining association rules between sets of items in large databases. In: *International Conference on Management of Data* (SIGMOD 93), (1993) pp. 207-216.
3. D. Angluin. Queries and concept learning. *Machine Learning* **2** (1988) 319-342.
4. A. Blum, L. Hellerstein, and N. Littlestone. Learning in the presence of finitely or infintely many irrelevant attributes. *Journal of Computer and System Sciences* **50** (1995) pp. 32-40.
5. A. Blum and P. Langley. Selection of relevant features and examples in machine learning. *Artificial Intelligence* **67** (1997) 245-285.
6. A. Blumer, A. Ehrenfeucht, D. Haussler and M. K. Warmuth. Occam's razor. *Information Processing Letters* **24** (1987) 377-380.

7. E. Boros, P.L. Hammer, T. Ibaraki and A. Kogan. Logical analysis of numerical data *Mathematical Programming* **79** (1997), 163-190.

8. E. Boros, P.L. Hammer, T. Ibaraki, A. Kogan, E. Mayoraz and I. Muchnik. An implementation of logical analysis of data. *IEEE Trans. on Knowledge and Data Engineering* **12** (2000) 292-306.

9. E. Boros, T. Horiyama, T. Ibaraki, K. Makino and M. Yagiura. Finding Small Sets of Essential Attributes in Binary Data. DIMACS Technical Report DTR 2000-10, Rutgers University, 2000; ftp://dimacs.rutgers.edu/pub/dimacs/TechnicalReports/-TechReports/2000/2000-10.ps.gz

10. E. Boros, T. Ibaraki and K. Makino. Error-free and best-fit extensions of a partially defined Boolean function. *Information and Computation* **140** (1998) 254-283.

11. E. Boros, T. Ibaraki and K. Makino. Logical analysis of binary data with missing bits. *Artificial Intelligence* **107** (1999) 219–264.

12. W. Brauer and M Scherf. Feature selection by means of a feature weighting approach. Technical Report FKI-221-97, Institute für Informatik, Technische Universität München, 1997.

13. N. Bshouty and L. Hellerstein. Attribute-efficient learning in query and mistake-bound models. *J. of Comput. Syst. Sci.* **56** (1998) 310-319.

14. R. Caruana and D. Freitag. Greedy attribute selection. In: *Machine Learning: Proceedings of the Eleventh International Conference*, (Rutgers University, New Brunswick, NJ 1994), pp. 28-36.

15. Y. Crama, P. L. Hammer and T. Ibaraki. Cause-effect relationships and partially defined Boolean functions. *Annals of Operations Research* **16** (1988) 299-326.

16. U. M. Fayyad, G. Piatetsky-Shapiro, P. Smyth and R. Uthurusamy. *Advances in Knowledge Discovery and Data Mining*, (AAAI Press/The MIT Press, 1996.)

17. M.A. Hall and L.A. Smith. Practical feature subset selection for machine learning. In: *Proceedings of the 21st Australasian Computer Science Conference* (Springer Verlag, 1998) pp. 181-191.

18. G. John, R. Kohavi and K. Pfleger. Irrelevant features and the subset selection problem. In: *Machine Learning: Proceedings of the Eleventh International Conference*, (Rutgers University, New Brunswick, NJ 1994), pp. 121-129.

19. K. Kira and L. Rendell. The feature selection problem: Traditional methods and a new algorithm. In: *Proceedings of the Tenth National Conference on Artificial Intelligence*, Menlo Park, (AAAI Press/The MIT Press, 1992), pp. 129-134.

20. N. Littlestone. Learning quickly when irreleveant attributes abound: a new linear-threshold algorithm. *Machine Learning* **2** (1988) 285-318.

21. H. Mannila and H. Toivonen. Multiple uses of frequent sets and condensed representations. In: *Proceedings of the 2nd International Conference on Knowledge Discovery and Data Mining*, (1996) pp. 189-194.

22. H. Mannila, H. Toivonen and A.I. Verkamo. Efficient algorithms for discovering association rules. In: *AAAI Workshop on Knowledge Discovery in Database* (U.M. Fayyad and R. Uthurusamy, eds.) (1994) pp. 181-192.

23. Y. Nesterov and A. Nemirovskii. *Interior-Point Polynomial Algorithms in Convex Programming*. SIAM Studies in Applied Mathematics, 1994.

24. J. R. Quinlan. Induction of decision trees. *Machine Learning* **1** (1986) 81-106.

25. L. G. Valiant. A theory of the learnable. *Communications of the ACM* **27** (1984) 1134-1142.

A Heuristic Optimal Reduct Algorithm

Keyun Hu, Lili Diao, Yuchang Lu and Chunyi Shi

(Computer Science Department, Tsinghua University, Beijing 100084, P.R.China)
hky@s1000e.cs.tsinghua.edu.cn, lyc@mail.tsinghua.edu.cn

Abstract   Reduct finding, especially optimal reduct finding, similar to feature selection problem, is a crucial task in rough set applications to data mining,   In this paper, we propose a heuristic reduct finding algorithm, which is based on frequencies of attributes appeared in discernibility matrix. Our method does not guarantee to find optimal reduct, but experiment shows that in most situations it does; and it is very fast.

Keywords   rough set, reduct, discernibility matrix, data mining

1 Introduction

The rough set theory provides a formal framework for data mining. It has several favorite features such as representing knowledge in a clear mathematical manner, deriving rules only from facts present in data and reducing information systems to its simplest form, etc.

Reduct is the most important concept in rough set application to data mining. A reduct is the minimal attribute set preserving classification accuracy of all attribute of original dataset. Finding a reduct is similar to feature selection problem. All reducts of a dataset can be found by constructing a kind of discernibility function from the dataset and simplifying it [2]. Unfortunately, It has been shown that finding minimal reduct or all reducts are both NP-hard problems. Some heuristics algorithms have been proposed. Hu gives an algorithm using significant of attribute as heuristics [4]. Some algorithms using genetic algorithm are also proposed. Starzyk use strong equivalence to simplify discernibility function [3]. However, there are no universal solutions. It's still an open problem in rough set theory.

In this paper, we propose a simple but useful heuristic reduct algorithm using discernibility matrix. The algorithm is based on frequencies of attributes appeared in discernibility matrix. Our method does not guarantee to find optimal reduct, but experiment shows that in most situations it does; And it is faster than finding one reduct (see section 5).

2 Related rough set concepts

This section recalls necessary rough set notions used in the paper. Detail description of the theory can be found in [2].

Definition 1 (information system) An information system is a ordered pair S=(U, A∪{d}), where U is a non-empty, finite set called the universe, A is a non-empty, finite set of conditional attributes, d is a decision attribute. $A \cap \{d\} = \Phi$. The elements of the universe are called objects or instances.

Information system contains knowledge about a set of objects in term of a predefined set of attributes. The set of objects is called concept in rough set theory. In order to represent or approximate these concepts, an equivalence relation is defined. The equivalence classes of the equivalence relation, which are the minimal blocks of the information system, can be used to approximate these concepts. Concept can be constructed from these blocks are called definable sets. As to undefinable sets, two definable sets, upper-approximation set and lower-approximation set are constructed to approximate the concept.

Definition 2 (Indiscernibility relation) Let $S=(U, A \cup \{d\})$ be an information system, every subset $B \subseteq A$ defines an equivalence relation IND(B), called an indiscernibility relation, defined as $IND(B)=\{(x,y) \in U \times U: a(x)=a(y)$ for every $a \in B\}$.

Definition 3 (Positive region) Given an information system $S=(U, A \cup \{d\})$, let $X \subseteq U$ be a set of objects and $B \subseteq A$ a selected set of attributes. The lower approximation of X with respect to B is $B_*(X)=\{x \in U:[x]_B \subseteq X\}$. The upper approximation of X with respect to B is $B^*(X) = \{x \in U: [x]_B \cap X \neq \Phi\}$. The positive region of decision d with respect to B is $POS_B(d)= \cup\{B_*(X) :X \in U/IND(d)\}$

The positive region of decision attribute with respect to B represents approximate quantity of B. Not all attributes are necessary while preserving approximate quantity of original information system. Reduct is the minimal set of attribute preserving approximate quantity.

Definition 4 (Reduct) An attribute a is dispensable in $B \subseteq A$ if $POS_B(d)= POS_{B-\{a\}}(d)$. A **reduct** of B is a set of attributes $B' \subseteq B$ such that all attributes $a \in B-B'$ are dispensable, and $POS_B(d)= POS_{B'}(d)$.

There are usually many reducts in an information system. In fact, on can show that the number of reducts of an information system may be up to $C^{|A|/2}_{|A|}$. In order to find reducts, discernibility matrix and discernibility function are introduced.

Definition 5 (discernibility matrix) The **discernibility matrix** of an information system is a symmetric $|U| \times |U|$ matrix with entries c_{ij} defined as $\{a \in A|a(x_i) \neq a(x_j)\}$ if $d(x_i) \neq d(x_j)$, Φ otherwise. A discernibility function can be constructed from discernibility matrix by or-ing all attributes in c_{ij} and then and-ing all of them together. After simplifying the discernibility function using absorption law, the set of all prime implicants determines the set of all reducts of the information system.

However, simplifying discernibility function for reducts is a NP-hard problem.

3 The principle

The heuristic comes from the fact that intersection of a reduct and every items of discernibility matrix can not be empty. If there are any empty intersections between some item c_{ij} with some reduct, object i and object j would be indiscernible to the reduct. And this contradicts the definition that reduct is the minimal attribute set discerning all objects (assuming the dataset is consistent).

A straightforward algorithm can be constructed based on the heuristic. Let candidate reduct set $R=\Phi$. We examine every entry c_{ij} of discernibility matrix. If their intersection is empty, a random attribute from c_{ij} is picked and inserted in R; skip the entry otherwise. Repeat the procedure until all entries of discernibility matrix are examined. We get the reduct in R.

The algorithm is simple and straightforward. However, in most times what we get is not reduct itself but superset of reduct. For example, there are three entries in the matrix: $\{a_1, a_3\}, \{a_2, a_3\}, \{a_3\}$. According the algorithm, we get the reduct $\{a1, a2, a3\}$ although it is obvious $\{a_3\}$ is the only reduct. Why that happens?

The answer is that our heuristic is a necessary but not sufficient condition for a reduct. The reduct must be a **minimal** one. The above algorithm does not consider this. In order to find reduct, especially shorter reduct in most times, we need more heuristics.

A simple yet powerful method is sort the discernibility matrix according $|c_{ij}|$. As we know, if there is only one element in c_{ij}, it must be a member of reduct. We can image that attributes in shorter and frequent $|c_{ij}|$ contribute more classification power to the reduct. After sorting, we can first pick up more powerful attributes, avoid situations like example mentioned above, and more likely get optimal or sub-optimal reduct.

The sort procedure is like this. First, all the same entries in discernibility matrix are merged and their frequency are recorded. Then the matrix is sorted according the length of every entry. If two entries have the same length, more frequent entry takes precedence.

When generating the discernibility matrix, frequency of every individual attribute is also counted for later use. The frequencies is used in helping picking up attribute when it is need to pick up one attribute from some entry to insert into reduct. The idea is that more frequent attribute is more likely the member of reduct. The counting process is weighted. Similarly, attributes appeared in shorter entry get higher weight. When a new entry c is computed, the frequency of corresponding attribute $f(a)$ are updated as $f(a)=f(a)+|A|/|c|$, for every $a \in c$; where $|A|$ is total attribute of information system. For example, let $f(a1)=3$, $f(a3)=4$, the system have 10 attributes in total, and the new entry is $\{a1,a3\}$. Then frequencies after this entry can be computed: $f(a1)=3+10/2=8$; $f(a3)=4+10/2=9$.

Empirical results present in later section shows that our algorithm can find optimal reduct in most times, and it's very fast once discernibility matrix is computed.

4 The Algorithm

This subsection presents the algorithm written in pseudo-code. The algorithm is designed according the principle given in previous subsection.

Input: an information system $(U, A\cup\{d\})$, where $A=\cup a_i$, $i=1,\ldots,n$.

Output: a reduct red

Red=Φ, count(a_i)=0, for i=1,...n.

Generate discernibility matrix M and count frequency of every attribute count(a_i);

Merge and sort discernibility matrix M;

For every entry m in M do

If (m$\cap$Red == Φ)

select attribute a with maximal count(a) in m

Red=Red∪{a}
Endif
EndFor
Return Red

Figure 1   A heuristic reduct algorithm

In line 2, when a new entry c of M is computed, count(a_i) is updated. count(a_i):=count(a_i)+n/|c| for every $a_i \in$ |c|. In line 3, Same entries are merged and M is sorted according the length and frequency of every entry. Line 4-9 traverses M and generates the reduct.

5 Implementation and complexity issues

In order to save space, every entry of discernibility matrix is implemented as a bit vector whose length equal to |A|. Every attribute is represented by one bit in the bit vector. A bit in the bit vector is set to 1 if corresponding attribute is present in the entry, 0 otherwise. Step 2 and step 3 are performed simultaneously in the implementation. Our implementation is based on standard template library (STL) in C++.

At step2, the cost for computing discernibility matrix is $O(|A||U|^2)$. In the worst case, there will be $|U|(|U|-1)/2$ entries in M, thus the sorting procedure in step 3 takes at most $O(|U|^2\log(|U|^2)) = O(2|U|^2\log(|U|))$. In fact, there are much less entries then the worst case for objects in the same class do not produce any entry.

Step4-step9 traverses M and generates reduct. Due to at most $|U|(|U|-1)/2$ entries in M and |A| items in each entry, the worst time complexity is also $O(|A||U|^2)$, though in practical applications it typical takes much less time than that of step2 for there are usually only a few entries left in M after step 3. So the total price is at most $O((|A|+\log U)|U|^2)$, which is less than complexity bound $O(|A|^3|U|^2)$ for finding a reduct in [1]. Empirical analysis also show that out algorithm is very fast (see below section).

6 Empirical Analysis

The algorithm is tested under a personal computer running windows 98 with pentium II 266 processor and 64Mb memory installed.

We have tested our algorithm on 45 UCI datasets [7]. All datasets are discretized using MLC utility [6]. In order to find whether our algorithm could find optimal reduct, we compute all reducts using bool reasoning methods as described in [2] for reference. Note that when we talk about optimal reduct we refer to the shortest reduct.

Twenty of 45 datasets have only one reduct. Our algorithm finds them successfully. These dataset are adult, australian, balance-scale, cars, cleve, diabetes, german-org, glass, heart, iris, led7, lenses, letter, monk1, monk2, monk3, parity5+5, pima, solar, and vehicle.

All reducts of three datasets can not be determined. The program runs for quite a few hours but there is no sign to end. We stopped the program. So we do not know whether our algorithm find the optimal reduct. These datasets are *led24, dna,* and *satimage.*

Results of the rest datasets are summarized in figure 2.

Dataset	Instances	Attributes	Values	All reducts	Optimal	Computing time(s)
anneal	598	39	126	30	Sub7(8)	1.92
auto	136	26	98	17	Yes(7)	0.05
breast	466	11	30	2	Sub6(7)	0.33
breastcancer	191	10	53	2	Yes(8)	0.06
chess	2130	37	75	14	Yes(24)	37.79
crx	490	16	55	4	Yes(12)	0.71
DNA	2000	181	363	-	Unknown(22)	162.64
german	666	21	67	5	Super10(11)	1.49
hepatitis	103	20	38	284	Sub7(8)	0.05
horse-colic	300	23	65	432	Yes(9)	0.44
hypothyroid	2108	26	54	2	Yes(12)	4.94
ionosphere	234	35	94	273	Sub7(9)	0.22
led24	200	25	58	-	Unknown(14)	0.71
mushroom	5415	23	127	306	Yes(4)	107.98
satimage	4435	37	190	-	Unkown(15)	145.34
shuttle	43500	10	175	6	Yes(6)	260.18
shuttlesmall	3866	10	59	4	Yes(5)	17.91
sonar	138	61	76	2	Yes(12)	0.16
soybean(s)	31	36	58	53	Yes(2)	1.38
soybean(l)	455	36	104	1094	Yes(9)	0.00
tic-tac-toe	638	10	29	7	Yes(7)	0.71
vote	300	17	50	2	Yes(8)	0.28
waveform40	300	41	72	4	Yes(12)	0.71
wine	118	14	35	56	Yes(4)	0.06
Zoo	67	17	43	37	Super4(5)	0.00
Total 25 datasets					Yes:16 sub:4 super:2 unkown: 3	

Figure 2   Summery of results of our algorithm

The leftmost column is dataset names. The 2nd, 3rd, 4th column are instance numbers, attribute numbers and attribute value numbers of corresponding dataset. The 5th column is the number of all reducts. The rightmost column is the computing time used by our algorithm. The 6th column is the results of our algorithm. The number in the bracket is the length of reduct our algorithm found. A yes before it indicting that what we found is optimal reduct. A superXX before it indicting that what we find is a superset of reduct, XX is the length of optimal reduct. A subXX indicting that what we find is a reduct, but not a shortest one, XX is the length of optimal reduct. And an unknown before it indicting all reducts can not determined.

For example, for dataset *auto*, all reduct algorithm find the following reducts (where the attribute names are coded as integers):
0 1 4 5 9 10 11 23; 0 1 4 5 9 10 11 14; 0 1 4 5 9 10 11 13; 0 1 4 5 8 10 11; 0 1 4 5 6 10 11 23 24; 0 1 4 5 6 10 11 20 23; 0 1 4 5 6 10 11 17 23; 0 1 4 5 6 10 11 16 23; 0 1 4 5 6 10 11 15 23; 0 1 4 5 6 10 11 14 24; 0 1 4 5 6 10 11 14 20; 0 1 4 5 6 10 11 14 17; 0 1 4 5 6 10 11 14 16; 0 1 4 5 6 10 11 14 15; 0 1 4 5 6 10 11 12 23; 0 1 4 5 6 10 11 12 14; 0 1 4 5 6 10 11 12 13;

Our algorithm find the optimal reduct: 0 1 4 5 8 10 11.

For dataset *german*, a super-reduct is obtained. All reducts are: 0 2 3 5 6 11 13 14 16 18; 0 1 3 5 6 8 9 11 13 16 18 19; 0 1 2 3 5 6 9 11 13 16 18; 0 1 2 3 4 5 6 8 11 13 14 16; 0 1 2 3 4 5 6 8 9 11 13 16. Our solution is 0 2 3 5 6 8 11 13 14 16 18.

For dataset *breast*, a sub-optimal reduct is found. All reducts are: 1 3 4 5 6 7 8; 1 2 4 5 6 8. Our algorithm has found first one.

From figure 1, we can see that our algorithm found most optimal reducts successfully. Even for the non-optimal situation, our algorithm can find satisfactory sub-optimal solution. And it is fast.

7 Conclusion

In this paper we propose an efficient heuristic optimal reduct algorithm. This algorithm makes use of frequency information of individual attribute in discernibility matrix, and develops a weighting mechanism to rank attributes. The method does not guarantee to find optimal reduct, but experiment shows that in most situations it does.

Further research direction includes enhancing our algorithm to incremental version, developing a more efficient weighting mechanism, etc.

Acknowledgments This research is supported by Natural Science Foundation of China, 985 research program of Tsinghua university and National 973 Fundamental Research Program.

References

1   J.W.Guan, D.A.Bell. Rough computational methods for information systems, Artificial intellignence, 105(1998)77-103

2   S.K.Pal, A.Skowron, Rough Fuzzy Hybridization- A new trend in decision-making, Springer, 1999

3   J.Starzyk, D.E.Nelson, K.Sturtz, Reduct generation in information systems, Bulletin of international rough set society, volume 3, 1998, 19-22

4   X.Hu, Knowledge discovery in databases: An attribute-oriented rough set approach, Ph.D thesis, Regina university, 1995

5   J.Deogun, S.Choubey, V.Raghavan, H.Sever. Feature selection and effective classifiers, Journal of ASIS 49, 5(1998), 403-414

6   Kohavi, R.,John, G., et al : MLC++: a machine learning library in C++, Tools with artificial intelligence (1994)740-743

7   Merz, C.J., Murphy, P. UCI repository of machine learning database. http://www.cs.uci.edu/ ~mlearn/MLRepository.html

A Note on Learning Automata Based Schemes for Adaptation of BP Parameters

M. R. Meybodi and H. Beigy

Computer Engineering Department
Amirkabir University of Technology
Tehran, Iran
email: beigy@ce.aku.ac.ir

Abstract. Backpropagation is often used as the learning algorithm in layered-structure neural networks, because of its efficiency. However, backpropagation is not free from problems. The learning process sometimes gets trapped in a local minimum and the network cannot produce the required response. In addition, The algorithm has number of parameters such learning rate (μ), momentum factor (α) and steepness parameter (λ). whose values are not known in advance, and must be determined by trail and error. The appropriate selection of these parameters have large effect on the convergence of the algorithm. Many techniques that adaptively adjust these parameters have been developed to increase speed of convergence. A class of algorithms which are developed recently uses learning automata (LA) for adjusting the parameters μ, α, and λ based on the observation of random response of the neural networks. One of the important aspects of learning automata based schemes is its remarkable effectiveness as a solution for increasing the speed of convergence. Another important aspect of learning automata based schemes which has not been pointed out earlier is its ability to escape from local minima with high possibility during the training period. In this report we study the ability of LA based schemes in escaping from local minma when standard BP fails to find the global minima. It is demonstrated through simulation that LA based schemes comparing to other schemes such as SAB, Super SAB, Fuzzy BP, ASBP method, and VLR method have higher ability in escaping from local minima.

1 Introduction

The multilayer feedforward neural network models with error back-propagation (BP) algorithm have been widely researched and applied [1]. Despite the many successful applications of backpropagation, it has many drawbacks. For complex problems it may require a long time to train the networks, and it may not train at all. It is pointed out by numerous researches that BP can be trapped in local minima during gradient descent and in many of these cases it seems very unlikely that any learning algorithm could perform satisfactorily in terms of computational requirements. Long training time can be the result of the non-optimum values for the parameters of the training algorithm. It is not easy to choose appropriate values for these parameters for a particular problem. The parameters are usually determined by trial and error and using the past experiences. For example, if the learning rate is too small, convergence can be very slow, if too large, paralysis and continuous instability can result. Moreover the best value at the beginning of training may not be so good later. Thus several researches have suggested algorithms for automatically adjusting the parameters of training algorithm as training proceeds, such as algorithms proposed by Arabshahi et al. [2], Darken and Moody [3], Jacobs [3], and Sperduti and Starita [4] to mention a few. Several learning automata (LA) based procedures have been recently developed [5][6][7]. In these methods variable structure learning automata (VSLA) or fixed structure learning automata (FSLA) have been used to find the appropriate values of parameters for the BP training algorithm. In these schemes either a separate learning automata is associated to each layer or each neuron of the network or a single automata is associated to the whole network to adapt the appropriate parameters. Through the computer simulations, it is shown that the learning rate adapted in such a way increases the rate of convergence of the network by a large amount.

When we use learning automata as the adaptation technique for BP parameters, the search for optimum is carried out in probability space rather than in parameter space as is in the case with other adaptation algorithms. In the standard gradient method, the new operation point lies within a neighborhood distance of the previous point. This is not the case for adaptation algorithm based on stochastic principles such as learning automata, as the new operating point is determined by probability function and is therefore not considered to be near the previous operating point. This gives the algorithm higher ability to locate the global minima. In this paper we study the ability of LA based schemes in escaping from local minima when standard BP fails to find the global minima. In this paper, It is demonstrated through simulation that LA based schemes comparing to the other schemes such as SAB [3], SuperSAB [3], adaptive steepness method(ASBP)[4], variable learning rate(VLR) method [8] and Fuzzy BP [2] have higher ability in escaping from local minima, that is BP parameter adaptation using LA bases scheme increases the likelihood of bypassing the local minimum.

The rest of the paper is organized as follows. Section 2 briefly presents basics of learning automata. Existing LA based adaptation schemes for BP parameters are described in section 3. Section 4 demonstrates through simulations the ability of LA based schemes in escaping from local minima. The last section is conclusion.

2 Learning Automata

Learning automata operating in unknown random environments have been used as models of learning systems. These automata choose an action at each instant from a finite action set, observe the reaction of the environment to the action chosen and modify the selection of the next action on the basis the reaction. The selected action serves as the input to the environment which in turn emits a stochastic response. The environment penalize the automaton with the penalty c_i, which is the action dependent. On the basis of the response of the environment, the state of the automaton is updated and a new action chosen at the next time instant. Note that the $\{c_i\}$ are unknown initially and it is desired that as a result of interaction with the environment the automaton arrives at the action which presents it with the minimum penalty response in an expected sense. If the probability of the transition from one state to another state and probabilities of correspondence of action and state are fixed, the automaton is said fixed-structure automata and otherwise the automaton is said variable-structure automata. Examples of the FSLA type that we use in this paper are Tsetline, Krinsky, TsetlineG, and Krylov automata. For more information on learning automata refer to [9].

3   LA Based Schemes For Adaptation of BP Parameters

In this section, we first, briefly describe LA based schemes for adaptation of BP parameters [5][6][7]. In all of the existing schemes, one or more automaton have been associated to the network. The learning automata based on the observation of the random response of the neural network, adapt one or more of BP parameters. The interconnection of learning automata and neural network is shown in figure 1. Note that the neural network is the environment for the learning automata. The learning automata according to the amount of the error received from neural network adjusts the parameters of the BP algorithm. The actions of the automata correspond to the values of the parameters being calculated and input to the automata is some function of the error in the output of neural network.

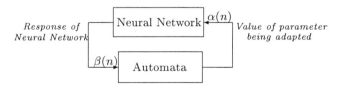

Fig. 1. Automata-neural network connection

Existing LA based procedures for adaptation of BP parameters can be classified into four groups which we call them group **A**, **B**, **C**, and **D**. In group **A** schemes, one automaton is used for the whole network whereas in group **B** schemes, separate automata one for each layer (hidden and output) are used [5]. Each group **A** and **B** depending on the type of automata used (fixed or variable structure) can be classified into two sub-groups. The parameter adapted by group **A** schemes will be used by all the links or neurons of the networks and therefore these schemes fall in the category of global parameter adaptation method, whereas group **B** schemes by adapting the parameter for each layer independently may be referred to as quasi-global parameter adaptation methods.

In a class **C** scheme one automata is associated to each link of the network to adjust the parameter for that link and in a class **D** scheme one automata is associated to each neuron of the network to adjust the parameter for that neuron. Group **C** and **D** schemes may be referred to as the local parameter adaptation methods. In [6] class **C** schemes are used for adaptation of learning rate and class **D** schemes are used for adaptation of steepness parameter. In class **C** and **D** schemes, the automata receives favorable response from the environment if the algebraic sign of derivative in two consecutive iterations is the same and receives unfavorable response if the algebraic sign of the derivative in two consecutive iterations alternates.

For the sake of convenience in presentation, we use the following naming conventions to refer to different LA based schemes in classes **A**, **B**, **C**, and **D**. Without loss of generality, we assume that in class **A** and class **B**, the neural network has one hidden layer.

$Automata - AX(\gamma)$ A scheme in class **A** for adjusting parameter γ which uses X structure LA *Automata*.

$Automata_1 - Automata_2 - BX(\gamma)$ A scheme in class **B** which uses X structure LA for hidden layer and X structure LA *Automata$_2$* for output layer.

$Automata - CX(\gamma)$ A scheme in class **C** for adjusting parameter γ which uses X structure LA *Automata*.

$Automata - DX(\gamma)$ A scheme in class **D** for adjusting parameter γ which uses X structure LA *Automata*.

The rate of convergence can be improved if both learning rate and steepness parameter are adapted simultaneously. Simultaneous use of class **C** and class **D** schemes for adaptation of learning rate and steepness parameters is also reported in [6]. A LA based scheme that simultaneously adapts learning rate and steepness parameter is denoted by $Automata_1 - Automata_2 - CDX(\mu, \lambda)$, if X structure LA is used and a LA based scheme which simultaneously adapt the learning rate and momentum factor is denoted by $Automata_1 - Automata_2 - CX(\eta, \alpha)$ when X structure LA is used. X denotes either fixed or variable structure automata. For all the LA based schemes reported in the literature, it is shown through simulation that the use of LA for adaptation of BP learning algorithm parameters increases the rate of convergence by a large amount [6].

4   LA Based Schemes and Local Minima

In this section, we examine the ability of the LA based schemes to escape from local minima. For this propose, we chose a problem in which local minima are occurred frequently [10]. This example considers the sigmoidal network for the

Table 1. Training set for given problem

Pattern	x	y	Desired output
A	0	0	0
B	1	0	1
C	1	1	0
D	0	1	1
E	0.5	0.5	0

XOR boolean function with the quadratic cost function and the standard learning environment. The training set of this problem is given in table 1.

The network which is used has two input nodes x and y, two hidden units, and one output unit. In this problem, if hidden units produce the lines a and b the local minima has been occurred and if hidden units produce the lines c and d the global minima occurred [10]. Figure 2 shows these configurations. The error surface of the network as a function of weights $w_{2,1,1}$ and $w_{1,1,1}$ is given in figure 3.

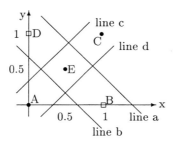

Fig. 2. Lines produced by hidden units

Depending on the initial weights, the gradient can get stuck in points where the error is far from being zero. The presence of these local minima is intuitively related to the symmetry of the learning environment. Experimental evidence of the presence of local minima is given in figure 3.

In order to show how well the LA based adaptation algorithm escapes local minima we test twelve different LA based algorithms, 4 from class **A**, 4 from class **B**, 1 from class **C**, 1 from class **D**, and 1 from class **CD**, and compare their results with the standard BP and five other known adaptation method: SAB, SuperSAB, VLR method, ASBP method, and fuzzy BP. The result of simulation for 20 runs are summarized in table 1. Note that for standard BP and also for standard BP when SAB or SuperSAB method is used to adapt the learning rate none of the 20 runs converges to the global minima. Among the non-LA based methods the ASBP method performs the best. For this scheme 7 out of 20 runs converges to global minima which is comparable to the some of

A Note on Covariances for Categorical Data

Takashi Okada

Center for Information & Media Studies, Kwansei Gakuin University

1-1-155 Uegahara, Nishinomiya, Japan 662-8501

okada@kwansei.ac.jp

Abstract. Generalization of the covariance concept is discussed for mixed categorical and numerical data. Gini's definition of variance for categorical data gives us a starting point to address this issue. The value difference in the original definition is changed to a vector in value space, giving a new definition of covariance for categorical and numerical data. It leads to reasonable correlation coefficients when applied to typical contingency tables.

1 Introduction

Covariances and correlation coefficients for numerical data express the strength of a correlation between a pair of variables. Such convenient measures have been expected for categorical data, and there have been many proposals to define the strength of a correlation [1]. However, none of these proposals has succeeded in unifying the correlation concept for numerical and categorical data.

Recently, variance and sum of squares concepts for a single categorical variable were shown to give a reasonable measure of the rule strength in data mining [2]. If we can introduce a covariance definition for numerical and categorical variables, more flexible data mining schemes could be formulated.

In this paper we propose a generalized and unified formulation for the covariance concept. Section 2 introduces Gini's definition of variance, and its limitations. A new definition of covariance is proposed in Section 3. Samples of covariance matrices and correlation coefficients are shown for typical contingency tables in Section 4.

2 Gini's Definition of Variance and its Limitations

Gini successfully defined the variance for categorical data [3]. He first showed that the following equality holds for the variance of a numerical variable x_i.

$$V_{ii} = \left(\sum_a (x_{ia} - \bar{x}_i)^2 \right) \Big/ n = \frac{1}{2n^2} \sum_a \sum_b (x_{ia} - x_{ib})^2 \quad , \tag{1}$$

where V_{ii} is the variance of the i-th variable, x_{ia} is the value of x_i for the a-th instance, and n is the number of instances.

Then, he gave a simple distance definition (2) for a pair of categorical values. The variance defined for categorical data was easily transformed to the expression at the right end of (3).

$$x_{ia} - x_{ib} \begin{cases} = 1 & \text{if } x_{ia} \neq x_{ib} \\ = 0 & \text{if } x_{ia} = x_{ib} \end{cases} , \tag{2}$$

$$V_{ii} = \frac{1}{2n^2} \sum_a \sum_b (x_{ia} - x_{ib})^2 = \frac{1}{2}\left(1 - \sum_r p_i(r)^2 \right) . \tag{3}$$

Here $p_i(r)$ is the probability that the variable x_i takes a value r. The resulting expression is the well-known Gini-index.

The above definition can be extended to covariances by changing $(x_{ia} - x_{ib})^2$ to $(x_{ia} - x_{ib})(x_{ja} - x_{jb})$ [4]. However, it does not give reasonable values relative to correlation coefficients. The difficulty can be seen in the contingency table example of Table 1. There are two variables, x_i and x_j, each of which takes three values. Almost all instances appear in the diagonal positions, and hence the data should have a high V_{ij}. The problem arises when we consider an instance at (t, v). Intuitively, this instance should decrease the strength of the correlation. However, there appears to be some positive contribution to V_{ij} between this instance and that at (r, u). It comes from the value difference pair, $(x_i: r/t, x_j: u/v)$, which is different from the major value difference pairs $(x_i: r/s, x_j: u/v)$, $(x_i: r/t, x_j: u/w)$ and $(x_i: s/t, x_j: v/w)$. This contradiction comes from (2) in that it does not discriminate between these four types of value difference pairs.

Table 1. A sample contingency table with high correlation.

		x_j		
		u	v	w
x_i	r	100	0	0
	s	0	100	0
	t	0	1	100

3 Generalized Covariance

We propose a scheme to generalize the definition of a covariance for categorical data. It employs Gini's variance definition (3) as the starting point, and introduces two additional concepts. The first is to represent the value difference as a vector in value space. The other is to regard the covariance as the extent of maximum overlap between vectors in two value spaces.

3.1 Vector Expression of a Value Difference

We employ a vector expression, $\overrightarrow{x_{ia}x_{ib}}$, instead of the distance, $x_{ia} - x_{ib}$, in the variance definition. When x_i is a numerical variable, the expression is a vector in one-dimensional space. The absolute value and sign of $(x_{ib} - x_{ia})$ give its length and direction, respectively.

Now let us think of a categorical variable, x_i, that can take three values, $(r\ s\ t)$. We can position these values at the three vertices of an equilateral triangle as shown in Figure 1. Then, a value difference is a vector in two-dimensional space. The length of every edge is set to 1 to adapt the distance definition of (2). If there are c kinds of values for a categorical variable, x_i, then each value can be matched to a vertex of the regular polyhedron in $(c$-1)-dimensional space.

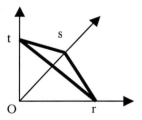

Fig. 1. Value space.

3.2 Definition of Covariance, V_{ij}

Our proposal for the V_{ij} definition is the maximum value of $Q_{ij}(L)$ while changing L, and $Q_{ij}(L)$ is defined by the subsequent formula,

$$V_{ij} = \max\left(Q_{ij}(L)\right) \quad , \tag{4}$$

$$Q_{ij}(L) = \frac{1}{2n^2} \sum_a \sum_b \left\langle \overrightarrow{x_{ia}x_{ib}} \left| L \right| \overrightarrow{x_{ja}x_{jb}} \right\rangle \quad . \tag{5}$$

Here, L is an orthogonal transformation applicable to the value space. The bracket notation, $<e|L|f>$, is evaluated as the scalar product of two vectors e and Lf (or $L^{-1}e$ and f). If the lengths of the two vectors, e and f, are not equal, zeros are first padded to the vector of the shorter length.

In general, L may be selected from any orthogonal transformation, but we impose some restrictions in the following cases.

1. When we compute the variance, V_{ii}, L must be the identity transformation, since two value difference vectors are in the identical space.

2. A possible transformation of L is (1) or (-1) when the vector lengths of e and f are unity. However, if both x_i and x_j are numerical variables, we always have to use the transformation matrix, (1), in order to express a negative correlation.

3.3 Assumed Properties for Bracket Notations

We assume several properties when using bracket notation, as follows. All these properties are easily understood as properties of a vector.

$$\left\langle \vec{rr} \middle| L \middle| \vec{uv} \right\rangle = \left\langle \vec{rs} \middle| L \middle| \vec{uu} \right\rangle = 0.0 \quad . \tag{6}$$

$$\left\langle \lambda \vec{rs} \middle| L \middle| \vec{uv} \right\rangle = \left\langle \vec{rs} \middle| L \middle| \lambda \vec{uv} \right\rangle = \lambda \left\langle \vec{rs} \middle| L \middle| \vec{uv} \right\rangle \quad . \tag{7}$$

$$\left\langle \vec{rs} \middle| L \middle| \vec{uv} \right\rangle = -\left\langle \vec{rs} \middle| L \middle| \vec{vu} \right\rangle = -\left\langle \vec{sr} \middle| L \middle| \vec{uv} \right\rangle = \left\langle \vec{sr} \middle| L \middle| \vec{vu} \right\rangle \quad . \tag{8}$$

$$\left\langle \vec{rs} \middle| L \middle| \vec{uv} \right\rangle + \left\langle \vec{rs} \middle| L \middle| \vec{vw} \right\rangle = \left\langle \vec{rs} \middle| L \middle| \vec{uw} \right\rangle \quad . \tag{9}$$

$$\left\langle \vec{rs} \middle| L \middle| \vec{uv} \right\rangle + \left\langle \vec{st} \middle| L \middle| \vec{uv} \right\rangle = \left\langle \vec{rt} \middle| L \middle| \vec{uv} \right\rangle \quad . \tag{10}$$

Furthermore, we can assume (11) without loss of generality, while (6) and (11) are alternative definitions for the original distance definition (2).

$$\left\langle \vec{rs} \middle| L \middle| \vec{rs} \right\rangle = 1.0 \quad . \tag{11}$$

4 Samples of Covariance Matrices

There is no way to prove the proposed covariance definition. Covariance matrices are derived for typical contingency tables to facilitate the understanding of our proposal.

4.1 2 x 2 Categorical Data

	X_j		
	u	v	
X_i r	n_{ru}	n_{rv}	$n_{r\cdot}$
s	n_{su}	n_{sv}	$n_{s\cdot}$
	$n_{\cdot u}$	$n_{\cdot v}$	n

Our first example is a simple 2 x 2 contingency table shown at the left, where $n_{r\cdot}$ and $n_{\cdot u}$ represent marginal distributions. The straightforward application of (5) to this table gives the following expressions for Q_{ii}.

$$Q_{ii}(L) = \frac{1}{2n^2}\left(n_{r\cdot}n_{r\cdot}\left\langle\overrightarrow{rr}\left|L\right|\overrightarrow{rr}\right\rangle + n_{r\cdot}n_{s\cdot}\left\langle\overrightarrow{rs}\left|L\right|\overrightarrow{rs}\right\rangle + n_{s\cdot}n_{r\cdot}\left\langle\overrightarrow{sr}\left|L\right|\overrightarrow{sr}\right\rangle + n_{s\cdot}n_{s\cdot}\left\langle\overrightarrow{ss}\left|L\right|\overrightarrow{ss}\right\rangle\right)$$
(12)
$$= \frac{1}{2n^2}2n_{r\cdot}n_{s\cdot}\left\langle\overrightarrow{rs}\left|L\right|\overrightarrow{rs}\right\rangle = \frac{n_{r\cdot}n_{s\cdot}}{n^2} \quad .$$

The resulting expression does not depend on L. V_{ii} and V_{jj} are given by (13) and by (14). These expressions are identical to those of Gini.

$$V_{ii} = n_{r\cdot}n_{s\cdot}/n^2 = \tfrac{1}{2}\left(1 - (n_{r\cdot}/n)^2 - (n_{s\cdot}/n)^2\right) \quad .$$
(13)
$$V_{jj} = n_{\cdot u}n_{\cdot v}/n^2 = \tfrac{1}{2}\left(1 - (n_{\cdot u}/n)^2 - (n_{\cdot v}/n)^2\right) \quad .$$
(14)

The same procedure gives Q_{ij} the following expression, where (8) is used to derive the second line.

$$Q_{ij} = \frac{1}{2n^2}\left(\begin{array}{c} n_{ru}n_{sv}\left\langle\overrightarrow{rs}\left|L\right|\overrightarrow{uv}\right\rangle + n_{rv}n_{su}\left\langle\overrightarrow{rs}\left|L\right|\overrightarrow{vu}\right\rangle \\ + n_{su}n_{rv}\left\langle\overrightarrow{sr}\left|L\right|\overrightarrow{uv}\right\rangle + n_{sv}n_{ru}\left\langle\overrightarrow{sr}\left|L\right|\overrightarrow{vu}\right\rangle \end{array}\right)$$
(15)
$$= \frac{1}{n^2}\left(n_{ru}n_{sv} - n_{rv}n_{su}\right)\left\langle\overrightarrow{rs}\left|L\right|\overrightarrow{uv}\right\rangle \quad .$$

Here, $\overrightarrow{rs}$ and $\overrightarrow{uv}$, are expressed by a vector with one element. The transformation matrix L can take the value (1) or (-1), a 1x1 matrix. Therefore, the expression of V_{ij} is given by the next formula.

$$V_{ij} = \frac{\left|n_{ru}n_{sv} - n_{rv}n_{su}\right|}{n^2} \quad .$$
(16)

The numerator of this formula is the critical term used to represent the extent of dependency between two variables. In fact, the correlation coefficient, defined by $V_{ij}/\sqrt{V_{ii}V_{jj}}$, is 1.0 (0.0) for completely dependent (independent) data, respectively.

4.2 2 x 3 Categorical Data

		x_j			
		u	v	w	
x_i	r	n_{ru}	n_{rv}	n_{rw}	$n_{r\cdot}$
	s	n_{su}	n_{sv}	n_{sw}	$n_{s\cdot}$
		$n_{\cdot u}$	$n_{\cdot v}$	$n_{\cdot w}$	n

V_{jj} takes the following expression,

$$V_{jj} = \tfrac{1}{2}\left(1-(n_{\cdot u}/n)^2 - (n_{\cdot v}/n)^2 - (n_{\cdot w}/n)^2\right) \quad . \quad (17)$$

Without loss of generality, the value difference vectors and the transformation, L, can be written as

$$\overrightarrow{rs} = \begin{pmatrix} 1 \\ 0 \end{pmatrix}, \quad \overrightarrow{uv} = \begin{pmatrix} 1 \\ 0 \end{pmatrix}, \quad \overrightarrow{uw} = \begin{pmatrix} \tfrac{1}{2} \\ \sqrt{3}\!/_2 \end{pmatrix}, \quad \overrightarrow{vw} = \begin{pmatrix} -\tfrac{1}{2} \\ \sqrt{3}\!/_2 \end{pmatrix}, \quad (18)$$

$$L(\theta,\sigma) = \begin{pmatrix} \cos\theta & \sin\theta \\ -\sin\theta & \cos\theta \end{pmatrix}\begin{pmatrix} 1 & 0 \\ 0 & -1 \end{pmatrix}^{\sigma}, \quad (19)$$

where the value of σ is 0 or 1, and the range of θ is from $-\pi$ to π. Using the upper (lower) sign for $\sigma = 1$ (0), $Q_{ij}(L)$ is given by

$$Q_{ij} = \frac{1}{n^2}\left\langle \begin{vmatrix} \begin{pmatrix} 1 \\ 0 \end{pmatrix} \end{vmatrix} \left(n_{ru}n_{sv} - n_{rv}n_{su}\right)\begin{pmatrix} \cos\theta \\ -\sin\theta \end{pmatrix} + \left(n_{ru}n_{sw} - n_{rw}n_{su}\right)\begin{pmatrix} (\tfrac{1}{2})\cos\theta \pm (\sqrt{3}\!/_2)\sin\theta \\ -(\tfrac{1}{2})\sin\theta \pm (\sqrt{3}\!/_2)\cos\theta \end{pmatrix} \right. \\ \left. + \left(n_{rv}n_{sw} - n_{rw}n_{sv}\right)\begin{pmatrix} -(\tfrac{1}{2})\cos\theta \pm (\sqrt{3}\!/_2)\sin\theta \\ (\tfrac{1}{2})\sin\theta \pm (\sqrt{3}\!/_2)\cos\theta \end{pmatrix} \right\rangle \quad (20)$$

$$= \cos\theta\left\{(n_{ru}n_{sv} - n_{rv}n_{su}) + (\tfrac{1}{2})(n_{ru}n_{sw} - n_{rw}n_{su}) - (\tfrac{1}{2})(n_{rv}n_{sw} - n_{rw}n_{sv})\right\}/n^2 \\ + \sin\theta\left\{0 + (\pm\sqrt{3}\!/_2)(n_{ru}n_{sw} - n_{rw}n_{su}) + (\pm\sqrt{3}\!/_2)(n_{rv}n_{sw} - n_{rw}n_{sv})\right\}/n^2 \quad .$$

This expression, (20), reduces to (15) if n_{rw} and n_{sw} are zero. Here, we examine two

(i)

		x_j		
		u	v	w
x_i	r	$n/3$	$n/3$	0
	s	0	0	$n/3$

$V_{ii} = \tfrac{2}{9}, \quad V_{jj} = \tfrac{1}{3},$

$V_{ij} = \tfrac{\sqrt{3}}{9}$ when $\theta = \pi\!/_2$, $\sigma = 0$,

$R_{ij} = 0.707$.

(ii)

		x_j		
		u	v	w
x_i	r	$n/6$	0	$n/6$
	s	$n/6$	$n/3$	$n/6$

$V_{ii} = \tfrac{2}{9}, \quad V_{jj} = \tfrac{1}{3},$

$V_{ij} = \tfrac{\sqrt{3}}{18}$ when $\theta = -\pi\!/_6$, $\sigma = 0$,

$R_{ij} = 0.354$.

specific contingency tables, (i) and (ii). The resulting correlation coefficients seem to have reasonable values in these cases. Shown at the right side are the value spaces of x_i and x_j, while (u, v, w) and (u', v', w') show vertices before and after the transformation, L, respectively. In the first case, the vector r→s shows maximum overlap with (u'→w' + v'→w'), and it corresponds to the observation from the contingency table. The same sort of overlap is found for (u'→v' + w'→v') in the second case.

4.3 3 x 3 Categorical Data

		x_j			
		u	v	w	
x_i	r	n_{ru}	n_{rv}	n_{rw}	$n_{r\cdot}$
	s	n_{su}	n_{sv}	n_{sw}	$n_{s\cdot}$
	t	n_{tu}	n_{tv}	n_{tw}	$n_{t\cdot}$
		$n_{\cdot u}$	$n_{\cdot v}$	$n_{\cdot w}$	n

V_{ii} and V_{jj} take the same expression as that of (17). (19) is used as the transformation, L, and the value difference vectors are set to the following forms,

$$\overrightarrow{rs}=\begin{pmatrix}1\\0\end{pmatrix},\quad \overrightarrow{rt}=\begin{pmatrix}\frac{1}{2}\\\frac{\sqrt{3}}{2}\end{pmatrix},\quad \overrightarrow{st}=\begin{pmatrix}-\frac{1}{2}\\\frac{\sqrt{3}}{2}\end{pmatrix},$$

$$\overrightarrow{uv}=\begin{pmatrix}1\\0\end{pmatrix},\quad \overrightarrow{uw}=\begin{pmatrix}\frac{1}{2}\\\frac{\sqrt{3}}{2}\end{pmatrix},\quad \overrightarrow{vw}=\begin{pmatrix}-\frac{1}{2}\\\frac{\sqrt{3}}{2}\end{pmatrix}. \tag{21}$$

Then, the following formula gives the expression for Q_{ij}.

$$Q_{ij}=\frac{\cos\theta}{n^2}\left\{\begin{aligned}&(n_{ru}n_{sv}-n_{rv}n_{su})+(\tfrac{1}{2})(n_{ru}n_{sw}-n_{rw}n_{su})-(\tfrac{1}{2})(n_{rv}n_{sw}-n_{rw}n_{sv})\\&+(\tfrac{1}{2})(n_{ru}n_{tv}-n_{rv}n_{tu})+(\tfrac{1}{4}\pm\tfrac{3}{4})(n_{ru}n_{tw}-n_{rw}n_{tu})+(-\tfrac{1}{4}\pm\tfrac{3}{4})(n_{rv}n_{tw}-n_{rw}n_{tv})\\&+(-\tfrac{1}{2})(n_{su}n_{tv}-n_{sv}n_{tu})+(-\tfrac{1}{4}\pm\tfrac{3}{4})(n_{su}n_{tw}-n_{sw}n_{tu})+(\tfrac{1}{4}\pm\tfrac{3}{4})(n_{sv}n_{tw}-n_{sw}n_{tv})\end{aligned}\right\}$$
$$+\frac{\sin\theta}{n^2}\left\{\begin{aligned}&0+(\pm\tfrac{\sqrt{3}}{2})(n_{ru}n_{sw}-n_{rw}n_{su})+(\pm\tfrac{\sqrt{3}}{2})(n_{rv}n_{sw}-n_{rw}n_{sv})\\&+(-\tfrac{\sqrt{3}}{2})(n_{ru}n_{tv}-n_{rv}n_{tu})+(\pm\tfrac{\sqrt{3}}{4}-\tfrac{\sqrt{3}}{4})(n_{ru}n_{tw}-n_{rw}n_{tu})+(\pm\tfrac{\sqrt{3}}{4}+\tfrac{\sqrt{3}}{4})(n_{rv}n_{tw}-n_{rw}n_{tv})\\&+(-\tfrac{\sqrt{3}}{2})(n_{su}n_{tv}-n_{sv}n_{tu})+(\mp\tfrac{\sqrt{3}}{4}-\tfrac{\sqrt{3}}{4})(n_{su}n_{tw}-n_{sw}n_{tu})+(\mp\tfrac{\sqrt{3}}{4}+\tfrac{\sqrt{3}}{4})(n_{sv}n_{tw}-n_{sw}n_{tv})\end{aligned}\right\}, \tag{22}$$

where upper and lower signs correspond to $\sigma = 0$ and 1, respectively.

When we are concerned with the contingency table on the next page, we get $R_{ij} = 1.0$ as expected. The resulting transformation, $\theta = 0$ and $\sigma = 0$, indicates the complete correspondence between two value sets, (r/u, s/v, t/w). The exchange of category names does not affect the R_{ij} value. That is, even if we move $n2$ to cell(t, v) and $n3$ to cell(s, w), the R_{ij} value remains equal to unity. In this case, the effect of the value exchange appears in the resulting values ($\theta = -\pi/6$ and $\sigma = 1$).

x_i		x_j		
		u	v	w
	r	$n1$	0	0
	s	0	$n2$	0
	t	0	0	$n3$

$$V_{ii} = V_{jj}$$
$$= (n1n2 + n2n3 + n3n1)/(n1 + n2 + n3)^2 ,$$
$$V_{ij} = V_{ii} \quad \text{when } \theta = 0, \sigma = 0 ,$$
$$R_{ij} = 1.0 \quad .$$

5 Conclusion

We proposed a new definition for the variance-covariance matrix that is equally applicable to numerical, categorical and mixed data. Calculations on sample contingency tables yielded reasonable results. When applied to numerical data, the proposed scheme reduces to the conventional variance-covariance concept. When applied to categorical data, it covers Gini's variance concept.

This current work does not give an explicit algorithm to compute the variance-covariance matrix. Furthermore, we do not discuss the statistical distribution of the sample variance and correlation coefficients. Nevertheless, this work is expected to open the door to a unified treatment for numerical and categorical data.

References

1. Takeuchi, K. et al. (eds.): Encyclopedia of Statistics (in Japanese). Toyo Keizai Shinpou Tokyo, (1990)

2. Okada, T.: Rule Induction in Cascade Model based on Sum of Squares Decomposition. In: Zytkow, J.M., Rauch, J. (eds.): Principles of Data Mining and Knowledge Discovery (PKDD'99). LNAI, Vol. 1704, Springer-Verlag (1999) 468-475

3. Gini, C.W.: Variability and Mutability, contribution to the study of statistical distributions and relations. *Studi Economico-Giuridici della R. Universita de Cagliari* (1912). Reviewed in: Light, R.J., Margolin, B.H.: An Analysis of Variance for Categorical Data. *J. American Statistical Association*, **66** (1971) 534-544

4. Okada, T.: Sum of Squares Decomposition for Categorical Data. *Kwansei Gakuin Studies in Computer Science*, **14** (1999) 1-6

A General Class of Neural Networks for Principal Component Analysis and Factor Analysis

Ying Han and Colin Fyfe

Applied Computational Intelligence Research Unit,
The University of Paisley,
Scotland.
email:ying.han,colin.fyfe@paisley.ac.uk

Abstract. We review a recently proposed family of functions for finding principal and minor components of a data set. We extend the family so that the Principal Subspace of the data set is found by using a method similar to that known as the Bigradient algorithm. We then amend the method in a way which was shown to change a Principal Component Analysis (PCA) rule to a rule for performing Factor Analysis (FA) and show its power on a standard problem. We find in both cases that, whereas the one Principal Component family all have similar convergence and stability properties, the multiple output networks for both PCA and FA have different properties.

1 Introduction

Principal Component Analysis (PCA) is a well-known statistical technique for finding the best linear compression of a data set. PCA uses the eigenvectors and corresponding eigenvalues of the covariance matrix of a data set. Let $\chi = \{\mathbf{x}_1, ..., \mathbf{x}_M\}$ be iid (independent, identically distributed) samples drawn from a data source. If each $\mathbf{x}_i$ is n-dimensional, $\exists$ at most n eigenvalues/eigenvectors. Let Σ be the covariance matrix of the data set; then Σ is $n \times n$. Then the eigenvectors, $\mathbf{e}_i$, are n dimensional vectors which are found by solving

$$\Sigma \mathbf{e}_i = \lambda_i \mathbf{e}_i \qquad (1)$$

where λ_i is the eigenvalue corresponding to $\mathbf{e}_i$. A second standard method is the technique of Factor Analysis (FA). PCA and FA are closely related statistical techniques both of which achieve an efficient compression of the data but in a different manner. They can both be described as methods to explain the data set in a smaller number of dimensions but FA is based on assumptions about the nature of the underlying data whereas PCA is model free.

We can also view PCA as an attempt to find a transformation from the data set to a compressed code, whereas in FA we try to find the linear transformation which takes us from a set of hidden factors to the data set. Since PCA is model free, we make no assumptions about the form of the data's covariance matrix. However FA begins with a specific model which is usually constrained by our prior knowledge or assumptions about the data set.

2 Artificial Neural Networks

Since the seminal work of Oja [5, 8, 6, 7], a great number of unsupervised neural networks have been shown to perform PCA. We investigate one biologially plausible network : the data is fed forward from the input neurons (the x-values) to the output neurons. Here the weighted summation of the activations is performed and this is fed back via the same weights and used in the simple Hebbian learning procedure. Consider a network with N dimensional input data and having M output neurons. Then the output of the ith output neuron is given by

$$y_i = \text{act}_i = \sum_{j=1}^{N} w_{ij} x_j \qquad (2)$$

where x_j is the activation of the jth input neuron, w_{ij} is the weight between this and the ith output neuron and act_i is the activation of the ith neuron. This firing is fed back through the same weights as inhibition to give

$$x_j(t+1) \leftarrow x_j(t) - \sum_{k=1}^{M} w_{kj} y_k \qquad (3)$$

where we have used (t) and $(t+1)$ to differentiate between activation at times t and $t+1$. Now simple Hebbian learning between input and output neurons gives

$$\Delta w_{ij} = \eta_t y_i x_j(t+1)$$
$$= \eta_t y_i \{x_j(t) - \sum_{l=1}^{M} w_{lj} y_l\}$$

where η_t is the learning rate at time t. This network actually only finds the subspace spanned by the Principal Components; we can find the actual Principal Components by introducing some asymmetry into the network [3].

We have previously shown[4] that, by not allowing the weights in the above network to become negative, i.e. enforcing the additional constraint, $w_{ij} \geq 0$ in our learning rules, our networks weights converge to identify the independent sources of a data set exactly. We have recently shown that this rectification may be used in general with PCA networks to create FA networks[1].

3 The new class of functions

It has recently been shown [12] that solutions of the generalised eigenvalue problem

$$A\mathbf{w} = \lambda B\mathbf{w} \qquad (4)$$

can be found using gradient ascent of the form

$$\frac{d\mathbf{w}}{dt} = A\mathbf{w} - f(\mathbf{w})B\mathbf{w} \tag{5}$$

where the function $f(\mathbf{w}) : R^n - \{0\} \to R$ satisfies

1. $f(\mathbf{w})$ is locally Lipschitz continuous
2. $\exists M_1 > M_2 > 0 : f(\mathbf{w}) > \lambda_1, \forall \mathbf{w} : \| \mathbf{w} \| \geq M_1$ and $f(\mathbf{w}) < \lambda_n, \forall \mathbf{w} : 0 < \| \mathbf{w} \| \leq M_2$
3. $\forall \mathbf{w} \in R^n - \{0\}, \exists N_1 > N_2 > 0 : f(\theta\mathbf{w}) > \lambda_1, \forall \theta : \theta \geq N_1$ and $f(\theta\mathbf{w}) < \lambda_n, \forall \theta : 0 \leq \theta \leq N_2$ and $f(\theta\mathbf{w})$ is a strictly monotonically increasing function of θ in $[N_1, N_2]$.

with λ_1 the greatest eigenvalue and λ_n the smallest. Taking $A = \Sigma = E(\mathbf{x}\mathbf{x}^T)$, and $B = I$, we return to the standard eigenvector problem which may be used to find the principal components of a data set. Since $y = \mathbf{w}.\mathbf{x}$, we have the instantaneous rule

$$\Delta\mathbf{w} \propto \mathbf{x}y - f(\mathbf{w})\mathbf{w}$$

For example, if we choose $f(\mathbf{w}) = ln(\mathbf{w}^T(t)\mathbf{w}(t))$ [12], we have:

$$\Delta w_j = \eta(x_j y_2 - \ln(\mathbf{w}^T\mathbf{w})\mathbf{w}) \tag{6}$$

Similarly, we can use:

$$\Delta w_j = \eta(x_j y - \ln(\sum_k \mid w_k \mid)w_j) \tag{7}$$

$$\Delta w_j = \eta(x_j y - \ln(\max_{1 \leq k \leq n} \mid w_k \mid)w_j) \tag{8}$$

$$\Delta w_j = \eta(x_j y - (\mathbf{w}^T\mathbf{w} - \phi)w_j) \tag{9}$$

$$\Delta w_j = \eta(x_j y - (\max_{1 \leq k \leq n} \mid w_k \mid -\phi)w_j) \tag{10}$$

$$\Delta w_j = \eta(x_j y - (\sum_k \mid w_k \mid -\phi)w_j) \tag{11}$$

The functions in (6)-(11) will be known as $f_1(), .., f_6()$ in the following and all provide iterative solutions to the maximisation of J_{PCA} which may either be defined in terms of minimisation of least mean square error or as best linear maximisation of variance.

Now (9) is simply the rule for the Bigradient algorithm with a single output [11] and so we now discuss the Bigradient algorithm.

4 Multiple Outputs

Now the bigradient algorithm [11] for multiple outputs may be viewed as the optimisation of three parts

1. The first part optimises the PCA criterion: e.g. it may be viewed as maximising the variance of the outputs of the neural network. The instantaneous
   optimisation is of

$$J_1 = \max_{\mathbf{w}}(\mathbf{w}.\mathbf{x})^2 \tag{12}$$

2. The second part ensures that the vector is of length 1. This constraint may
   be thought of as optimising

$$J_2 = \min_{\mathbf{w}}(1 - \mathbf{w}.\mathbf{w})^2 \tag{13}$$

3. The third part ensures that each weight vector is orthogonal to every other
   weight vector:

$$J_3 = \min_{\mathbf{w}} \sum_{i \neq j}(\mathbf{w}_i.\mathbf{w}_j)^2 \tag{14}$$

This suggests turning the argument in the last section on its head. If each of
these rules using the derivatives of J_1 and either that of J_2 (the one neuron
bigradient algorithm) or any of the other equivalent functions, $f_i()$, finds the
first principal component, can we adjust each rule by inserting a term ensuring
that J_3 is also optimised so that all weights learn to respond to different inputs.
This gives us a learning rule

$$\Delta\mathbf{w}_i = \eta(\mathbf{x}y_i - f(W)\mathbf{w}_i - \sum_{k \neq i}(\mathbf{w}_k.\mathbf{w}_i)\mathbf{w}_i) \tag{15}$$

where we have used $\mathbf{w}_i$ as the ith weight vector and W as the matrix of all weight
vectors.

To this end, we perform a series of simple experiments: we generate artificial data such that x_1 is a sample from a Gaussian distribution with standard
deviation 1 (i.e. N(0,1)), x_2 is drawn from N(0,2) etc so that the input with the
highest variance is clearly the last. In our experiments we chose 5 inputs and 3
outputs and began the simulation with a learning rate of 0.0001 which decreased
to 0 in the course of 100000 iterations. Typical results are shown in Table 1. If
the principal subspace spanned by the first three PCs is found, there will be
zeros in the first two positions in the weight vector (as for $f_4()$).

We see that there are three distinct groups of results

1. The first three functions fail to find the subspace of the first three Principal
   Components. Extensive experimentation with different learning rates, initial
   conditions and number of iterations have all resulted in similar results.
2. The fourth function is exactly the usual bigradient algorithm. As expected it
   finds the subspace of the first three Principal Components (though it should
   be noted that the normalisation is far from secure).
3. The fifth and sixth functions are the most interesting: they also find the
   subspace but more interestingly actually seem to be able to identify the
   actual Principal Components themselves.

The first thing to point out is that the equivalence of the six functions in the
one neuron case no longer exists in the multiple neuron case. The fifth and sixth
functions are different in that they use the absolute value of the weights.

Function $f_1()$		Function $f_2()$	
$\mathbf{w}_1$	-1.6 1.6 -1.1 -1.1 0.4	$\mathbf{w}_1$	-1.6 1.6 -1.1 -1.1 0.4
$\mathbf{w}_2$	2.2 2.1 1.3 1.1 7.6	$\mathbf{w}_2$	2.2 2.1 1.3 1.1 7.6
$\mathbf{w}_3$	-3.0 -4.8 -1.3 -0.2 2.9	$\mathbf{w}_3$	-3.0 -4.8 -1.3 -0.2 2.9
Function $f_3()$		Function $f_4()$	
$\mathbf{w}_1$	-1.6 1.6 -1.1 -1.1 0.4	$\mathbf{w}_1$	0 0 1.5 0.9 -1.6
$\mathbf{w}_2$	2.2 2.1 1.3 1.1 7.6	$\mathbf{w}_2$	0 0 -1.2 1.4 -1.6
$\mathbf{w}_3$	-3.0 -4.8 -1.3 -0.2 2.9	$\mathbf{w}_3$	0 0 0 1.7 2.1
Function $f_5()$		Function $f_6()$	
$\mathbf{w}_1$	0 0 -0.1 -6.2 0	$\mathbf{w}_1$	0 0 -0.1 -6.0 0
$\mathbf{w}_2$	0 0 -0.1 0 9.2	$\mathbf{w}_2$	0 0 -0.1 0 9.0
$\mathbf{w}_3$	0 0 -4.0 0.1 0	$\mathbf{w}_3$	0 0 -3.9 0.1 0

Table 1. Converged vectors for three outputs and five inputs using each of the functions $f_1(), ..., f_6()$. The first three functions fail to find the Principal Subspace. The last three find the Subspace, and the last two come close to finding the Principal Components themselves.

5 Multiple outputs and Non-negativity

This last finding is interesting to us in the light of our previous changes to a PCA network which transformed it into a Factor Analysis network by enforcing a positivity constraint on the weights. Thus we use the same learning rules as in Section 4 but impose the constraint that we cannot have negative factor loadings.

The benchmark experiment for this problem is due to Földiák [2]. The input data here consists of a square grid of input values where $x_i = 1$ if the ith square is black and 0 otherwise. However the patterns are not random patterns: each input consists of a number of randomly chosen horizontal or vertical lines. The important thing to note is that each line is an independent source of blackening a pixel on the grid: it may be that a particular pixel will be twice blackened by both a horizontal and a vertical line at the same time but we need to identify both of these sources. We again find that $f_6()$ in its multiple output (bigradient) form is the best at finding the independent components, even outperforming the original bigradient algorithm with the non-negativity constraint. We do however have to loosen the force with which each weight vector repels its neighbours by

$$\Delta\mathbf{w}_i = \eta(\mathbf{x}y_i - f(W)\mathbf{w}_i - \gamma \sum_{k \neq i}(\mathbf{w}_k.\mathbf{w}_i)\mathbf{w}_i) \qquad (16)$$

where $\gamma < 1$.

6 Conclusion

We have reviewed a new class of one neuron artificial neural networks which had previously been shown to find the first Principal Component of a data set. In the one neuron case, it has been stated that the members of this class of networks are all equivalent in terms of convergence and stability (this is readily confirmed experimentally). We have extended this class of neural networks by amending the learning rule so that each neuron learns to respond to a different section of the data - the Principal Subspace is found - by using a method suggested by the bigradient algorithm. However now we see that the class of functions is no longer homogeneous in terms of its convergence; clearly the interaction between the criteria is having a differential effect. Interestingly two of the members of the class find the actual principal components of the data set.

We have also implemented the rectification of the weights which transformed a PCA network to a FA network and again found that some functions find the underlying factors of the data set while others do not.

Future work will investigate deflationary algorithms [10] and lateral inhibition [9].

References

1. D. Charles and C. Fyfe. Discovering independent sources with an adapted pca network. In *Proceedings of The Second International Conference on Soft Computing, SOCO97*, Sept. 1997.
2. P. Földiák. *Models of Sensory Coding*. PhD thesis, University of Cambridge, 1992.
3. C. Fyfe. Introducing asymmetry into interneuron learning. *Neural Computation*, 7(6):1167–1181, 1995.
4. C. Fyfe. A neural net for pca and beyond. *Neural Processing Letters*, 6(1):33–41, 1997.
5. E. Oja. A simplified neuron model as a principal component analyser. *Journal of Mathematical Biology*, 16:267–273, 1982.
6. E. Oja. Neural networks, principal components and subspaces. *International Journal of Neural Systems*, 1:61–68, 1989.
7. E. Oja, H. Ogawa, and J. Wangviwattana. Principal component analysis by homogeneous neural networks, part 1: The weighted subspace criterion. *IEICE Trans. Inf. & Syst.*, E75-D:366–375, May 1992.
8. Erkki Oja and Juha Karhunen. On stochastic approximation of the eigenvectors and eigenvalues of the expectation of a random matrix. *Journal of Mathematical Analysis and Applications*, 106:69–84, 1985.
9. J. Rubner and P. Tavan. A self-organising network for principal-component analysis. *Europhysics Letters*, 10(7):693–698, Dec 1989.
10. T.D. Sanger. Analysis of the two-dimensional receptive fields learned by the generalized hebbian algorithm in response to random input. *Biological Cybernetics*, 1990.
11. L. Wang and J. Karhunen. A unified neural bigradient algorithm for robust pca and mca. *International Journal of Neural Systems*, 1995.
12. Qingfu Zhang and Yiu-Wing Leung. A class of learning algorithms for principal component analysis and minor component analysis. *IEEE Transactions on Neural Networks*, 11(1):200–204, Jan 2000.

Generalised Canonical Correlation Analysis

Zhenkun Gou and Colin Fyfe

Applied Computational Intelligence Research Unit,
The University of Paisley,
Scotland.
email:zhenkun.gou,colin.fyfe@paisley.ac.uk

Abstract. Canonical Correlation Analysis [3] is used when we have two data sets which we believe have some underlying correlation. In this paper, we derive a new family of neural methods for finding the canonical correlation directions by solving a generalized eigenvalue problem. Based on the differential equation for the generalized eigenvalue problem, a family of CCA learning algorithms can be obtained. We compare our family of methods with a previously derived [2] CCA learning algorithm. Our results show that all the new learning algorithms of this family have the same order of convergence speed and in particular are much faster than existing algorithms; they are also shown to be able to find greater nonlinear correlations. They are also much more robust with respect to parameter selection.

1   Canonical Correlation Analysis

Canonical Correlation Analysis is a statistical technique used when we have two data sets which we believe have some underlying correlation. Consider two sets of input data; $\mathbf{x}_1$ and $\mathbf{x}_2$. Then in classical CCA, we attempt to find the linear combination of the variables which give us maximum correlation between the combinations. Let

$$\mathbf{y}_1 = \mathbf{w}_1 \mathbf{x}_1 = \sum_j w_{1j} x_{1j}$$

$$\mathbf{y}_2 = \mathbf{w}_2 \mathbf{x}_2 = \sum_j w_{2j} x_{2j}$$

where we have used $\mathbf{x}_{ij}$ as the jth element of $\mathbf{x}_1$. Then we wish to find those values of $\mathbf{w}_1$ and $\mathbf{w}_2$ which maximise the correlation between $\mathbf{y}_1$ and $\mathbf{y}_2$. Then the standard statistical method (see [3]) lies in defining:

$$\Sigma_{11} = E\{(\mathbf{x}_1 - \mu_1)(\mathbf{x}_1 - \mu_1)^T\}$$
$$\Sigma_{22} = E\{(\mathbf{x}_2 - \mu_2)(\mathbf{x}_2 - \mu_2)^T\}$$
$$\Sigma_{12} = E\{(\mathbf{x}_1 - \mu_1)(\mathbf{x}_2 - \mu_2)^T\}$$
$$\text{and } K = \Sigma_{11}^{-\frac{1}{2}} \Sigma_{12} \Sigma_{22}^{-\frac{1}{2}} \tag{1}$$

where T denotes the transpose of a vector and $E\{\}$ denotes the expectation operator. We then perform a Singular Value Decomposition of K to get

$$K = (\alpha_1, \alpha_2, ..., \alpha_k)D(\beta_1, \beta_2, ..., \beta_k)^T \tag{2}$$

where α_i and β_i are the standardised eigenvectors of KK^T and $K^T K$ respectively and D is the diagonal matrix of eigenvalues. Then the first canonical correlation vectors (those which give greatest correlation) are given by

$$\mathbf{w}_1 = \Sigma_{11}^{-\frac{1}{2}}\alpha_1 \tag{3}$$

$$\mathbf{w}_2 = \Sigma_{22}^{-\frac{1}{2}}\beta_1 \tag{4}$$

with subsequent canonical correlation vectors defined in terms of the subsequent eigenvectors, α_i and β_i.

2 A neural implementation

A previous 'neural implementation' [2] of CCA was derived by phrasing the problem as that of maximising

$$J = E\{(y_1 y_2) + \frac{1}{2}\lambda_1(1 - y_1^2) + \frac{1}{2}\lambda_2(1 - y_2^2)\}$$

where the λ_i were motivated by the method of Lagrange multipliers to constrain the weights to finite values. By taking the derivative of this function with respect to both the weights, $\mathbf{w}_1$ and $\mathbf{w}_2$, and the Lagrange multipliers, λ_1 and λ_2 we derive learning rules for both:

$$\Delta w_{1j} = \eta x_{1j}(y_2 - \lambda_1 y_1)$$
$$\Delta \lambda_1 = \eta_0(1 - y_1^2)$$
$$\Delta w_{2j} = \eta x_{2j}(y_1 - \lambda_2 y_2)$$
$$\Delta \lambda_2 = \eta_0(1 - y_2^2) \tag{5}$$

where w_{1j} is the jth element of weight vector, $\mathbf{w}_1$ etc. If we consider the general problem of maximising correlations between two data sets which may be have an underlying nonlinear relationship, we can use some nonlinear function, for example tanh(), to train the output neurons. So, the outputs y_3 and y_4 can be calculated from:

$$y_3 = \sum_j w_{3j} \tanh(v_{3j}x_{1j}) = \mathbf{w_3 g_3} \tag{6}$$

$$y_4 = \sum_j w_{4j} \tanh(v_{4j}x_{2j}) = \mathbf{w_4 g_4} \tag{7}$$

The weights $\mathbf{v}_3$ and $\mathbf{v}_4$ are used to optimise the nonlinearity, which gives us extra flexibility in maximising correlations. The maximum correlation between y_3 and y_4 was found by maximising the function:

$$J = E\{(y_3 y_4) + \frac{1}{2}\lambda_3(1 - y_3^2) + \frac{1}{2}\lambda_4(1 - y_4^2)\}$$

We may now use the derivative of this function with respect to the weights, $\mathbf{w}_3$ and $\mathbf{w}_4$, the Lagrange multipliers, λ_1 and λ_2 and also the weights $\mathbf{v}_3$ and $\mathbf{v}_4$, to derive learning rules for both:

$$\Delta w_{3i} = \eta \mathbf{g}_{3i}(y_4 - \lambda_3 y_3)$$
$$\Delta v_{3i} = \eta \mathbf{x}_{1i}\mathbf{w}_{3i}(y_4 - \lambda_3 y_3)(1 - \mathbf{g}_3^2)$$
$$\Delta w_4 = \eta \mathbf{g}_{4i}(y_3 - \lambda_4 y_4)$$
$$\Delta v_{4i} = \eta \mathbf{x}_{2i}\mathbf{w}_{4i}(y_3 - \lambda_4 y_4)(1 - \mathbf{g}_{4i}^2) \tag{8}$$

We note that both the linear and the nonlinear rules use a two-phase approach - the λ parameter updates interleave with the updates of the weights. In the next section, we will derive a much simplified learning rule and show that the new learning rule outperforms this set of rules.

3   CCA and the Generalised Eigenvalue Problem

Now it may be shown [1] that an alternative method of finding the canonical correlation directions is to solve the generalised eigenvalue problem

$$\begin{bmatrix} 0 & \Sigma_{12} \\ \Sigma_{21} & 0 \end{bmatrix} \begin{bmatrix} \mathbf{w}_1 \\ \mathbf{w}_2 \end{bmatrix} = \rho \begin{bmatrix} \Sigma_{11} & 0 \\ 0 & \Sigma_{22} \end{bmatrix} \begin{bmatrix} \mathbf{w}_1 \\ \mathbf{w}_2 \end{bmatrix} \tag{9}$$

where ρ is the correlation coefficient. Intuitively since $\Sigma_{ij} = E(\mathbf{x}_i\mathbf{x}_j)$ we are stating that $\mathbf{w}_2$ times the correlation between $\mathbf{x}_1$ and $\mathbf{x}_2$ is equal to the correlation coefficient times the weighted (by $\mathbf{w}_1$) variance of $\mathbf{x}_1$. Now this has multiple solutions since we are not constraining the variance of the outputs to be 1. If $\mathbf{w}_1^*$ and $\mathbf{w}_2^*$ are solutions to (9), then so are $a\mathbf{w}_1^*$ and $a\mathbf{w}_2^*$ for all real a. Thus this method will find the correct correlation vectors but not with a unique magnitude.

It has recently been shown [4] that solutions of the generalised eigenvalue problem

$$A\mathbf{w} = \lambda B\mathbf{w} \tag{10}$$

can be found using gradient ascent of the form

$$\frac{d\mathbf{w}}{dt} = A\mathbf{w} - f(\mathbf{w})B\mathbf{w} \tag{11}$$

where the function $f(\mathbf{w}) : R^n - \{0\} \to R$ satisfies

1. $f(\mathbf{w})$ is locally Lipschitz continuous
2. $\exists M_1 > M_2 > 0 : f(\mathbf{w}) > \lambda_1, \forall \mathbf{w} :\| \mathbf{w} \| \geq M_1$ and $f(\mathbf{w}) < \lambda_n, \forall \mathbf{w} : 0 <\| \mathbf{w} \| \leq M_2$
3. $\forall \mathbf{w} \in R^n - \{0\}, \exists N_1 > N_2 > 0 : f(\theta\mathbf{w}) > \lambda_1, \forall \theta : \theta \geq N_1$ and $f(\theta\mathbf{w}) < \lambda_n, \forall \theta : 0 \leq \theta \leq N_2$ and $f(\theta\mathbf{w})$ is a strictly monotonically increasing function of θ in $[N_1, N_2]$.

Taking $\mathbf{w} = [\mathbf{w}_1^T \mathbf{w}_2^T]^T$, we find the canonical correlation directions $\mathbf{w}_1$ and $\mathbf{w}_2$ using

$$\frac{d\mathbf{w}_1}{dt} = \Sigma_{12}\mathbf{w}_2 - f(\mathbf{w}_1)\Sigma_{11}\mathbf{w}_1$$

$$\frac{d\mathbf{w}_2}{dt} = \Sigma_{21}\mathbf{w}_1 - f(\mathbf{w}_2)\Sigma_{22}\mathbf{w}_2$$

Using the facts that $\Sigma_{ij} = E(\mathbf{x}_i\mathbf{x}_j^T), i, j = 1, 2$, and that $y_1 = \mathbf{w}_1.\mathbf{x}_1$, we may propose the instantaneous rules

$$\Delta\mathbf{w}_1 = \mathbf{x}_1 y_2 - f(\mathbf{w}_1)\mathbf{x}_1 y_1$$

$$\Delta\mathbf{w}_2 = \mathbf{x}_2 y_1 - f(\mathbf{w}_2)\mathbf{x}_2 y_2$$

For example, if we choose $f(\mathbf{w}) = ln(\mathbf{w}^T(t)\mathbf{w}(t))$, we have:

$$\Delta w_{1j} = \eta x_{1j}(y_2 - \ln(\mathbf{w}_1^T\mathbf{w}_1)y_1)$$

$$\Delta w_{2j} = \eta x_{2j}(y_1 - \ln(\mathbf{w}_2^T\mathbf{w}_2)y_2) \tag{12}$$

This algorithm is simpler then that used previously [2], in that we don't need to adjust the parameter λ any more. In the similar manner, we can use:

$$\Delta w_j = \eta x_j(y_i - \ln(\sum_j | w_j |)y_i) \tag{13}$$

$$\Delta w_j = \eta x_j(y_i - \ln(\max_{1 \leq j \leq n} | w_j |)y_i) \tag{14}$$

$$\Delta w_j = \eta x_j(y_i - (\mathbf{w}^T\mathbf{w} - \phi)y_i) \tag{15}$$

$$\Delta w_j = \eta x_j(y_i - (\max_{1 \leq j \leq n} | w_j | -\phi)y_i) \tag{16}$$

$$\Delta w_j = \eta x_j(y_i - (\sum_j | w_j | -\phi)y_i) \tag{17}$$

The functions (12)-(17) will be known as $f_1(), .., f_6()$ in the following. These new algorithms only have a one-phase operation; there is no additional λ parameter to update.

It may be argued however, that the rule (15) is equivalent to the update of the λ parameter in the previous section. This is only superficially true: firstly, the derivations are quite different; secondly, the ϕ parameter in (15) must satisfy the constraint that it is greater than the greatest eigenvalue of the covariance matrix of the input data whereas the rule of the previous section used the equivalent parameter to ensure that the variances of the outputs were bounded. The need for a larger value of ϕ in (15) has been verified experimentally. Nevertheless, we have experimented with the functions $f_1(), ..., f_6()$ in the nonlinear case equivalent to 5

$$y_3 = \sum_j w_{3j}tanh(v_{3j}x_{1j}) = \mathbf{w}_3\mathbf{g}_3 \tag{18}$$

$$y_4 = \sum_j w_{4j}tanh(v_{4j}x_{4j}) = \mathbf{w}_4\mathbf{g}_4 \tag{19}$$

to get the nonlinear update equations y_3 and y_4 used

$$\Delta w_3 = \eta g_3(y_4 - f(w)y_3)$$
$$\Delta v_{3i} = \eta x_{1i} w_{3i}(y_4 - f(w)y_3)(1 - g_3^2)$$
$$\Delta w_4 = \eta g_4(y_3 - f(w)y_4)$$
$$\Delta v_{4i} = \eta x_{2i} w_{4i}(y_3 - f(w)y_4)(1 - g_4^2) \tag{20}$$

4 Simulations

4.1 Artificial Data

To compare this new family of algorithms with the existing neural algorithm, we will use the artificial data reported in [2]. We generated an artificial data set to give two vectors x_1 and x_2. x_1 is a 4 dimensional vector, each of whose elements is drawn from the zero-mean Gaussian distribution, N(0,1); x_2 is a 3 dimensional vector, each of whose elements is also drawn from N(0,1). In order to introduce correlations between the two vectors, x_1 and x_2, we generate an additional sample T from N(0,1) and add it to the first elements of each vector and then divide by 2 to ensure that there is no more variance in the first elements than in the others. Thus there is no correlation between the two vectors other than that existing between the first elements of each. All simulations have used an initial learning rate of 0.001, which is decreased linearly to 0 over 100,000 iterations.

The weights' convergence is shown in Figures 1 and 2. The convergence is given as the angle between the weights at each iteration in our simulation and that of the optimal set of weights i.e.(1,0,0,0) for x_1 and (1,0,0) for x_2. In each figure, we graph two lines to express the convergence of w_1 and w_2. Comparing Figures 1 and 2, we can see the new algorithm converges much faster than the existing algorithm and is very stable.All of the learning algorithms of our class have the same order of convergence speed, which means the order of convergence speed does not depend on the specific form of $f(w)$. The learning algorithms are robust to implementation error on $f(w)$. The simple $f(w)$ reduces the implementation complexity.

4.2 Real Data

Again, in order to compare our family of methods with those reported earlier, we use data taken from [3]. The data set consists of 88 students who sat 5 exams, 2 of which were closed book exams while the other 3 were open book exams. Thus we have a two dimensional x_1 and a three dimensional x_2. To illustrate the non-uniqueness of the correlation vectors and the effect of the parameter we show in Table 1 a set of results. In our experiment, the learning rate was 0.0001 and the iterations was 50000.

In Table 1, w_1 vector consists of the weights from the closed-book exam data to y_1 while the w_2 vector consists of the weights from the open-book exam data to y_2. We note the excellent agreement between the methods.

Standard statistics maximum correlation	0.6630			
$\mathbf{w}_1$	0.0260 0.0518			
$\mathbf{w}_2$	0.0824 0.00081 0.0035			
Existing neural network maximum correlation	0.6962			
$\mathbf{w}_1$	0.0260 0.0518			
$\mathbf{w}_2$	0.0824 0.0081 0.0035			
New neural network maximum correlation	0.6790			
$\mathbf{w}_1$	0.0270			
$\mathbf{w}_2$	0.0810 0.0090 0.0040			

Table 1. Correlation and Weight Value of the Real Data Experiment

4.3   Random Dot stereograms

Becker (1996)has developed the idea about that one of the goals of sensory information processing may be the extraction of common information between different sensors or across sensory modalities. Becker experimented this idea on a data set which is an abstraction of random dot stereograms, just like Figure3. The two different neural units should learn to extract features that are coherent across their inputs. If there is any feature in common across the two inputs, it should be discovered, while features that are independent across the two inputs will be ignored. We wish to find the maximum linear correlation between $\mathbf{y}_1$ and $\mathbf{y}_2$ which are themselves linear combinations of $\mathbf{x}_1$ and $\mathbf{x}_2$. In order to find these, we require two pairs outputs and the corresponding pairs of weights($\mathbf{w}_1$,$\mathbf{w}_2$) and ($\mathbf{w}_3$,$\mathbf{w}_4$). The learning rules for w_3 and w_4 in this experiment are analagous to those for $\mathbf{w}_1$ and $\mathbf{w}_2$; at each presentation of a sample of input data, a sample competition between the products $\mathbf{y}_1\mathbf{y}_2$ and $\mathbf{y}_3\mathbf{y}_4$ determine which weights will learn on the current input samples: if $\mathbf{y}_1\mathbf{y}_2 \succ \mathbf{y}_3\mathbf{y}_4$, $\mathbf{w}_1$,$\mathbf{w}_2$ are updated, else $\mathbf{w}_3$, $\mathbf{w}_4$ are updated.

Using a learning rate of 0.001 and 100000 iterations with $f_1()$, the weights converge to the vectors shown in Table 2. The first pair of withts $\mathbf{w}_1$ and $\mathbf{w}_2$

$\mathbf{w}_1$	-0.004	1.649	-0.004	0.000
$\mathbf{w}_2$	0.000	-0.004	1.649	-0.003
$\mathbf{w}_3$	0.000	0.010	1.649	0.016
$\mathbf{w}_4$	0.016	1.649	0.018	0.000

Table 2. The converged weights of Random dot stereograms

have identified the second element of $\mathbf{x}_1$ and the third element of $\mathbf{x}_2$ as having maximum correlation while other inputs are ignored (the weithts from these are approximately 0). This corresponds to a right shift. This first pair of outputs has a (sample) correlation of 0.542. Similarly the second pair of weights has identified the third element of $\mathbf{x}_1$ and the second element of $\mathbf{x}_2$ as having maximum correlation while other inputs are ignored. The second pair has a (sample)correlation of 0.488 and corresponds to an identification of left shift.

5 Nonlinear correlations

We investigate the general problem of maximising correlations between two data sets when there may be an underlying nonlinear relationship between the data sets: to compare with previous experiments [2], we generate artificial data according to the prescription:

$$x_{11} = sin\theta + \mu_1 \tag{21}$$
$$x_{12} = cos\theta + \mu_2 \tag{22}$$
$$x_{21} = \theta - \pi + \mu_3 \tag{23}$$
$$x_{22} = \theta - \pi + \mu_4 \tag{24}$$

where θ is drawn from a uniform distribution in $[0,2\pi]$ and μ_i,i=1,...,4 are drawn from the zero mean Gaussian distribution N(0,0.1). Equations (21)and(22)define a circular manifold in the two-dimensional input space while Equations (23) and (24) define a linear manifold within the input space where each manifold is only approximate due to the presence of noise(μ_i,i=1,...,4). The subtraction of π in the linear manifold equations is merely to centre the data. Thus $\mathbf{x}_1 = (x_{11}, x_{12})$ lies on or near the circular manifold $x_{11}^2 + x_{12}^2 = 1$ while $\mathbf{x}_2 = (x_{11}, x_{12})$ lies on or near the line $x_{21} = x_{22}$. We wish to test whether the new algorithm can find correlations between the two data sets and the test whether such correlations are greater than the maximum linear correlations. To do this we train two pairs of output neurons:

• we train one pair of weights $\mathbf{w_1}$ and $\mathbf{w_2}$ using rules (12);

• we train a second pair of outputs, y_3 and y_4 which are calculated using 19 The correlation between y_1 and y_2 neurons was maximised using the previous linear operation (12)while that for y_3 and y_4 are maximised using 20.

We use a learning rate of 0.001 for all weights and learn over 100 000 iterations. We did not attempt to optimize any parameters for the existing or the new algorithm. In the linear case, the network finds a linear correlation between the data sets similar to that found by the Lai and Fyfe method. However in the nonlinear case our family of networks find a greater correlation.

	existing	$f_1()$	$f_2()$	$f_3()$	$f_4()$	$f_5()$	$f_6()$
linear	0.452		0.444	0.452	0.452	0.452	0.452	0.452
nolinear	0.702		0.859	0.859	0.859	0.863	0.831	0.814

Table 3. linear and nonlinear correlations

In Table 3, we can see the new algorithms find the same correlation as the existing algorithms in the linear case and can find greater nonlinear correlations than the existing algorithm.

6 Conclusion

We have derived a neural implementation of Canonical Correlation Analysis and shown that it is much more effective than previous neural implementations of CCA. In particular, it

- is much faster than previous algorithms
- is much less dependent on selection of optimal parameter values than previous methods.

The new methods constitute a very robust family of neural implementations of CCA.

We have also extended the method to nonlinear correlations and shown that this family of methods robustly finds greater correlations than is possible with linear methods.

References

1. J.O.Ramsay and B.W.Silverman. *Functional Data Analysis*. Springer, 1997.
2. P. L. Lai and C. Fyfe. A neural network implementation of canonical correlation analysis. *Neural Networks*, 12(10):1391–1397, Dec. 1999.
3. K. V. Mardia, J.T. Kent, and J.M. Bibby. *Multivariate Analysis*. Academic Press, 1979.
4. Qingfu Zhang and Yiu-Wing Leung. A class of learning algorithms for principal component analysis and minor component analysis. *IEEE Transactions on Neural Networks*, 11(1):200–204, Jan 2000.

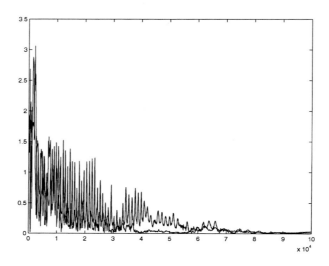

Fig. 1. Convergence on Artificial data using existing algorithm.

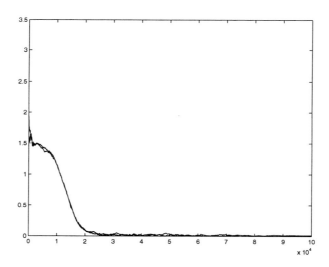

Fig. 2. Convergence on Artificial data using new algorithm with $f_1()$.

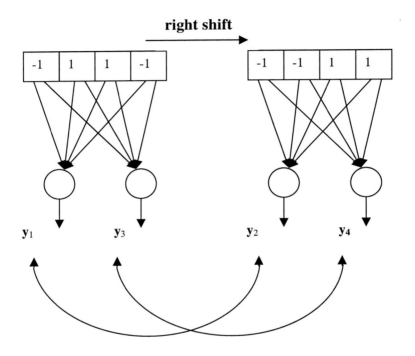

Fig. 3. The random dot stereogram data and network.

Integrating KPCA with an Improved Evolutionary Algorithm for Knowledge Discovery in Fault Diagnosis

Ruixiang Sun[1], Fugee Tsung[1], and Liangsheng Qu[2]

[1] Department of Industrial Engineering and Engineering Management,
Hong Kong University of Science and Technology,
Clear Water Bay, Kowloon, Hong Kong, China
{sunrx, season}@ust.hk
[2] Institute of Diagnostics and Cybernetics,
Xi' an Jiaotong University, Xi' an, Shaanxi 710049, China
lsqu@xjtu.edu.cn

Abstract. In this paper, a novel approach to knowledge discovery is proposed based on the integration of kernel principal component analysis (KPCA) with an improved evolutionary algorithm. KPCA is utilized to first transform the original sample space to a nonlinear feature space via the appropriate kernel function, and then perform principal component analysis (PCA). However, it remains an untouched problem to select the optimal kernel function. This paper addresses it by an improved evolutionary algorithm incorporated with Gauss mutation. The application in fault diagnosis shows that the integration of KPCA with evolutionary computation is effective and efficient to discover the optimal nonlinear feature transformation corresponding to the real-world operational data.

1 Introduction

In last decade, knowledge discovery, or data mining has attracted more and more attention in the field of automatic information processing. Although it is still in the infancy, knowledge discovery has been successfully applied in many areas, such as market data analysis [1], process monitoring and diagnosis [2], and financial engineering. In these areas, there are mountains of data collected every day. How to automatically analyze such volumes of data and then to make appropriate decisions remains a hard problem. Knowledge discovery highlights the techniques that can extract knowledge from data. There are many technologies, such as neural networks [3], rough sets [4] and genetic algorithms [5], [6], individual or synergistic, applied in knowledge discovery.

As we know, principal component analysis (PCA) has played an important role in dimensionality reduction, noise removal, and feature extraction of the original data sets as a pre-processing step in knowledge discovery. It is implemented with ease and effective in most common cases. However, for some complicated cases in industrial processes, especially nonlinearity, PCA exhibits bad behavior because of its linearity nature. A modified PCA technique, called kernel principal component analysis (KPCA) [7], [8], has been emerging to tackle the nonlinear problem in recent years. KPCA can efficiently compute principal components in high-dimensional feature spaces by the use of integral operator and nonlinear kernel functions. For a given data set, it is the key step to select a corresponding optimal kernel function in order to obtain the optimal nonlinear feature transformation. This paper addresses the unsolved problem using evolutionary computation.

Evolutionary computation, mainly composed of four branches: genetic algorithms (GA), genetic programming (GP), evolution strategies (ES), and evolutionary programming (EP), has developed to be a powerful intelligent optimization tool employed extensively in complex real-world problems, such as face recognition, structure design, and shop job scheduling. The paper proposes an improved evolutionary algorithm, which incorporates with Gauss mutation operator. Afterwards, it is used to solve the optimal selection of kernel functions when we perform KPCA.

The organization of the paper is as follows. The mathematical basis and the relationship between PCA and KPCA are reviewed in Section 2. An improved evolutionary algorithm is detailed in Section 3. Then, the integration of KPCA and the improved evolutionary algorithm for feature extraction in fault diagnosis is given in Section 4. At last, the conclusions are summarized in Section 5.

2   PCA and KPCA

2.1   Principal Component Analysis

PCA is an orthogonal transformation technique of the initial coordinate system in which we describe our data. The transformed new coordinate system can describe the data using a small number of principal components (PCs) while retaining as much of the variation as possible. Thus, it can extract effective features from original variables, especially for redundant, correlated variables.

Given a known data matrix D, representing M observations of N variables as

$$D = \begin{bmatrix} x_{11} & x_{12} & \dots & x_{1N} \\ x_{21} & x_{22} & \dots & x_{2N} \\ & \dots\dots & & \\ x_{M1} & x_{M2} & \dots & x_{MN} \end{bmatrix}. \tag{1}$$

Denote one observation as a column vector $X_k = \{x_{k1}, x_{k2}, \dots, x_{kN}\}^T$, $k=1,2,\cdots,M$, where $X_k \in R^N$, $\sum_1^M X_k = 0$, i.e. the mean value of each variable is set to zero. The superscript T denotes the transpose operation of the vector. Thus, PCA, in essence, is to diagonalize the covariance martrix

$$C = \frac{1}{M} \sum_{j=1}^M x_j x_j^T. \tag{2}$$

Then solve the eigenvalue equation
$$\lambda \mathbf{v} = C\mathbf{v}, \tag{3}$$
where λ is the eigenvalue and $\mathbf{v}$ is the corresponding eigenvector.

We can obtain the solutions to Eq. (3) by the method of linear algebra. Then we obtain the PCs, which are linear combinations of the original variables.

2.2 Kernel Principal Component Analysis

PCA exhibits a good performance when dealing with linear problems. However, for complex nonlinear problems, PCA can not exhibit such a good performance. Kernel principal component analysis (KPCA) is an emerging technique to address the nonlinear problems on the basis of PCA. KPCA is a superset of PCA, and it involves two major operations: first mapping the original data space to a feature space via the pre-selected kernel function, and then performing PCA in that feature space.

For the given data matrix D in Eq. (1), the covariance matrix C in KPCA now is altered to

$$\bar{C} = \frac{1}{M}\sum_{i=1}^{M}\phi(\mathbf{x}_i)\phi(\mathbf{x}_i)^T, \tag{4}$$

where $\phi: R^N \to F$ is the mapping function from N-dimensional data space R^N to certain feature space F.

So, the eigenvalue equation is expressed as:

$$\lambda \mathbf{v} = \bar{C}\mathbf{v}. \tag{5}$$

If we perform the mapping with explicit expression of $\phi: R^N \to F$, then in general, we will face the puzzle of 'curse of dimensionality'. It can be solved by computing dot products in feature space via kernel function [8]. From Eq. (4) and (5), we can obtain:

$$\lambda(\phi(\mathbf{x}_k) \cdot \mathbf{V}) = (\phi(\mathbf{x}_k) \cdot \bar{C}\,\mathbf{V}) \quad k = 1,2,..., M. \tag{6}$$

The eigenvector $\mathbf{V}$ can be expressed as:

$$\mathbf{V} = \sum_{j=1}^{M}\alpha_j\phi(\mathbf{x}_j). \tag{7}$$

where $\alpha = (\alpha_1, \alpha_2,...,\alpha_M)^T$ is the coefficient column vector.

Combine Eq. (4), (6), and (7), we obtain:

$$\lambda\sum_{j=1}^{M}\alpha_j(\phi(\mathbf{x}_k) \cdot \phi(\mathbf{x}_j)) = \frac{1}{M}\sum_{j=1}^{M}\alpha_j(\phi(\mathbf{x}_k) \cdot \sum_{i=1}^{M}\phi(\mathbf{x}_i)(\phi(\mathbf{x}_i) \cdot \phi(\mathbf{x}_j))) \tag{8}$$

$$k = 1,2,..., M$$

If we define a square matrix K with M rows and M columns as

$$K_{ij} = (\phi(x_i) \cdot (\phi(x_j)), \tag{9}$$

then Eq.(8) can be simplified as

$$M\lambda K\alpha = K^2\alpha. \tag{10}$$

In order to obtain the solutions to Eq. (10), we can solve the eigenvalue problem,

$$M\lambda\alpha = K\alpha. \tag{11}$$

In group one, we only consider the data sequence as a 9-state structural sequence and use squared distance functions which are provided by a class of positive semidefinite quadratic forms. For example, $\mathbf{u} = (u_1, u_2, \cdots, u_p)$ denotes the p-dimensional observation of each different distance of patterns in a state on an object that is to be assigned to one of the g prespecified groups, then, for measuring the squared distance between $\mathbf{u}$ and the centroid of the ith group, we can consider the function [1] $D^2(i) = (\mathbf{u} - \bar{\mathbf{y}})' \mathbf{M}(\mathbf{u} - \bar{\mathbf{y}})$ where $\mathbf{M}$ is a positive semidefinite matrix to ensure the $D^2(i) \geq 0$.

On the value-point pattern discovery, we use local polynomial techniques on a given the bivariate data $(X_1, Y_1), \cdots, (X_n, Y_n)$. We can replace the weighted least squares regression function in section 2.2 by

$$\sum_{i=1}^{n} \ell\{Y_i - \sum_{j=0}^{p} \beta_j (X_i - x_0)^j\} K_h(X_i - x_0)$$

where $\ell(\cdot)$ is a loss function. For the purpose of predicting future values, we use a special case of the above function with $\ell_\alpha(t) = |t| + (2\alpha - 1)t$.

Then we combine those two local polynomial models to obtain final results.

3   Experimental Results

There are three steps of experiments for the investigation of "Exchange Rates Patterns" between the U. S. dollar and the Australian dollar [4] . The data consist of daily exchange rates for each business day between 3 January 1994 and 9 August 1999. The time series is plotted in figure 1. All experiments were done on our Unix system and Windows NT 4.0; prototype was written in Awk language.

Modelling DTS: Since the difference between every successive pair of time points in this DTS is a constant: $t_{i+1} - t_i = c$, we may view the structural base as a set of vector sequence $\mathbf{X} = \{\mathbf{X_1}, \cdots, \mathbf{X_m}\}$, $\mathbf{X_i} = (s1, s2, s3, s4, s5, s6, s7, s8, s9)^T$ denotes the 9 dimensional observation on an object that is to be assigned to a prespecified group. Then the structural pattern searching becomes local linear regression in multivariate setting. We may also view the value-point process data as bivariate data $(X_1, Y_1), \cdots, (X_n, Y_n)$. This is one-dimensional local polynomial modelling. So the pattern searching problem in a DTS can be formulated as multilevel local polynomial analysis.

Dealing with Structure: We are investigating the sample of the structural base to test the naturalness of the similarity and periodicity on Structural Base distribution. The size of this discrete-valued time series is 1257 points. We only consider 8 states in the state-space of structural distribution[5]: $\mathcal{S} = \{s1, s2, s3, s4, s6, s7, s8, s9\}$.

---

[4] The Federal Reserve Bank of New York for trade weighted value of the dollar = index of weighted average exchange value of U.S. dollar against the Australian dollar: `http://www.frbchi.org/econinfo/finance/finance.html`.

[5] in this case study, the state 5 (i.e, s5) is an empty state

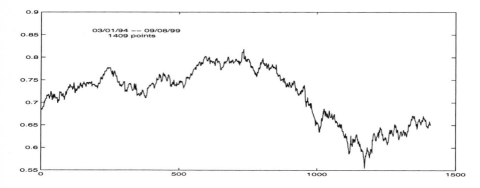

Fig. 1. 1409 business exchange rates between the U.S. dollar and the Australian dollar.

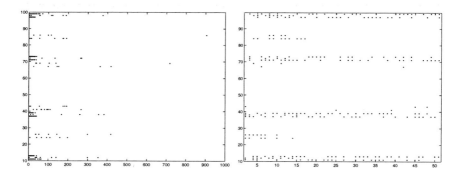

Fig. 2. Left: plot of the distance between same state for all 8 states in 1257 business days. Right: plot of the distance between same state for all 8 states in first 50 business days.

In Figure 2, the x-axis represents the distances between patterns and the y-axis represents different patterns (e.g., the pattern (s1, s2) is represented at point 12 on the y-axis). This explains two facts: (1) there exists a hidden periodic distribution which corresponds to patterns on the same line with different distances, and (2) there exist partial periodic patterns on and between the same lines. To explain this further, we can look at the plot of distances between of the patterns at a finer granularity over a selected portion of the daily exchange rates. For example, in the right of Figure 2 the dataset consists of daily exchange rates for the first 50 business days, with each point representing the distance of patterns of various forms. And between some combined pattern classes there exist some similar patterns.

In summary, some results for the structural base experiments are as follows:

- Structural distribution is a hidden periodic distribution with a periodic length function $f(t)$ (there are techniques available to approximate to the form of this function such as higher-order polynomial functions).
- There exist some partial periodic patterns based on a distance shifting.
- For all kinds of distance functions there exist a cubic curve: $y = a + \frac{b}{x} + \frac{c}{x^2}$, where a, c and $x > 0$, $b < 0$.

Dealing with Values: We now illustrate our method to analyse and to construct predictive intervals on the value-point sequence for searching patterns. The linear regression of value-point of X_t against X_{t-1} explains about 99% of the variability of the data sequence, but it does not help us much in analysis and predicting future exchange rates. In the light of our structural base experiments, we have found that the series $Y_t = X_t - X_{t-2}$ has non-trivial autocorrelation. The correlation between Y_t and Y_{t-1} is 0.4898. Our analysis is focused on the series Y_t, which is presented in the left of Figure 3. It is scatter plot of lag 2 differences: Y_t against Y_{t-1}. We obtain the exchange rates model according to the nonparametric quantile regression theory:

$$Y_t = 0.4732Y_{t-1} + \varepsilon_t$$

From the distribution of ε_t, the $\varepsilon(t)$ can be modelled as an $AR(2)$

$$\varepsilon_t = 0.2752\varepsilon_{t-1} - 0.4131\varepsilon_{t-2} + e_t$$

with a small $Var(e_t)$ (about 0.00041) to improve the predictive equation.

For prediction of future exchange rates for the next 150 business days, we use the simple equation $Y_t = 0.4732Y_{t-1}$ with an average error -0.000057. In the right of Figure 3 the actually observed series and predicted series are shown. Some results for the value-point of experiments are as follows:

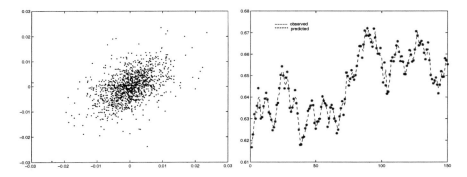

Fig. 3. Left: Scatter plot of lag 2 differences: Y_t against Y_{t-1}. Right:Plot of future exchange rates only for 150 business days by using the simple equation $Y_t = 0.4732$ Y_{t-1}

- There does not exist any full periodic pattern, but there exist some partial periodic patterns based on a distance shifting.
- There exist some similarity patterns with a small distance shifting.

Using Multilevel Local Polynomial Model: By embedding pure value results of local polynomial model into structure pattern model, we have the following combined results on exchange rates as follows:

- There does not exist any full periodic pattern but there exist some partial periodic patterns.
- There exist some similarity patterns with a small distance shifting.
- Temporal patterns can be predicted only for near future (in a window of a few months) based on past data.

4 Conclusion

This paper has presented a multilevel-local polynomial model for finding patterns in discrete-valued time series. The method guarantees finding different patterns if they exist with structural and valued probability distribution of a real-dataset. The results of preliminary experiments are promising and we are currently applying the method to large realistics data sets.

Acknowledgements

This research has been supported in part by an Australian Research Council (ARC) grant and a Macquarie University Research Grant (MURG). Support has also been provided by the Cooperative Research Centre for Advanced Computational Systems (ACSys) established under the Australian Government's Cooperative Research Centres Program.

References

1. T. W. Anderson. *An introduction to Multivariate Statistical Analysis*. Wiley, New York, 1984.
2. C. Bettini. Mining temportal relationships with multiple granularities in time sequences. *IEEE Transactions on Data & Knowledge Engineering*, 1998.
3. J. W. Han, Y. Yin, and G.Dong. Efficient mining of partial periodic patterns in time series database. *Ieee Trans. On Knowledge And Data Engineering*, 1998.
4. J.Fan and I.Gijbels, editors. *Local polynomial Modelling and Its Applications*. Chapman and hall, 1996.
5. Michael K. Ng and Zhexue Huang. Temporal data mining with a case study of astronomical data analysis. In G. Golub, S. H. Lui, F. Luk, and R. Plemmons, editors, *Proceedings of the Workshop on Scientific Computing 97*, pages 258–264. Springer-Verlag, Hong Kong, March 1997.

First Experiments for Mining Sequential Patterns on Distributed Sites with Multi-Agents

Ioan Alfred Letia, Florin Craciun, Zoltan Köpe, and Alexandru Lelutiu

Technical University of Cluj-Napoca
Department of Computer Science
Baritiu 28, RO-3400 Cluj-Napoca, Romania

Abstract. We consider the problem of mining sequential patterns over several large databases placed at different sites. Experiments carried out on synthetic data generated within a simulation environment are reported. We use several agents capable to communicate with a temporal ontology.

1 Introduction

Much effort has been recently put into trying to turn the data available in the enormous amount of databases around us into useful knowledge [7], among other means, by:

a multistrategy methodology for *conceptual data exploration*, by which we mean the derivation of high-level concepts and descriptions from data through symbolic reasoning involving both data and background knowledge.

There are many current research issues in this area including *learning over multiple databases and the World Wide Web* and [8]:

Optimizing decisions rather than predictions. The goal here is to use historical data to improve the choice of actions in addition to the more usual goal of predicting outcomes.

Making rational decisions requires knowledge of the phenomena in the application domain and sequential patterns play an important role. Mining sequential patterns over a large database of customer transactions was aimed at first to provide valuable information to businesses, such as customer buying patterns and stock trends [1, 5, 9]. Mining generalized sequential patterns [9] has been given a more efficient solution [6]. Temporal features in the mining models or processes can provide accurate information about an evolving business domain [2], but can also benefit other application areas.

Another approach to face distribution is by the deployment of various agents, eventually specialized on various tasks working together toward a common high-level goal [3, 10]. We describe a model and operations for the process of distributed database mining by multi-agents and report some experiments showing how the basic operations we propose perform on synthetic data.

2   Information Marketplace Environment

The scenario we have chosen to study the strategy of agents is an information marketplace with several customers collecting infons that appear and disappear. Infons are carriers of information characterized by its utility value varying in the range 1 to 4. The customers have various interests shown by the utility value of the infons they collect. A sample of our synthetic world showing possible changes in the marketplace for the time steps τ=0,1,2,3 is illustrated in figure 1. All infons appear randomly, one in a square of the grid, with a life span described

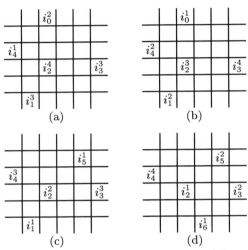

Fig. 1. Segment of the information marketplace at times (a) τ=0, (b) τ=1, (c) τ=2 and (d) τ=3.

by the sequence

$$i_k^1 \rightarrow i_k^2 \rightarrow i_k^3 \rightarrow i_k^4 \rightarrow i_k^4 \rightarrow i_k^4 \rightarrow i_k^3 \rightarrow i_k^2 \rightarrow i_k^1$$

for infon i_k, that is its utility increases in time up to the maximum and then decreases again until 1, and in the next time step it disappears.

2.1   Mining Task

We assume that have customer C_0 interested in infons of utility 3 and 4, customer C_1 interested just in infons of maximum utility, customer C_2 interested in infons of increasing utility value and customer C_3 interested in infons of decreasing utility. The transactions that have been realized over the time interval [0..3] by customers C_0, C_1, C_2, C_3 in the segment of the information market world depicted by figure 1 are shown in table 1. The transactions that have been realized over time on a location of information market are saved into a log file.

Table 1. Data-sequence database example.

Customer	Time	Items	Customer	Time	Items
C_0	0	i_1^3, i_2^4, i_3^3	C_2	0	i_3^3, i_4^1
C_0	1	i_2^3, i_3^4	C_2	1	i_4^2
C_0	2	i_3^3, i_4^3	C_2	2	i_4^3, i_5^1
C_0	3	i_4^4	C_2	3	i_5^2, i_6^1
C_1	0	i_2^4	C_3	0	i_0^2, i_1^3, i_2^4
C_1	1	i_3^4	C_3	1	i_0^1, i_1^2, i_2^3
C_1	3	i_4^4	C_3	2	i_1^1, i_2^2
			C_3	3	i_1^1, i_2^1

Table 2. Log file example.

Time	Items	Customer
0	i_1^3	C_0, C_3
1	i_1^2	C_3
2	i_1^1	C_3
3		

In table 2 are shown transactions for infon i_1 location from figure 1. From these distributed log files we intend to extract the customers behavior by distributed mining.

2.2 Conceptual Agent

Our agents are based on the following algorithm for discovery of frequent episodes in event sequences [4, 5]. This algorithm has two phases, generation of candidates and validation of generated candidates:

```
Input: a set E of event types, an event sequences S over E,
 a window width Win, and a frequency threshold Min.
Output: The collection R(S,Win,Min) of frequent episodes.
Algorithm:
L := 1; //current length
CurrCandidates := generation of candidate episodes with length L;
while (CurrCandidates != {}) do
  CurrResult := validation of CurrCandidates based on Min;
  L := L +1;
  //Result will contain the frequent episodes with all values of L
  Result := Result U CurrResult;
  CurrCandidates := generation of candidate episodes with length L;
end
output Result;
```

The algorithm starts from the most general episodes, i.e. episodes with only one event ($L = 1$) and continues until it cannot generate new candidates. On each level the algorithm first computes a collection of candidate episodes, and then checks their frequencies from the event sequence database. The crucial point in the candidate generation is given by the following lemma: *If an episode is frequent in an event sequence, then all sub-episodes are frequent.* The main idea of validation phase is to move the window Win over the event sequence S and count the appearances of a candidate. When these appearances are more than given threshold Min, the candidate is validated. The algorithm works with two kind of episodes:

- *serial episodes* noted as $S(AB)$: it occurs in a sequence only if there are events of types A and B that occur in this order in the sequence.
- *parallel episodes* noted as $P(AB)$: no constraints on the relative order of A and B are given.

The generation phases are the same for both event types, but validation phases are different. Serial candidate episodes are validated by using state automata that accept the candidate episodes and ignore all other input.

3   Multi-Agent System

Our agents perform a distributed data mining. Each agent analyses a site and can cooperate with other agents. Cooperation is possible because they use an any-time algorithm for data mining. The algorithm can be suspended and then resumed, after each phase of length L. Communication between agents are based on simple messages, formed as a combination of serial and/or parallel episodes (e.g. P(S(FE)S(BC))). They don't transfer large data, but only results of their mining. The agents must use the same ontology for event symbols. Also the agents keep the episodes extracted from a site and then can use them on other site. A multi-agent for data mining avoid the expensive operation to move the whole data on a site.

4   Experimental Results

Table 3. Log File fragment

Time	Infon	Customer	Time	Infon	Customer
2	A	C_4	28	B	C_3
14	F	C_3	29	C	C_1,C_3
15	B	C_1	30	A	C_4
16	C	C_4	33	E	C_3
17	A	C_4	36	B	C_1

Our experiments consist of two phases. First we generated synthetic data within a simulated environment and then we used data mining agents to analyze the data. In data generation phase we used the information marketplace environment with $80X80$ grid dimensions. The number of infons remains constant all the time. When an infon becomes zero, it moves randomly to another free grid location. We defined four kinds of customer behavior, C_1, C_2, C_3, C_4, as a combination of serial and/or parallel episodes. These behaviors are shown in lines with label "Generated" from table 4, where $A = (4, \downarrow)$, $B = (2, \uparrow)$, $C = (3, \uparrow)$, $D = (3, \downarrow)$, $E = (1, \downarrow)$, $F = (1, \uparrow)$ and a pair (V, T) represents an infon with value V and evolution trend T. Executing their behavior the customer accesses different grid location. For each grid location we generated a log file. A log file fragment is shown in table 3. These distributed log files are inputs for data mining agents. Table 4 shows what data mining agents have extracted from three different log files.

Table 4. Types of behavior

Behavior Type	Behavior Description (generated and extracted)
C1	Generated: S(BAC)
C1	Log1: P(C), P(A), P(B), S(C), S(A), S(B), S(CB), S(AB)
C1	Log2: P(C), P(A), P(B), S(C), S(A), S(B), S(CC), S(CA), S(CCC), S(CCA), S(CCCA)
C1	Log3: P(C), P(A), P(B), S(C), S(A), S(B), S(AA)
C2	Generated: S(CAD)
C2	Log1: P(C), P(A), P(D), P(CA), P(CD), P(AD), S(C), S(A), S(D), S(CD), S(AD)
C2	Log2: P(C), P(A), P(D), P(CA), P(AD), S(C), S(A), S(D)
C2	Log3: P(C), P(D), P(CD), S(C),S(A), S(D), S(CC), S(CD), S(AD)
C2	Log3: P(C), P(D), P(CA), S(C),S(A), S(D), S(CC), S(CD), S(AD)
C3	Generated: P(S(FE)S(BC))
C3	Log1: P(B), P(C), P(E), P(F), P(BC), P(BE), P(CE), P(EF), P(BCE), S(B), S(C), S(E), S(F)
C3	Log2: P(B), P(C), P(E), P(F), P(BC), P(BE), P(CE), P(EF), P(BCE), S(B), S(C), S(E), S(F)
C3	Log3: P(B), P(C), P(E), P(F), P(CE), P(EF), S(B), S(C), S(E), S(F)
C3	Log3: P(B), P(C), P(E), P(F), P(BC), P(BE), P(CE), P(EF), S(B), S(C), S(E), S(F)
C4	Generated: P(CA)
C4	Log1: P(C), P(A), P(CA), S(C), S(A), S(CC)
C4	Log2: P(C), P(A), P(AC), S(C), S(A), S(AA), S(AC), S(AAA)
C4	Log3: P(C), P(A), P(CA), S(C), S(A), S(AA)

Only customer behavior C_4 has been completely extracted. The other behaviors has been partially extracted. At local level extracted behaviors are correct, but at information marketplace level these behaviors are incomplete. The local information are incomplete, so it is necessary a cooperation mechanism between agents.

5 Conclusions

It has been shown that meta-learning can improve accuracy while lowering per transaction losses [10]. Therefore distribution of mining can reduce significantly communication and contribute to the scaling up of various methods. Intelligent agents should be able to take advantage of higher-level communication on their common mining tasks by using an appropriate ontology. This is our next step in the search of more flexible mining on distributed sites.

References

1. R. Agrawal and R. Srikant: Mining sequential patterns. In *International Conference on Database Engineering*, pages 3–14, Washington, D.C., 1995. IEEE Computer Society Press.
2. C. Bettini, X. Sean Wang, and S. Jajodia: Testing complex temporal relationships involving multiple granularities and its application to data mining. In *Proceedings of the Fifteenth ACM Symposium on Principles of Database Systems*, volume 15, pages 68–78, New York, NY 10036, USA, 1996. ACM Press.
3. D.W. Cheung, V.T. Ng, A.W. Fu, and Y. Fu: Efficient mining of association rules in distributed databases. *IEEE Transactions on Knowledge and Data Engineering*, pages 911–922, Dec 1996.
4. Luc Dehaspe and Hannu Toivonen: Discovery of frequent Datalog patterns. *Data Mining and Knowledge Discovery*, 3, 1999.
5. H. Mannila, H. Toivonen, and A. I. Verkamo: Discovering frequent episodes in sequences. In U. M. Fayyad and R. Uthurusamy, editors, *Proceedings of the First International Conference on Knowledge Discovery and Data Mining (KDD-95)*, pages 210–215, Montreal, Canada, August 1995. AAAI Press.
6. F. Masseglia, F. Cathala, and P. Poncelet: The PSP approach for mining sequential patterns. In J.M. Zytkow and M. Quafafou, editors, *Principles of Data Mining and Knowledge Discovery*, LNAI 1510, pages 176–184, 1998.
7. Ryszard S. Michalski and Kenneth A. Kaufman: Data mining and knowledge discovery: A review of issues and a multistrategy approach. In R.S. Michalski, I. Bratko, and M. Kubat, editors, *Machine Learning and Data Mining*, pages 71–112. John Wiley, 1998.
8. T.M. Mitchell: Machine learning and data mining. *Communications of the ACM*, 42(11), Nov 1999.
9. R. Srikant and R. Agrawal: Mining sequential patterns: Generalizations and performance improvements. In *Proceedings of the 5th International Conference on Extending Database Technology*, Avignon, France, 1996.
10. S. Stolfo, A. Prodromidis, S. Tselepsis, W. Lee, D. Fan, and P. Chan: JAM: Java agents for meta-learning over distributed databases. In *Proceedings of the 3rd International Conference on Knowledge Discovery and Data Mining*, 1997.

Nonlinear and Noisy Time Series Prediction Using a Hybrid Nonlinear Neural Predictor

[1]Seng Kah Phooi, [1]Man Zhihong, [2]H. R. Wu

[1] School of Engineering, The University of Tasmania, Hobart 7001, Australia
[2] School of Computer Science & Software Engineering, Monash University, Australia
Email: kp_seng@utas.edu.au ,Tel: 0011-61-3-62262925, Fax: 0011-61-3-62267863

Abstract – A hybrid nonlinear time series predictor that consists a nonlinear sub-predictor (NSP) and a linear sub-predictor (LSP) combined in a cascade form is proposed. A multilayer neural network is employed as the NSP and the algorithm used to update the NSP weights is Lyapunov stability-based backpropagation algorithm (LABP). The NSP can predict the nonlinearity of the input time series. The NSP prediction error is then further compensated by employing a LSP. Weights of the LSP are adaptively adjusted by the Lyapunov adaptive algorithm. Signals' stochastic properties are not required and the error dynamic stability is guaranteed by the Lyapunov Theory. The design of this hybrid predictor is simplified compared to existing hybrid or cascade neural predictors [1]-[2]. It is fast convergence and less computation complexity. The theoretical prediction mechanism of this hybrid predictor is further confirmed by simulation examples for real world data.

1. Introduction

Financial forecasting is an example of a signal processing problem which is challenging due to small sample sizes, high noise, non-stationarity and non-linearity. Neural networks (NN) have been very successful in a number of signal processing applications including the prediction of the real-world data e.g. sunspot time series [5] and financial forecasting [6]. Many types of NN structures have been introduced in [7] and this is a good reference for the time series analysis or prediction. In practice, many of the time series include both nonlinear and linear properties and the amplitude of the time series are usually continuous. Therefore it is useful to use a combined structure of linear and nonlinear models to deal with such signals.

In this paper, we propose a hybrid predictor with Lyapunov adaptive algorithms. It consists of the following sub-predictors: (1) A NSP, which consists of a multilayer neural network (MLNN) with a nonlinear hidden layer and a linear output neuron. The algorithm used to update the weights is LABP [8]. (2) A LSP, which is a conventional finite-impulse-response (FIR) filter. Its weights are adaptively adjusted by the Lyapunov adaptive algorithm [9]. The NSP that includes nonlinear functions can predict the nonlinearity of the input time series. However the actual time series contains both linear and nonlinear properties, hence the prediction is not complete in some cases. Therefore the NSP prediction error is further compensated for by employing a LSP after the NSP. In this paper the prediction mechanism and the role of the NSP and LSP are theoretically and experimentally analyzed. The role of the NSP is to predict the nonlinear and some part of the linear property of the time series. The LSP works to predict the NSP prediction error. Lyapunov functions are defined for these prediction errors so that they converge to zero asymptotically. The signals' stochastic properties are not required and the error dynamic stability is guaranteed by the Lyapunov Theory. The design of this hybrid predictor is simplified compared to existing hybrid or cascade neural predictors [1]-[2]. It is fast convergence and less computational complexity. Furthermore predictability of the hybrid predictor for noisy time series is investigated. Computer simulations using nonlinear sunspot times series and other conventional predictor models are demonstrated. The theoretical analysis of the predictor mechanism is confirmed through these simulations.

2. A Hybrid Structure of Neural Network-Fir Predictor

Figure 1 illustrates the proposed hybrid predictor structure that is the cascade form of MLNN and FIR filter. The actual time series contains both linear and nonlinear properties and its amplitude is usually continuous value. For these reasons, we combine nonlinear and linear predictors in a cascade form. The nonlinear prediction problem can be described as follow: A set of the past samples $x(n-1),.....,x(n-N)$ is transformed into the output, which is the prediction of the next coming sample $x(n)$. Therefore we employ a MLNN called a NSP in the first stage. It consists of a sigmiodal hidden layer and a single output neuron. The NSP is trained by the supervised leaning algorithm called LABP [8]. This means the NSP itself acts as a single nonlinear predictor.

In reality it is rather difficult to generate the continuous amplitude and to predict linear property. Hence a linear predictor is employed after the NSP to compensate for the linear relation between the input samples and the target. A FIR filter is used for this purpose, which will be called a Linear Sub-predictor (LSP). The LSP is trained by Lyapunov theory-based adaptive filtering algorithm (LAF) [9]. The same target or the desired time series is used for both NSP and the LSP. Hence the nonlinear and some part of linear properties of the input signal can be predicted by the NSP and the remaining part is predicted by the LSP. The current sample, $x(n)$ is used as the desired response, $d(n)$ for both the NSP and the LSP.

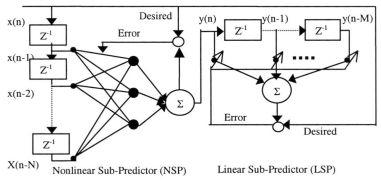

Fig. 1 Structure of the hybrid predictor

3. Nonlinear Sub-predictor (NSP)

The architecture of the MLNN considered is shown in Figure 1. Hence for convenience of presentation, we describe the LABP algorithm with the that $L = 2$, implying one hidden layer. The algorithm can be extended easily to cases when $L \neq 2$ The input $x(n)$ is a sampled signal: $x(n)= \{x(n-1),... x(n-N)\}$ or $x(n) = \{x_n, x_{n-1}, ...,x_{n-N} \}$ and the output is a scalar $y_{NSP}(n)$. The purpose of this neural network is to adjust the neural weights in order to achieve error between the network output $y_{NSP}(n)$ and the desired output $d(n)$ converge to zero asymptotically. Let $W_{j,i}^{(1,)}(n)$ denote the connection weight between the i'th neuron in the input layer, $l=0$ and j'th neuron in the hidden layer, $l=1$(for $i = 1$, 2, ...N; $j = 1, 2, ...M$). Let $S_j(n)$ and $F_j(\cdot)$ be the output and the activation function of the j'th neuron in the hidden layer, respectively. $W_{1j}^{(2)}(n)$ denotes the connection weight between the j'th neuron in the hidden layer and the neuron in the output layer $y(n)$, $l=2$. Then we have the following system equations:

$$y_{NSP}(n) = \sum_{j=1}^{M} W_{1j}^{(2)} S_j(n) \tag{3.1}$$

$$S_j(n) = F_j\left(\sum_{i=1}^{N} W_{ji}^{(1)} x_i(n) \right) \tag{3.2}$$

where $j = 1, 2, ...,M$ and $i = 1, 2, ..., N$.

Substituting (3.2) into (3.1) gives

$$y_{NSP}(n) = \sum_{j=1}^{M} W_{1j}^{(2)}(n) F_j\left(\sum_{i=1}^{N} W_{ji}^{(1)} x_i(n) \right) \tag{3.3}$$

where $F(\bullet) = \dfrac{1}{1 + e^{-\alpha(\bullet)}}$

The prediction error for NSP is computed as follow,

$$e_{NSP}(n) = d(n) - y_{NSP}(n) \tag{3.4}$$

The weight vectors of the MLNN can be updated using the following expressions:

$$W_{1j}^{(2)}(n) = W_{1j}^{(2)}(n-1) + \Delta W_{1j}^{(2)}(n) \tag{3.5}$$

and $\quad W_{ji}^{(1)}(n) = W_{ji}^{(1)}(n-1) + \Delta W_{ji}^{(1)}(n) \tag{3.6}$

where $\Delta W_{1j}^{(2)}(n) = \dfrac{1}{S_j(n)} \dfrac{1}{M}\left[d(k) - \sum_{j=1}^{M} W_{1j}^{(2)}(n) S_j(n) \right] \tag{3.7}$

$$\Delta W_{ji}^{(1)}(n) = \left[-W_{ji}^{(1)}(n-1) + \dfrac{1}{N} \dfrac{1}{x_i(n)} g_j(u(n)) \right] \tag{3.8}$$

$$u(n) = \dfrac{1}{M} \dfrac{1}{W_{1j}(n)} d(n) \tag{3.9}$$

$$g_j(\bullet) = F_j^{-1}(\bullet)$$

The detailed derivation and design of the LABP algorithm can be found in [8].
To prevent the singularities problem due to zero values of $x_i(n)$ and $\Delta W_{1j2}(n)$, those weights updated law $\Delta W_{j,i}^{(1)}(n)$ and $\Delta W_{1j}^{2}(n)$ (3.7) (3.8) can be modified as follow

$$\Delta W_{1j}^{(2)}(n) = \dfrac{1}{S_j(n)} \dfrac{1}{M}\left[d(n) - \sum_{j=1}^{M} W_{1j}^{(2)}(n) S_j(n) \right] \tag{3.10}$$

$$\Delta W_{ji}^{(1)}(n) = \left[-W_{ji}^{(1)}(n-1) + \dfrac{1}{N} \dfrac{1}{x_i(n) + \lambda_1} g_j(u(n)) \right] \tag{3.11}$$

where $\quad u(n) = \dfrac{1}{M} \dfrac{1}{W_{1j}(n) + \lambda_2} d(n) \tag{3.12}$

The smaller values of λ_1 and λ_2 contribute smaller error $e_{NSP}(n)$.

4. Linear Sub-predictor (LSP)

The linear sub-predictor (LSP) consists a conventional finite-impulse-response (FIR) filter. It can be characterized by the difference equation

$$y_{LSP}(n) = \sum_{i=0}^{K-1} h_i(n) y_{NSP}(n-i) \tag{4.1}$$

The difference equation in (4.1) can be rewritten in vector form as

$$y_{LSP}(n) = H^T(n) Y_{NSP}(n) \tag{4.2}$$

where $H(k) = [h_k(0), h_k(1), ..., h_k(N-1)]^T$

$Y_{NSP}(n) = [y_{NSP}(n), y_{NSP}(n-1), ..., y_{NSP}(n-K+1)]^T$

The LSP's coefficient vector is updated by the LAF algorithm [11].

$$H(n) = H(n-1) + g(n)\alpha(n) \tag{4.3}$$

where $g(n)$ is the adaptation gain and $\alpha(n)$ is the a priori estimation error defined as

$$\alpha(n) = d(n) - H^T(n-1) Y_{NSP}(n) \tag{4.4}$$

The adaptation gain $g(n)$ in (4.3) is adaptively adjusted using Lyapunov stability theory as (4.5) so that the error $e_{LSP}(n) = d(n) - y_{LSP}(n)$ asymptotically converges to zero.

$$g(n) = \frac{Y_{NSP}(n)}{\| Y_{NSP}(n) \|^2} \left(1 - \kappa \frac{| e_{LSP}(n-1) |}{| \alpha(n) |} \right) \tag{4.5}$$

where $0 \le \kappa < 1$. To avoid singularities, (4.5) can be modified as (4.6)

$$g(n) = \frac{Y_{NSP}(n)}{\lambda_3 + \| Y_{NSP}(n) \|^2} \left(1 - \kappa \frac{| e_{LSP}(n-1) |}{\lambda_4 + | \alpha(n) |} \right) \tag{4.6}$$

where λ_3, λ_4 are small positive numbers and $0 \le \kappa < 1$, then the prediction error $e_{LSP}(n)$ asymptotically converges to a ball centered on the origin that the radius of the ball depends on λ_3, λ_4. According to [10], the prediction error $e_{LSP}(n)$ will not converge to zero if the adaptive gain $g(n)$ is adjusted using expression (4.6), but it will converge to a ball centred at the system origin. Again, the convergence rate is affected by the choice of κ. The radius of the ball depends on the values of λ_3 and λ_4. Generally, the smaller λ_3 and λ_4 are, the smaller the error $e_{LSP}(n)$ is.

Prediction Analysis: The role of LSP is to predict the prediction error caused by the NSP [3],[4]. It analysis can be summarized as follow: From the expression (3.4), we rewrite (3.4) as

$$y_{NSP}(n) = d(n) - e_{NSP}(n) \tag{4.8}$$

Due to the LSP is the FIR structure with K taps, its output $y_{LSP}(n)$ can be expressed as

$$y_{LSP}(n) = h_0 y_{NSP}(n) + h_1 y_{NSP}(n-1) + ... + h_{K-1} y_{NSP}(n-K+1) \tag{4.9}$$

By substituting the expression (4.8) into (4.9), we get

$$y_{LSP}(n) = h_0(d(n) - e_{NSP}(n)) + h_1 y_{NSP}(n-1) + ... + h_{K-1} y_{NSP}(n-K+1) \tag{4.10}$$

$$= h_0 d(n) + [-h_0 e_{NSP}(n) + h_1 y_{NSP}(n-1) + ... + h_{K-1} y_{NSP}(n-K+1)]$$

Let

$$y^*(n) = h_1 y_{NSP}(n-1) + ... + h_{K-1} y_{NSP}(n-K+1) \tag{4.11}$$

With the assumption that $h_0 \approx 1$, the expression (4.10) can be rewritten as

$$y_{LSP}(n) = d(n) - [e_{NSP}(n) - y^*(n)] \tag{4.12}$$

Therefore the final prediction error can be expressed as

$$e_{final}(n) = e_{LSP}(n) = d(n) - y_{LSP}(n) = e_{NSP}(n) - y*(n) \qquad (4.13)$$

Hence, the function of LSP is to predict the prediction error resulted from the NSP. The contribution of the NSP and the LSP in the overall performance of the proposed hybrid prediction can be measured by the following ratio

$$R = P_{NSP}/P_{LSP} \qquad (4.14)$$

Where P_{NSP} and P_{LSP} are the power of the NSP output and LSP output respectively. The normalized root mean square error (NRMSE) [3],[4] is used to express the prediction error so that they can be used for comparison. It is calculated as

$$NRMSE = \sqrt{MSE / P_{input}} \qquad (4.15)$$

where MSE: the mean squared error of NSP or LSP. P_{input} is the input signal power.

5. Simulation Results Using Hybrid Model

Nonlinear Times Series - Simulations have been done for a one-step ahead prediction of 2 examples: Sunspot data and Chaotic data. Sunspot data is used as a benchmark for many years by researchers. Data file of the Sunspot times series is download from [11]. It consists the sunspot data from the year 1700 to 1999 (300 Samples). Fig. 2 shows the plots of the sunspot time series. Fig. 3 illustrate the plot of the output of the hybrid predictor for sunspot time series (1950-1999). Fig. 4 and 5 show the square predictor error of NSP, $e_{NSP}^2(n)$ and LSP, $e_{LSP}^2(n)$ respectively.

Comparison With Other Models - In this section, the prediction performance of the proposed hybrid predictor, a linear FIR predictor and a nonlinear MLNN predictor with a linear output neuron are compared for the Sunspot time series. Comparison using different kinds of predictor was demonstrated in [3]. The simulation results using the Sunspot time series are tabulated in Table 1. Compared to those models, the proposed hybrid predictor has the minimum prediction errors in both cases. The linear predictor does not perform well due to the high nonlinearity in the time series.

6. Conclusion

A hybrid nonlinear time series predictor that consists the NSP and the LSP combined in a cascade form is proposed. The NSP is a MLNN and the algorithm used to update NSP weights is Lyapunov stability-based backpropagation algorithm (LABP). The nonlinearity and some part of linearity of the input time series is predicted by NSP. The LSP then further predict the NSP prediction error. Weights of the LSP are adaptively adjusted by the LAF. Lyapunov functions are defined for these prediction errors and convergence to zero asymptotically is desired to achieve. Signals' stochastic properties are not required and the error dynamic stability is guaranteed by the Lyapunov Theory. The design of this hybrid predictor is simplified compared to exiting hybrid or cascade neural predictors. It is fast convergence and less computation complexity. Predictability for the noisy time series is also investigated. Properties of these predictors are analyzed taking the nonlinearity of the time series into account. Hence the prediction mechanism and the role of the NSP and LSP of the hybrid predictor have been theoretically and experimentally analyzed and clarified.

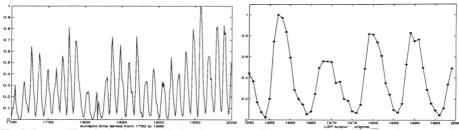

Fig. 2: Sunspot Time Series from 1700 to 1999

Fig. 3: Predictor output waveforms for Sunspot data using the proposed hybrid predictor (1950-1999) '___ original data', ' * predictor output data'

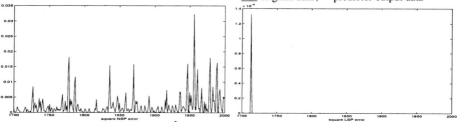

Fig. 4: The NSP square output error, $e_{NSP}^2(n)$

Fig. 5: The LSP square output error, $e_{LSP}^2(n) \times 10^{-5}$

Model	Proposed Hybrid Predictor	MLNN Predictor (BP)	Linear FIR predictor(LMS)
NRMSE	4.6×10^{-4}(NRMSE of LSP)	0.092	0.2897
	0.091 (NRMSE of NSP)		

Table 1: Comparison of NRMSE among different models for sunspot data

References

[1] Simon Haykin, "Nonlinear Adaptive Prediction of Nonstationary Signals", IEEE Trans. Signal Processing, Vol. 43, No. 2, February, 1995.
[2] Jens Baltersee, Jonathon A. Chambers, "Nonlinear Adaptive Prediction of Speech With A Pipeline Recurrent Neural Network", IEEE Trans. Signal Processing, Vol. 46, No. 8, August, 1998.
[3] Ashraf A.M.K, Kenji N, "A Cascade Form Predictor of Neural and FIR Filters and Its Minimum Size Estimation Based on Nonlinearity Analysis of Time Series", IEICE Trans. Fundamentals, Vol. E81-A, No. 3, March, 1998.
[4] Ashraf A.M.K, Kenji N, "A Hybrid Nonlinear Predictor: Analysis of Learning Process and Predictability for Noisy Time Series", IEICE Trans. Fundamentals, Vol. E82-A, No. 8, August, 1999.
[5] A.S. Weigend, D. E. Rumelhart, "Generalization through minimal networks with application to forecasting", Proc. INTERFACE'91: Computing Science and Statistics, ed. Elaine Keramindas, pp. 362-370, Springer Verlag, 1992.
[6] Steve Lawrence, Ah Chung Tsoi, C. Lee Giles, "Noisy Time Series Prediction using Symbolic Representation and Recurrent Neural Network Grammatical Inference", Technical report, UMIACS-TR-96-27 and CS-TR-3625, Institute for Advanced Computer Studies , University of Maryland.
[7] A.S. Weigend, N.A. Gershenfeld, "Times series prediction: Forecasting the future and understanding the past", Proc. V. XV, Santa Fe Institute, 1994.
[8] Zhihong Man, Seng Kah Phooi, H.R. Wu, "Lyapunov stability-based adaptive backpropagation for discrete and continuous time systems", 2nd International Conference on Information, Communications and signal processing, ICICS'99, pp. paper no. 376, 1999.
[9] Man ZhiHong, H.R.Wu, W.Lai and Thong Nguyen, "Design of Adaptive Filters Using Lyapunov Stability Theory", The 6th IEEE International Workshop on Intelligent Signal Processing and Communication Systems, vol, pp. 304-308, 1998.
[10] Slotine, J-J. E. and Li, W. Applied nonlinear control, Prentice-Hall, Englewood Cliffs, NJ, 1991.
[11] http://www.astro.oma.be/SIDC/index.html

Genetic Programming Prediction of Solar Activity

Romuald Jagielski

School of Information Technology
Swinburne University of Technology
Victoria, Australia
RJagielski@swin.edu.au

Abstract. For many practical applications, such as planning for satellite orbits and space missions, it is important to estimate the future values of the sunspot numbers. There have been numerous methods used for this particular case of time series prediction, including recently neural networks. In this paper we present genetic programming technique employed to sunspot series prediction. The paper investigates practical solutions and heuristics for an effective choice of parameters and functions of genetic programming. The results obtained expect the maximum in the current cycle of the smoothed series monthly sunspot numbers is 164 ± 20, and 162 ± 20 for the next cycle maximum, at the 95% level of confidence. These results are discussed and compared with other predictions.

1 Introduction

Planning high frequency communication links and space-related activities undertaken by NASA and other organizations, requires prediction of solar activity, and in particular, to estimate the sunspot numbers for the oncoming years.

The sun undergoes periods of high activity, when many solar flares and coronal mass ejection take place, followed by relatively quiet periods of low activity. One way to investigate solar activity is to measure systematically the number of sunspots - during the active periods this number is high and goes down again later (the cycle last about 11 years).

The sunspots affect also the conditions on the Earth, for example, it may disrupt radio communication. Possibly, there is a relation between sunspots and the Earth climate.

The characteristics of the sunspot number series are similar to those frequently occurring in financial and economic models (they contain sudden irregular variations, cycles and trends), therefore the solution for this problem extends beyond astrophysics, radio communication and space services.

Time series prediction is one of the most prevalent functions of any serious business operation. The model used here is the univariate model, which uses the past series to predict the future values. Unfortunately, univariate models omit cause variables and the prediction is based solely on the discovered pattern in historical data (some statisticians are quite sceptical about certain practices used in prediction, for example Moroney [1] calls one chapter of his book "Prediction and Fortune Telling"). Since the phenomenon of sunspots is not entirely understood, it seems that there is some justification in the choice of this model. A great number of methods exist for forecasting generally, and some were specifically developed for the sunspot number series [3].

In this paper, we discuss genetic programming, a variation of evolutionary computation, applied to this type of prediction. Genetic programming, developed by John Koza [4] is inspired by evolution, and operates on a population of individuals, which in this case are computer programs. These individuals participate in a simulated evolutionary process and, as a result of it, an optimal or near optimal solution emerges.

The program used in this investigation has been written in C++ and uses C-like syntax trees (i.e. programs) to represent solutions (i.e. individuals). The initial population consists of programs that are randomly generated syntax trees. These programs are created as hierarchical compositions of primitives - non-terminals (or functions) and terminals (variables or constants). A node on the syntax tree represents a terminal or a function. The selection of primitives is a very significant step in genetic programming. The set of primitives may include arithmetic and Boolean operators, mathematical functions, conditional and iterative operators and any other functions predefined by the user.

Evolutionary computing is a repetitive process of transforming populations of programs by means of reproduction, crossover and mutation. As a termination condition, the number of generations can be chosen and the best program that appears in any generation is the solution.

2 Representation of the time series prediction problem for genetic programming

In Figure 1 an example of an evolved program as a solution for the sunspot number series prediction is shown (exactly in the form as it was generated by our software).

GPvalue =   // value of the following program:
((w[3])+((((((w[227])/((w[118])+(w[161])))/(-37.1942))/(((((
(w[258])/((((((((((((((((((w[120])+((w[326])-
w[78])))/((w[106])*(w[95])))/((w[106])*(w[95])))+
((w[140])+(w[8])))*(w[16]))*
(w[51]))+((w[263])+(w[16])))-((w[210])+(w[116])))
-((w[316])-(w[197])))+(((w[40])/(((((((((((w[71])-((
w[100])-((((((w[46])-(w[109]))+((w[206])-(w[286])))
/(w[193]))*(((((w[105])+((w[140])+
(w[8])))+((w[37])*(w[260])))/((w[37])-(w[84])))-
(w[91])))-((w[276])-(w[333]))))))*((w[255])+(w[134]
)))-(((w[7])/(w[99]))*(((w[16])
+(w[50]))/((w[224])*(((((w[300])*(w[245]))/(((
w[153])-(w[173])))+((w[52])/(w[281])))+((w[37])
/(w[166])))))))-((w[289])*(w[41])))+((w[326])-(

---

[1] Moroney, M.J. "Facts from Figure" Penguin Books, 1964

w[78])))/((w[226])*(w[63])))+((w[173])/(w[30])))
+w[68])+(((((w[75])*(w[109]))/((w[131])/(w[99])
))/(((w[118])+(w[161])))))))+(((w[73])-(w[78]))+(
w[129])))-((w[16])+(w[50])))/((w[75])+(w[245]))))
-(w[306])))*(((w[131])/(w[225]))+(w[6])))/((w[4])
+(w[121])))/((w[194])+(w[276])))*((w[49])+(
w[173])))/((w[254])-(w[158])))*((w[71])/(w[243])))
/(w[225]))+(w[263])))-((w[16])+(w[245])))/((w[75])+
(w[245])))/((((w[134])+(w[258])*(w[109]))))-(
(w[16])+((w[16])+(w[50]))))/(58.37)))
; // end of the Gpvalue

Figure 1. A sample solution - a program that returns predicted sunspot number

Each program is an expression and when evaluated it returns a real number – a sunspot number (called in Figure 1 *GPvalue*). The excessive number of brackets makes these programs hard to read but they are legitimate C functions and they can be included in an ANSI C or C++ program. The variables, the operators and constants will be explained shortly.

The time series data is a sequence of numbers $n[t_1], n[t_2],...,n[t_i],...,n[t_{max}]$, and usually no additional information about the meaning of the series and the best prediction period *lag* is available. The aim is to find the best prediction of the unseen continuation of the unavailable sequence. We will attempt to evolve the solution using a certain number (smaller than *lag*) of values directly preceding time t_j , that is a "window" $w[t_{j-lag}]...,w[t_{j-1}]$ with j going through a part or the whole series (the result presented in Figure 1 is an expression of elements $w[t_j]$ of such a window).

We will seek a solution in a form of a polynomial of high degree, therefore the used operators are the standard arithmetic operators: "+", "-", "*", "/" (slightly modified to ensure the closure property, for example allowing division by 0). The experiments with other operators, such as trigonometric function *sin* and *cos*, and *if-then* did not contribute anything better (after all it is possible to find a high-degree polynomial that can fit any data perfectly).

The set of terminal includes also constants, initially real numbers generated randomly. In the process of evolution, mutation may change them.

The parameter *lag*, that determines the period of time taking into consideration for a single prediction has been chosen after many experiments as *lag*=140 which for monthly data corresponds roughly to one cycle. This means that prediction of a value of time t_{140} has been calculated using values selected from time $t_{139}, t_{138},...,t_0$. Note that not all the values have to be present, and some may be used many times. Strictly speaking, this parameter is not particularly important– solutions with a big *lag* would include more variables, many of them irrelevant.

3 Data

The history of observing sunspots is very long, but since invention of the telescope, quite systematic records are kept. There is a commonly accepted definition of an average sunspot number, called Wolf Sunspot Number that takes into consideration

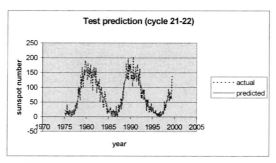

Figure 2. Test prediction of cycles 21-22

such factors as spots grouping and observing conditions. The available data goes back as far as 1750, but as it has been shown, the earlier records are not very reliable [2]. We will follow other researches and use observations starting from 1850. The data used here are monthly actual and monthly smoothed sunspot numbers, available for example from Sunspot Index Data Centre in Royal Observatory of Belgium. The Figure 2 shows a small part of the actual data. The smoothed data used here is so called "13-month running mean". The smoothing for month n is obtained from the following formula:

$$\overline{R}_n = \frac{1}{24}\sum_{i=-6}^{5} R_{n+i} + \frac{1}{24}\sum_{i=-5}^{6} R_{n+i}$$

where R_n is the actual value month n.

The solutions were evolved here using samples of smoothed data, selected randomly with the sampling rate around 10%. For testing predictions, cycles 21 and 22 were used (this corresponds roughly to the period 1975 –1999). In many applications of evolutionary techniques testing is not a necessary step – the fitness indicates the quality of the solution. However here, taking into consideration random character of sampling, the solution was additionally tested each time when "better-so-far" result was obtained.

4 Experiments and results

To evolve solutions we used sampling techniques. The fitness of each program was calculated for three different samples (a greater number of samples increases considerably the number of evaluations – k samples means, practically, k times longer time of computing). Each sample consists of 200 randomly selected points from the training data set (consisting of around 1500 cases), and this number of times the solution was evaluated. The final fitness was ten taken as the average value over all samples. This approach, which may be thought as a version of cross validation for big data sets, was chosen to minimise overspecialisation (or overfitting effect). Overfitting is the major problem we face in time series prediction – genetic

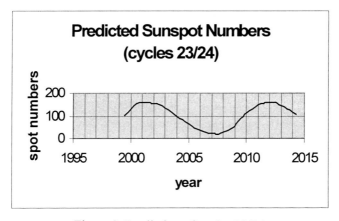

Figure 3. Prediction of cycles 23/24

programming is extremely good for symbolic regression (finding a function that fits a given set of points), but there is no guarantee that the evolved program has the capability for generalisation. The method describe above and used in this work seems to deal with this problem quite well. Using smoothing data instead actual sunspot numbers also helps to fight overspecialisation.

We conducted a number of experiments, trying to establish the best parameters for genetic programming to get the best results. Table 1 shows selected results of best ten predictions.

These programs has been evolved under the following conditions:

- fitness function: mean squared error (MSE);
- population size : 10 000;

Run	maximum cycle 23	year	maximum cycle 24	year	MAD
1	179	2001.12	170	2012.02	1.8
2	172	2001.09	183	2012.02	1.8
3	151	2001.02	164	2011.05	3.5
4	197	2001.08	151	2011.01	7.6
5	150	2001.03	152	2012.01	1.7
6	153	2000.07	148	2010.02	2.7
7	155	2000.07	162	2010.02	2.7
8	154	2000.07	148	2010.02	2.7
9	167	2000.05	173	2011.09	2.4
10	167	2000.05	170	2011.09	2.5
Average:	164.5	2000.57	162.1	2011.04	2.94

Table 1. Results of ten runs (maxima of cycles 23 and 24 and Mean Absolute Deviation of the testing prediction)

- selection method: 10% population selected using the tournament method with the size of a group equals to 4;
- crossover: one point cross-over;
- mutation: terminals, with probability 0.01;
- maximum number of generations: 80;
- lag randomly selected in each experiment from interval $140 \pm n$, $0 < n < 70$ (a value between one cycle and one and half cycle).

When it was necessary to do so, in the situation when actual data was not available yet, the predicted results were smoothed and then used for further prediction.

One particular solution is shown in Figure 1.

In the Figure 3 the prediction (average from ten runs) for the cycles 23 and 24 is shown. The maximum 164.5 ± 20 of cycle 23 is expected to be in July 2000, and the maximum 162.1 ± 20 of cycle 24 is predicted at January 2011. The average Mean Absolute Deviation is 2.94. All these results are within distribution independent confidence interval 95%, (as defined in [5]).

This prediction for maximum of cycle 23 differs little from value 154 ± 21, obtained by Hathaway at al. [3] who performed very comprehensive research using a various classical and specialised techniques. The results obtained from neural networks (maximum 130 with uncertainty ± 30-80 by Conway et al. [2]) differ more from our results but admittedly, they have to their disposition less data available in 1998. In addition, in these two reported cases [1, 2] of neural network prediction the annual mean sunspot numbers were used, simplifying the computation for the cost of accuracy.

The Solar Cycle prediction Panel of Space and Environment Centre issued a report that predicts the smoothed monthly maximum of Cycle 23 as 159 to occur between January 2000 and June 2001, which lays in boundary of our results.

There is possible to employ a different approach to predicting longer intervals. So far the presented results were obtain from month by month prediction, that is, to predict a sunspot number at time t_0 the previous values from series $t_{lag},...,t_2, t_1$ were used. It is much harder to obtain a good accuracy for predicting for longer period ahead. In Figure 4 we show results of prediction 1, 2 and 6 year ahead for cycle 23

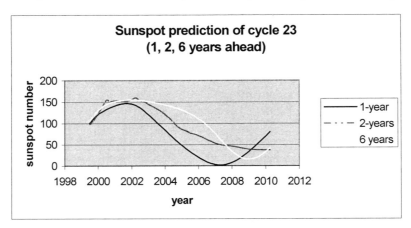

Figure 4. Prediction of cycle 23 1, 2 and 6 year ahead

and the beginning of cycle 24 (the expression "x year ahead" means here that in process of training and testing the data from months preceding $12*x$ was excluded from the process of evolving the solution and prediction).

5 Conclusion

We have used genetic programming for prediction the solar activity measured as monthly Wolf number. The results compare favourably with other extended research, when classical methods and neural networks were used for sunspot number prediction. Genetic programming is a non-linear data driven and adaptive technique that appears useful for forecasting. The paper proposes practical solutions for genetic programming approach to the problem of time series prediction.

References

1. Calvo, R.A., H.A. Ceccatto, R.D. Piacentini: Neural Network Prediction of Solar Activity, The Astrophysical Journal, 444, May 10 (1995) 916-921
2. Conway, A.J., K.P. Macpherson, G.Blacklaw, J.C.: A neural network prediction of solar cycle 23, Journal of Geophysical Research, vol.103, No.A12, Dec 1 (1988) 733-29, 742
3. Hathaway, D.H., R.M. Wilson, E.J. Reichmann: A synthesis of solar cycle prediction techniques, Journal of Geophysical Research – Space, Vol.104, No.A10 (1999)
4. Joselyn, J.A. , J.B.Anderson, Coffey H. K.Harvey. D.Hathaway, G.Heckman, E.Hildner, W.Mende, K.Schatten, R.Thompson, A.W.P.Thompson and O.R.White: Panel achieves consensus prediction of Solar Cycle 23, EOS, Trans.Amer.Geophys.Union, 78, (1997) 205, 211-212
5. Koza, J.: Genetic Programming. On the Programming of Computers by Means of Natural Selection, The MIT Press (1992)
6. Masters, T.: Neural, Novel & Hybrid Algorithms for Time Series Prediction, Wiley (1995)

Interpretation of the Richardson Plot in Time Series Representation

William Blackburn, Miguel Segui Prieto and Alfons Schuster

Faculty of Informatics, University of Ulster, Newtownabbey, BT37 0QB, Northern Ireland.
wt.blackburn@ulst.ac.uk

Abstract

In fractal analysis of a time series, the relationship between series length and ruler length may be represented graphically as a Richardson Plot. Fractal dimension measures can be estimated for particular ranges of ruler length, supported by the graphical representation.

This paper discusses Richardson Plots which have been obtained for several types of time series. From these, patterns have been identified with explanations. There is particular focus on local maxima and minima. Significant influences found present are described as *gradient* and *vertex effects*. The task - and implications - of partitioning the range of ruler lengths in determining fractal dimension measures is briefly addressed.

1. Introduction

Historically, the discovery of mathematical structures that did not fit the patterns of Euclid and Newton raised doubts about the appropriateness of the term Exact Sciences often associated with mathematics. These patterns and structures caused a revolution led by mathematicians such as Cantor, Peano, Von Koch and Sierpinski. Cantor conceived a set known as *Cantor's Dust* [7], constructed by dividing one-dimensional line segments, which seemed to bend the concept of dimension. Nevertheless, it was not until the 1960's when this phenomenon was extensively studied. Mandelbrot associated these shapes with forms found in nature, defining them as *fractals* [9].

The observation of fractal shapes in nature spawned considerable work in trying to model them with a particular class of mathematical equations. These equations are composed of basic elements which, when the equations are iterated, give birth to new elements similar in some aspect to the originals. This peculiarity is known as *self-similarity* and has been associated with shapes such as the *Koch snowflake*[4,5,9]. Richardson [10,13] showed how estimates of the lengths of international borders obtained by the Hausdorff approach[5] were inversely related to the length of the ruler used. Plotting these estimates against ruler length on a log-log graph - which became known as a Richardson Plot - produced a near linear association. Mandelbrot [9,10] interpreted the slope of this line to be a measure of the geometric dimensionality of the boundary. This value is fractional and lies between 1 and 2. Mandelbrot[9] used the term *fractal dimension*.

More generally a fractal dimension (FD) attempts to measure an object/figure at different scales, in order to extract a relation factor from these measurements[2,9]. This concept is itself a special case of a general dimension defined by Hausdorff[5], which permits the use of this measure (FD) even with sets which may not necessarily be self-similar over a wider range of space or time, such as the time series considered in this paper.

Kaye[7] has described how fine particles may be classified by the fractal dimension of their rugged boundaries. Kaye also showed how natural boundaries can possess two distinct fractal scalings leading to two fractal dimensions. These occur as two distinct straight sections on the log-log plot of length estimate against ruler length. Kaye used the terms *textural fractal dimension* (TFD) and *structural fractal dimension*(SFD) to describe the measures associated with short and longer rulers respectively.

Approaches to *normalisation* vary. Kaye normalised both length and ruler size using the maximum *Feret's diameter*, while the maximum horizontal distance (observed time) of a time series has been used elsewhere to normalise length only [6,14].

Caution has been advised in the interpretation of a Richardson Plot. For example, Avenir[1] referred to data lines fitted at coarse resolution exploration to shapes with a high aspect ratio as *fractal rabbits*. Kaye[7,8] also advised a restriction on the size of ruler to less than 30% of a maximum Feret's diameter in exploring a rugged profile, and further that if the aspect ratio is greater than 3, any low-value fractal should be treated warily.

2. Method

Several time series models were studied, including series with a small number of vertices and others sampled from negative exponential, random or sinusoidal distributions. Each comprised 200 observations.

For each series a procedure to estimate length from the first to the last value was followed, after Hausdorff[5]. This may be explained by reference to the graph. On the graph of each, all the points were joined in series by straight lines. Then starting at the (left) first observed value, an arc of a fixed size r (ruler) was drawn. The first interception on the joined series of this arc became the next position from where the arc of this radius was drawn again. This process continued until the 200th observation was covered. An appropiate measurement (C_r) was taken at the end of the series when the remaining part was less than a full ruler length. A count N_r of the number of completed rulers of length r was determined. A length $L_r = N_r \cdot r + C_r$ was recorded. This whole process was repeated with different sizes of ruler. Normalisation was not applied. The Richardson Plot was constructed for each model - this represents log L_r against log r from the above process.

Where calculated, fractal dimension measures were estimated from 1-m where m was the slope of a linear regression model fitted over an appropiate range of rulers.

The covering and other computational procedures were implemented as algorithms in Borland C++ and the graphics were studied using SPSS Version 9.0.

3. Observations

The Richardson Plots observed generally displayed decreasing trend left to right - the gradient was small initially, then steepening and finally decreasing to zero.

Several causes of variation from this general shape may be highlighted. One feature, named a *gradient effect*, is explained by a steep fall in the time series, whereby an incrementally longer ruler is associated with a significant reduction in contribution to total length. This effect was particularly prominent in graphs of random time series with steeply descending links between some points. A significant reduction in ruled length was also observed when there was a convex pattern in a sequence of decreasing plotted values. This was named a *curvature effect*.

Volatility was evident in the profiles of many of the Richardson Plots. One cause was named the *vertex effect*. Figure 1 illustrates this for a simple time series where the observations lie on two connected straight lines of equal length.

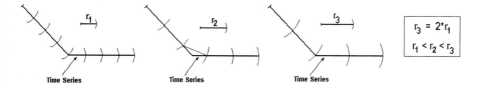

Figure 1: Vertex effect

In Figure 1 although ruler length r_2 lies between r_1 and r_3 in size, the corresponding measured time series lengths L_1 and L_3 are both greater than L_2. As L_1 and L_3 cover the series exactly, they correspond to local maxima on the Richardson Plot. Any other size of ruler which exactly covers the series to the vertex (say the left half) will also lead to a local maximum - for example $r_3/3$, $r_3/4$, etc. Furthermore, if r_2 cuts at equal distance either side of the vertex, L_2 corrresponds to a local minimum on the Richardson Plot. The model exhibited in Figure 2 further illustrates this effect.

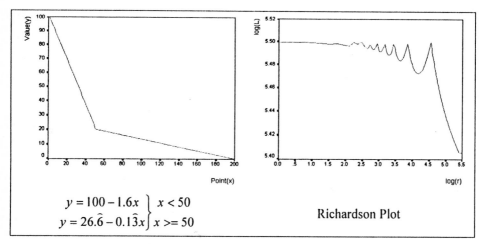

$$y = 100 - 1.6x \quad \rbrace \quad x < 50$$
$$y = 26.\overline{6} - 0.1\overline{3}x \rbrace \, x >= 50$$

Richardson Plot

Figure 2 : Effect of vertex in a time series on corresponding Richardson Plot

The Richardson Plots for observations drawn from a series of exponential functions with increasingly negative exponents are summarised in Figure 3. The progressive appearance and prominence of the local maxima and minima over the series can be observed. This can be attributed to the vertex effect.

In Figures 1 - 3 the mirror image of each series about the line connecting the start and end points have a corresponding Richardson Plot identical to that displayed.

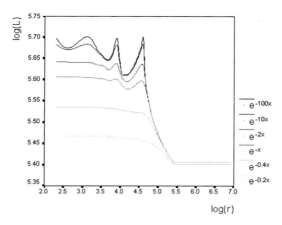

Figure 3 : Vertex effect on exponential series

Where a distinctive summit occurs in the original time series, increasing ruler size r may lead to a local maximum in the measured length L_r. In Figure 4, a short ruler r_1 provides a total series length L_1. Increasing the size of the ruler causes a decrease in measured total length initially, but if the summit is pronounced, a longer ruler r_n may produce a longer L_n, whereas a still longer ruler r_{n+1} leads to a shorter L_{n+1}. We refer to this as a *peak effect*, a development of the vertex effect (skewness in the summit as illustrated will add a curvature effect). Likewise a corresponding trough in the original time series will also lead to a corresponding local maximum on the Richardson Plot, a *valley effect*.

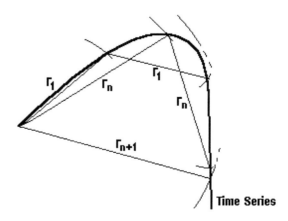

Figure 4: Peak effect

In a time series displaying a regular wave pattern (with amplitude small relative to the time scale) and a linear trend the occurrences and causes of local minima and maxima are readily identifiable. In Figure 5, for example, a ruler of length half the period of the cycle - or integer multiples of same - will correspond to local minima on the Richardson Plot.

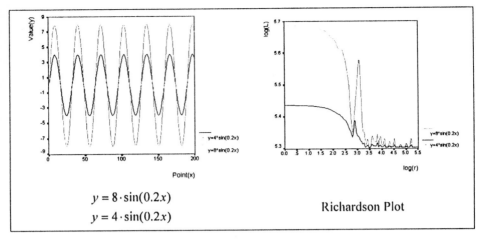

Figure 5: Cyclical time series with linear trend and associated Richardson Plot

Obviously with a time series having many segments of unequal length and varying patterns at different scales of enlargement the interpretation of volatility from the general shape of the associated Richardson Plot is more complex. Such volatility will influence the values of extracted fractal dimension measures such as TFD and SFD.

Further comparative studies were made using an approximation to the Hausdorff approach in which instead of placing the ruler along the time series it measures horizontally[6,14]. This method yielded significantly different Richardson Plots (practitioners tend to support employing a particular method throughout their related analyses and interpret derived fractal dimensions on a comparative basis). Figure 6 provides an illustrative example for a randomly generated time series. Associated TFD and SFD measures will differ in actual and relative order of size (the difference between the graphs in values represented on the vertical axes is due to normalisation used and does not affect the derived measures).

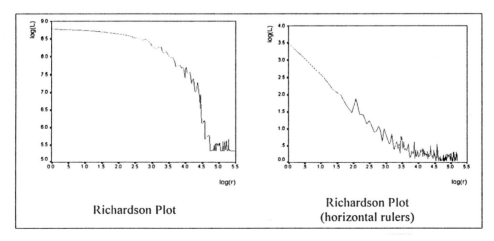

Figure 6: Comparison of Richardson Plots for random time series

4. Future Directions

Ongoing investigation includes study of the criteria and process for selecting boundaries in grouping the rulers, for example in determining TFD and SFD values. Some approaches might include identifying boundaries on the basis of maximising the linear correlation coefficient for each set of related points, partitioning to create maximum difference in gradient between say TFD and SFD, development of a guidance/expert system to support for example coping with local maxima and minima, or automated profile analyser with associated report generator.

The approach so far has used linear interpolation in covering the series using a particular ruler - the potential of non-linear interpolation merits consideration, particularly as a potential approach to reduce the related vertex effect.

Further current and planned studies include comparison with other related methods of analysis, such as rescaled range analysis (Hurst Exponent). Application to a continuous series of observations would facilitate comparison with associated methods such as wave analysis. Also the potential in convergence studies involving for example telecommunications and financial data [3,11,12] is being assessed.

References

[1] Avnir D. *Proceedings of Annual Meeting*, Materials Research Society, 1984
[2] Barnsley M. *Fractals Everywhere* -2nd ed.-. Boston; London: Academic Press, 1993
[3] Chorafas D. *Chaos Theory in Financial Markets*, Probus, 1994
[4] Edgar G.A. *Measure, Topology and Fractal Geometry*. Springer-Verlag: Undergraduate Texts in Mathematics, 1990
[5] Elert G. *The Chaos Hypertextbook*. http:/www.hypertextbook.com/chaos
[6] Gough N. A.J. *Fractal Analysis of Foetal Heart Rate Variability*, Physiol. Meas. 14, pp 309-315, 1993
[7] Kaye B. H. A *Random Walk Through Fractal Dimensions*, VCH, 1989
[8] Kaye B. H. *Fractal Rabbits are Real - Sometimes!* Lecture Notes, Laurentian University, 1984
[9] Mandelbrot B. *The Fractal Geometry of Nature*, WH Freeman & Co., 1977
[10] Mandlebrot B. *How Long is the Coast of Britain, Statistical Self-Similarity and Fractional Dimension*, Science 155, pp636-638, 1967
[11] Peters E. E. *Chaos and Order in the Capital Markets*, J.Wiley&Sons Inc., 1991
[12] Peters E. E. *Fractal Market Analysis*, J.Wiley&Sons Inc., 1994
[13] Richardson L. F. *The Problem of Contiguity: An Appendix to Statistics of Deadly Quarrels*, General Systems Yearbook 6, pp 139-87, Systems Science Institute, University of Louisville, 1961
[14] Schuster A. *Fractal Dimension of New-Born Heart Rate Variability*, Preliminary Project Report, Northern Ireland Bio-Engineering Centre, University of Ulster, 1994

B.

FINANCIAL ENGINEERING

Wavelet Methods in PDE Valuation of Financial Derivatives

M.A.H. Dempster, A. Eswaran & D.G. Richards

Centre for Financial Research

Judge Institute of Management

University of Cambridge

Email: {mahd2, ae206, dgr22}@cam.ac.uk

Web: www-cfr.jims.cam.ac.uk

Abstract. We investigate the application of a wavelet method of lines solution method to financial PDEs. We demonstrate the suitability of a numerical scheme based on biorthogonal interpolating wavelets to financial PDE problems where there are discontinuities or regions of sharp transitions in the solution. The examples treated are the Black Scholes PDE with discontinuous payoffs and a 3-dimensional cross currency swap PDE for which a speedup over standard finite difference methods of two orders of magnitude is reported.

1   Introduction

What are wavelets ? Wavelets are nonlinear functions which can be scaled and translated to form a basis for the Hilbert space $L^2(\mathbb{R})$ of square integrable functions. Thus wavelets generalize the trignometric functions given by $e^{ist}(s \in \mathbb{R})$ which generate the classical Fourier basis for L^2. It is therefore not surprising that wavelet and fast wavelet transforms exist which generalize the time to frequency map of the Fourier transform to pick up both the space and time behaviour of a function [11]. Wavelets have been used in the field of image compression and image analysis for quite some time. Indeed the main motivation behind the development of wavelets was the search for fast algorithms to compute compact representations of functions and data sets based on exploiting structure in the underlying functions. In the solution of PDE's using wavelets [1, 4, 5, 18, 19] functions and operators are expanded in a wavelet basis to allow a combination of the desirable features of finite-difference methods, spectral methods and front-tracking or adaptive grid approaches. The advantages of using wavelets to solve PDE's that arise in finance are that large classes of operators and functions which occur in this area are sparse, or sparse to some high accuracy, when transformed into the wavelet domain. Wavelets are also suitable for problems with multiple spatial scales (which occur frequently in financial problems) since they give an accurate representation of the solution in regions of sharp transitions and combine the advantages of both spectral and finite-difference methods.

In this paper we implement a wavelet method of lines scheme using biorthogonal wavelets to solve the Black Scholes PDE for option values with discontinuous payoff structures and a 3-dimensional cross currency swap PDE based on extended Vasicek interest rate models. We demonstrate numerically the advantages of using a wavelet based PDE method in solving these kind of problems. The paper is organized as follows. In Section 2 we give a brief introduction to wavelet theory. In Sections 3 and 4 we give an explanation of wavelet based PDE methods and explain the biorthogonal wavelet approach in more detail. Sections 5 and 6 contain respectively the problems and numerical results for the Black Scholes and cross currency swap PDEs and Section 7 concludes and describes research in progress.

2   Basic Wavelet Theory

We now give a brief introduction to wavelets for real valued functions of a real argument. Further detail can be found in the cited references and [6] and we shall extend the concepts needed for this paper to higher dimensions in the sequel.

Daubechies based wavelets

Consider two functions: the scaling function ϕ and the wavelet function ψ. The *scaling function* is the solution of a *dilation equation*

$$\phi(x) = \sqrt{2} \sum_{k=0}^{\infty} h_k \phi(2x - k), \tag{1}$$

where ϕ is normalised so that $\int_{-\infty}^{\infty} \phi(x)dx = 1$ and the *wavelet function* is defined in terms of the scaling function as

$$\psi(x) = \sqrt{2} \sum_{k=0}^{\infty} g_k \phi(2x - k). \tag{2}$$

We can build up a *orthonormal basis* for the *Hilbert space* $L^2(\mathbb{R})$ of (equivalence classes of) square integrable functions from the functions ϕ and ψ by dilating and translating them to obtain the *basis functions*:

$$\phi_{j,k}(x) = 2^{-j/2} \phi(2^{-j}x - k) = 2^{-j/2} \phi\left(\frac{x - 2^j k}{2^j}\right) \tag{3}$$

$$\psi_{j,k}(x) = 2^{-j/2} \psi(2^{-j}x - k) = 2^{-j/2} \psi\left(\frac{x - 2^j k}{2^j}\right). \tag{4}$$

In the above equations j is the *dilation* or *scaling parameter* and k is the *translation parameter*. All wavelet properties are specified through the coefficients $H := \{h_k\}_{k=0}^{\infty}$ and $G := \{g_k\}_{k=0}^{\infty}$ which are chosen so that dilations and translations of the wavelet ψ form an orthonormal basis of $L^2(\mathbb{R})$, i.e.

$$\int_{-\infty}^{\infty} \psi_{j,k}(x)\psi_{l,m}(x)dx = \delta_{jl}\delta_{km} \qquad j,k,l,m \in \mathbb{Z}_+, \tag{5}$$

where $\mathbb{Z}_+ := \{0, 1, 2, \dots\}$ and δ_{jl} is the Kronecker delta function.

Under these conditions for any function $f \in L^2(\mathbf{R})$ there exists a set $\{d_{jk}\}$ such that

$$f(x) = \sum_{j \in \mathbb{Z}_+} \sum_{k \in \mathbb{Z}_+} d_{jk} \psi_{j,k}(x), \tag{6}$$

$$d_{jk} := \int_{-\infty}^{\infty} f(x)\psi_{j,k}(x)dx. \tag{7}$$

It is usual to denote the spaces spanned by $\phi_{j,k}$ and $\psi_{j,k}$ over the parameter k, with j fixed by

$$\mathbf{V}_j := span_{k \in \mathbb{Z}_+} \phi_{j,k} \qquad \mathbf{W}_j := span_{k \in \mathbb{Z}_+} \psi_{j,k}. \tag{8}$$

In the expansion (6) functions with arbitrary small scales can be represented, however in practice there is a limit on how small the smallest structure can be.

(This could for example be dependent on a required grid size in a numerical computation as we shall see below.) To implement wavelet analysis on a computer, we need to have a bounded range and domain to generate approximations to functions $f \in L^2(\mathbb{R})$ and thus must limit H and G to *finite* sets termed *filters*. Approximation *accuracy* is specified by requiring that the wavelet function ψ satisfies

$$\int_{-\infty}^{\infty} \psi(x) x^m dx = 0 \qquad (9)$$

for $m = 0, \dots, M - 1$, which implies exact approximation for polynomials of degree $M - 1$. For *Daubechies wavelets* [6] the number of coefficients or the *length* L of the filters H and G is related to the number of vanishing moments M in (9) by $2M = L$. In addition elements of H and G are related by $g_k = (-1)^k h_{L-k}$ for $k = 0, \dots, L-1$ and the two finite sets of coefficients H and G are known in the signal processing literature as *quadrature mirror* filters. The coefficients H needed to define compactly supported wavelets with high degrees of regularity can be derived [6] and the usual notation to denote a Daubechies based wavelet defined by coefficients H of length L is D_L. Therefore on a computer an approximation subspace expansion would be in the form of a finite direct sum of finite dimensional vector spaces as

$$\mathbf{V_J} = \mathbf{W}_0 \oplus \mathbf{W}_1 \oplus \mathbf{W}_2 \oplus \cdots \oplus \mathbf{W}_{J-1} \oplus \mathbf{V}_0,$$

and the corresponding orthogonal wavelet series *approximation* to a continuous function f on a compact domain is given by

$$f(x) \approx \sum_k d_{0,k} \psi_{0,k}(x) + \cdots + \sum_k d_{J-1,k} \psi_{J-1,k}(x) + \sum_k s_{0,k} \phi_{0,k}, \qquad (10)$$

where J is the number of *multiresolution components* (or *scales*) and k ranges from 0 to the number of coefficients in the specified component. The spaces W_j and V_j are termed *scaling function* and *approximation subspaces* respectively. The coefficients $d_{0,k}, \dots, d_{J-1,k}, s_{0,k}$ are termed the *wavelet transform coefficients* and the functions $\phi_{J,k}$ and $\psi_{J,k}$ are the *approximating wavelet functions*. Some examples of basic wavelets are the *Haar wavelet* which is just a square wave (the indicator function of the unit interval), the *Daubechies wavelets* [6] and *Coiflet wavelets* [2].

Biorthogonal wavelets

Biorthogonal wavelets are a generalization of orthogonal wavelets first introduced by Cohen, Daubechies and Feauveau [3]. Biorthogonal wavelets are symmetric and do not introduce phase shifts in the coefficients. In biorthogonal wavelet analysis we have four basic function types $\phi, \psi, \tilde{\phi}$ and $\tilde{\psi}$. The functions ϕ and ψ are termed *mother* and *father* wavelets and the functions $\tilde{\phi}$ and $\tilde{\psi}$ are the *dual wavelets*. The father and mother wavelets are used to compute the wavelet coefficients as in the orthogonal case, but now the *biorthogonal wavelet approximation* of a continuous function on a compact domain is expressed in terms of the dual wavelet functions as

$$f(x) \approx \sum_k d_{0,k}\tilde{\psi}_{0,k}(x) + \cdots + \sum_k d_{J-1,k}\tilde{\psi}_{J-1,k}(x) + \sum_k s_{0,k}\tilde{\phi}_{J,k}. \tag{11}$$

In signal processing ϕ and ψ are used to *analyze* the signal and $\tilde{\phi}$ and $\tilde{\psi}$ are used to *synthesize* the signal. In general biorthogonal wavelets are not mutually orthogonal, but they do satisfy *biorthogonal* relationships of the form

$$\int \phi_{j,k}\tilde{\phi}_{j',k'}(x)dx = \delta_{j,j'}\delta_{k,k'}$$

$$\int \phi_{j,k}\tilde{\phi}_{j',k}(x)dx = 0$$

$$\int \psi_{j,k}\tilde{\phi}_{j,k'}(x)dx = 0$$

$$\int \psi_{j,k}\tilde{\psi}_{j',k'}(x)dx = \delta_{j,j'}\delta_{k,k'}, \tag{12}$$

where j, j', k, k' range over appropriate finite sets of integers.

3 Wavelets and PDE's

Wavelet based approaches to the solution of PDE's have been presented by Xu and Shann [21], Beylkin [1], Vasilyev *et al* [18,19], Prosser and Cant [14], Dahmen *et al* [5] and Cohen *et al* [4]. There are two main approaches to the numerical solution of PDEs using wavelets. Consider the most general form for a system of parabolic PDEs given by

$$\frac{\partial u}{\partial t} = F(x, t, u, \nabla u)$$

$$\Phi(x, t, u, \nabla u) = 0, \tag{13}$$

which describe the time evolution of a vector valued function u and the boundary conditions are possibly algebraic or differential constraints. The *wavelet-Galerkin* method assumes that the wavelet coefficients are functions of time. An appropriate wavelet decomposition for each component of the solution is substituted into (13) and a Galerkin projection is used to derive a nonlinear system of ordinary differential-algebraic equations which describe the time evolution of the wavelet coefficients. In a *wavelet-collocation* method (13) is evaluated at collocation points of the domain of u and a system of nonlinear ordinary differential-algebraic equations describing the evolution of the solution at these collocation points is obtained.

If we want the numerical algorithm to be able to resolve all structures appearing in the solution and also to be efficient in terms of minimising the number of unknowns, the *basis* of active wavelets and consequently the *computational grid* for the wavelet-collocation algorithm should adapt dynamically in time to reflect local changes in the solution. This adaptation of the wavelet basis or computational grid is based on analysis of the wavelet coefficients. The contribution of a particular wavelet to the approximation is significant if and only if the nearby structures of the solution have a size comparable with the wavelet scale. Thus using a *thresholding* technique a large number of the fine scale wavelets may be dropped in regions where the solution is smooth. In the wavelet-collocation method every wavelet is uniquely associated with a collocation point. Hence a collocation point can be omitted from the grid if the associated wavelet is omitted from the approximation. This property of the *multilevel* wavelet approximation allows local grid refinement up to a prescribed small scale without a drastic increase in the number of collocation points. A fast adaptive wavelet collocation algorithm for two dimensional PDE's is presented in [18] and a spatial discretization scheme using bi-orthogonal wavelets is implemented in [12–14]. The wavelet scheme is used in the latter to solve the *reacting Navier-Stokes* equations and the main advantage of the approach is that when the solution is computed in wavelet space it is possible to exploit sparsity in order to reduce storage costs and speed up solution times. We will now explain the wavelet-collocation method in greater detail.

The biorthogonal wavelet approach

The main difference in using biorthogonal systems is that we have both *primal* and *dual* basis functions derived from primal and dual scaling and wavelet functions. Biorthogonal wavelet systems are derived from a *paired* hierarchy of approximation subspaces

$$\cdots \mathbf{V}_{j-1} \subset \mathbf{V}_j \subset \mathbf{V}_{j+1} \cdots$$
$$\cdots \tilde{\mathbf{V}}_{j-1} \subset \tilde{\mathbf{V}}_j \subset \tilde{\mathbf{V}}_{j+1} \cdots .$$

(Note that here increasing j denotes refinement of the grid, although some authors in the wavelet literature use an increasing scale index j to indicate its coarsening.) For periodic discretizations $dim(\mathbf{V}_j) = 2^j$. The basis functions for these spaces are the *primal* scaling function ϕ and the *dual* scaling function $\tilde{\phi}$. Define two *innovation spaces* $\mathbf{W}_j$ and $\tilde{\mathbf{W}}_j$ such that

$$\mathbf{V}_{j+1} := \mathbf{V}_j \oplus \mathbf{W}_j$$
$$\tilde{\mathbf{V}}_{j+1} := \tilde{\mathbf{V}}_j \oplus \tilde{\mathbf{W}}_j \tag{14}$$

where $\tilde{\mathbf{V}}_j \perp \mathbf{W}_j$ and $\mathbf{V}_j \perp \tilde{\mathbf{W}}_j$. The innovation spaces so defined satisfy

$$\bigoplus_{j=0}^{\infty} \mathbf{W}_j = \mathbf{L}^2(\mathbb{R}) = \bigoplus_{j=0}^{\infty} \tilde{\mathbf{W}}_j \tag{15}$$

and the innovation space basis functions are ψ and $\tilde{\psi}$.

Biorthogonal Interpolating wavelet transform

The *biorthogonal interpolating wavelet transform* [8,9] has basis functions

$$\phi_{j,k}(x) = \phi(2^j x - k)$$

$$\psi_{j,k}(x) = \phi(2^{j+1} x - 2k - 1)$$

$$\tilde{\phi}_{j,k}(x) = \delta(x - x_{j,k}), \tag{16}$$

where $\delta(.)$ is the Dirac delta function. The wavelets are said to be *interpolating* because the primal scaling function ϕ to which they are related satisfies

$$\phi(k) = \begin{cases} 1 & k = 0, \\ 0 & k \neq 0. \end{cases}$$

The *projection* of a function f onto a space of scaling functions $\mathbf{V}_j$ is given (discretizing $[0,1]$) by

$$P_{\mathbf{V}_j} f(x) = \sum_{k=0}^{2^j} s^f_{j,k} \phi^{\square}_{j,k}(x), \tag{17}$$

where $s^f_{j,k}$ is defined as $< f, \tilde{\phi}_{j,k} >$ in terms of a suitable inner product and $\phi^{\square}$ is used to denote a *boundary* or *internal wavelet* given by

$$\phi^{\square}_{j,k}(x) = \begin{cases} \phi^L_{j,k}(x) & k = 0, \ldots, M - 1 \\ \phi_{j,k}(x) & k = N, \ldots, 2^j - M \\ \phi^R_{j,k}(x) & k = 2^j - M + 1, \ldots, 2^j. \end{cases} \tag{18}$$

Fast biorthogonal wavelet transform algorithm

The projection of a function f onto a *finite dimensional* scaling function space $\mathbf{V}_j$ is given as above by

$$P_{\mathbf{V}_j} f(x) = \sum_k < f(u), \tilde{\phi}_{j,k}(u) > \phi_{j,k}(x)$$

$$= \sum_k f(k/2^j) \phi_{j,k}(x)$$

$$= \sum_k s^f_{j,k} \phi_{j,k}(x), \tag{19}$$

where $s^f_{j,k} = f(k/2^j)$. The coefficients at resolution level j must be derived using

$$P_{\mathbf{W}_j} f(x) = P_{\mathbf{V}_{j+1}} f(x) - P_{\mathbf{V}_j} f(x)$$

$$\sum_l d^f_{j,l} \psi_{j,l}(x) = \sum_m s^f_{j+1,m} \phi_{j+1,m}(x) - \sum_n s^f_{j,n} \phi_{j,n}(x). \tag{20}$$

An arbitrary *wavelet coefficient* $d^f_{j,m}$ can be calculated from

$$d^f_{j,m} = s^f_{j+1,2m+1} - \sum_n s^f_{j,n} \phi(m - n + 1/2) = s^f_{j+1,2m+1} - \sum_n \Gamma_{mn} s^f_{j,n}, \tag{21}$$

where Γ is a square matrix of size $2^j \times 2^j$ for periodic discretizations defined by

$$\Gamma_{mn} := \phi(m - n + 1/2).$$

Because of the compact support of the primal scaling function this matrix has a band diagonal structure. The primal scaling function can be defined through the use of the *two scale* relation

$$\phi(x) = \sum_{\xi \in \Xi} \phi(\xi/2) \phi(2x - \xi). \tag{22}$$

where Ξ is a suitable subset of $\mathbb{Z}_+$. The smoothness of the primal scaling function is dictated by its $(M - 1)^{st}$ degree polynomial span which in turn depends on the $M + 1$ non-zero values of $\phi(\xi/2)$. The values $\phi(\xi/2)$ can be calculated using a explicit relation as in [13]. Fast transform methods for the evaluation of the wavelet and scaling function coefficients are given in [15, 17].

Irrespective of the choice of primal scaling function the transform vector that arises from the wavelet transform will have a structure of the form given below:

$$\{s^f_{J,0}, s^f_{J,1}, s^f_{J,2} \cdots \qquad \cdots s^f_{J,2^J-1}\}^T$$

$$\downarrow$$

$$\{d^f_{J-1,0}, \cdots, d^f_{J-1,2^{J-1}-1} \qquad | s^f_{J-1,0}, s^f_{J-1,1} \cdots s^f_{J-1,2^{J-1}-1}\}^T$$

$$\downarrow$$

$$\{d^f_{J-1,0}, \cdots, d^f_{J-1,2^{J-1}-1}, | d^f_{J-2,0}, \qquad \cdots d^f_{J-2,2^{J-2}-1} | s^f_{J-2,0} \cdots s^f_{J-2,2^{J-2}-1}\}^T$$

$$\downarrow$$

$$\{d^f_{J-1,0}, \cdots, | \cdots d^f_{J-P-1,0}, \qquad \cdots d^f_{J-P-1,2^{J-P-1}-1} | s^f_{J-P-1,0} \cdots s^f_{J-P-1,2^{J-P-1}-1}\}^T$$

$$\mathbf{W}_{J-1} \oplus \mathbf{W}_{J-2} \oplus \mathbf{W}_{J-3} \oplus \qquad \cdots \qquad \mathbf{V}_{J-P}$$

$$\tag{23}$$

involving P resolution levels and a finest discretization of 2^J.

Algorithm complexity

The number of of floating point operations required for the fast biorthogo-nal wavelet transform algorithm for P *resolution* levels is $2M \sum_{j=J-P}^{J} 2^j = 2^{J-P} M \{2^{P+1} - 1\}$. This comes from the fact that we require $2M$ filter coefficients to define the primal scaling function ϕ which spans the space of polynomials of degree less than $M - 1$. The calculation of the wavelet coefficients $d_{j,k}^f$ for a given resolution j can be accomplished in $2(M - 1) + 1$ floating point operations. The sub sampling process for the scaling function coefficients $s_{j,k}^f$ requires a further 2^j operations and a total of $2^{j+1} M$ operations are required per resolution j. Thus for fixed J and P the complexity of the fast interpolating wavelet transform algorithm is $O(M)$ [15]. Since the finest resolution in a PDE spatial grid of N points is $J = \log_2 N$, for fixed M and P the complexity of the transform is $O(N)$.

Decomposition of differential operators

If we define $\partial_J^{(n)}$ by

$$\partial_J^{(n)} f(x) := P_{V_J} \frac{d^n}{dx^n} P_{V_J} f(x),$$

then repeated application of the approximation subspace decomposition gives us

$$\partial_J^{(n)} f(x) := \left(P_{V_{J-P}} + \sum_{j=J-P}^{J-1} P_{W_j} \right) \frac{d^n}{dx^n} \left(P_{V_{J-P}} + \sum_{j=J-P}^{J-1} P_{W_j} \right) f(x). \quad (24)$$

For example, the decomposition of the first derivative operator $\frac{d}{dx}$ is given by

$$\partial_J = \left(P_{V_{J-P}} + \sum_{j=J-P}^{J-1} P_{W_j} \right) \frac{d}{dx} \left(P_{V_{J-P}} + \sum_{j=J-P}^{J-1} P_{W_j} \right), \quad (25)$$

where $\partial_J := W \partial_J^1 W^{-1}$ and W and W^{-1} are matrices denoting the forward and inverse transforms with

$$\partial_J^1 = P_{V_J} \frac{d}{dx} P_{V_J}. \quad (26)$$

We can analyze ∂_J^1 instead of ∂_J without loss of generality because the forward and inverse transforms are exact up to machine precision. The matrix ∂_J^1 has a band diagonal structure and can be treated as a finite difference scheme for analysis. The biorthogonal expansion for $\frac{df}{dx}$ requires information on the interaction between the differentiated and undifferentiated scaling functions along with information about both the primal and dual basis functions. Using the sampling nature of the dual scaling function ∂_J^1 can be written as

$$\partial_J^1 = 2^J \sum_{\alpha,k} s_{J,k}^f \frac{d\phi^\square}{dx} \big|_{x=\alpha-k}, \qquad (27)$$

and using equation (18) we get

$$\partial_J^1 = \begin{cases} 2^J \sum_{\alpha,k} s_{J,k}^f \frac{d\phi^L}{dx} \big|_{x=\alpha-k} \phi_{J,\alpha}^L(x) & k = 0, \dots, M-1 \\ 2^J \sum_{\alpha,k} s_{J,k}^f \frac{d\phi}{dx} \big|_{x=\alpha-k} \phi_{J,\alpha}(x) & k = M, \dots, 2^J - M \\ 2^J \sum_{\alpha,k} s_{J,k}^f \frac{d\phi^R}{dx} \big|_{x=\alpha-k} \phi_{J,\alpha}^R(x) & k = 2^J - M + 1, \dots, 2^J. \end{cases} \qquad (28)$$

The entire operator ∂_J^1 can be determined provided the values of $r_{\alpha-k}^{(1)} = \frac{d\phi}{dx}\big|_{x=\alpha-k}$ can be obtained. An approach to determining filter coefficients for higher order derivatives is given in [13].

Extension to multiple dimensions

The entire wavelet multiresolution framework presented so far can be extended to several spatial dimensions by taking straightforward tensor products of the appropriate 1D wavelet bases. The imposition of boundary conditions on nonlinearly bounded domains is nontrivial, but these are fortunately rare in derivative valuation PDE problems which are usually Cauchy problems on a strip.

The fast biorthogonal interpolating wavelet transform used with wavelet collocation methods for problems posed over d-dimensional domains exhibits better complexity than its alternatives. Indeed, since one basis function is needed for each collocation point, using a spatial grid of n points in each dimension there are $N := n^d$ points in the spatial domain to result in transform complexity $O(n^d)$ – versus $O(n^d \log_2 n)$ for the *Fast Fourier Transform* (where applicable), $O(n^{2d})$ for an *explicit* finite difference scheme and $O(n^{3d})$ for a *Crank-Nicholson* or *implicit* scheme (which makes these methods impractical for $d > 2$, *cf.* [7]).

4 Wavelet Method of Lines

In a traditional finite difference scheme partial derivatives are replaced with algebraic approximations at grid points and the resulting system of algebraic equations is solved to obtain the numerical solution of the PDE. In the *wavelet method of lines* we transform the PDE into a vector system of ODEs by replacing the spatial derivatives with their wavelet transform approximations but retain the time derivatives. We then solve this vector system of ODEs using a suitable stiff ODE solver. We have implemented both a fourth order Runge Kutta method and a method based on the backward differentiation formula (LSODE) developed at the Lawrence Livermore Laboratories [16]. The fundamental complexity of this method is $O(\tau n^d)$ for space and time discretizations of size n and τ respectively over domains of dimension d (*cf.* §3, [16]).

An example

Consider a first order nonlinear hyperbolic *transport* PDE defined over an interval $\Omega = [x_l, x_r]$:

$$\frac{\partial u}{\partial t} = \frac{\partial u}{\partial x} + S^{u/\rho} \qquad x \notin \partial\Omega$$

$$\frac{\partial u}{\partial t} = -\chi^L(t) \qquad\qquad x = x_l$$

$$\frac{\partial u}{\partial t} = -\chi^R(t) \qquad\qquad x = x_r.$$

The numerical scheme is applied to the wavelet transformed counterpart of the above equations

$$\frac{\partial}{\partial t}\wp_{J-P}^{J-1} u = -\partial_J^{(1)} u + \wp_{J-P}^{J-1} S^{u/\rho} \qquad x \notin \partial\Omega,$$

where $\wp_{J-P}^{J-1} := \left(P_{\mathbf{V}_{J-P}} + \sum_{i=J-P}^{J-1} P_{\mathbf{W}_i} \right)$ and $\partial_J^{(1)}$ is the standard decomposition of $\frac{d}{dx}$ defined as $\wp_{J-P}^{J-1} \frac{d}{dx} \wp_{J-P}^{J-1}$. In using the multiresolution strategy to discretize the problem we represent the domain $P+1$ times, where P is the number of different resolutions in the discretization, because of the P wavelet spaces and the coarse resolution scaling function space $\mathbf{V}_{J-P}, P \geq 1$. In the transform domain each representation of the solution defined at some resolution p should be supplemented by boundary conditions and [15] shows how to impose boundary conditions in the both the scaling function spaces and the wavelet spaces.

5   Financial Derivative Valuation PDEs

In this section we introduce briefly the PDEs for financial derivative valuation and the products we have valued using the wavelet method of lines described above. More details may be found in [7, 20].

Black Scholes products

We have applied wavelet methods to solve the Black Scholes PDE for a vanilla European call option and two binary options. The *Black Scholes* quasilinear parabolic *PDE* is given by

$$\frac{\partial C}{\partial t} + \frac{1}{2}\sigma^2 S^2 \frac{\partial^2 C}{\partial S^2} + rS\frac{\partial C}{\partial S} - rC = 0 \tag{29}$$

where S is the *stock price*, σ is *volatility*, r is the *risk free rate* of interest. We transform (29) to the *heat diffusion* equation

$$\frac{\partial u}{\partial \tau} = \frac{\partial^2 u}{\partial x^2} \quad \text{for} \quad -\infty < x < \infty, \quad \tau > 0$$

with the transformations

$$S := Ke^x, \quad t := T - \frac{2\tau}{\sigma^2}$$

$$C := e^{-1/2(k-1)x - 1/4(k+1)^2\tau} Ku(x, \tau)$$

where $k = 2r/\sigma^2$, K is the *exercise price* and T is the *time to maturity* of the option to be valued. The boundary conditions for the PDE depend on the specific type of option. For a vanilla *European call option* the boundary conditions are:

$$C(0, t) = 0, \quad C(S, t) \sim S \quad \text{as} \quad S \to \infty$$

$$C(S, T) = \max(S - K, 0).$$

The boundary conditions for the transformed PDE are:

$$u(x, \tau) = 0 \quad \text{as} \quad x \to -\infty,$$

$$u(x,\tau) = e^{1/2(k+1)x+1/4(k+1)^2\tau} \quad \text{as} \quad x \to \infty,$$

$$u(x,0) = \max(e^{1/2(k+1)x} - e^{1/2(k-1)x}, 0).$$

The first type of binary option that we solved was the *cash-or-nothing call* option with a payoff given by

$$\Pi(S) = B\mathcal{H}(S - K),$$

where $\mathcal{H}$ is the Heaviside function, i.e the payoff is B if at expiry the stock price $S > K$. The boundary conditions for this option in the transformed domain are

$$u(x,\tau) = 0 \quad \text{as} \quad x \to -\infty,$$

$$u(x,\tau) = \frac{B}{K}e^{\frac{1}{2}(k-1)x+\frac{1}{4}(k+1)^2\tau} \quad \text{as} \quad x \to \infty,$$

$$u(x,0) = e^{\frac{1}{2}(k-1)x}\frac{B}{K}\mathcal{H}(Ke^x - K).$$

The second binary option we solved was a *supershare call* [20] option that pays an amount $1/d$ if the stock price lies between K and $K + d$ at expiry. Its payoff is thus

$$\Pi(S) = \frac{1}{d}(\mathcal{H}(S - K) - \mathcal{H}(S - K - d))$$

which becomes a *delta function* in the limit $d \to 0$. The initial boundary condition for this option is

$$u(x,0) = \frac{1}{dK}e^{\frac{1}{2}(k-1)x}(\mathcal{H}(Ke^x - K) - \mathcal{H}(Ke^x - K - d)).$$

For all of the above options the solution is transformed back to real variables using the transformation

$$C(S,t) = K^{\frac{1}{2}(k+1)}S^{\frac{1}{2}(1-k)}e^{\frac{1}{8}(k+1)^2\sigma^2(T-t)}u(\log(S/K), 1/2\sigma^2(T - t)),$$

where $k = 2r/\sigma^2$. There are closed form solutions for all the above options (see for example [20]). The Black Scholes solution for the vanilla European call option is

$$C(S,t) = SN(d_1) - Ke^{-r(T-t)}N(d_2)$$

$$d_1 := \frac{\log(S/K) + (r + \frac{1}{2}\sigma^2)(T - t)}{\sigma\sqrt{(T - t)}}$$

$$d_2 := \frac{\log(S/K) + (r - \frac{1}{2}\sigma^2)(T - t)}{\sigma\sqrt{(T - t)}}.$$

The solution for a cash or nothing call is

$$C(S, t) = Be^{-r(T-t)}N(d_2).$$

The solution for the supershare option is

$$C(S, t) = \frac{1}{d}e^{-r(T-t)}(N(d_2) - N(d_3))$$

$$d_3 := d_2 - \frac{\log(1 + \frac{d}{K})}{\sigma\sqrt{T - t}}.$$

Cross currency swap products

A *cross currency swap* is a derivative contract between two counterparties to exchange cash flows in their respective domestic currencies. Such contracts are an increasing share of the global swap markets and are individually structured products with many complex valuations. With two economies, i.e one domestic and one foreign, there are different term structure processes and risk preferences in each economy and a rate of currency exchange between them. We will model the interest rates in single factor a extended Vasicek framework.

To value any European-style derivative security whose payoff is a measurable function with respect to a filtration $\mathcal{F}_T$ we may derive a PDE for its value. The *domestic* and *foreign bond prices* and *exchange rate* are specified in terms of the driftless Gaussian state variables X_d, X_f and X_S whose corresponding processes $\mathbf{X}_d$, $\mathbf{X}_f$ and $\mathbf{X}_S$ are sufficient statistics for movements in the term structure dynamics. Let $V = V(X_d, X_f, X_S, t)$ be the *domestic value function* of a security with a terminal payoff measurable with respect to $\mathcal{F}_T$ and no intermediate payments, and assume that $V \in C^{2,1}\left(\mathbb{R}^3 \times [0, T)\right)$. Then the *normalised domestic value* process, defined by

$$V^*(t) := \frac{V(t)}{P_d(t, T)}, \tag{30}$$

satisfies the quasilinear parabolic PDE with time dependent coefficients given by

$$-\frac{\partial V^{\bullet}}{\partial t} = \frac{1}{2}\lambda_d^2\frac{\partial^2 V^{\bullet}}{\partial X_d^2} + \frac{1}{2}\lambda_f^2\frac{\partial^2 V^{\bullet}}{\partial X_f^2} + \frac{1}{2}H^{SS}\frac{\partial^2 V^{\bullet}}{\partial X_S^2} + H^{df}\frac{\partial^2 V^{\bullet}}{\partial X_d\partial X_f} + H^{dS}\frac{\partial^2 V^{\bullet}}{\partial X_d\partial X_S} + H^{fS}\frac{\partial^2 V^{\bullet}}{\partial X_f\partial X_S},$$

$$(31)$$

on $\mathbb{R}^3 \times [0, T]$. Here the functions H^{SS}, H^{df}, H^{dS} and H^{fS} are defined by

$$H^{SS}(s) := G_d^2(s)\lambda_d^2(s) + G_f^2(s)\lambda_f^2(s) + \sigma_S^2(s) - 2\rho_{df}(s)G_d(s)\lambda_d(s)G_f(s)\lambda_f(s)$$

$$+2\rho_{dS}(s)G_d(s)\lambda_d(s)\sigma_S(s) - 2\rho_{fS}(s)G_f(s)\lambda_f(s)\sigma_S(s)$$

$$H^{df}(s) := \rho_{df}(s)\lambda_d(s)\lambda_f(s)$$

$$H^{dS}(s) := \lambda_d(s)\left[G_d(s)\lambda_d(s) - \rho_{df}(s)G_f(s)\lambda_f(s) + \rho_{dS}(s)\sigma_S(s)\right]$$

$$H^{fS}(s) := \lambda_f(s)\left[\rho_{df}(s)G_d(s)\lambda_d(s) - G_f(s)\lambda_f(s) + \rho_{fS}(s)\sigma_S(s)\right] \qquad (32)$$

and the volatility is of the form

$$\sigma_k(t, T) = [G_k(T) - G_k(t)]\lambda_k(t) \quad k = d, f. \qquad (33)$$

$$G_k(t) := \frac{1 - e^{-\xi_k t}}{\xi_k}, \quad \lambda_k(t) = e^{\xi_k t}\kappa_k(t) \qquad k = d, f, \qquad (34)$$

for some *mean reversion rates* ξ_d and ξ_f, where $\kappa_k(t)$ is the *prospective variability* of the short rate. For the derivation of the PDE and further details of the extended Vasicek model see [7]. For a standard European-style derivative security we solve the PDE with the appropriate boundary conditions.

The most common type of cross-currency swap is the exchange of floating or fixed rate interest payments on *notional principals* Z_d and Z_f in the domestic and foreign currencies respectively. We can also have a short rate or *diff swap* where payments are swapped over $[0, T]$ on a domestic principal, with the floating rates based on the short rates in each country. A *LIBOR currency swap* is a swap of interest rate payments on two notional principals where the interest rates are based on the LIBOR for each country. The swap period $[0, T]$ is divided into N periods and payments are denoted by p_j. Now we describe precisely the deal that we are going to value which differs from that of [7], see also [10].

Fixed-for-fixed cross-currency swap with a Bermudan option to cancel

The cross-currency swap tenor is divided into N_{cpn} *coupon periods*. The start and end dates for these periods are given by $T_0, \ldots, T_{N_{cpn}}$ and cashflows are exchanged at coupon period end dates $T_1, \ldots, T_{N_{cpn}}$. Typically, the swap cashflows consist of coupon payments at annualized rates on notional amounts Z_d for the first currency Z_f for the second currency. In addition, notional amounts Z_d and Z_f may be exchanged at the swap start and/or end dates. The size of a coupon payment is given by: *coupon rate × notional amount × coupon period day count*. Both interest rates R_f and R_d are *fixed* at the outset of the contract, as opposed to those for a LIBOR swap where they are floating [7]. There is no path-dependence in the payoffs, i.e. the path taken is not relevant because the payoff is fully determined by component values at the payment date. Payments p_j are made at at the end of each period at time t_j^- of size

$$p_j = \delta_j \left(S(t_j^-) R_f Z_f - m - Z_d R_d \right),$$

where m is the *margin* to the issuing counterparty. This is the terminal condition for the period $[t_{j-1}, t_j)$. The *value* of the deal is the sum of the present values of all payments.

When the contract has a *Bermudan option to cancel*, one of the counterparties is given an option to cancel all the future payments at times $t_1, \ldots, t_n$. Typically $t_1, \ldots, t_n$ are set a fixed number of calendar days before the start date of each period, i.e $t_1 = T_{N_{cpn}-1-n} - \Delta, \ldots, T_{N_{cpn}-1} - \Delta$, where Δ is the *notification period*. We assume that net principal amounts $(Z_d - S(0)Z_f))$ are paid at time 0 and at time t_N if the option is *not* cancelled, or at time t_{k+1} if the option is cancelled. The *terminal condition* at t_N^- is given by

$$V(t_N^-) = \delta_N \left(S(t_N^-) Z_f (1 + R_f) - m - Z_d (R_d + 1) \right). \tag{35}$$

When the option to cancel is exercised at t_k, we exchange coupon payments due on $T_{N_{cpn}-2-n+k}$ and notional amounts. The holder of the option will terminate the deal if the expected future value of the deal is less than the termination cost. Thus the decision at time $t_{k+1-\Delta}$ is to *continue* if

$$P_d(t_{k+1} - \Delta, t_{k+1}^-) V(t_{k+1}) < S(t_{k+1} - \Delta) Z_f P_f(t_{k+1} - \Delta, t_{k+1}^-) - P_d(t_{k+1} - \Delta, t_{k+1}^-) Z_d.$$

The deal is valued by dynamic programming backward recursion, solving the PDE for the last period using the terminal condition (35) and stepping backwards in time using the condition

$$V(t_{k+1} - \Delta) = \min\{P_d(t_{k+1} - \Delta, t_{k+1}^-)V(t_{k+1}),$$

$$S(t_{k+1} - \Delta)Z_f P_f(t_{k+1} - \Delta, t_{k+1}^-) - P_d(t_{k+1} - \Delta, t_{k+1}^-)Z_d\}$$

for earlier periods. We then add on the exchange of principals at time 0.

6 Numerical Results

The numerical results using a 1D and 3D implementation of the wavelet method of lines algorithm and the LSODE stiff vector ODE solver [16] are given below. In each case the numerical deal values are compared with a standard PDE solution technique and the known exact solution. Practical speed-up factors are reported which increase with both boundary condition discontinuities and spatial dimension.

European call option

Stock price: 10   *Strike price*: 10   *Interest rate*: 5%   *Volatility*: 20%   *Time to maturity*: 1 Year

The exact value of this option is: **1.04505**.

Comparing tables 1 and 2 shows a speedup of **1.9**.

Table 1. Wavelet Method of Lines Solution

Space Steps	Time Steps	Value	Solution Time in Seconds
64	60	1.03515	.05
128	100	1.04220	.10
256	200	1.04502	.13
512	200	**1.04505**	**.30**
1024	200	1.04505	.90

Table 2. Crank-Nicolson Finite Difference Method

Space Steps	Time Steps	Value	Solution Time in Seconds
64	60	1.03184	.02
128	100	1.04184	.04
256	200	1.04426	.09
512	200	1.04486	.16
1024	200	1.04501	.30
2000	200	**1.04505**	**.57**

Cash-or-nothing call

The option with the same parameters as the European call.

The payoff is $B.\mathcal{H}(S - K)$, where $B := 3$ is the cash given, with a single discontinuity.

The exact value of this option is: **1.59297**.

Comparing tables 3 and 4 shows a speed up of **2.5**.

Table 3. Wavelet Method of Lines Solution

Space Steps	Time Steps	Value	Solution Time in Seconds
128	100	1.49683	.10
256	200	1.54904	.13
512	200	1.59216	.30
1024	400	**1.59288**	**1.02**

Table 4. Crank-Nicolson Finite Difference Scheme

Space Steps	Time Steps	Value	Solution Time in Seconds
128	200	1.46296	.04
256	400	1.53061	.10
512	400	1.56391	.18
1024	400	1.58046	.31
2048	800	1.58872	1.35
4096	800	**1.59285**	**2.56**

Supershare call

Stock price: 10   *Strike price*: 10   *Parameter* d: 3   *Interest rate*: 5%   *Volatility*: 20%

Time to maturity: 1 Year

The option pays an amount $1/d$ if the stock price lies between K and $K + D$ i.e. the option has a payoff $1/d.(\mathcal{H}(S - K) - \mathcal{H}(S - K - D))$ with two discontinuities. The exact value of this option is: **0.13855.**

Comparing tables 5 and 6 shows a speed up of **4.9**.

Table 5. Wavelet Method of Lines Solution

Space Steps	Time Steps	Value	Solution Time in Seconds
128	100	0.12796	.10
256	200	0.13310	.14
512	200	0.13808	.30
1024	400	**0.13848**	**1.04**

Table 6. Crank-Nicolson Finite Difference Scheme

Space Steps	Time Steps	Value	Solution Time in Seconds
128	200	0.12369	.04
256	400	0.13290	.09
512	400	0.13435	.16
1024	400	0.13666	.34
2048	800	0.13787	1.35
4096	800	0.13800	2.56
8000	800	**0.13835**	**5.11**

Cross Currency Swap

Domestic fixed rate: 10%, *Foreign fixed rate:* 10%

The exact value of this option is: **0.0**

Comparing tables 7 and 8 shows a speed up exceeding **81**.

Table 7. Wavelet Method of Lines Solution

Discretization	Value	Solution Time in Seconds
20 X 8 X 8 X 8	-0.00082	1.2
20 X 16 X 16 X 16	-0.00052	6.54
20 X 32 X 32 X 32	-0.00047	40.40
40 X 64 X 64 X 64	**-0.00034**	**410.10**
100 X 128 X 128 X 128	-0.00028	4240.30
160 X 256 X 256 X 256	-0.00025	53348.10

Table 8. Explicit Finite Difference Scheme

Discretization	Value	Solution Time in Seconds
20 X 8 X 8 X 8	-0.00109	0.28
20 X 16 X 16 X 16	-0.00101	1.70
20 X 32 X 32 X 32	-0.00074	16.82
40 X 64 X 64 X 64	-0.00058	188.10
100 X 128 X 128 X 128	-0.00046	2421.6
160 X 256 X 256 X 256	**-0.00038**	**33341.8**

7   Conclusions and Future Directions

The wavelet method of lines performs well on problems with one spatial dimension and discontinuities or spikes in the payoff. For example in the supershare option the wavelet method requires a lower discretization than the Crank Nicolson finite difference scheme for equivalent accuracy (3 decimal places), as the discontinuities in the payoff can be resolved better in wavelet space. We also see that for the (prototype) cross currency swap PDE in 3 spatial dimensions the wavelet method outperforms the (tuned) explicit finite difference scheme by approximately two orders of magnitude – a very promising result. One of the important things to note is that $O(N)$ wavelet based PDE methods generalize $O(N \log N)$ spectral methods without their drawbacks. This lower basic complexity feature of the wavelet PDE method makes it suitable to solve higher dimensional PDEs. Further, to improve basic efficiency of the method we are currently implementing an adaptive wavelet technique in which the wavelet coefficients are thresholded at each time step (*cf.* §3). This should result in an improvement in both speed and memory usage because of sparse wavelet representation. Such a technique has resulted in a further order magnitude speedup in other applications [18]. Future work will thus involve applying the wavelet technique to solve cross currency swap problems with two and three factor interest rate models for each currency to result in solving respectively 5 and 7 spatial dimension parabolic PDEs.

References

[1] BEYLKIN, G. (1993). Wavelets and fast numerical algorithms. Lecture Notes for Short Course, AMS 93.

[2] BEYLKIN, G., R. COIFMAN AND V. ROKHLIN (1991). Fast wavelet transforms and numerical algorithms. *Comm. Pure and Appl. Math* **44** 141–183.

[3] COHEN, A., I. DAUBECHIES AND J. FEAUVEAU (1992). Biorthogonal bases of compactly supported wavelets. *Comm. Pure Appl Math* **45** 485–560.

[4] COHEN, A., S. KABER, S. MULLER AND M. POSTEL (2000). Accurate adaptive multiresolution scheme for scalar conservation laws. Preprint, LAN University Paris.

[5] DAHMEN, W., S. MULLER AND T. SCHLINKMANN (1999). On a robust adaptive multigrid solver for convection-dominated problems. Technical report, RWTH Aachen. IGPM Report No 171.

[6] DAUBECHIES, I. (1992). *Ten Lectures on Wavelets*. SIAM, Philadelphia.

[7] DEMPSTER, M. A. H. AND J. P. HUTTON (1997). Numerical valuation of cross-currency swaps and swaptions. In *Mathematics of Derivative Securities*, eds. M. A. H. Dempster and S. R. Pliska. Cambridge University Press, 473 – 503.

[8] DESLAURIERS, G. AND S. DUBUC (1989). Symmetric iterative interpolation processes. *Constr. Approx* **5** 49–68.

[9] DONOHO, D. (1992). Interpolating wavelet tansforms. Presented at the NATO Advanced Study Institute conference, Ciocco, Italy.

[10] MAGEE, B. (1999). Pay attention to interest. *Risk* (October) 67–71.

[11] POLIKAR, R. The wavelet tutorial. http://www.public.iastate.edu/~ rpolikar/wavelet.html.

[12] PROSSER, R. AND R. CANT (1998). Evaluation of nonlinear terms using interpolating wavelets. Working paper, CFD laboratory, Department of Engineering, University of Cambridge.

[13] PROSSER, R. AND R. CANT (1998). On the representation of derivatives using interpolating wavelets. Working paper, CFD laboratory, Department of Engineering, University of Cambridge.

[14] PROSSER, R. AND R. CANT (1998). On the use of wavelets in computational combustion. Working paper, CFD laboratory, Department of Engineering, University of Cambridge.

[15] PROSSER, R. AND R. CANT (1998). A wavelet-based method for the efficient simulation of combustion. *J. Comp. Phys* **147** (2) 337–361.

[16] SCHIESSER, W. (1991). *The Numerical Method of Lines.* Academic Press, Inc.

[17] SWELDENS, W. (1996). Building your own wavelets at home. ACM SIGGRAPH Course Notes.

[18] VASILYEV, O., D. YUEN AND S. PAOLUCCI (1996). A fast adaptive wavelet collocation algorithm for multi-dimensional PDEs. *J. Comp. Phys* **125** 498–512.

[19] VASILYEV, O., D. YUEN AND S. PAOLUCCI (1997). Wavelets: an alternative approach to solving PDEs. Research Report, Supercomputer Institute, University of Minnesota.

[20] WILMOTT, P., S. HOWISON AND J. DEWYNNE (1995). *The Mathematics of Financial Derivatives.* Cambridge University Press.

[21] XU, J. AND W. SHANN (1992). Galerkin-wavelet methods for two-point boundary value problems. *Numerische Mathematik* **63** 123–144.

Fast Algorithms for Computing Corporate Default Probabilities

Amir Atiya

Caltech 136-93,Pasadena, CA 91125, USA, Email: amir@deep.caltech.edu

Abstract. In this paper we consider the corporate default problem. One of the well-known approaches is to model the dynamics of the assets of the firm, and compute the probability that the assets fall below a threshold (which is related to the firm's liabilities). When modeling the asset value dynamics as a jump-diffusion process (the most realistic model), a serious computational problem arises. In this paper we propose a fast method for computing the default probability. The new method achieves significant acceleration over the available approach.

1 Introduction

There are two main approaches for corporate default prediction. The first approach uses financial statement data as inputs and uses a neural network or a regression model to predict the binary outcome default/no default (see for example [1]). The premise here is that the financial statement data such as revenues, earnings, debt, etc reflect the fundamental health of the firm. The other approach, invented by Merton [2] (see also [3]), is more of a "first principles approach". It is based on modeling the value of the firm's assets. The ability of the firm to fulfill its credit obligations is greatly affected by the relative value of the firm's assets to its liabilities. By modeling the asset value as some process such as a Brownian motion, the probability of default can be obtained by computing the probability that the assets will fall below some threshold that is related to the firm's liabilities. The advantage of such a model is that it gives the probability of default, rather than simply a default prediction. That can help in quantifying the risk for a credit portfolio. The drawbacks of such a model is the computational load involved in computing the default probability through lengthy Monte Carlo procedures. There are no closed-form solutions, except for the simple Brownian motion asset dynamics model. The more realistic jump diffusion process needs a computationally extensive simulation. In this paper we propose a fast Monte Carlo procedure to compute the default probability for such a model. The proposed procedure achieves several orders of magnitude speed-up over the conventional approach.

2 Description of the Problem

Merton [4] considered the jump-diffusion process, defined as

$$dx = \mu dt + \sigma dw - adq \tag{1}$$

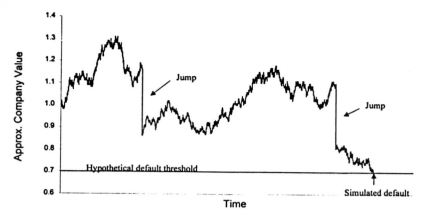

Figure 1: The evolution of the firm's asset value which follows a jump-diffusion process

where x is the log of the asset value (the asset value is a log-normal process), and μ, σ and a represent respectively the drift term, the volatility of the diffusion component, and the jump magnitude (which could be a constant or random). The jump instances are typically governed by a Poisson process, say of rate λ. The diffusion term represents the gradual day-to-day changes in the firm's prospects and value. On the other hand, the jump term represents sudden events, for example the loss of a major contract, or even gradual events that accummulate but are released by the management (to the investors and debtors) in one shot.

Let the initial condition be $x(0) = x_0$. Assume that we would like to estimate the probability of default in some interval $[0, T]$ (T could represent the horizon of the debt). We can assume that the default threshold is zero (we can always translate x to achieve that).

3 Overview of the Method

The main problem with evaluating the default probability is that no analytical solution is known for the level crossing problem for a jump diffusion process. Hence we have to resort to simulations to solve our problem. Generating the diffusion process using a Monte Carlo simulation is very slow and impractical, especially in view of the fact that we have to perform the Monte Carlo simulation for every debt instrument in the portfolio, and this whole procedure has to be repeated many times if the parameters of the model have to be tuned. A known rule of thumb is to use a time sampling rate of 6 points a day, that is $6 \times 250 = 1500$ points a year. So for example if the horizon of the debt is 5 years, we have to evaluate 7500 points for every Monte Carlo iteration.

The method we propose is also a Monte Carlo-type method. The distinction here is that we typically have to evaluate 6 or 7 points every Monte Carlo iteration, thus it is several orders of magnitude faster than the plain Monte Carlo approach. The method is also very flexible. It can handle the following cases:

1) the case when the shock magnitudes obey a certain density rather than constant a.
2) the case when the shocks are correlated accross debt instruments.
3) the case when the shocks obey a different density from Poisson, they obey a Poisson density with time varying rate of arrival, or if they are serially correlated. For example one might consider the case where shocks occur in bursts.

The basic idea of the method is that first we generate the shock instances from the Poisson distribution. In between any two shocks the state variable follows a pure diffusion process. But, we know that for a diffusion process the level crossing problem has a closed form solution. The level crossing problem is often referred to as the first passage problem (see [5]). A closed form solution exists only for a diffusion process [6]. We utilize this solution and combine it with whether the shocks have caused default to obtain an estimate for the default probability for this particular run. We repeat this experiment in a Monte Carlo fashion, and compute the average to obtain our estimate of the default probability. Since typically there will be about 6 or 7 shocks for the horizon considered, we need to perform only this amount of computations per Monte Carlo iteration. The details of the method are described in the next section.

4 Details of the Proposed Method

Consider Figure 2 for the definitions of the variables. As we mentioned, we generate the shock times $T_1, T_2, \cdots$ from a Poisson distribution. Then we generate the state variables at the times $T_1, T_2, \cdots$ immediately before the shock (say $x(T_1^-), x(T_2^-), \cdots$). These are generated from a Gaussian distribution with appropriate mean and standard deviation. Consider for example that we would like to generate $x(T_i^-)$. Since we know the value of $x(T_{i-1}^+)$ (the value of the state at T_{i-1} but immediately after the shock), and we know that the process from $x(T_{i-1}^+)$ to $x(T_i^-)$ is a Brownian motion, we generate $x(T_i^-)$ from a Gaussian density of mean $x(T_{i-1}^+) + c(T_i - T_{i-1})$ and standard deviation $\sigma\sqrt{T_i - T_{i-1}}$.

Once we generate the data, we check whether any of the $x(T_i^-)$ or $x(T_i^+)$ is below the default threshold zero. If yes, we declare that for this particular Monte Carlo run default was certain (i.e. we consider $P_{def} = 1$). If default has not occurred, then we have to check each of the intervals in between the shocks (T_{i-1}, T_i) and estimate the probability of default $P_{def}(i-1, i)$ in these (or to be precise the probability that $x(t)$ goes below the default threshold in these intervals).

Let K be 1 + the number of shocks. To simplify the notation, let $T_K = T$, i.e. all T_i's are the shock times except the last one, which equals T. Once all the

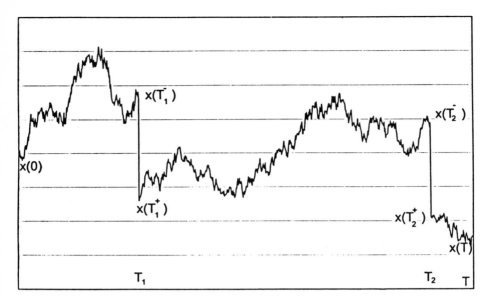

Figure 2: Definition of the used variables

intervals are considered, the probability of default in the whole interval $[0, T]$ can be obtained as

$$P_{def} = 1 - \Pi_{i=1}^{K}\left[1 - P_{def}(i - 1, i)\right] \tag{8}$$

It can be proved that the inter-jump default probabilities are given by:

$$P_{def}(i - 1, i) = \begin{cases} e^{-\frac{2x(T_i^-)x(T_{i-1}^+)}{\sigma^2 \tau}} & \text{if } x(T_i^-) > 0 \\ 1 & \text{if } x(T_i^-) \le 0 \end{cases} \tag{()}$$

The following is a summary of the algorithm:

1) Generate T_i according to the Poisson distribution, by generating inter-jump times $T_i - T_{i-1}$ from an exponential density.

2) For $j = 1$ to M perform the following Monte Carlo runs (Steps 3-7):

3) Starting from $i = 1$ to K (K is $1 +$ the number of jumps that happen to fall in $[0, T]$), perform the following: a) Generate $x(T_i^-)$ from a Gaussian distribution of mean $x(T_{i-1}^+) + c(T_i - T_{i-1})$ and standard deviation $\sigma\sqrt{T_i - T_{i-1}}$. (Let $x(T_0^+)$ be the starting state $x(0)$). b) Compute $x(T_i^+)$ as $x(T_i^-) - a$.

4) If any of $x(T_i^-), x(T_i^+)$ are below zero (the default threshold), then set $P_{def}^{(j)} = 1$. Go to 3) for another cycle.

5) If $x(T_i^-), x(T_i^+)$ are all positive, then perform Steps 6 and 7.

6) For $i = 1$ to $K - 1$ compute

$$P_{def}(i - 1, i) = e^{-\frac{2x(T_i^-)x(T_{i-1}^+)}{\sigma^2 \tau}}$$

7) Compute

$$P_{def}^{(j)} = 1 - \Pi_{i=1}^{K}\left[1 - P_{def}(i-1, i)\right]$$

8) If $j = M$, i.e. we have completed all cycles of the Monte Carlo simulation, obtain estimate of the default probability:

$$P(\text{default in } [0, T]) = \frac{1}{M}\sum_{j=1}^{M} P_{def}^{(j)}$$

5 Simulations

We have tested the proposed algorithm using artificial data. We considered a case with $\mu = 0.05$, $\sigma = 0.3$, $\lambda = 0.3$, and $a = 0.3$. The prediction horizon is $T = 5$, and the initial value $x(0) = 1$. All time units are considered in years. In addition to our method, we simulated the plain Monte Carlo approach (i.e. simulating the actual path of the jump-diffusion process in a Monte Carlo fashion. we used a time step of 0.001 (very close to the rule of thumb).

For both the proposed method and the standard Monte Carlo method, we ran 1000 runs. The actual default probability was 0.2565. The standard Monte Carlo obtained an RMS error of 0.014 in a computational time of 200.9 CPU time. On the other hand, the proposed method obtained an RMS error of 0.011 in computational time of 3.4 CPU time. One can see the superiority of the proposed method, especially in computational speed.

References

1. M. Odom and R. Sharda, "A neural network model for bankruptcy prediction" *Proc of IEEE Int. Conf. on Neural Networks*, pp. 163-168, 1990.
2. R. Merton, "On the pricing of corporate debt: the risk structure of interest rates", *J. Finance*, Vol. 29, pp. 449-470, 1974.
3. F. Longstaff and E. Schwartz, "A simple approach to valuing risk fixed and floating rate debt", *J. Finance*, Vol. 50, pp. 789-819, 1995.
4. R. Merton, "Option pricing when the underlying stock returns are discontinuous", *J. Financial Economics*, Vol. 3, pp. 125-144, 1976
5. F. Knight, *Essentials of Brownian Motion and Diffusion*, American Mathematical Society, Providence, RI, 1981.
6. M. Domine, "First passage time distribution of a Wiener Process with drift concerning two elastic barriers", *J. Appl. Prob.* Vol. 33, pp. 164-175, 1996.

Variance-Penalized Reinforcement Learning for Risk-Averse Asset Allocation

Makoto Sato and Shigenobu Kobayashi

Tokyo Institute of Technology, 4259 Nagatsuta, Midori-ku, Yokohama, JAPAN
{satom@fe., kobayasi@}dis.titech.ac.jp

Abstract. The tasks of optimizing asset allocation considering transaction costs can be formulated into the framework of Markov Decision Processes(MDPs) and reinforcement learning. In this paper, a risk-averse reinforcement learning algorithm is proposed which improves asset allocation strategy of portfolio management systems. The proposed algorithm alternates policy evaluation phases which take into account the mean and variance of return under a given policy and policy improvement phases which follow the variance-penalized criterion. The algorithm is tested on trading systems for a single future corresponding to a Japanese stock index.

1 Introduction

Asset allocation and portfolio management deal with the tasks of constructing the optimal distribution of capital to various investment opportunities including stocks, foreign exchanges and others. If transaction cost for changing allocations must be considered, it can be formulated into a Markov Decision Problem to maintain profitable portfolio for a given risk level in dynamic market [5].

Reinforcement learning [9] finds reasonable solutions (policy) for large state space MDPs by using various function approximators like neural networks, linear regression and so on. Typical reinforcement learning algorithms (e.g. Q-Learning[10], ARL [2]), however, do not care risks of a policy. Although several techniques has been developed for reflecting the given risk level [4][7], they do not estimate the variance of return.

The authors derived a temporal difference (TD) algorithm for estimating the variance of return under a policy in MDPs [3]. In this paper, we simplify the TD algorithm by making use of characteristics of the MDPs formulated in [6]. This simplification allows decision making rely on two value functions no matter how many assets must be concerned. And we propose a policy iteration algorithm using the TD algorithm and variance-penalized policy criterion [11]. Then we test the algorithm using neural networks on the real world task of trading futures corresponding to a Japanese stock index.

2 A MDPs formulation for Portfolio Management

Markov Decision Processes (MDPs) [8] provide sequential decision making models in stochastic environments. MDPs can be described by a state space $\mathcal{X}$! "an

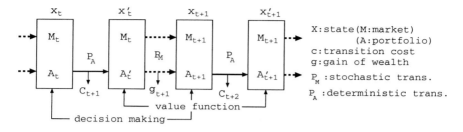

Fig. 1. A MDPs formulation for Portfolio Management

action space $\mathcal{U}(x)$ of admissible control actions for every state $x \in \mathcal{X}$, a transition function $\mathcal{P}$, an immediate reward function $\mathcal{R}$ and a policy μ of a decision maker (agent). The agent iterates the environment by observing state $x_t \in \mathcal{X}$, selecting action $u_t \in \mathcal{U}(x_t)$, being evolved to next state x_{t+1}, and receiving immediate reward $r_{t+1} \in \Re$.

[6] formulated asset allocation into Markov decision problem under the following assumptions: the agent is not able to influence the market by its trading actions and the agent has an infinite time horizon (Figure 1). In this formulation, state $x_t = (M_t, A_t)$ consists of element M_t which characterizes the market and element A_t which characterizes the allocation of the capital at time t. Action space $\mathcal{U}(x)$ corresponds to the set of all admissible transactions on A_t. Immediate reward r_{t+1} consists of transaction cost c_{t+1} and g_{t+1} characterizing the gain of wealth from time t to $t+1$.

The agent aims to maximize some utility function on the discounted sum of reward for infinite horizon (i.e. return $R_t = \sum_{t=0}^{\infty} \gamma^t (c_{t+1} + g_{t+1})$). Q-Learning, which is a typical reinforcement learning algorithm, aims to maximize the expected return. Therefore it is an essential problem how estimates the expected return for each state x and action a under policy μ. Typically, Q-$value$(i.e. $Q^\mu(x, u) = E\{R_t | x_t = x, u_t = u, \mu\}$) and $state$-$value$(i.e. $V^\mu(x) = E\{R_t | x_t = x, \mu\}$) are estimated.

By introducing intermediate state (M_t, A'_t), state transition is resolved into deterministic transition $\mathcal{P}_A$ and uncontrollable Markov chain $\mathcal{P}_M$. Since the agent knows the deterministic transition function and cost function in asset allocation tasks, one optimal value function $Q^*(M, A')$ is simply needed for optimal decision making. The agent can obtain the optimal policy μ^* by the following optimality equation:

$$\mu^*(M, A) = \arg \max_u [c(A, \mathcal{P}_A(A, u)) + Q^*(M, A')].$$

In this formulation, Q-Learning estimates Q-$values$ for each M and A' using the following equation and stochastic approximation algorithms:

$$Q^\mu(M_t, A'_t) = E[g_{t+1} + \gamma[c(A_{t+1}, A'_{t+1}) + Q^\mu(M_{t+1}, A'_{t+1})]],$$

where $g_{t+1} = g(M_t, A'_t, M_{t+1}), A' = \mathcal{P}_A(A, \mu(M, A))$. If learning algorithms demand an improved policy, it can be obtained by the following operation:

$$\mu_{new}(M_t, A_t) = arg \max_u [c(A_t, u) + Q^\mu(M_t, A'_t)].$$

This learning algorithm (QLU algorithm [6]) converges to the optimal *Q-values* under the standard conditions and can be extended to large state space asset allocation by using function approximators. Besides, since this formulation simply needs one value function, it can be extended to the tasks in which many assets must be considered. But QLU has a disadvantage not to care risks of the decisions.

3 Variance-penalized Reinforcement Learning

Within the MDPs formulation for portfolio management in Figure 1, a central problem is how estimates the value functions of the intermediate state for given policy μ. Since an agent can predict the transaction cost and the resultant asset allocation for each admissible transaction, if the agent can evaluate the values of the intermediate state, the most profitable transaction can be determined from the evaluated values and costs.

We introduce to the framework the variance-penalized criterion which is one of risk-averse criterion. Values of the intermediate states are evaluated by the following:

$$E\{R|M, A', \mu\} - \alpha Var\{R|M, A', \mu\},$$

where R is return and α is a non-negative tradeoff parameter between risk and return. Here, we define $q^\mu(M, A') = Var\{R_t|M_t = M, A'_t = A', \mu\}$ and call it the *q-value* of state (M, A') for policy μ. Now, the central problem is estimations of the *q-value* function.

For any MDPs, the variance of return R, for any state x and action u, holds the following bellman equation:

$$q^\mu(x_t, a_t) = E[(r_{t+1} + \gamma V^\mu(x_{t+1}) - Q^\mu(x_t, a_t))^2 + \gamma^2 v^\mu(x_{t+1})],$$

where $q^\mu(x, u) = Var\{R_t|x_t = x, u_t = u, \mu\}$ and $v^\mu(x) = Var\{R_t|x_t = x, \mu\}$. By stochastic approximation algorithms using the above equation (TD algorithm), the estimated $q(x, u)$ converges to $q^\mu(x, u)$ for any x and u [3].

For the simplified MDPs in Fig.1, *q-values* and *Q-values* holds the following equation:

$$q^\mu(M_t, A'_t) = E[(g_{t+1} + \gamma(c(A_{t+1}, A'_{t+1}) + Q^\mu(M_{t+1}, A'_{t+1})) - Q^\mu(M_t, A'_t))^2$$
$$+ q^\mu(M_{t+1}, A'_{t+1})].$$

$q^\mu(M, A')$ also can be estimated by stochastic approximation. If the *Q-value* and *q-value* functions are obtained for policy μ, the new policy is obtained as follows:

$$\mu_{new}(M_t, A_t) = arg \max_u [c(A_t, u) + Q^\mu(M_t, A'_t) - \alpha q^\mu(M_t, A'_t)]. \tag{1}$$

1. collect samples of M_t and M_{t+1} from training data set, random asset allocation A_t' and $\mu(M_{t+1}, A_{t+1})$.

2. train Q-value function using the following targets for each sampled t:

$$Q^\mu(M_t, A_t') \leftarrow g_{t+1} + \gamma(c(A_t', A_{t+1}') + Q^\mu(M_{t+1}, A_{t+1}')).$$

3. train q-value function using the following targets for each sampled t:

$$q^\mu(M_t, A_t') \leftarrow (g_{t+1} + \gamma(c_{t+1} + Q^\mu(M_{t+1}, A_{t+1}')) - Q^\mu(M_t, A_t'))^2$$
$$+ q^\mu(M_{t+1}, A_{t+1}').$$

4. generate policy μ_{new} by equation (1) and evaluate it by some measure.

5. if μ_{new} is superior to μ, update μ, the Q-value and q-value functions and go to 1, otherwise break.

Fig. 2. Variance-penalized Policy Iteration for Portfolio Management

Unfortunately, under the variance-penalized criterion, there does not exist a simple optimality equation such like Bellman optimality equation. This means that μ_{new} is not guaranteed to superior to μ. Thus, policy μ_{new} must be evaluated by some performance measure before replaces μ. In asset allocation, performances of trading results on training data or validation data can be such a measure. Note that incremental learning algorithms are not suitable for the criterion because they generate candidates of new policy at each time.

Figure 2 shows the QqPI learning algorithm. Since the QqPI requires only two value tables or neural networks as function approximators independent of the number of assets to be considered, it can be extended to large-scaled tasks. Because the training of q-values requires the estimated Q-values, the training of q-value function had better carry out after the training of Q-value function.

4 Experiments

The framework of learning described above is also available for trading systems dealing with a single security. In this section we tested our algorithm on a task of trading futures which behaves like a Japanese stock index.

At each time t, Our agent can take one of long, neutral and short positions (i.e. $pos_t \in \{-1 : long, 0 : neutral, 1 : short\}$). The agent observes the N-nearest histories of prices and trading volumes of the security (i.e. $H_t = \{pri_t, \ldots, pri_{t-N+1}\}, vol_t, \ldots, vol_{t-N+1}\}$).

The reward r_{t+1} is calculated by the following:

$$r_{t+1} = g_{t+1} + c_{t+1},$$
$$= pos_t(\frac{pri_{t+1}}{pri_t} - 1) + TC(|pos_t - pos_{t-1}|)(1.0 + pos_{t-1}(\frac{pri_{t+1}}{pri_t} - 1)),$$

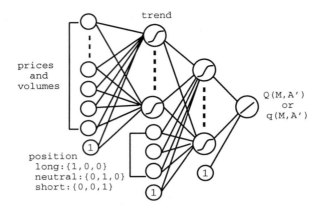

Fig. 3. The Neural Network Architecture

where, TC (actually 0.2%) denotes the transaction cost and r_{t+1} means the rate of increase of wealth (W) from time t to $t+1$ (i.e. $r_{t+1} = W_{t+1}/W_t - 1$). If the agent invests a fixed fraction of accumulated wealth in each long or short trade, return R_t correspond to,

$$R_t = r_{t+1} + \gamma r_{t+2} + \gamma^2 r_{t+3} + \cdots,$$
$$= (\frac{W_{t+1}}{W_t} - 1) + \gamma(\frac{W_{t+2}}{W_{t+1}} - 1) + \gamma^2(\frac{W_{t+3}}{W_{t+2}} - 1) + \cdots. \tag{2}$$

Our reinforcement learning agent aims to maximize Eq.(2).

Fig.3 shows our network architecture. A pre-trained network for predicting trend [1] yields market status M_t from H_t. pos_t is transformed into the portfolio part A'_t by standard binary transformation. M_t and A'_t compose the state space.

We used two neural networks as function aproximators for both *Q-value* and *q-value* functions. The trend-predict network had 40-40-2 units and the output units are sigmoidal. The value-approximate networks had 5-10-1 units and the output units are linear. These networks are trained by back-propagation(2-fold cross-validation). *Q-value* and *q-value* are sampled from short trajectories which begin with random time and position.

We applied QqPI to the Japanese stock index data (Jan.,1992-Sep.,2000) with various α. We divided the data into training set (Jan.,1992-Dec,1996), validation set (Jan.,1997-Dec.,1998) and test set (Jan.1999-Sep.2000). The training set are used for tuning weights of the neural networks. The policy evaluation measure based on the simulation results on the training set and validation set. The best policies were applied to the test set. Table.1 shows that the proposed algorithm with adequate tradeoff parameter learned stable policies.

5 Conclusion and Future Work

A risk-averse reinforcement learning method has been proposed for improving asset allocation policy of portfolio management systems. The algorithm was tested on the real data and showed valid results. But more experiments are needed with various feature extraction methods. Fundamental trading and multi-asset tasks are other future directions.

Table 1. Comparison of the capital gains

Tradeoff param.	Training set	Validation set	Test set
$\alpha = 0.0$	29.2 %	0.8%	26.2%
$\alpha = 0.2$	61.8 %	12.4 %	18.9%
$\alpha = 0.4$	59.4 %	13.3 %	9.4 %

References

[1] Baba, N.: A user friendly decision support system for dealing stocks using neural network. Proc. of IJCNN, Vol.1, (1993) 762-765.

[2] Mahadevan, S.: Average reward reinforcement learning: foundations, algorithms, and empirical results. Machine Learning, vol.22, (1996) 159-196.

[3] Makoto, S., Hajime, K., Shigenobu, K.: TD algorithm for the variance of return and mean-variance reinforcement learning. Journal of Japanese Society for Artificial Intelligence, (in Japanese, To appear).

[4] Moody, J., Saffell, M.: Reinforcement learning for trading systems and portfolios. Proc. of KDD-98, (1998) 279-283.

[5] Neuneier, R.: Optimal asset allocation using adaptive dynamic programming. Proc. of NIPS 9, MIT Press (1996).

[6] Neuneier, R.: Enhancing Q-Learning for optimal asset allocation. Proc. of NIPS 10, MIT Press (1997) 936-942.

[7] Neuneier, R., Mihatsch, O.: Risk sensitive reinforcement learning. Proc. of NIPS 11, MIT Press (1998) 1031-1037.

[8] Puterman, M.L.: Markov Decision Processes. John Wiley & Sons, Inc., New York, (1994).

[9] Sutton, R. S., Barto, A. G.: Reinforcement Learning: An Introduction. MIT Press, (1998).

[10] Watkins, C.: Learning from delayed rewards. PhD thesis, King's College, UK(1989).

[11] White, D. J.: Mean, variance, and probabilistic criteria in finite Markov decision processes: A review. Journal of Optimization Theory and Applications, vol.56(1), (1988) 1-29.

Applying Mutual Information to Adaptive Mixture Models

Zheng Rong Yang† and Mark Zwolinski‡

†Department of Computer Science, Exeter University, Exeter EX4 4PT, UK
Z.R.Yang@ex.ac.uk
‡Department of Computer Science and Electronics, Southampton University,
Southampton SO17 1BJ, UK

Abstract. This paper presents a method for determine an optimal set
of components for a density mixture model using mutual information.
A component with small mutual information is believed to be independent from the rest components and to make a significant contribution
to the system and hence cannot be removed. Whilst a component with
large mutual information is believed to be unlikely independent from the
rest components within a system and hence can be removed. Continuing
removing components with positive mutual information till the system
mutual information becomes non-positive will finally give rise to a parsimonious structure for a density mixture model. The method has been
verified with several examples.

1 Introduction

Many pattern recognition systems need to discover the underlying probability
density function for the purpose of efficient decision making. Density mixture
model is a powerful tool for pattern recognition. The basic computational element of a density mixture model is a component that has a nonlinear mapping
function. Suppose that a set of components is $\Theta = \{\theta_k, k = 1, \ldots, m\}$ and a
component function of component θ_k is $K(\theta_k)$, a density mixture model is then
a mixture of mixing component functions on Θ, $\varphi = \Sigma \omega_k K(\theta_k)$, where ω_k is
a mixing coefficient of component θ_k satisfying $\omega_k \in \Re$ and $\Sigma_{k=1}^{m} \omega_k = 1$. One
of the popular component functions is Gaussian $K(\theta_k) = N(\vec{\mu}_k, \sigma_k^2)$ [2], [5], [7],
[10], [12], [13], [14], [16] such as Parzen estimator [8], where $\vec{\mu}_k \in \Re^d$ and σ^2 are
the center and the variance of the component θ_k respectively and d is dimension. Since these non-parametric methods fix all the observation patterns as the
centers of components, it leads to time and space inefficiency. To overcome this,
parsimonious structures are desirable [12], [13], [14], [16].

Given a set of patterns Ω, instead of exhaustively searching for all the possible subsets of Ω, the Kullback-Leibler distance, $J = \int p(\vec{x}) ln(p_r(\vec{x})/p(\vec{x}))$,
has been employed to select the best representation (an optimal subset) of Ω
($\Omega^* \subset \Omega$) [5]. $p(\vec{x})$ is the Parzen estimator, which fixes all patterns from Ω
as the centers of components and $p_r(\vec{x})$ is a reduced Parzen estimator, which
employs a subset of Ω. This method assumes that there is a best representation
of Ω. If Ω does not contain a best representation, the method will not be able to
give an accurate density estimator. Moreover, this method fixes the number of
components for a density mixture model. In general regression neural network,

the centers of components were sought through employing a forgetting function dynamically [12], [13]. Covariance matrix was also used for probabilistic neural network [14]. These methods avoided fixing original patterns as the centers of components, but the learning mode is homoscedastic, which is not robust for most real applications. Since heteroscedastic training of the Parzen estimator using the Expectation-Maximization (EM) algorithm frequently falls into a local minimum [15], a robust statistical method called the Jackknife was used to build a robust estimator [16]. But how to determine an optimal set of components for a density mixture model is a trial-and-error method in that procedure [16].

All the above work selected components using the information contained in the patterns rather than using the information contained in the components themselves. It is therefore not easy to make these techniques adaptive. A decision-to-add-one rule was therefore developed to select an optimal set of components using the information from both patterns and components [9]. The decision to create a new component was determined by whether a new pattern contains information, which is not found in the existing components. If a data space is not well ordered, the computational cost of reconstruction may be large. Moreover, this method is very sensitive to noise.

This paper presents a new method, which determines an optimal set of components by investigating the relationship between components. If two components are mutually dependent their relationship will be strong. Hence mutual information [11] could be used to measure whether one component is strongly dependent on the rest components. If a component has small mutual information with respect to the rest components in a system, the component is assumed to be independent from the rest components. Thus the component makes a significant contribution to the system and hence cannot be removed. If the mutual information of a component is large it is not independent from the rest components in a system and removing it will not significantly change the system probability density function. Continuing removing components with the largest and positive mutual information until system mutual information becomes non-positive, an optimal set of components can be found. The probability density function constructed by a density mixture model using this optimal set of components will be an approximation to the true probability density function.

2 Density mixture model

Both the greatest gradient and the maximum likelihood can be used to estimate the parameters of a density mixture model. It has been shown that the maximum likelihood method is a fast training procedure for some cases [15]. Suppose that there are n patterns and m components, each of which has a Gaussian probability density function. Let ω_k, $\vec{\mu}_k$ and $\beta_k = 1/\sigma_k^2$ be the mixing coefficient, the center and the smoothing parameter for component θ_k respectively, a density mixture model is $p(\vec{x}) = \sum_{k=1}^{m} \omega_k p(\vec{x}|\theta_k)$, where $p(\vec{x}|\theta_k) = (\beta_k/\pi)^{d/2} exp(-\beta_k \|\vec{x} - \vec{\mu}_k\|^2)$. A logarithmic likelihood function by considering an optimization term is $\hat{L} = ln \prod_{i=1}^{n} p(\vec{x}_i) + \lambda(\Sigma_{k=1}^{m} \omega_k - 1)$. Let the derivatives of the log likelihood function with respect to each parameter be zero leads to an estimate of the centers, variances, the mixing coefficients of the components: $\vec{\mu}_k = \Sigma_{i=1}^{n} \gamma_{i,k} \vec{x}_i$, $(\beta_k)^{-1} = 2\Sigma_{i=1}^{n} \gamma_{i,k} \|\vec{x}_i - \vec{\mu}_k\|^2/d$ and $\omega_k = \Sigma_{i=1}^{n} \xi_{i,k}$ respectively, where $\xi_{i,k} = \omega_k p(\vec{x}_i|\theta_k)/p(\vec{x}_i)$ and $\gamma_{i,k} = \xi_{i,k}/\Sigma_{l=1}^{n} \xi_{l,k}$.

3 Mutual information theory

Mutual information theory is used to measure the information shared among objects and aims to minimize the entropy within a system [11]. It has been applied to a number of areas [1], [3], [4], [6]. If the information shared between two objects is small, the two objects are likely to be independent. Otherwise the two objects are likely to be dependent on each other. The necessity of a component is therefore determined by the mutual information between the component and the rest components within a system. If the mutual information of a component is large, that component is unlikely to make a significant contribution to the system probability density function because it is not independent from the rest components and this component can be removed from the system. The mutual information is a difference between initial and conditional uncertainty.

Let Θ be the component space, $\theta_i \in \Theta$ and $\theta_j \in \Theta$ are two components and $p(\theta_i)$ and $p(\theta_j)$ are the probabilities of the components θ_i and θ_j. The initial uncertainty of θ_i is $H(\theta_j) = -p(\theta_i)ln(\theta_i)$. This initial uncertainty is measured when θ_i is isolated. Let $p(\theta_i|\theta_j)$ the conditional probability of $p(\theta_i)$ given $p(\theta_j)$. The conditional uncertainty of θ_i with respect to the rest components is $H(\theta_i|\Theta^{-i}) = -\Sigma p(\theta_j)p(\theta_i|\theta_j)ln(p(\theta_i|\theta_j))$, where $\theta_j \in \Theta^{-i}$ and $\Theta^{-i} = \Theta - \{\theta_i\}$. This conditional uncertainty measures the information of θ_i given the condition that the rest components in Θ (denoted by Θ^{-i}) exist in the same system. The mutual information of θ_i with respect to the rest components is then the difference between the initial uncertainty of θ_i and the conditional uncertainty of θ_i, $I(\theta_i, \Theta^{-i}) = H(\theta_i) - H(\theta_i|\Theta^{-i})\Sigma i(\theta_i, \theta_j)$, where $\theta_j \in \Theta^{-i}$ and $i(\theta_i, \theta_j) = p(\theta_i, \theta_j)ln(p(\theta_i, \theta_j)/p(\theta_i)p(\theta_j))$. The joint probability $p(\theta_i, \theta_j)$ can be computed by a geometrical method: divide a space into a set of hyper-cubes, probability density is computed by dividing the number of components within a hyper-cube over the volume of a hyper-cube [1]. In this paper, $p(\theta_i, \theta_j)$ is calculated by applying Bayesian rule, $p(\theta_i, \theta_j) = p(\theta_i|\theta_j)p(\theta_j)$ or $p(\theta_i, \theta_j) = p(\theta_j|\theta_i)p(\theta_i)$. The system mutual information is defined as $I(\Theta) = \Sigma p(\theta_i)I(\theta_i, \Theta^{-i})$, where $\theta_i \in \Theta$. The system mutual information indicates whether a system has arrived at a stable point where all the components in the system are mutually independent. The component mutual information $I(\theta_i, \Theta^{-i})$ denotes whether θ_i has a significant and independent contribution to the system probability density function. The mutual relationship $i(\theta_i, \theta_j)$ measures the mutual relationship between a specific pair of components (θ_i and θ_j) or the probability that θ_i and θ_j exist within a system at the same time. If they are mutually dependent the mutual information between them will be large. There are three possible values for $i(\theta_i, \theta_j)$; negative, zero and positive. A zero value means that they are mutually independent $p(\theta_i, \theta_j) = p(\theta_i)p(\theta_j)$. A negative value of mutual information means that they can be regarded as much less dependent because $p(\theta_i, \theta_j) < p(\theta_i)p(\theta_j)$. A positive value means that they are mutually dependent $p(\theta_i, \theta_j) > p(\theta_i)p(\theta_j)$. Only in this situation, one of the two components will be considered to remove from a system.

panies are plotted year by year. Whether a ratio possesses a stable profile or not can therefore be visualised. In Figure 1, the solid lines represent the mean ratios of non-failed companies; the dotted lines are the mean ratios of failed companies. The ratios plotted in Figure 1 and 2 have stable profiles. On the other hand, the ratios shown in Figure 3 and 4 do not possess stable profiles.

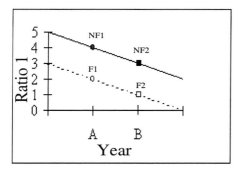

Figure 1: Stable profiles

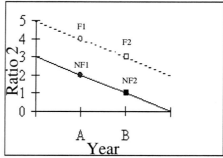

Figure 2: Stable profiles

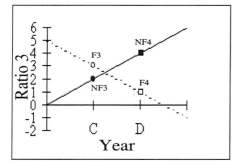

Figure 3: Non-stable profiles

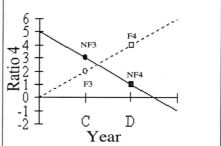

Figure 4: Non-stable profiles

The impact of profile stability of financial ratios on the relationship between company performance and financial ratios is analysed by combining ratios to see whether a combination results in a consistent decision rule, or a linear decision space.

The impact of profile stability of financial ratios on the relationship between company performance and financial ratios is analysed by combining ratios to see whether a combination results in a consistent decision rule, or a linear decision space. At the first, the situation shown in Figure 1 and 2 is considered where ratio 1 and ratio 2 have stable profiles. If the sampling years are fixed at A and B, four companies are selected as shown in Figure 1 and 2, where F1 and F2 are two failed companies, NF1 and NF2 are two non-failed companies. Each of them has two ratios; there are therefore eight points in Figure 1 and 2 shown as squares and circles. For example, the non-failed company at year A is marked as 'NF1' and has the value 4 for ratio 1 and the value 2 for ratio 2. Combining these two ratios together, a two-dimensional data space is formed as shown in Figure 5. It can be seen that the combination leads to a linear relationship between company performance and financial ratios because the decision space composed of these two ratios is linearly divided into two half parts, each of them represents one particular group of companies, failed or non-failed companies. The closer to the right down corner, the better (stronger) the company performance, the closer to the left top corner, the worse (weaker) the company performance. A linear relationship is therefore satisfied. Hence a combination of two ratios possessing stable profiles comprises a linear relationship between company performance and financial ratios.

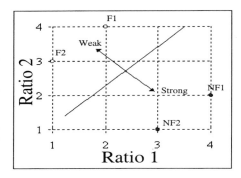 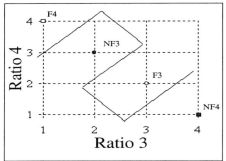

Figure 5: Combination of Ratio 1 and Figure 6: Combination of Ratio 3 and
2   4

Now consider the situation shown as in Figure 3 and 4, where ratio 3 and ratio 4 do not possess stable profiles. If the sampling years are fixed at C and D, another four companies named as F3, F4, NF3 and NF4 are selected where F1 and F2 are two failed companies and NF1 and NF2 are two non-failed companies. Each of them has two ratios shown as eight points in Figure 3 and 4. Ratio 3 and ratio 4 can be combined into another two-dimensional data space, see Figure 6. It can be seen that the combination of these two ratios results in a nonlinear relationship between company performance and financial ratios because there is no linear decision space like that in Figure 6. Therefore whether financial ratios have stable profiles or not is the cause of whether the relationship between company performance and financial ratios is linear or not.

3 The empirical result

Financial statements of 2408 UK companies from 1989 to 1994 were collected in this study. Among this set of data, there are 2244 non-failed companies and 164 failed companies. Thirty-three ratios were calculated based on this raw data, see Table 1. Among these 33 ratios, there are nine liquidity ratios, nine assets structure ratios, 12 profitability ratios and three gearing ratios. Liquidity ratios are used to indicate the possibility of the short-term survival of a company [6]. They show whether a company is able to meet its immediate obligations and whether a company has enough money to pay back its credits. Gearing ratios (or capital structure) are used to indicate extent to which company is expected to experience financial risk [4]. Profitability ratios are used for measuring whether a company is able to earn an acceptable return to continue its business by the contributions from income, capital, assets and funds [6]. Asset structure (or activity) ratios usually help managers and outsiders to judge how effectively a company manages its assets [4].

The analysis result is shown in Table 2. It can be seen that 19 ratios do not have stable profiles, where 58 percent of profitability ratios, 56 percent of liquidity ratios, 67 percent of gearing ratios and 56 percent of assets structure ratios do not possess stable profiles. Therefore the relationship between company performance and financial ratios is nonlinear in this particular industry.

Table 1 The 33 Key Ratios

RATIOS	CLASSIFICATION	DEFINITIONS
(CA-STK)/CL	Liquidity	CA:current assets
DBT/EQT	Gearing	DBT:debt; EQT:equit
TU/EQT	Assets structure	TU:turnover
PAT/TA	Profitability	PAT:profit after taxes
(STL+LTL)/TA	Gearing	STL:short term loan
PAT/CL	Liquidity	CL:current liabilities
FA/TA	Assets structure	FA:fixed assets
WC/TA	Assets structure	WC:working capital
(PBIT+DEP)/TA	Profitability	PBIT:profit before ints and taxes
(PBIT+DEP)/EQT	Profitability	STK:stock and work in progres
PBIT/TA	Profitability	DEP:depreciate
CA/TA	Assets structure	TA:total assets
CL/TA	Assets structure	LTL:long term loan
(CA-STK)/TA	Assets structure	
PBIT/EQT	Profitability	
FA/EQT	Gearing	
PBT/EQT	Profitability	PBT:profit before interest
PBIT/(TA-CL)	Profitability	
PBIT/CL	Liquidity	
PBIT/TU	Profitability	
CA/CL	Liquidity	
PAT/(NA+STL)	Profitability	NA:net assets
CA/NA	Assets structure	
TU/NA	Assets structure	
STL/PBIT	Liquidity	
PBIT/(NA+STL)	Profitability	
DBT/CRD	Liquidity	CRD:creditor
CL/CA	Liquidity	
PBIT/CA	Profitability	
NCI	Assets structure	NCI:no-credit intervals
cash flow/CL	Liquidity	
CA/TL	Liquidity	
PBT/avg CL	Profitability	

Table 2 The analysis result of stable profiles

DEFINITION	TOTAL	INSTABLE	percent
Profitability	12	7	58
Liquidity	9	5	56
Gearing	3	2	67
Assets structure	9	5	56
Total	33	19	58

Two ratios (PAT/TA and (PBIT+DEP)/TA) with stable profiles are plotted in Figure 7 and 8 and two ratios (DBT/EQT and CA/NA) without stable profiles are plotted in Figure 9 and 10. In Figure 3, the filled circles indicate the mean values of the non-failed companies and the open circles denote the mean values of the failed companies.

Figure 11 is a combination of two financial ratios (PAT/TA and (PBIT+DEP)/TA) both having stable profiles. It can be seen that a straight line can be drawn to separate failed and non-failed companies without any difficulty. Therefore the relationship between company performance and financial ratios is linear if only consider these two ratios for decision making. Figure 12 is a combination of one financial ratio (PAT/TA) with a stable profile with other financial ratio (CA/NA) without a stable profile. It can be seen that this combination still results in a linear relationship between company performance and financial ratios if only consider these two ratios for decision making. Figure 13 shows a combination of two financial ratios (DBT/EQT and CA/NA) both having non-stable profiles. As expected that this combination leads to a nonlinear relationship between company performance and financial ratios because it is impossible to separate failed and non-failed companies by one straight line if only consider these two ratios. Considering put all the 33 ratios for decision making (UK construction companies evaluation), it can be concluded that the decision space would be very complex and it does need to access the ability of nonlinear techniques such as neural networks.

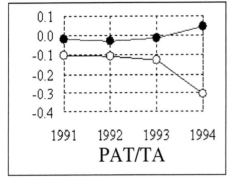

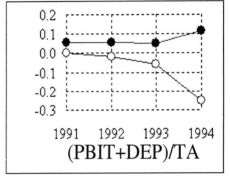

Figure 7: A ratio with a stable profile

Figure 8: Another ratio with a stable profile

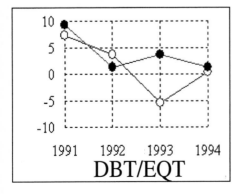

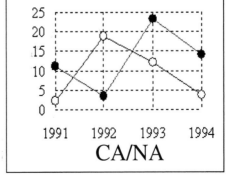

Figure 9: A ratio without a stable profile

Figure 10: Another ratio without a stable profile

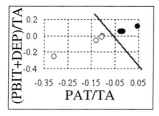 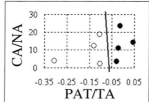 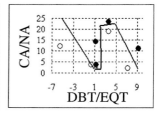

Figure 11: Combination 1 Figure 12: Combination 2 Figure 13: Combination 3

Summary

This study indicates that profile stability of financial ratios is the main cause of the complexity of the relationship between company performance and financial ratios. The analysis on the data set collected from UK companies gives the evidence that the relationship between company performance and financial ratios is indeed nonlinear. From this, it can be seen that univariate analysis is unable to evaluate company performance when such a complexity presents. The non-stable profiles lead to non-consistent decision rules between failed and non-failed companies. This causes nonlinearity. Hence using nonlinear techniques such as neural networks for company performance evaluation based on company financial ratios is expected to produce better results. The further work will include the variances of ratios in study.

References

[1] Altman E.I., Financial ratios, discriminant analysis and the prediction of corporate failure, J. of Finance (1968) 589-609.

[2] Blum M., Failing Company Discriminant Analysis, J. of Accounting Research (1974) 1-25.

[3] Deakin E.B., A discriminant analysis of predictors of business failure, J. of Accounting Research (1972) 167-179.

[4] Edum-fotwe F., Price A. and Thorpe A., A review of financial ratio tools for predicting contractor insolvency, Construction Management and Economics **14** (1996) 189-198.

[5] Lau A.H., A five-state financial distress prediction model, J. of Accounting Research 25)1987) 125-138.

[6] Lev B., Financial Statement Analysis, A New Approach, Prentice-hall, Inc. Englewood Cliffs, NJ (1974).

[7] Pinches G.E., Mingo K.A. and Caruthers J.K., The stability of financial patterns in industrial organisation, The J. of Finance (1977) 389-395.

[8] Robertson J., Research directions in financial ratio analysis, Management Accounting (1984) 30-31.

[9] Salchenberger L.M., Cinar E.M. and Lash N.A., Neural networks: a new tool for predicting thrift failures, Decision Sciences **23** (1992) 899-916.

[10] Storey D., Keasey K., Watson R. and Wynarczyk P., The Performance of Small Firms, Croom Helm (1988).

[11] Trigueiros D. and Taffler R., Neural networks and empirical research in accounting, Working Paper, London Business School, Ver. 23.2.95 (1995).

Modeling of the German Yield Curve
by Error Correction Neural Networks

Hans-Georg Zimmermann[1], Ralph Neuneier[1], and Ralph Grothmann[2]

[1] SIEMENS AG, Munich, Germany
[2] University of Bremen, Germany

Abstract. In this paper we introduce a new recurrent network architecture called ECNN, which includes the last model error measured as an additional input. Hence, the learning can interpret the models misfit as an external shock which can be used to guide the model dynamics afterwards. As extentions to the ECNN, we present a concept called overshooting, which enforces the autoregressive part of the model, and we combine our approach with a bottleneck coordinate transformation to handle high dimensional problems (variants-invariants separation). Finally we apply the ECNN to the German yield curve. Our model allows a forecast of ten different interest rate maturities on forecast horizons between one and six months ahead. It turns out, that our approach is superior to more conventional forecasting techniques.

1   Modeling Dynamic Systems by Error Correction

If we have a complete description of all external forces u_t influencing a deterministic system y_t, Eq. 1 would allow us to identify temporal relationships by setting up a memory in form of a state transition equation s_t. Unfortunately, our knowledge about the external forces u_t is usually limited and the observations made, are typically noisy. Under such conditions learning with finite datasets leads to the construction of incorrect causalities due to learning by heart (over-fitting). The generalization properties of such a model are very questionable.

$$\begin{aligned} s_t &= f(s_{t-1}, u_t) \\ y_t &= g(s_t) \end{aligned} \qquad (1)$$

If we are unable to identify the underlying dynamics of the system due to unknown influences, we can refer to the observed model error at time period $t - 1$, which quantifies the misspecification of our model. Handling this error flow as an additional input, we extend Eq. 1 obtaining Eq. 2, where y_{t-1} denotes the output of the model at time period $t - 1$.

$$\begin{aligned} s_t &= f(s_{t-1}, u_t, y_{t-1} - y_{t-1}^d) \\ y_t &= g(s_t) \end{aligned} \qquad (2)$$

Keep in mind, that if we had a perfect description of the dynamics, the extension of Eq. 2 would be no longer required, since the model error at $t - 1$ would be equal to *zero*. In case of imperfect information, the model uses it's own error flow as a measurement of unexpected shocks. This is similar to the MA part of an *linear* ARIMA model. Working with state space models, we can skip the use of delayed error corrections.

1.1 Error Correction Neural Networks

An neural network implementation of the error correction equations (Eq. 2) can be formulated as

$$
\begin{aligned}
s_t &= \tanh(As_{t-1} + Bu_t + D\tanh(Cs_{t-1} - y_{t-1}^d)) \\
y_t &= Cs_t
\end{aligned}
\tag{3}
$$

$$
\frac{1}{T} \cdot \sum_{t=1}^{T} \left(y_t - y_t^d\right)^2 \rightarrow \min_{A,B,C,D}
\tag{4}
$$

The neural network of Eq. 3 stated in an error correction form measures the deviation between the expected value Cs_{t-1} and the related observation y_{t-1}^d. The term Cs_{t-1} recomputes the last output y_{t-1} and compares it to the observed data y_{t-1}^d. The transformation D is necessary in order to adjust different dimensionalities in the state transition equation. While matrix B introduces external information u_t to the system, the model error is utilized by D. For numerical reasons, we included $\tanh(\cdot)$ nonlinearity. The system identification (Eq. 4) is a parameter optimization task adjusting the weights of matrices A, B, C, D.

1.2 Unfolding in Time of Error Correction Neural Networks

In a next step we want to translate the formal description of Eq. 3 into a recurrent network architecture, which unfolds over several time steps using shared weights, i. e. the weight values are the same at each time step of the unfolding [5]. We call this architecture *Error Correction Neural Network (ECNN)* (see Fig. 1).

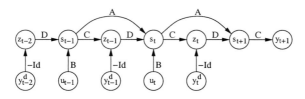

Fig. 1. Error Correction Neural Network

The ECNN architecture (Fig. 1) is best to understood if one analyses the dependency between s_{t-1}, u_t, $z_t = Cs_{t-1} - y_{t-1}^d$ and s_t.

We have two input types: $(i.)$ the external inputs u_t directly influencing the state transition and $(ii.)$ the targets y_t^d. Only the difference between the internal expected y_t and the observation y_t^d has an impact on state transition. Note, that $-Id$ is an negative identity matrix frozen during the learning.

At time period $t + 1$, there is no compensation y_{t+1} of the internal expected value y_{t+1}^d, and thus the system offers a forecast. This design also allows an elegant handling of missing values: if there is no compensation of the internal expected value $y_t = Cs_{t-1}$ the system automatically creates a replacement y_t^d.

The output clusters of the ECNN which generate error signals during the learning are the $z_{t-\tau}$. Have in mind, that the target values of the sequence of output clusters $z_{t-\tau}$ are *zero*, because we want to optimize the compensation mechanism between the expected value $y_{t-\tau}$ and its observation $y_{t-\tau}^d$.

1.3 Overshooting in Error Correction Neural Networks

An obvious generalization of the ECNN in Fig. 1 is the extension of the autonomous recurrence in future direction $t + 1, t + 2, \cdots$ (see Fig. 2). We call this extension *overshooting* (see [5] for more details).

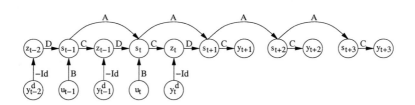

Fig. 2. Combining Overshooting and Error Correction Neural Networks

Note, that overshooting generates additional valuable forecast information about the dynamical system and acts as a regularization method for the learning. Furthermore, overshooting influences the learning of the ECNN in an extended way: A forecast provided by the ECNN is based on a modeling of the recursive structure of a dynamical system (coded in the matrix A) and the error correction mechanism which is acting as an external input (coded in C, D). Now, the overshooting enforces the autoregressive substructure allowing long-term forecasts. Of course, in the overshooting we have to provide the additional output clusters $y_{t+1}, y_{t+2}, \ldots$ with target values in order to generate error signals for the learning. Note, that due to *shared weights* overshooting has the same number of parameters as the basic ECNN (Fig. 1).

2 Variants-Invariants Separation combined with ECNN

In this section we want to integrate the dimension reduction concept of coordinate transformation (so called variants-invariants separation) into the ECNN (Fig. 3) in order to model high dimensional dynamical systems (see [5]).

The separation of variants-invariants can be realized by a bottleneck neural network (left hand-side of Fig. 3).The compressor F separates into variants and invariants, while the decompression is done by matrix E reconstructing the complete dynamics.

Combining the latter concept with ECNN (Fig. 3), the compressor / decompressor network seems to be disconnected from the ECNN, however this isn't true: Since we use *shared weights* the two subsystems influence each other without having an explicit interconnection.

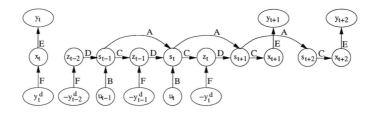

Fig. 3. Combining Variance - Invariance Separation and Forecasting

Thus, the ECNN has to predict a coordinate transformed low dimensional vector x_t instead of the high dimensional vector y_t. Note, that the ECNN requires $-y_t^d$ as inputs in order to generate $-x_t^d$ in the z_t layer. This allows the compensation of the internal forecasts $x_t = Cs_{t-1}$ by the transformed target data $-x_t^d = F(-y_t^d)$.

3 Application: Yield Curve Forecasting by ECNN

Now, we apply the ECNN combined with the separation of variants-invariants (see Fig. 3) to the German bond market to forecast the complete yield curve (REX1 - REX10).

Our empirical study can be characterized as follows: We are working on the basis of monthly data from Jan. 1975 to Aug. 1997 [266 data points] to forecast monthly, quarterly and semi-annual changes of the German yield curve, i. e. predicting interest rate shifts of REX1 to REX10 for these forecast horizons simultaneously. The data is divided into *two* subsets: the training set covers the time period from Jan. 91 to Aug. 95 [234 data points], while the generalization set covers the time from Oct. 95 to Dec. 97 [32 data points].

Since we are interested in forecasting 1, 3 and 6 months changes of the German yield curve, the applied ECNN uses 6 month of background information to model the present time state and includes an overshooting environment of *six* month, i. e. there are *six* autonomous iterations of the dynamical system. In our experiments we found, that for the German yield curve only 3 variants are important. Furthermore, composing the internal state of the ECNN of 8 neurons, allows a fairly good description of the underlying dynamics. We trained the ECNN until convergence with the *vario-eta* learning algorithm using a small batch size of 15 patterns (see [2]).

As a further decision, we composed a data set of external factors in order to forecast the German yield curve. Considering economical trends, inflation, stock markets and FX-rates of Germany, USA and Japan, we obtained 9 economic indicators. Note, that the *preprocessing* of the input data is basically done by calculating the *scaled momentum* of the time series (see [2]).

In order to measure the performance of our ECNN, we compare its forecasts to those of *two* benchmarks: The *first* one refers to a naive strategy which assumes that an observed trend of the interest rate development will last for more than one time period. The *second* one is a 3-layer MLP with one input layer, a hidden layer consisting of 20 neurons with $\tanh(\cdot)$ activation function and one output layer with a squared cost function simultaneously predicting the complete German yield curve for the 3 forecast horizons. The input signals, preprocessing, time scheme and data sets correspond to the dispositions described above. We trained the network until convergence with pattern-by-pattern learning using a small batch size of 1 pattern (see [2]).

The performance of the models is measured by their realized potential, which is defined as the ratio of the accumulated model return to the maximum possible accumulated return. The accumulated return refers to a simple trading strategy using the particular yield curve forecasts, e. g. we sell bonds if we expect rising interest rates. Proceeding this way, we would expand our net capital balance in case of an higher interest rate level using the price shifts of the bonds.

The empirical results are summarized in Fig. 4. It turns out, that the ECNN combined with variants-invariants separation is superior to both benchmarks. This is especially true for longer forecast horizons, e. g. 6 month ahead. Comparing the two benchmarks, it becomes obvious that the naive strategy achieves better results forecasting short-term maturities (REX 1 to REX 5), while the 3-layer MLP dominates in forecasting long-term maturities (REX 6 to REX 10). The latter observation, which is true for every forecast horizon investigated, can be seen as the consequence of the short-term trend behavior of the interest rates. Interestingly the ECNN reaches a steady forecasting quality over the complete yield curve, i. e. there is *no* drawback in forecasting long-term instead of short-term maturities. The latter is due to the fact of the variants-invariants separation. The ECNN realizes nearly 60% of the maximum reachable performance, considering monthly and quarterly yield curve forecasts. For the long-term forecast horizon, it turns out, that the ECNN is able to achieve up to 80% of the potential accumulated return. Note, that the other benchmarks are far behind these results.

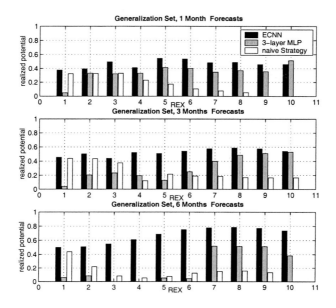

Fig. 4. Realized potential of each trading strategy.

4 Conclusion

We introduced an ECNN architecture, which is able to handle external shocks without changing the identified dynamics of the underlying system. The ECNN can be extented by overshooting as well as a variants-inveriants separation, which allows the modeling of high dimensional, noisy dynamical systems. The empirical results indicate, that the performance of the ECNN is superior to more conventional forecasting techniques.

The described algorithms are integrated in the *Simulation Environment for Neural Networks*, SENN, a product of Siemens AG.

References

1. S. Haykin. *Neural Networks. A Comprehensive Foundation.* Macmillan College Publishing, New York, 1994. second edition 1998.
2. Ralph Neuneier and Hans Georg Zimmermann. How to Train Neural Networks. In *Neural Networks: Tricks of the Trade*, pages 373–423. Springer, Berlin, 1998.
3. B. Pearlmatter. Gradient Calculations for Dynamic Recurrent Neural Networks: A survey, In IEEE Transactions on Neural Networks, Vol. 6, 1995.
4. L. R. Medsker and L. C. Jain. Recurrent Neural Networks: Design and Application, CRC Press international series on comp. intelligence, No. I, 1999.
5. H. G. Zimmermann and R. Neuneier. Neural Network Architectures for the Modeling of Dynamical Systems. In J. F. Kolen and St. Kremer, editors, *A Field Guide to Dynamical Recurrent Networks*, IEEE Press, 2000.

Feature Selection for Support Vector Machines in Financial Time Series Forecasting

L. J. CAO and FRANCIS E. H. TAY

Department of Mechanical & Production Engineering, National University of Singapore,10 Kent Ridge Crescent, 119260, Singapore. Email: mpetayeh@nus.edu.sg

Abstract. This paper deals with the application of saliency analysis to Support Vector Machines (SVMs) for feature selection. The importance of feature is ranked by evaluating the sensitivity of the network output to the feature input in terms of the partial derivative. A systematic approach to remove irrelevant features based on the sensitivity is developed. Five futures contracts are examined in the experiment. Based on the simulation results, it is shown that that saliency analysis is effective in SVMs for identifying important features.

1   Introduction

Over the recent past years, support vector machines (SVMs) have been receiving increasing attention in the regression estimation area due to their remarkable characteristics such as good generalization performance, the absence of local minima and sparse representation of the solution [1,2]. However, within the SVMs framework, there are very few established approaches for identifying important features. The issue of feature selection for SVMs is recently discussed in [3]. There it has been stated that feature selection is better to be performed in SVMs if many features exist, as this procedure can improve the network performance, speed up the training and reduce the complexity of the network.

This paper proposes saliency analysis (SA) to SVMs for selecting important features. The SA measures the importance of features by evaluating the sensitivity of the network output with respect to the weights (weight-based SA) or the feature inputs (derivative-based SA). Based on the idea that important features usually have large absolute values of connected weights and unimportant features have small absolute values of connected weights, the weight-based saliency analysis is to detect irrelevant weights by evaluating the magnitude of weights, and then remove the features emanating these irrelevant weights [4]. This method is also extended into other types of weight-pruning by using a penalty term in the cost function to remove irrelevant features [5]. The derivative-based SA measures the importance of features by evaluating the sensitivity of the network output with respect to the feature inputs based on the partial derivative [6]. To irrelevant features which provide little information on the prediction, the output produces a small value of saliency metric which indicates that the network output is insensitive to those features. On the contrary, to significant features which contribute much to the prediction, the output will produce a large value of saliency metric. As the weights of SVMs lie in a high dimensional feature space, and the magnitude of weights is a measure of the importance of the high dimensional feature inputs, rather than the original feature inputs, in this paper only the derivative-based SA is developed for SVMs.

This paper is organized as follows. In section 2, we briefly introduce the theory of SVMs in the regression estimation. In section 3, the method of saliency analysis is described. Section 4 gives the experimental results, followed by the conclusions in the last section.

2   Theory of SVMs for Regression Estimation

Given a set of data points $G = \{(X_i, d_i)\}_i^N$ (X_i is the input vector, d_i is the desired value, and N is the total number of data patterns), SVMs approximate the function by

$$y = f(X_i) = \sum_{i=1}^{N} W\phi(X_i) + b \tag{1}$$

where $\{\phi(X_i)\}_{i=1}^N$ are the high dimensional feature spaces which are nonlinearly mapped from the input space X_i. The coefficients W and b are estimated by minimizing

$$R_{SVMs}(C) = C\frac{1}{N}\sum_{i=1}^{N} L_\varepsilon(d_i, y_i) + \frac{1}{2}\|W\|^2 \tag{2}$$

$$L_\varepsilon(d, y) = \begin{cases} |d - y| - \varepsilon & |d - y| \geq \varepsilon \\ 0 & \textit{otherwise} \end{cases} \tag{3}$$

The first term $C\frac{1}{N}\sum_{i=1}^{N} L_\varepsilon(d_i, y_i)$ is the empirical error, which are measured by using the ε-insensitive loss function (3). The second term $\frac{1}{2}\|w\|^2$ is the regularization term. C and ε are referred to as the regularized constant and tube size.

To get the estimations of W and b, equation (2) is transformed to the primal function (4) by introducing the positive slack variables ζ_i and ζ_i^*.

Minimize: $$R_{SVMs}(W, \zeta^{(*)}) = \frac{1}{2}\|W\|^2 + C\sum_{i=1}^{N}(\zeta_i + \zeta_i^*) \tag{4}$$

Subjected to: $d_i - W\phi(X_i) - b_i \leq \varepsilon + \zeta_i$, and $\zeta^{(*)} \geq 0$

$$W\phi(X_i) + b_i - d_i \leq \varepsilon + \zeta_i^*$$

Finally, by introducing Lagrange multipliers and exploiting the optimality constraints, the decision function (1) has the following explicit form [7]:

$$f(X, a_i, a_i^*) = \sum_{i=1}^{N}(a_i - a_i^*)K(X, X_i) + b \tag{5}$$

In function (5), a_i and a_i^* are the so-called Lagrange multipliers, and $K(X_i, X_j)$ is defined as the kernel function. Any function that satisfies Mercer's condition [7] can be used as the kernel function.

Based on the Karush-Kuhn-Tucker (KKT) conditions of quadratic programming, only a number of coefficients ($a_i - a_i^*$) will assume nonzero, and the data points associated with them have approximation errors equal to or larger than ε, and are referred to as support vectors. According to (5), it is evident that support vectors are the only elements of the data points that are used in determining the decision function.

3 Saliency Analysis of SVMs

As illustrated in (5), the decision function in SVMs is expressed as:

$$y_i = \sum_{j=1}^{N_s} (a_j - a_j^*) K(x_j, x_i) + b$$

where N_s is the number of support vectors. So the network output is dependent on the converged Lagrange multipliers $(a_j - a_j^*)$ and the used kernel $K(x_j, x_i)$.

The sensitivity of the network output to the input is approximated by the derivative:

$$\frac{\partial y_i}{\partial x_k} = \frac{\partial(\sum_{j=1}^{N_s} (a_j - a_j^*) k(X_j, X_i) + b)}{\partial x_k}$$

$$= \frac{\partial \sum_{j=1}^{N_s} (a_j - a_j^*) k(X_j, X_i)}{\partial x_k} + \frac{\partial b}{\partial x_k}$$

$$= \sum_{j=1}^{N_s} (a_j - a_j^*) \frac{\partial k(X_j, X_i)}{\partial x_k} \tag{6}$$

(i) To the Gaussian function $k(X_j, X_i) = e^{\frac{\sum_{l=1}^{K}(x_{il} - x_{jl})^2}{\sigma^2}}$, then

$$\frac{\partial k(X_j, X_i)}{\partial x_{ik}} = -\frac{2}{\sigma^2} (x_{ik} - x_{jk}) e^{\frac{\sum_{l=1}^{K}(x_{il} - x_{jl})^2}{\sigma^2}}.$$ In this case,

$$\frac{\partial y_i}{\partial x_{ik}} = -\frac{2}{\sigma^2} \sum_{j=1}^{N_s} (a_j - a_j^*)(x_{ik} - x_{jk}) e^{\frac{\sum_{l=1}^{K}(x_{il} - x_{jl})^2}{\sigma^2}}.$$

(ii) To the polynomial kernel $k(x_j, x_i) = (\sum_{l=1}^{K} x_{il} x_{jl} + 1)^d$, then

$$\frac{\partial k(X_j, X_i)}{\partial x_{ik}} = d(\sum_{l=1}^{K} x_{il} x_{jl} + 1)^{d-1} x_{jk}.$$ In this case, $\frac{\partial y_i}{\partial x_{ik}} = d \sum_{j=1}^{N_s} (a_j - a_j^*) x_{jk} (\sum_{l=1}^{K} x_{il} x_{jl} + 1)^{d-1}.$

(iii) To the 2-layer tangent kernel $k(x_j, x_i) = \tanh(\beta_0 \sum_{l=1}^{K} x_{il} x_{jl} + \beta_1)$, then

$$\frac{\partial k(X_j, X_i)}{\partial x_{ik}} = \frac{4\beta_0 x_{jk}}{(e^{\beta_0 \sum_{l=1}^{K} x_{il} x_{jl} + \beta_1} + e^{-(\beta_0 \sum_{l=1}^{K} x_{il} x_{jl} + \beta_1)})^2}.$$ In this case,

$$\frac{\partial y_i}{\partial x_{ik}} = \sum_{j=1}^{N_s} \frac{4(a_j - a_j^*)\beta_0 x_{jk}}{(e^{\beta_0 \sum_{l=1}^{K} x_{il} x_{jl} + \beta_1} + e^{-(\beta_0 \sum_{l=1}^{K} x_{il} x_{jl} + \beta_1)})^2}.$$

The derivative of the output to the input can be calculated for any type of kernel function according to (6), and the value depends on the input feature x_{ik}, the support vectors X_j as well as the converged Lagrange multipliers ($a_j - a_j^*$).

Then, the saliency metric of each feature is calculated as the absolute average of the derivative of the output to the input over the entire training data sample, which is:

$$s_k = \sqrt{\frac{\sum_{i=1}^{N} \left| \frac{\partial y_i}{\partial x_{ik}} \right|}{N}} \tag{7}$$

Other calculations could be $s_k = \sqrt{\dfrac{\sum_{i=1}^{N} (\frac{\partial y_i}{\partial x_{ik}})^2}{N}}$ and $s_k = \max\limits_{i=1,...N}\{\frac{\partial y_i}{\partial x_{ik}}\}$ [8].

After calculating the saliency value, a criterion needs to be set up to determine how many features could be removed from the whole feature set. This paper uses a simple threshold method. The features with saliency value lower than the threshold are deleted while those with saliency value larger than the threshold are retained, as a small value of saliency in comparison with others means that the corresponding input does not significantly contribute to the network output and therefore could be disregarded from the overall feature set. A systematic procedure for eliminating insignificant features is outlined as follows.

1. Train SVMs using full feature set.

2. Calculate s_i by (6) and (7) for each candidate feature.

3. Rank s_i in a descending order as $s_1' > s_2' > ... > s_K'$, where $s_1' = \max\limits_{m_1}\{s_i\}$, $s_2' = \max\limits_{\substack{i \neq m_1 \\ m_2}}\{s_i\}, ...,$ and $s_K' = \max\limits_{\substack{i \neq m_1,...,m_{K-1} \\ m_K}}\{s_i\}$.

4. Choose a proper threshold ε.

5. If $s_i' > \varepsilon$ and $s_{i+1}' < \varepsilon$, delete the features corresponding to the saliency value $s_{i+1}', ..., s_K'$.

4   Experiment Results

Five real futures contracts collated from the Chicago Mercantile Market are examined in the second series of experiments. They are the Standard&Poor 500 stock index futures (CME-SP), United Sates 30-year government bond (CBOT-US), Unite States 10-year government bond (CBOT-BO), German 10-year government bond (EUREX-BUND) and French government stock index futures (MATIF-CAC40). The daily closing prices are used as the data set. And the original closing price is transformed into a five-day relative difference in percentage of price (RDP).

The input variables are constructed from 3 lagged transformed closing prices which is obtained by subtracting a 15-day exponential moving average from the closing price (x_1, x_2, x_3) and 14 lagged RDP values based on 5-day periods

($x_4, \ldots, x_{17}$). These indicators are referenced from Thomason [9], but more numbers of indicators that are believed to involve redundant information are used here for the purpose of feature selection. The output variable RDP+5 is obtained by first smoothing the closing price with a 3-day exponential moving average, as the application of a smoothing transform to the dependent variable generally enhances the prediction performance of neural network. Each data set is partitioned into three parts according to the time sequence. The first part is for training, the second part for validating which is used to select optimal kernel parameter for SVMs, and the last part for testing. There are a total of 907 data patterns in the training set, 200 data patterns in both the validation set and the test set in all the data sets.

The Gaussian function is used as the kernel function of SVMs. The kernel parameter, C and ε are selected based on the smallest normalized mean squared error (NMSE) on the validation set. The NMSE is calculated as

$$NMSE = \frac{1}{n * \delta^2} \sum_{i=1}^{n} (d_i - y_i)^2 \tag{8}$$

$$\delta^2 = \frac{1}{n-1} \sum_{i=1}^{n} (d_i - \overline{d})^2$$

where $\overline{d}$ denotes the mean of d_i. The values of δ^2, C and ε slightly vary in futures due to the different market behaviors of the futures. The Sequential Minimal Optimization algorithm [10] is implemented and the program is developed using VC$^+$ language.

The selected features are reported in Table 1. As it is unknown whether the irrelevant features have been correctly deleted, the selected features are used as the inputs of SVMs to retrain the network. The NMSE of the test set for the full feature set and the selected feature set is given in Table 2. It is evident that there is smaller NMSE on the test set in the selected feature setthan that of using full feature set. The result is consistent in all of the five contracts. This indicates that saliency analysis is effective in selecting important features for SVMs.

5 Conclusions

The saliency analysis for ranking the importance of features has been developed for SVMs by evaluating the partial derivative of the output to the feature input over the entire training data samples. The threshold method is applied to delete irrelevant features from the whole feature set. According to the simulation results by using five real futures contracts, it can be concluded that saliency analysis is effective in SVMs for selecting important features. By deleting the irrelevant features, the generalization performance of SVMs is greatly enhanced.

There are still some aspects that require further investigation. Although using a simple threshold method for determining how many unimportant features are deleted works well in this study, more formal methods need to be explored for complex problems.

References

1. Muller, R., Smola, J. A., Scholkopf, B.: Prediction Time Series with Support Vector Machines. In Proceedings of International Conference on Artificial Neural Networks (1997) 999
2. Vapnik, V. N., Golowich, S. E., Smola, A. J.: Support Vector Method for Function Approximation, Regression Estimation, and Signal Processing. Advances in Neural Information Processing Systems 9 (1996) 281-287
3. Barzilay, O., Brailovsky, V. L.: On Domain Knowledge and Feature Selection Using a SVM. Pattern Recognition Letters 20 (1999) 475-484.
4. Steppe, J. M., Bauer, Jr. K.W.: Feature Saliency Measures. Computers Math. Application 33 (1997) 109-126
5. Reed, R.: Pruning algorithms — a survey. IEEE Transactions on Neural Networks 4 (1993) 940-947
6. Ruck, D. W., Rogers, S. K., Kabrisky, M.: Feature Selection Using a Multi-layer Perceptron. Journal of Neural Network Computing 2 (1990) 40-48
7. Vapnik, V. N.: The Nature of Statistical Learning Theory. Springer-Verlag, New York 1995
8. Zurada, J. M., Malinowski, A., Usui, S.: Perturbation Method for Deleting Redundant Inputs of Perceptron Networks. Neurocomputing 14 (1997) 177-193
9. Thomason, M.: The Practitioner Methods and Tool. Journal of Computational Intelligence in Finance 7(3) (1999) 36-45
10. Smola, A. J., Scholkopf, B.: A tutorial on Support Vector Regression. NeuroCOLT Technical Report TR, Royal Holloway College, London, UK 1998

Table 1. The selected features in the five futures contracts.

Futures	Selected features
CME-SP	$x\ ,x_2,x\ ,x_7,x_{12}$
CBOT-US	$x_1,x_2,x\ ,x_0\ ,x_{12}\ x_6$
CBOT-BO	$x_1,x_2,x\ ,x_8\ x_9,x_0\ ,x_{12}$
EUREX-BUND	$x_1,x_2,x\ ,x_6,x_{12}\ x_7$
MATIF-CAC40	$x_1,x_2,x\ ,x_9,x_{12}\ x_7$

Table 2. The NMSE on the test set of the selected features and full futures.

Features	Full features	Selected features
CME-SP	0.9629	0.8442
CBOT-US	1.1643	1.0501
CBOT-BO	1.1853	0.9936
EUREX-BUND	1.4762	1.0792
MATIF-CAC40	1.1582	0.9584

ε-Descending Support Vector Machines for Financial Time Series Forecasting

L. J. CAO and FRANCIS E. H. TAY

Department of Mechanical & Production Engineering, National University of Singapore, 10 Kent Ridge Crescent, 119260, Singapore. Email: mpetayeh@nus.edu.sg

Abstract. This paper proposes ε-descending support vector machines (ε-DSVMs) to model non-stationary financial time series. The ε-DSVMs are obtained by taking into account the problem domain knowledge of non-stationarity in the financial time series. Unlike the original SVMs which use the same tube size in all the training data points, the ε-DSVMs use the tube whose value decrease from the distant training data points to the recent training data points. Three real futures which are collected from the Chicago Mercantile Market are examined in the experiment, and it is shown that the ε-DSVMs consistently forecast better than the original SVMs.

1 Introduction

Financial time series are inherently noisy and non-stationary [1, 2]. The non-stationary characteristic means that the distribution of financial time series changs over time. This will lead to gradual changes in the dependency between input and output variables. In the modeling of financial time series, the learning algorithm used should take into account this characteristic. Usually, the information provided by the recent data is weighted more heavily than that of the distant data [3].

Recently, support vector machine (SVM) developed by Vapnik and his co-workers in 1995 [4] as a novel neural network technique has received increasing attention in the area of regression estimation [5,6] due to its remarkable generalization performance. SVMs implement the Structural Risk Minimization principle which seeks to minimize an upper bound of the generalization error rather than minimize the empirical error as commonly implemented in other neural networks. Another key property of SVMs is that training SVMs is equivalent to solving a linearly constrained quadratic programming. Consequently, the solution to the problem is only dependent on a small subset of training data points called support vectors. Using only support vectors, the same solution of the decision function can be obtained as using all the training data points.

What are support vectors? In regression estimation, they are the training data points which associated approximation errors are equal to or larger than ε, the so-called tube size. That is, they are the data points lying on or outside the ε-bound of the decision function. In usual case, the number of support vectors decreases as ε increases. In the case of a wide tube where there are few support vectors, the decision function can be represented very sparsely. However, too wide a tube will also depreciate the estimation accuracy as ε is equivalent to the approximation accuracy placed on the training data points. In the standard SVMs, ε is used as a constant value and selected empirically.

In this paper, the authors propose ε-descending SVMs (ε-DSVMs) to model financial time series by associating the relationship between support vectors and ε with the non-stationary characteristic of the financial time series. The ε-DSVMs use the tube whose value will decrease from distant training data to recent training data to deal with the structural changes of the financial time series. There are two reasons for this modification. Firstly, since support vectors are a decreasing function of ε, by using a smaller ε the recent data will have greater probability of converging to the determinant support vectors and thus be obtained more attention in the representation of the decision function than the distant data. Secondly, from the approximation accuracy point of view, the recent data will be approximated more accurately than the distant data. This is desirable according to the non-stationarity of the financial time series. The proposed method is illustrated experimentally using three real futures contracts. The experiment shows great improvement by the use of ε-DSVMs.

This paper is organized as follows. Section 2 gives a brief introduction of SVMs in the regression estimation. Section 3 presents the ε-DSVMs. Section 4 gives the experimental results together with the data preprocessing technique. Section 5 concludes the work done.

2   Theory of SVMs for Regression Estimation

Given a set of data points $G = \{(x_i, d_i)\}_i^n$ (x_i is the input vector, d_i is the desired value, and n is the number of training data points), SVMs approximate the function using the following form:

$$y = f(x) = \sum_{i=1}^{n} w_i \phi_i(x) + b \tag{1}$$

where $\{\phi_i(x)\}_{i=1}^n$ are the high dimensional feature spaces which are nonlinearly mapped from the input space x. The coefficients $\{w_i\}_{i=1}^n$ and b are estimated by minimizing the regularized risk function (2).

$$R_{SVMs}(C) = C \frac{1}{n} \sum_{i=1}^{n} L_\varepsilon(d_i, y_i) + \frac{1}{2}\|w\|^2 \tag{2}$$

$$L_\varepsilon(d, y) = \begin{cases} |d - y| - \varepsilon & |d - y| \geq \varepsilon \\ 0 & otherwise \end{cases} \tag{3}$$

The first term $C \frac{1}{n} \sum_{i=1}^{n} L_\varepsilon(d_i, y_i)$ is the empirical error, which are measured by using the ε-insensitive loss function (3). The second term $\frac{1}{2}\|w\|^2$ is the regularization term. C and ε are referred to as the regularized constant and tube size.

To get the estimations of $\{w_i\}_{i=1}^{n}$ and b, equation (2) is transformed to the primal function (4) by introducing the positive slack variables ζ_i and ζ_i^{*}.

$$\text{Minimize: } R_{SVMs}(w, \zeta^{(*)}) = \frac{1}{2}\|w\|^2 + C\sum_{i=1}^{n}(\zeta_i + \zeta_i^{*}) \qquad (4)$$

Subjected to: $d_i - w\phi(x_i) - b_i \le \varepsilon + \zeta_i$, and $\zeta^{(*)} \ge 0$
$$w\phi(x_i) + b_i - d_i \le \varepsilon + \zeta_i^{*}$$

Finally, by introducing Lagrange multipliers and exploiting the optimality constraints, the decision function (1) has the following explicit form [4]:

$$f(x, a_i, a_i^{*}) = \sum_{i=1}^{n}(a_i - a_i^{*})K(x, x_i) + b \qquad (5)$$

In function (5), a_i and a_i^{*} are the so-called Lagrange multipliers. They satisfy the equalities $a_i * a_i^{*} = 0$, $a_i \ge 0$ and $a_i^{*} \ge 0$ where $i = 1,...,n$, and they are obtained by maximizing the dual function of (4), which has the following form:

$$R(a_i, a_i^{*}) = \sum_{i=1}^{n}d_i(a_i - a_i^{*}) - \varepsilon\sum_{i=1}^{n}(a_i + a_i^{*}) - \frac{1}{2}\sum_{i=1}^{n}\sum_{j=1}^{n}(a_i - a_i^{*})(a_j - a_j^{*})K(x_i, x_j) \qquad (6)$$

with the following constraints: $\sum_{i=1}^{n}(a_i - a_i^{*}) = 0$, $0 \le a_i \le C$, and $0 \le a_i^{*} \le C, i = 1,2...n$

$K(x_i, x_j)$ is defined as the kernel function. Any function that satisfies Mercer's condition [4] can be used as the kernel function. Based on the Karush-Kuhn-Tucker (KKT) conditions of quadratic programming, only a number of coefficients ($a_i - a_i^{*}$) will assume nonzero, and the data points associated with them have approximation errors equal to or larger than ε, and are referred to as support vectors. According to (5), it is evident that support vectors are the only elements of the data points that are used in determining the decision function.

3 ε-Descending Support Vector Machines (ε-DSVMs)

In $\mathcal{E}$-DSVMs, instead of a constant value, the tube size ε adopts the following exponential function.

$$\varepsilon_i = \varepsilon_0 \frac{1 + \exp(a - 2a * i/n)}{2} \qquad (7)$$

Where n is the total number of training data patterns, with $i = n$ being the most recent observation and $i = 1$ being the earliest observation. a is the parameter to control the descending rate. The ideas of $\mathcal{E}$-DSVMs are, firstly, to give the recent data higher chance of converging to support vectors and secondly, to place higher approximation accuracy on the recent data than the distant data, therefore paying more attention to the recent information than the distant information since the recent information is more important than that of the distant data in the non-stationary financial time series.

The behaviors of the weight function can be summarized as follows (some examples are illustrated in Fig. 1):

(i)   When $a \to 0$, then $\underset{a \to 0}{Lim}\, \varepsilon_i = \varepsilon_0$. In this case, the weights in all the training data points are equal to 1.0.

(ii)   When $a \to \infty$, then $\underset{a \to \infty}{Lim}\, \varepsilon_i = \begin{cases} \infty & i < \dfrac{n}{2} \\ \dfrac{1}{2}\varepsilon_0 & i \geq \dfrac{n}{2} \end{cases}$. In this case, the weights for the first half of the training data points are increased to an infinite value while the weights for the second half of the training data points are equal to 0.5.

(iii)   When $a \in [0,\infty]$ and a increases, the weights for the first half of the training data points will become larger while the weights for the second half of the training data points will become smaller.

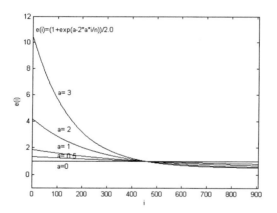

Fig. 1. Weights function of ε-DSVMs.

In ε-DSVMs, the regularized risk function has the original form but the constraints are changed according to (8) whereby every training data point corresponds to different tube size ε_i.

$$R_{SVMs}(w,\zeta^{(*)}) = \frac{1}{2}\|w\|^2 + C\sum_{i=1}^{n}(\zeta_i + \zeta_i^*)$$

$$\text{Subjected to:} \begin{array}{l} d_i - w\phi(x_i) - b_i \leq \varepsilon_i + \zeta_i \\ w\phi(x_i) + b_i - d_i \leq \varepsilon_i + \zeta_i^* \end{array} \tag{8}$$

Thus, the dual function becomes as (9) with the original constraints.

$$R(a_i,a_i^*) = \sum_{i=1}^{n} d_i(a_i - a_i^*) - \sum_{i=1}^{n}\varepsilon_i(a_i + a_i^*) - \frac{1}{2}\sum_{i=1}^{n}\sum_{j=1}^{n}(a_i - a_i^*)(a_j - a_j^*)K(x_i,x_j) \tag{9}$$

Constraints: $\sum_{i=1}^{n}(a_i - a_i^*) = 0$, $0 \leq a_i \leq C$, and $0 \leq a_i^* \leq C, i = 1,2...n$

4   Experiment Results

Three real future contracts collected from the Chicago Mercantile Market are examined in the experiment. They are the Standard&Poor 500 stock index futures (CME-SP), United Sates 30-year government bond (CBOT-US) and German 10-year government bond (EUREX-BUND). The daily closing prices are used as the data set. The original closing price is transformed into a five-day relative difference in percentage of price (RDP). The input variables are constructed from four lagged RDP values based on 5-day periods and one transformed closing price which is obtained by subtracting a 15-day exponential moving average from the closing price. The output variable RDP+5 is obtained by first smoothening the closing price with a 3-day exponential moving average. Then, all the data points are scaled into the range of [-0.9,0.9] as the data points include both positive values and negative values. There are a total of 907 data patterns in the training set and 200 data patterns in both the validation set and the test set in all the three data sets.

The Gaussian function is used as the kernel function of the SVMs. Both δ^2 and C are chosen as 10 as these values produced the smallest normalized mean squared error (NMSE) on the validation set. The NMSE is calculated as

$$NMSE = \frac{1}{n * \delta^2} \sum_{i=1}^{n} (d_i - y_i)^2 \qquad (10)$$

$$\delta^2 = \frac{1}{n-1} \sum_{i=1}^{n} (d_i - \overline{d})^2$$

where $\overline{d}$ denotes the mean of d_i. With respect to ε_0, a range of reasonable values from 0.001 to 0.1 are studied. The Sequential Minimal Optimization algorithm [7,8] is implemented and the program is developed using VC$^+$ language.

Table 1 gives the results of ε - DSVMs and the original SVMs for the three futures. It can been seen that there are smaller converged NMSE in the ε-DSVMs than those of the original SVMs in all the investigated ε_0. The result is also irrespective of the futures. Fig. 2 gives the predicted and actual values of RDP+5 on the test data points. It is obvious that ε -DSVMs forecast more closely to the actual values and capture the turning points better than the original SVMs.

5   Conclusions

This paper proposes a modified version of SVMs to model financial time series by incorporating the non-stationary characteristic of financial time series into SVMs. These modified SVMs use the non-constant tube which sizes decrease from the distant training sample data to the recent training sample data in an exponential form. The simulation results demonstrated that the ε -DSVMs is more effective in modeling financial time series by considering the structural changes of the financial time series.

Future work will involve a theoretic analysis of the ε -DSVMs. More sophisticated weights function which can closely follow the dynamics of financial time series will be explored for further improving the performance of support vector machines in financial time series forecasting.

Table 1. The NMSE of ε - DSVMs and the original SVMs.

ε_0	CME-SP		CBOT-US		EUREX-BUND	
	ε -DSVMs	SVMs	ε -DSVMs	SVMs	ε -DSVMs	SVMs
0.001	0.8910	0.9512	1.0902	1.1745	1.1794	1.2603
0.005	0.8841	0.9545	1.0907	1.1750	1.1976	1.2697
0.01	0.9023	0.9447	1.0697	1.1784	1.1870	1.2599
0.05	0.8961	0.9508	1.0992	1.1658	1.2052	1.2522
0.1	0.9172	0.9550	1.0911	1.1767	1.2058	1.2534

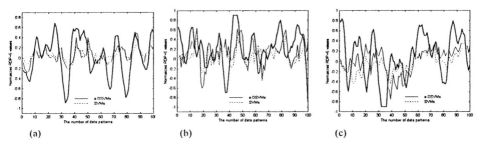

(a)   (b)   (c)

Fig. 2. Predicted and actual values of RDP+5. (a) CME-SP. (b) CBOT-US. (c) EUREX-BUND.

References

1. Hall, J. W.: Adaptive Selection of U.S. Socks with Neural Nets. Trading On the Edge: Neural, Genetic, and Fuzzy Systems for Chaotic Financial Markets, Wiley, New York (1994)
2. Yaser, S. A. M., Atiya, A. F.: Introduction to Financial Forecasting. Applied Intelligence 6 (1996) 205-213
3. Refenes, A. N. Bentz, Y., Bunn, D. W., Burgess, A. N., Zapranis, A. D.: Financial Time Series Modelling with Discounted Least Squares Back-propagation. Neurocomputing 14 (1997) 123-138
4. Vapnik, V. N.: The Nature of Statistical Learning Theory. Springer-Verlag, New York 1995
5. Muller, R., Smola, J. A., Scholkopf, B.: Prediction Time Series with Support Vector Machines. In Proceedings of International Conference on Artificial Neural Networks (1997) 999
6. Vapnik, V. N., Golowich, S. E., Smola, A. J.: Support Vector Method for Function Approximation, Regression Estimation, and Signal Processing. Advances in Neural Information Processing Systems 9 (1996) 281-287
7. Smola, A. J., Scholkopf, B.: A tutorial on Support Vector Regression. NeuroCOLT Technical Report TR, Royal Holloway College, London, UK 1998
8. Smola, A.J.: Learning with Kernels. PhD Thesis, GMD, Birlinghoven, Germany 1998

Classifying Market States with WARS

Lixiang Shen[1] and Francis E. H. Tay[2]

Department of Mechanical and Production Engineering, National University of Singapore
10 Kent Ridge Crescent, Singapore 119260
{[1]engp8633, [2]mpetayeh}@nus.edu.sg

Abstract. In this paper, a new indicator - *WARS (Weighted Accumulated Reconstruction Series)* at classifying the state of financial market, either trending state or mean-reverting state, was presented. Originated from the computation of Entropy, this new indicator was found to be able to reflect the market behavior accurately and easily. The algorithm of generating *WARS* and its meaning related to Entropy were introduced and some comparison results between *WARS* and the *Daily Profit Curve* were listed. As a new indicator, *WARS* also can be used to build a trading system - to provide buy, sell and hold signals. Through the application on S&P 500 index, it was verified to be effective and was a promising indicator.

1   Introduction

One of the basic tenets put forth by Charles Dow in the Dow Theory [1] is that security prices do trend. Trends are often measured and identified by "trendlines" and they represent the consistent change in prices (i.e., a change in investor expectations). In the Fig. 1 and Fig. 2, rising trend and falling trend were illustrated.

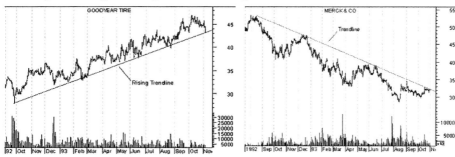

Fig. 1. Rising Trend   **Fig. 2.** Falling Trend

A principle of technical analysis is that once a trend has been formed, it will remain intact until broken [2]. The goal of technical analysis is to analyze the current trend using trendlines and then either invest with the current trend until the trendline is broken, or wait for the trendline to be broken and then invest with the new (opposite) trend. For trading, it is very important to know the current market state – either in the rising trend or in the falling trend. So our work was focussed on searching for indicators that can reflect the fluctuation of price or index in the financial markets. An indicator, called *Weighted Accumulated Reconstruction Series* (*WARS*), has been constructed and found to have interesting characteristics. It can reflect the trend of the changes in price. The indicator was able to make use of more information contained in the data than moving average and therefore may be able to better reflect the state of the price or index.

2 Weighted Accumulated Reconstruction Series (*WARS*)

The idea of generating *Weighted Accumulated Reconstruction Series (WARS)* came from the computation of Entropy. The concept of Entropy was first proposed by Shannon [3] in the Information Theory as a measure of the complexity of a system. Up to now, this concept has been applied in the economic domain to measure the production flexibility [4], customer requirements [5], and processing cost of administrating the production facility [6]. In the capital market, a derivative of information entropy - Kolmogorov Entropy, was applied to measure how chaotic a system is based on the analysis of real-time price or index [7, 8, 9, 10, 11, 12]. By calculation of Kolmogorov Entropy, the predictability of the price changes or returns is studied. Kapur and Kesavan [13] even used the Kullback's Minimum Cross-Entropy Principle to minimise the risk in portfolio analysis.

The Shannon Entropy, represented by *Ent(S)*, of a system is defined as:

$$Ent(S) = -\sum_{i=1}^{k} P(C_i, S) \log(P(C_i, S)) . \tag{1}$$

where C_i presents the *i*th event in system S, i = 1, 2, ..., k;

$P(C_i,S)$ is the *a priori* probability of event C_i's occurrence in *S*.

From the above definition in Eq. 1, the distribution of the system must be known before the System Entropy is calculated. But in practice, usually the distribution of the system may not be known in advance. The easiest way to solve this problem is to accumulate this series and it will follow the exponential function for a positive series. Following this idea, the algorithm to construct the new indicator is formulated in.

Step 1: Normalize every value of this series between -1 to 1 (to remove amplitude effect off the series)

$$x_i = x_i / \max(|x_i|); \qquad\qquad (i = 1, 2, ..., \text{Win\_length}) \tag{2}$$

Step 2: Subtract the first value of a series (to keep all the intervals at the same beginning, the origin of coordinates).

$$x_i = x_i - x_1; \qquad\qquad (i = 1, 2, ..., \text{Win\_length}) \tag{3}$$

Step 3: Subtract the mean value from the whole series.

$$x_i = x_i - Mean\_x ; \qquad\qquad (i = 1, 2, ..., \text{Win\_length}) \tag{4}$$

where: $Mean\_x = \dfrac{1}{n}\sum_i x_i$

Step 4: Reconstruct a new series (*WARS*) by means of weighted accumulating the original one.

$$Weight_j = \frac{1 + 2 + \cdots + j}{1 + 2 + \cdots + Win\_length}. \qquad\qquad (j = 1, 2, ..., \text{Win\_length}) \tag{5}$$

$$y_1 = \frac{1}{1 + 2 + \cdots + n} x_1 ;$$

$$\cdots$$
$$y_n = \frac{1}{1+2+\cdots+n}x_1 + \frac{1+2}{1+2+\cdots+n}x_2 + \cdots + \frac{1+2+\cdots+n}{1+2+\cdots+n}x_n \; . \tag{6}$$

In this process, the more recent points have more contribution to *WARS*.

Step 5: Calculate the area of this interval and get its absolute value.

$$Area = |y_1 + y_2 + \cdots + y_n| \; . \tag{7}$$

The trending and mean-reverting states were distinguished according to the area value. If the area value is greater than 0, then market is in a trending state, else the market is in a mean-reverting state.

In Figure 3, three curves representing up-trending, down-trending and mean-reverting series were drawn. After *weighted accumulated reconstruction*, the corresponding three curves were drawn in Figure 4.

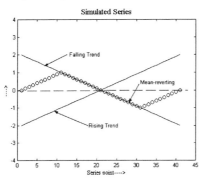

Fig. 3. The illustration of Accumulated Reconstruction Series

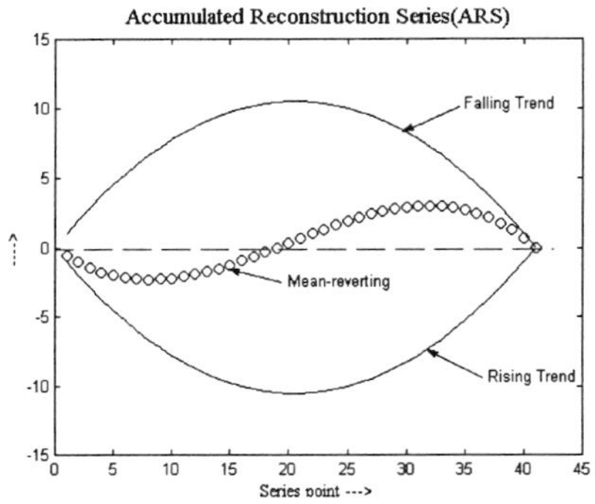

Fig. 4. The illustration of Accumulated Reconstruction Series

During the process of generating *WARS*, the original series was rolled and the *area* of every interval was calculated iteratively. For instance, if there are 10 points in a series; and *Win_length* is chosen as 4. From the 1st point to the 4th point the first area value is calculated. From the 2nd point to the 5th point the second area value is obtained. This process is repeated and eventually six points are obtained to construct *WARS*. The length of *WARS* equals to the length of original series less *Win_length*.

3 Comparison of *WARS* and *Daily Profit Curves*

For a large company, usually a certain strategy will be adopted to direct its operation in the financial market. Further, the *equity curve* of a period will be used to evaluate the pros and cons of this strategy [14]. If the *equity curve* goes up, the company is making a profit and vice versa. The generation of the *equity curve* will not be introduced in this paper. This was taken to be a given information. For the testing of the new indicator, 15 historical futures data supplied by Man-Drapeau Research Pte Ltd (Singapore) were selected. The *WARS* was generated from the *daily close price*. For the convenience of comparison of the above two curves, the *equity curve* was first changed to *daily profit curve* by using the following method:

$$y_i = x_i - x_{i-1}. \qquad (i = 1, 2, \ldots, n) \tag{8}$$

Then the *moving average curve* [15] was calculated for both *WARS* and *Daily Profit Curve*. The correlation coefficient of *WARS* and the *Daily Profit Curve* was calculated to evaluate their similarity.

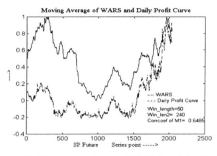

Fig. 5. The comparison of *WARS* and *Daily Profit Curve* for SP Futures

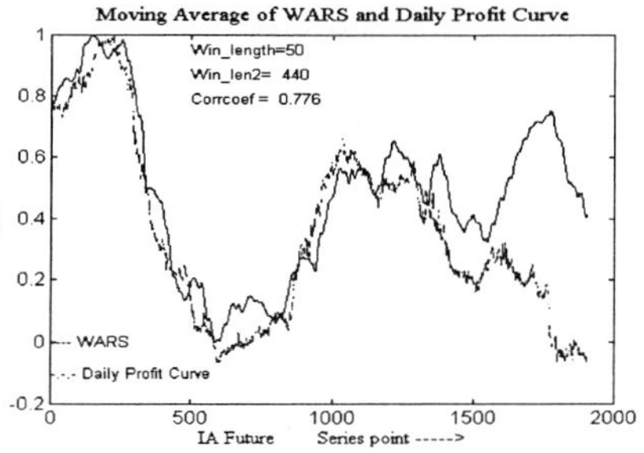

Fig. 6. The comparison of *WARS* and *Daily Profit Curve* for IA Futures

In Figures 5 - 6, the two curves were rescaled between -1 and 1 so that they can be compared directly. The solid line curve in Figures 5 - 6 represented *WARS* while the other curve represented the *Daily Profit Curve*. In these Figures, the two curves, *WARS* and *Daily Profit Curve* were found to have similar shape. It was clear that *WARS* reflected the fluctuation of *Daily Profit Curve*. From the correlation coefficient, the value was always larger than 0.6 (sometimes almost equal to 0.95). Thus *WARS* reflected the changing of *Daily Profit Curve* quite well.

From the generation of *WARS*, its meaning in the financial market can be interpreted as follows: *WARS* was generated by using the closing price in a period. If within this period, the price changes in a trending way, either up-trending or down-trending, *WARS* will maintain its large value or it may go up. When the price fluctuates in a mean-reverting way, *WARS* will go down or remain as a small value. Indirectly, it continuously reflects the changing of price. From the view of entropy, it can be simply interpreted as follows: The market states can be represented as 1 - up-trending, 0 -mean-reverting and -1 - down-trending. When the market falls in the trending state (either 1 or -1), the entropy of market equals to 0, corresponding to large value of *WARS*, close to 1. The mean-reverting state (0) is composed of up-trending and down-trending states, when the entropy of market equals to $\log 2$ ($Ent = -(\frac{1}{2}\log\frac{1}{2} + \frac{1}{2}\log\frac{1}{2})$), corresponding to a small value of *WARS*, close to 0. It is easy to understand the above results. When the market moves in a trending way, the system is more certain than in a mean-reverting state, in which the direction of price cannot be determined, i.e. more uncertainty contained in this system.

4 Using *WARS* to Generate Trading System

Based on the previous analysis, in this section, *WARS* was used to generate a trading system. The trading system [16] was built in the following steps:
- Calculate *WARS* using historical data.

- Determine the threshold value for buying and selling action according to the value of *WARS* calculated using training data set.
- Generate the trading signals as follows:
  If value of *WARS* > threshold of buying, then buy at the next day's opening price
  If value of *WARS* < threshold of selling, then sell at the next day's opening price
  If value of *WARS* is in between the thresholds, then no action is taken - hold.

  Figure 7 depicts such a trading system using S&P500 index. The time interval of data was daily. The *WARS* was calculated based on 5-day-Win_length.

CME-SP 500

Fig. 7. Trading system generated using *WARS* on S&P 500 index

From the Figure 7, it can be seen that *WARS* gave correct trading signals at suitable time when the market changed gradually, from Jan. 1993 to Oct. 1997. But when the market changed dramatically, from Nov. 1997 to Apr. 1999, some signals given were lagging behind the change of price. This indicated that *WARS* is a reactive indictor. The trading performance was illustrated in Table 1.

Table 1. Trading system performance based on the indicator *WARS* on S&P 500

Training Data Set	Testing Data Set
Training period:	Testing period:
01/04/1988 - 12/31/1992	01/01/1993 - 08/12/1999
max_*WARS*_area = 0.022152	Net_profit = 873.649963
min_*WARS*_area = -0.034170	max_win = 325.150024
threshold_buy = 0.003378	max_loss = -37.000000
threshold_sell = -0.015396	Trading_number = 14
Mean_*WARS*_area = 0.000446	Winning_Trade = 9
Std_*WARS*_area = 0.005593	Sharpe_ratio = 0.522271

There were altogether 14 trades in this index, among which 9 of them were profitable. From these results, it can be seen that this new indicator is effective in differentiating the market states and so it can be used to trace the changing market and provide the trading signals.

5 Concluding Remarks

A new indicator - *Weighted Accumulated Reconstruction Series* (*WARS*) is presented. In comparison with the *Daily Profit Curve*, *WARS* can indicate the *Daily Profit Curve* accurately and easily. In addition, *WARS* can be used to build a trading system. Through the application on S&P 500 index, it can be seen that this indicator is effective and promising. Further, *WARS* can be used to reflect the uncertainty of the market. When the magnitude of *WARS* approaches 1, the market is a strong trending state and therefore more investment can be done.

Although *WARS* is very similar in behaviour to the *Daily Profit Curve,* there are still many factors affecting the final results, such as the parameters: *Win_length* and *Moving Average Interval*. These issues will be further studied in the future

References

1. Bishop, G. W.: Charles H. Dow and the Dow theory. New York, Appleton-Century-Crofts (1960)
2. Achelis, S. B.: Technical Analysis from A to Z: covers every trading tool - from the Absolute Breadth Index to the Zig Zag. Probus Publisher, Chicago (1995)
3. Shannon, C. E. and Weaver,W.: The mathematical theory of communication. Urbana: University of Illinois Press (1949)
4. Frizelle, G. and Woodcock, E.: Measuring Complexity as an Aid to Developing Operational Strategy. International Journal of Operations and Production Management 15 (1995) 26-39
5. Johnston, R. B.: From Efficiency to Flexibility: Entropic Measures of Market Complexity and Production Flexibility. Complexity International 3 (1996)
6. Ronen, B. and Karp R.: An Information Entropy Approach to the Small-Lot Concept. IEEE Transactions on Engineering Management 41 (1994) 89-92
7. Barkoulas J. and Travlos N: Chaos in an emerging capital market? The case of the Athens Stock Exchange. Applied Financial Economics 8 (1998) 231-243
8. Mayfield E. and Mizrach B.: On Determining the Dimension of Real-Time Stock-Price Data. Journal of Business & Economic Statistics 10 (1992) 367-374
9. Frank, M. and Stengos, T.: Measuring the Strangeness of Gold and Silver Rates of Return. Review of Economic Studies 56 (1989) 553-567
10. Chen, S.-H.: Elements of Information Theory: A Book Review. Journal of Economic Dynamics and Control 20 (1996) 819-824
11. Chen, S.-H and Tan, C.-W.: Measuring Randomness by Rissanen's Stochastic Complexity: Application to Financial Data. In: Dowe, D., Korb, K. and Oliver, J. (eds.): Information, Statistics and Induction in Science. World Scientific, Singapore (1996) 200-211
12. Chen, S-H and Tan, C.-W.: Estimating the Complexity Function of Financial Time Series: An Estimation Based on Predictive Stochastic Complexity. Journal of Management and Economics 3 (1999)
13. Kapur, J. and Kesavan, H.: Entropy optimization principles with applications, Boston: Academic Press (1992)
14. Hampton, J.: Risk Management: the Equity Curve Revisited. Journal of Computational Intelligence in Finance 6 (1998) 47-50
15. Webster, A. L.: Applied Statistics for Business and Economics. 2nd ed. McGraw-Hill Inc. (1995)
16. Pardo, R.: Design, Testing, and Optimization of Trading Systems. John Wiley & Sons Inc. (1992)

"Left Shoulder" Detection in Korea Composite Stock Price Index Using an Auto-Associative Neural Network

Jinwoo Baek and Sungzoon Cho

Department of Industrial Engineering, Seoul National University,
San 56-1, Shillim-Dong, Kwanak-Gu, 151-742, Seoul, Korea
E-mail : baekhana@snu.ac.kr , zoon@snu.ac.kr

Abstract. We propose a neural network based "left shoulder" detector. The auto-associative neural network was trained with the "left shoulder" patterns obtained from the Korea Composite Stock Price Index, and then tested out-of-sample with a reasonably good result. A hypothetical investment strategy based on the detector achieved a return of 124% in comparison with 39% return from a buy and hold strategy.

1. Introduction

Technical analysts use certain stock chart patterns and shapes as signals for profitable trading opportunities [6]. Many professional traders claim that they consistently make trading profits by following those signals. Recently there have been efforts to identify "change point" with data mining technique [3].

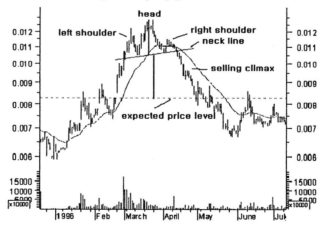

Figure 1. Head and shoulder formation

One of the best known chart patterns is "Head and Shoulder Formation" (HSF) [7] (see Figure 1). The HSF is believed to be one of the most reliable trend reversal patterns. Especially "Left Shoulder"(LS) of HSF is a starting event of HSF. In particular, if we can detect an LS of HSF, it can be used to make profitable trading like buying stocks in individual stock market. With a detection of "Head" of HSF, a short sale makes a profitable trading.

Generally technical analysts try to detect HSF manually after the fact. The process is obviously subjective and the prediction is often incorrect. However, it is possible to accurately detect HSF from historical data.

Thus, a pattern classification method such as a neural network is an ideal candidate. The detection problem can now be formulated as a 2-class problem. A neural network is trained with LS patterns and non-LS patterns. Then, given a new input data, or a current situation, the network tries to classify it as an Ls of HSF or a non-LS of HSF. A problem with this approach is the inability to collect a sufficient number of "non-LS" patterns. This is a well known problem of "partially-exposed environment" in pattern classification where training data from one class are very few or non-existent. Related problems include counterfeit bank note detection and typing pattern identity verification [1].

Recently, Auto-Associative Neural Network (AANN) has been proposed to be quite effective in partially-exposed environment [1]. AANN is basically a neural network whose input and target vectors are the same. In session 2 the details of AANN are reviewed and the reason of LS detection is provided.

The proposed detection process is as follow. First, the LS patterns are identified in historical database. Second, they are used to train AANN. Third, the trained AANN is used as an LS detector. An input pattern is compared with the output. If they are similar enough, the input pattern is classified as LS. Otherwise it is classified as non-LS. The LS signal could result in "buy" recommendation while non-LS signal results in "sell" or other action recommendation (see Figure 2).

Figure 2. System framework

2. Auto-associative neural network as an LS detector

AANN should reproduce an input vector at the output with a least error[2]. Let F denote an auto-associative mapping function, x_i an input vector and y_i an output vector. Then network F is usually trained to minimize the mean square error given by the equation:

$$E = \sum_{i=1}^{N} \left\| x_i - y_i \right\|^2 = \sum_{i=1}^{N} \left\| x_i - F(x_i) \right\|^2 .$$

Mapping function F can be separated into F_1 and F_2, that is $F(.) = F_2(F_1(.))$ where F_1 is a dimension reduction process and F_2 a dimension expansion process. Dimension reduction is achieved by projecting the vectors in the input space onto a subspace captured by the set of weights in the network part for F_1. Dimension expansion is achieved by mapping the lower dimensional vectors onto a hypersurface captured by the set of weight in the network part for F_2. Generally subspace and hypersurface are nonlinear because of the nonlinearity in the transfer function.

Historical financial data have particular trends and characteristics. They tend to repeat themselves. The financial situations that correspond to LS of HSF are assumed to have unique characteristics. If the core information can be incorporated into the network input variables, the unique characteristics can be captured by the subspace of AANN embodied by the transformation at the hidden layers. Once AANN is trained with LS data sets, any LS data that shares common characteristic will result in a small error at the output layer while non-LS data will result in a large error at the output layer. With an appropriate threshold, the AANN can be used to detect the occurrence of the LS.

3. Data collection and neural network training

We used Korea Composite Stock Price Index (KOSPI) data from April 1,1977 to July 24, 2000 for experiment. The KOSPI is a kind of a market-value weighted index, similar to S&P 500 and TOPIX [8]. The base date is January 4, 1980 with the base index of 100. For each trading day i, let opening index denote $O(i)$, high $H(i)$, low $L(i)$, closing $C(i)$, net change $N(i)$, volume $V(i)$ and turnover $M(i)$. Various moving averages of 20 days and 5 days were calculated as follows:

$$C_{MA}^{20}(i) = \frac{1}{20} \sum_{j=i-19}^{i} C(j) , C_{MA}^{5}(i) = \frac{1}{5} \sum_{j=i-4}^{i} C(j) , N_{MA}^{20}(i) = \frac{1}{20} \sum_{j=i-19}^{i} N(j) ,$$

$$V_{MA}^{20}(i) = \frac{1}{20} \sum_{j=i-19}^{i} V(j) , M_{MA}^{20}(i) = \frac{1}{20} \sum_{j=i-19}^{i} M(j) .$$

We used a total of 10 input variables $[O(i) - C_{MA}^{20}(i)]$, $[H(i) - C_{MA}^{20}(i)]$, $[L(i) - C_{MA}^{20}(i)]$ $[C(i) - C_{MA}^{20}(i)]$, $[N(i) - N_{MA}^{20}(i)]$, $[V(i) - V_{MA}^{20}(i)]$, $[M(i) - M_{MA}^{20}(i)]$, $[C(i) - C_{MA}^{5}(i)]$, $C(i)$ and $\log(C(i)/C(i-1))$. Combining daily data with moving averages can reduce the number of input variables effectively, while maintaining historical information. Reducing the number of input variables helps to prevent overfitting [4].

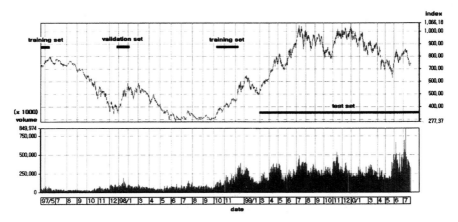

Figure 3. KOSPI data set from 1997 to 2000

Figure 3 displays KOSPI data used in this experiment. Trading days before March 1999 were used for training while those days after were used for testing. Since only those days constituting LS were used for actual training and validation, however, only 86 days and 27 days were actually used to train and validate AANN, respectively.

LS days were manually selected by one of the authors basically. The criteria used are as following:

-Choose selling climax that is defined as a local maximum over 30 day periods (see Figure 1).

-Draw neckline with head and shoulder.

-Collect data corresponding to LS (For more details of term, refer to [5],[6]).

The AANN used has a 10L-12N-7N-12N-10L structure where L denotes a linear transfer function while N denotes a nonlinear transfer function (tangent sigmoid used). A 5 layer network with nonlinear transfer functions can perform better dimension reduction than a 3 layer network[2]. A gradient descent was employed to minimize the error function with an early stopping method to prevent overfitting. The experiment was performed on MATLAB 5.3

4. Results

Figure 4 shows the KOSPI during the test period as well as the network's prediction of LS indicated by thick bars. A threshold of 0.3 was empirically determined based on the performance with the training set.

We employed two classification measures of False Rejection Rate (FRR) and False Acceptance Rate (FAR) and a financial measure of return rates. Let us define $D(i)$, $L(i)$ as following:

$$D(i) = \begin{cases} 0 & \text{if classified as non - LS at ith day} \\ 1 & \text{if classified as LS at ith day} \end{cases} \quad L(i) = \begin{cases} 0 & \text{if non - LS at ith day} \\ 1 & \text{if LS at ith day} \end{cases}$$

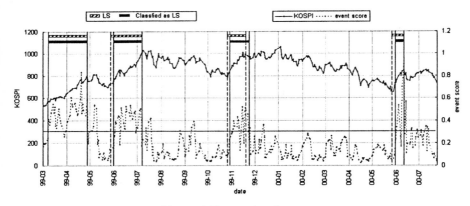

Figure 4. The results of test set

The classification measures and FRR and FAR are defined as

$$\text{FRR} = \left(\sum_{i=1}^{n} L(i) - \sum_{i \in \{i | L(i)=1\}}^{n} D(i)\right) \Big/ \sum_{i=1}^{n} L(i) \quad \text{and} \quad \text{FAR} = \sum_{i \in \{i | L(i)=0\}}^{n} D(i) \Big/ \left(n - \sum_{i=1}^{n} L(i)\right)$$

where n is the total number of test set.

The proposed approach is evaluated based on a financial measure of return rate. Let us envision a hypothetical investment strategy based on LS signal, i.e. $D(i)$. The so called LS strategy dictates "buy" when $D(i)$ changes from 0 to 1 and "sell" when $D(i)$ changes from 1 to 0. For the comparison buy and hold strategy was also evaluated:

$$\text{Return of LS strategy} = \sum_{i \in \{i | D(i)=1\}}^{n} (O(i+2) - O(i+1)) \Big/ O(1)$$

$$\text{Return of Buy and Hold} = (C(n) - O(1))/O(1).$$

We assumed that one buys or sells at the next day's opening price and that the market is perfectly liquid with no transaction cost.

The Performance of AANN in test set (March 2, 1999-July 24, 2000) is given in Table 1. There is a trade off between FRR and FAR. If the threshold of event score increases, FAR becomes smaller and FRR becomes lager. The Return of LS strategy is 124%, three times as much as the return of buy and hold strategy.

Table 1. Performance of AANN in test set

Measurement	Value (total 348 days)
False Rejection Rate	22.2 % (20 days / 90 days)
False Acceptance Rate	9.6 % (25 days / 258 days)
Return of LS strategy	124 % (648.2 points /524.9 points)
Return of Buy and Hold	39 % (203.9 points / 524.9 points)

5. Conclusions

In this paper, we proposed a neural network based detector of "left shoulder" in "head and shoulder formations". The auto-associative neural network was trained with the "left shoulder" patterns obtained from the Korea Composite Stock Price Index for 23 months (April 1997-February 1999). And then tested on out-of-sample period of March 1999-July 2000. The preliminary result was surprisingly good given the fact that the training period coincided with the worst financial crisis of the nation's history. A hypothetical investment strategy based on the detector achieved a return of 124% in comparison with 39% return from a buy and hold strategy.

There are several limitations in this work. First, the performance criteria used have a lot to be desired. False Acceptance Rate and False Reject Rate are problematic since they simply count the number of days, thus unfairly give more weight to detection of slowly arising left shoulder. Second, the left shoulder detection leads to market entry signal. Even more important is to find a way to give market exit signal. Detection of head or right shoulder may help. Third, KOSPI itself is not tradable. But KOSPI 200, a subset of KOSPI, is. Futures and options use it as an underlying asset.

It will be worthwhile to investigate whether a network trained with KOSPI data can detect LS in other data sets such as KOSPI 200 or other individual equity stocks. And it will be also useful to detect such widely used chart patterns as symmetrical triangles, descending triangles, ascending triangles, double bottoms, double top and rising wedges [7].

Acknowledgements

This research was supported by Brain Science and Engineering Research Program sponsored by Korean Ministry of Science and Technology and by the Brain Korea 21 Project to the first author.

References

1. S. Cho, C. Han, D. Han, & H. Kim.(2000). Web based Keystroke Dynamics Identity Verification using Neural Network. *Journal of Organizational Computing and Electronic Commerce. In print*
2. C. Bishop.(1995). Neural networks for pattern recognition. *Oxford: clarendon press.*
3. V. Guralnik, J. Srivastava.(1999). Event Detection from time Series Data. *KDD-99 Proceeding of the fifth ACM SIGKDD International Conference on Knowledge Discovery and Data Mining. pp 33-42.*
4. G. Deboeck.(1994). Trading on The Edge. *John Wiley & Sons, Inc.*
5. W.Eng.(1988). The Technical Analysis of Stocks, Options & Futures. *McGraw-Hill.*
6. TradeTalk company.(2000). http://www.tradertalk.com/tutorial/h&s.html.
7. Borsanaliz.com company.(2000). "Tools for technical analysis stock exchange" , http://www.geocities.com/wallstreet/floor/1035/formations.htm
8. Korea Stock Exchange.(2000). "KOSPI & KOSPI 200", http://www.kse.or.kr.

C.
AGENTS

A Computational Framework
for Convergent Agents

Wei Li
Department of Computer Science
Beijing University of Aeronautics and Astronautics
Beijing 100083, China

Abstract

As a computational approach, a framework is proposed for computing
the limits of formal theory sequences. It defines a class of agents, called
convergent agents. The approach provides a method to generate a new
theory by the limit of some sequence of theories, and also has potential applications to many scientific and engineering problems. As applications of
the framework, some convergent agents are discussed briefly, e.g., GUINA,
which can learn new versions from the current versions of a theory and
some external samples, and the learned versions converge to the truth one
wants to know.

Keywords: Formal theory sequence, Limit, Convergent agent, Inductive inference, Algebraically closed fields.

1 Introduction

There is a class of agents which have the following computational characters:
each agent would constantly access some countably infinite external data $S_1, S_2,$
$\cdots, S_k, \cdots$ as its inputs; and for the kth computation round, it generates Γ_k as
its output. The outputs form an infinite sequences: $\Gamma_1, \Gamma_2, \cdots, \Gamma_k, \cdots$, and the
sequence is convergent to a certain limit. The following example demonstrates
the feature:

Given a data set stored on a network, it can be expressed as a language
$E = \{w_1, w_2, \cdots\}$, and given its non-terminals V (in fact, this restriction can
be removed) and terminals T, the question is: How to construct a grammar
$G = (V, T, P, S)$ such that $E = L(G)$? The problem may be solved in an
evolutionary way as follows:

1. At the beginning, We choose an initial grammar $G_0 = (V, T, P_0, S)$ where
   P_0 is a set of production rules and can be viewed as our first guess of the
   rules.

2. We then check if $w_1 \in L(G_0)$, if yes then check if $w_2 \in L(G_0)$, $\cdots$,
   otherwise we have $w_1 \notin L(G_0)$. Let α be the sentential form obtained by
   (partial) from-bottom-up parsing analysis of w_1 in G_0, then there are two
   possibilities:

(a) If $L((V, T, P_0 \cup \{S \to \alpha\}, S)) \neq \emptyset$, then let $P_1 = P_0 \cup \{S \to \alpha, S \to w_1\}$. Thus, we get a new grammar $G_1 = (V, T, P_1, S)$ by adding new productions.

(b) If $L((V, T, P_0 \cup \{S \to \alpha\}, S)) = \emptyset$, then we have to constract P_0 by deleting some rules from P_0, which contradicts $S \to \alpha$ and get P_0'.

3. Generally, for G_{k-1}, we check if $w_k \in L(G_{k-1})$, if yes then check if $w_{k+1} \in L(G_{k-1})$, $\cdots$, otherwise either add new productions, i.e., $P_k := P_{k-1} \cup \{S \to \alpha, S \to w_k\}$ to get a new grammar G_k, or revise it as in the sub-case 2.a. Here α is the sentential form obtained by (partial) from-bottom-up parsing analysis of w_k in G_{k-1}.

The above process can be easily specified by an agent which we call *Analysis* (G_0, E). Let $E_k = \{w_1, \cdots, w_k\}$. It will generate a sequence of grammars: $G_0, G_1 = Analysis(G_0, E_1), \cdots, G_k = Analysis(G_{k-1}, E_k), \cdots$, where $\cup_{i=1}^{\infty} E_i = E$. If E is finite, then *Analysis* will stop in finite steps. If E is infinite, then the *Analysis* may execute forever, but in many cases, the sequence $\{G_n\}$ will have a "limit" G. The computational properties of *Analysis* are listed as follows informally:

(1) *Analysis* is a Turing machine. It takes the current grammar G_k and some parts of the data E_{k+1} to be analyzed as its inputs, and outputs a new grammar G_{k+1}. (2) The input E to *Analysis* is countably infinite. (3) At the beginning, a grammar G_0 can be taken as an initial grammar to feed *Analysis*. (4) In each computational round, *Analysis* takes the current grammar G_{k-1} and external data E_k as its inputs, and generates a new grammar G_k. In other words, external information E is involved in the computation process. (5) The outputs of every round of *Analysis* form a sequence $\{G_k\}$. (6) The computational process is rational if the grammar sequence $\{G_k\}$ is convergent to some limit G and $L(G) = E$.

From now on we call the agents with the computational characters described above convergent agents. The purpose of the paper is to formalize these characters and to demonstrate them by examples.

2 Limits of Theory Sequences and Convergent Agents

In this section, we will define convergent agents based on the classical computation model–Turing machine and the notion of the limit given in (Li, 1992).

In the rest of the paper, we use the following standard notations: $\mathcal{L}$ is a first order language, Γ is a finite theory, $\Gamma = \{A_1, \cdots, A_m\}$, where A_i's are formulas of $\mathcal{L}$, and $Th(\Gamma) = \{A \mid \Gamma \vdash A\}$ is the theory closure of Γ. For given two theories Γ_1 and Γ_2, we define $\Gamma_1 \equiv \Gamma_2$ iff $Th(\Gamma_1) = Th(\Gamma_2)$. A sequence of formal theories is denoted by $\Gamma_0, \Gamma_1, \cdots, \Gamma_k, \cdots$ or by $\{\Gamma_k\}$.

Definition 2.1. (Li, 1992) Let $\Gamma_0, \Gamma_1, \cdots, \Gamma_k, \cdots$ be a sequence of formal theories.

$$\Gamma^* \equiv \bigcap_{n=1}^{\infty} \bigcup_{m=n}^{\infty} \Gamma_m, \qquad \Gamma_* \equiv \bigcup_{n=1}^{\infty} \bigcap_{m=n}^{\infty} \Gamma_m$$

are called the upper limit and lower limit of the above sequence respectively. $\Gamma_0, \Gamma_1, \cdots, \Gamma_k, \cdots$ is convergent iff $\Gamma_* \equiv \Gamma^*$. The limit of a convergent sequence is denoted by $\lim_{k \to \infty} \Gamma_k$.

Now, we are ready to give the following definition of a computation model for computing the limit of theory sequences in the first order languages.

Definition 2.2. (Convergent agent) Let Γ and S_k be finite sets of sentences in first order languages, and

$$\Gamma_0 = \Gamma, \ \Gamma_k = \varphi(\Gamma_{k-1}, S_k), \text{ for } k \geq 1,$$

where φ is a procedure (which can be expressed by a Turing machine). Let $S = \cup_{k=1}^{\infty} S_k$, and define

$$\varphi(\Gamma, S) = \begin{cases} \lim_{k \to \infty} \Gamma_k, & \text{if } \lim_{k \to \infty} \Gamma_k \text{ exists}, \\ undefined, & \text{otherwise}. \end{cases}$$

Then, $\varphi(\Gamma, S)$ is called a **convergent agent**, Γ is called an initial theory.

Remark: (1) Note that in general, $\varphi(\Gamma, S)$ is not a result produced by the procedure φ because S is infinite and cannot be an input of a Turing machine. In fact, in each round of computation of φ, the output of φ is some Γ_k which is an approximation of $\varphi(\Gamma, S)$ and may not equal to $\varphi(\Gamma, S)$. Strictly speaking, the real numbers defined by power series such as e and π are defined formally by convergent agents. Informally, the limit can be viewed as a result of a generalized Turing machine which allows infinite inputs and produces infinite convergent sequence. (2) S_k is a formal description of the principle of observability of the world, which says that data of a scientific problem can be got whenever necessary. In practice, S_k can be example sets (training sets) from huge databases on the networks. (3) If for some $k, \varphi(\Gamma_k, S_{k+1})$ does not halt, then $\Gamma_{k+1} = \bot$, where $\bot$ denotes *undefined computation*. Thus, for this case, $lim_{k \to \infty} \Gamma_k$ does not exist.

Note that if $S = \emptyset$, then the convergent agent defines the classical computation by a Turing machine. In other words, it defines computations in closed world. The various resolution procedures are the typical examples for this case, and they are used as a framework for theorem proving. If $S \neq \emptyset$, then the convergent agent defines a class of computations, or say, it defines computations in open world. The proofs of Lingenbuam's theorem, the extentions used in default logic, and the problems of knowledge base maintenance, specification capturing, the rationality of inductive reasoning, and a class of agents used in the Internet can be defined by the convergent agents (Li, 1999) and (Li and Ma, 2000).

3 Convergent Agent GUINA for Inductive Inference and its Rationality

We show in this section that the inductive processes can be modeled in the proposed framework. In (Li, 1999), a convergent agent called GUINA was introduced to generate convergent inductive sequences. In other words, GUINA can be viewed as an effort to model automated learning systems.

First, we need some basic definitions for presenting GUINA. A model $\mathbf{M}$ is a pair of $< M, I >$, where M is a domain, I is an interpretation. Sometimes, $\mathbf{M}_\wp$ is used to denote a model for a scientific problem $\wp$. $Th(\mathbf{M}_\wp)$ denotes the set of all true sentences of $\mathbf{M}_\wp$ and is a countable set. The interpretation of the Herbrand universe of L under $M_\wp$ is called the Herbrand universe of $M_\wp$, and is denoted by $\mathbf{H}_{M_\wp}$. The interpretation of a Herbrand sequence of L of $M_\wp$ is called a complete instance sequence of $M_\wp$, it is denoted by $\mathcal{E}_M$, sometimes by $\{A_m\}$ if no confusion can occur.

Suppose that $\mathcal{E}_M \equiv A_m\}$ is the only thing which we know about $\mathbf{M}$ and Γ is an initial version of a theory (or say an initial guess)to be started. Furthermore, we suppose that the inductive generalization, inductive sufficient condition, and revision rules are the only rules allowed to be used, see (Li 1999). The reason of introducing revision rule is because there is no guarantee that an inductive consequence would never meet a rejection by samples. In this sense, an inductive inference system is rational only if the sequence of versions of theories eventually converge to the truth of the problem. Thus, the rationality of inductive systems should be expressed by the question: Does there exist a convergent agent that for every sequences $\{\Gamma_n\}$ generated by the agent, such that $\Gamma_1 = \Gamma$ and

$$\lim_{n \to \infty} Th(\Gamma_n) = Th(\mathbf{M}_\wp)?$$

In what follows, we describe such a convergent agent GUINA briefly. Our goal is to obtain all true sentences of $\mathbf{M}$ by using GUINA which takes $\mathcal{E}_M$ and Γ as its inputs. An informal description of GUINA can be as follows, and its formal definition is in (Li, 1999).

Let $\Gamma_1 = \Gamma$. Γ_{n+1} will be defined as follows:

1. If $\Gamma_n \vdash A_i$ for some i, then $\Gamma_{n+1} = \Gamma_n$;

2. If $\Gamma_n \vdash \neg A_i$, since A_i is positive sample and it must be accepted ($\neg A_i$ has met a rejection by facts A_i), Γ_{n+1} is a maximal subset of Γ_n which is consistent with A.

3. If neither 1 nor 2 can be done, then Γ_{n+1} is defined by the induction rules (see, (Li, 1999)) as below:

    (a) If $A_i = B(t)$ and the inductive generalization rule can be applied, then Γ_{n+1} is $\{A_i, \forall x.B(x)\} \cup \Gamma_n$;

(b) Otherwise, if $A_i = B$ and exists A, such that $\Gamma_n \vdash A \supset B$, and the inductive sufficient condition rule can be applied for A, then Γ_{n+1} is $\{A, A \supset B, B\} \cup \Gamma_n$;

(c) If neither case (a) nor case (b) can be done, then Γ_{n+1} is $\{A_i\} \cup \Gamma_n$.

The following theorem shows that GUINA is a convergent agent, and the proof can be found in (Li, 1999).

Theorem 3.1. Let $\mathbf{M}_\wp$ be a model for a specific problem $\wp$, $Th(\mathbf{M}_\wp)$ be the set of its all true sentences, $\mathcal{E}_{M_\wp}$ be its complete instance sequence, and Γ be a theory. If the sequence $\{\Gamma_n\}$ is generated by GUINA from $\mathcal{E}_{M_\wp}$ and Γ, then $\{\Gamma_k\}$ is convergent, and

$$\lim_{k \to \infty} Th(\Gamma_k) = Th(\mathbf{M}_\wp).$$

4 Convergent Agents over Algebraically Closed Fields

As we have seen in Section 3, there is a problem in GUINA, which is as follows. Given the current theory Γ and a statement A, how to determine (1) $\Gamma \vdash \neg A$ or (2) $\Gamma \vdash A$ or (3) $\Gamma \not\vdash A$ and $\Gamma \not\vdash \neg A$. For the first order predicate logic, there is no decision algorithm for solving this problem. In order to avoid this situation, in (Li and Ma, 2000a) and (Li and Ma, 2000b), we investigated the computational aspects of convergent agents in Algebraically Closed Fields (ALC). ALC is a typically complete and decidable theory, in ALC there can be a decision algorithm to solve this problem. The main reasons for study of convergent agents over ALC is that it has the following advantages:

(1) It has strong expressive powers in the sense that many scientific problems can be specified in its scope. (2) Since ALC is categorical, i.e., all of its models are isomorphic, we can choose a specific model, e.g., the complex number field, when involving semantic approaches, that is, there is no need of the unification. (3) In ALC, the formal theories can be syntactically transformed into the systems of polynomial equations, and some metric can be defined to allow that convergent agents can compute analytically in a way like numeric computations. Therefore, some symbolic and algebraic computation techniques and numeric computation techniques developed by (Wu, 1986) and (Cucker and Smale, 1999) can be used to compute the limits of theory sequences symbolically and numerically.

5 Concluding Remarks

Recently, with the rapid developments of the Internet techniques and applications, it has been required to establish fundamental frameworks to deal with the running processes and massive unstructured data stored on the networks. For example, search engines should intelligently suit their users whose interests are gradually changing and developing, the semantics of unstructured information contained in home pages should be made precisely in an evolutionary way, and the knowledge hidden in massive data should be discovered in some non-monotonic mining processes, and so on. We believe that the solutions of these problems would rely heavily on powerful analytic concepts and methods, such as limits, calculus, measures, and gradually expansion. The convergent agents as a computational framework could provide solutions to these problems. In fact, introducing convergent agents is to model automated reasoning systems.

Acknowledgements

I thank Shilong Ma for valuable discussions on the paper. The research is supported by the National 973 Project of China under the grant number G1999032701.

6 References

1. Blum, L., Cucker, F., Shub, M. and Smale, S., *Complexity and Real Computation*, Springer-Verlager, 1998.

2. Chang, C.C, and Keisler, H.J., *Model Theory*, third edition, North-Holland Publishing Company, 1990.

3. Li, W., *An Open Logic System*, Science in China (Scientia Sinica) (series A), No.10, (in Chinese), 1992, 1103-1113.

4. Li, W., *A Logical Framework for Evolution of Specifications*, Programming Languages and Systems, (ESOP'94), LNCS 788, Sringer-Verlag, 1994, 394-408.

5. Li, W., *A logical Framework for Inductive Inference and Its rationality*, Advanced Topics in Artificial Intelligence, Fu, N.(eds.), LNAI 1747, Springer, 1999.

6. Li, W. and Ma, S., *A Framework for Analytic-Intelligent Agents*, Proceedings of the International Conference on Artificial Intelligence, Las Vegas, USA, June 26-29, 2000, CSREA Press, 691-697.

7. Li, W. and Ma, S., *Limits of Theory Sequences over Algebraically Closed Fields and Applications*, Technical Report, The National Lab. of Software Development Environment, Beijing University of Aeronautics and Astronautics, 2000.

8. Reiter, R., *A Logic for Default Reasoning*, Artificial Intelligence, 13(1980), 81-132.

9. Wu, W., *On Zeros of Algrbraic Equations—An Application of Ritt's Principle*, Kexue Tongbao, 31(1986), 1-5.

Multi-agent Integer Programming

Jiming Liu[1] and Jian Yin[2]

[1]Department of Computer Science, Hong Kong Baptist University, Kowloon Tong
Hong Kong; jiming@comp.hkbu.edu.hk
[2]Department of Computer Science, Zhongshan University, Guangzhou, 510275, P. R. China
issjyin@zsu.edu.cn

Abstract. Many real-life optimization problems such as planning and scheduling require finding the best allocation of scarce resources among competing activities. These problems may be modeled and solved by means of mathematical programming. This paper explores a distributed multi-agent approach to mathematical programming, and demonstrates the approach in the case of integer programming. The important characteristics of the multi-agent approach consist in that the behavior-based computation performed by the agents is parallel and goal-driven in nature, and has low time complexity.

Keywords. Multi-agents; Integer programming; Behavior-based computation.

1 Introduction

A multi-agent system is a system of interacting heterogeneous agents with different reactive behaviors and capabilities. Some examples of multi-agent systems include an artificial-life agent system for solving large-scale constraint satisfaction problems developed by Han, Liu, and Cao [4], an evolutionary agent system for solving theorem-proving problems by Yin, Liu, and Li [5], and a reactive behavior-based image feature extraction system by Liu, Tang, and Cao [6]. As one of the most active research areas in Distributed Artificial Intelligence, multi-agent approaches have shown to have a great potential in solving problems that are otherwise difficult to solve. This is primarily due to the fact that many real-life problems are best modeled using a set of interacting agents instead of a single agent [1-3]. In particular, multi-agent modeling allows to cope with natural constraints like the limited processing power of a single agent and to benefit from the inherent properties of distributed systems like robustness, redundancy, parallelism, adaptability, and scalability.

This paper explores a distributed multi-agent approach to mathematical programming, and in particular, demonstrates the approach in the case of integer programming. The motivation behind this work lies in that many real-life optimization problems such as planning and scheduling require finding the best allocation of scarce resources among competing activities under certain hard constraints. Such problems may be modeled and solved by means of mathematical programming.

2 Problem statement

In what follows, let us first take a look at a typical integer linear-programming problem:

(IP_0) minimize $z=\sum_j c_j x_j$

subject to $\sum_j a_{ij} x_{ij}$ $[\leq$ or $=$ or $\geq] b$, $i=1,2,\ldots,m$

and $x_j \geq 0$, x_j integer, $j=1,2,\ldots,n$.

where n is the number of variables and m is the number of constraints.

In order to solve the above problem, generally speaking we can first eliminate the integer constraints and obtain a problem as follows:

$(IP_0^{'})$ minimize $z=\sum_j c_j x_j$

subject to $\sum_j a_{ij} x_{ij}$ $[\leq$ or $=$ or $\geq] b$, $i=1,2,\ldots,m$

and $x_j \geq 0$

We call $IP_0^{'}$ is a relaxation of IP_0. Obviously, every feasible solution to IP_0 is also a feasible solution to $IP_0^{'}$. We can apply a simplex method to solve $IP_0^{'}$, and therefore obtain a lower bound on the optimal value for IP_0. If the solution happens to contain all integer components, it will be optimal for the original problem. Else, we obtain a non-integer solution. Let x_k is a non-integer component, its value is a. Suppose that a_1 is the maximum integer less than a, and a_2 is the minimum integer greater than a. Adding

$x_k \leq a_1$ and $x_k \geq a_2$ into the constraints of integer programming respectively, we can construct two new linear programming problems. The two new problems are as follows:

(IP$_1$) minimize $z = \sum_j c_j x_j$

subject to $\sum_j a_{ij} x_{ij}$ [$\leq$ or $=$ or $\geq$] b , i=1,2,...,m

$x_k \leq a$

and $x_j \geq 0$, x_j integer, j=1,2,...,n.

(IP$_2$) minimize $z = \sum_j c_j x_j$

subject to $\sum_j a_{ij} x_{ij}$ [$\leq$ or $=$ or $\geq$] b , i=1,2,...,m

$x_k \geq a_2$

and $x_j \geq 0$, x_j integer, j=1,2,...,n.

The above process of constructing new problems by adding constraints is called branching. The linear programs that result from branching are called sub-problems of IP$_0$. In other words, in order to solve IP$_0$, we only need to solve sub-problems IP$_1$ and IP$_2$. Based on the idea of branching, we have designed a reactive behavior-based, distributed multi-agent approach to solving an integer-programming problem. An overview of this approach is given in the following section.

3 An overview of the multi-agent system

The general design of our multi-agent system contains three key elements: a goal of the system, agent environments, and a behavioral repository for the distributed agents in reproduction, reaction, and communication. We will refer to each of the distributed agent as G.

Specifically, the reactive behaviors of an agent can be described as follows:

1. Reproduction

Each agent G can be reproduced into two agents G_1 and G_2. They will have the same goal as G, but not the same environments. We call G a parent agent, and its reproductions G_1 and G_2 offspring agents. An agent can be a parent agent and an offspring agent at the same time.

2.Action

An agent G is always keeping on computing and evaluating its current state until either a goal state has been successfully achieved or a termination condition is satisfied.

3.Communication

Let us illustrate agent communication through an example. Suppose that there is agent G in environment E. It begins to compute its goal at the current state. If the result is false, it will start to reproduce and generate offspring agents. Let G_1 and G_2 be two reproduced agents. When G reproduces, its environment E will also be divided into two sub-environment E_1 and E_2, which serve as the environments for G_1 and G_2, respectively. Next, G_1 and G_2 compute their goal in their own environments. If any of them can successfully reach a goal state, it will send this result to its parent agent G, else it will continue to reproduce. On the other hand, the parent agent will decide whether or not its goal state is achieved based on the results returned by G_1 and G_2. It will also decide when to stop the reactions of G_1 and G_2.

4 Multi-agent integer programming

Now, let us consider how the above agent model can be applied to solve an integer-programming problem. First, we regard the constraints of problem IP_0 as the environment of an agent and the optimal solution of IP_0 as its goal. At the first step, G executes its reaction, i.e., solving the relaxation problem of IP_0 by means of a simplex method. If G can reach its goal state, that is, the result of its reaction satisfies the integer constraints, then G stops, else G begins to reproduce G_1 and G_2, which correspond to sub-problems IP_1 and IP_2. In a similar fashion, the reproduced agents continue to react and reproduce.

As in our implementation, the data structure for each agent is defined as follows:

Define a variable z to store the optimal objective value, let $z=+\infty$.

1. Goal and environment:

Assign the optimal solution of integer programming to the goal of G and the constraints to the environment of G (only for the root agent). Define a variable z_L to store the result of the agent's reaction.

2. Reaction:

A simplex procedure is performed to solve the relaxation problem of Goal, and

(1) If the solution satisfies the integer constraints, then $z_L \leftarrow$ optimal value. If there is no feasible solution, then $z_L \leftarrow +\infty$. In these two cases, if the agent is a root agent, then $z=z_L$ and stop, else send z_L to its parent agent and then stop.

(2) If the solution contains a non-integer component, then the agent sends the result to its parent agent with a non-integer label (for the root agent, let parent agent be itself).

3. Reproduction:

If a solution component x_k is non-integer and its value is a, let a_1 be the maximum integer less than a and a_2 be the minimum integer greater than a, then agent G begins to reproduce its offspring agents, G_1 and G_2. Both hold the same goal as G. Their environments are derived by adding constraints $x_k \leq a_1$ and $x_k \geq a_2$ to the environment of G, respectively.

4. Communication:

Parent agent G_p communicates with its offspring agent G_s according to the following rule:

Let z_L be the result of G_s being sent back to G_p,

(1)   if z_L is a non-label result then $z \leftarrow \min(z, z_L)$

(2)   if z_L is a label result then,

   if $z_L > z$ then stop G_s

   else request G_s to reproduce

The process of solving an integer-programming problem begins with the reaction of a root agent, and stops when no agent can reproduce. At this time, if $z=+\infty$ then there is no optimal solution for the integer programming problem, else z is the optimal value found.

4.1 Time complexity

We have implemented the above multi-agent integer programming system. We note that if an integer programming problem is solved with a sequential processing method, the required time complexity would be O(n), but on the other hand, with our proposed model, the time complexity would become O(log n).

5 An illustrative example

In this section, we present a walkthrough example of applying the above-mentioned approach:

(IP_0) minimize $z=-x_1-5x_2$ $(IP_0^{'})$ minimize $z=-x_1-5x_2$

subject to   subject to

$x_1-x_2 \geq -2$ $x_1-x_2 \geq -2$

$5x_1+6x_2 \leq 30$ $5x_1+6x_2 \leq 30$

$x_1 \leq 4$ $x_1 \leq 4$

$x_1,x_2 \geq 0$ $x_1,x_2 \geq 0$

x_1,x_2 integers

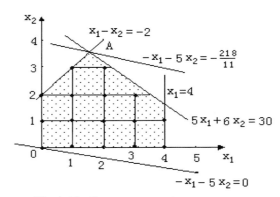

Fig. 1. The linear programming problem

First, we assign the optimal solution and constraints of IP_0 to the goal and environment of agent G. Initially, we set the goal state of G to be false.

Because the goal state is false, G begins to execute its reaction, solving $IP_0^{'}$ by means of a simplex method. For the sake of illustration, here we solve $IP_0^{'}$ by using a graphical method. As shown in Figure 1, the optimal solution point is A. The solution component is $x_1=18/11$, $x_2=40/11$, and the optimal value is $z_L =-218/11$, which is a lower bound for IP_0.

Because the solution component is non-integer, e.g., x_1 is a non-integer, we obtain two integers 1 and 2, and then agent G begins to reproduce agents G_1, G_2, their goals are the same as G, and their environments are different by adding constraints of $x_1 \leq 1$ and $x_1 \leq 2$, respectively.

G_1 and G_2 continue to react to their goals under the supervision of their parent G, until the goals are reached or the termination condition is satisfied.

6 Conclusion

In this paper, we have described a novel distributed agent approach to solving integer-programming problems. The key ideas behind this approach rest on three notions: Goal, Environment, and Reactive behavior. Each agent can only sense its local environment and applies some behavioral rules for governing its reaction. While presenting the agent model, we also provided an illustrative example.

The advantage of the proposed approach can be summarized as follows:

1. The reproduction and computation of agents are parallel in nature.
2. The process of distributed computation is goal-driven.
3. The time complexity is $O(\log n)$.

Reference

1. Clement, B. and Durfee, E., Scheduling high-level tasks among cooperative agents, in Proceedings of the Third International Conference on Multiagent Systems, ICMAS'98, 1998.
2. Decker, K. and Li, J., Coordinated hospital patient scheduling, in Proceedings of the Third International Conference on Multiagent Systems, ICMAS'98, 1998.
3. Seghrouchni, F., and Haddad, S., A recursive model for distributed planning, in Proceedings of the Second International Conference on Multiagent Systems, ICMAS'96, 1996.
4. Han, J., Liu, J., and Cai, Q., From ALIFE agents to a kingdom of N queens, in Jiming Liu and Ning Zhong (ed.), Intelligent Agent Technology: Systems, Methodologies, and Tools, The World Scientific Publishing Co. Pte, Ltd., 1999, 110-120.
5. Yin, J., Liu, J., and Li, S., A reasoning model based on evolutionary agents, in Proceedings of the 5th International Conference for Young Computer Scientists, ICYCS'99, 1999, 532-536.
6. Liu, J., Tang, Y. Y., and Cao, Y. C., An evolutionary autonomous agents approach to image feature extraction, IEEE Trans. on Evolutionary computation, 1997, 1(2):141-159.

Building an Ontology for Financial Investment

Zili Zhang, Chengqi Zhang, and Swee San Ong
School of Computing and Mathematics
Deakin University, Geelong Victoria 3217, Australia
{zili, chengqi, ong}@deakin.edu.au

Abstract. Intelligent agent technologies hold great promise for the financial services and investment industries such as portfolio management. In financial investment, a multi-agent system approach is natural because of the multiplicity of information sources and the different expertise that must be brought to bear to produce a good recommendation (such as a stock buy or sell decision). The agents in a multi-agent system need to coordinate, cooperate or communicate with each other to solve a complex problem. However, ontologies are a key component in how different agents in a multi-agent system can communicate effectively, and how the knowledge of agents can develop. This paper presents a case study in building an ontology in financial investment. The lessons we learned from the construction process are discussed. Based on our ontology development experience and the current development of ontologies, a framework of next generation ontology construction tools, which is aimed to facilitate the ontology construction, is proposed.

1 Introduction

An intelligent agent is an encapsulated computer system that is situated in some environment and that is capable of flexible, autonomous action in that environment in order to meet its design objectives. Intelligent agent technologies hold great promise for the financial services and investment industries such as portfolio management. A collection of intelligent agents can be programmed to actually enter the Internet and carry out a sequence of instructions, searching through a number of sources to locate predetermined information, and making decisions based on these information.

In financial investment, the tasks are dynamic, distributed, global, and heterogeneous in nature. Take the financial portfolio management as an example, the task environment has the following interesting features: (1) the enormous amount of continually changing, and generally unorganized, information available; (2) the variety of kinds of information that can and should be brought to bear on the task (market data, financial report data, technical models, analysts' reports, breaking news, etc.); (3) the many sources of uncertainty and dynamic change in the environment. To deal with problems such as portfolio management, a multi-agent system approach is natural because of the multiplicity of information sources and the different expertise that must be brought to bear to produce a good recommendation (such as a stock buy or sell decision). When solving a complex problem, the agents in a multi-agent system need to coordinate, cooperate, and communicate with each other. However, ontologies are a key component in how different agents in a multi-agent system can communicate effectively, and how the knowledge of agents can develop.

An *ontology* is a theory of a particular domain or sphere of knowledge, describing the kinds of entity involved in it and the relationships that can hold among different entities. An ontology for finance, for example, would provide working definitions of concepts like money, banks, and stocks. This knowledge is expressed in computer-usable formalisms; for example, an agent for personal finances would draw on its finance ontology, as well as knowledge of your particular circumstances, to look for appropriate investments.

Building an ontology for finance was initially motivated by our ongoing financial investment advisor project. As part of this project, we have built a multi-agent system called *agent-based soft computing society*[1]. In this society, there are three kinds of agents–problem solving agents, serving agents, and soft computing agents. They work together to solve some problems in finance such as portfolio selection by using soft computing technologies as well as financial domain knowledge. A financial ontology is essential for these agents to communicate effectively.

Although intelligent agent technology holds great promise for the financial services and investment industries, up to now, there are not many papers published or products announced in financial field. Some typical multi-agent systems (by no means all) in finance include the Warren System[2][3], the Banker and Investor Agent System[4], and the Distributed Financial Computing System[5] etc. For these multi-agent systems in finance, there are not corresponding financial ontologies being used. It is no doubt that if there exists such a finance ontology, the development of financial multi-agent application systems should be much easier. The same situation is held for other application fields.

Interest in ontologies has grown as researchers and system developers have become more interested in reusing or sharing knowledge across systems. There are some general-purpose upper ontologies such as CYC and Wordnet and some domain-specific ontologies that focus on the domains of discourse such as chemicals ontology and air campaign planning ontology (refer to [6] for an overview of the recent development of the field of ontologies in artificial intelligence). Until now, very few financial ontologies have been reported. In the Larflast project, a financial domain ontology is under construction and will be used for learning finance terminology(*http://www.linglink.lu/hlt/projects/larflast-inco/ar-99/ar99. html* and [7]). In I3 (Intelligent Integration of Information, *http://dc.isx.com/I3*) project, there is a *financial ontology and databases* group. They are creating ontologies of financial knowledge in Loom (a kind of knowledge-representation language) that describe the contents of existing financial databases. We failed to find an existing financial ontology that can be (re)used in multi-agent environment. The lack of financial ontology that can be (re)used directly motivated us to build such an ontology.

In this paper, we will describe the development of the financial ontology as well as lessons we learned from the developing process. Based on these discussions, a framework of the next generation of ontology construction tools is proposed.

The remainder of the paper is organized as follows. Section 2 deals with the details of our financial ontology construction. The lessons we learned from the development process are discussed in Section 3. In Section 4, a framework of the next generation of ontology construction tools is proposed. Finally, Section 5 is concluding remarks.

2 Construction of Financial Ontology

We use *Ontolingua* to construct our financial ontology. *Ontolingua* is an ontology development environment that provides a suite of ontology authoring and translation tools and a library of modular reusable ontologies. For details on Ontolingua, visit *http://ontolingua.stanford.edu*. Ontolingua is based on a top ontology that defines terms such as *frames, slots, slot values,* and *facets*. When we build the ontology using Ontolingua, we must define the terms such as *portfolio, security, share, stock, bond* etc. by determining the slots and giving the slot values. Before we can do this, we face a hard knowledge-acquisition problem. Like knowledge-based-system development, ontology development faces a knowledge-acquisition bottleneck.

Because we are not experts in financial domain, we first read some books in finance to get some basic concepts in financial investment. We then held preliminary meetings with financial experts to look for general, not detailed, knowledge. After this, we studied the documentation very carefully and tried to learn as much as possible about the domain of expertise (finance). Having obtained some basic knowledge, we started by looking for more general knowledge and gradually moved down into the particular details for configuring the full ontology. We extracted the set of terms and their relationships, and then defined the attributes and their values. At the later stage of knowledge-acquisition, we submitted these to financial experts for inspection. During knowledge acquisition, we used the following set of knowledge-acquisition techniques in an integrated manner[9]: (1) Non-structured interviews with experts to build a preliminary draft of the terms, definitions, a concept classification, and so on; (2) Informal text analysis to study the main concepts in books and handbooks; (3) Formal text analysis. We analyzed the text to extract attributes, natural-language definitions, assignation of values to attributes, and so on; (4) Structured interviews with the expert to get specific and detailed knowledge about concepts, their properties, and their relationships with other concepts; (5) Detailed reviews by the expert. In this way, we could get some suggestions and corrections from financial experts before coding the knowledge.

This is a time consuming and error containing process. Obviously, more efficient construction tools are needed. After we acquire the knowledge, we manually code the knowledge with Ontolingua. Some terms of our financial ontology written in Ontolingua are as follows:

```
;;; Securities
(Define-Class Securities (?X) "A term that covers the paper
certificates that are evidence of ownership of bonds, debentures,
 notes and shares."
:Def (And (Relation ?X)))


;;; Share
(Define-Class Share (?X) "A unit of equity capital in a company."
:Def (And (Securities ?X)))
```

Currently, you can log in to *Ontolingua* and check the *financial investment ontology* in the unloaded category. To use this ontology, we adopt the *Open Knowledge Base Connectivity* (OKBC) protocol[11] as a bridge between the agents in our financial investment advisor multi-agent system and the financial ontology. Although we build this ontology mainly used in multi-agent systems, any other systems can access the ontology through the OKBC. This enables the reuse of this ontology. The ontology constructed by using Ontolingua is in *Lisp* format. Before we can access the ontology through OKBC, we must translate the ontology into OKBC format. This can be accomplished automatically by using the ontology server.

3 Discussions–Lessons Learned

By analyzing the ontology construction process described in Section 2 (it is a typical procedure followed by most researchers in this area), we can extract the following two points: (1) switching directly from knowledge acquisition to implementation; (2) manually coding the required knowledge for the domain of interest. It is these two points that cause the following disadvantages or problems:

First, the primary current disadvantage in building ontologies is the danger of developing ad-hoc solutions. Usually, the conceptual models describing ontologies are implicit in the implementation codes. Making the conceptual models explicit usually requires reengineering. Ontological commitments and design criteria implicit and explicit in the ontology code. All these imply that the built ontologies may contain errors, inconsistencies etc. Second, domain experts and human end users have no understanding of formal ontologies codified in ontology languages. Third, as with traditional knowledge bases, direct coding of the knowledge-acquisition result is too abrupt a step, especially for complex ontology. Finally, ontology developers might have difficulty understanding implemented ontologies or even building new ontologies. This is because traditional ontology tools focus too much on implementation issues rather than on design problems.

The source of these problems is the absence of an explicit and fully documented conceptual model upon which to formalize the ontology. To this end, some researchers have proposed ontological engineering[9]. Central to ontological engineering is the definition and standardization of a life cycle ranging from requirements specification to maintenance, as well as methodologies and techniques that drive ontology development. They have developed a framework called *Methontology* for specifying ontologies at the knowledge level, and an *Ontology Design Environment* (ODE). The knowledge acquisition result is not coded by target language, but represented by an *intermediate representations*. The knowledge in intermediate representation can be automatically converted to Ontolingua codes by using ODE. Using Methontology and ODE can alleviate some of the problems mentioned above. For example, at the later stage of our financial ontology development, only following the idea of ontological engineering (not accessing the ODE) speeds up the ontology construction. To overcome the difficulties mentioned in [8], more powerful tools or frameworks are still essential.

4 Framework of Next Generation Ontology Construction Tools

Ontology construction is difficult and time consuming and is a major barrier to the building of large-scale intelligent systems and software agents. It is clear that the creation of easy-to-use tools for creating, evaluating, accessing, using, and maintaining reusable ontologies by both individuals and groups is essential. Based on our ontology building experience and a relatively profound analysis of the current development of ontologies, we propose that the next generation ontology construction tools should include the following capabilities: Assemble and extend modules from ontology repositories; Adapt and reconcile ontologies; Extract and taxonomize terms from other sources; Semi-autonomously synthesize ontologies based on the use of terms in natural language documents; Merge overlapping ontologies; Visualize ontologies; Detect inconsistencies; Browse and retrieve ontologies; Translate and reformulate.

Currently, a research group at Stanford University is building ontology development and use technology that addresses seven (out of nine) of these needs[10]. We can use the current visualization technologies to visualize the spatial relationships, temporal relationships, concept/document associations, and complex, aggregate patterns etc. in ontologies. The theory of logic programming is a possible solution for adaptation and reconciliation of ontologies. Hence, our framework of next generation ontology construction tools is reasonable and actual. Tools with such capabilities will facilitate the rapid, accurate development of variety ontologies, and multi-agent systems as well as other knowledge based systems will also be better enabled for knowledge sharing and have much better interaction.

5 Concluding Remarks

Ontologies play a key role in how different agents in a multi-agent system can communicate effectively, and how the knowledge of agents can develop. Until now, there are few collections of ontologies in existence; most of them are still under development. The same is true for ontologies in finance. To this end, we started to build a financial ontology used in multi-agent systems. We used Ontolingua as our construction tool. Other systems can access this ontology through OKBC. Currently, the construction of this financial ontology is still in progress.

Experience with the financial ontology development and a relatively profound analysis of currently ontology research have led us to an extended and refined set of ideas regarding the next generation ontology construction tools. We proposed that the next generation ontology construction tools should have adapting and reconciling, visualizing ontologies, and detecting inconsistencies etc. nine capabilities. A framework with these nine capabilities is reasonable and actual. Tools with such capabilities will facilitate the rapid, accurate development of variety ontologies, and multi-agent systems as well as other knowledge based systems will also be better enabled for knowledge sharing and have much better interaction.

References

1. C. Zhang, Z. Zhang, and S. Ong, An Agent-Based Soft Computing Society, Proceedings of RSCTC'2000, LNAI,Springer, 2000, 621-628.
2. K. Sycara, K. Decker, A. Pannu, M. Williamson, and D. Zeng, Distributed Intelligent Agents, IEEE Expert, Vol. 11, No. 6, 1996, 36-46.
3. K. P. Sycara, K. Decker and D.Zeng, Intelligent Agents in Portfolio Management, in: N. R. Jennings and M. J. Wooldridge (Eds.), *Agent Technology: foundations, Applications, and Markets,* Springer, Berlin, 1998, 267-281.
4. K. krishna and V. C. Ramesh, From Wall Street to Main Street: Reaching out to Small Investors, Proceedings of the 32nd Annual Hawaii International Conference on System Sciences, 1999.
5. J. Yen, A. Chung, et al., Collaborative and Scalable Financial Analysis with Multi-Agent Technology, Proceedings of the 32nd Annual Hawaii International Conference on System Sciences, 1999.
6. B. Chandrasekaran, J. R. Josephson, and V. R. Benjamins, What Are Ontologies, and Why Do We Need Them? IEEE Intelligent Systems and Their Applications, January/February 1999, 20-26.
7. S. Trausan-Matu, Web Page Generation Facilitating Conceptualization and Immersion for Learning Finance Terminology, *http://rilw.emp.paed.uni-muenchen.de/99/papers/Trausan.html.*
8. D. S. Weld (Ed.), The Role of Intelligent Systems in NII, *http://www.aaai.org/Resources/Policy/nii.html,* 47-50.
9. M. F. Lopez, A. Gomez-Perez, J. P. Sierra, and A. P. Sierra, Building a Chemical Ontology Using Methontology and the Ontology Design Environment, IEEE Intelligent Systems and Their Applications, January/February 1999, 37-46.
10. R. Fikes and A. Farquhar, Distributed Repositories of Highly Expressive Reusable Ontologies, IEEE Intelligent Systems and Their Applications, March/April 1999, 73-79.
11. V. K. Chaudhri et al., OKBC: A programmatic Foundation for Knowledge Base Interoperability, Proc. AAAI'98, AAAI Press, 1998.

A Multi-Agent Negotiation Algorithm for Load Balancing in CORBA-Based Environment

Kei Shiu Ho and Hong-Va Leong

Department of Computing, Hong Kong Polytechnic University,
Hung Hom, Hong Kong

Abstract. The original event service of the Common Object Request Broker Architecture (CORBA) suffers from several weaknesses. Among others, it has poor scalability. Previously, we have proposed a framework, called SCARCE, which extends the event service to tackle the problem in a transparent manner. Scalability is improved through an agent-based load balancing algorithm. In this paper, we propose two new features to the algorithm that can further enhance its stability and performance.

1 Introduction

In many applications, such as video conferencing and Internet radio, the same piece of data is being disseminated from a single source to multiple receivers, effecting a multicasting model. Honoring this, the Object Management Group has proposed the event service [3], which defines a framework for decoupled and asynchronous message passing between distributed CORBA objects. In the event service, both the senders and the receivers, referred to as the suppliers and the consumers respectively, are connected to an event channel, which is actually an ordinary CORBA object. A supplier sends out data by invoking the "push" method of the event channel object, to be collected by the consumers on the other end.

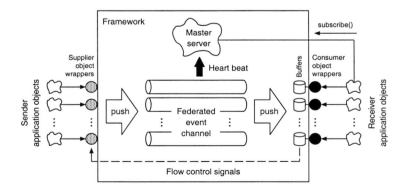

Fig. 1. The SCARCE framework.

Despite its flexibility, the event service suffers from several shortcomings [4]. Among others, it has poor scalability. Unicasting is often needed to emulate multicasting in many existing networking environments. Consequently, the efficiency of communication is degraded when the number of consumers and/or suppliers increases. To tackle this, we have previously extended the original event service into a new framework, known as SCARCE (SCAlable and Reliable Event service) [1] (see Fig. 1). Scalability is improved through the concept of federated channels (see Fig. 2). Precisely, event channels are replicated on-demand which are interconnected to give a two-level structure and the total load is shared among the replica through an agent-based dynamic load balancing algorithm.

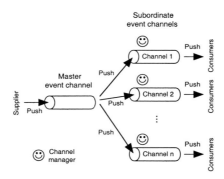

Fig. 2. Federated event channel in SCARCE.

2 Dynamic Load Balancing in SCARCE

With reference to Fig. 2, each subordinate event channel is associated with an agent, known as the channel manager. Upon the creation of every event channel, the master server (in Fig. 1) will "broadcast" the object references of the new channel and its channel manager to all the existing managers. Periodically, a channel manager, say A, will pick up another channel manager B from the list of channel managers it knows. If the load of B is greater than that of A, A will notify one of its clients to switch to the channel managed by B.

Our initial experience with SCARCE reveals that although the dynamic load balancing algorithm is effective in most cases, transient overloading may not be resolved quick enough, and a high fluctuation of performance is observed occasionally. In view of this, we propose two extensions to the original algorithm. First, an adaptive approach is applied for adapting the frequency at which a channel manager attempts to unload its clients. This makes the system more responsive to spontaneous overloading. On the other hand, instead of involving two agents only in each unloading interaction, multiple agents can negotiate together. This has the advantage that fewer unloading operations will be needed, thereby reducing negotiation overhead. At the same time, it helps to reduce the fluctuation in load.

3 Extensions to the Dynamic Load Balancing Algorithm

3.1 Interaction Frequency

It is intuitive enough that with high interaction frequency, the load in the whole system will be more balanced, and it takes a shorter time to bring the system to a more stable state, upon a transient bursty arrival of clients, or the failure of an event channel object. It also takes a shorter period to relieve the load of existing channel objects should a new channel be added. The cost paid is the high interaction cost between the channel managers.

We discover initially in our experiments that if the frequency of interaction is too high, the system will become unstable and fluctuation of load levels is observed. On the other hand, if the frequency is too low, the system will not be responsive enough in case the load level of a channel is being jerked up suddenly (due to factors such as network congestion). Furthermore, whether the frequency is too high or too low is also dependent on the load of the system as a whole. For a lightly loaded system, a shorter interaction period will be preferred, since clients can get migrated to a lightly loaded channel within a short period. On the other hand, a longer interaction period will be more appropriate in a heavily loaded system, since the cost for interaction could be too high, compared with the cost saved by migrating clients to lighter-loaded channels.

In view of this, we propose to perform an adaptive mechanism in SCARCE to determine the operational interaction frequency, in such a way that the interaction period can take advantage of the overall system loading. Our rationale is that, the effectiveness of load balancing interaction is measured by the amount of clients transferred per interaction. The more clients transferred per interaction, the more effective is the interaction and the higher frequency is more likely to benefit the system performance before reaching the local maximum. Initially, the interaction period is set to a default parameter τ_{max}. Let n be the number of clients transferred in the previous interaction. If n is equal to 0, $\tau_i = \tau_{max}$. Otherwise, $\tau_i = \tau_{i-1} \times \frac{\omega}{n}$, where $\omega \leq 1$ is a constant weight. We also curb the range of τ_i to stay within a prescribed system bound $\tau_i \in [\tau_{min}, \tau_{max}]$. So if $\tau_i < \tau_{min}$, we will set τ_i to τ_{min}.

3.2 Location Mechanism

The location mechanism is required to determine the channel or a set of channels to take over one or more transferred clients. In the original SCARCE design, load negotiation is performed between a pair of channel managers. Furthermore, only one client is migrated per interaction at most. In such a case, the initial negotiation cost is $2r$ and the transfer cost is $r+T$, where r is the roundtrip delay and T the cost of migrating a client. A simple generalization is to transfer $n \geq 1$ clients per interaction, thus bringing the cost to $3r + nT$. A natural question is to whether such a pairing is effective. Again generalizing, one can consider the negotiation of load among $m \geq 2$ channel managers per interaction. This gives rise to a more complicated communication structure, but perhaps a more effective transfer as more clients can be migrated from a heavily loaded channel within one single interaction to one or more lightly loaded channels. Furthermore, with such an arrangement, the interaction frequency can be reduced as well.

With more than two channel managers, one can naturally adopt an m-to-m communication structure (everyone being equal), or a ring structure (with one initiator), or a star structure (with one initiator/coordinator). Intuitively, the cost with the m-to-m structure is very high, since there are totally $\frac{m(m-1)}{2}$ interaction pairs that the number of socket connections is demanding. With the ring structure, the cost is mr for initial negotiation and the cost of transfer is at least $r + nT$ and at most $(m-1)(r+nT)$, depending on where the transferred clients finally go to. With the star structure, the cost is $2(m-1)r$ for initial negotiation and between $r + nT$ and $(m-1)r + nT$ for transfer.

The advantage of the ring configuration is that it is as flexible as the fully connected configuration, since all clients can be migrated to any channel along the ring, though the number of steps can be more than one. A simple algorithm can roughly balance the workload within two rounds of propagation. Initiator first negotiates with channel managers along the ring, each of them reporting their workload. Upon collecting the workload of all members, the initiator (with sender-initiated algorithms) computes the average load and sends the excessive loads to the next member. A member with fewer clients than the average takes up some extra load to make up to the average and passes on the rest. A member with more clients than the average will give out its excessive load.

The star configuration has the advantage of simplicity. The coordinator can also compute the average and migrate off the excessive tasks to the selected channels directly. However, the coordinator will have a higher workload than the ring configuration.

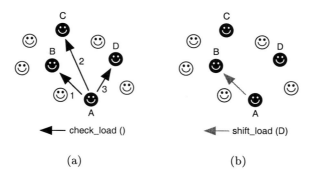

Fig. 3. Multi-agent negotiation for dynamic load balancing.

In our modification of SCARCE, we adopt the star configuration due to its simplicity and flexibility. Similar to the original design, at most one client can be migrated per interaction. Consider the example as shown in Fig. 3. Here, the value of m is equal to 4. Channel manager A acts as the coordinator, and the other members include channel managers B, C and D. A starts the negotiation by collecting the load information of B, C and D by invoking the operation "check_load()" (see Fig. 3(a)). It then compares the load levels of all channels involved. Suppose that the channel monitored by B is the most heavily loaded one whereas the load of the channel monitored by D is the lightest. If the load of B exceeds that of D by more than a threshold fraction θ,[1] A will notify B to unload one of its clients to D via the operation "shift_load(D)" (see Fig. 3(b)).

4 Experiment

In this section, we report the result of an initial experiment with the modified dynamic load balancing algorithm. Here, n is set to 1, meaning that only one client can be transferred per interaction. The value of the parameter ω used for adapting the interaction period is equal to 0.95, and the values of τ_{max} and τ_{min} are set to 5 seconds and 1 second, respectively. Load negotiation is performed among a group of 3 channel managers each time (so the value of m is equal to 3), which are arranged in a star configuration.

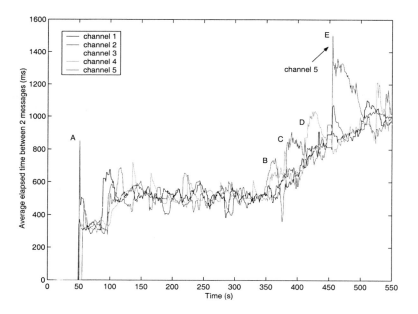

Fig. 4. Result of the experiment.

---

[1] Note that if the value of θ is too small, the system will become unstable, whereas if it is too large, the responsiveness of the load balancing algorithm will be sacrificed. In the experiment, θ is set to 10%, which is determined empirically.

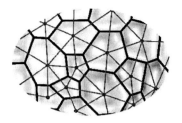

Fig. 1. Voronoi Diagrams & Delaunay Triangulations

of color switching. With the analogy of soap froth, the energies (or business clout) of an agent are defined as

$$\varepsilon_{\text{same}} \propto \alpha \sigma L_{\text{same}}$$
$$\varepsilon_{\text{diff}} \propto \gamma \sigma L_{\text{diff}} \tag{4}$$

where $\varepsilon_{\text{same}}$, $\varepsilon_{\text{diff}}$ are the interaction energies of the boundary shared by the same and different color agents, respectively. L_{same}, L_{diff} are the lengths of the boundary shared by the same and different color agents. σ is the intrinsic strength of the agent (i.e. the surface tension of real soap froth). α and γ are the strengths of the bonding energy of the same and different colors. We define a relative strength parameter of different color interaction to same color interaction as $x = \gamma/\alpha$. The energy of an agent i is then equal to the difference of the weighted same color interaction energies and the weighted different color interaction energies.

$$E_i = m_{\text{same}}\varepsilon_{\text{same}} - m_{\text{diff}}\varepsilon_{\text{diff}} \tag{5}$$

where m_{same} and m_{diff} are the number of neighboring agents belonging to the same and different groups.

Let P_i be the probability of customers originally belonging to the agent i decide to switch to an agent of different color, and $Q_i = 1 - P_i$ be the probability of customers that will not switch their affiliation. The color pattern on the cellular network evolves according to the Boltzmann distribution of switching probability as

$$P_i = \frac{e^{-\beta E_i}}{\displaystyle\sum_{\eta \in M_i} e^{-\beta E_\eta}} \tag{6}$$

where M_i is the set of neighboring agents of the agent i and β is the noise factor.

4 Results

Four hundred points are randomly generated on a square region of two- dimensional plane. Using Delaunay triangulation described above, we can compute the

Voronoi tessellation. To avoid the boundary and finite size effect, the square region is cut into four quadrants and then are duplicated on complementary sides. Based on the switching dynamics, the system undergoes 1000 Monte Carlo steps. From our previous results, the system attains to different phases [10] with the variation of the noise factor β and the relative strength interaction ratio x. Inside the phase diagram, different phases of colonization of monopolies and fair market are found existing in the multi-agent system.

To examine the configuration of the distribution of agents in detail. We observe that when color dominance appears, the majority agents (those with the dominant color) like to coalesce together to form a larger cluster. Minority agents (those with color different from the dominant color) can still survive between the large clusters inside the system. Indeed, we observe that the probability of agents in decagons with the dominant color is much higher than in squares, which are smaller. In the Figure 2, it shows that majority agents mainly dominates in the large cells while most minority agents surviving in the smaller cells.

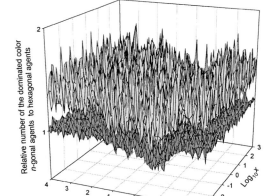

Fig. 2. Minority of agents presents in smaller sizes of cells

5 Discussions

This phenomenon can be explained by considering the model of multi-agent system. The driving force of an agent acquiring business in the market is the minimization of the cost and the maximization of the profit. By the Equation 4, the interaction energy is proportional to the length of the same color and different color bubbles. It implies that the cost is correlated with the amount of the customers. The more customers open for competition, the larger the interaction energy between the agents. Therefore majority agents have a larger energy in bigger cells to convert the customers on the perimeter to change their affiliation, thereby switch color to the dominant color.

On the other hand, for small cells, the perimeter is also small, implying that the smaller amount of customers does not appear sufficiently attractive to the majority agents to spend resources over them. This provides an opportunity for the minority agents to survive in the smaller cells. These results elucidate why small size companies are still able to operate in the market even under the strong influence of big companies. However, if the company does not have sufficient resources to compete against others, especially the big companies, it is hard to survive in the major market.

Acknowledgments

K.Y. Szeto acknowledged that the work described in this paper was partially supported by a grant from the Research Grants Council of the Hong Kong Special Administrative Region, China (Project No. HKUST6123/98P, HKUST6144/00P).

References

1. Engelen, G., White, R., Uljee, I., and Drazan, P.: Using Cellular Automata for Integrated Modelling of Socio-Environmental Systems. Environmental Modelling and Assessment. **34** (1995) 203–214
2. Lor, W.K.F., and De Wilde, P.: Soap Bubbles and the Dynamical Behavior of Multi-Agent Systems. Proccedings of Asia-Pacific Conference on Intelligent Agent Technology. (1999) 121–130
3. Szeto, K.Y., and Tam, W.Y.: Universal Topological Properties of Layers in Soap Froth. Phys.Rev. E. **53** (1996) 4213–4216
4. Szeto K.Y., Aste,T., and Tam, W.Y.: Topological Correlations in Soap Froth. Phys.Rev.E. **58** (1998) 2656–2659
5. Szeto, K.Y., and Tam, W.Y.: Lewis' Law vs Feltham's Law in Soap Froth. Physica A. **221** (1995) 256–262
6. Von Neumann, J.: Discussion. Metal Interfaces. (1952) 108–110
7. Stavans, J., Domany, E., and Mukamel, D.: Universality and Pattern Selection in Two-Dimensional Cellular Structures. Europhysics Letters. **15** (1991) 479–484
8. Szeto, K.Y., and Tam, W.Y.: Edge Scaling of Soap Froth. Physica A. **254** (1998) 248–256
9. Okabe, A., Boots, B., and Sugihara, K.: Spatial Tessellations: Concepts and Applications of Voronoi Diagrams, John Wiley, Chichester, England. (1992)
10. Lor, W.K.F., and Szeto, K.Y.: Switching Dynamics of Multi-Agent Systems: Soap Froths Paradigm. International Joint Conference on Neu-ral Networks, 2000. (to appear)

Combining Exploitation-Based and Exploration-Based Approach in Reinforcement Learning

Kazunori Iwata[1], Nobuhiro Ito[2], Koichiro Yamauchi[1], and Naohiro Ishii[1]

[1] Dept. of Intelligence and Computer Science, Nagoya Institute of Technology,
Gokiso-cho, Showa-ku, Nagoya 466-8555, Japan
{kiwata,yamauchi,ishii}@egg.ics.nitech.ac.jp
[2] Dept. of Electrical and Computer Engineering, Nagoya Institute of Technology,
Gokiso-cho, Showa-ku, Nagoya 466-8555, Japan
itoh@elcom.nitech.ac.jp

Abstract. Watkins' Q-learning is the most popular and an effective model-free method. However, comparing model-based approach, Q-learning with various exploration strategies require a large number of trial-and-error interactions for finding an optimal policy. To overcome this drawback, we propose a new model-based learning method extending Q-learning. This method has separated EI and ER functions for learning exploitation-based and exploration-based model, respectively. EI function based on statistics indicates the best action. The another ER function based on the information of exploration leads the learner to well-unknown region in the global state space by backing up in each step. Then, we introduce a new criterion as the information of exploration. Using combined these function, we can effectively proceed exploitation and exploration strategies and can select an action which considers each strategy simultaneously.

1 Introduction

Reinforcement learning is an effective learning in unknown environment, where a supervisor cannot support the learner. The learner learns an optimal behavior through trial-and-error interactions with a dynamic environment. In reinforcement learning problem, each time the learner performs an action in its environment, a trainer may provide a reward or penalty to indicate the desirability of the resulting state [1]. The learner is told only the reward, but is not told whether or not the action of selected is best. This means that the learner must explicitly explore its environment. So, the learner must balance between exploitation and exploration.

Many reinforcement learning algorithms has been proposed in Markov Decision Processes (MDP) environments, these algorithms can be classified into two methods, model-free method and model-based method. Model-free methods learn a policy or value function without explicitly representing a model of the controlled system. Model-based methods learn an explicit model of the system simultaneously with a value function and policy [2]. Atkeson et al. [2] compared these two methods according to two measures of data and computing efficiently and showed that model-based methods is more efficient than model-free methods.

Q-learning [3] is the most popular and an effective model-free method. However, comparing model-based approach, Q-learning with various exploration strategies [4],[5],[6] need a large number of trial-and-error interactions for finding an optimal policy. To overcome this drawback, we propose a new model-based learning method extending Q-learning. This method has separated EI and ER functions for learning exploitation-based and exploration-based model, respectively. EI function based on statistics indicates the best action. The another ER function based on the information of exploration leads the learner to well-unknown region in the global state space by backing up in each step. Then, we introduce a new criterion as the information of exploration. Using combined these function, we can effectively proceed exploitation and exploration strategies and can select an action which considers each strategy simultaneously.

2   Q-learning

In this paper, we consider only the case in MDP environments which state set $\mathbf{S}$ and action set $\mathbf{A}$ are finite. In MDP, the transition probability p and the expected reward r depend only on current state and action, not on earlier states or actions [1].

Watkins' Q-learning [3] is the most popular and an effective model-free method. In Q-learning, the learner works estimating and evaluating following Q-value from its experiences $\langle s_t, a_t, s_{t+1}, r_{t+1} \rangle$.

$$Q(s_t, a_t) \leftarrow (1 - \alpha)Q(s_t, a_t) + \alpha(r_{t+1} + \gamma \max_{a' \in \mathbf{A}} Q(s_{t+1}, a')) \qquad (1)$$

, where $\alpha(0 \leq \gamma \leq 1)$ denotes a learning rate and $\gamma(0 \leq \gamma \leq 1)$ is a discounted factor which controls the rate between immediate reward r_{t+1} and further one. Each Q-value will eventually converge to the true Q-value Q^* for all state s and action a [3]. Selecting an action is based on current Q-values. Two selecting method which controls an exploitation vs. an exploration is well-known [4],[5],[6].

ϵ-greedy With probability ϵ, an action is selected randomly. On the other hand, the best action which has the largest Q is selected with $1 - \epsilon$ probability.

Boltzmann exploration The probability $p(a \mid s)$ of taking action a in state s defined as follows:

$$p(a \mid s) \overset{\mathrm{D}}{=} \frac{\exp^{Q(s,a)/T}}{\sum_{a' \in \mathbf{A}} \exp^{Q(s,a')/T}} \qquad (2)$$

, where T is a temperature parameter which can be decreased over time to decrease exploration.

3   EI and ER combined Learning

In this section, we explain our exploitation-based and exploration-based combined learning (combined learning) algorithm extending above Q-learning. In our learning, we adapt a model-based approach using EI and ER functions. Let us start with describing how to build exploitation-based and exploration-based model formulating EI and ER functions, respectively. Then, we will describe the combined function Q_{comb} of these functions. Furthermore, we will discuss the weight parameter which connects between EI and ER functions.

3.1   EI and ER functions

First, EI function represents the mean of the expected sum of reward which the learner will receive if the learner executes the optimal policy in state s. We define it recursively as

$$x_{EI}(s_t, a_t) \leftarrow (1 - \alpha)x_{EI}(s_t, a_t) + \alpha \max_{a \in \mathbf{A}} EI(s_{t+1}, a) \tag{3}$$

$$EI(s_t, a_t) \leftarrow \tilde{r}(s_t, a_t) + \gamma x_{EI}(s_t, a_t) \tag{4}$$

, where $\tilde{r}(s, a)$ is the weighted mean of reward. Recall α and γ denotes a learning rate and a discount factor, respectively. The approximate EI function is approaching to the true EI function EI^* asymptotically with many episodes.

Second, ER function denotes the expected worth of taking explorational actions about current transition and further one. We express it recursively as equation below.

$$x_{ER}(s_t, a_t) \leftarrow (1 - \alpha)x_{ER}(s_t, a_t) + \alpha \sum_{a \in \mathbf{A}} ER(s_{t+1}, a) \tag{5}$$

$$ER(s_t, a_t) \leftarrow e(s_t, a_t) + \gamma x_{ER}(s_t, a_t) \tag{6}$$

The exploration-based information $e(s, a)$ is a important factor to realize efficient exploration. In the next section, we introduce a new criterion in detail.

In each step, to calculate above EI and ER functions, the learner needs to update some adequate statistics as follows:

$$\sum r(s_t, a_t) \leftarrow (1 - \alpha) \sum r(s_t, a_t) + r_{t+1} \tag{7}$$

$$\sum r^2(s_t, a_t) \leftarrow (1 - \alpha) \sum r^2(s_t, a_t) + r_{t+1}^2 \tag{8}$$

Using these statistics, we can calculate the weighted mean $\tilde{r}(s, a)$ of reward and the weighted variance $\tilde{\sigma}^2(s, a)$ of reward as follows [7] :

$$\tilde{r}(s, a) = \frac{\sum r(s, a)}{\tilde{n}(s, a)} \tag{9}$$

$$\tilde{\sigma}^2(s, a) = \frac{1}{\tilde{n}(s, a)}(\tilde{r}^2(s, a) - \frac{(\tilde{r}(s, a))^2}{\tilde{n}(s, a)}) \tag{10}$$

, where $\tilde{n}(s, a) = \sum_{t=1}^{n(s,a)}(1 - \alpha)^{t-1}$ and $n(s, a)$ denotes the number of selected action a in state s. Thus, the EI and ER functions has a different information are learned separately. With many episodes, EI and ER informations propagate from the goal to the start. This means that EI and ER functions lead to the best policy and well-unknown region in the global state space, respectively.

3.2 Exploration-based information

Now that we discussed ER function's work. In ER function, the exploration-based information $e(s, a)$ has a important role to realize efficient exploration.

Suppose the stochastic reward $r(s, a)$ follow a normal distribution, the weighted variance of maximum likelihood estimate $\tilde{r}(s, a)$ satisfies below by Cramer-Rao's inequality.

$$V[\tilde{r}(s, a)] \geq \frac{\tilde{\sigma}^2(s, a)}{\tilde{n}(s, a)} \qquad (11)$$

We use its minimum as exploration-based information, that is,

$$e(s, a) \overset{\text{D}}{=} \frac{\tilde{\sigma}(s, a)}{\sqrt{\tilde{n}(s, a)}} \qquad (12)$$

3.3 Combined Function

Instead of Q-value in Q-learning, we use the following combined function $Q_{comb}(s, a)$ of EI and ER functions for evaluating and planning.

$$Q_{comb}(s, a) \overset{\text{D}}{=} EI(s, a) + \omega(s, a)ER(s, a) \qquad (13)$$

, where $\omega(s, a)$ is the weight parameter which controls a ratio between exploitation and exploration. In this way, we consider exploitation-based and exploration-based informations simultaneously.

3.4 Control Weight

In this section, we take a close look at the weight parameter. Consider the learner reaches a state s. To encourage behavior that tests long-untried actions, we use Sutton's "bonus" concept [5] as $\omega(s, a)$. If the action a has not been tried in m step, we define the weight parameter $\omega(s, a)$ as

$$\omega(s, a) \overset{\text{D}}{=} \kappa\sqrt{m} \qquad (14)$$

, where κ is a small parameter.

4 Experiments

We examined the performance of our learning method in experiment and compare with above Q-learning and Sutton's Dyna-Q+ [5]. To compare briefly, we employed ϵ-greedy selection for these algorithms. In each algorithm, ϵ is decayed by $\epsilon \leftarrow \frac{1}{\log(2+episode)}$ and the discount factor γ was set to 0.95. We set the other parameters of each algorithm as follows.

Q-learning The learning rate α is decayed by $\alpha \leftarrow \frac{1}{\log 2(2+episode)}$.

Dyna-Q+ The learning rate α is decayed by $\alpha \leftarrow \frac{1}{\log 2(2+episode)}$. The iterations number N was set to 5. The bonus reward parameter κ was set to 0.2.

Combined learning The learning rate α is decayed by $\alpha \leftarrow \frac{1}{\log 2(2+episode)}$. The parameter κ was set to 7.5.

To compare each performance in delayed-reward environment, we tested these algorithm on Sutton's environment [8] (Task1) as Figure 1 and Tree-type environment (Task2) as Figure 2. These environments have a difference characteristic each other in delayed-reward. In each Figure, circles represent the states of environment, narrow arrows are state transitions, the upper number of narrow arrow represents action, and the lower number of narrow arrow represents the probability of state transition. Wide arrows with the number 10 represent reward.

5 Results

Let us compare combined learning performance to the other performances. Result1 as Figure 3 represents the average reward received over a sequence of 300 steps, averaged over 50 runs. Result2 as Figure 4 represents the average reward received over a sequence of 600 steps, averaged over 50 runs. X-axis shows the number of steps and Y-axis shows the average reward per step. From each result, we can found the superiority of combined learning. We can see that, in both case, combined learning is much efficient than the other algorithm in delayed-reward environment.

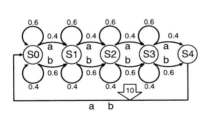

Fig. 1. Sutton's Environment [8]

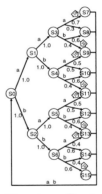

Fig. 2. Tree-type Environment

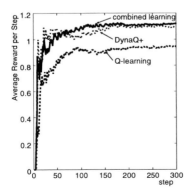

Fig. 3. Performance for Task1

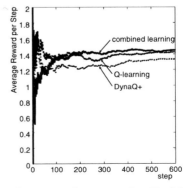

Fig. 4. Performance for Task2

6 Conclusions

We proposed a new model-based approach extending Q-learning. This method has EI and ER functions for evaluating exploitation-based and exploration-based information, respectively. These functions are learned separately by backing up in each step. Using combined these function, we can effectively proceed exploitation and exploration strategies and can take an action which consider each information simultaneously. We tested the performance of our learning, comparing with the other learning algorithm in two environments. As shown in each result, we found the superiority of our learning.

In summary, our findings for EI and ER combined learning as follows : First, backing up the exploitation and exploration information, combining learning effectively leads the learner to the best action in exploration strategy and well-unknown region in global state space in exploration strategy. This means the combined learning efficiently proceeds exploitation and exploration strategies. Second, we can consider exploitation and exploration informations simultaneously. Third, this algorithm is relatively easy to implement. Therefore, it is a flexible and useful on various applications.

References

1. Tom Mitchell, *Machine Learning*, McGraw Hill, p367-390, 1997.
2. Atkeson, C. G. and J. C. Santamaria, J. C., *A comparison of direct and model-based reinforcement learning*, International Conference on Robotics and Automation, 1997.
3. Watkins, C.J.C.H., Dayan, *P.Technical Note : Q-learning*, Machine Learning 8, p55-68, 1992.
4. Leslie Pack Kaelbling, Michael L.Littman, Andrew W.Moore, *Reinforcement Learning : A Survey*, Journal of Artificial Intelligence Research 4, p237-285, 1996.
5. Sutton R., Barto A., *Reinforcement Learning : An Introduction*, MIT Press, 1998.
6. S. D. Whitehead and D. H. Ballard, *Learning to perceive and act by trial and error*, Machine Learning, 7, p45-83, 1991.
7. Feller, W. *An Introduction to Probability Theory and Its Applications*, Modern Asia Editions, 1960.
8. Richard S. Sutton, *Temporal Credit Assignment in Reinforcement Learning*, PhD thesis, University of Massachusetts, Amherst, Massachusetts, 1984.

A Probabilistic Agent Approach to the Traffic Jam Problem

Duncan McKay and Colin Fyfe

Applied Computational Intelligence Research Unit,
The University of Paisley,
Scotland.
email:duncan.mckay,colin.fyfe@paisley.ac.uk

Abstract. Artificial life simulations of social situations are a relative new field which aims to model situations which are too complex to be analytically investigated. In this paper, we develop commuter-agents with simple probabilistic models of the world and show that such agents can develop cooperation which aids the society as a whole. We show that there are situations in which the more powerful agents are sometimes forced by their greater knowledge into taking a lower utility than the weaker ones. In the last series of experiments we show that agents which have the ability to predict others' road usage can materially improve the utility of the population as a whole.

1 Introduction

Wang and Fyfe [2] suggested an interesting N-player game based upon a simple simulation of traffic flow in a city, where players decide whether to take the car or bus every morning with different payoffs depending upon their opponent's choices. They used an evolutionary approach and showed that cooperation in the society as a whole could evolve to the extent that an individually selfish population evolved to the Nash equilibrium point where no individual could improve his utility by changing his mode of transport within the current population. Here, we look at an alternative probabilistic approach to the problem using probabilistic agents to represent the commuters in the game.

Firstly, we expect our agents to behave rationally, that is they always choose the action that maximises their expected utility based upon the information available to them. Each agent also has a view of the world based on his memory of his previous experiences in the world. Each individual can calculate the probability that there will be i car users in the rest of the population from $P(\text{other cars} == i) = \frac{c}{ML}$ where c is the number of times he remembers i other users to have used the car in his memory space of ML memories. Using the maximum likelihood number of cars, he can then calculate his utility if he should take the car or the bus. Each agent begins with a prior probability for each i equal to $\frac{1}{N-1}$.

If we constrain every agent to use the same model and initialisation, we would expect that each agent would always take the same decision as every other agent in every round, as they are all making rational decisions based upon identical evidence. To bring about individuality, we need to introduce differing design aspects in the agents, such as those suggested below:

Different histories - players could be allowed to have different memory lengths. The players with longer memories may be able to assign more accurate probabilities to events and therefore calculate more accurate expected utilities.

Additional information - this is one of the most common aspects of probabilistic game theory. Some players will have a more complex game representation than other players i.e. players may model additional events and therefore have a different level of evidence compared to the other players.

We have previously investigated imperfect information in the Iterated Prisoner's Dilemma [1] which may be considered an abstraction of such social problems as traffic flow. In this paper, we shall examine the effect of the different modelling attributes in a series of experiments and show that, counter intuitively, it is not always the agent with greatest processing power who gains most from social interactions.

2   Experimental Investigation - History Lengths

Initially, we define 10 identical agents to take part in the game, all having a memory length of 1 - that is, they may only remember the result of the single previous round. Each agent uses the same utility evaluation functions:
$U(car) = 100-(10*m)$, and $U(bus) = 60-(4*m)$
where m represents the number of agents in the population who use cars.

The maximum utility for the entire population exists when every player takes the bus - however, each player will only take the decision that maximises their own personal utility. Each agent can maximise their personal utility by taking the car if there are 6 or less other car users. It is easily shown that the Nash Equilibrium point for this utility function is around 7 car users; at this point it does not pay a bus user to switch to car use nor a car user to switch to bus use.

When all agents had a single-round memory, we observe that all players choose the car in the first round, and thereafter strictly alternate between car and bus every round, with every agent always mimicking one another. Every agent scores an average utility of 35 per round, with the overall population average utility being 350.

In experiment 2, we then individualise memory size, the first agent having length 1, the second 2, and so on, we find that the average population utility score tends towards 350 as in the previous experiment, however car and bus journeys are differently distributed amongst the agents. In total, car journeys represent 70.5% of trips, which is close to the Nash equilibrium described earlier.

If we examine the converging behavior of our agents, we can clearly see how each agent's strategy dovetails with the other players. The players who gain the highest individual utilities are agents 2,6,9 and 10, who quickly tend to take the car almost every journey. However, it is interesting to note that agent 4 switches

Experiment 2				Experiment 3			
Agent	Memory	Takes Car	Ave. Utility	Agent	Memory	Takes Car	Ave. Utility
1	1	0.49	29.78	1	1	0.12	31.06
2	2	0.96	38.76	2	3	0.87	36.64
3	3	0.53	30.04	3	5	0.14	31.1
4	4	0.06	31.62	4	7	0.11	31.22
5	5	0.53	30.1	5	9	0.96	37.96
6	6	0.98	38.86	6	11	0.96	37.9
7	7	0.55	30.5	7	13	0.97	38.1
8	8	0.98	38.86	8	15	0.98	38.3
9	9	0.99	39.0	9	17	0.98	38.3
10	10	0.98	38.8	10	19	0.98	38.3

Table 1. The left table shows the number of times each agent (with different memory lengths - Experiment 2) takes the car and his average utility during the experiment. The right table shows corresponding results for Experiment 3.

to take the bus every turn, but this strategy is still an improvement on agent 1, who has the shortest memory length and performs most poorly - he simply alternates between taking the car and bus every turn. However, we also see that agent 5 switches to this same strict alternating strategy after turn 13, as does agent 7 after turn 21. The overall population of agents quickly settle down to an alternating pattern of car use after turn 21, where there are 9 car drivers on the even turns and 5 car drivers on the odd turns.

If we change the memory lengths (Experiment 3) so that the first agent has memory length 1, second 3, third 5, and so on with agent 10 having a memory length of 19. All agents in the population have odd-valued memory lengths. After 100 turns, we found the following:

- Average Total Utility: 358.88
- Average Car Journeys: 0.707
- Average Bus Journeys: 0.293

We can see that the utility in this experiment was slightly higher than previously, although the number of overall car journeys was very similar. Results are shown in the right half of Table 1. Again we observe that some agents continually choose to take the bus, whilst the others choose to always take the car and score more highly. If we examine the actual number of cars per turn, we observe an equilibrium being reached, although this time stability is obtained at 7 cars after 31 turns.

Repeating this experiment with memory lenghts 2, 4, 6 etc. so that all memory lengths are even-valued, we obtain similar results.

Initially, it would appears as if there is a definite relationship between increased memory length and greater utility gain: the agents with longer memories tend to gain higher utilities. However in Experiment 4, we change the pay-off functions to

$U(car) = 100-(10*m)$ and $U(bus) = 80-(4*m)$

so that now, relatively fewer cars can be used before using the bus represents higher utility gain.

Experiment 4				Experiment 5			
Agent	Memory	Takes Car	Ave. Utility	Agent	Memory	Takes Car	Ave. Utility
1	3	0.45	55.9	1	2	0.82	67.68
2	4	0.43	56.56	2	4	0.89	67.74
3	3	0.45	55.9	3	6	0.92	68.28
4	4	0.43	56.56	4	8	0.93	68.7
5	3	0.45	55.9	5	10	0.07	63.06
6	4	0.43	56.5	6	12	0.1	62.82
7	3	0.45	55.9	7	14	0.07	62.88
8	4	0.43	56.56	8	16	0.05	62.88
9	3	0.45	55.9	9	18	0.05	62.88
10	50	0.03	63.34	10	20	0.05	62.88

Table 2. The left table shows the number of times each agent (with second payoff function - Experiment 4) takes the car and his average utility during the experiment. The right table shows corresponding results for Experiment 5.

The left half of Table 2 shows that again the agent with the greater memory obtains the best utility, this time recognising to take the bus more frequently. It should also be noted that this time, the number of cars being used quickly converges to a steady 4 cars per turn which is close to the Nash equilibrium.

However, in Experiment 5, we again use this new payoff scheme and show that increased memory length does not always resultant in greater individual utility (right half of Table 2). Again the number of car users in the population quickly converges to 4 per turn, but this time, the six agents with the largest memories choose to take the bus and score less individually than the four shorter-memory agents who choose to take the car. This can be explained if we consider that the shorter-memory agents behave 'stupidly' and take the car because they believe it will always give higher utility, whereas the longer-memory agents would like to be able to take the car but have the information available to realise that with the more selfish agents always selecting the car, they should take the bus. The shorter-memory agents score more highly but not as a result of more complex reasoning than the other agents.

3 Experimental Investigation - Additional Information

In this section, we examine an extended agent model that makes use of an additional node which estimates the number of drivers based on an associated conditional probability from the previous day's car drivers. In modelling terms, this is different from varying the memory length in that this is a qualitative modelling change and not simply a quantitative change. We would expect this new agent to be able to take advantage of cyclical behaviour patterns in other agents. The conditional probabilities connecting the node representing predicted cars and the parent previous count node are again determined by the statistics available in the agent's memory space, with a uniform prior being used where no data is available. Initially, we will experiment with only one 'enhanced' agent in the population, the remaining agents following the simple model.

We use our original pay-off scheme U(car) = 100-(10*m) and U(bus) = 60-(4*m). Agent 1 will be defined as the agent using the enhanced model.

- Average Total Utility: 261.12
- Average Car Journeys: 0.708
- Average Bus Journeys: 0.292

Agent	Memory	Takes Car	Ave. Utility
1 (E)	10	0.51	28.2
2-10	10	0.73	25.88

Table 3. The single enhanced agent (numbered 1) has greater utility than any of the other 9.

We can see (Table 3) that Agent 1 obtains a higher utility than the others, and is able to better select when to take the bus when he predicts that the others will be following an alternating pattern and will take the car on that particular turn. In fact, when the pattern of car use is studied, we find that Agent 1 is able to ascertain that following a day when everyone takes the car, the other agents will try to take the car again the following day, and takes the bus for maximum benefit to himself.

We now recreate one of our earlier experiments using differing memory lengths, combined with all agents using the improved model to see how the results compare.

- Average Total Utility: 358.84
- Average Car Journeys: 0.709
- Average Bus Journeys: 0.291

Comparing Table 4 with the previous experiment with only one modified agent Table 3, we can see that although the average number of car journeys is almost identical, the overall total utility for the whole population is much higher. This is caused by the agents being able to select the car at different times, due to all agents having more varied levels of information. It is interesting to note that in this experiment agents 1, 4 and 5 become regular bus users, but in an earlier experiment with the same pattern of memory lengths and older model, it was agents 1, 2 and 3 who were the bus users. It would appear that the change of model causes a different synchronisation of agent behaviour in both experiments.

Agent	Memory	Takes Car	Ave. Utility
1 (E)	2	0.16	31.66
2 (E)	4	0.96	37.76
3 (E)	6	0.91	37.36
4 (E)	8	0.10	31.0
5 (E)	10	0.12	31.22
6 (E)	12	0.94	37.72
7 (E)	14	0.96	37.82
8 (E)	16	0.98	38.1
9 (E)	18	0.98	38.1
10 (E)	20	0.98	38.1

Table 4. When all agents are enhanced, the payoff to the population increases.

4 Conclusion

Artificial life simulations of social situations is a new area of research which brings the advantages of diversity and parallelism in simulations to situations which are not readily analysed. In this paper, we have paralleled a recent set of experiments using genetic algorithms to evolve cooperation in a population of commuters. However, our agents are probabilistic agents who are totally self seeking and yet manage to develop strategies which include accepting lower utilities which favours the population as a whole.

One interesting finding in this paper is that the most powerful commuters (those with greatest memories) do not always gain the greatest utilities; they are able to see that there is no individual gain in short sighted greed and so they rightly opt for bus-use which helps the rest of the population too. This aspect of forced altruism is an area of future research.

We have also shown that agents with a capacity to predict the number of car users in any situation is more capable of gaining greater utilities than the first simple population. Such agents have meta-capabilities in that they can predict the change in car-use in other road users; in particular such agents can identify cyclical use of cars/buses. Again this aspect of meta-information is worthy of future research; in particular, the effect of this meta-information on the synchronisation seen in groups of agents' strategies.

References

1. M. Chapman, G. Manwell, and C. Fyfe. Imperfect information in the iterated prisoner's dilemma. In C. Fyfe, editor, *Engineering Intelligent Systems, EIS2000*. ICSC Press, June 2000.
2. T. Z. Wang and C. Fyfe. Simulating responses to traffic jams. *(Submitted)*, 2000.

Round-Table Architecture
for Communication in Multi-agent Softbot Systems

Pham Hong Hanh[1] and Tran Cao Son[2]

[1] State University of New York at New Paltz
Department of Computer Science
75 S. Manheim Blvd. Suite 6, NY 12561-2440
pham@mcs.newpaltz.edu

[2] Stanford University, Knowledge Systems Laboratory
Gates CS Building, 2A, CA 94305
tson@KSL.Stanford.EDU

Abstract. This paper proposes a new communication architecture which is based on a round-table mechanism. Communication channels are preliminarily defined according to the matching of agent requests. A channel connects an agent to a queue of matched agents with the same interests and is scheduled to become periodically active based on their proportions in total demand and the amount of available resources. The order to activate channels and the sequence of agents in matched queues are defined based on agent time constraints. Our evaluation shows that the proposed model achieves a good balance of performance and quality of service compared with the other methods and is especially useful when the number of agents is large and the capacity of systems is limited.

1 Introduction

Agent technology is predicted as one of the most efficient tools to conduct business via Internet in an automatic, fast, and low-cost way. Softbots are programs which can act autonomously to fulfill user tasks. In multi-agent systems, which are based on softbots, agents can be distributed on different hosts, they interact and cooperate with each other through communication. Thus, agent communication architectures have significant influences on system performance and quality of service.

The development of agent communication systems for agent-based software involves: (i) define formal languages for representing commands and the transferred information; (ii) design communication architectures which include interaction mechanisms and communication models; (iii) develop local planning systems for each agent which define when and what commands or information should be exchanged with other agents to achieve given goals. While there are many systems designed for (i) and (iii), (ii) receives less attention and yet to be developed.

In this paper we concentrate on communication architectures, i.e. (ii). In the next section, we discuss issues of multi-agent communication in softbot-based systems. Then, a new architecture for agent communication is described in section 3. In order to compare the proposed architecture with the others, an estimation is carried out in section 4. Finally, conclusion is given in section 5.

2 Communication in Agent-based Softbot Systems

General layout of a multi-agent softbot system and its communication management can be illustrated as in Fig.1. Requirements and goals in developing agent communication architectures can be stated as follows:

Given: n agents A1, A2, ..., An with Q service-request categories C={C1,C2,..C$_Q$}. Each agent Ai , i=1..n, characterizes by a set of data (Ti, Si, Di), where:

- Ti is the period of time for which the agent is scheduled to live.
- Si shows what services the agent are interested in, their deadlines are also given.
- Di is other data such as sizes of messages, message box's address etc.

Requirements: Design a model and mechanisms for agents {A1, A2, ..., An} to exchange messages based on their interests and needs given in Si, i=1..n. The goal is to guarantee reliability while maintaining good performance and quality of service such as response time, privacy, and customization.

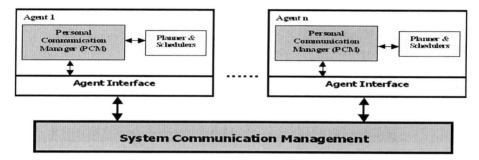

Fig. 1. Softbot Communication

Existing architectures for agent communication can be grouped into the following categories: *Yellow-pages* (YP)[1], *Contract-Net* (CN)[9], *Pattern-based* (PB)[4], and *Point-to-point* (PP) [2]. A study in [6] shows that most of them use either fixed numbers of communication channels [1],[9] or generates channels based on agent requests without any control and consideration of system capacity [2],[4]. Thus, when the number of agents is large [1][10], PP and PB make system crush while YP and CN give long response times, and all of them suffer from agent starvation. That is because these systems use standard interprocess communication mechanisms of low-level middlewares or operating systems, which do not consider other information about agents, such as their interests, deadlines of requests, or agent life time.

3 Round-Table Architecture

To overcome these shortcomings, we propose a new communication architecture. Our goals are (i) to take it into account the limited capacity of the host system and agent deadlines; and (ii) to achieve a good balance between the workload of agents and the workload of communication manager. We propose to have a combination of centralized management unit (CMU) and autonomous management (AM) by each agent. Besides, the system resources such as memory and CPU's time will be divided fairly between agents according to the deadlines of requests and agent live times.

3.1 Communication Model

Our model can be illustrated as in Fig 2. It consists of: (i) Database; (ii) Round Table; (iii) Agent Personal Dispatchers (built in each agent). System Data stores: agent IDs, pointers to message boxes and their status. For security, System Data can be accessed only by CMU, not available for agents. Agent Data is formed at the registration when the agent enters the system, and is accumulated based on the information submitted to the CMU during agent life. It has the following form:

- A_1: Life time T_1, service interest $S_1=\{(R_1^1, t_1^1), ...,(R_1^{D1}, t_1^{D1})\}$; ...
- A_n: Life time T_n, service interest $S_n=\{(R_n^1, t_n^1), ...,(R_n^{Dn}, t_n^{Dn})\}$.

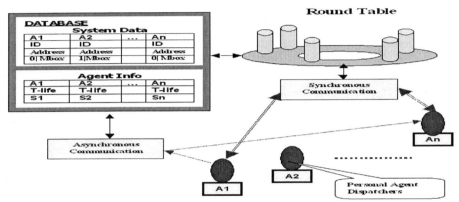

Fig. 2. Communication Management Components

An agent communicates with the others by sending messages. The communication management is carried out by Agent Personal Dispatchers (APD) and CMU which provide agents two alternatives of communication (Fig.3): (i) Synchronous; and (ii) Asynchronous. *In asynchronous mode*, an agent X sends a message directly to a known target agent Y at any time when it needs. This message is stored in the receiver Y's message box. *In synchronous mode*, an agent can use services of Round-Table mechanism to create a communication channel to a queue of agents who have the same interests. Protocols for synchronous communication are described in details in [6]. First, the agent sends a request to CMU, which contains data about his interests. The CMU defines the matched queue for the given request. Then, a seat for this agent in the Round Table is defined by its own APD. Next, a permanent communication channel is automatically established between the agent and the queue and is activated by the rules of the Round Table, which are described in the next section. Since then, this agent will send/receive messages synchronously within a given period of time defined by the Round Table mechanism. Algorithms for APD and CMU in synchronous mode are described in [6].

3.2 Structure of Round Table

Round Table is a mechanism which matches agents according to their interests and then creates communication channels between the matched ones. Unlike other communication mechanisms, communication channels in this model are established with consideration of agent time constraints. Round Table also controls the number of channels based on the available resources: threads and memory. Round Table has Q double *queues of services* and virtually a chain of seats (Fig.3.). The Q queues $\{R_1, R_2, ..., R_Q\}$ are formulated based on agent interests given in Si, i=1..n. In each queue Rj, j=1..Q, we have two subqueues: (i) $R^+(j)$ - a list of agents interested in providing the service Cj; and (ii) $R^-(j)$ - a list of agents interested in demanding the service Cj.

- $R^+(j)=\{\{A^1, t_j^1\}, \{A^2, t_j^2\}, ... \{A^{u(j)}, t_j^{u(j)}\}\}$
- $R^-(j)=\{\{A^{1*}, t_j^{1*}\}, \{A^{2*}, t_j^{2*}\}, ... \{A^{u(j)*}, t_j^{u(j)*}\}\}$

Where, $A^k \in AS=\{A_1, A_2, ..., A_M\}$, k=1...u(j) or k=1...u(j)*; AS is the set of agents who use Round-Table mechanism; t_j^k is the time constraint for the given request of agent A^k concerning service Cj, either in providing or demanding.

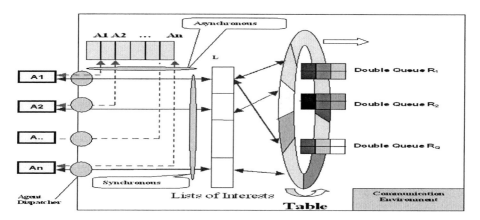

Fig. 3. Round-Table for Agent Communication

Every agent, who wants to use the Round Table for synchronous communication, has an entry to the Round Table mechanism. There are M entries to the Round Table at the given time. Each entry has its *queue of requests* which is a *list of interests* of the given agent Ai: $L^i =\{L^i_{[1]}, L^i_{[2]}, .. L^i_{[Hi]}\}$, where Hi is the number of requests of the given agent, i=1..M. This list is maintained by APD and is sorted based on the deadlines of the requests given in S_i. On the other side, assume that Mc is the maximal number of channels, which can be created using the available resources. Then, the total number of seats in the Round Table is Mc. These seats are distributed to the agents by the following law: each queue of service Rj, i.e. a sector of the Round table for agents interested in Cj, receives Δ_j seats which is defined as follows:

$$\Delta j = \frac{Mc \times Kj}{\sum_{i=1}^{Q} Ki}$$

where, Kj, j=1..Q, is the number of agents interested in Cj. Thus, Mc channels would be distributed to Q queues of services by the following rule:

$$Mc = \sum_{j=1}^{Q} \Delta j = \sum_{j=1}^{Q} \frac{Mc \times Kj}{\sum_{i=1}^{Q} Ki}$$

A request from a list of requests of an agent is matched to a queue of service by local APD. Receiving this request from APD, the central management unit CMU checks if there is a free seat in the matched sector, i.e. queue of service. If so, the seat is granted and a communication channel is created. If no more seat is available then CMU creates a waiting queue W(j) for the given sector, j=1..Q. Requests from W(j) gain seats according to the priorities of requests $L^i[h]$, h=1..Hi, which are defined by:

$$PL^i[h] = F(Ti, t^i_h) - Age(Ti).$$

where, F is some function defined by CMU ; Ti is life time of agent Ai; $Age(Ti)$ is an aging function which increases priority of an agent by the time the agent name is in the system. We use this technique to avoid agent starvation; t^i_h is the deadline of request $L^i[h]$ of agent Ai.

For each queue of service Rj, j=1..Q, Δj channels are given to agents who have shortest life times. The order of potential target agents in a subqueue $R^+(j)$ or $R^-(j)$ is defined by their priorities as the following:

$$PTA^{j(+/-)}[p] = G(T_p, t^p_j).$$

where, G is a function; T_p is life time of agent A^p; t^p_j is the deadline of agent A_p interest in Cj; $p = 1..u(j)/u(j)*$. More protocols and algorithms of Round Table mechanism are described in [6].

4 Comparative Evaluation

In order to estimate the performance of the proposed model we use the following criteria: (i) *Cost of EC:* time complexity spent for establishing communication network, usually for matching agents and filtering messages; (ii) *Maximal Number of Channels:* the possible highest number of channels in the agent communication system at a time; (iii) *Density:* the maximal average number of channels to/from an agent. Performance characteristics of PP, PB, CN, and YP methods, described in [7], and of the new architecture are shown in Table. 1.

Table 1. Performance Characteristics

Methods	Cost of EC	Maximal Number of Channels	Density
Point-to-Point	0	$(n-1) \times n/2$	$(n-1) \to m*$
Pattern-Based	$Q \times n$	$Q \times n$	$Q \to m*$
Contact-Net	0	n	1
Yellow-Pages	$Q \times n$	n	1
Round-Table	$Q \times n$	Mc	$(Q/2+1) \to m*$

(m* is the number of agents which matched the requests of a given agent)

We use a set of fuzzy values {VL,L,M,H,VH} stand for {Very Low, Low, Medium, High, Very High} for measuring quality of service with the following criteria: Agent workload; Agent response time; Privacy; Customization. A comparison of PP, PB, CN, YP, and RT architectures is shown in Fig. 4. Note that in our architecture an agent can have both synchronous and asynchronous communication simultaneously. It gives agents more freedom and flexibility. The asynchronous communication is good for one-to-one negotiation, while synchronous communication with Round Table mechanism would be suitable for surveys.

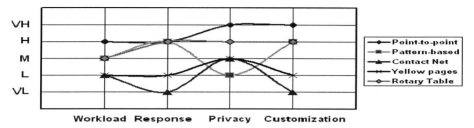

Fig. 4. Fuzzy Comparison of PP, PB, CN, YP in term of Quality of Service

5 Conclusion

We have proposed a new architecture for agent communication which considers system and time constraints and is able to scale itself to adapt to the limitation including the change of system capacity. Thus, this architecture would be especially useful in agent-based systems with large size or system running on hosts with limited resource. Our analysis and evaluation show that it also achieves a good balance of system performance and quality of service. In the future we intend to embed the given architecture into an e-business system for mobile services which is proposed in [5] by VTT Electronics of Finland.

6 Acknowledgment

This work is supported by the Research Creative Award N00-01 from the State University of New York at New Paltz.

References

1. Bradshaw J. et al, Agents for the Masses, *IEEE Intelligent Systems*, p53-63, March-April 1999.
2. Jamali J., Thati P., and Agha G., An Actor-Based Architecture for Customizing and Controlling Agent Ensembles, *IEEE Intelligent Systems*, p38-44, March-April 1999.
3. Kiniry Joseph and Zimmerman Daniel, A Hands-on look at Java Mobile agents, *IEEE Internet Computing*, July-August1997.
4. Ma Moses. Agents in E-commerce, *ACM Communications* , p79-80, March 1999.
5. Palola M., Heikkinen M., Constructing Mobile Web Services on a software agent platform, proceeding of the *International Conference on Internet Computing*, p323-329, June 26 - 29, 2000.
6. Pham H. Hanh, Agent Communication, TR-2000-06-01 Tech. Report, *SUNY at New Paltz*, 2000.
7. Pham H. Hanh, Nguyen Hien, Nguyen V.Hop, Environment and Means for Cooperation and Interaction in E-commerce Agent-based Systems, proceeding of the *International Conference on Internet Computing* (IC'2000), Las Vegas, p253-259, June 26 - 29, 2000.
8. Pham H. Hanh, Worasing R. , and Thanadee U., "Distributed Multi-level Adaptation for Dynamic Multi-Agent Systems", in the Proceeding of 22nd *IEEE Conference on Systems, Man, and Cybernetics* (SMC'99), October-1999.
9. Smith R.G., The contract Net protocol: High-level Communication and Control in a Distributed problem Solver, *IEEE Tran. On Computers*, V29-N12, p1104-1113, 1980.
10. Yamamoto G. and Nakamura Y., Architecture and Performance Evaluation of a Massive Multi-Agent System, *Autonomous Agents'99*, Seattle USA, p319-325, 1999.

Mobile Agents for Reliable Migration in Networks

DongChun Lee[1], Byeongkuk Jeon[2], and Yongchul (Robert)Kim[3]

[1] Dept. of Computer Science Howon Univ., Korea
ldch@sunny.howon.ac.kr
[2]Dept.of Office Automation WonJu Nat'l College, Korea
[3]Embedded System Team LGIS RD Center, Korea
robertkim@lgis.com

Abstract. Mobile agents are autonomous objects that can migrate from one node to other node of a computer network. Due to communication nodes failures, mobile agents may be blocked or crashed even if there are other nodes available that could continue processing. To solve it, we propose a scheme with the path reordering and backward recovery to guarantee migration of mobile agents in networks.

1 Introduction

Mobile agents are autonomous objects that can migrate from node to node of a computer network and provide to users which have executed themselves using databases or computation resources of hosts connected by network. To migrate the mobile agent, it is needed a virtual place so-called the mobile agent system to support mobility [1]. Many prototypes of mobile agent systems have been proposed in several different agent systems such as Odyssey [2], Aglet [3], AgentTCL
, Mole[5], and so forth. However, most systems are rarely ensuring its migration for a fault of communication nodes or a crash of hosts to be caused during touring after a mobile agent launches. That is, when there are some faults such as a destruction of the nodes or the mobile agent systems, mobile agents may be destroyed to block or orphan state even if there are available other nodes that continue processing. Because of the autonomy of mobile agents, there is no natural instance that monitors the progress of agent execution.

2 Previous Mobile Agent For Migration

Mobile agents are migrated autonomously according to the relevant routing schedule, and then accomplished their goals. Figure 1 depicts how a node repository can use for implementation instead of transaction message queue for agents. Assume that an agent moves from a node to the consecutive node along the path N1 N2...N(k-1) Nk (where Ni is a network node, Hi is a host, Ri is an agent repository). As an agent may visit the same node several times Ni and Nj (1<=i, j<=k) may denote the same or different nodes. Assume further that an agent is stored in a repository when it is accepted by the agent system for execution. Except Nk, each other node performs the following sequence of operations on Transaction Ti such as Get (agent); Execute (agent); Put (agent); Commit. Get removes an agent from the node's repository. Execute performs the received agent locally. Put places it on the repository of the host that will be visited the right next time. Three operations are performed within a transaction and hence consisted of the atomic unit of work.

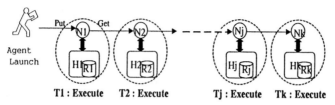

Agent
Launch

T1 : Execute   T2 : Execute   Tj : Execute   Tk : Execute

Fig.1.A migration path of a mobile agent.

In Fig. 1, we assume to happen a failure in a particular node Ni within the migration path of the mobile agent. Though the node Ni of the host Hi of node Ni lives, the agent can't migrated. Inversely, though the node Ni can be communicated with the previous node N (i-1), the agent can't occasionally migrate if the host Hi does not operate in the agent system. In the above cases, the agent never arrives by the last node Nk. the agent at previous host Hi-1 needs to receive user's assertion. In the worse case, if a shared host on the multiple agents launched occurs to crash on executing (launching), the agents will block or destroy.

3   Proposed Scheme

We describe an scheme for the agent system to support reliable migration of mobile agents even if it dose happen some failures hosts on the cluster of computer networks. The scheme adapts 'fault types' such that agents are not able to migrate more continuously.

3.1   Reordering of The Whole Path

The mobile agent is impossible to migrate to the destination node by the fault of node or host crash. Fig. 2(a) supposes that there is a migration path corresponding with an agent's routing schedule and some faulty nodes, such as N3, N4, and N7. An agent migrates and executes from node N1 to N2 sequentially, but it is blocked at the host of node N2 until the node N3 is recovered. If the node N3 dose not recovered, the agent may be orphan or destroyed by the particular host. To solve this situation is for the agent to skip the fault node N3 that includes on the migration path and move the address of node N3 to the last one of the migration path. Hence, the node N2 successfully connects the next other node N4 without any fault. As the same method is also applied to other nodes, the agent's migration path has reordered. This solution changes the previous migration path by connecting with normal nodes except that some nodes have the particular fault. Afterward, the agent retries to connect each certain fault node after it waits for the time-stamp to assign by the mobile agent system. If the certain fault node is recovering during the time-stamp, the agent succeeds to the migration. Otherwise, the address of the fault node will be discarded.Fig. 2(b) shows that all migration path for the mobile agent is changed by this scheme.

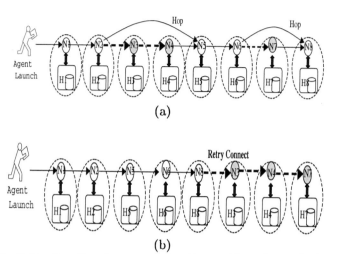

(a)

(b)

Fig.2. Faults of nodes on a migration path and reordering

The Path Reordering executes connecting to communicate with the mobile agent system. If the agent doesn't connect the destination node, it succeeds with connecting the right next node, after the failed address is moved to the last one of routing table and that will be retried to connect about the node. When it does reconnect each failed destination address, it does wait for the time-stamp to be assigned by the mobile agent system to connect. If it does fail again, it does ignore this address, and repeat to connect the next fault node. And then, if it does adapt to more than twice times failed node, a mobile agent may be occurred loophole for connection. So it limits to retry. Although it is connected, if each host of nodes errors the mobile agent system, it is adapted equally. In this way, algorithm 1 offers automatically to reorder the migration path.

Algorithm 1.Path Reordering

```
For each agent's routing-table {
  extract a target address and fail_checked information;
  if(no more a target address)backward multicastes'Agent_Fire'
      signal to successful_target nodes;
  if(is it a fail_checked_address) {
      wait the agent during some system_timestamp;
      try to connect Socket to the address;
```

```
    if (success){ call goAgent;
                exit;
    } else { notify to user the address is unavailable;
            ignore the address;
    } }
else if (not a fail_checked_address) {
    try to connect Socket to the destination node;
    if (success) { call goAgent;
                exit;
    } else { notify to user;
        move the current failed_address to last in the routing-table;
        set the fail_checked information;
    } } }
```

3.2 Backward Recovery

In Fig. 3, we suppose that migrated agents execute autonomously at the host H5. If the host H5 of node N5 crashes, all agents at that host are blocked or destroyed. To prevent it, when an agent migrates after it ends its job at a previous host, the agent's clone leave equally itself at that host. Then, the clone is unconditionally waiting for an acknowledge signal 'ACK' that reaches from the next host. If the signal 'ACK' doesn't reach within the time-stamp from the next host H5, the cloned agent waiting for at the host H4 has automatically activated since it resolves to any hindrance. Then, it is passed by the node N5 and hops to the next node N6. If the migrated agent faults at the host H6 on execution, it will be repeated the same method. However, the running agent in a host H5 is destroyed by being clashed, and at the same time if the prior node N4's host occurs succeeding fault, the cloned agent has already copied the prior host H3 wakes up and re-runs. This is so-called Backward Recovery.

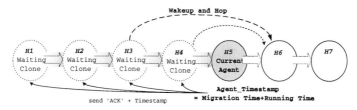

Fig.3.An example of Backward Recovery

The Backward Recovery is as follows: The agent system leave the clone of the agent being already passed at all hosts from source to current node and each clone is waiting during it's own time-stamp. Here in, the time-stamp of each clone is maximum at source, the next will be less reflecting the migration and execution time of the prior, and so forth. Since an agent is launch, it's time-stamp accumulates informing to every clone of the prior hosts it's own moving and running time before it depart for the current host. Therefore, clones are waiting during the time-stamp. Each clone spontaneously revives and redoes the path reordering regarding that host as clashed if none received any signal from next host. At the last node's host, the agent system broadcasts a signal 'Agent_Fire' to be destined all copied of the agent except the faulty nodes and failed hosts until reaching the destination.

Algorithm 2.A Backward Recovery

```
Wating Clones Check {
  for each sleeped_Clone
    if (empty a Clone_timestamp) notify to user;
      call wakeup Clone; }
goAgent {
 send the agent;
   wait the agent's 'ACK' signal during send_timestamp;
   if ( 'ACK') { clones the agent;
       call sleepAgent; }
   else call wakeupAgent;
        } arriveAgent { send 'ACK' to the previous_node;
           execute the agent;
             } sleepAgent {
                 for each cloned_agent {
                 add agent_timstamp to system_ time-stamp;
                 add the agent to the sleeped_list;
                 sleep the agent;
               }
} wakeupClone {
  for the sleeped_list find a cloned_agent;
  remove it from the sleep_list;
  if('Agent_Fire')remove the cloned_agent;
  else {
    move the current failed_address to last in the routing-table;
    set the fail_checked information;
     call arrangePath at the algorithm 1;
         }
    }
```

4   An Implementation

Our scheme is implemented in the JAva Mobile Agent System (JAMAS) that we developed. As shows in Fig. 4, the JAMAS consists of Graphic User Interface, Agents Mobile Service component, Agents Execution Environment component, and Agents Repository to provide the naming transparency of agents. In addition, it may be executing one more systems within a host

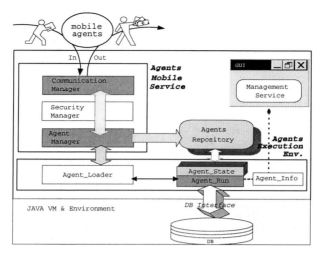

Fig.4. The architecture of JAMAS

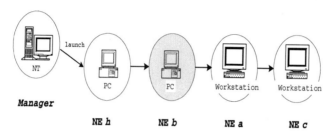

Fig.5. A routing path having a fault NE b

We show to experiment with an agent which manages some NE (network elements). The following figures show the progress that the sample agent as a role of MIB (Management Information Base) browser is migrated and executed according to the routing schedule. Fig. 5 depicts the routing path of the sample agent such as NEh, NEb, NEa, NEc, and we assume faulty at the host NEb. The network manager fetches the prepared agent and specifies routing addresses of it to migrate. So, clicking the 'Go' button on the manager's window to launch it, the agent starts on a tour to get the MIB information of each NE on behalf of the network manager.

Fig.6 shows screen shots of results of the mobile agent. The agent tracer GUI shows what nodes have faulty and how to migrate continuously in the network. The executed agent at the host IP address 172.16.53.21 of the first node NEh does migrate to the second node NEb. Due to a particular fail, the agent has been hopped and migrated at the third node NEa. On completing the execution at the last node NEc, it results information of reconnection to the faulted node NEb on the reordered path. Finally, Fig.7 realizes execution of the agent at each NE. Fig. 7 (a) as a screen capture of the host NEh, shows hopping by connection failure at the next NEb after the launched agent normally progresses. That is, due to fail the host, the agent passes to next one. Thereafter, Fig. 7(b), (c) capture executing of the agent at the hosts NEa, NEc. Then it is adapted to the our scheme. Therefore, the agent has toured for all nodes having no faults before that it does re-connect with the fault nodes.

Fig.6.Agent_Tracer GUI

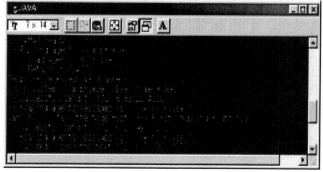

(a) AScreen shot of executing at the NEh

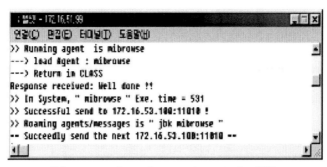

(b) screen shot of executing at the NEa

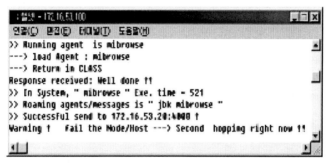

(c) A screen shot of executing at the NEc and attempting migration of the second at the NEb

Fig.7.Fault-tolerable execution of a mobile agent at each NE

5   Conclusions

We discuss a fault-tolerable scheme with the path reordering and backward recovery to ensure the migration of mobile agents in networks. The proposed scheme not only affords to avoid faults of communication nodes or hosts of mobile agents, but also affects to agents' life span.

References

1. OMG, "Mobile Agent Facility Interoperability Facilities Specification(MAF)", OMG
2. General Magic, "Odyssey", and URL: http://WWW.genmagic.com/agents/
3. IBM,"The Aglets Workbench", URL: http://www.trl.ibmco.jp/aglets
4. Robert S.G, "AgentTCL: A Flexible and Secure Mobile-Agent System", TR98-327, Dartmouth Col. June 1997
5. J.Baumann,"A Protocol for Orphan Detection and Termination in Mobile Agent Systems", TR-1997-09,Stuttgart Univ. Jul.,1997.

D.

INTERNET APPLICATIONS

A Construction of the Adapted Ontology Server in EC

Hanhyuk Chung[1], Joong-min Choi[2], Jun-ho Yi[1], Junghyun Han[1], Eun-seok Lee[1]

[1] School of Electrical and Compuiter Engineering, SungKyunKwan Univ.(SKKU)
300 Chunchun-dong Jangahn-gu Suwon-si Kunggi-do South Korea
bellows@seopo.skku.ac.kr
jhvi@yurim.skku.ac.kr
han@ece.skku.ac.kr
eslee@seopo.skku.ac.kr
[2] Department of Computer Science and Engineering, HanYang Univ.
1271 Sa-1 Dong, Ansan-si, Kyunggi-do, South Korea
Department of Computer
jmchoi@cse.hanyang.ac.kr

Abstract. Ontology is an essential element for the agent system. The agent can share its knowledge and communicate with each other with it. As the agent system is more widely applied, the importance of ontology is increasing. Though there were some approaches to construct ontology, it was too far to satisfy practical needs. In this paper we have constructed an Ontology Server, which provides ontology adapted in electronic commerce (EC), and have applied it to comparative shopping system.

1. Introduction

Ontology[5,6,7] is essential for the agent system[4,5]. The explicit specification about Knowledge can be represented by the ontology. Not only among agents, but also between user and system, ontology is crucial for communication and interoperation. Though there were some approaches to the construction of ontology[8,9,10,11], it was too far to be applied to a real field. Their ontology was too general and independent of any specific domain, so it only described very abstract concept. Therefore we propose some characters, which should be held by the ontology adapted in EC[1,2,3].

- Ontology can be translated. In EC, there are many shopping sites. To communicate and to execute a role, it needs that agent can translate its knowledge into another ontology especially in EC. So we decide to construct standard ontology, which can be translated into local terms. Of course, inversion is also possible.
- Ontology should be practical. In EC, it is very important how ontology details. If ontology presents only abstract concept, then it is not possible for agent to perform its part exactly. On the contrary, if its description is too detailed, it is hard to gain fully efficiency for the real use

2. Ontology feature

Our goal for an ontology adapted in EC, makes the ontology have some particular feature.

2.1 Domain specific

First we have tried to build generous ontology, which is independent of domain. But Generality hinders expressing fully. It cannot satisfy practical and useful needs. We hope that ontology have the power enough to be used in real field, so we determine that our ontology is dependent on domain.

2.2 Ontology type

We classify ontology by its type on behalf of the use and the convenience. Its applying field changes slightly with its types. Types are divided with two axes. One of them is about the time of use. it divides into analysis time and search time. When searching, ontology is mainly used to build the interface, which can communicate between user and agent. In analyzing, agent gathers data and analyzes it. Of course, some ontology is used in both times. The other is about how to use. As you noticed, there are mainly two input types on Web. One is the subjective input type like text, and the other is the selective input type like combo. Fig. 1.depicts the type classification and distribution. There are also some ontology lying cross the axis of the time of use.

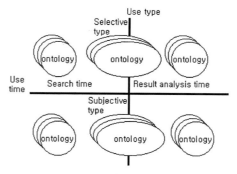

Fig. 1. Two axes for classifying ontology

2.3 Ontology relation

There are many synonyms on the Web. But it is hard for agent to understand its meaning. To communicate with each other, translation is necessary. We reach a conclusion to construct the standard ontology for translation facility. Because it is better building central point to connect than giving each terms an ability to change into each other. We designate this as a relation. The relation determines the power of performance and expression, so it is requested careful choosing the strategy about it. The most important factor of the strategy is the values, included in selective type's ontology. Because the diversity of value is too extreme, it raises a serious problem about making a relation. So it has n:n relation. On the other hand, in the same domain, ontologies are similar, so it can easily have 1:1 relation. Fig. 2 shows one case in which there is a relation between site A and site B, and the relation of values is more complex than ontology

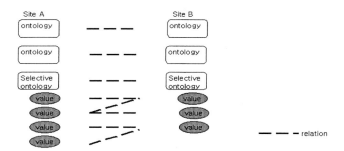

Fig. 2. The relation of ontology between Site A and Site B

3   Ontology Server

In Ontology Server, a standard ontology was built. And that must be based on the Web site to be applied in the real field and to get the usefulness and practicality. So it is necessary the standard ontology has the objective and concrete property. Ontology Server provides a manager with the editor. The detailed explanation follows

1   Gathering from Web

First of all, we need the local terms used in site. The standard ontology can be built based-on that. Gathering Agents are in charge of this process. They collect local terms as well as other information, and classify the ontology type. Once this process is done, all information is stored in the database.

2   Making a relation

As referred previously, making a relation is not only an important job, but also a substantial and challenging problem like many other ontology projects. Ontology Server provides an editor, which browses the stored information and makes a relation.

3   Modifying or rebuilding the standard ontology

On making a relation, it may occur that a need of modifying or rebuilding standard ontology. Because a standard ontology may have some faults, or new ontology may appear.

4   Servicing the standard ontology

After all process is done, the standard ontology is serviced to other agents. And the translator is automatically generated for translation.

4   Implement

4.1   System architecture

All system(in Fig. 3) is developed with JAVA, and MySQL is used as a database. Ontology Server on Linux machine performs a role of constructing standard ontology and servicing it. Fig. 4 shows an editor with two panels. On the left the current standard ontology is displayed and on the other panel local terms is presented. With that a manager builds a relation. All information are stored in Ontology Server. User Agent executes a search by user's request. Gathering Agent residing in server-side gathers the relevant information from Web, and analyzes it. Fig. 5 presents Gathering Agent, which analyzes one game site.

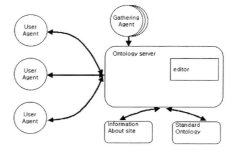

Fig. 3. System architecture

Fig. 4. An example of editor in Ontology Server

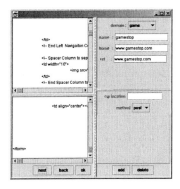

Fig. 5. An example of Gathering Agent's view

4.2 Search process

The search process is similar with the traditional real-time comparative shopping[2,3]. But the interface changes dynamically with user's choice. So a user can have a lot of search functions like selection. But the ordinary system only provides a keyword search. A user can not only search more conveniently and precisely but also get more abundant result. Because the description of site's product attribute is stored in the ontology server, a user agent can analyze search result with it Traditional system only shows minimum result like name and cost. When user's choice is determined, User agent converts it into local forms fitted in each site with translator. And adversely the result of site is transformed into standard ontology. User agent shows this result to the user. So user can get it more fluently. This process is described in Fig. 6,

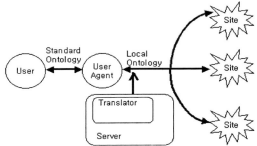

Fig. 6. The execution of User Agent

5. Result and related Work

We show that the adapted ontology in EC, is applied usefully. User interface is changed dynamically as domain changes, therefore the search can be achieved more precisely, and result has more attribute than that of ordinary comparative shopping system with information in ontology server. A user gains more profit and, reduces time and effort to search. While our system proves that ontology's performance and application in EC is remarkably successful, there are also revealed a number of limitations. The ontology relation and standard ontology needs hand-coding, and it is a chronic problem as other ontology projects have. It may be short from objectivity. Needless to say, WWW is less agent-friendly, so Gathering Agent has a trouble in the analysis.

Acknowledgement

This work was supported by the Brain Korea 21 Project.

References

1. R.Kalakota and A. B. Whinston.: Reading in Electronic Commerce. Addison Wesley Publishing Company. (1997)
2. Robert B.Doorenbos, Oren Etzioni, and Daniel S.Weld.: A Scalable Comparison-Shopping Agent for the World-Wide Web. Proceedings of the first international conference on Autonomous agents. (1997) 39-48
3. H. S. Nwana, J. Rosenschein, T. Sandholm, C. Sierra, O. Maes, and R. Guttman.: Agent-mediated electronic commerce: Issues, challenges and some view points. In Proceedings of the Second International Conference on Autonomous Agents. ACM Press. New York (1998) 189-196
4. P. Maes, R. H. Guttman, and A. G. Moukas.: Agents that buy and sell. Communication of the ACM, (1999)
5. Alper Caglayan, Colin Harrison.: Agent sourcebook. WILEY & sons,Inc. (1997)
6. Munindar P. Singh.: Agent Communication Languages: Rethinking the Principles. IEEE Computer, Vol.31, No12. (1998) 40-47
7. Tim Finin, Jay Weber.: DRAFT Specification of the KQML Agent-Communication Language. The DARPA Knowledge Sharing Initiative External Interfaces Working Group,. June. (1993)
8. Kuhanandha Mahalingam, Dr.Michael N.Huhns.: An Ontology Tool for Query Formulation in an Agent-Based Context. Proceedings of the Second IFCIS International Conference on Cooperative Information Systems. (1997) 170-178
9. Adam Farquhar, Ricard Fikes.: The Ontolingua Server: a Tool for Collaborative Ontology Construction. Proceeding on KAW '96 http://ksi.cpsc.ucalgary.ca/KAW/KAW 96/farquhar/farquha r .html. (1996)
10. Kilian stoffel, Merwyn Taylor and Jum Hendler.: Efficient Management of Very Large Ontologies. AAAI Fourteenth National Conference on Artificial Intelligence. (1997)
11. Natalya Fridman Noy and Mark A.Musen.: SMART : Automated Support for Ontology Merging and Alignment. KAW '99 Twelfth Workshop on Knowledge Acquisition, Modeling and Managemen. (1999)
12. J.Ben Schafer, Joseph Konstan, John Riedl.: Recommender Systems in E-Commerce. Proceedings of the ACM Conference on Electronic Commerce (1999)

A Design and Implementation of Cyber Banking Process and Settlement System for Internet Commerce

Moon-Sik Kim[1], Eun-Seok Lee[1]

[1]School of Electrical and Computer Engineering, SungKyunKwan Univ.(SKKU)
300 Chunchun-dong Jangahn-gu Suwon-si Kyunggi-do South Korea
mskimdqn@thrunet.com
eslee@seopo.skku.ac.kr

Abstract. In this paper, we suggest, design and implement a cyber banking process and settlement system for Internet-commerce. The proposed system employs the concept of OPOI(One Process One Input), the basic concept of Korean BankERP System we have already developed. The system can be used for all kind of transaction like B2B, B2C and C2C. We have actually applied the system to handle real-world transactions by an alliance with a major leading bank in Korea, and confirmed its effectiveness

1. Introduction

With the explosive proliferation of Internet, E-Commerce (EC) has drawn the attention of the most part of company and customer as either infrastructure or business model for all kind of business transaction. In actual fact the EC brings a lot of benefits to both buyer and seller in an economic aspect[1]. In spite of those, however, the EC has some critical problems such as the complexity in payment settlement system. One of the most important elements on Internet e-business is cyber banking process and settlement system. The existing system requires the sellers for management on the system and network cost that make the indirect cost increase. By this reason of the cost from the process and settle comparably high imposed on product/service price, the existing system is not proper to act for the small amount transaction and limitedly applied not for the whole range of transaction[4]. The well-known existing systems are as follows, which have the same common problems mentioned above: Digicash[3, HRER 1], Cyber Cash [HRER 2], Mondex [HRER 3], Enipay [HRER 4], Netcheck [HRER 5], e-check [HRER 6], SFNB [HRER 7], TeleBank [HRER 8], CYBank [HRER 9], egg [HRER 10], fleetBoston [HRER 11] and so on.

The Cyber Banking Process and Settlement System suggested in this paper is adopted as a Korean BankERP System and a banking system model currently. The proposed system is to act as a broker between seller and purchaser due to its convenience, safety and reliability in use. So it can effectively assist all kind of transactions like B2C, B2B, C2C and so on. It gives advantage to the seller reducing the direct/indirect cost of system management, network, O&M(Operation and Maintenance) and etc[5,8]. Its low commission rate makes the small amount transaction active. It allows the purchaser to simply access the system without use of card or additional equipment. It is the first system designed and implemented in Korea for Cyber Banking Processing and Settlement on the Internet e-business.

In Chapter 2, a Cyber Banking Process and Settlement System is suggested, Chapter 3 describes the system architecture and functions. Chapter 4 describes implementation and evaluation. Chapter 5 is conclusion.

2. Business Process of Cyber Banking Process and Settlement System

Internal integration business process and settlement business process of the system is defined as follows:

2.1 Internal Integration Business Process: OPOI

The applicable BankERP of this system has OPOI (One Process One Input) concept, which process by one input of account date and management data. Bank has various processes of traditional deposit, loan and credit, import/export, fund and head office/branch and etc. The bank processes may be divided into two categories – account process and due-date process. The account process is based on the debit and credit to the account and due-date process has time deposit, installments, loans, import and export and fund and etc. These process types are shown in Figure1.

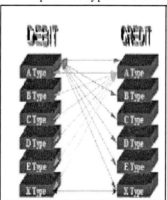

A Type: Account process

B Type: time deposit, loans, funds

C Type: import, export, foreign remittance

D Type: installments,

E Type: trust

X Type: other processes, settlement of

Fig. 1. Knowledge Map of the OPOI

(1) A type of process is transferable to A, B, C, D, E and X type of process.
(2) B, C, D and E types of process are not transferable each other but only to A type.
(3) X type of process is transferable to A and X type.

2.2 Business Process of Cyber Banking Process and Settlement System

The system consists of four parties; sellers (shopping malls and others), purchasers, strategic alliance banks and system owner who operates the system. Each party's function is as below:

(1) Operating Owner of Cyber Banking Process and Settlement System: he will establish servers, DB and network necessary to the system operation. He will open cyber accounts of sellers and purchasers upon their request/subscription and processes the payment and settlement. He shall provide with firewall, cryptograph and insurance securing the safety and reliability of system, so that the system will have security solution. In strategic alliance with traditional banks, he shall prepare reservation fund account in the name of the owner at the strategic alliance bank that supports users prompt and safe cash in-out. The owner and strategic alliance bank shall come into a contract for fund management in order to make safe management about the money income to the reservation fund account. In case of buy & sell, some trading commission shall be imposed to the seller.

(2) Seller: Seller shall open account to receive the payment from purchaser in the System. The seller may request to debit after reasonable period of time from the account

(3) Purchaser: Purchaser shall open account in it for the purpose of payment and credit cash amount to the account via existing traditional bank – account transfer, home banking, internet banking, etc. When he credit to the account he shall inform to the owner. When he needs to debit, upon his request the money will transfer from cyber account to the real account in the traditional bank.

(4) Strategic alliance bank: the bank shall open reservation fund account of the system by the contract between the owner and assist the money in-out of seller and purchaser on the real time basis and control the owner's debit at front office of bank.

The above four parties' process flows are as follows (see Figure2):

① Cyber account open by seller and purchaser

② Purchaser's cash credit to the reservation fund account at the alliance bank and notice to the owner his credit. The alliance bank informs to the owner real-timely the transaction of debit and credit of the reservation fund account.

③ Purchaser buys from and/or subscribes to the seller's site

④ Purchaser accept the payment of product/service to the owner's site

⑤ Owner makes the payment transfer from purchaser's account to seller's and notify and confirm its transaction to sell.

⑥ Seller delivers the product/service to purchaser

⑦ Seller requests the payment to his designated bank account.

⑧ Purchaser requests the debit his amount in cyber account to his designated bank account

⑨ Owner submits payment order to alliance bank to make money transfer from the reservation fund account to the requesting seller and purchaser's account.

⑩ Alliance bank does transfer to the designated bank account of seller and purchaser upon the owner's payment order.

⑪ Alliance bank notifies daily transaction details of reservation fund account to owner. Owner shall check daily correspondence between the balance amount of the reservation fund account and whole accounts at cyber bank.

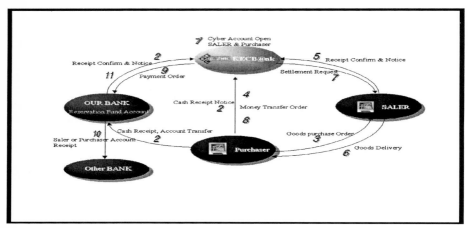

Fig. 2. Cyber Banking Process and Settlement System

3. System Architecture

The system architecture (see figure 3), as a type of 3 ties client/server[10], consists of WEB server (see figure 4), Application server and DB server (see figure 5). WEB Server consists of WWW Server (Apache Server), WEB Page, Security certification server, WEB Brokerage Application Server and Service distribution Gateway. Application Server consists of account transfer system, account information system. DB Server consists of Data DB, Memory DB and History DB. 1 tie is accessible by users via web browsers (Netscape, Explore) on the internet, 2 tie has WEB Servers, WEB Gateway, WEB Service Broker, Firewall, Security Certification support the user's safe use. Application Server run financial application program, 3 tie is RDBMS that stores all the data of users in the data base. Language are JAVA, UNIX, CCGI and HTML, operation system UNIX, LINUX and Window98, Database ORACLE RDBMS, Security System is 128bit SSL[6,11, HRER 12] model. Network protocol is TCP/IP for internal server telecommunication and X.25 for alliance bank telecommunication.

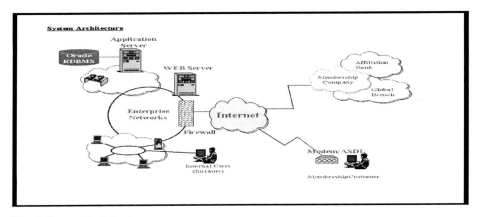

Fig. 3. System Architecture

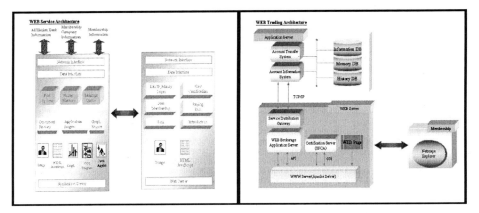

Fig. 4. Web service Architecture   **Fig. 5.** Web Trading Architecture

4. Implement Business Process of Cyber Banking Process and Settlement System and evaluation

4.1 Implementation

The process has been implemented with application of BankERP System that this paper mainly concerned. Application Design is using Power Designer.

Major process of the system (1) Cyber account inquiry (2) money transfer from bank account to Cyber account (3) transfer from cyber account to banks account, (4) transfer from cyber account to cyber account (5)Payment at seller's site. The details as follow: (1) Cyber account check is to inquire account in and transaction details and balance periodically (2) money transfer from bank account and cyber account is to input cash to the cyber account. (3) Money transfer from cyber account to bank account is to seller's payment out put and user's cash payback. (4) Transfer from cyber account to cyber account is for a user's money transfer within the cyber bank (5) at Seller's site, purchaser does one click payment from cyber account after user purchase

4.2 Evaluation

Cyber Banking Process and Settlement System this paper suggests is to support convenient, safe, prompt and reliable banking settlement in the internet EC. Since the system is in the beginning stage of commercial practice, it is not easy to physically evaluate the effectiveness but possible to do by comparing with other existing systems. The other existing system is based on real account at the bank via internet tool and limited in its service to simple credit, deposit, loan and transfer. They are found not enough to represent as settlement system for EC. They are not allow to monitor real-timely account in-out and impose high commission rate in small amount transaction. Credit Card system is open to the risk of card and personal data reveal and malicious use by others. And it also impose high commission rate to its users and is inconvenient to possess and possible to miss. In the contrary Cyber Banking Process and Settlement System is utilizing cyber account and make settlement ready by One Click on the internet. It assists the seller and purchaser to direct trade and commission rate is comparatively lower than others. It is very easy for seller and purchaser to be equipped with system. It has most less problem. Except credit card system, all other system is not able to deal the deferred payment but the system is able to do like credit card system. All other system does not allow the payback of balance amount in the account but the system allow the payback at any time as the user wants. The system does need no additional equipment or facility but only need Web Browser to access internet, which lessens the user's investment and maintenance cost and more economical than other systems. The low rate of commission rate encourages the transaction to be active whatever the amount is big or small. Since the system begins its service with a strategic alliance with major leading bank in Korea, it is proven its effectiveness. This system is the first system applied Korean BankERP which is possibly to be also proven its effectiveness. So far its service has been shown quite satisfactory.

5. Conclusion

This paper suggests, designs and implements the first Korean business process model of Cyber Banking Process and Settlement System which has been in commercial operation and increased its use-ability by an alliance with major bank in Korea. The system gives lot of benefits to the users; for seller it is necessary for no additional equipment or facility but low rate of commission and safe and prompt settlement to its cyber account simultaneously at the trading, for purchaser it supports easily to access by only web browser and make payment safely and promptly and also be guaranteed for any possible loss at the procurement by the system, for alliance bank, it operates the reservation fund which gives certain profit to the bank and it warrants reliability to other user. It is confident the system will represent as a model of cyber settlement system and contribute EC to actively expand in the near future. The next mission is the first cyber bank establishment upgrading the system by Korean BankERP application in combination with off-line and on-line banks.

References

[1] E.S.Lee, "Agent-based Electronic Commerce – Tutorial," International Conference on Electronic Commerce (ICEC'98), (April. 1998).
[2] E.S.Lee, "Application of Agent Technologies to EC," The Magazine of the IEEK, Vol.26, No.1, pp.61-70 (Jan. 1999).
[3] Patiwat Panurach, "Money in Electronic Commerce: Digital cash, Electronic Fund Transfer, and Ecash," Communications of ACM, vol.39, No.6, 1996.
[4] N. Asokan, Phillipe A. Janson, Michael Steiner, Michael waidner, "The state of the art in electronic payment systems," IEEE computer, 1997.
[5] Bernard s. Hirsch, "Reflections on a system Integration Project for Internet Banking," Technical report, Hewlett Packard Company, 1997. => http://hpme.sprynet.com
[6] Chaum,D., "Achieving Electronic Privacy," Scientific American, pp.96-101, 1992.
[7] McChesney, M. c., "Banking in Cyberspace: An Investment in Itself," IEEE spectrum, vol.34, No.2, pp.54-59, 1997.
[8] Robert orfali & D. Harkey, Client/Server Programming with Java and Corba, wiley, 1997.
[9] Anup k. Ghosh, E-Commerce Security : Weak Links, Best Defenses, wiley, 1998.

<Hypertext References>
[HREF 1] http://www.digicash.com
[HREF 2] http://www.cybercash.com/cybercash/services/
[HREF 3] http://www.mondexusa.com/
[HREF 4] http://www.inicis.com/html/ini/inipay/
[HREF 5] http://nii.sis.edu/info/netcheque
[HREF 6] http://www.fstc.org/projexts/echeck/
[HREF 7] http://www.sfnb.com
[HREF 8] http://www.telebankonline.com/
[HREF 9] http://www.cybank.net/aboutcyb.htm
[HREF 10] http://www.egg.com/
[HREF 11] http://www.fleet.com/
[HREF 12] http://www.ssl.com/

A Shopping Agent That Automatically Constructs Wrappers for Semi-Structured Online Vendors

Jaeyoung Yang[1], Eunseok Lee[2], and Joongmin Choi[1]

[1] Department of Computer Science and Engineering, Hanyang University
1271 Sa-1-dong, Ansan, Kyunggi-do 425-791, Korea
{jyyang, jmchoi}@cse.hanyang.ac.kr
[2] School of Electrical and Computer Engineering, Sungkyunkwan University
300 Chunchun-dong, Suwon, Kyunggi-do 440-746, Korea

Abstract. This paper proposes a shopping agent with a robust inductive learning method that automatically constructs wrappers for semi-structured online stores. Strong biases assumed in many existing systems are weakened so that the real stores with reasonably complex document structures can be handled. Our method treats a logical line as a basic unit, and recognizes the position and the structure of product descriptions by finding the most frequent pattern from the sequence of logical line information in output HTML pages. This method is capable of analyzing product descriptions that comprise multiple logical lines, and even those with extra or missing attributes. Experimental tests on over 60 sites show that it successfully constructs correct wrappers for most real stores.

1 Introduction

A shopping agent is a mediator system that extracts the product descriptions from several online stores on a user's behalf. Since the stores are heterogeneous, a procedure for extracting the content of a particular information source called a *wrapper* must be built and maintained for each store. A wrapper is generally consists of a set of extraction rules and the code to apply those rules[5].

In some systems such as TSIMMIS[4] and ARANEUS[2], extraction rules for the wrapper are written by humans. Wrapper induction[5] has been suggested to automatically build the wrapper through learning from a set of resource's sample pages. However, most previous systems were unable to cover many real stores since they relied on some strong biases, imposing too much restrictions on the structure of documents that can be analyzed. For example, ShopBot[3] assumes that product descriptions reside on a single line, and HLRT[5] can not handle the cases with noises such as missing attributes. STALKER[6] algorithm deals with the missing items or out-of-order items, but it is not fully automatic in the sense that users need to be involved in the preparation of training examples. ARIADNE[1] is a semi-automatic wrapper generation system, but its power of automatic wrapper learning is limited since heuristics are obtained mainly from the users rather than through learning.

In this paper, we propose a shopping agent with a simple but robust inductive learning method that automatically constructs wrappers for semi-structured on-line stores. Strong biases that have been assumed in many systems are weakened so that real-world stores can be handled. Product descriptions may comprise multiple logical lines and may have extra or missing attributes. Our method treats a logical line as a basic unit, and assigns a category to each logical line. The HTML page of a product search result is converted into a sequence of logical line categories. The main idea of our wrapper learning is to recognize the position and the structure of product descriptions by finding the most frequent pattern containing the price information. This pattern is regarded as the extraction rule of the wrapper.

2 Overview of Comparison Shopping Agent

Our wrapper learning method is implemented in a prototype comparison shopping agent called MORPHEUS. The overall architecture of MORPHEUS is shown in Fig. 1. It consists of several modules including the wrapper generator, the wrapper interpreter, and the uniform output generator.

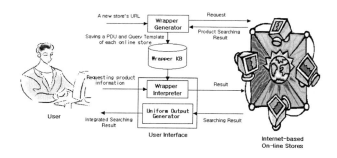

Fig. 1. The overall architecture of MORPHEUS

The *wrapper generator* is the main learning module that constructs a wrapper for each store. In fact, the wrapper generator learns two things. First, it learns how to query a particular store by recognizing its query scheme. An HTML page containing a searchable input box is analyzed and a query template is generated. Second, it learns how to extract a store's content. Product descriptions in the store's search result pages are recognized and their repeating pattern is determined. The *wrapper interpreter* is a module that executes learned wrappers to get the current product information. This module forms several actual queries by combining each store's query template with the keywords that the user actually typed in, and sends them to the corresponding shopper sites. The search results from the stores are then collected and fed to the uniform output generator module. The *uniform output generator* integrates search results from several stores and generates a uniform output.

3 Learning Wrappers for Online Stores

One key function of the wrapper generator is to learn the format of product descriptions in result pages from successful searches. Each page contains one or more product descriptions that matched the sample query. A product description is composed of a sequence of items that describe the attributes of the product. For example, a bookstore displays search results in which the attributes of a product include the booktitle, the author, the price, and/or the reader's review.

Wrapper learning has to find the starting and ending position of the list of product descriptions in the entire result page, and to recognize the pattern of a product description. To do this, our method is divided into three phases.

In the first phase, the HTML source of the page is broken down into logical lines. A logical line is conceptually similar to a line that the user sees in the browser, so the algorithm recognizes each logical line by examining HTML's delimiter tags such as `<br>`, `<p>`, `<dd>`, `<hr>`, `<table>`, `<td>`, and `<tr>`.

The second phase of the algorithm is to categorize each logical line and assign it the corresponding category number. Currently, we maintain 5 categories including TEXT, PRICE, LTAG, TITLE, and TTAG, and their category numbers are 0, 1, 2, 3, and 8, respectively. Here, TITLE denotes the product name, PRICE denotes the price, TTAG denotes table tags such as `<tr>`, LTAG denotes the HTML tags other than TTAG used in logical line breaking, and TEXT denotes a general string that is not recognizable as one of the above four categories. We use simple heuristics for this category assignment. For example, TITLE is assigned to a logical line when the line contains one of the keywords in the sample query, and PRICE is assigned by recognizing a dollar sign $ (or some other symbol that represents the price unit) and a digit. Fig. 2 shows the HTML source of a product description that is obtained from the Amazon bookstore by the query "Korea", along with assigned category numbers for logical lines.

```
<a href="/exec/obidos/ASIN/3540618724/qid=95863                          3
6791/sr=1-3/103-6540613-6072633">Advances in Cryptology-Asiacrypt
'96 : International Conference on the Theory and Applications of
Cryptology and Information Security Kyongju, Korea,)</a>
<br>                                                                     2
by K. Kim(Editor), Tsutomu Matsumoto (Editor). Paperback (November      0
1996)
</td>                                                                    8
</tr>                                                                    8
<tr>                                                                     8
<td valign=top width=50%>                                               8
<font face=verdana,arial,helvetica size=-1> Our Price:$73.95            1
```

Fig. 2. An HTML source for a book and the categories for logical lines

After the categorization phase, the entire page can be expressed by a sequence of category numbers. The third phase of our algorithm then finds a repeating pattern in this sequence. It first finds the pattern of each product description unit(PDU) and counts the frequency of each distinct pattern to get the most frequent one. Finding the next candidate PDU is done by searching for PRICE first, and then backtracks in the sequence to search for TITLE, despite it is generally assumed that the TITLE attribute appears before the PRICE attribute in a PDU. This is because the reliability of the heuristics for correctly recognizing PRICE is higher than that of the heuristics for recognizing TITLE. The subsequence of logical lines between TITLE and PRICE becomes the resulting pattern of a PDU. A pseudocode for this algorithm is given below.

```
seq ← the input sequence of logical line categories;
seqStart ← 1; /* initial position for pattern search */
numCandPDUs ← 0; /* number of distinct PDU pattern */
while (true) {
        /* find the next candidate PDU */
        priceIndex ← findIndex(seq, seqStart, PRICE);
        titleIndex ← findIndexReverse(seq, priceIndex, TITLE);
        currentPDU ← substring(seq, titleIndex, priceIndex);
        if (currentPDU == NULL) then exit the while loop; /* no more PDUs */
        if (currentPDU is already stored in candPDUs array)
        then the frequency count of currentPDU is incremented by 1;
        else { save currentPDU in candPDUs array;
                increment numCandPDUs by 1; } /* a new PDU pattern */
        seqStart ← priceIndex+1; /* starting point for searching next PDU */
}
mostFreqPDU ← the element of candPDUs array with maximum frequency;
return(mostFreqPDU);
```

For Amazon, the learned PDU pattern is 32088881 as shown in Fig 2. In the shopping stage, the wrapper interpreter module applies the learned PDU pattern to modify noisy PDUs with different attributes by ignoring extra attributes or putting dummy values for missing attributes.

4   Experimental Results

We implemented MORPHEUS and built a Web interface as shown in Fig 3(a) so that the user can select a store that is to be learned. Learned stores are added to the store list from which the comparison shopping can be done.

To evaluate the performance, we have tested MORPHEUS for 62 real online stores as to whether correct wrappers can be generated. We assume that a proper test query is given in the learning phase so that the output page with reasonably many matched products can be produced. In order to verify whether the correct wrapper is generated, the result of wrapper learning is displayed as in Fig. 3(b). In this display, the learned PDU pattern along with the product names and their corresponding prices are shown. If this data is consistent with the one that is

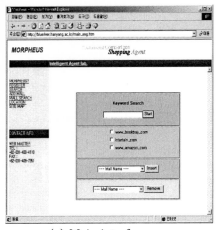

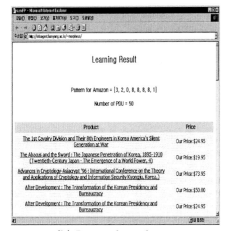

(a) Main interface   (b) Learned result

Fig. 3. MORPHEUS Interfaces

obtained by directly accessing the store site, it can be regarded that the correct wrapper is really generated.

Table. 1 shows the test data for some of the 62 sites that have been tested. During the test, we have collected some relevant information for each output page of the site such as the test query used in learning, the learned PDU pattern, the number of PDUs, and the number of MF-PDUs(most frequent PDUs). In this experiment, the proposed wrapper generation algorithm works satisfactorily with succeeding in 58 out of 62 stores. A few sites such as www.dsports.com failed to get a PDU pattern since it contains some unnecessary product information in the header of the output page.

Table 1. Experiment data during wrapper generation for some of 62 sites

Store URL	test query	PDU pattern	No. of total PDUs	No. of MF-PDUs
www.more.com	gift	388088088088121	7	7
www.jewelryweb.com	ring	320222288880881888808821	18	18
www.softwarebuyLine.com	school	320808020808088081	40	29
www.1cache.com	video	32088021	10	10
www.etronixs.com	video	32088021	10	10
www.egghead.com	compaq	38080881	44	36
www.bookbay.com	java	3202021	17	17
intertain.com	java	321	133	133
www.more.com	gift	388088088088121	7	7
www.amazon.com	java	32088881	50	26
⋮	⋮	⋮	⋮	⋮

5 Discussion and Future Work

We have developed a robust method for automatic wrapper generation in the domain of comparison shopping, and the test results have shown that it successfully constructs correct wrappers for most real stores.

The characteristics of our method in comparison to previous researches are summarized as follows. First, the strong biases assumed in many existing systems are weakened so that the real stores with reasonably complex document structures can be handled. Second, we do not exploit the domain knowledge. This makes the learning algorithm simple and domain independent, and it still works satisfactorily. Third, learning in MORPHEUS is processed quickly since it does not incorporate a separate module for removing redundant fragments such as the header, tail, and advertisements.

There are also some limitations in our current system. First, we have assumed that a proper keyword is given for the test query by humans. Heuristics for providing a proper test query automatically should be investigated. Second, each product description must contain the price attribute. We think that this is not a severe restriction since most stores that produce semi-structured product information contains the price attribute, with only a few exceptions. Nonetheless, this restriction may reduce the generality of the algorithm since it cannot be applied to other domains that do not require the price information. One solution might be that the feature attribute that must exist in a product description may be specified as a parameter to the algorithm, rather than hard-coded in the program. Third, we only extract the price information from a product description that may contain several other attributes. Extracting non-price information by exploiting proper domain knowledge(or the ontology) is under progress.

References

1. Ambite, J., Ashish, N., Barish, G., Knoblock, C., Minton, S., Modi, P., Muslea, I., Philpot, A., Tejada, S.: ARIADNE: A System for Constructing Mediators for Internet Sources. ACM SIGMOD International Conference on Management of Data (1998) 561–563
2. Atzeni, P., Mecca, G., Merialdo, P.: Semi-structured and Structured Data in the Web: Going Back and Forth. ACM SIGMOD Workshop on Management of Semi-structured Data (1997) 1–9
3. Doorenbos, R., Etzioni, O., Weld, D.: A Scalable Comparison-Shopping Agent for the World Wide Web. First International Conference on Autonomous Agents (1997) 39–48
4. Hammer, J., Garcia-Molina, H., Nestorov, S., Yerneni, R., Breunig, M., Vassalos, V.: Template-based wrappers in the TSIMMIS system. ACM SIGMOD International Conference on Management of Data (1997) 532–535
5. Kushmerick, N., Weld, D., Doorenbos, R.: Wrapper Induction for Information Extraction. International Joint Conference on Artificial Intelligent (1997) 729–735
6. Muslea, I., Minton, S., Knoblock, C.: A Hierarchical Approach to Wrapper Induction. Third International Conference on Autonomous Agents (1999) 190–197

Real-Time Web Data Mining and Visualisation

Bai Li and Ni Guohua
School of Computer Science & Information Technology
The University of Nottingham
Nottingham, NG8 1BB
UK
bai@cs.nott.ac.uk gxn@cs.nott.ac.uk

Abstract. This paper presents new services for intelligent monitoring and visualising user accesses to a university's web site. These are based on the use of data mining techniques to process data recorded in the web log files and visualise it. The system is to be used by the University of Nottingham's web server to monitor the interests of potential students and to predict the student numbers and their geographical distributions for the next academic year. The system could be adapted for other academic and commercial web sites to assist intelligent decision making.

1. Introduction

This paper reports the innovative research that applies data mining techniques to the data collected from web log files access to discover subtle relationships and patterns to assist decision making. Recently there have been many successful applications of data mining techniques to industrial and business domains. However little is reported of data mining applications in academic institutions at the time of writing.

The research aims at applying data mining techniques in the context of academic institutions. At the centre of the research is a real-time web traffic analysis and monitoring system for the University of Nottingham's web server. The research seeks to transform the web into an environment where users are aware of the presence of each other and the web server is aware of the presence and the interests of its users so to monitor and control user accesses more effectively. The system provides graphical and textual representations of web access by users from all over the world. Our work has been motivated by the need of universities to know the interests of their users and the access demands for their web servers at different times round the clock, so to provide better services for the users. Monitoring web access not only allows a university to know its potential students but also to know the strength and limitations of its server structure. It is important for universities to know their who potential students might be and what they are interested in the university.

The University of Nottingham excels in its teaching and research as one of the leading academic institutions in the UK. The number of potential applicants to the university, home or overseas, is ever increasing. More and more potential applicants are using the University's web site to get information about courses and other matters. However at the moment the only way to estimate users' interests in the University is by counting the number of hits of the University's web pages. This can be misleading as undoubtedly the hits could have been due to some casual users exploring the web. The access counters alone cannot tell what user's interests are.

To analyse user access we start with the web server log files. Though these server log files are rich in information, the data is itself usually in plain text format with comma delimiters, abbreviated and cryptic. It is difficult and time-consuming to make sense of it. The volume of information is also overwhelming: a 1MB log file typically contains 4000 to 5000 URL requests, along with the IP address of the request, the date and time of the request, and the encoding language of the users' browser.

2. Real-time Web Access Data Visualisation

The first step is to transfer all the entries of the web log file into a SQL database. No information was lost in this process. Data mining programs are then applied to the database to visualise the relevant data and extract its meaning.

2.1. Data Visualisation Against Map Images
Users are classified according to their geographical distributions. Because the users may not have registered with the University so their distributions have to be estimated according to the difference of users' local time and the time of the server. The users are then placed into appropriate time zones and displayed against a GIS map, as shown in Figure 1 below. The database is updated each time a new access request is received by the web server and the screen is refreshed with the new entry added to the appropriate time zone. For registered users of the web site, their countries and their exact locations in the country is known so they can be added to the total numbers in the locations.

Figure 1. User distributions

2.2 Data Visualisation Using Dynamic Mapping
The visualisation part of the system was also implemented using ArcXML to create dynamic mapping. It is no trivial task to create dynamic mapping of real time data onto a GIS map and automatically display it on the web. The usual way of doing this is to hard code the hyperlinks on a map image. Web browsers only support HTML and XML documents, they can't display GIS layers.

We use ArcXML and ASP to create dynamic mapping of data onto a GIS map and automatically display the map on the web, see Figure 2.

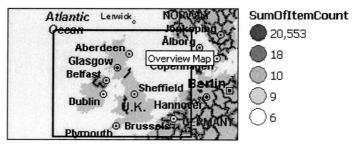

Figure 2. Dynamic mapping for hits display

First we developed a simple renderer (a dynamic chart) using ArcXML. It reads ASP variables to provide the framework for filling polygons, drawing lines, displaying points, symbols and text labels. Example of symbols and text labels are shown in Figure 3.

Figure 3. Display layers

GIS software can superimpose different layers on top of one another and display them all on a map. The problem is ArcXML only allows one symbol layer or one label layer to be mapped onto a renderer. Also web browsers can display one renderer on the same position of a page. This is the reason why the system uses ASP via ODBC to retrieve data from the SQL database for the renderer, rather than using ArcXML to call the data directly. For example, if there are two data items, one is 'Glasgow' for creating a label and one is the number of hits 4464 for creating the symbol (pink coloured circle). A renderer can read only one column of data from the database. If it reads 'Glasgow', it will not be able to read the number of hits. Using an ASP variable with value 'Glasgow4464' the system creates a renderer display and both the label and symbol layouts are displayed on the renderer.

2.3 Visualising Failed Access Attempts

Apart from displaying successful access of a web site, those waiting or failed attempts to access the web can also be displayed by making use of the information stored in the error log file. Figure 4 shows textually the successful and failed accesses to a few web pages of the web site over a period of 60 minutes. Each of the three digit numbers in the columns represents up to 10 users currently using the web site. Some web servers and databases have a limit to the number of access allowed at the same time. Page usage analysis is useful for identifying user interest and for improving the site design: pages attracting no traffic may be removed and some resources may be clustered to improve network traffic.

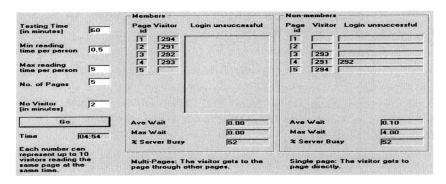

Figure 4. Page accesses

2.4 Visualising Web Server Usage

Similarly server traffic and the access behaviour of each user can be displayed and rules concerning user interests can be derived based on his/her access display, see Figure 5. Users in each geographical location are further classified into different subject categories such as education, MBA, IT sectors etc., to assist user interest analysis.

Hits	Target_Page
20448	/index.asp
41	/Webmaster/Visitors/graphichour.asp
31	/Webmaster/serverval.asp
8	/Webmaster/Sessionsrecord.asp

Top 4 of Course Web Sites(%)

MBA	IT	English	Accounting
91	78	67	56

Figure 5.   Page hit account and the top 4 course web pages

We broke down web server log report into two categories: information for web administrators and information for the administrators of the University or its departments. Web administrators need information such as what pages are most often accessed and what links are followed and where the problems lie. The administrators of the University are more interested in attracting users with the web contents.

3. Data Mining

Data mining techniques can be categorised into three categories: classification, association, and sequence. Extracting association rules from data allows to see the relationships hidden in the data. For example, the presence of some IP addresses in the log file may imply the presence of other IP addresses. The role of classification in data mining is to develop rules to group data together based on certain common features.

3.1 Classification. Available data for this is IP addresses discovered from the log database. Classification rules classify IP addresses into two groups. Let T_2 be a set of

IP addresses belong the University, T_1 be a group of IP addresses which do not belong to the University.

T_1 = Non-university IP address
T_2 = University IP address (128.243.00.00)

Also, the languages of users' browsers could be categorised into different groups. Let L be a set of languages: L_1 = UK English, L_2= US English and $L_{3.....n}$ = other languages.

3.2 Association. This involves rules that associate one attribute of a relation with another. For example, an association rule could be of type (T_1) AND (L_1) → (URL = ENGLISH.HTML). This rule associates the IP address and the language of the users' browser to the type of courses he/she is interested. Other example associations are

IF $U_{(1,4)}$ = Overseas users → Course site including English support (225.225.12. 33)
IF $U_{(1,1)}$ = Local users → Course site without English support (199.127.0.10)

In table 1 below there is a user whose IP address is 225.225.12.33 and whose browser encoding language was Spanish and the time difference was 1 hour. This means that the user is from another country who wanted to know the detail of our MBA courses and English support. The user whose IP address is 199.127.0.10 and whose browser encoding language is *gb-en* (UK English) and no time difference is a local user, and he/she is more interested in the service of the University and the course modules.

Table 1. $U_{(t,l)}$ Log File Database

Grope of IP addresses	URL
128.243.233.23	Modules, Society
225.225.12.33	English, MBA, CSIT
199.127.0.10	Modules, Library, Sports, IT support

* U is a set of URL, t is a group of IP address and l is a group of browser encoding languages

We know that certain users will visit a page and will not continue traversing the hyperlinks contained in that page. For example, IT courses are as popular as MBA courses, but MBA fees are much higher than IT courses, so over 70% of the users were directed to IT courses instead. All these analyses provide an insight into the behaviour of users and the usage of the site's resources.

3.3 Creating Rules. Previous work on quantifying the "usefulness" or " interesting" of a rule focused on how much the support of a rule is more than that of the support of the antecedent and the consequent of the rule. We implemented Piatetsky-Shapiro's idea, as X➜ Y is not interesting if support (X → Y) ≈ support (X) × support (Y). Consider the following rule:

$U_{(1,4)}$ → English Support

If "Non-University's IP addresses" is a parent of "English Support", and over 15% of users of "Non-University's IP addresses", we would expect the rule: $U_{(1,4)}$ → English Support to have 2% support and 70% confidence. If the actual support is around 2% and 70%, respectively, the rule can be considered redundant since it does not convey any additional information and is less general than the first rule.

The problem of discovering generalised association rules can be decomposed into four steps as show below. Let I be a set of IP addresses, I1 the University IP address, I2 the set of other IP addresses.

- Determine L_1 (language) and I from the log database with a minimum support α
This is to find UK visitors regardless they are current students of the University or not.

- Generate the candidate 2-item set C_2 from I_1 and I_2.
This is to create two child nodes, one for I1 with L1, the other for I2 with L1

- Let F be a set of frequent URLs, which are not used to generate C_2. Scan all of database tables to decide the real L_1 and obtain L_2 from C_2. If a transaction belongs to F, then it is filtered out for the information of any 2-item set in L_2.

- Perform the remaining steps in the same way to find L_n for $n>=2$
To determine the locations of visitors whose language is in L2. This involves comparing time differences. Repeat to create the next two nodes (C2).

4. References

[1] U. M. Fayyad, G. Piatetsky-Shapiro, P. Smyth, and R. Uthurusamy, Advances in Knowledge Discovery and Data Mining. AAAI/MIT Press, 1996.
[2] M. S. Chen, J. S. Park, and P.S. Yu, Data mining for path traversal patterns in a web environment, Proce. 16th Int. Conf. On Distributed Computing Systems, May 1996.
[3] M Perkowitz and O. Etzioi, Adaptive sites: Automatically learning from user ccess patterns. In Proc. 6th Int. World Wide Web Conf., Santa Clara, California, April 1997.
[4] Ramakrishnan Srikant, Rakesh Agrawal: Mining generalized rules. Future Generation Computer Systems 13 (1997) 161-180
[5] R. Cooley, B. Mobasher, J. Srivastava: Web Mining: Inforamtion and Pattern Discovery on the WWW. IEEE (1997) 558-567
[6] James Pitkow: In search of reliable usage on the WWW. Computer Networks and ISDN Systems 29 (1997) 1343-1355
[7] Steve Benford, Dave Snowdon, Chris Brown, Gail Reynard, Rod Ingram: Visualising and populating the Web. Computer Networks and ISDN Systems 29 (1997) 1751-1761

WebGuide: Filtering and Constraining Site Browsing through Web Walker Techniques

Djamel Fezzani and Jocelyn Desbiens

INRS-Télécommunications, Place Bonaventure
900 de la Gauchetière Ouest,
Montréal, Québec, H5A 1C6 Canada
{fezzani, desbiens}@inrs-telecom.uquebec.ca
http://www.inrs-telecom.uquebec.ca/users/desbiens/

Abstract. A flexible constraint-posting architecture for Web site filtering from the field of knowledge representation has been transferred to the domain of Web constrained browsing. The architecture defines an interpreter that accepts declarative constraint formulae which it uses to filter urls to which declarative actions are applied.

1 Introduction

A *walker* is a computer program that systematically browses the Web, building indexes as it follows every link it can find. Walkers can read about a thousand pages per second, and many of them read every word on every page. The walker then feeds the information it has gathered into a searchable database. Probably the two most useful of these types of search engines are Alta Vista and HotBot. These are both great for "needle-in-a-haystack" type searches - very specific information like exact quotes, phrases or names of people and places.

In Mallery, 1996, a Web walker for the Hypertext Transfer Protocol (HTTP) was implemented using a control architecture. *W4* uses a declarative and extensible vocabulary of constraints to characterize traversals of Web structures. Starting from a root resource, the walker recursively follows all hyperlinks whose associated resource satisfies the constraints guiding the walk. As the walker traverses the structure it performs operations that are specified in a declarative and extensible action vocabulary.

The purpose of this paper is to describe how, for research and pedagogical reasons, we reengineered and reused this *W4* filtering walker technology to constrain user's browsing for a local experimental educational Web site. Section 2 and 3 explains the logical and software framework. Section 4 gives a detailed description of the filtering mechanism.

2 CL-HTTP

It is known that a Web site is accessible to the users via an Internet access and software called Web server. Due to the nature of the distance supervision problem

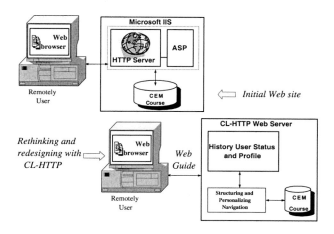

Fig. 1. Exporting urls with `CL-HTTP`

that requires intelligent and flexible manipulation of data and the AI based techniques needed to solve the problem, the Common Lisp HTTP server (aka `CL-HTTP` (Mallery, 1994)) was the prime choice rather than other standard non-programmable HTTP servers. This tool was tailored to meet user requirements and to create modules capable of performing the following:

- detect the trace of students' learning process,
- identify the students' profile and their needs in terms of pedagogical materials,
- propose and sometimes impose to these students, the training mode that meets their profile and courses which will be most adequate for them, and
- evaluate the students' learning process and predict their achievement.

These objectives are met according to the functional system, which controls user's Web navigation independently of the course design stage.

3 Constrained Web Walking

3.1 W4

As the World Wide Web has grown, Web walkers have settled into two general applications: site maintenance and high-volume indexing. In these roles, the walkers have been tuned for specific activities that are applied uniformly over Web regions.

The *W4* constraint-guided Web walker is a second generation Web walker intended for traversing well-specified regions of the World Wide Web and performing any variety of actions. Control of the walk is specified with an extensible vocabulary of constraints that limit enumeration of Web resources. Actions applied to each accepted resource are specified by an extensible action vocabulary. Conditional branching in constraints and actions makes possible adaptive responses to Web topology. Most importantly, constraint and action abstractions enforce a separation of control from action as they encourage reuse of control and action abstractions. *W4* extends the abstractions of this server and basic client to accessing Web resources and walking Web structures.

3.2   Using *W4* as a Template

The initial hypothesis we made was that using traditional teaching methods through the Web would save time and effort, and could provide itself a novel and innovative delivery medium. This statement was merely too simplistic. Time and space resources were certainly saved; however students seemed uncomfortable assuming a bigger part of the responsibility for their course success/failure. Indeed, in most instances, teachers and students are miles apart during most of the instructional process and never meet face-to-face at all. As a result, students become responsible for both the course content and the process by which they acquire and manage this content without supervision.

With respect to these considerations and based on the filtering model of *W4*, we developed a system that is powerful enough to structure and provide intelligently pedagogical material to the students according to their profile and their history. This system, called *WebGuide*, is a actually prototype including intelligent tutoring methods allowing teachers to organize and constraint navigation of the supervised Web site by the students. Teachers and authors use this tool to manage and monitor students' learning process. Students choose transparently the training mode, which best meets their profile.

4   *WebGuide*: Constrained Browsing

4.1   Exporting URLs

Writing Common Lisp functions that compute responses to incoming HTTP requests is the main feature of the CL-HTTP. Response functions compute a reply to the HTTP methods `get` or `post`. Before returning HTML to the user, they must arrange for an appropriate status code and appropriate headers to be returned. A response function becomes accessible only after an associated url is exported with `export-url`. An example exported url follows:

```
(export-url #u"/cl-http/cem/index.html"
            :html-computed
            :authentification-realm :minimum-security
            :expiration '(:no-expiration-header))
```

4.2   Scanning and Mapping Web Site

The first step in the process of filtering navigation on a Web site is to build a list of all meaningfull urls and to export them through the CL-HTTP `export-url` mechanism. This task can be accomplished, for instance, by a Web walker. Each targeted url is remapped automatically as soon as it is scanned by the walker (see Figure 1).

4.3 Basic Mechanism and User Profile

Trapping the requested user url via the `redirect-to-html` keyword and redirecting it to *WebGuide* for further processing is the basic mechanism used for harnessing the navigation on the site. In other words, the user url:

```
(export-url #u"/cl-http/cem/index.html"
            :html-computed
            :authentification-realm :minimum-security
            :response-function #'redirect-to-html
            :expiration '(:no-expiration-header))
```

is mapped to the computed url:

```
(export-url #u"/cl-http/cem/@index.html"
            :html-file
            :pathname "/dev/cem/index.html"
            :authentification-realm :minimum-security
            :expiration '(:no-expiration-header))
```

if the current set of constraints is satisfied. If this the case, the url will displayed in the browser (see Figure 1).

The enabling of actions and activities for a particular user is made possible through the definition and activation of user profiles. Each potential user owns a set of properties defining the type of ressources he may or may not access. Creation of user profile is done by calling the `make-client` macro. For instance,

```
(make-client :user-name "smith"
             :password "john"
             :email-address "smith@inrs-telecom.uquebec.ca"
             :status "teacher")
```

There are currently four categories of users: student, professor, author, and administrator, each having its own set of properties.

4.4 Constraints

Constraints are instances of constraint types. Constraint types serve as templates governing the behavior of constraint instances. They hold general-purpose functionality governing their instances while their instances store specializing parameters. Circumstance constraint types are special constraints that operate on collections of constraints, and thus, accept arguments which are constraint structures. Among other things, these constraint types implement logical operations and conditional branching over constraint structures. For instance, the following macro call:

```
(define-constraint-type
  check-if-professor
  (:url
    :documentation "Shows report page when user is a professor.")
  (constraint activity url user)
  (equalp (client-status (find-client (user-name user))) "professor")
```

defines a constraint (called `check-if-professor`) that is satisfied only when the current user belongs to the professor category as shown in Figure 2.

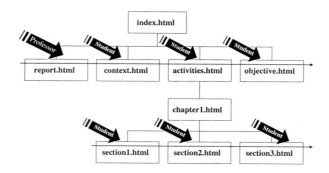

Fig. 2. Constraint applied to the professor or student category

4.5 Actions

Each activity contains a set of actions that are applied to urls that have passed its associated constraint set. Actions are instances of action types, whose behavior is parameterized by their arguments. Primary actions are the basic kind of action. These perform some operation on a url. An example is an action that writes HTML describing the current url to the client stream. For instance, the following macro call:

```
(define-action-type
 redirect-output
 (:encapsulating
  :class encapsulating-action-type
  :documentation "An action that redirects a page on STREAM.")
  (action activity url stream user)
  (let* ((url-address (url:name-string url))
  (slash (search "/" url-address :from-end t))
  (url-prefix (subseq url-address 0 (1+ slash)))
  (url-suffix (subseq url-address (1+ slash))))
  (setf (client-history (find-client user)) (pushnew url (client-history (find-client user))))
  (redirect-request http::*server* #u(concatenate 'string url-prefix "@" url-suffix))))
```

defines an action (called `redirect-output`) that implements the basic redirection mechanism (see Figure 3).

4.6 Activities

Activities collect a set of constraints to guide a site walk and a set of actions that are performed on visited urls. A site walk is initiated by applying the generic function `walk` to a url and an activity. One can think of an activity as a complex argument to a function, containing a number of interrelated parameters that are invoked in different ways during a recursive process. Rather than pass all these arguments separately, here they are bundled into named objects that can be reused. Activities can be defined with `define-activity` or they can be created on the fly with the macro `with-activity`. In each case, textual specifications for constraints and actions are passed to routines that allocate corresponding objects used during the walk. For instance, the following code:

```
(defmethod redirect-to-html ((url url:authentication-mixin) stream)
 (let ((realm (url:authentication-realm url))
       (capabilities (url:capabilities url))
       (authorization (get-raw-header :authorization))
       (user (current-user-object)))
```

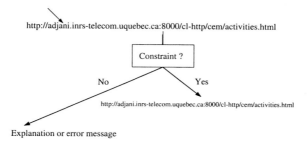

Fig. 3. Basic redirection mechanism

```
(declare (ignore realm capabilities authorization))
(or
 (with-activity
    ("display"
     :constraints '((or (check-user-path ,user) (check-if-professor ,user)))
     :actions '((redirect-output () ,stream ,user)))
   (walk url activity))
 (with-activity
    ("explain"
     :constraints '((not (check-user-path ,user)))
     :actions '((signal-error () ,stream)))
   (walk url activity)))))
```

defines two activities. The first one (`display`) actually displays the current url if the user has fulfilled the mandatory class requirements or if he is a teacher. The second activity explains to the user why the url request has failed.

5 Conclusion

In this paper we have described the re-engineering of a Web walker that uses a set of constraints to characterize traversals of Web structures and performs actions specified in the action vocabulary. This system, called *WebGuide*, provides an environment for creating and reusing abstractions that constrains regions browsing of any given Web site and perform actions over them. The initial dictionary provided with *WebGuide* can be extended to support intelligent agents performing resource management of Web sites. Future works will concern privacy and information confidentiality which were not part of the actual prototype design.

References

Fezzani, D., Desbiens, J., Abdelhak, R., Ghazel, A.: Internet-Based Solution for Tele-learning: the PRICAT Experience. Proceedings of the 4th World Multiconference on Systemics, Cybernetics and Informatics, Orlando, Florida, July 22-26, 2000, pp. 374-379.

Mallery, J.C.: A Common Lisp Hypermedia Server. Proceedings of the First International Conference on the World-Wide Web, Geneva, CERN, 1994.

Mallery, J.C., Blumberg A.C. and Vincent C.R.: A Constraint-Guided Web Walker for Specialized Activities. Proceedings of the Dynamic Objects Workshop at Object World East, Boston, Massachusetts, May 5-6, 1996.

Topic Spotting on News Articles with Topic Repository by Controlled Indexing

Taeho C. Jo, Jerry H. Seo, and Hyeon Kim

KORDIC (Korea Research & Development Information Center)
P.O.Box122, Yusong-Gu, Taejon, 305-350, South Korea
tcjo@netian.com, jerry@kordic.re.kr

Abstract. Topic spotting is the task of assigning a category to the document, among the predefined categories. Topic spotting is called text categorization. Controlled indexing is the procedure of extracting the informative terms reflecting its contents, from the text. There are two kinds of repositories, in the proposed scheme of topic spotting; one is the integrated repository for controlled indexing and the other is topic repository for topic spotting. Repository is constructed by learning the texts, and consists of terms and their associated information: the total frequency and IDF (Inverted Document Frequency). An unknown text is represented into the list of informative terms by controlled indexing referring the integrated repository and the category corresponding to the largest weight is determined as the topic (category) of the text. In order to validate, the news articles from the site, "http://www.newspage.com" are used as examples, in the experiment of this paper.

1 Introduction

Topic spotting is the process of assigning the topic most related with its contents to the document among predefined ones [1]. Topic spotting is identical to text. There is a task similar as topic spotting, called text routing. Text routing is the process of retrieving documents related with the topic or the category given as a query [1]. On contrary, topic spotting or text categorization is the process of retrieving the topic or topics related with the document given as a query [1].

The researches about the technique of automatic topic spotting have been progressed. In 1995, Wiener proposed the application of the most common neural network model, backpropagation, to topic spotting in the thesis of master of the University of Colorado [1]. In his thesis, text is represented into feature vector, of which the features are the selected terms [1]. In 1995, Yang proposed noise reduction to improve efficiency the application of LLSF (Linear Least Square fit) to topic spotting. Noise reduction is the process of eliminating the terms not representing the contents and functioning grammatically [2]. In 1996, Kalt proposed the new probability model for text categorization [3]. In this scheme, text is represented into feature vector and the new probability model estimates the probability of each category [4]. Cohen proposed the hybrid model combining of sleeping expert model and RIPPER considering the context in the text [5]. Lewis proposed the first trainable linear models, Widrow-Hoff algorithm and Exponential Gradient algorithm [5]. Larkey proves through his experiments that the combined model is superior to the individual model of K-Nearest Neighbor, Bayesian classifier, and relevance feedback [6]. In 1997, Joachims proposed the application of SVM (Support Vector Machine) to text categorization, in order to mitigate the curse of dimension [7]. Sahami, Hearst, and Saund proposed the combination of supervised learning model and unsupervised learning model to text categorization [8]. In 1999, Yang proved that K-Nearest Neighbor and LLSF are superior to WORD in the performance of text categorization [9], and apply the techniques of text categorization to event tracking, which mean the decision whether the article focuses on a particular event, or not [10]. In the above schemes of text categorization, the text is represented into the feature vector, of which features are the selected term. But such representation has the problem, called the curse of dimension, which means that too large dimension of the feature vector makes the performance of text categorization poor. In order to avoid this problem, Jo proposed that a text is represented into the list of informative terms instead of a feature vector for text categorization [11]. But this scheme was validated in the only toy experiment, in which categories are politics, sports, and business. Its precision is reach more than 95% [11]. The scheme of text categorization proposed in [11] is applied to a function, automatic knowledge classification, which reinforces the product of KMS (Knowledge Management System), what is called KWave.

In [11], the used jargon was not academic, because the paper was written just after the development of the module of the product for text categorization. And the experiment was very small; the predefine categories are politics, sports, and business. The number of documents for training is only 300, and the number of documents for test only 30. In this paper, the jargon for text categorization will be changed to more academic and the experiment to validate the scheme of text categorization proposed in the literature [11] will be done to more close to real experiment. The number of categories is increased from 3 to 9, the number of documents for training is increased from 300 to near 1000, and the number of documents for testing is increased from 30 to 90. In the jargons for topic spotting, "back data" is changed to "repository", "integrated backdata" is changed to "integrated repository", "categorical back data" is changed to "topic repository", and "keyword filtering" is changed to "controlled indexing [12]". The goals of this paper are two; one is that the scale of the experiment is increased to validate the scheme of topic spotting proposed in [11] and the other is that the jargons of the proposed scheme used in [11] is changed to more academic. Therefore, this paper is the Revised Version of the literature [11].

In the organization of this paper, in the next section controlled indexing will be described, and in the third section, the scheme of topic spotting will be described. In the 4th section, the scheme is validated its result will be presented through the experiment. In 5th section, the meaning of this paper and the orientation of the future research will be mentioned.

2 Controlled Indexing

Controlled indexing is the process of representing the given text into the list of informative terms, terms reflecting its content. The process of document indexing retrieves a list of terms included in the text. The terms representing its contents are selected based on a particular measurement. The process of controlled indexing is presented like the figure 1.

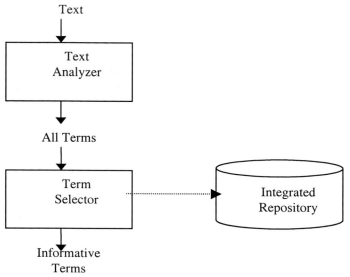

Fig. 1. This process is the controlled indexing proposed in this paper.

As presented in the figure 1, text is represented into the list of all terms contained in itself by text analyzer. Term selector selected terms representing its content enough with the reference to the integrated repository. The integrated repository is the tabular form consisting of term, its frequency, and its IDF (Inverted Document Frequency). It is constructed by learning texts. The texts for constructing the integrated repository are called training documents or training texts.

3 Topic Spotting

In this section, topic spotting , for which the text is represented into the list of informative terms, will be described. the process of topic spotting is represented like the figure 2.

Text is represented into the list of informative terms by controlled indexing mentioned in the previous section. The learning process of each topic repository is identical to that of the integrated repository. But the difference from the integrated repository is summarized in the table 1.

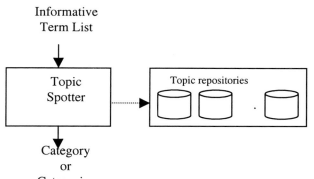

Fig. 2. This process is the topic spotting proposed in this paper.

Table 1. The difference between Integrated and Topic Repository

	Integrated Repository	Topic Repository
training texts	Unlabeled	Manually Labeled
Number	Single	#predefined topics
Function	selecting informative terms	assigning probability of each category
Weight	substantial weight	categorical weight

In the table 1, the number of topic repository is same to the number of the predefined topics, while the integrated repository is given single. The training documents for each topic repository should belong to the homogenous topic. In other words, all training documents for topic repositories should be labeled manually. By referring the topic repositories, the categorical weights of each informative term are computed. The measurement, categorical weight, is the degree in which the term reflects the category. For example, the terms, "Clington", "President", or "Minister", have the high categorical weights of politics, because they are included mainly in the news articles about politics. But these terms have the low categorical weight of sports, because they are inlcuded very little in the news aricles about sports.

4 Experiment & Results

In this section, the experiment of topic spotting and the result of the validation of the proposed of topic spotting will be presented. The corpus of this experiment is the set of news articles from 1st May 1999 to 15th July. The web site of the news articles is "http://www.newspage.com". The categories of the news articles are like the following this.
- Business
- Healthcare Regulation
- Migration
- Pharmacy

- Politics
- Pulbic
- Sports
- Wireless communication
- WeirdNuz

The integrated repository is constructed by learning the training documents: 1000 news articles regardless of their categories (inlcuding the categories not listed above). The number of training documents for topic repositories is given 100 news articles per topic. The total number of training documents for these repositories becomes 900. And the number of news articles for testing is 10 per topic.

The informative terms are selected by ranking terms in the descending order of substantial weight. The rank thresolds are 5, 10, 15, 20, 25, and 30. The substnatial weight of each term is computed by the simple equation, in this experiment.

$$SW(t_i) = F(f_i, tf_i, idf_i) = \frac{f_i}{tf_i + idf_i} \quad (5)$$

$$SW(t_i) = F(f_i) = f_i \quad (6)$$

Note that if there is no identical term in the integrated repository, the equation (6) is applied to the computation of the substantial weight of each term.

To each informative term, the categorical weight is cmputed by the following equation.

$$cw_{ij} = F(SW_i, tf_{ij}, idf_{ij}) = tf_{ij} + idf_{ij} \quad (7)$$

If there is no identical term in the topic repository to an informative term, the categorical weight, cw_{ij}, is 0. In this experiment, only one category corresponding to the largest value of probability is assigned to each news article. The measurment of the performance in topic spotting is the precision expressed like the following this.

$$Pecision = \frac{The \ Number \ of \ News \ Articles \ Correctly \ Classified}{The \ Number \ of \ News \ Articles \ for \ Testing} \quad (8)$$

The result of topic spotting is presented like figure 3.

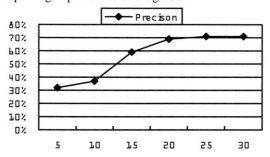

Figure 3. The Result of Topic Spotting

In the figure 3, the x-axis means the number of informative terms, and the y-axis means the precision. In the interval between 10 and 20, the precision of the topic spotting is increased outstandingly, and in the interval between 20 and 30, the precision is increased very little. The figure 3 presents that the efficient number of the informative terms is 20.

5 Conclusion

The scheme of topic spotting proposed in the [11] is described more formally and validated in the experiment, which the number of categories is increased from 3 to 9, and the number of test documents is increased from 30 to 90. In the experiment of the literature [11], the precision of topic spotting is even more than 95%. If the domain of corpus is extended, the precision is reduced from 95% or 71%. The equations computing substantial weight and categorical weight of each term can be developed in several. It is important to the optimal equation of substantial weight and categorical weight, which generate the maximal precision. And it is necessary to extend the experiment for the validation of the proposed scheme and the comparison with other techniques of topic spotting should be more extended. In the future, the proposed scheme will be validated and compared with other techniques in the experiment using Reuters-21578 collection as test bed. This technique is applied to the development of the component of topic spotting for the product of KMS (Knowledge Management System), what is called KWave..

References

1. E. D. Wiener, A Neural Network Approach to Topic Spotting in Text, the Faculty of the Graduate School of the University of Colorado (1995) Master of Thesis.
2. Y. Yang, Noise Reduction in a Statistical approaches to Text Categorization, The Proceedings of SIGIR 95 (1995) 256-263.
3. T. Kalt and W.B. Croft, A New Probabilistic Model of Text Classification and Retrieval, downloaded from http://ciir.cs.umass.edu/info/psfiles/irpubs/irnew.html, (1996) IR-78.
4. W.W. Cohen and Y. Singer, Context-sensitive learning methods for text categorization, The Proceedings of SIGIR 96 (1996) pp306-315.
5. D.D. Lewis, R.E. Schapire, J.P. Callan, and R. Papka, Training Algorithms for Linear Text Classifiers, The Proceedings of SIGIR 96 (1996) pp298-305.
6. D.D. Lewis, R.E. Schapire, J.P. Callan, and R. Papka, Training Algorithms for Linear Text Classifiers, The Proceedings of SIGIR 96 (1996) pp298-305.
7. T. Joachims, Text Categorization with Support Vector Machines: Learning with Many Relevant Features, Dortmund University (1997) LS-8 Report 23.
8. M. Sahami, M. Hearst, and E. Saund, Applying the Multiple Case Mixture Model to Text Categorization, Proc. ICML 96 (1996) appearing
9. Y. Yang, An Evaluation of Statistical Approaches to Text Categorization, Information Retrieval Journal (1999) 69-90
10. Y. Yang, J. Carbonell, R. Brown, T. Pierce, B.T. Archibald, and X. Liu, A Study on Learning Appraches to Topic Detection and Tracking, IEEE Expert, Special Issue on Application of Intelligent Information Retrieval, (1999), appearing

Validating the Behavior of Self-Interested Agents in an Information Market Scenario

Ioan Alfred Letia[1], Florin Craciun[1], and Zoltan Köpe[1]

Technical University of Cluj-Napoca,
Department of Computer Science
Baritiu 28, RO-3400 Cluj-Napoca, Romania
{letia,florin,kzoltan}@cs-gw.utcluj.ro

Abstract. We describe some experimental results within a scenario in a simulation framework we are developing to enable experimentation of multi-agents behavior, measured by the total utility that agents can gather during a given time horizon. In this scenario the population of self-centered agents performs in an $80{\times}80$ grid with objects carrying information (infons) of varying utility that several autonomous agents are trying to obtain. This model is an abstraction for a real world information marketplace where agents simply cannot cooperate all the time for various practical reasons. The aim of this work is to show how we can validate the connection of agent local behavior to global behavior in various environmental situations.

Keywords: multi-agent systems, modeling issues, large-scale agent population, validation by simulation

1 Introduction

For self-interested agents, that simply maximize their own utility, it is desirable that reasonable local behavior should lead to global reasonable behavior [3, 4]. But if agents are untruthful or deceitful just to increase their utility by any means then harm might arise to the whole society. It is therefore important to evaluate basic behavior of large agent societies in assumed environments. Of the two forms of cooperation: (i) deliberate and contractual, and (ii) emergent (non contractual and even unaware), we are concerned here with the second one.

The goal to resist exploitation by malevolent agents has seen some results in probabilistic reciprocity schemes [7] and prescriptive strategies that promote and sustain cooperation among self-interested agents. Exhaustive experiments are reported on emergent cooperation in an information marketplace for agents acting in various alternatives of the iterated prisoner's dilemma [1].

For modeling multiple agents under uncertainty we have chosen ICL (independent choice logic) [6]. Inspired by decision/game theory, it constitutes a solid foundation for evaluating multi-agent behavior over a time horizon. Our simulation framework materializes this approach.

We have constructed a model of multi-agents to experiment how a large number of agents behave. As illustrative scenario a world resembling an information marketplace has been implemented. The agents in this scenario cooperate in a random fashion, capturing in this way the real world where, for various reasons, agents are not always able to do it, even when trying hard. By simulating various kinds of encounters between the agents we expect to evaluate those strategies that are favorable for particular agents and also how to counteract unacceptable behavior of some agents in a more realistic world.

2　Agent Model

For the the scenario of the information marketplace we use the theory of practical rationality with dynamic obligation hierarchies [2] to describe what agents have to do. A statement of the form $Pref(a,\phi,\psi)(i)$ says that agent a prefers ϕ to ψ for the interval i. $PFObl(a,\phi)(i)$ states that ϕ is among a's *prima facie* obligations for interval i.

$Pref(a,PFObl(a,\phi),PFObl(a,\psi))(i)$ says that, for interval i, ϕ is a more important *prima facie obligation* for agent a than ψ. A *realisable prima facie obligation* for an agent a for interval i is a *prima facie obligation* of a's for interval i which a can realize on interval i.

The agent always has a set of *obligations* with *preferences*, defining a partial order over the set of obligations. The obligation pair for which no preference is given is considered *indifferent*. An agent a prefers ϕ to ψ during the time interval $[i_1, i_2]$ if the agent a prefers $\phi \wedge \neg\psi$ to $\psi \wedge \neg\phi$ during the time interval $[i_1, i_2]$. Obligations define the way the agent should behave in all situations. An obligation is *realisable* if there is some plan e by means of which a can achieve ϕ for i: At any given time step some of the obligations will seem realizable, even if they are not. Due to the uncertainty of the environment estimating realizability does not yield a unique value. In this way, the realizability of an obligation acts as a filter in generating the set of *realisable prima facie obligations*. Of all the obligations in the hierarchy, the most preferred is selected for fulfillment.

2.1　Conceptual Agent

The scenario we have chosen to study the strategy of agents is a grid world with several agents trying to collect infons that appear and disappear. Infons are carriers of information characterized by its utility value varying in the range 1 to 4. The agents try to maximize the global utility value of all infons they can collect. A sample showing possible changes in the grid world for time $t=0,1,2,3$ is illustrated in figure 1.

All infons appear randomly, one in a square of the grid, with a life span described by the sequence

$$i_k^1 \rightarrow i_k^2 \rightarrow i_k^3 \rightarrow i_k^4 \rightarrow i_k^3 \rightarrow i_k^2 \rightarrow i_k^1$$

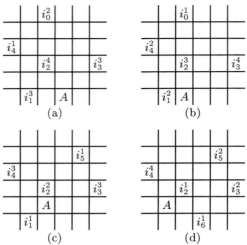

Fig. 1. Sample of grid world at time (a) $t=0$, (b) $t=1$, (c) $t=2$ and (d) $t=3$.

for infon i_k, that is its utility increases in time up to the maximum and then decreases again until 1, and in the next time step it disappears. Every self-interested agent A tries to get infons i_k^j, where j is the utility of the infon, to increase its own overall utility as much as possible. We can see in figure 1 that agent A steps westwards at time step 0 to get the infon i_1 at time $t=1$ when adjacent to it. Agents prefer collecting infons with higher utility value,

$$utility(i_k) > utility(i_j) \rightarrow Pref(a,get(i_k),get(i_j))$$

but it is their overall utility that they try to maximize.

For a given state of the infon world an agent can establish which infons it can collect and which not. Some preferences of the agent A in the states shown in figure 1 are as follows.

$$Pref(A,PFObl(get(i_2)),PFObl(get(i_1)))[0..2]$$
$$Pref(A,PFObl(get(i_2^4)),PFObl(get(i_3)))(0)$$
$$Pref(A,PFObl(get(i_3)),PFObl(get(i_2)))[1..3]$$
$$Pref(A,PFObl(get(i_2)),PFObl(get(i_4)))[0..1]$$
$$Pref(A,PFObl(get(i_4)),PFObl(get(i_2)))[2..3]$$

The preferences on *prima facie obligations*, the *realisable prima facie obligations* and those that have been realized over the interval [0..3] by agent A of figure 1 are shown in table 1. Here we can see the change of preferences in time and also the change of their realizability. Our agent A has been able to collect infons i_1^2 and i_2^2 both with utility value 2.

3   Simulation Framework

Various simulation tools have been developed for the study of multi-agent behavior, including coordination and survivability [8]. Our simulation framework

Table 1. Agent preferences, realizable and realized obligations over the interval $[0..3]$.

τ	Preferences on prima facie obligations	RPFObl	Real
0	$i_1 \prec i_2$ $i_3 \prec i_2$ $i_4 \prec i_2$ $i_5 \prec i_2$ $i_4 \prec i_1$ $i_5 \prec i_1$ $i_4 \prec i_3$ $i_5 \prec i_3$ $i_4 \prec i_5$	i_1 i_2 i_3 i_4	
1	$i_0 \prec i_3$ $i_1 \prec i_3$ $i_2 \prec i_3$ $i_4 \prec i_3$ $i_0 \prec i_2$ $i_1 \prec i_2$ $i_4 \prec i_2$ $i_0 \prec i_1$ $i_0 \prec i_4$	i_1 i_2 i_4	i_1^2
2	$i_1 \prec i_3$ $i_2 \prec i_3$ $i_5 \prec i_3$ $i_1 \prec i_4$ $i_2 \prec i_4$ $i_5 \prec i_4$ $i_1 \prec i_2$ $i_5 \prec i_2$	i_2 i_4 i_5	
3	$i_2 \prec i_4$ $i_3 \prec i_4$ $i_5 \prec i_4$ $i_6 \prec i_4$ $i_2 \prec i_3$ $i_6 \prec i_3$ $i_2 \prec i_5$ $i_6 \prec i_5$	i_2 i_4 i_5	i_2^2

is developed with Swarm [5], extended with a choice space and a utility space to observe global agent behavior [6].

3.1 Evaluation of Agent Behavior

The expected utility for agent a under strategy profile σ over an entire time horizon is [6]

$$\epsilon(a, \sigma) = \sum_\tau p(\sigma, \tau) \times u(\tau, a)$$

where $p(\sigma, \tau)$ is the probability of the world τ under strategy profile σ and $u(\tau, a)$ is the utility of the world for agent a. The strategy profile σ depends on the choices made by the agent a according to its obligations and also its perception of the current world.

3.2 Experimental Agent

The experimental environment consists of several infons with varying utility value on an 80×80 grid. An agent can collect an infon when it is situated in a square adjacent to its own square. All agents can see just a part of the entire grid world given by the parameter S, representing the number of squares in all directions (North, South, East, West). The agent always executes the most important goal among its set of goals:

```
pref(A, O1,O2)          :- pfobl(A,O1), pfobl(A,O2), prefer(A,O1,O2).
prefthan(A,V,X,Y, L) :- findall(O,pref(A,O,o(V,X,Y)), L).
noreallist(_,[]).
noreallist(A,[H|T])    :- not(real(A,H)), noreallist(A,T).
mostpref(A,o(V,X,Y)) :- pfobl(A,o(V,X,Y)), real(A,o(V,X,Y)),
                        prefthan(A,V,X,Y,L), noreallist(A,L).
```

where o(V,X,Y) is an obligation to collect the infon with current utility V, on the grid with current coordinates (X,Y). The realizability of an obligation is currently calculated by a pessimistic estimation of the evolution of infons. Agents assume that infon evolution is linear, although in fact this could be in steps.

An agent step is achieved in five stages:

- **Prima Facie Obligation** or *what the agent should do*: what the agent can see with a given vision (number of squares from its current position), that is obligations the agent is imposed to fulfill.
- **Preferences** or *what order the agent wants on tasks*: a partial ordering relation on the infons seen by the agent. This relation makes use of the current utility of the infons and their position on the grid.
- **Realizable** or *what tasks the agent believes possible to be realized*: subset of obligations realizable, that is there is a free path to that infon and the infon will not disappear from the grid in that time.
- **Obligation** or *the goal of the agent at a given step*: the most preferred obligation in the set of realizable obligations.
- **Action** or *how the agent fulfills the current goal*: the action that the agent will execute to fulfill the most preferred obligation.

These stages can be visualized to allow the designer to eventually analyze how local behavior influences global behavior. An agent cycle in its interaction with the world is achieved in three execution phases: (i) *perception*, (ii) *reasoning* and (iii) *acting*, during which the world does not change.

4   Simulation Results

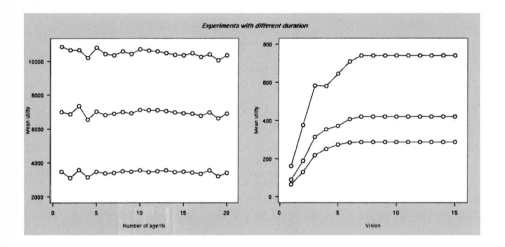

Fig. 2. (a) Agent behavior vs. number of agents (b) Agent behavior vs. vision.

Initially the agents a distributed at random on the grid. In figure 2 (a) it is shown the influence of vision on the average utility collected by an agent. Each experiment was carried out with a varying number of infons and agents.

We notice a threshold from which average utility increases very slowly with the increase in vision.

Figure 2 (b) shows how average utility collected by an agent varies with the number of agents on the grid. Both the number of infons and the vision of agents was varied. We notice significant variation when the number of agents is small, when the conflicts on obligations is not significant. When the number of agents is increased the number of conflicts increases and the agents have difficulty in resolving conflicts. This indicates a threshold where more coordination will prove beneficial.

5   Conclusions

Instead of just designing good social laws, strategies for interactions with other agents that can promote and sustain cooperation among self-interested agents have already been reported [7]. Simulation was also used to provide ability and flexibility when modeling complex interaction among heterogeneous agents [8] Our abstract scenario for the information marketplace can easily be extended with other parameters describing in a concise manner the real world. The simulation framework we are developing is more general as it allows various logical specifications of agents to be included and experimented with. Our next step will be inclusion of various kinds of agents defined in the literature and the measurement of their performance in terms of individual and overall utility.

References

1. Aaron A. Armstrong and Edmund H. Durfee. Mixing and memory: Emergent cooperation in an information marketplace. In Y. Demazeau, editor, *Proceedings of the 3rd International Conference on Multi-Agent Systems (ICMAS-98)*, pages 34–41, Paris, France, July 1998. IEEE Computer Society Press.
2. John Bell and Zhisheng Huang. Dynamic obligation hierarchies. In P. MacNamara and H. Praken, editors, *Proceedings of ΔEON'98*, pages 127–142, 1998.
3. N. R. Jennings, K. Sycara, and M. Wooldridge. A roadmap of agent research. *Autonomous Agents and Multi-Agent Systems*, 1(1):7–38, 1998.
4. Victor R. Lesser. Reflections on the nature of multi-agent coordination framework and its implications for an agent architecture. *Autonomous Agents and Multi-Agent Systems*, 1(1):89–111, 1998.
5. M. Minar, R. Burkhart, C. Langton, and M. Askenazy. The Swarm simulation system: A toolkit for building multi-agent simulations. Technical report, Santa Fe Institute, 1996. http://www.santafe.edu/projects/swarm/.
6. David Poole. The independent choice logic for modelling multiple agents under uncertainty. *Artificial Intelligence*, 94(1-2):7–56, 1997.
7. Sendip Sen. Reciprocity: A foundational principle for promoting cooperative behavior among self-interested agents. In *Proceedings of the 2nd International Conference on Multi-Agent Systems (ICMAS-96)*, pages 315–321, Kyoto, Japan, 1996.
8. R. Vincent, B. Horling, T. Wagner, and V. Lesser. Survivability simulator for multi-agent adaptive coordination. In P. Fishwick, D. Hill, and R. Smith, editors, *International Conference on Web-Based Modeling and Simulation*, pages 114–119, San Diego, CA, 1998.

Discovering User Behavior Patterns in Personalized Interface Agents

Jiming Liu, Kelvin Chi Kuen Wong, and Ka Keung Hui

Department of Computer Science, Hong Kong Baptist University, Kowloon Tong, Hong Kong
{jiming,kckwong,kkhui}@comp.hkbu.edu.hk

Abstract. In human-computer interaction, user interface events can be recorded and organized into sequences of episodes. By computing their implication networks, episode frequencies, and some heuristic measures of interestingness, we can readily derive some application-specific episode association rules. In order to demonstrate the proposal method, we have developed a personalized interface agent that can take into consideration interface events in analyzing user goals. It can then delegate on behalf of the user to interact with the software based on the recognized plans. In order to adapt to different users' needs, the agent can personalize its assistance by learning user profiles. Currently, we have used the *Microsoft Word* as a test case. By detecting and analyzing the patterns of user behavior in using *Word*, the agent can automatically assist the users in certain *Word* tasks. The pattern association can be achieved at several levels, i.e., text-level (phrase association), paragraph-level (formatting association), and document-level (style and source association).

1   Introduction

The ease with which a software system can be effectively operated by users is to a large extent determined by the design and complexity of a user interface. This paper explores the application of an interface agent that records the events of human-computer interaction (HCI) and discovers the consistent patterns of user behavior. Thereafter, the agent can provide just-in-time assistance to a user by predicting the most likely plan of the user and delegates part of the plan on behalf of the user.

The advantages of incorporating an agent in the user interface are: (1) the interface is no longer static as it reacts to different situations and requirements, (2) the interface is seamlessly personalized as it learns the behavior patterns as well as styles of individual users, and (3) the software system can be manipulated in a semi-autonomous manner that significantly reduces the amount of intervention required.

Earlier examples of user interface agents include Letizia [1] and Let's Browse [2]. These agents assist a user in browsing the World Wide Web by tracking user behavior and anticipating items of interest. These systems analyze user behavior by means of matching the keywords in the Web documents, whereas in our case, the agent will recognize user action plans by tracing and analyzing the action sequences of the user.

Our approach discovers the rules that can best describe and predict user behavior by finding frequently occurred episodes in user action sequences. Such an approach is inspired by the earlier work Window Episode (WINEPI) and Minimal Occurrence Episode (MINEPI) [3, 4]. In order to reliably detect patterns from a limited number of observed sequence data samples, we employ a method of inducing implication networks [5, 6]. This method constructs a dependence relationship between two ordered events based on statistical testing.

2   Problem statement

In our work, we regard the events of a user interface as episodes E_I, and capture all the sequences of episodes S_i as a user is interacting with an application through the interface. Therefore, we can reduce the problem of finding user patterns in HCI into that of discovering frequent episodes α_i out of the sequences of events S_i.

Figure 1 presents a schematic diagram of the above problem: Given the sequences of events, S_1, S_2, ..., find out some significant frequent episodes α_i by applying some statistical tests on the sequences. In the figure, the frequent episodes are $\alpha_1: E_1 \Rightarrow E_2$, which expresses a co-occurrence that event E_1 will be followed by event E_2, and $\alpha_2: E_3 \Rightarrow E_5 \Rightarrow E_2$.

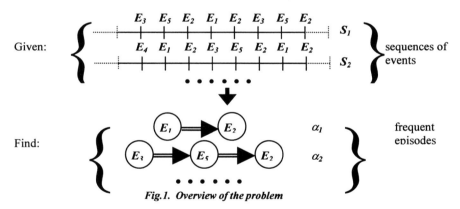

Fig.1. *Overview of the problem*

3   Discovering user behavior patterns

In what follows, we will describe how to find and use consistent behavior patterns in HCI. Throughout our descriptions, we will use *MSWord* as our test case to illustrate how our approach works.

Specifically, we will develop a capability of Episode Identification and Association (EIA) in our user interface agent, which is called as Personalized Word Assistant (PWA). Figure 2 provides an overview of PWA.

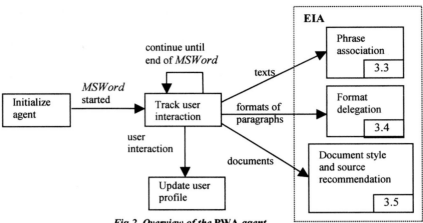

Fig.2. Overview of the PWA agent

3.1 Window episode (WINEPI)

In HCI, an event E is a pair of action type and occurrence time (H, t). a sequence S is defined as (s, T_s, T_e) where s is an event sequence, T_s is the starting time, and T_e is the ending time. In order to discover frequency episodes from an event sequence, a time window will be defined that divides a long sequence into a number of shorter sequences. For each window, we also consider it as a set W of events. W is defined as (w, t_s, t_e) where w is an event sequence, t_s is the starting time, and t_e is the ending time. Moreover, the time difference $t_s - t_e$ is called the width of the window W, and it is denoted by $width(w)$.

The frequency of an episode is defined as the fraction of windows in which the episode occurs. That means, given an event sequence s and the window width is limited by win, the frequency of an episode E in s is:

$$Fr(E, s, win) = \left|[w \in W(s, win) \mid E \text{ occurs in } w]\right| \tag{1}$$

To be a frequent episode, it has to pass two tests: One is a frequency threshold test and another is a confidence threshold test, as given below, respectively:

$$\frac{fr(\mathbf{E}_a \Rightarrow \mathbf{E}_b, s, win)}{fr(\mathbf{E}_a, s, win)} \geq \min\_fr \tag{2}$$

$$\frac{fr(\mathbf{E}_a, s, win)}{|\mathbf{W}(s, win)|} \geq \min\_conf \tag{3}$$

3.2 Implication relations

Sometimes, an interface agent may need to discover frequent episodes with limited information. In order to deal with this situation, we utilize an implication induction algorithm [5, 6]. For each implication relation $E_a \Rightarrow E_b$, this algorithm computes the lower bound of a *(1-α_c)* confidence interval around the measured conditional probability p_{min}. Suppose that there have been N_{error} number of observations that violate $E_a \Rightarrow E_b$, Thus, based on the binomial distribution $Bin(N_{error}, p_{min})$, it tests whether or not the probability of errors is less than a threshold, that is:

$$P(x \leq N_{error}) < \alpha_c \tag{4}$$

where α_c is the alpha error of this conditional probability test. If X is the frequency of the occurrence, then X satisfies a binomial distribution, whose probability function $p_x(k)$ and distribution function $F_x(k)$ are given below:

$$p_x(k) = \binom{n}{k} p_{min}^k (1 - p_{min})^{n-k} \tag{5}$$

$$F_x(k) = p(X \leq k) = \sum_{i=0}^{k} \binom{n}{i} p_{min}^i (1 - p_{min})^{n-i} \tag{6}$$

3.3   Phrase association

The first level of assistance in the implemented PWA agent is called *phrase association*. At this level, PWA considers word(s) as an episode and a sequence of words as an event sequence. With a bag-of-word text document representation, it readily finds out the frequency counts of the words (episodes). By using the above-mentioned algorithms of EIA, it discovers various associations among words. If there is one word in an episode, we call it 1-gram. If there are two words, we call it 2-gram. The n-gram representation can consider up to five words in an episode. The PWA agent will provide assistance to a user whenever it detects a phrase association.

3.4   Format delegation

The second level of EIA is called *format delegation*. At this level, it concentrates on the delegation of formatting and finds consistent formats in paragraphs. When a user changes certain part of a paragraph format, and continues to perform the same operations elsewhere, the PWA agent will detect a format change pattern between F_1 and F_2, i.e., discover a frequent episode, $F_1 \Rightarrow F_2$. With those detected frequent episodes, the agent can automatically delegate the task of applying the consistent format changes in other paragraphs.

3.5   Document style and source recommendation

The third level of assistance is called *document style and source recommendation*, which is concerned with discovering relevant styles and sources for a certain document. Among various documents, there may be many different styles. The PWA agent first categorizes the documents into different styles. That is, the documents with similar styles are clustered and a template style will be created. Therefore, whenever the PWA agent detects that a user is about to create certain style, it can automatically make style template recommendations.

At the same time, document source recommendation locates and suggests various relevant document sources to the user. Whenever the user is writing some document, the agent will search both the local (file system) and global (WWW) for related contents. Both searches will apply the same methods of determining which document is to be associated, that is, document categorization based on feature selection [7, 8, 9, 10] text weighting based on Term Frequency and Inverse Document Frequency (TFIDF) [11].

4   Experimentation

In order to validate the effectiveness of the PWA agent in offering personalized interface assistance, we have designed and conducted two experiments, both involving real users handling real documents.

4.1   Experiment 1

In this experiment, we have one group of 10 users participating in the test. They are asked to write documents with the help of the PWA agent. First, the users have to decide which kinds of documents will be written in the experiment, and at the same time, provide some of the documents that are considered to be relevant and are written by them before. After the user profiles have provided such information, PWA will then try to build user profiles for the individual users at the above-mentioned first two levels. Thereafter the experiment starts - the users begin to write their documents. During the experiment, we record the number of suggestions offered and the number of acceptances. The averages are shown in Table 1. Both levels of suggestions have quite high percentage of correctness: 75% for phrase association and 86% for format delegation.

	Phrase association	Format delegation
Average number of suggestions	175.14	83.24
Average number of acceptances	131.14	71.49

Table 1. Results of phrase association and format delegation

4.2   Experiment 2

In the second experiment, we have two groups of users (G_1 and G_2) participating in the test. One group of 5 users (G_1) will write a document with the help of the PWA agent. And the other group of 5 users (G_2) will write the document without the assistance of the agent. There are two sets of documents (D_1 and D_2) for the test, the context of the documents are very similar. First of all, the agent prepares user profiles for the G_1 users by storing and learning their related documents. The G_1 users will write documents with the PAW agent, while the G_2 users will write by themselves without the help of PWA. Similar to Experiment 1, the total processing time and the number of operation steps are recorded. The results of the two groups are shown in Table 2. G_1 (with PWA) preformed better than G_2 (without PWA) in both results.

	G_1 (with PWA)	G_2 (without PWA)
Averaged total processing time	8 minutes and 56 seconds	11 minutes and 59 seconds
Averaged number of operation steps	253	401

Table 2. Results of G_1 and G_2

5   Conclusion

In this paper, we have described an interface agent that records the events of human-computer interaction (HCI) and discovers the consistent patterns of user behavior. As experimentally validated in the case of *MSWord*, the interface agent can effectively carry out the different levels of Episode Identification and Association (EIA), and thereafter, provide just-in-time assistance to users by predicting the most likely plan of the user and delegates part of the plan on behalf of the user.

References

[1] Henry Lieberman. Letizia: An agent that assists web browsing. 1995.
    http://lieber.www.media.mit.edu/people/lieber/Lieberary/Letizia/Letizia-AAAI/Letizia.html
[2] Adriana Vivacqua, Henry Lieberman, Neil Van Dyke. Let's browse: A collaborative web browsing agent. 1997.
    http://lieber.www.media.mit.edu/people/lieber/Lieberary/Lets-Browse/Lets-Browse.html
[3] A. Inkeri Verkamo Heikki Mannila, Hannu Toivonen. Discovery of frequent episodes in event sequences. 1997.
[4] Heikki Mannila, Hannu Toivonen. Discovering generalized episodes using minimal occurrences. 1997.
[5] Jiming Liu, Michel C. Desmarais. A method of learning implication networks from empirical data: algorithm and Monte-Carlo simulation-based validation. 1997.
[6] Michel C. Desmarais, D. A. Maluf, and Jiming Liu, User-expertise modeling with empirically derived probabilistic implication networks. In the International Journal of User Modeling and User-Adapted Interaction, vol. 5, no. 3-4, pp. 283-315, 1996.
[7] Dunja Mladeic, Marko Grobelnik. Feature selection for classification based on text hierarchy. 1999.
[8] Dunja Mladeic, Marko Grobelnik. Feature selection for unbalanced class distribution and naïve bayes. 1999.
[9] Dunja Mladeic, Marko Grobelnik. Word sequences as features in text-learning. 1999.
[10] Dunja Mladeic, Marko Grobelnik. Assigning keywords to documents using machine learning. 1999.
[11] Thorsten Joachims. A probabilistic analysis of the Rocchio algorithm. 1996.

An Agent-Based Personalized Search on a Multi-search Engine Based on Internet Search Service*

Min-Huang Ho[1], Yue-Shan Chang[2] Shyan-Ming Yuan[1] Winston Lo[3]

[1]Department of Computer and Information Science,National Chiao Tung University,
Hsin-Chu, Taiwan 31151, R.O.C.
smyuan@cis.nctu.edu.tw
[2]Department of Electronic Engineering, Ming-Hsin Institute of Technology
1 Hsin-Hsing Road, Hsin-Fong, Hsin-Chu, Taiwan 304 R.O.C.
ysc@mhit.edu.tw
[3]Department of Computer and Information Science, Tung Hai University
Taichung, Taiwan, R.O.C.
winston@cis.thu.edu.tw

Abstract. The Internet Search Service (ISS) was proposed to support an uniform interface for searching on the World Wide Web. Based on this service, a multi-search engine named Octopus had been built. In order to provide more services, such as personal functionality, we provide personalized search for users. In this paper, the policies of personalized search are described. In addition, in order to keep the advantages of the ISS, a personal information-filtering agent is added into the Octopus instead of modifying the architecture or interface of ISS. The *feedback mechanism* is in cooperation with the *filtering mechanism* to achieve the functionality of personalized search in a search engine.

1. Introduction

Most of search engines and multi-search engines [1,2] are developed only for WWW users, not for application programs that need to exploit data from the web. They also have no an uniform interface while accommodating new and powerful search engines in future, so that most multi-search engines are less the extensibility.

We have proposed an uniform interface - Internet Search Service (ISS) [3] that follows the COSS of OMG's CORBA [4] to solve the problem described above. And, an experimental ISS-based multi-search engine termed Octopus has been built. With that Octopus can accommodate new search engines easily and support application programs to exploit data from the Internet.

Most returned results from search engines could be not useful for users even if these results are ranked higher index. Search engines with the function of personalized search are strongly necessary for experts. Some well-known search

---

* This work was supported by Ministry of Education's Program of Excellence Research under Grant 89-E-FA04-1-4.

engines have supported this function, such as SavvySearch, MyYahoo etc. The main reason of personalized search is to offer most suitable query results to user.

This paper will describe the design and implementation for supporting personalized search in the Octopus. In Octopus, an *absolutely irrelevant filtering approach* used to support the personalized search.

In order to balance system load and user requirement, the filtering mechanism is divided into three levels – URL, Description/Context, and Content respectively. In addition, the *feedback mechanism* is in cooperation with the *filtering mechanism* to achieve the functionality of personalized search in a search engine.

This kind of search service is favorable for WWW user, not for application programs. Therefore, this function is independent of the ISS. To support such service is only to redesign the architecture of Octopus. The original advantages of ISS should be reserved in providing other functionality. All the interfaces will be not modified. The major contribution of the paper is providing an approach to support the personalized search service based on the ISS without change its interface of the Octopus.

2. Related Works

A variety of search tools are offering the means of personalizing or customizing their sites to the individual user, such as Excite, Lycos, MyYahoo etc. The advantage of these tools like "push" services and provide you with up-to-date information tailored to your desires with little ongoing active effort on your part. But, how much information do you want to reveal about yourself?

Famous multi-search engine that supports optimal search is the SavvySearch [2]. It automatically tracks the effectiveness of each search engine in responding to previous queries and creates a meta-index for future queries to decide which search engines are more adequate. Because one of major factors of adjusting the meta-index is the number of visitors, according to the meta-index to make the search plan is not adequate individual users.

Amalthaea [6] is a multi-agent information filtering and discovery system. In the system, the information discovery agents refer to their history logs and check if the information-filtering agent that has been the most profitable for doing requests. If no, it proceeds to the next preferred filtering agent and check again. If yes, that request is selected. The drawback of Amalthaea likes the SavvySearch.

Many other researches have been proposed their architecture to support personalized search [5, 7]. These solutions are based on proprietary technique that is not easy to be applied by other application programs.

3. Personalized Search Supports

The ISS is designed by following the style of CORBA's COSS. Its major goal is providing an uniform interface for most search engines. The details of ISS Octopus's scenario please refer to [3]. In the section, we describe the personalized support on the Octopus.

3.1 Design principle

In keeping the advantage of the ISS, a personal information-filtering agent is added into the Octopus instead of modifying architecture or interface of ISS when adding personal functionality. Figure 1 shows the preliminary design of the Octopus with personalized search. The major difference between this architecture with original Octopus version is adding a personal information-filtering agent that used to filter users favor. Such design philosophy is in order to reduce the search overhead when similar query is requested repeatedly.

The *feedback mechanism* is in cooperation with the *filtering mechanism* to achieve the functionality of personalized search. The latter used to find out adequate results, while the former let the user to respond what his/her favor is. In this paper, two mechanisms are adapted *implicit feedback approach* and *absolutely irrelevant filtering approach* respectively.

Using *implicit feedback approach* instead of explicit one is in order to go with the filtering mechanism properly. The *absolutely irrelevant filtering approach* is based on the custom of user in searching information from large amount of URLs and descriptions. In generally, users will first visit those deemed more suitable of URLs and skip the others that symbolize irrelevant. The visited web page may represent the page is interested by user in some extent. To analyze those fully irrelevant URLs or descriptions may find out more relevant to what don't he/she want than relevant approach and act as the filtering basis. This is the spirit of *absolutely irrelevant filtering approach.*

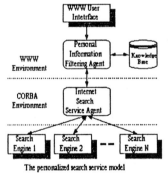

The personalized search service model

Figure 1. The preliminary architecture of supporting personalized search

We can utilize classical Boolean model of Information Retrieval [8] to explain the concept. If $\bar{K}_i$ is the set of relevant terms and $\bar{K}_j$ is the set of non-relevant terms. Then $K = \bar{K}_i \cup \bar{K}_j$ will be all of terms that are included in returned results or documents. And $K - \bar{K}_j$ will be more relevant terms. So that we use *absolutely irrelevant filtering approach* to filter the non-relevant terms will get more relevant terms.

In the design, the *personal information-filtering agent* analyzes the factor of these non-relevant URLs or web pages and stores it into knowledge base for future searching requests. The knowledge base keeps personal filtering information. When the *Search Engine Agent* replies the user request, then the *Information-Filtering Agent* will filter the result in accordance with the personal filtering information.

3.2 Level of Filtering

The filtering mechanism is the corpus in supporting personalized search. In order to balance system load and user requirement, the filtering mechanism is divided into three levels – URL, Description/Context, and Content respectively.

1. URL: This is a simplest filtering level. This level filters the URLs of result that are selected and non-visited by user, into personal database. Those non-visited URLs imply absolutely irrelevant and act as filtering base for future searching request. Because this level is simplest, it has slightest overhead.
2. Description/Context: Almost all returned results of search engines consist of URL and description. In the level, *filtering mechanism* analyzes vocabulary in description that excludes *non-stop term[1]* of all the non-visited web sites and applies the *index model* [8] to create an index for each term. When the index of certain term exceeds the pre-determined *cutoff threshold*, the *filtering mechanism* will keep it into the *list of filtering terms* and stores the analyzed results into *filtering base*. When an user issues a search request with this filtering level, the *Information Filtering Agent* will utilize the filtering base to filter the query result and to discard those irrelevant results.
3. Content: The same technology as second level is applied to this level with the exception of analyzed target is the full content of web site. Because the size of analysis is the largest in three levels, the overhead is also largest.

All of filtering level is based on the *implicit feedback mechanism* that feed back the selected web sites implicitly. The detailed description is in next subsection.

3.3 Architecture of Personalized Search

Figure 2 shows the detail architecture in supporting the functionality of personalized search in Octopus. Based on ISS, some components are added into the system to support this function, such as *User Profile, Filtering Database, Feedback mechanism,* and *Result processing mechanism* etc. Follows describe the system scenario. The system first checks user identifier through *User Profile*. Once the user passes the check, the system will generate a query page for user to post the query string and wait for query request. Then, *Result Filter* will look for the query result from *Result Cache*. If missing the expected information, then *Query Page Generator* will submit this request to ISS's mediator for searching new information and get the result through the *Result Aggregator*. The *Result Filter* thereat filters the results based

---

[1] It means the non-terminal vocabulary, such as "be" verb, auxiliary verb, pronoun, adverb, and prefix etc.

on the information of personal profile and filtering database and passes the filtered results to user. Once the user receives the results, *Feedback Mechanism* is activated to monitor the user's feedback.

When a user wants to visit the web page through *Result Display* page, the visiting process will physically link to server's CGI program that can log the visited history and redirect the visited URL to the web site. The recorded information just represents that the URLs are related. So that the situation to filter those irrelevant information are the user complete a review session after visit those related web pages and press the "Next Page" or "Back" bottom.

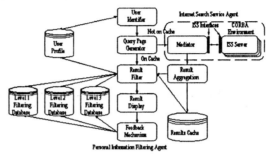

Figure 2. The detail architecture of supporting personalized search

3.4 Implementation and Performance Evaluation

Octopus's underlying system is run on two platforms (a SPARC and a Windows NT). The ORB of this system is IONA's Orbix 2.02, which is a full implementation of CORBA specification.

Table 1. The overhead of Octopus with personalized search in two representative search engines (sec)

# of Returned	20	40	60	80	100	120	140	160	180	200
AltaVista	4.88	6.84	7.27	12.82	16.47	18.78	21.1	25.27	26.07	37.02
A.V. Mediator	5.31	7.41	7.7	13.45	17.22	19.58	22.42	26.64	27.95	39.65
Overhead	0.43	0.57	0.57	0.63	0.75	0.8	1.32	1.37	1.88	2.63
Yahoo	1.37	2.91	4.71	6.31	10.05	14.18	17.91	21.1	25.45	38.94
Y. Mediator	1.74	3.38	5.07	6.81	10.47	14.58	18.42	21.64	25.95	39.65
Overhead	0.37	0.47	0.36	0.5	0.42	0.4	0.51	0.54	0.5	0.7

A new user must register his/her personal information. It also has to select the *filtering level* and *cutoff threshold* before issue the searching request. We performed some preliminary measurements to assess the overhead of Octopus system with personalized search function, as shown in table 1. There are two search engines used to assess the overhead of Octopus, Altavista and Yahoo respectively. The first row shows the number of returned item from the search engine. From the result, though the overhead of Internet is unpredictable in most of situations, it is obviously that our system is efficiency. The average of total overhead is about 6.5%. We believe that the major overhead are filtering the returned references and networking overhead of CORBA. But these operations are parallel execution, the overhead will not increase linearly, i.e., it will not rapidly increase with the number of search engines increase.

4. Discussions and Conclusions

In this paper, we have described the policy of supporting personalized search based on ISS. We also have implemented these functions into Octopus. In order to keep advantages of ISS, a personal information-filtering agent is added into the Octopus instead of modifying architecture or interface of ISS. In Octopus, an *absolutely irrelevant feedback approach* used to support the personalized search.

Many advantages of using the ISS to build a multi-search engine have been raised in [3]. There are other advantages that are discovered in the design. First, a personal information-filtering agent is added into the Octopus instead of modifying architecture of interface of ISS when adding personal functionality. We believe this design is more suitable to exploit useful data in the other application. Second, because the interface of ISS is based on the distributed object-oriented technique and the modules of personalized search are implemented as replaceable components. It is ease to replace these components when a new and more suitable algorithm is proposed. Third, each user with specific domain has individual profile in Octopus. It might avoid the Octopus return unsuitable results to users. Finally, because the filtering mechanism is divided into three levels, it can balance the load and the user requirement.

Reference:

1. Erik Selberg and Oren Etzioni, "The MetaCrawler architecture for resource aggregation on the Web", IEEE Expert, Jan.-Feb. 1997, pp.11-14
2. Daniel Dreilinger, Adele E. Howe, "Experiences with Selecting Search Engines Using Metasearch", ACM Transaction on Information System, Vol.15, No.3, July 1997, Pages 195-222.
3. Yue-Shan Chang, Shyan-Ming Yuan, Winston Lo, "A New Multi-Search Engine for querying Data through Internet Search Service on CORBA," Intl. J. of Computer Networks, Vol.34, No.3, Aug. 2000, pp.467-480.
4. Object Management Group, Inc. The Common Object request Broker (CORBA): Architecture and Specification, v2.0, November 1995.
5. Chia-Hui Chang, Ching-Chi Hsu, "Enabling Concept-Based Relevance Feedback for Information Retrieval on the WWW", IEEE Transactions on Knowledge and Data Engineering, Vol. 11, No. 4, July/August 1999, pp595-609.
6. Alexandros Moukas and Pattie Maes, "Amalthaea: An Evolving Multi-Agent Information Filtering and Discovery System for the WWW", Autonomous Agents and Multi-Agent System, Vol. 1, pp.59-88, 1998.
7. L. Ardissono, C. Barbero, A. Goy, G. Petrone, "An agent architecture for personalized Web stores", in Proc. of AGENT'99, pp. 182-189.
8. B. Y. Ricardo and R. N. Berthier, "Modern Information Retrieval", Addison Wesley, 1999.

A Case-Based Transformation
from HTML to XML
– An Extended Abstract –

Masayuki Umehara[1] and Koji Iwanuma[2]

[1] Graduate School of Electrical Engineering and Computer Science,
Yamanashi University,
4-3-11 Takeda, Kofu-shi, 400-8511, JAPAN
`mon@iw.media.yamanashi.ac.jp`
[2] Department of Computer Science and Media Engineering, Yamanashi University,
4-3-11 Takeda, Kofu-shi, 400-8511, JAPAN
`iwanuma@iw.media.yamanashi.ac.jp`

Abstract. Recently, a huge quantity of HTML documents have been created in Internet, which really constitute a treasury of information. HTML, however, is designed mainly for reading with browsers, and not suitable for machine processing, whereas XML was proposed as a solution for this problem. In this paper, we give a case-based transformation method from HTML documents to XML ones. There are many series of HTML pages in actual Web sites, and each page of a series usually has a quite similar structure with each other. Therefore a case-based transformation must be a promising method in practice for a semi-automatic transformation from HTML to XML. Throughout experimental evaluations, we show this case-based method achieved a highly accurate transformation, i.e., 85% of actual 80 pages can be transformed in a correct way, with this case-based method.

1 Introduction

In order to utilize a tremendous amount of information in Internet, machine processing of HTML documents has been becoming quite important. HTML, however, is designed mainly for reading with browsers, thus not suitable for machine processing. A wrapper is an information extraction technology for HTML, but it is difficult to automatically develop and maintain wrappers [8]. Recently XML was proposed as a solution for this problem [7, 13]. We are addressing the problem by transforming from HTML documents to XML ones. Unfortunately, full automatic transformation from HTML to XML is also extremely difficult, because it absolutely needs to understand the meaning of HTML documents. On the other hand, there are indeed many series of HTML pages in actual Web sites. Each page of a series usually has a quite similar structure with each other. Therefore a case-based transformation must be a promising method for such an HTML-page series in practice [9].

In this paper, we give a case-based transformation method from HTML documents to XML ones. The transformation method consists of two phases: a sample-analyzing phase and an XML-document-generating phase. Given a series of HTML documents and a sample transformation from an HTML document among the series into an XML document, the case-based method first analyses both of the syntactic and semantic features embedded in the sample transformation, and next automatically transforms the remaining HTML pages of the series into XML documents by using the information extracted from the sample. We adopt a vector model of term weighted frequency for approximating the meaning of HTML documents, and also use both of headlines and a parsing-tree as syntactical information.

The rest of this paper is structured as follows: Section 2 explains the sample-analyzing phase. Section 3 shows the generating phase of XML documents. Section 4 discusses our method throughout experimental evaluations with actual HTML documents collected from Internet, followed by some conclusions in section 5.

2 Analyzing a sample transformation

HTML documents are transformed into XML ones with a sample transformation. A given sample HTML document is called a *sample H-document* and a given sample XML document is called a *sample X-document*. The other HTML documents among a given series, which will be transformed into XML, are called *target H-documents*. For example, Fig. 1 depicts a sample pair of HTML and XML documents of a transformation, Fig. 2 shows a target H-document.

```
<HTML>
  <HEAD>
   <TITLE>Spa Guide</TITLE>
  </HEAD>
  <BODY>
   <H1>Shirahone spa</H1>
    <H2>Charge</H2>
     <P>500 yen</P>
    <H2>Business Hours</H2>
     <P>From 10:00 to 17:00</P>
  </BODY>
</HTML>
```

```
<!ELEMENT spa_guide
    (name, charge, business_hours)>
<!ELEMENT name (#PCDATA)>
<!ELEMENT charge (#PCDATA)>
<!ELEMENT business_hours
                    (#PCDATA)>

<spa_guide>
  <name>Shirahone spa</name>
  <charge>500 yen</charge>
  <business_hours>From 10:00 to
              17:00</business_hours>
</spa_guide>
```

Fig. 1. A sample pair: The left is a sample H-document. The right is a sample X-document.

```
<HTML>
  <HEAD>
   <TITLE>Spa Guide</TITLE>
  </HEAD>
  <BODY>
   <H1>Fefukigawa spa</H1>
    <H2>Charge</H2>
     <P>600 yen</P>
    <H2>Business Hours</H2>
     <P>From 10:00 to 19:00</P>
  </BODY>
</HTML>
```

Fig. 2. A target H-document.

In the sample-analyzing phase, we investigate some features of texts in a sample H-document and a relationship between a sample H-document and a transformed XML document.

2.1 Analyzing features of texts in a sample H-document

We divide the text part into several blocks. A *text block* is defined as a text part enclosed with a pair of HTML tags. Specially, text blocks in a sample H-document are called *s-blocks*.

For example, text blocks of an HTML document in Fig. 1 are "Spa Guide", "Shirahone spa", "Charge", and so on.

Next, we analyze each s-block on two aspects: syntactic structure and semantic information.

Analyzing syntactic features. We consider here the headlines embedded in a sample H-document and also uses the parsing-tree information. A *headline* is defined as an s-block which is enclosed with <H> tags in sample H-document. A *headline of an s-block B* is defined as a headline appearing immediately before *B*. A *parsing-tree path of an s-block B* is defined as a path from the root to *B* on an HTML parsing-tree.

For example, Fig. 3 is a parsing-tree of an HTML document shown in Fig. 1. Therefore, the s-block "500 yen" in Fig. 2 has the headline "Charge" and the parsing-tree path "HTML – BODY – P".

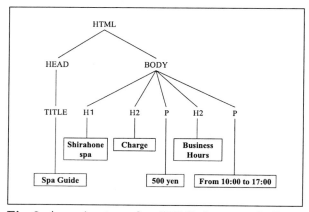

Fig. 3. A parsing-tree of an HTML document in Fig. 1.

Analyzing semantic features. We consider a term vector as the meaning of an s-block. A text block would be represented by a term vector of the form $V_d = (w_1, w_2, ..., w_n)$, where each w_i corresponds to the weight of the term i [3, 10]. We use WIDF (*Weighted Inverse Document Frequency*) [10, 11]. The WIDF weight of a term t in a s-block d is defined as follows:

$$\text{WIDF}(d, t) = \frac{\text{TF}(d, t)}{\sum_{i=1}^{N} \text{TF}(d_i, t)}, \tag{1}$$

where $\text{TF}(d, t)$ is the number of occurrences of the term t in the s-block d, and i ranges over s-blocks in the sample H-document.

2.2 Analyzing a relationship between HTML and XML documents in a sample pair

In a sample pair, each s-block in the sample H-document is embedded into the sample X-document, and is enclosed with a pair of XML tags. We call such a enclosing XML tag an *E-tag*. To analyze a relationship between a sample H-document and a X-document, we make up a table consisting of the correspondence relations between E-tags and the enclosed s-blocks.

3 Generating XML document

In the second phase, we generate an XML document from a target H-document by using the analysis result of a sample pair.

At first, we divide a target H-document into several text blocks, which are called *t-blocks*, and analyze features of each t-block with the same method as in analyzing s-blocks of a sample H-document.

Next, we generate a skeleton of an XML document according to the DTD data in a given sample X-document. Namely, we produce E-tags with a null text data if the DTD indicates that the E-tags should have a text content.[1] Otherwise we just produce XML tags, according to the definition in DTD.

For example, Fig. 4 is an XML skeleton generated from the DTD in a sample X-document in Fig. 1.

```
<spa_guide>
    <name>          </name>
    <charge>        </charge>
    <business_hours>        </business_hours>
</spa_guide>
```

Fig. 4. A generated skeleton of XML document according to the DTD in Fig. 1.

At last, we assign an optimal t-block to a null text column enclosed by E-tags in a generated XML skeleton. The optimal t-block for an E-tag is the t-block which is the most similar to an s-block enclosed with the E-tag in a given sample X-document.

We consider a synthetic similarity measure between two text blocks, which consists of syntactic and semantic measures.

3.1 Calculating similarity measure

We formalize a semantic similarity between two text blocks which would be obtained by comparison of the term vectors. We consider both of the *cosine* of the angle and the ratio of the length of two vectors. Thus, a semantic similarity between vectors V_i and V_j, $Sim(V_i, V_j)$ is defined as

$$Sim(V_i, V_j) = \frac{\sum_{k=1}^{n}(w_{ik} \times w_{jk})}{\sqrt{\sum_{k=1}^{n}(w_{ik})^2} \times \sqrt{\sum_{k=1}^{n}(w_{jk})^2}} \times \frac{\min(|V_i|, |V_j|)}{\max(|V_i|, |V_j|)}, \qquad (2)$$

where w_{ik} means the k-th element of the term vector V_i. The greater the value of $Sim(V_i, V_j)$ is, the greater the similarity between two text blocks is. Notice that $0 \leq Sim(V_i, V_j) \leq 1$.

Two text blocks can be regarded as more similar if the corresponding headlines and the parsing-tree paths are identical with each other. Thus, the *synthetic*

---

[1] At this point, we can not yet decide which t-block should be embedded in a text-data-column of an E-tag.

similarity between text blocks T_i and T_j, $S(T_i, T_j)$ is defined as

$$S(T_i, T_j) = \begin{cases} Sim(V_i, V_j) + \alpha + \beta & \text{if both of the headlines and the} \\ & \text{parsing-tree paths are identical} \\ & \text{with each other.} \\ Sim(V_i, V_j) + \alpha & \text{if only the headlines are identical.} \quad (3) \\ Sim(V_i, V_j) + \beta & \text{if only the parsing-tree paths are} \\ & \text{identical.} \\ Sim(V_i, V_j) & \text{otherwise.} \end{cases}$$

where V_i means the term vector of the text block T_i, and α and β are some constant numbers. Notice that $0 \leqq S(T_i, T_j) \leqq 1 + \alpha + \beta$.

For example, Fig. 5 shows a generated XML document from a HTML page in Fig. 2, where some appropriate t-blocks fill null text columns in the XML skeleton shown in Fig. 4.

```
<!ELEMENT spa_guide(name, charge, business_hours)>
<!ELEMENT name (#PCDATA)>
<!ELEMENT charge (#PCDATA)>
<!ELEMENT business_hours (#PCDATA)>
<spa_guide>
    <name>Fefukigawa spa</name>
    <charge>600 yen</charge>
    <business_hours>From 10:00 to 19:00 </business_hours>
</spa_guide>
```

Fig. 5. A generated XML document from a target H-document in Fig. 2.

4 Evaluations

This section describes some experiments to evaluate the performance of the case-based transformation method from HTML to XML. We tested the proposed case-based method with 80 actual HTML documents of 8 series. The *accuracy* is evaluated by

$$accuracy = a/b * 100, \tag{4}$$

where a is the number of text blocks which are enclosed with a pair of correct E-tags, b is the total number of text blocks in the generated XML document.

Results. Table 1 shows the results of the experiments, where *Series* is a name of a series of HTML documents, dn is the number of transformed target H-documents in a series, tn is an average of the number of terms appearing in each s-block.

We achieved a highly accurate transformation, i.e., 85% of actual 80 pages can be transformed in a correct way, with this case-based method.

5 Conclusions

We proposed a new case-based transformation method from HTML documents to XML ones. We used 80 actual HTML documents of 8 series for the experimental evaluation, which showed that the proposed method accomplished high accuracy. The case-based transformation should simplify the task of Internet information extraction, and is quite valuable for practical applications.

415

Table 1. A result of evaluation.

Series	dn	tn	average of b	average of a	average of accuracy
[4] (in Japanese)	4	12.6	5.0	4.8	95
[14] (in Japanese)	12	26.0	3.0	3.0	100
[5] (in Japanese)	4	35.6	8.0	7.8	97
[15] (in Japanese)	8	6.0	5.0	4.5	90
[4] (in Japanese)	5	25.6	10.0	8.0	80
[12] (in Japanese)	11	9.6	6.0	4.7	79
[2] (in Japanese)	8	26.7	3.0	2.1	71
[1] (in English)	20	2	4	5.0	80
[6] (in English)	8	14.6	8.0	7.1	89
TOTAL	80				85

As a future research, we are planing to extend the case-base transformation method in order to improve the accuracy. On the other hand, it is, unfortunately, impossible to avoid transformation errors completely within the case-based method. Therefore we are planing to develop on interactive editor for support the transformation.

Acknowledgements

This work was partially supported by Telecommunications Advancement Organization of Japan(TAO).

References

1. ACM Home Page: Calendar of Upcoming Events, http://www.acm.org/events/coe.html, 1999
2. Faculty of Engineering Yamanashi University: http://www-eng.yamanashi.ac.jp/teachers.html, 1999 (in Japanese)
3. G. Salton, M. J. McGill: *Introduction to Modern Information Retrieval*, McGraw-Hill, 1983
4. HotSpa Tour: http://www.iijnet.or.jp/act/hotspa/asasina/index.html, 1999 (in Japanese)
5. JTB: Guides Separated for Each Prefecture, Travel Japan Site, http://www.jtb.co.jp/TJsite/library/library.html, 1999 (in Japanese)
6. JTB: Guides Separated for Each Prefecture, Travel Japan Site, http://www.jtb.co.jp/TJsite/library/library_e.html, 2000
7. M. Murata, A. Momma, K. Arai: *Introduction XML*, Nihon Keizai Shimbun, Inc., 1998 (in Japanese)
8. Nicholas Kushmerick: Regression testing for wrapper maintenance, *AAAI-99*, pp. 74-79, 1999
9. S. Russell, P. Norvig: *Artificial Intelligence A Modern Approach*, Prentice-Hall, 1995
10. T. Tokunaga, M. Iwayama: Text Categorization based on Weighted Inverse Document Frequency, *Information Processing Society of Japan, NL*, 100-6, March 1994 33–40
11. Takenobu Tokunaga: *Information Retrieval and Natural Language Processing*, University of Tokyo Press, 1999 (in Japanese)
12. VECTOR SOFT LIBRARY: http://www.vector.co.jp/vpack/filearea/win/, 1999 (in Japanese)
13. XML/SGML salon: *Perfect Guide for Standard XML*, Gijyutsu-Hyoron Co, 1998 (in Japanese)
14. YAHOO! JAPAN NEWS: http://news.yahoo.co.jp/headlines/top/, 1999 (in Japanese)
15. Yamanashi sightseeing guide: http://www.pref.yamanashi.jp/shouko/kanko/kankou/index-j.html, 1999 (in Japanese)

Persistent DOM: An architecture for XML repositories in relational databases

Richard Edwards and Sian Hope

School of Informatics, University of Wales, Bangor,
Dean Street, Bangor, Gwynedd LL57 1UT, United Kingdom
email: rich@sees.bangor.ac.uk

Abstract. A generic architecture for the storage and retrieval of XML documents in relational databases is proposed. Documents are stored as node trees to facilitate retrieval and manipulation using an interface that conforms to the Document Object Model (DOM) specification of the World Wide Web Consortium (W3C). This approach offers many benefits, including the ability to leverage DOM programming techniques for the manipulation of XML documents that would otherwise be prohibitively large for persistence in memory.

1 Introduction

The Extensible Markup Language (XML) [1], a data formatting recommendation proposed by the W3C as a simplified form of the Standard Generalized Markup Language (SGML), is becoming the de facto standard for the platform-independent representation of information and its transfer between and within web-enabled applications.

XML is a meta-language that facilitates the creation and formatting of domain- or application-specific conceptual models and document markup languages in which the language elements (consisting of a start tag and an end tag, `<foo> ... </foo>`, or an empty tag, `<foo/>`) can be defined by Document Type Definitions (DTDs) or XML Schema Definitions (XSD) [2]. Alternatively, XML documents may be entirely self-describing.

XML documents that conform to the rules of XML mark-up are called "well-formed"; for example, each document must have a single top-level (root) element, and all tags must be correctly nested (for an example document see figure 1). A number of additional instructions are permitted, such as comments, processing instructions, unparsed character data and entity references. Tags can also contain attributes in the form of name and value pairs, with the values enclosed in quotation marks.

One essential aspect of XML is that it allows semantically-rich content to be abstracted away from the presentation layer afforded by languages such as Hyper Text Markup Language (HTML). Companion recommendations such as the Extensible Stylesheet Language (XSL) [4] allow information from XML files to be rendered into other text formats, including HTML for display on browser platforms, and other formats such as Rich Text Format (RTF) and LaTeX.

1.1   Node trees

Any well-formed XML document can be portrayed as a hierarchical node tree in which the nodes represent tag elements, text, or supporting information such as processing instructions and comments. Figure 1 shows an example XML document and figure 2 shows the corresponding node tree. The labelling of each

```
<wml>
  <card id="cFirst" title="First card" newcontext="true">
   <p align="center">
    <img src="/images/logo.wbmp" alt="Logo" align="middle"/>
    <br/> Welcome!
   </p>
   <p> <a href="#cSecond">Next card</a> </p>
  </card>
  <card id="cSecond" title="Second card">
   <p align="center"> Some content...</p>
  </card>
</wml>
```

Fig. 1. Sample XML

node with two numerical coordinates (designated x and y) by walking around the node tree from the root node, downwards and from left to right, provides simple algebraic methods of navigation, for example:

1. The next sibling (x', y') of any given node (x, y) has $x' = y + 1$.
2. The first child (x', y') of any given node (x, y) has $x' = x + 1$.
3. The set of nodes that originate from any given node (x, y) have $x < x' < y-1$.

1.2   The Document Object Model

The Document Object Model (DOM) proposed by the W3C [3] provides an application programming interface (API) for XML and HTML documents. The model defines a logical structure for such documents, and the API facilitates document access and manipulation. A DOM object internalises an XML (or HTML) document as a node tree, and exposes methods for the creation, retrieval and manipulation of its nodes. On completion of processing, the DOM object can be serialised as XML.

1.3   Parsing XML

There are two XML parsing approaches in common usage; one involves an event-based model and the other a compilation model. In the compilation method the XML document is encapsulated as a DOM object, providing rich functionality through the methods of the DOM API, but with limitations commensurate with

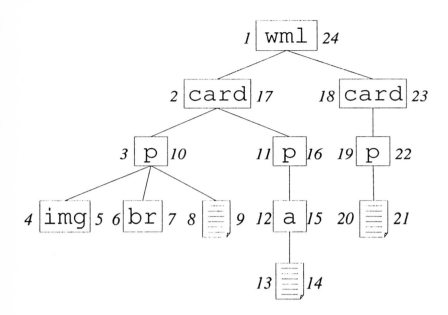

Fig. 2. Sample XML document represented as a node tree

the amount of available memory and the CPU-intensive nature of this approach. In practice, documents with a size in excess of more than a couple of megabytes can become unwieldy and impractical. This is a significant problem for real-world applications handling non-trivial data files.

The event-based model, the Simple API for XML (SAX), offers an alternative that does not have the same limitation regarding large documents, but may provide less functionality for the application developer. SAX uses a serial-access mechanism with element-by-element processing. The XML document is scanned in a sequential fashion and key events (such as an element being encountered) trigger callback methods. Serial access allows for any size of file, but does not provide the same immediacy of contextual information as DOM encapsulation affords.

Both parsing approaches can optionally include validation of the supplied XML against a DTD or XSD. At the very least, they must ensure that the supplied document is well-formed.

2 XML and Databases

XML documents are generally considered as belonging to one of two categories; data-centric and document-centric [5, 6]. Typically, data-centric XML documents contain structured information (of varying types) extracted from databases and other conventional data sources. In contrast, document-centric XML documents use XML markup to add semantics to irregularly structured text-based information. These distinctions are not rigid, and XML documents that display the characteristics of both are increasingly common.

A number of technologies for storing XML documents are currently available. Many database vendors offer some degree of XML support in the latest releases of their products, although these solutions are not yet mature, and either store XML documents as single entities, or require the user to map their schemas to specific database tables. "Native XML" databases (which can store any well-formed XML document without recourse to restructuring them to suit a different underlying storage model) are in the early stages of commercial release, although at the time of writing, these systems are restricted in terms of the hardware platforms they support and may also be prohibitively expensive.

A suitable compromise for many organisations will be to extend their current storage solutions to accommodate XML, in order to leverage the stability and scalability of their existing platforms and take advantage of their in-house expertise. Relational databases are a particular case in point, not least because organisations may wish to link information from relational sources into XML documents.

A number of studies have proposed strategies for storing XML data in relational databases; see, for example, [7, 8]. Florescu and Kossmann measured query performance for a variety of mapping schemes, in which XML data is modelled as edge-labelled graphs; for the purposes of their study it was not necessary to maintain the distinction between attributes and sub-elements. Their models were designed to maximise query performance, with less emphasis on facilitating efficient updates and serialisation of whole documents.

Our proposed architecture can accommodate data from any well-formed XML document, even if schema information is not available, and maintains the distinction between attributes and sub-elements. The architecture facilitates programmatic traversal and manipulation of XML node trees through an API that exposes methods which conform to the DOM recommendation of the W3C.

2.1   Persistent DOM (pDOM)

This section outlines our XML repository architecture. Document loading is achieved in two stages using a SAX parser. The first pass ensures the XML is well-formed prior to any database activity. The second pass involves the following activities:

1. A logical database transaction is commenced. The document loading process is undertaken as a single transaction to ensure that is succeeds or fails as a single unit.
2. Stored procedures in the database are invoked to insert data into the appropriate tables.
3. Upon successful completion, the transaction is committed.

The first action of the parser-instantiated database transaction is an insert to the doc table. The document is given an arbitrary numerical identifier doc_id, which is stored along with the URI of the source document and some version control information.

Node identifiers (an arbitrary node_id plus the x and y indices), the node type, the depth of the node in the tree, and a pointer to the x value of the node's nearest neighbours are stored in the node table. Element names and text are stored in node_leaf (namespaces are stored separately in node_namespace_leaf). Attribute information, namespace, name and value are stored in the four tables with names prefixed with attribute_

In the tables suffixed with leaf_, the leaf_text field has a varchar(255) datatype. Although many RDBMS platforms support longer varchar fields, even free text objects, the 255 byte character field represents the "lowest common denominator". Since XML element and attribute names, namespaces, values and text can exceed 255 characters, there is a paging mechanism; data is broken up into a linked list of 255 character pages (each identified by a sequential leaf_id). A full listing of tables and columns is provided in table 1.

Table 1. XML repository tables; primary key columns are indicated by *.

Static tables (column list...)
node_type (node_type_id*, description, left_delimiter, right_delimiter)

Dynamic tables (column list...)
doc (doc_id*, root_node_id, source, date_loaded, contributor_id)
node (node_id*, x_index, y_index, node_type, owner_doc_id, depth, parent_node_id, prev_sibling_node_id, next_sibling_node_id, first_child_node_id, node_size)
element_namespace_leaf (node_id*, leaf_id*, leaf_text)
element_name_leaf (node_id*, leaf_id*, leaf_text)
attribute (node_id*, attribute_id*)
attribute_namespace_leaf (node_id*, attribute_id*, leaf_id*, leaf_text)
attribute_name_leaf (node_id*, attribute_id*, leaf_id*, leaf_text)
attribute_value_leaf (node_id*, attribute_id*, leaf_id*, leaf_text)
text_leaf (node_id*, leaf_id*, leaf_text)
comment_leaf (node_id*, leaf_id*, leaf_text)
entity_reference_leaf (node_id*, leaf_id*, leaf_text)
pi_data_leaf (node_id*, leaf_id*, leaf_text)
pi_target_leaf (node_id*, leaf_id*, leaf_text)

To facilitate programmatic access to documents stored in the repository (or components thereof), a pDOM Java class has been developed. A pDOM object connects to the repository when it is instantiated, and disconnects when it is destroyed. The pDOM API provides DOM-compliant methods; the methods address nodes in the repository database, whereas DOM parser methods typically address nodes in memory. The pDOM API will allow system developers to scale up DOM-based solutions simply by loading documents into the repository and instantiating pDOM objects instead.

2.2 Current and further work

Current work is focussed on the following issues:

1. Performance enhancements, including improved text storage capabilities, and strategies for priming the RDBMS cache with nearest-neighbour nodes.
2. Methods for handling concurrent document manipulation.
3. Standards-based querying capabilities.
4. Server-side code using XSL transformations (XSLT) to convert XML data from the repository into other formats.
5. Validation of documents with DTDs and XSDs stored in the same (or companion) repositories.

3 Acknowledgements

The authors would like to thank Mike Malloch (Know-Net) and Tony Eastwood (PrismTechnologies) for useful discussions, and Stef Ghazzali for trialling the repository.

References

1. W3C: Extensible Markup Language (XML) Version 1.0. http://www.w3.org/TR/1998/REC-xml-19980210 (1998)
2. W3C: XML Schema. http://www.w3.org/XML/Schema.html (2000)
3. W3C: Document Object Model (DOM) Level 2 Specification. http://www.w3.org/TR/DOM-Level-2 (2000)
4. W3C: XSL Transformations (XSLT) Version 1.0. http://www.w3.org/TR/xslt-19991116 (1999)
5. Abiteboul, S., Buneman, P., Suciu, D.: Data on the Web: From Relations to Semistructured Data and XML. Morgan Kaufmann Publishers (2000)
6. Bourret, R. P.: XML Database Products. http://www.rpbourret.com/xml/ (2000)
7. Florescu, D., Kossmann, D.: Storing and Querying XML Data using an RDBMS. Bulletin of the Technical Committee on Data Engineering, **22**(3) (1999) 27–34
8. Zhang, X., Lee, W. C., Mitchell, G.: Metadata-Driven Approach to Integrating XML and Relational Data. http://davis.wpi.edu/dsrg/xmlrdbms/summer-2000/archive/GTE-paper.ps (2000)

E.

MULTIMEDIA
PROCESSING

Automatic News Video Caption Extraction and Recognition

Xinbo Gao and Xiaoou Tang

Department of Information Engineering
The Chinese University of Hong Kong
Shatin, Hong Kong
{xgao, xtang}@ie.cuhk.edu.hk

Abstract. Caption graphically superimposed in news video frames can provide important indexing information. The automatic extraction and recognition of news captions can be of great help in querying topics of interest in a digital news video library. To develop such a system for Chinese news video, we present algorithms for detection, extraction, binarization and recognition of Chinese video captions. Experimental results show that our caption processing scheme is effective and robust and significantly improves video caption OCR results.

1 Introduction

The ongoing proliferation of digital image and video databases has led to an increasing demand for systems that can query and search large video databases efficiently and accurately. Manual annotation of video is extremely time-consuming, expensive, and unscalable [1]. Therefore, automatic extraction of video descriptions is desirable in order to annotate and search large video databases. Text present in video frames is a valuable description of video content information. Automatic extraction and recognition of video text can provide an efficient approach to systematically label and annotate video content.

The automatic extraction of caption text in the video frames has attracted much attention in content-based information retrieval. Some practical systems have been constructed for VOD [2–4]. However, current research almost exclusively focuses on extraction and recognition of English texts. Little work can be found on Chinese characters, which has very unique structures compared to English characters. In this paper, we use Chinese news video as a test-bed to address the problem of Chinese caption extraction and recognition.

Compared with OCR from document images, caption extraction and recognition in video presents several new challenges [3]. First, the caption in a video frame is often embedded in complex backgrounds, making caption extraction and separation difficult. The second problem is low resolution of the characters, since most video caption characters are made fairly small to avoid occluding interesting objects in the frame. Lastly, the low resolution character image is further degraded by lossy compression scheme typically used for video compression.

With these problems in mind, we have designed a system for extraction and recognition of Chinese caption in news video programs. The system consists

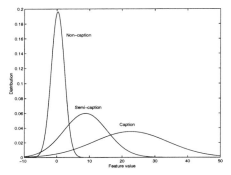

Fig. 1. The partition of a frame.   **Fig. 2.** The distribution of blocks.

of four modules, caption detection, caption extraction, character binarization, and Chinese OCR. We use the news program of Hong Kong to evaluate the performance of our system.

2 Caption Detection

According to a priori knowledge of news video, the captions always position in the center of the screen. We need only look at the central section of the video frame to detect whether a caption line appears. For the news video of Hong Kong TVB station, each frame is digitized to 288×352 pixels and the size of the character ranges from 14×14 to 20×20 pixels. To detect whether a caption line exists in the central part of the frame, we first divide the central section of the frame into 24 blocks as shown in Fig.1. Let the central part of each frame for a given video sequence denoted by $F_t, t = 1, 2, \cdots, T$, each block is represented as $B_t^i, i = 1, 2, \cdots, 24$. The task is then trying to find the blocks that contain caption text.

Chinese characters primarily consist of four types of basic strokes, *i.e.*, horizontal stroke, vertical stroke, up-right-slanting and up-left-slanting stroke [4]. These stroke segments contain rich high frequency energy in the four directions. To extract the directional frequency information in each block, we use a single-level wavelet transform to decompose the image segment into four directional components. They provide approximation to the original image block and the details in horizontal, vertical and diagonal directions. We use the Haar wavelets since they are computationally efficient and are suitable for local detection of line segment [2].

For each smoothed block $B_t^i, i = 1, 2, \cdots, n$ of a given video frame, the single-level Haar wavelet decomposes the image into four subbands,

$$W_H : B_t^i \rightarrow \begin{pmatrix} A_t^i(u,v) & H_t^i(u,v) \\ V_t^i(u,v) & D_t^i(u,v) \end{pmatrix} \tag{1}$$

where $A_t^i(u,v)$ is the approximation of the block image $B_t^i(x,y)$, and H_t^i, V_t^i and D_t^i are the details of the image in horizontal, vertical and diagonal directions respectively. For each $M \times N$ subband image, we calculate the average energy as the feature value,

$$E_t^i(d) = \frac{4}{M \times N} \sum_u \sum_v (d_t^i(u,v))^2, \qquad d \in \{H, V, D\} \tag{2}$$

In addition, we also compute the conventional edge feature $E_t^i(B)$ directly from the binary edge map of the original block B_t^i. $E_t^i(B)$ is calculated by counting the edge pixel number of the edge map.

Since the caption regions contain line strokes in all the four directions, they have large values for all the features simultaneously. While, for the background blocks, only a subset of the features has relatively large values, indicating certain edge like structures in a particular direction. To obtain a more stable and distinguishable feature, we integrate the four features into a single feature by the multiplication of the four features,

$$\eta_t^i = \prod_{d \in \{H, V, D, B\}} E_t^i(d), \qquad i = 1, 2, \cdots, n, \ t = 1, 2, \cdots, T \tag{3}$$

After selecting the features, we use a simple second order statistical classifier to identify the caption blocks. Let the caption block and non-caption block denoted by Φ_c and Φ_n respectively, a given block B_t^i with feature value η_t^i is classified as Φ_c or Φ_n according to the following rule,

$$\Re : B_t^i \rightarrow \begin{cases} \Phi_c & \text{if } \|\eta_t^i - \mu_c\|/\sigma_c \leq \|\eta_t^i - \mu_n\|/\sigma_n \\ \Phi_n & \text{if } \|\eta_t^i - \mu_c\|/\sigma_c > \|\eta_t^i - \mu_n\|/\sigma_n \end{cases} \tag{4}$$

where μ_c and μ_n are the means and σ_c and σ_n are the variances of the two categories, and $\|\cdot\|$ is a certain norm.

Since we do not assume to know the exact location and height of the caption line, the block height is chosen to be small enough that at least one block is fully occupied by captions. Some blocks straddle between caption lines and non-caption space. We put these blocks in a new category, semi-caption category Φ_s. Therefore we have three categories. With 7200 training blocks, we obtain the sample distribution of three categories as shown in Fig.2. The blocks labeled as semi-caption and caption will form the potential caption regions.

3   Caption Extraction

After the caption and semi-caption blocks are identified, they are merged into caption regions. The next step is to locate and separate caption lines and individual characters.

In traditional document OCR, the text lines are separated by horizontal projections. However, this technique is not suitable for video captions, since a video frame usually contains very complex background. To reduce the influence of the complex background, we use a set of mathematical morphology operations

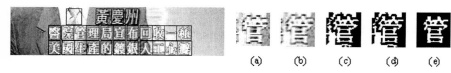

Fig. 3. The located characters.

Fig. 4. An example of character binarization.

to detect the contour of the characters. Assuming that a binarized caption image is denoted by R_c, the contour map of R_c is extracted by

$$e(R_c) = R_c - R_c \circ S, \qquad R_c \circ S = (R_c \ominus S) \oplus S \qquad (5)$$

where S is an isotropic structuring element, $R_c \circ S$ is opening of R_c by S, which is defined by an erosion operator followed by a dilation operator. A smoothing filter is first applied on the contour map to eliminate extraneous fragments and to connect broken character segments. Then a simple threshold can locate caption boundaries in the horizontal projection of the smoothed image.

For the obtained caption line, a vertical projection can be used to locate the individual characters. However, it is difficult to select a proper threshold to locate all the characters. A high threshold will lead to character loss, while a low threshold will lead to character merging. Our strategy is first to guarantee the low character loss rate, then to re-segment the merged characters with heuristic rules. Fig.3 shows the located characters marked with boxes. We see that except a false character, all the characters are located exactly. The false character will be excluded in the recognition step.

4 Character Binarization

Although we have obtained the individual characters, they can not be fed into an OCR classifier directly, since the extreme low resolution is insufficient for recognition and the character is still blended with a complex background. Before separating the character from the background, we first increase the resolution of the character image by a factor of four through interpolation. Even though this does not add new information to the gray scale image, it does help to smooth the characters in the binary image.

We show the character binarization steps through an example character shown in Fig.4. Fig.4 (a) gives a typical character in a non-uniform background. Using a spline interpolation function, we obtain the image with higher resolution in (b). We then binarize the interpolated image with a fixed threshold to get the binary image in (c). Apparently, some background regions still remain in the binary image. Fortunately, a bright character on a bright background always has a black profile around it to help the audience to read the character. Based on this observation, a region connectivity analysis scheme is proposed to eliminate the remaining background residues.

Because of background noise the character often connects the background residues with small bridges even though there is a black profile around the character. To break the bridges across the character and the background, we adopt a set of morphological processing techniques, the opening operation and H-break operation. The opening eliminates small noise particles, while preserves the global shape of the objects. The H-break operation mainly eliminates the H-connected pixels. Both of them are effective in cutting off the connection between the character and the background.

After the morphological operations, we label all the connected-components in the binary image. We then remove a connected component that is too small in size. If a connected component connects the periphery of the character image, it is also declared as background and filtered out. Through these processes, we finally obtain the binary character with clear background shown in Fig.4(e).

Since there exist several successful commercial OCR packages, we do not intend to implement a new OCR system. After a clear binary character is extracted from the video frame, we use the OCR classifier, TH-OCR LV, for final character recognition. Our purpose is to test whether our character extraction methods can efficiently obtain binary characters clear enough for regular printed optical character recognition.

5   Experimental Results

We evaluate the system using the TVB news programs aired by the Hong Kong Jade station. Video data is encoded in MPEG1 format at 288×352 resolution. Three 30-mintue programs are used in the experiments.

Evaluation of caption detection: Through the training process, we first get the parameters of classifier, then classify 1272 test image blocks. The obtained confusion matrix for the caption detection is shown in Table 1. The results are very good in terms of separating non-caption from caption and semi-caption parts, which is the main purpose of this classification.

	Φ_n	Φ_s	Φ_c
Non-caption	94.72%	5.28%	0%
Semi-caption	0%	88.66%	11.34%
Caption	0%	0%	100%

Candidate	With Pp	Without Pp
1	86.11%	15.27%
2	90.27%	18.75%
3	92.36%	20.83%

Table 1. The confusion matrix of caption detection.

Table 2. The OCR results with and without preprocessing.

Evaluation of caption extraction: The second data set is used to evaluate the caption extraction. The caption extraction includes the caption line separation and individual character separation. We get the *precision* rate of 93% for all the extracted characters. Although some false characters are extracted they can be further excluded by the following OCR procedure. Fig.5(a) presents an example of the characters extracted from news video. Looking at the 4 false characters, we find that they often have similar features as real characters.

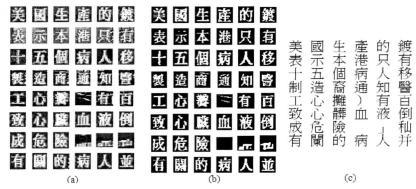

Fig. 5. An example of extraction, binarization and recognition of video characters.

Evaluation of character binarization and OCR: Using our algorithms, we binarize the extracted individual character from the complex background. An example is shown in Fig.5(b). Although several small strokes in some characters are lost in the process, most characters are correctly binarized. Finally, we obtain average recognition rate of 15% for characters without any preprocessing and 86% for the binary characters extracted using our algorithms. Fig.5(c) shows an example of recognition result. Table 2 shows the comparison between with and without our preprocessing for the correct rates of first one, two and three candidates. The results show that the preprocessing improves the correct recognition rate significantly.

6   Conclusion

We have presented an effective Chinese caption processing system. Overall OCR rate is improved significantly through our processing scheme. With this system, one can realize the automatic annotation of news video and provide indexing text file for a news retrieval system. Accurate video OCR is valuable not only for conventional video libraries, but also for other new types of video content understanding applications, such as matching faces to names and identifying advertisements.

References

[1] Shim J.C., Dorai C., Bolle R.: Automatic text extraction from video for content-based annotation and retrieval. In Proc. of ICPR'98 (1998) 618–620.

[2] Li H.P., Doemann D., and Kia O.: Automatic text detection and tracking in digital video. IEEE Trans. on Image Processing, **9(1)** (2000) 147–156.

[3] Sato T., Kanade T., *et. al.*: Video OCR: Indexing digital news libraries by recognition of superimposed captions. ACM Multimedia Systems, Special Issue on Video Libraries (1998) 1–11.

[4] Ariki Y., Matsuura K., and Takao S.: Telop and flip frame detection and character extraction from TV news articles. In Proc. of ICDAR'99 (1999) 701–704.

Advanced Multilevel Successive Elimination Algorithms For Motion Estimation in Video Coding

Soo-Mok Jung, Sung-Chul Shin, Hyunki Baik, Myong-Soon Park

Internet Computing Laboratory,

Department of Computer Science and Engineering Korea University,

An-Am Dong, Sung-Buk Gu, Seoul, 136-701, Korea

{jsm, scshin, gibson, myongsp}@iLab.korea.ac.kr

Abstract. In this paper, we present advanced algorithms to reduce the computation cost of block matching algorithms for motion estimation in video coding. Advanced Multilevel Successive Elimination Algorithms are based on Multilevel Successive Elimination Algorithm for Block Matching Motion Estimation [1] and Successive Elimination Algorithm [2]. Advanced Multilevel Successive Elimination Algorithms consist of three algorithms. The second algorithm is useful not only for Multilevel Successive Elimination Algorithm but also for all kinds of block matching algorithms. The efficiency of the proposed algorithms was verified by experimental results.

1   Introduction

There is considerable temporal redundancy in consecutive video frames. Motion estimation and compensation techniques have been widely used in image sequence coding schemes to remove temporal redundancy. The accuracy and efficiency of motion estimation affects the efficiency of temporal redundancy removal.

Motion estimation methods are classified into two classes of block matching algorithms (BMA)[3] and pel-recursive algorithms (PRA)[4]. Due to their implementation simplicity, block matching algorithms have been widely adopted by various video coding standards such as CCITT H.261, ITU-T H.263, and MPEG. In BMA, the current image frame is partitioned into fixed-size rectangular blocks. The motion vector for each block is estimated by finding the best matching block of pixels within the search window in the previous frame according to matching criteria.

Although Full Search (FS) algorithm finds the optimal motion vector by searching exhaustively for the best matching block within the search window, its high computation cost limits its practical applications. To reduce computation cost of FS, many fast block matching algorithms such as three step search, 2-D log search, orthogonal search, cross search, one-dimensional full search, variation of three-step search, unrestricted center-biased diamond search, and circular zonal search have been developed. As described in [5], these algorithms rely on the assumption that the motion-compensated residual error surface is a convex function of the displacement motion vectors, but this assumption is rarely true [6]. Therefore, the best match obtained by these fast algorithms is basically a local optimum. In other words, most fast algorithms reduce computation cost at the expense of the accuracy of the motion estimation.

Without this convexity assumption, Successive Elimination Algorithm (SEA) proposed by Li and Salari [2] reduces the computation cost of the FS. To reduce the computation cost of SEA, X. Q. Gao etc. proposed Multilevel Successive Elimination Algorithm (MSEA) [1]. This paper presents Advanced Multilevel Successive Elimination Algorithms (AMSEA). The motion estimation accuracy of AMSEA is identical to that of FS and the computation cost of MSEA is reduced by using AMSEA.

2   Multilevel Successive Elimination Algorithm

Let $f_c(i,j)$ and $f_p(i,j)$ denote the intensity of the pixel with coordinate (i,j) in the current frame and the previous frame respectively. Assume that the size of a block (Y component of the macro block in H.263) is NxN pixels, the search window size is $(2M+1)x(2M+1)$ pixels, and the matching criteria function is Sum of Absolute Difference (SAD) which is the distortion between two blocks. Let $\mathbf{B}_c^{(i,j)}$ and $\mathbf{B}_p^{(i,j,x,y)}$ denote the target block and compared block in the current frame and the previous frame with the top left corners at (i,j) and $(i-x, j-y)$ respectively. $\mathbf{B}_c^{(i,j)}$ is the target block which requires motion vector.

$$\mathbf{B}_c^{(i,j)}(m,n)= f_c(i+m, j+n) \qquad (1)$$

$$\mathbf{B}_p^{(i,j,x,y)}(m,n) = f_p(i-x+m, j-y+n) \qquad (2)$$

where x and y represent two components of a candidate motion vector, $-M \leq (x,y) \leq M$ and $0 \leq (m,n) \leq N-1$. The SAD between the two blocks is defined as:

$$SAD(x,y) = \sum_{m=0}^{N-1} \sum_{n=0}^{N-1} | \mathbf{B}_c^{(i,j)}(m,n) - \mathbf{B}_p^{(i,j,x,y)}(m,n) | \qquad (3)$$

The goal of motion estimation is to find the best pair of indices (x,y) so that the following sum of absolute difference is minimized, as follows:

$$d = \min_{x,y} SAD(x,y) \qquad (4)$$

Applying mathematical inequality $| \, \|\mathbf{X}\|_1 - \|\mathbf{Y}\|_1 \, | \leq \|\mathbf{X} - \mathbf{Y}\|_1$ [7] for $\mathbf{X}= \mathbf{B}_c^{(i,j)}$ and $\mathbf{Y}= \mathbf{B}_p^{(i,j,x,y)}$ gives

$$| R - M(x,y) | \leq SAD(x,y) \qquad (5)$$

where, $R = \|\mathbf{B}_c^{(i,j)}\|_1 = \sum_{m} \sum_{n}^{N-1\,N-1} \mathbf{B}_c^{(i,j)}(m,n)$, $\qquad M(x,y) = \|\mathbf{B}_p^{(i,j,x,y)}\|_1 = \sum_{m} \sum_{n}^{N-1\,N-1} \mathbf{B}_p^{(i,j,x,y)}(m,n)$,

$$SAD(x,y) = \|\mathbf{B}_c^{(i,j)} - \mathbf{B}_p^{(i,j,x,y)}\|_1 = \sum_{m} \sum_{n}^{N-1\,N-1} |\mathbf{B}_c^{(i,j)}(m,n) - \mathbf{B}_p^{(i,j,x,y)}(m,n)|$$

R and M(x,y) are sum norms and are pre-computed using the efficient procedure described in [1].

In MSEA, each block is partitioned into several sub-blocks. First, the block is partitioned into four sub-blocks with size N/2 x N/2. Then each sub-block is partitioned into four sub-blocks with size N/4 x N/4. This procedure can be repeated until the size of the sub-blocks become 2x2. The maximum level of such partition is $L_{max}=\log_2^N-1$ for the blocks with size N x N. The MSEA with L-level partition, $0 \leq L \leq L_{max}$, is called L-level MSEA, and the SEA[2] corresponds to the 0-level MSEA.

At lth level of the L-level partition, where $0 \leq l \leq L$, the number of the sub-blocks is $S_l= 2^{2l}$, and each sub-block is of size N_l x N_l, where $N_l = N/2^l$. If we denote

$$SAD\_SB_l = \sum_{u=0}^{2^l-1} \sum_{v=0}^{2^l-1} |R_l^{(u,v)} - M_l^{(u,v)}(x,y)| \tag{6}$$

where $R_l^{(u,v)} = \sum_{m=0}^{N_l-1} \sum_{n=0}^{N_l-1} \mathbf{B}_c(m+uN_l, n+vN_l), \quad M_l^{(u,v)}(x,y) = \sum_{m=0}^{N_l-1} \sum_{n=0}^{N_l-1} \mathbf{B}_p(m+uN_l, n+vN_l)$

[1] shows that equation (5) can be expressed as equation (7) for L-level MSEA.

$$SAD\_SB_0 = |R\text{-}M(x,y)| \leq \ldots \leq SAD\_SB_{l-1} \leq SAD\_SB_l \leq \ldots \leq SAD(x,y) \tag{7}$$

where $0 \leq l \leq L$.

L-level MSEA procedure is as follows:

1   select initial candidate motion vector within the search window in the previous frame.

2   calculate SAD at the selected point, current minimum SAD(curr_min_SAD) = SAD

3   select another candidate motion vector among the rest of the search points

4.0 calculate the SAD_SB_0 at the selected search point

    if (curr_min_SAD $\leq$ SAD_SB_0) goto 7

4.1 calculate the SAD_SB_1 at the selected search point

• if (curr_min_SAD $\leq$ SAD_SB_1) goto 7

•

4.L calculate the SAD_SB_L at the selected search point

    if (curr_min_SAD $\leq$ SAD_SB_L) goto 7

5   calculate the SAD at the selected search point

    if (curr_min_SAD $\leq$ SAD) goto 7

6   curr_min_SAD=SAD

7   if (all the search points in the search window are not tested?)   goto 3

8   minimum SAD=curr_min_SAD, calculate motion vector

The MSEA speeds up the process of finding the motion vector by eliminating hierarchically impossible candidate motion vectors in the search window before their SAD calculation.

3   *Proposed* Advanced Multilevel Successive Elimination Algorithms

3.1 Further Computational Reduction

Partial distortion elimination (PDE) [8] is an effective speedup technique used in vector quantization to find the best reconstruction vector from a set of vector code-words. PDE technique in SAD calculation is the strategy employed in the full search performed in the Telenor implementation of Test Model 1.4a distributed as part of the H.263 standardization effort.

In MSEA, PDE technique was used in SAD calculation. But, PDE technique was not used in SAD_SB_l calculation. So, PDE technique can be used with the L-level MSEA to reduce the computations further where SAD_SB_l must be computed. In equation (6), if at any sub-blocks the partially evaluated sum exceeds the current minimum SAD, the point (x,y) cannot be the optimum motion vector and the remainder of the sum does not need to be calculated. We denote our PDE technique used in SAD_SB_l calculation as PDE_{sb} to differentiate from PDE technique used in SAD calculation (symbolized: PDEsad). While it is not efficient to test the partial sum against the current minimum SAD every time an additional term is added, a reasonable compromise is to perform the test after each sub-block row as shown in table 1. In 3-level MSEA, a block consists of 8 sub-block rows and each sub-block row consists of 8 sub-blocks. So, 8 times PDE test is executed in SAD_SB_3 calculation.

The standard video sequence, "salesman.qcif", was used in experiment and we tested 100 frames of the sequence. The block size was 16x16 pixels (N=16). The size of search window was 31x31 pixels (M=15) and only integer values for the motion vectors were considered. All our experiments (3.1, 3.2, 3.3) were executed under these conditions.

Experimental results are shown in table 1 and table2. In table 1, "x row" means that the PDE_{sb} test is executed at each x-th sub-block row and simple notation $MSEA_L$ means L-level MSEA. In tables, "m.e." means matching evaluation that require SAD calculation, "avg. # of rows" means the number of calculated row in SAD calculation before partial distortion elimination. Overhead(in rows) is the sum of all the computations such as the sum norm computations by using the efficient method described in [1], the computations of step 4, the computations of PDE_{sb} etc. but except for SAD calculation. In tables, "in rows" means that the computations are represented in order of 1 row SAD computations.   It is important to notice that with the MSEA, the efficiency of the procedure depends on the order in which the candidate motion vectors are searched, and that the most likely candidates should be tested first. This eliminates the maximum number of candidates. In our experiment, we used spiral search pattern to find the motion vector.

The method MSEA+PDE$_{sb}$, which incorporates the MSEA with PDE$_{sb}$, reduces the computations of MSEA by 0.4%, 2.8%, 6.2% for MSEA$_1$, MSEA$_2$, and MSEA$_3$ respectively for this fairly large search window.

Table 1. Computations of the MSEA$_3$+PDE$_{sb}$ for several PDE$_{sb}$ test points

Algorithm	Avg. # of m.e./frame	Avg. # of rows/m.e.	Overhead (in rows)	Total (in rows)
MSEA$_3$+PDE$_{sb}$ (1 row)	242.3	14.39	27,479.6	30,966.3
MSEA$_3$+PDE$_{sb}$(2 row)	242.3	14.39	27,719.9	31,206.6
MSEA$_3$+PDE$_{sb}$(4 row)	242.3	14.39	28,277.9	31,764.6

Table 2. Computations of the FS algorithm and MSEA with PDE$_{sb}$

Algorithm	Avg. # of m.e./frame	Avg. # of rows/m.e.	Overhead (in rows)	Total (in rows)	Computations reduction
FS	77,439.0	16.00	0.00	1,239,024.0	
FS+PDEsad	77,439.0	4.36	6135.0	343,596.8	
MSEA$_0$(SEA)	24,995.6	5.79	8653.9	153,378.4	
MSEA$_1$	8,769.7	7.84	14,851.5	83,605.9	
MSEA$_1$+PDE$_{sb}$	8,769.7	7.84	14,530.3	83,284.7	0.4%
MSEA$_2$	1,589.1	10.33	23,552.8	39,968.2	
MSEA$_2$+PDE$_{sb}$	1589.1	10.33	22,434.5	38,849.9	2.8%
MSEA$_3$	242.3	14.39	29,510.6	32,997.3	
MSEA$_3$+PDE$_{sb}$	242.3	14.39	27,479.6	30,966.3	6.2%

3.2   Adaptive SAD Calculation

SAD calculation requires very intensive computations. SAD calculation must be done at many matching evaluation points per frame as shown in table 2. To find the method reducing the computations of SAD calculation, we investigated absolute difference values of $|\mathbf{B}_c^{(i,j)}(m,n) - \mathbf{B}_p^{(i,j,x,y)}(m,n)|$ for $0 \le m,n \le N-1$. There are 256 absolute difference values at each block. These values range from 0 to maximum pixel intensity value. One outstanding feature is that large absolute difference vales are centered together. This property is shown in table 3. If we calculate SAD from large absolute difference vales to small absolute difference values, partial distortion elimination in SAD calculation can be done very early. So, the computations of SAD calculation can be reduced.

To calculate SAD adaptively for each block, we divided each block into 4 sub-blocks with size of 8x8 pixels and sampled 8 points at each sub-block and calculated the sum of absolute difference for the sampled pixels for each sub block as shown in Fig. 1. Sampling points at each sub-block must be chosen to represent the SAD of its sub-blocks. The sum of sampled absolute difference values at each sub-blocks are sorted to determine the order of sub-blocks to be used in SAD calculation. First of all, we calculated SAD at the sub-block of which the sum of sampled absolute difference values is greatest, and then we calculated SAD at the sub-blocks following the ordered sequence.

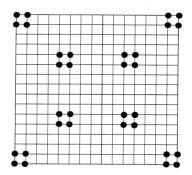

Fig. 1. Block division and sampling

As maximum to minimum SAD ratio increases, the partial distortion elimination is achieved early in Adaptive SAD Calculation algorithm. Table 3 shows that a considerable portion of the blocks have a ratio that is very large. The total blocks of table 3 that are checked for 100 frames are 7,734,000. Adaptive SAD Calculation algorithm(symbolized: SAD_{adap}) reduces the computations by 10.6%, 7.2%, 6.2%, 3.0%, 0.4% for FS+PDEsad, $MSEA_0$, $MSEA_1$, $MSEA_2$, and $MSEA_3$ respectively.

Table 3.   The distribution of blocks according to the ratio of
(maximum SAD of sub-blocks/minimum SAD of sub-blocks)

≥10	≥8	≥6	≥4	≥2	≥1.8	≥1.6	≥1.4	≥1.2	≥1.0
2.1%	1.6%	3.2%	9.1%	41.6%	10.0%	11.2%	11.3%	8.0%	1.8%

Table 4. Computations of Adaptive SAD Calculation algorithm

Algorithm	Avg. # of m.e./frame	Avg. # of rows/m.e.	Overhead (in rows)	Total (in rows)	Computations reduction
FS+SAD$_{adap}$	77,439.0	3.90	5,095.4	307,107.5	10.6%
MSEA$_0$+SAD$_{adap}$	24,995.6	5.27	10,631.2	142,358.0	7.2%
MSEA$_1$+SAD$_{adap}$	8769.7	7.16	15,603.2	78,394.3	6.2%
MSEA$_2$+ SAD$_{adap}$	1,589.1	9.50	23,673.2	38,769.7	3.0%
MSEA$_3$+ SAD$_{adap}$	242.3	13.87	29,521.0	32,881.7	0.4%

Adaptive SAD Calculation algorithm can be combined with not only MSEA but also all kinds of block matching algorithms to reduce the computations of motion estimation.

3.3   Elimination Level Estimation

As shown in MSEA procedure step 4, if a search point is eliminated at l-level, L-level MSEA checks SAD_SB$_0$, SAD_SB$_1$, …, SAD_SB$_l$ sequentially and then eliminate the search point at l-level where $0 \le l \le L+1$. In Elimination Level Estimation algorithm, step4.($L+1$) is equal to step5 of the MSEA. If we can estimate the elimination level l, where $0 \le l \le L+1$, of a search point in L-level MSEA, we can reduce the computations because   4.0, 4.1, … 4.(l-1) procedures are not necessary.

The estimation result can be classified into five groups as follow:

case1,   *hit1*: when the estimated elimination level (EEL) is 0 and EEL is equal to the practical elimination level(EL)

case2,   *hit2*: when EEL is greater than 0 and EEL is equal to EL

case3,   *acceptable miss1*: EEL is 0 and EEL is smaller than EL

case4,   *acceptable miss2*: EEL is greater than 0 and EEL is smaller than EL case5, *non-acceptable miss*: EEL is greater than EL

There is a profit when the estimation result is *hit2* or acceptable *miss2* cases. *Hit1* and *acceptable miss1* cases cannot reduce computations. There is a loss when the estimation result is *non-acceptable miss* case because it increases computations. The loss is approximately 4 times greater than the profit between two levels whose difference is 1 level. One incorrect estimation loss compensates the profit incurred by 4 times correct estimation. So, the estimation method requires a very high level of correctness. To achieve this aim, we use a very concrete estimation function as (8).

In this algorithm, the motion vector search pattern is as shown in fig. 2 which is modified from the spiral search pattern. Black circle represents the search point at which MSEA is executed and white circle represents the search point that requires elimination level estimation. Motion vector search sequence is as the number ordering sequence in fig.2. At search point 19, search points 2, 10, 11, 19 are the search points of which the elimination levels were calculated and point 20 is the search point which requires the elimination level estimation, we denote a search point which requires elimination level estimation such as point 20 as an estimation search point. We denote practical elimination level of search point 10 and estimated elimination level of search point 20 to EL(10) and EEL(20) respectively. We used equation (8) as estimation function.

$$EEL(20)=\min(EL(10),\ EL(2),\ EL(11),\ EL(19))\qquad(8)$$

The correctness of this estimation function is excellent as shown table 5, but there is estimation overhead. To reduce the overhead of the estimation function, four points are divided into two groups {10, 2} and {11, 19}. Points {10, 2} are lower left side points of point 20 and upper right side points of point 37. Points {11, 19} are upper right side points of point 20 and lower left side points of point 42. We can express equation (8) as follow:

$$EEL(20)=\min(lside(20),\ uside(20))\qquad(9)$$

where $lside(20)=\min(EL(10),\ EL(2))$, $uside(20)=\min(EL(11),\ EL(19))$

The grouping technique is useful when the following operation is done. If EL(10) is equal to 0, then setting EEL(20), EEL(40), EEL(65), EEL(37), lside(20), uside(37), lside(40), and uside(65) to zero. So, if one of neighbor points is zero then estimation is unnecessary. If all of the neighbor points are not zero, estimated elimination level can be found easily by equation (9)

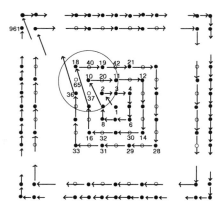

Fig. 2. Motion vector search pattern in search window for Elimination Level Estimation algorithm

As shown in table 5, the hit (*hit1+hit2*) ratio of estimation is 89% and (*hit1+hit2+acceptable miss1+acceptable miss2*) ratio is nearly 100% and *non-acceptable miss* ratio is nearly 0%. So, the correctness of estimation function used in this algorithm is reliable. As shown in table 6, Elimination Level Estimation algorithm reduces the computations of MSEA by 0.3%, 1.3%, 1.9%, 2.1% for $MSEA_0$, $MSEA_1$, $MSEA_2$, and $MSEA_3$ respectively. Although the correctness of estimation is reliable, the reduction of computations is small because of most blocks are eliminated at level 0 and estimation overhead and the loss incurred by incorrect estimation is larger than the profit incurred by correct estimation. Fig. 7 shows the number of blocks that are eliminated at each when 3-level MSEA is used. The total blocks for 100 frames are 7,734,000. Applying this algorithm to a video sequence of which the elimination rate at level 0 is small and the elimination rate at upper level is large then the performance of this algorithm will increase.

Table 5.   Elimination level estimation results

Algorithm	Case1	Case2	Case3	Case4	Case5
$MSEA_0$+EL estimation	2,245,282	807,943	296,204	0	171
$MSEA_1$+ELestimation	2,245,282	713,052	296,204	94,855	207
$MSEA_2$+EL estimation	2,245,282	681,906	296,204	125,982	226
$MSEA_3$+EL estimation	2,245,282	681,537	296,204	126,351	226

Table 6. Computations of MSEA combined with Elimination Level Estimation algorithm

Algorithm	Avg. # of m.e./frame	Avg. # of rows/m.e.	Overhead (in rows)	Total (in rows)	Computations reduction
$MSEA_0$+ELestimation	24,997.3	5.79	8,148.9	152,883.3	0.3%
$MSEA_1$+ELestimation	8,770.1	7.84	13,741.5	82,499.1	1.3%
$MSEA_2$+ELetimation	1,589.2	10.33	22,791.3	39,207.7	1.9%
$MSEA_3$+ELestimation	242.4	14.39	28,815.3	32,303.4	2.1%

Table 7.   The number of elimination blocks at each level for MSEA3

	Level 0	Level 1	Level 2	Level 3	at m.e.
Elimination block	5,244,345 (67.8%)	1,622,582 (21.0%)	718,063 (9.3%)	134,679 (1.7%)	14,331 (0.2%)

at m.e.: eliminated at matching evaluation

4   Conclusions

Advanced Multilevel Successive Elimination Algorithms, which are improved version of the Multilevel Successive Elimination Algorithm, have been proposed to reduce the computation cost of block matching algorithms for motion estimation in video coding.

Further Computation Reduction and Elimination Level Estimation algorithms are only useful in MSEA, but Adaptive SAD Calculation algorithm can be combined with not only the MSEA but also all kinds of block matching algorithms to reduce computations. This AMSEA can provide computations reduction over the MSEA, while keeping the same motion estimation accuracy as the FS.

AMSEA are very efficient solution for video coding applications that require both very low bit-rate and good coding quality.

References

1. X. Q. Gao, C.J. Duanmu, and C.R. Zou: A Multilevel Successive Elimination Algorithm for Block Matching Motion Estimation. IEEE Trans. Image Processing, Vol. 9, No.3, pp.501-504, Mar. 2000.

2. W. Li and E. Salari: Successive elimination algorithm for motion estimation. IEEE Trans. Image Processing, vol. 4, No.1, pp. 105-107, Jan. 1995.

3. J. R. Jain and A. K. Jain: Displacement measurement and its application in interframe image coding. IEEE Trans. Commun., vol. COMM-29, pp. 1799-1808, Dec. 1981.

4. A. N. Netravali and J. D. Robbins: Motion compensated television coding: Part I. Bell Syst. Tech. J., vol. 58, pp. 631-670, Mar. 1979.

5. B. Liu and A. Zaccarin: New fast algorithms for the estimation of block motion vectors. IEEE Trans. Circuits Syst. Video Technol., vol. 3, no. 2, pp. 148-157, Apr. 1993.

6. K. H. K. Chow and M. L. Liou: Genetic motion search algorithm for video compression. IEEE Trans. Circuits Syst. Video Technol., vol. 3, pp. 440-445, Dec. 1993.

7. T. M. Apostol: Mathematical Analysis. Reading, MA: Addison-Wesley, 1975

8. A. Gersho and R. M. Gray, Vector Quantization and Signal Compression. Boston, MA: Kluwer, 1991.6

News Content Highlight via Fast Caption Text Detection on Compressed Video

Weiqiang Wang   Wen Gao   Jintao Li   Shouxun Lin

Institute of Computing Technology,Chinese Academy of Science, 100080, BeiJing, China
{wqwang, wgao, jtli, sxlin} @ict.ac.cn

Abstract. Captions present in video frames play an important role in understanding video content. This paper presents a fast algorithm to automatically detect captions in MPEG compressed video. It is based on statistics features of caption text's chrominance components. The paper also discusses its principle and speed-up mechanism in detail. We have successfully exploited the technique to automatically construct the pictorial catalogue, a new content representation. Experiment results show the proposed caption detection algorithm has not only the ideal accuracy 96.6% and recall 100%, but also a detection speed of faster than real time.

1 Introduction

In the field of content-based visual information retrieval (CBVIR), automatic detection of high level visual features is a significant topic. Text present in video frames plays an important role in understanding video content. In many classes of video, text is often overlapped on original natural video, such as news, documentaries, etc, to form concise annotation of relevant video clips. Gargi et al [1] call it caption text, to distinguish from scene text which occurs naturally in the 3-D scene.

Some research efforts have been made to detect text in video. [2] proposed an algorithm to detect text region in video frames. They first exploited the feature of clustered sharp edges for a typical text region, to determine those candidates. Then consistent detection of the same region over a certain period of time was applied to verify them. The algorithm requires no priori knowledge, completely based on analysis of frame images, so it can be applied in all classes of video. But since it operates on original images, intensive decode computation results in its relative low detection speed. [3] proposed a caption detection algorithm in MPEG compressed domain. Based on the assumption that caption appearance and disappearance often occur in the middle of a video shot, a similar technique as [4] was applied to compute inter-frame content difference in caption regions. At the same time, the algorithm identified and ignored the large content difference caused by shot transition, to locate caption appearance and disappearance events. But our observation of CCTV news shows existence of caption text commonly covers multiple shots. So the algorithm in [3] is no longer applicable in the context. In this paper, we propose a fast algorithm that automatically detects caption text in MPEG compressed video. Our approach is based on statistics features of caption texts' chrominance components.

The rest of the paper is organized as follows. Section 2 first gives a more general model about video overlap operation and discusses the principle of the algorithm. Then its details are described. Last we address the speed-up mechanism further. In section 3, we apply the algorithm to automatically construct a pictorial catalogue and experiment results are given. Section 4 concludes the paper.

2 Caption Text Detection in compressed MPEG video

2. 1 Overlap Modal of Video objects and Principle of the Proposed Algorithm

Many multimedia applications involve various manipulations and compositings of video signal, including translation, overlap, etc. During the editing stage of production or live broadcast, some annotating text is often overlapped on frames in a clip. Let N, S represent a background object and a foreground object before overlapping respectively. Many types of overlapping can exist between them. Opaque overlapping requires substituting the pixels of the object S for those of the object N, while semi-transparent overlapping requires a linear combination of them, based on a transparency factor α ($0 \leq \alpha \leq 1$), i.e.,

$$P[i, j] = \alpha N[i, j] + (1 - \alpha) S[i, j] \tag{1}$$

where $P[i,j]$, $N[i,j]$, $S[i, j]$ are the pixels of the new object, the background object and the foreground object at position (i, j). When $\alpha = 0$, we get a result of opaque overlapping.

A more complicated mixture of the two overlap modes aforementioned exists, i.e., partial pixels of the object P are produced through opaque overlapping, let these pixels form a set λ, while the rest pixels are produced through semi-transparent overlapping, the corresponding pixels set is π, $\pi \cap \lambda = \phi$. We can establish a model for this overlapping, as formula (2).

$$P[i, j] = \alpha \cdot M[i, j] \cdot N[i, j] + (1 - \alpha) \cdot M[i, j] \cdot S[i, j] + \overline{M[i, j]} \cdot S[i, j] \tag{2}$$

where function $M[i, j]$ and $\overline{M[i, j]}$ are defined as the following:

$$M[i, j] = \begin{cases} 1 & (i, j) \in \pi \\ 0 & (i, j) \in \lambda \end{cases} \quad \overline{M[i, j]} = \begin{cases} 0 & (i, j) \in \pi \\ 1 & (i, j) \in \lambda \end{cases} \tag{3}$$

This kind of overlapping is common in CCTV news programs. Text region in a caption object S forms the set λ, while text background region in the object S corresponds to the set π. Here we can consider S as a binary image, i.e.,

$$S[i, j] = \begin{cases} b & (i, j) \in \pi \\ a & (i, j) \in \lambda \end{cases} \tag{4}$$

Where a and b are text and text background colors in the caption object S. From (4), formula (2) can be converted to (5)

$$F[i,j] = \begin{cases} \alpha N[i,j] + (1-\alpha) \cdot b & (i,j) \in \pi \\ a & (i,j) \in \lambda \end{cases} \tag{5}$$

In the Y-Cb-Cr color space, a component of each pixel is an integer from 0 to 255. So, for a pixel in the region π, its corresponding component value must range from $(1-\alpha) \cdot b$ to $(1-\alpha) \cdot b + 255\alpha$ after overlapping, while for a pixel in the set λ the result is a constant a. Since each pixel in the caption text region $\pi \cup \lambda$ has the property, we can expect if we calculate the average v of all the pixels in the region $\pi \cup \lambda$, then v will also belong to a specific range. Usually when a person selects the colors a and b for the object S, they should form a strong contrast against those of common natural background objects.

The above analysis results have been verified by our observation of CCTV news.

2. 2 Detection of Caption Text

Applying the algorithm in [4], we can extract a DC image for each frame in MPEG video with minimal decoding. The DC in each block is equal to the average of the pixels in that block. Through interactively choosing caption text regions as input samples, we can obtain the following important information, (i) the caption text region T, (ii) the dynamic distribution ranges of DC values in T. (iii) the dynamic distribution ranges of the average and standard variance of the DC values in T.

Since existence of caption text in video generally continues no less than 3 seconds, the algorithm detects only all the I frames, which can speed up the detection process. The details of the proposed algorithm are described in the following,

① Initialization. Open the video document fp, obtain the sequence number $CurFrmNum$ of the first I frame, and the GOP length gl of the MPEG stream.

②Extract DC images $X_{cb} = \{x_{ij}^{cb}\}$ and $X_{cr} = \{x_{ij}^{cr}\}$ for the chrominance components Cb and Cr,, from the frame with the sequence number $CurFrmNum$.

③ Suppose T represents the caption text region, b_{ij} is the region of the element whose index is (i,j) in DC image X_{cb} and X_{cr}. Let $C_{cb} = \{c_{ij}^{cb} \mid c_{ij}^{cb} = x_{ij}^{cb}, b_{ij} \subseteq T\}$, $C_{cr} = \{c_{ij}^{cr} \mid c_{ij}^{cr} = x_{ij}^{cr}, b_{ij} \subseteq T\}$. Calculate $F = (r_s^{cb}, r_e^{cb}, avg^{cb}, sd^{cb}, r_s^{cr}, r_e^{cr}, avg^{cr}, sd^{cr})$, where

$$r_s^{cb} = \min_{d \in C_{cb}} d \text{ , } r_e^{cb} = \max_{d \in C_{cb}} d, avg^{cb} = \frac{1}{|C_{cb}|} \sum_{d \in C_{cb}} d, sd^{cb} = \sqrt{\frac{1}{|C_{cb}|} \sum_{d \in C_{cb}} (d - avg^{cb})^2}, r_s^{cr} = \min_{d \in C_{cr}} d \text{ , }$$

$$r_e^{cr} = \max_{d \in C_{cr}} d \text{ , } avg^{cr} = \frac{1}{|C_{cr}|} \sum_{d \in C_{cr}} d \text{ , } sd^{cr} = \sqrt{\frac{1}{|C_{cr}|} \sum_{d \in C_{cr}} (d - avg^{cr})^2} \text{ , where } |c| \text{ represents}$$

the cardinal number of the set C.

④If $[r_s^{cb}, r_e^{cb}] \subseteq [v_s^{cb}, v_e^{cb}]$, $avg^{cb} \in [avg_s^{cb}, avg_e^{cb}]$, $sd^{cb} \in [sd_s^{cb}, sd_e^{cb}]$, $[r_s^{cr}, r_e^{cr}] \subseteq [v_s^{cr}, v_e^{cr}]$, $avg^{cr} \in [avg_s^{cr}, avg_e^{cr}]$, $sd^{cr} \in [sd_s^{cr}, sd_e^{cr}]$ all hold, then caption text exists in the frame with sequence number $CurFrmNum$, where $[v_s^{cb}, v_e^{cb}]$, $[v_s^{cr}, v_e^{cr}]$, $[avg_s^{cb}, avg_e^{cb}]$, $[avg_s^{cr}, avg_e^{cr}]$, $[sd_s^{cb}, sd_e^{cb}]$, $[sd_s^{cr}, sd_e^{cr}]$ are the dynamic ranges of different components in the feature vector F, which are obtained through the interactive off-line statistical process aforementioned. Besides the features in F, relation features between two chrominance components' statistical data can also be found and utilized, to improve detection accuracy. For example, we observed that in CCTV news there exist such relation features $avg^{cb} \geq avg^{cr}$ and $sd^{cb} \geq sd^{cr}$.

⑤ To eliminate noises, the system declares a caption appearance event, if and only if it consistently detects captions in W_s consecutive I frames, and represents the start frame of the caption event by $STextFrmNum$. Similarly, Only when in W_e consecutive I frames, the system does not find captions, the disappearance event will be declared, and outputs the detection result $(STextFrmNm, ETextFrmNm)$, where $ETextFrmNum$ represents the end frame of the caption event. W_s and W_e are system parameters, we choose $W_s = W_e = 3$ in our system.

⑥ $CurFrmNum = CurFrmNum + gl$. If the end of the document is not met then goto ②. Otherwise the file fp is closed, and the whole algorithm exits.

2. 3 Speed up Detection Process

In the algorithm aforementioned, frames are sampled according to the granularity of a GOP, to detect appearance and disappearance of captions. If we apply a larger granularity to sample frames, the number of frames detected will greatly reduce, thus the detection speed will increase. Since a caption is used to annotate content of a relevant clip, it should stay enough time to make watchers notice it and be impressed, especially in news, so we can use the granularity $\varepsilon \cdot gl$ to detect caption events, where ε is an integer more than 1 and called a granularity factor.

If minimal resident time of a caption in a video stream is τ, it is easy to prove that if the frame sample granularity $l < \tau$ is used, then at least one frame in each clip containing a caption will be checked. So the algorithm will not miss detection of any caption due to too large frame sample granularities. Similarly, if minimal time interval between two consecutive clips with different captions is μ, it will hold that if the frame sample granularity $l < \mu$, then at least one frame in each clip with no caption will be checked. So the algorithm will not mistake different captions as the same caption due to too large frame sample granularities. Thus when the current frame does not contain caption and the system is ready to detect next caption appearance event, the granularity factor ε_1 chosen should satisfy $\varepsilon_1 \cdot gl < \tau$, i.e., $\varepsilon_1 < \dfrac{\tau}{gl}$. Similarly, when the current frame contains a caption and the caption's disappearance event is to be detected, the granularity factor ε_2 chosen should satisfy $\varepsilon_2 < \dfrac{\mu}{gl}$. From the aforementioned, we know that when the system chooses a sample granularity l to detect caption text, it assumes the τ and μ of a MPEG stream satisfy $l < \tau$, $l < \mu$. In practical applications, the assumption is easy to be satisfied, since some priori knowledge can help us to choose a suitable l, or a friendly human-machine interface can be designed to flexibly set the parameter l.

3 Experiments

Owing to the constraint of Internet bandwidth, people hope computers can extract minimal video data to summarize essential content of the corresponding video document, to alleviate network burden and reduce cost of network traffic. Many abstraction representations of video content have been proposed, such as storyboard, scene transition graph, pictorial summary, etc. The paper suggests a new form to present essence of news content, called pictorial catalogues. It is a group of frame images arranged in a time order and each image contains a caption to annotate a news item. Its construction is based on detection of caption text in news video.

Our observation of CCTV news shows that almost each news item clip contains a caption overlapped on some consecutive frames to annotate the clip. Usually, CCTV News lasts half-hour and includes about 20 news items. So using a pictorial catalogue is attractive, since it can present a user only about 20 images to make him understand the essential news content of that day well.

Table 1. The Experiment Results of Detecting Captions over the Test Set

Sequences	Number of frames	Total captions (S)	Output of detection (D)	False (E)	missed (U)
News0	44965	19	20	1	0
News1	44770	22	22	0	0
News2	45106	21	23	2	0
News3	44913	19	19	0	0
News4	36339	17	19	2	0
News5	59610	18	18	0	0
News6	44447	16	16	0	0
News7	49775	12	12	0	0
Sum total	369925	144	149	5	0

We use 8 days' CCTV news MPEG streams as a test set, to verify the validity of the proposed algorithm. All experiments are done on the PC with a PIII-450 CPU and 64M memories. The MPEG streams have a frame rate of 24 f/s with the frame dimension 720×576 pixels. The whole test set contains 369925 frames and lasts about 4.5 hours. The experiment results are tabulated in table 1. Based on the statistics in table 1, the accuracy of detecting captions $P = 1 - \dfrac{E}{D} = 1 - \dfrac{5}{149} = 96.6\%$ and the

recall $R = 1 - \dfrac{U}{S} = 1 - \dfrac{0}{144} = 100\%$ can be calculated. It is ideal that the algorithm has

the recall 100% and high accuracy. Because it is easy work for a user to select few images not containing caption from a small number of images through an interaction tool. Figure 1 gives a small part of a pictorial catalogue generated by the algorithm for news3. Table 2 tabulates the system's runtime of partial streams under the different granularities. Though the decoding engine embedded in the system has only performance of 8 f/s over the MPEG-2 streams, table 2 implies our algorithm has the performance of faster than real time. This is mainly because the whole detection process completely operates in the compressed domain and some mechanisms of speed up are introduced in the system.

Fig. 1. An Example of Pictorial Catalogues (News3)

Table 2. Detection Time of Partial Streams under the Different Granularities

Sequences	Time(s) g=1	Time(s) g=2	Time(s) g=3	Time(s) g=4	
News5	615	344	240	191	here g represents the granularity factor.
News6	370	206	148	109	
News7	483	286	171	134	

4 Conclusions

The paper proposes a fast caption detection algorithm in the compressed domain. We successfully applied the technique in constructing pictorial catalogues of CCTV news video. Our experiment results show the proposed algorithm has not only the ideal accuracy and recall, but also very fast detection speed. So it has significant application value. Its disadvantage is that it needs to establish the color distribution model of caption through an off-line interaction tool. So it is suitable to be applied in news video, since many properties of caption text have relative stability.

References

1. U. Gargi, S. Antani and R. Kasturi, "Indexing Text Events in Digital Video Databases", 14th International Conference on Pattern Recognition, 1998 (ICPR'98).
2. M.A. Smith and T. Kanade, "Video Skimming and Characterization through the Combination of Image and Language Understanding Techniques", IEEE conference on Computer Vision and Pattern Recognition, June, 1997, pp. 775-781
3. B.L. Yeo and B. Liu, "Visual Content Highlighting via Automatic Extraction of Embedded Captions on MPEG Compressed Video", in SPIE Digital Video Compression: Algorithms and Technologies, Vol. 2668, Feb. 1996, pp. 38-47
4. B.L. Yeo and B. Liu, "Rapid Scene Analysis on Compressed Videos", in IEEE Transactions on Circuits and Systems for Video Technology, Vol. 5, No. 6, December 1995.pp. 533-544.

Texture-Based Text Location for Video Indexing

Keechul Jung and JungHyun Han

School of Electrical and Computer Engineering
Sung Kyun Kwan University, Suwon, 440-746, Korea
{kjung, han}@ece.skku.ac.kr
http://graphics.skku.ac.kr

Abstract. This paper proposes texture-based text location methods with a neural network (NN) and a Support Vector Machine (SVM). Both a NN and an SVM are employed to train a set of texture discrimination masks for the given texture classes: text region and non-text region. In these two approaches, feature extraction stage is not used as opposed to most traditional text location schemes, and discrimination filters for several environments can be automatically constructed. Comparisons between NN/SVM-based text location methods and a connected component method are presented.

1 Introduction

Text location has been studied for many applications including document analysis, text-based video indexing, multimedia systems, digital libraries, and vehicle number plate recognition [2-5,7,8]. Recently, researchers have proposed various methods for the text-based retrieval of video documents. Automatic text location for video documents is very important as a preprocessing stage for optical character recognition. However, text region location in complex images may suffer from low resolution of characters unlike black characters in white documents [2].

There are two primary methods for text location. The first method uses a connected component analysis [5,8]. This is not appropriate for video documents because it is based on the effectiveness of the segmentation which guarantees that a character is segmented as one connected component separated from other objects. On the other hand, texture-based methods are based on the observation that texts in video images have distinct textural properties, and use Garbor filters, wavelet decomposition, and spatial variance [4,6,7]. In this method, the text location can be posed as a texture classification problem where the problem-specific knowledge is available prior to the classification. This use of texture information for text location is sensitive to character font size and style. Therefore in a complex situation with various font styles, sizes, and colors, it is difficult to manually generate a texture filter set.

This paper presents texture-based text location methods using an NN and an SVM, which are employed to train a set of texture discrimination masks for the given texture classes: text region and non-text region. An NN and an SVM have several similar aspects. These two approaches use no feature extraction stage as opposed to most traditional text location schemes, and discrimination filters for several applications can be automatically constructed. Comparisons between NN/SVM-based texture discriminations and a connected component method are presented. As shown in the experimental results, NN and SVM have a trade-off in time and accuracy.

The remainder of the paper is organized as follows. Chapter 2 describes the proposed NN-based method and SVM-based method. Experimental results are shown in Chapter 3. Chapter 4 presents some final conclusions and outlines future work.

2 Texture-based Text Location Methods

This chapter presents NN/SVM-based text location methods and compares the performance with connected component method. The proposed text location system operates in two stages: First, it applies a NN or an SVM to classify the pixels in the input image, that is, feature extraction and the pattern recognition stages are integrated in those classifiers. The classified image is a binary image in which the pixels classified as text are black and those classified as non-text are white. Then it post-processes (eliminates noises then places bounding boxes) filtered outputs.

2.1 NN-based Text Locations

This section presents a NN-based text location method. A neural network is used to classify the pixels of input images. To this end, the NN-filter is applied at each location in the image. That is, the neural network examines local regions looking for text pixels that may be contained in a text region.

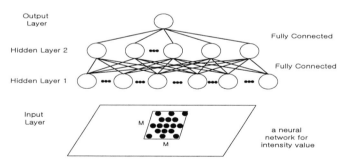

Fig. 1. A three-layer feed-forward neural network [6]

An input image is segmented into text and non-text classes using a multi-layer feed-forward neural network classifier which receives the intensity values of a given pixel and its neighbors as input. The activation values of the output node are used to determine the class of a given central pixel. A classified image is obtained as a binary image in which the text pixels are black [4]. Fig. 1 describes the architecture of the neural network-based classifier. Adjacent layers are fully connected, the nodes on the hidden layer operate as a feature extraction masks, and the output layer is used to determine the class of a pixel: text or non-text. The input layer receives the intensity values of the pixels, at predefined positions inside an M×M window over an input frame [6]. To investigate the properties of the masks, the frequency response of these masks must be demonstrated. To illustrate the frequency responses of the hidden nodes, the image shown in Fig. 2-(a) was considered [6]. Fig. 2-(b)-(e) is the outputs of the first hidden layer's nodes when applied to Fig. 2-(a). For good visualization, the output images were smoothed and the contrast of the images enhanced. These images show that each hidden node has its special orientation and localized frequency.

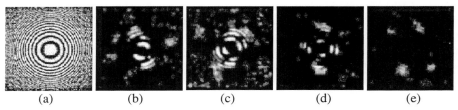

| (a) | (b) | (c) | (d) | (e) |

Fig. 2. Frequency responses (b)-(e) of hidden nodes when applied to 128×128 image in (a)

2.2 SVM-based Text Locations

A Support Vector Machine has been recently proposed as a method for pattern classification and nonlinear regression [1]. For several pattern classification applications SVMs have been shown to provide a better generalization performance than traditional techniques such as neural networks. In this chapter we present a brief description for the SVM and the text location method using an SVM.

Consider a two-class pattern classification problem. Let the training set of size N be $\{(\mathbf{x}_i, d_i)\}_{i=1}^{N}$, where $\mathbf{x}_i \in R^p$ is the input pattern for the i th example and $d_i \in \{-1,+1\}$ is the corresponding desired response. The non-linear SVM first performs a nonlinear mapping $\phi : R^p \rightarrow H$. Let $\phi(\mathbf{x})$ denote a set of non-linear transformations from the input space R^p to the feature space H. An SVM can be trained to construct a hyperplane $\mathbf{w}^T\phi(\mathbf{x})+b=0$ for which the *margin of separation* is maximized [1]. Using the method of Lagrange multipliers, this hyperplane can be represented as:

$$\sum_{i=1}^{N} \alpha_i d_i \phi^T(\mathbf{x}_i)\phi(\mathbf{x}) = 0 \tag{1}$$

where the auxiliary variables α_i s are Lagrange multipliers. These α_i s can be found by solving the following problem:

$$\text{Maximize } Q(\alpha) = \sum_{i=1}^{N} \alpha_i - \frac{1}{2}\sum_{i,j=1}^{N} \alpha_i \alpha_j d_i d_j K(\mathbf{x}_i, \mathbf{x}_j) \tag{2}$$

where $K(\mathbf{x}_i, \mathbf{x}_j)$ is the inner-product kernel defined by:

$$K(\mathbf{x}_i, \mathbf{x}_j) = \phi^T(\mathbf{x}_i)\phi(\mathbf{x}_j), \tag{3}$$

subject to the constraints:

$$\sum_{i=1}^{N}\alpha_i d_i = 0, \; 0 \le \alpha_i \le C \text{ for } i=1,2,\ldots,N \tag{4}$$

where C is a constant balancing contributions from the first and second terms. This performs a similar role with the regularization parameter in the radial basis function and affects the generalization performance of SVM. The value of this parameter is determined empirically to be 10.

An SVM is trained to classify each pixel in the input image into text or non-text by analyzing the textural properties of its local neighborhood. No texture feature extraction scheme is explicitly incorporated. Instead the intensity level values of the raw pixels are directly fed to the classifier. The proposed method utilizes a small window to scan the image and classify the pixel located in the center of window as text or non-text using an SVM.

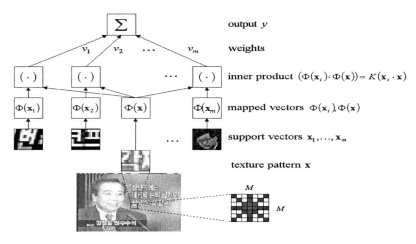

Fig. 3. SVM architecture for text detection

Fig. 3 shows a three-layer feed-forward network architecture of an SVM as a text detector. The input to the network directly comes from the intensity level values of the M×M (typically 13×13) window in the input image. However, instead of using all the pixels in the window, a configuration for autoregressive features is used [6]. The hidden layer applies nonlinear mapping ϕ from the input space to the feature space H and computes the dot product between its input and support vectors. These two operations are performed in a single step by using the kernel function K. For the kernel function, a polynomial kernel is used. The sign of the output y obtained by weighting the activation of the hidden layer, represents the class of the central pixel in the input window. For training, +1 was assigned for the text class and −1 for the non-text class. Accordingly, if the SVM's output of a pixel is positive, it is classified as text. To detect texts in an image, the detection window is shifted over all locations in the image. As a result of classification, a classified image is obtained as binary images in which the text pixels are black.

3 Experimental Results

The database for this experiment was composed of two sets. One included image data, and the other video data. The images were all scanned using a Hewlett Packard Scanjet 5100C flat-bed scanner. A total of 100 scanned images were used for the experiments. The scanned images came from a variety of journals and magazines. The resolution of the images was 150 DPI. The proposed text location method was applied to 12 video clips. Each video clip had a running time of 2~3 minutes. 1000 key frames with a size of 320×240 were automatically selected using a simple key frame extraction technique. Of these frames, 50 video frames and several images were used in the initial training process, and the others were used in the testing process. This paper focuses on super-imposed and horizontally aligned text in video frames and complex images. No prior knowledge of resolution, text location, and font styles is assumed. However the horizontal alignment of text is required.

Fig. 4. Example of text location

Text rectangles are identified by performing a profile analysis and merging certain rectangles. Owing to the restriction that texts may be aligned horizontally in input images, a simple heuristic method is used to align bounding boxes. Figure 4 shows examples of the text location [4]. The detection rates and processing times for a neural network and a support vector machine are shown in Table 1, compared with those of the connected component analysis method [8]. It is clear that the proposed methods exhibited a superior performance than the connected component method. The most important texts with sufficiently large font sizes were successfully located by the proposed system.

Table 1. Performance comparisons

Methods	Detection rates (%)	Processing times (sec.)
NN	86.3	3.5
SVM	91.2	7.0
Connected Component Method	73.8	1.2

4 Conclusions

This chapter presents a summary of the proposed text location methods. In addition, some continuing problems are noted, which need to be addressed in future work. It has been shown that a neural network and a support vector machine can be trained for supervised text location in images. The proposed text location method can be distinguished from other algorithms by the following properties: (1) discrimination filters for several applications can be automatically constructed; (2) the input image is directly processed instead of extracting some feature vectors; (3) they allow for the easy implementation of a parallel system. The main limitation of the current system is its running time. It may be useful to modify the architecture of the filtering network or the input window size automatically. The relatively low number of false detections shows the excellence of an SVM for text location, however, in real-time application, the rather longer processing time of an SVM advocates its use as a second-stage processor, which only investigates a doubtful region that has already been identified by a faster yet less reliable first-stage text detector, for example a neural network or a connected component method.

Acknowledgement

This work was supported by grant No. 1999-2-515-001-5 from the Basic Research Program of the Korea Science & Engineering Foundation.

References

1. Kim, K.I., Jung, K., Park, S.H., and Kim, H.J., Supervised Texture Segmentation using Support Vector Machine. *IEE Electronics Letters*, Vol. 35, No.22, (1999) pp. 1935-1937, October.
2. Jun Ohya, Akil Shio, and Shigeru Akamatsu, Recognizing Characters in Scene images. *IEEE Transactions on Pattern Analysis and Machine Intelligence*, Vol. 16, No. 2, Feb. (1994).
3. Tan, C.L. and NG, P.O., Text Extraction using Pyramid. *Pattern Recognition*, Vol. 31, No. 1, (1998) pp. 63-72.
4. Jeong, K. Y., Jung, K., Kim, E. Y., and Kim, H. J., Neural Network-based Text Locating for news video Indexing. *Proc. of ICIP*. (1999).
5. Jain, A.K. and Yu, B., Automatic Text Location in Images and Video Frames. *Pattern Recognition*, Vol. 31, No. 12, (1998) pp. 2055-2076.
6. Jain, A.K. and Karu, K., Learning Texture Discrimination Masks. *IEEE Trans. on PAMI*, Vol. 18, No. 2, (1996) pp. 195-205.
7. Park, S.H., Jung, K., etc., Locating Car License Plates using Neural Networks. *Electronics Letters*, Vol. 35, No. 17, (1999) pp. 1475-1477.
8. Kim, E.Y., Jung, K., etc., Automatic Text Region Extraction Using Cluster-based Templates, *4th International Conference on Advances in Pattern Recognition and Digital Techniques(ICAPRDT)*, (2000) pp. 418~421.

Video Segmentation by Two Measures and Two Thresholds

DaLong LI[#], HanQing Lu[1#], DongZhang[*]

[#]National Lab of Pattern Recognition, *Hanwang Co,
Institute of Automation, Chinese Academy of Sciences
{luhq dlli} @nlpr.ia.ac.cn

Abstract. Video partitioning is a key issue in video classification that facilitates the management of video resources. The video partitioning involves the detection of boundaries between uninterrupted segments (video shots). Shot boundaries can be classified into two categories, gradual transition and abrupt change. Detection of a gradual transition is considered to be difficult. Few methods have been reported for gradual transition detection. In this paper, a new approach called Two Measures Two Thresholds (TMTT) is proposed. The method requires the use of two measures and consequently two thresholds. By comparing the gray level histogram difference of consecutive frames with a smaller Threshold (Ts), possible shot boundaries are located. Then false boundaries are discarded by comparing their color ratio histogram with another threshold that is used to measure the similarity of content of the frames. The efficiency of TMTT is promising according to the analysis of some experimental results.

1   Introduction

It has become important to archive and access multimedia information in several important application fields such as VOD (video on demand), DLI (digital library). Of all the media types, video is the most challenging one, because it combines all the other media information into a single bit stream. The most popular method is text-based. Unfortunately the content of the videos is so abounded that the key words can not express all information. So it is urgent to browse and retrieve video sequences directly by their content.

The primary task before browsing and retrieval is to systematize video that has an obvious structure hierarchy, i.e. *video, shot,* and *frame.* A video is made up of shots; a shot is an uninterrupted segment of screen time, space and graphical configurations. According to the duration of shot boundaries, there are two types: camera breaks and gradual transitions. Basically there are two kinds of gradual transition: wipe and dissolve. A wipe is a moving boundary line crossing the screen such that one shot gradually replaces another; a dissolve superimposes two shots where one shot gradually lightens while the other fades out slowly. Detection of camera breaks has received considerable attention and it has been done very successfully. Unfortunately the detection of the gradual transition is rather unsatisfactory. Yeo and Liu suggested looking for the "plateau" [1] and Zhang et al proposed a twin-comparison algorithm [2] to search the gradual transitions. Step-variable algorithm was proposed by Wei Xiong and John Chung-Mong Lee [3]. Lifang Gu suggested a linear model based method to detect dissolves [4]. Model based video segmentation is suggested in our paper [5]. In another paper, I proposed an algorithm called STDD [6] to detect shot boundaries. The algorithm can detect both camera breaks and gradual transitions.

---

[1] The corresponding author

STDD significantly improves the detection performance. However the choice of threshold is still difficult and this effects the performance of the algorithm greatly. Also since STDD needs to compare backwards, it is difficult to work real-time. In recognizing the necessity to associate the merits of different measures, I expressed the idea " Multi-scale hierarchy video segmentation "in the paper [7]. Actually TMTT can be regards as an implement of the idea.

The rest of the paper is organized as follows. In Section 2, TMTT is introduced. Color Ratio Histogram and Gray Level Ratio Histogram are reviewed in section 3. Experimental results and discussions are reported in Section 4.

2   Shot Boundary Detection: TMTT

The algorithm is easy to understand. Fig.1 shows the figure used to illustrate the algorithm. The figure is supposed to stand for the gray level difference of consecutive frames. The length of the transition distinguishes the gradual transition and camera break. Then we compare the content of the frames in each pair of possible gradual transitions by gray level ratio histogram. As to possible camera break such as b_1, frame b_1 and b_1+1 are to be compared.

$$RHD(m,n) = \sum_i | Hm(i) - Hn(i) |$$

Then compare RHD with a threshold T_b, if it is lower than T_b, that means that they are still inside a shot and there is no shot shift. Otherwise it is a shot boundary. False transitions are mainly caused by illumination variation. Sudden illumination variation may be mistaken as abrupt transition and gradual illumination variation is easily be regarded as wipe or dissolve. Both of them will be marked as the boundaries at the first step of the TMTT, but they are discarded after the second step when ratio histogram is used. The thresholds are selected dynamically according to the idea in the paper [10].

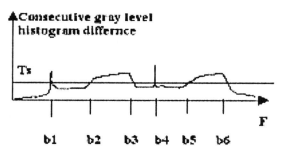

Fig. 1. Four boundaries including two false boundaries are found by thresholding the curve with the Threshold T_s . b_1 and b_4 are the possible camera breaks while (b_2, b_3) and (b_5, b_6) are the possible gradual transitions.

The algorithm can be formulated in the following:

1.   H={ h_0, h_1, h_2, h_3, ... , h_i, ...}, where h_i is the gray level histogram of frame i.

2. $HD(m,n) = \sum_{i=0}^{255} | Hm(i) - Hn(i) |$

3. $D = \{ d_i \mid d_i = HD(i, i+1), i=0,1,2,\ldots \}$
4. $PB = \{ pb_0, pb_1, pb_1, pb_2, pb_3, \ldots, pb_i, \ldots \}$
   $pb_i = \{ k \mid d_k > T_s, k \text{ is continuous} \} = \{ g_0, g_1, g_2, \ldots, g_t \}$
5. $TB = \{ tb_0, tb_1, tb_2, tb_3, \ldots, tb_i, \ldots \}$
   $tb_i = pb_i$ if $rhd(pb_i(g_0), pb_i(g_t)+1) > T_b$
   $$rhd(m,n) = \sum_i \mid RHm(i) - RHn(i) \mid$$

   $RH(i)$ is the gray level ratio histogram of the i th
   frame.
6. Camera Breaks $= \{ tb_i \mid t=0 \}$
   Gradual Transitions $= \{ tb_i \mid t > 0, M_0 < t < M_1 \}$
   t is the lasting time of the gradual transition.
   M_0 is the minimum length for a gradual transition. M_1 is the maximal length for a gradual transition.

The length of the transition can be used to discard some false gradual transitions. We denote M_0 as the minimum length for a gradual transition, M_1 as the maximal length for a gradual transition. And lgt stands for the length of a transition. When it is less than M_0 or larger than M_1, these frames are not corresponding to a gradual transition. Thus some kind of camera motion (for example panning) inside a shot will not be alarmed as a gradual transition.

3   Color Ratio Histogram and Gray Level Ratio Histogram

The important thing in video segmentation is that a suitable metric should be selected to measure the difference between frames. Many were proposed such as pixel- or block-based temporal image difference [8 9] or gray and color histogram. Histogram has been widely used because it is simple to compute and it is insensitive to object motion. However they are sensitive to illumination variations. Color ratio histogram was adopted in shot detection [10]. Unfortunately, the computing cost is rather high. To reduce the computing cost, we use gray level ratio histogram as the measurement. The computing procedure is similar to that of the color ratio histogram.

Though illumination may cause it change greatly, we still use gray level histogram first since generally illumination variation does not occur frequently [7]. Therefore it is not economic to calculate ratio histogram each time. It is used to measure the content similarity of two frames that are marked as the possible shot boundary.

Still a problem remains that neither color ratio histogram nor Gray Level Histogram can solve. Firstly let us review what makes the content inside a shot changes. It is illumination, object motion, camera motion. The illumination and object motion can not affect color ratio histogram. But some camera motions do alter color ratio histogram. It is not easy to distinguish the changes introduced by camera movements such as panning or zooming from those due to special-effect transitions.

4   Experimental Results and Discussion

TMTT has been validated by experiments with several video sequences which include features related to film producing and editing such as lighting condition variation, object and camera motion.

Fig.2 shows an example of how TMTT works. Table 1 gives the detected boundaries. This sequence is taken from a TV news report. There are many illumination variations due to the photo-chemistry-flash of journalists who took photograph on a ceremony. These illumination variations cause the sudden change in the gray level histogram. However there is no false alarms made. Three boundaries are located correctly. There are two camera breaks and one gradual transition(wipe).

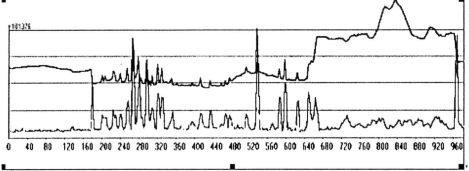

Fig.2. In the figure, there are three curves. The highest curve stands for the difference of the average gray level of two consecutive frames, the higher stands for that of the gray level histogram and the last one stands for that of the gray level ratio histogram. As we can see that the second curve is just the one as expected in Fig.1. The reason to draw the curve of the average gray level of two consecutive frames is to test the assumption that the process of dissolve is linear [4].

Table 1. The segmented shots of the video.(2 camera breaks and 1 wipe)

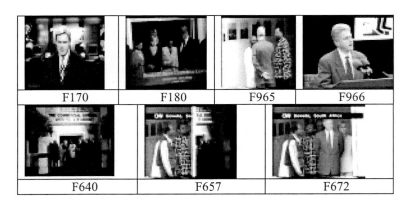

To investigate the tolerance and accuracy of gradual transition detection, we perform recall-precision to evaluate the results. Denote A_i as the number of frames due to action i ; B_i as the number of detected frames in class i ; C_i as the number of correctly detected frames in class i. Then

$Recall(i)=C_i/A_i$

$Precision(i)=C_i/B_i$

Where $i \in$ {camera breaks, gradual transitions}

Table 2. detection results. D: correct detection; M: missed detection; F: false alarms.

Video sequences	Camera break D M F	Gradual transition D M F
1(6878 frames)	25 0 0	13 0 1
2(7855 frames)	24 0 3	12 3 2
Recall	1.00	0.89
Precision	0.94	0.89

It is easy to see that TMTT recalls all the camera breaks. Some smooth gradual transitions are missed. Unfortunately there are some false alarms. Knowledge of camera motion or dissolve and wipe will be employed to get ride of them. False camera break is due to the sudden movement of the camera. Table 3 gives the examples. First the camera is from a distance away, then it moves to near the actors; therefore the content of the picture changes abruptly, which makes a false camera break alarm. Again when the camera moves to a distant away and the content of the picture changes from the actors to the desert. Another false camera break is made. False gradual transitions are mainly due to panning. In the second line of the table there is an example. First the camera is focused on the Monkey King who is drawing the horse, then gradually the camera becomes focused on the monk on the back of the horse. The content of the picture changes gradually, so the sequences are marked as a gradual transition. But actually there is no shot shift. Very smooth shot shift is very likely to be missed. In the third line of the table, the transition from the horse to the bird is missed.

Table 3. The failure of the TMTT

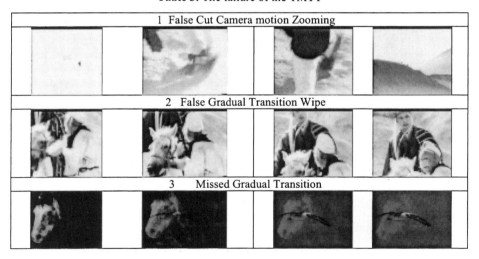

TMTT is able to detect both camera breaks and gradual transitions precisely with two measures and two thresholds. The recall rate is improved greatly. Very few shot boundaries are missed. However an additional process is necessary to identify dissolve or wipe from the false alarms. It is impossible to distinguish wipe and dissolve from camera motions by histogram that can not reflect the regulation of wipe or dissolve. One of the possible solutions is suggested in my paper [7].

Further work is focused on how to distinguish dissolve and wipe from camera motions in other ways. What is more, another metric that can reflect dissolve or wipe is to be proposed. The computation of the metric should be efficient.

Acknowledgements

This work is sponsored by the National Key Basic Research Program (Project G1998030500) and the National High-Technology Research and Development Program (Project 863-306-QN99-2).

References

[1] B.L.Yeo and B.Liu.: Rapid scene analysis on compressed video. IEEE Trans. Circuits Systems Video techol. 5,1995,533-544.

[2] H.J.Zhang, A. KanKanhali,and S.W.Smoliar.: Automatic partitioning of full-motion video. ACM Multimedia Systems 1,1993,10-28

[3] Wei Xiong and John Chung-Mong Lee.: Efficient Scene Change Detection and Camera Motion Annotation for Video Classification. Computer Vision and image Understanding Vol.71.No.2.Augest.pp166-181,1998.

[4] Lifang Gu, Ken Tsui and David Keightley. : Dissolve Detection in MPEG Compressed Video. IEEE International Conference on Intelligent Processing Systems October 28-31, 1997,Beijing, China.

[5] Dalong Li, H.Q.Lu. : Model based video segmentation. to appear in the Proc. of the IEEE Workshop on Signal Processing System, October 11-13, 2000 , Lafayette, Louisiana, USA.

[6] Dalong Li , H.Q.Lu and H.Q.Liang. : Efficient Video segmentation by STDD. Proc. International Conference on Modeling and Simulation, Pittsburgh, USA, 2000.

[7] Dalong Li, H.Q.Lu. : Multi-Scale Hierarchy Video Segmentation. Proc. the 1st IEEE EIT conference, Chicago, USA, 2000.

[8] K.Otsuji, Y.Tonomura and Y.Ohba.: Video browsing using brightness data. Proc. SPIE Conf. Visual Communications and Image Processing, pp.980-989,Nov 1991

[9] A.Nagasaka and Y.Tanaka,Automativ. : video indexing and full-video search for object appearances. Proc.2nd Visual Database Systems,pp119-133,October 1991

[10] W.X.Kong, X.F.Ding, H.Q.Lu and S.D.Ma.: Improvement of Shot Detection Using Illumination Invariant Metric and Dynamic Threshold Selection. International Conference on Visual information System(Visual'99) Netherland, 1999

Ink Retrieval from Handwritten Documents

Thomas Kwok, Michael P. Perrone, and Gregory Russell

IBM T.J. Watson Research Center, Yorktown Heights, NY 10598, USA
{kwok,mpp,gfr}@ibm.us.com

Abstract. This paper compares several information retrieval (IR) methods applied to the problem of retrieving specific words from a handwritten document. The methods compared include variants of the Okapi formula and Latent Semantic Indexing (LSI); recognition-based retrieval; and keyword search. One novel aspect of the work presented is that it uses the output stack of a Hidden Markov Model (HMM) handwriting recognizer with a 30,000-word lexicon to convert each handwritten word into a document which is then used for document retrieval. Preliminary experiments on a database of 1158 words from 75 writers indicate that the keyword search has superior precision and recall for text queries, and that ink queries result in minor performance reductions.

1   Introduction

The value of computerized storage of handwritten documents would be greatly enhanced if they could be searched and retrieved in ways analogous to the methods used for text documents. If precise transcripts of handwritten documents exist, then IR techniques can be applied; however, such transcripts are typically too costly to generate by hand, and machine recognition methods for automating the process of transcript generation are far from perfect. Thus, such transcripts are usually incomplete and/or corrupted by incorrect transcriptions.

One approach to handling these problems is to rely on the redundancy of the target documents to compensate for the noise in transcription [4]; however, this may not work if document word redundancy is low, and it does not allow for handwritten queries. Another approach uses template matching between query ink and document ink [1, 2, 5]; however, this can be very slow if the number of documents to be searched is large and the match method is very complex; also, it does not allow for text queries. Others have used ink simply to annotate text documents for IR [3] but do not handle IR of handwritten documents.

The approach presented here avoids the weaknesses of previous methods by using a statistical classifier to convert each ink word of a handwritten document into a set of scores, one associated with each of the possible text translations of the ink. This set of scores is termed a "stack". In practice, each ink word in each document is converted into a stack. This step need only be done once. Each word of an ink query is likewise converted into a stack; while each word of a text query is converted into a trivial stack by giving a maximum score to the query word and a minimum score to all other stack entries. (*i.e.*, we assume no error in entering a text query; though this assumption could be easily relaxed.)

In this paper we focus only on single-word queries and documents, since these form the basis for advanced retrieval tasks. In future work, we will consider more complex queries and documents.

2   Stack Retrieval Methods

Let $\mathcal{W}$ be the set of all possible words and let $\mathcal{I}$ be a given handwritten occurrence of $w \in \mathcal{W}$. We define the **stack** associated with $\mathcal{I}$ as the vector $\boldsymbol{S}(\mathcal{I}) = (S_1(\mathcal{I}), S_2(\mathcal{I}), \ldots)$ where $S_i(\mathcal{I})$ is the score of $\mathcal{I}$ given w_i, the i-th word of $\mathcal{W}$, according to some machine recognition system. In this paper we used an HMM [7] trained on an unconstrained, writer-independent data set to calculate $S_i(\mathcal{I})$ as a measure of the HMM's probability of $\mathcal{I}$ given w_i. In practice, we threshold $S_i(\mathcal{I})$ to disregard low scores which results in stacks averaging ~ 16 non-zero entries. For the rest of the paper, we drop explicit reference to $\mathcal{I}$.

Stack retrieval methods work by defining a measure between the stack from a query and the stacks from a database. The measure is used to rank each database stack relative to each query stack. Documents are then retrieved in their ranked order. The precision and recall of various measures can be compared based on the rankings. We now define some retrieval methods

The keyword measure is analogous to standard keyword searches of text documents; however in our case, for a keyword, w_i, a stack is retrieved only if its corresponding stack score, S_i, is above a threshold. The retrieved stacks are then ranked by their relative S_i scores. This approach assumes that the query was entered as text rather than ink.

The recognition measure (and all subsequent measures) assumes that the query was entered as ink and has been converted into a stack. The stack word with the highest score is then used as text entry to the keyword method (Sec. 2). Clearly this method can not work as well as the keyword measure with the correct word; however it will benefit from the fact that even though a query may be recognized incorrectly, the incorrect word will probably exist in other stacks of the same word. More importantly, this method allows the user to write a query; in some circumstances, this may be the preferred method of entry (*e.g.* PDA's.)

The Okapi measure [9] between a query stack, $\boldsymbol{q}$, and a document stack, $\boldsymbol{d}$, is given by

$$O(\boldsymbol{q}, \boldsymbol{d}) = \sum_i \frac{f(i, \boldsymbol{d}) f(i, \boldsymbol{q}) g(\boldsymbol{d}, \boldsymbol{D})}{C_1 + C_2 L(\boldsymbol{d})/A + f(i, \boldsymbol{d})} \tag{1}$$

where the inverse document frequency is given by

$$g(\boldsymbol{d}, \boldsymbol{D}) = \log \left(\frac{N - n(\boldsymbol{d}, \boldsymbol{D}) + 0.5}{n(\boldsymbol{d}, \boldsymbol{D}) + 0.5} \right), \tag{2}$$

N is the number of documents in the database; $\boldsymbol{D}$ is the set of all document stacks; $L(\boldsymbol{d})$ is the length of stack $\boldsymbol{d}$ (i.e. the number of scores above a threshold);

$f(i, d)$ is the term frequency of the i-th word in d which we define as the normalized recognition score of the i-th word times $L(d)$; $f(i, q)$ is the query term frequency; $A = \frac{1}{N} \sum_{d \in D} L(d)$ is the average length of all stacks; $n(d, D)$ is the number of ink documents associated with D which have the same ground-truth text label as d; and C_1 and C_2 are tunable parameters. In general, ground-truthed text labels to not exist; so the stacks must be used to estimate $n(d, D)$. In our use of the Okapi formula, we have not optimized the free parameters but have chosen instead to use values that have been successfully used elsewhere [6, 8] ($C_1 = 0.5$ and $C_2 = 1.5$) since Okapi is known to be fairly robust to these parameters.

The correlation measure between a query stack, q, and a document stack, d, is given by

$$C(q, d) = \frac{q \cdot d}{q \cdot q + d \cdot d} \tag{3}$$

which is always between 0 and 0.5. The correlation is used to rank the database stacks.

The cosine measure between a query stack, q, and a document stack, d, is given by

$$\cos(q, d) = \frac{q \cdot d}{\sqrt{(q \cdot q)(d \cdot d)}} \tag{4}$$

which is always between 0 and 1. The cosine is then used to rank the database stacks. The q and d can be pre-normalized to reduce computation. This is the same measure used in LSI [10].

3   Experiments

In order to compare the IR performance of the various methods outlined above, a database of 1158 unconstrained, handwritten ink words (580 unique word labels) from sentences of 75 writers was converted into stacks using multistate, Bakis-topology HMMs [7]. The scores in the stacks correspond loosely to the log-likelihoods of the data given words. A beam search algorithm was used to prune out unlikely words from a lexicon of 30,000 words resulting in stacks ranging in length from 2 to 20 words with an average of 16. Each stack was associated with a visual ground-truthed "correct" word label.

All of the experiments reported in this paper are carried out using leave-one-out cross-validation queries in which each word was removed from the database in turn and used as a query against the remainder with the exception of words which only appear once in the database (445 words) which were not used as queries since one can not retrieve documents that do not exist. Results were then tallied over all queries.

For each query, q, we calculated recall and precision as follows:

$$\text{Recall}(q, D_q, \theta) = \frac{nc(q, D_q, \theta)}{n(q, D_q)} \tag{5}$$

$$\text{Precision}(\boldsymbol{q}, \boldsymbol{D}_q, \theta) = \frac{nc(\boldsymbol{q}, \boldsymbol{D}_q, \theta)}{nr(\boldsymbol{q}, \boldsymbol{D}_q, \theta)} \tag{6}$$

where $\boldsymbol{D}_q$ is the set of all document stacks without the stack $\boldsymbol{q}$, $nr(\boldsymbol{q}, \boldsymbol{D}_q, \theta)$ is the number of stacks retrieved from $\boldsymbol{D}_q$, $nc(\boldsymbol{q}, \boldsymbol{D}_q, \theta)$ is the number of correct stacks retrieved from $\boldsymbol{D}_q$, and θ is a threshold used to truncate the document rankings that are generated for each query. The averages over all queries of the recall and precision for all θ are reported in the figures.

4 Results

Fig. 1A compares the precision vs. recall curves for the keyword, recognition keyword, Okapi, cosine, correlation factor and LSI measures. Our first observation is that keyword performs better than recognition keyword - as expected, there is a significant penalty for making the query more flexible (*i.e.* including ink queries.) More surprising is the observation that the recognition keyword performs significantly better than Okapi, correlation factor, cosine and LSI[1] which are comparable methods to much of current IR research. Since these results are on a database of 75 different writers, experiments on data from a single writer are likely to be better due to increased similarity of the ink.

Fig. 1B shows how the recognition keyword measure can be significantly improved by knowing whether or not the HMM correctly recognized the ink query. As one might expect, when the query is known to be correctly recognized by the HMM, the precision/recall performance is virtually the same as the keyword measure. This suggests that one way to improve ink query retrieval performance is to display the recognition results for the query to the user for verification before performing retrieval. If the recognition is incorrect, the user could optionally correct it.

In addition to straightforward ranking, we can also use a threshold on the stack scores to prune stacks out of the query-based rankings. The rationale for doing this is that stacks are less likely to correspond to the correct word as scores decrease. Figs. 2AB and 3A show how the precision/recall curve for the keyword, recognition keyword and Okapi measures improves as score cutoff threshold increases. Note that the precision improvement comes at cost to recall. The improvement in Okapi doesn't quite match that of the keyword and recognition keyword, but in the low recall domain, it is closer. Also note that excessive pruning severely degrades performance.

Fig. 3B shows a similar plot for the keyword measure using a rank cutoff to prune stacks. Rank pruning improves precision and recall more than score pruning. This is because the majority of the correct words are in the top two stack positions and for nearly all stacks containing the correct word, the correct word occurs in one of the top five stack positions. This suggests that this method can be made even faster at little loss to performance by only creating stacks of

---

[1] Following heuristics in the LSI literature, we chose to use an 800 dimensional LSI factor subspace. No optimization was performed.

length five. It further suggests that by combining rank and score thresholding, we may be able to improve precision while minimizing the recall degradation.

5 Summary

We have described a new IR method for ink documents based on the idea of converting individual words into stack documents and defining a stack measure for constructing a ranking for document retrieval. The method compares favorably to existing stack measures; can be used in both text and ink retrieval mode; and is fast because the stack comparison process is fast and the stack generation process for the ink database need only be performed once and can therefore be performed off-line and in advance. In the future, we will apply these techniques to more complex ink queries and ink documents.

Acknowledgements

The authors would like to thank Alain Biem, Martin Franz, Ken Ocheltree, John Pitrelli, Gene Ratzlaff, Greg Russell and Jay Subrahmonia of the IBM T.J. Watson Research Center for useful discussions, and John Pitrelli for meticulous proofreading.

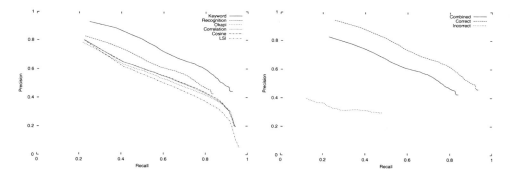

Fig. 1. Precision vs. recall: comparison (Fig. A, left) and for recognition keyword when the query is known to be recognized correctly and incorrectly. (Fig. B, right)

References

[1] Aref, W., Barbara, D., Vallabhaneni, P.: The Handwritten Trie: Indexing Electronic Ink. Proceedings of the SIGMOD (1995) 151-162
[2] El-Nasan, A. Nagy, G.: Ink-Link. Proceedings of the ICPR (2000) [to appear]
[3] Golovchinsky, G., Price, M., Schilit, B.: From Reading to Retrieval: Freeform Ink Annotation as Queries. Proceedings of the SIGIR (1999) 19-25

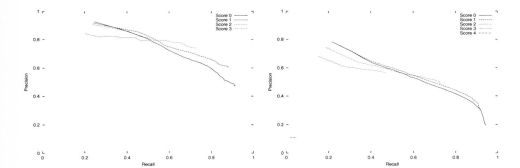

Fig. 2. Precision vs. recall dependence on score cut-off threshold for keyword (Fig. A, left) and recognition measure (Fig. B, right)

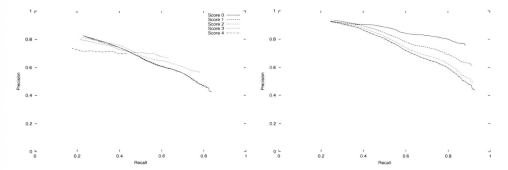

Fig. 3. Precision vs. recall dependence on score cut-off threshold for Okapi (Fig. A, left) and on rank cutoff for keyword (Fig. B, right)

[4] Nielsen, J., Phillips, V., Dumais, S.: Information Retrieval of Imperfectly Recognized Handwriting. `http://www.useit.com/papers/handwriting_retrieval.html` (1993)

[5] Lopresti, D., Tompkins, A.: On the Searchability of Electronic Ink. Proceedings of the IWFHR (1998)

[6] Ponte, J., Croft, W.: A Language Model Approach to Information Retrieval. Proceedings of the SIGIR (1998) 275-281

[7] Subrahmonia, J., Nathan, K., Perrone, M.: Writer Dependent Recognition of On-Line Unconstrained Handwriting. Proceedings of the ICASSP (1996) 3478-3481

[8] Turtle, H., Croft, W.: Efficient Probabilistic Inference for Text Retrieval. Proceedings of the RIAO (1991)

[9] Robertson, S., Walker, S., Jones, M., Hancock-Beaulieu, Gatford, M.: Okapi at TREC-3. Proc. TREC-3 (1995)

[10] Deerwester, S., Dumais, S., Furnas, G., Landauer, T., Harshman, R.: Indexing by Latent Semantic Analysis. J. of American Society for Information Science. (1990) 41:391-407

An Off-Line Recognizer
for Hand-Written Chinese Characters

P.K. Wong

Department of Computing
Hong Kong Institute of Vocational Education (Sha Tin)
Vocational Training Council
21 Yuen Wo Road, Sha Tin, N.T., Hong Kong
spkwong@vtc.edu.hk

Abstract. An off-line hand-written Chinese character recognizer supporting a vocabulary of 4,616 Chinese characters, alphanumerics and punctuation symbols has been reported. Trained with a sample for each character from each of 100 writers and tested on texts of 160,000 characters written by another 200 writers, the average recognition rate is 77.2%. Two statistical language models have been investigated in this study. Their performances in terms of their capabilities in upgrading the recognition rate by 8.8% and 12.0% respectively when used as postprocessors of the recognizer.

1 Introduction

Chinese characters are complex patterns of strokes. The bit-map of a character image can be segmented into a number of regions each of which consists of either purely white or purely black pixels. An unknown character image is recognized by identifying its regions to that of the templates. The structural information of an image in terms of the inter-relationship between its regions is represented statistically. The location and size of a region are stochastic. Even if a pixel is known to belong to a particular region, the cellular features [1] considered as a feature vector, observed at the pixel are still stochastic and different feature vectors can be observed at different pixels of the same region. A region is not characterized by just the distribution of feature vectors observed at its pixels, but by the stochastic relationship between it and its neighbor regions also as well as its location and size. The totality of such stochastic properties of a region defines a codeword. Hence, a codeword and a region are synonymous. A character as a collection of regions corresponds therefore to a codebook.

2 Contextual Vector Quantization Character Recognizer

A character image is abstracted into a matrix of cellular feature vectors $\mathbf{O} = [\mathbf{o}_{i,j}]$ with $\mathbf{o}_{i,j}$ observed at pixel (i,j). Each $\mathbf{o}_{i,j}$ is modeled as a realization of a random vector observable in $z_{i,j}$ which is the region where pixel (i,j) is located. $z_{i,j}$ takes one of the K qualitative values $\{G_1, G_2, \cdots, G_K\}$ each of which is a region of the character. Each region is characterized by three sets of attributes: $\{Pr(z_{i,j} = G_k), Pr(\mathbf{o}_{i,j} \mid G_k), Pr(z_{m,n} = G_l \mid z_{i,j} = G_k)\}$. m and n are integers equal to $i - 1$ to $i + 1$ and $j - 1$ to $j + 1$ respectively indexing the regions of the immediate neighbors of pixel (i,j). If these attributes of a region are fitted into the framework of a codeword, then a character is modeled by a codebook. Matching an unknown to a character becomes quantizing $\mathbf{O}$ with the codebook of the character. $Pr(z_{m,n} = G_l \mid z_{i,j} = G_k)$ supplies the contextual information and that leads to the name Contextual Vector Quantization (CVQ).

$\mathbf{O}$ is quantized by quantizing each of its pixels individually. Pixel (i,j) is quantized to $z_{i,j}$ in order to maximize the posterior probability $\Pr(z_{i,j}|\mathbf{O})$. In order to reduce the complexity of the problem, $z_{i,j}$ is chosen to maximize $\Pr(z_{i,j}|\mathbf{o}_{i,j}, \mathbf{o}_{\eta_{i,j}})$, where $\eta_{i,j}$ is the immediate neighborhood of pixel (i,j). Under the assumption that feature vectors in the same neighborhood are related to each other through the regions they belong to only, one then has this posterior probability proportional to:

$$\sum_{z_{\eta_{i,j}}} \left\{ \Pr(z_{i,j}, z_{\eta_{i,j}}) \cdot \prod_{(m,n) \in \eta_{i,j}^+} Pr(\mathbf{o}_{m,n}|z_{m,n}) \right\} \tag{1}$$

where the summation is over all admissible values of $z_{\eta_{i,j}}$ defining the region membership of the pixels in the prescribed neighborhood $\eta_{i,j}$ of pixel (i,j). $\eta_{i,j}^+$ is the union of $\eta_{i,j}$ and (i,j). Even with this simplification, analytical progress is barred in general, because $\Pr(z_{i,j}, z_{\eta_{i,j}})$ is unavailable in closed form. For further simplification, it is assumed that $z_{m,n}$'s, where $(m,n) \in \eta_{i,j}$, are mutually independent given $z_{i,j}$. So,

$$\Pr(z_{i,j}, z_{\eta_{i,j}}) = \Pr(z_{i,j}) \cdot \prod_{(m,n) \in \eta_{i,j}} \Pr(z_{m,n}|z_{i,j}) \tag{2}$$

A CVQ method can be derived as follows. Given a character image with observed feature vectors $[\mathbf{o}_{i,j}]$, assign each $\mathbf{o}_{i,j}$ to region G_k if

$$G_k = argmax_{z_{i,j}} Pr(z_{i,j}) \cdot Pr(\mathbf{o}_{i,j}|z_{i,j}) \cdot$$
$$\prod_{(m,n) \in \eta_{i,j}} \sum_{z_{m,n}} \Pr(z_{m,n}|z_{i,j}) \cdot Pr(\mathbf{o}_{m,n}|z_{m,n}) \tag{3}$$

where the term on the second line of Eq.(3) represents the contribution of contextual information. The argument of the $argmax_{z_{i,j}}$ function:

$$Pr(z_{i,j}) \cdot Pr(\mathbf{o}_{i,j}|z_{i,j}) \cdot$$
$$\prod_{(m,n) \in \eta_{i,j}} \sum_{z_{m,n}} \Pr(z_{m,n}|z_{i,j}) \cdot Pr(\mathbf{o}_{m,n}|z_{m,n}) \tag{4}$$

is a pseudo-likelihood measurement of quantizing $\mathbf{o}_{i,j}$ to region G_k.

Upon matching an unknown image to a character template ω for identification, regions of the unknown image are matched to regions of ω. That in turn, is accomplished by identifying a region of ω for each pixel of the unknown image to be quantized to. That avoids segmenting an unknown image into regions explicitly and then matching them as a random graph as in [2]. This process of region identification for each pixel considers not just the pixel in question, but its neighboring pixels and the most suitable regions they belong to as well. Thus, recognizing a character becomes identifying the codebook that yields the minimum quantization error (measured in terms of the inverse of a pseudo-likelihood function) to the unknown image.

This algorithm has been implemented in an off-line writer independent handwritten character recognizer supporting a vocabulary of 4,616 Chinese characters, alphanumerics and punctuation symbols [3]. The codebook for each character is trained with 100 samples written by 100 writers. When tested on 160,000 characters written by another 200 writers, the recognition rate is 77.2%

3 Post-Processing Language Models

If the input is a syntactically and semantically sound sequence of characters, its linguistic information can provide a useful basis for improving the recognition rate [4]. The second phase of the character recognizer is thus a language model which endows the recognizer with linguistic (just statistical at present) knowledge of Chinese. For each character image, the language model chooses the most suitable one out of the n-best candidates proposed by the image recognizer in order to arrive at a sequence of characters which is linguistically sound according to some criteria. There are two statistical language models experimented in this study as a post-processor of the image recognizer. They select a candidate according to its capability to form words with its neighboring images.

3.1 Lexical Analysis of a Lattice of n-best Candidates

The lexical analytic statistical language model bases on the usage frequency of each word in a large lexicon. This lexicon must cover most, if not all, of the Chinese words actively used in modern texts such as journals, newspapers, and literature. In order to determine the statistics of word-pairs, to enrich the lexicon of its vocabulary and to improve the estimates of word usage frequencies, a large Chinese text corpus of over 63 million characters has been acquired. The first step towards gathering such statistics is to segment text lines into words because different from texts in English, there is no explicit word marker in Chinese texts.

Maximum matching [5] is one of the most popular structural segmentation algorithms for Chinese texts. This method favors long words and is a greedy algorithm in nature, hence, sub-optimal. Segmentation may start from either end of the line without any difference in segmentation results. In this study, the forward direction is adopted. The major advantage of maximum matching is its efficiency while its segmentation accuracy can be expected to lie around 95%.

Most Chinese linguists accept the definition of a word as the minimum unit that is semantically complete and can be put together as building blocks to form a sentence. However, in Chinese, words can be united to form compound words, and they in turn, can combine further to form yet higher ordered compound words. As a matter of fact, compound words are extremely common and they exist in large numbers. It is impossible to include all compound words into the lexicon but just to keep those which are frequently used and have closely united word components. A lexicon, WORDDATA, was acquired from the Institute of Information Science, Academia Sinica in Taiwan. There are 78,410 word entries in this lexicon, each associated with a usage frequency. Due to cultural differences of the two societies, there are many words encountered in the text corpus but not in the lexicon. The latter must therefore be enriched before it can be applied to perform any lexical analysis. The first step towards this end is to merge a lexicon constructed in China into this one made in Taiwan, increasing the number of word entries to 85,855. This extended lexicon is then applied to segment the text corpus into words. In this process, when a word of a single character is encountered, word usage frequencies will be considered to decide if the single character should not be combined with it neighboring characters to form other words on the expense of the length of neighboring words. In this word segmentation process, words used in the text corpus but not found in the lexicon will be considered to be added to the latter which is eventually enriched to encompass 87,326 words.

The image recognizer supplies the n-best candidates for each character image scanned. A line of text as a sequence of m images delimited by a pair of punctuation symbols correspond to m by n candidates. Starting from the first image position, the longest word that can be formed with a candidate of the image as the first character of the word is accepted. This repeats starting from the next image position lying beyond the last image of the word just formed until the end of the line is reached.

As n increases, the number of coincidental word formations increases also, thus bringing down the recognition rate instead of upgrading it. On the other hand, for pages poorly recognized, n must be large enough to include the true candidate. A compromise on the optimal choice of n is reached by experimenting the effect of n on the recognition rates on another 100 pages earmarked for language model tuning. Consequently, n is chosen to be 6. The recognition rate over the test text of 160,000 characters is upgraded to 86% from 77.2%.

3.2   A Language Model of Word Class Bigram Statistics

The limitation of maximum matching word segmentation as a language model is its failure to capture the inter-dependence of words in a line of text. The use of bigram statistics in a language model is a step towards overcoming this shortcoming. Since there are over 80,000 words in the lexicon, the number of parameters in such a language model will be astronomical. A common practice is to employ the bigram statistics between word-classes instead. If a sequence of character images $\mathbf{o}_1, ..., \mathbf{o}_T$ is segmented into $\mathbf{o}_1^{w_1}, ..., \mathbf{o}_{k_1}^{w_1}, \mathbf{o}_1^{w_2}, ..., \mathbf{o}_{k_2}^{w_2}, ...,$

$\mathbf{o}_1^{w_h}, ..., \mathbf{o}_{k_h}^{w_h}$ correpsonding to a word sequence of $w_1, ..., w_h$ which in turn, belonging to word-classes $s_1, ..., s_h$ respectively, the soundness of the segmentation is measured in terms of:

$$L = p(s_0 \mid s_h) \prod_{i=1}^{h} p(s_i \mid s_{i-1}) p(\mathbf{o}_1^{w_i}, ..., \mathbf{o}_{k_i}^{w_i} \mid s_i) \tag{5}$$

where s_0 is a word-class of punctuation symbols appearing before and after the sequence of character images. $p(s_i \mid s_{i-1})$ and $p(s_0 \mid s_h)$ can be collected from the segmented text corpus while the suitability of $\mathbf{o}_1^{w_i}, ..., \mathbf{o}_{k_i}^{w_i}$ forming a word w_i in s_i is defined as:

$$p(\mathbf{o}_1^{w_i}, ..., \mathbf{o}_{k_i}^{w_i} \mid s_i) = p(w_i \mid s_i) \prod_{j=1}^{k_i} p(\mathbf{o}_j^{w_i} \mid c_j^{w_i}) \tag{6}$$

Here, word w_i is a character sequence $c_1^{w_i}, ..., c_{k_i}^{w_i}$. $p(w_i \mid s_i)$ is computed from the segmented text corpus. $p(\mathbf{o}_j^{w_i} \mid c_j^{w_i})$ is a measure of similarity between the observed image $\mathbf{o}_j$ and the character $c_j^{w_i}$ of the word w_i supplied by the image recognizer. The principle of dynamic programming is employed to determine the optimal segmentation of the character images into words.

Originally, words in WORDDATA are grouped into 192 syntactic/semantic word-classes with each word belonging to mostly one but up to four word-classes. In this investigation, each word is assigned the membership of the most important class indicated in WORDDATA. A natural and objective criterion in measuring the soundness of any clustering is that all members within a cluster should have a similar pattern of associations with all clusters. From the text corpus, the probability of observing word w_j of s_i placed before any word of class s_q, can be computed for all q. Associated with word w_j of s_i, there is therefore a probability vector $\mathbf{p}_j^{s_i}$ of 192 components, viz., $p_{j_k}^{s_i}$ for $k = 1, 2, ..., 192$. $p_{j_k}^{s_i}$ is the probability of seeing w_j of class s_i before any word of class s_k in an average line of the corpus. Since each word belongs to one class only in this investigation, there is no ambiguity if the superscript s_i is dropped in $\mathbf{p}_j^{s_i}$ and its components. These vectors are normalized so that they lie on the surface of a unit hyper-sphere.

The centroid $\mathbf{C_i}$ of class s_i is defined as a unit vector along the direction of the average probability vector of all the words (weighted by the prior probability of the word) of the class. With this concept in mind, the homogeneity of class s_i, a word-class of M_i words, can be defined as:

$$H_i = \sum_{j=1}^{M_i} P(w_j) \mathbf{C}_i \cdot \mathbf{p}_j^{s_i} \tag{7}$$

Various thresholds are chosen over a number of iterations so that any word-class with a homogeneity below it will be split into two as in ISODATA, except that the feature space is confined to a unit hyper-sphere surface. A newly formed word-class with a homogeneity still below the threshold will be further split repeatedly. At the end of an iteration corresponding to a particular homogeneity threshold, the effect of the word-class bigram statistics language model on the recognition of the 100 earmarked pages is measured. Finally, 470 word-classes are formed and bigram statistics between them are collected from the text corpus when the process converges.

The word-class splitting process discussed above is hierarchical. To mitigate the ill effect caused by any mis-classification of words in WORDDATA, after the number of classes has stabilized at 470, each word is re-assigned to a word-class whose centroid has the minimum inner product with the probability vector of the word. As soon as a word has been re-assigned, the centroids of the two word-classes affected are updated accordingly. With the newly defined word memberships, the probability vector of each word is re-computed by going over the text corpus again and so are the homogeneities of all word-classes consequently. This process repeats over several iterations. The average recognition rate is upgraded to 89.2% after the word-class reassignment process.

4 Discussion

An off-line hand-written Chinese character recognizer supporting a vocabulary of 4,616 Chinese characters, alphanumerics and punctuation symbols has been reported. For the blocks of related news lines with 9 candidates for each image, the average recognition rate using the language model as a post processor is 87.13% compared to 77.2% achieved by the recognizer without language model. It shows that the language model is very effective in helping the recognizer to select suitable character candidates.

References

1. T.H. Hildebrandt & W.T. Liu, "Optical Recognition of Handwritten Chinese Characters: Advances since 1980", *Pattern Recognition*, Vol. 26, No. 2, pp. 205-225, 1993.
2. A.K.C. Wong & M. You, "Entropy and Distance of Random Graphs with Application to Structural Pattern Recognition", *IEEE Trans. on PAMI*, Vol. 7, No. 5, pp. 599-609, 1985.
3. S.L. Leung, P.C. Chee, Q. Huo & C. Chan; "Contextual Vector Quantization Modeling of Handprinted Chinese Character Recognition"; *Procs. of IEEE International Conference on Image Processing*, pp. 432-435, Washington, D.C., Oct. 1995.
4. K.T. Lua, "From Character to Word – An Application of Information Theory", *Computer Processing of Chinese and Oriental Languages*, Vol. 4, No. 4, pp. 304-313, March 1990.
5. Y. Liu, Q. Tan and K.X. Shen, "The Word Segmentation Rules and Automatic Word Segmentation Methods for Chinese Information Processing (in Chinese)", *Tsinghua University Press and Guangxi Science and Technology Press*, page 36, 1994.

Bayesian Learning for Image Retrieval
Using Multiple Features

Lei Wang, Kap Luk Chan[†]

School of Electrical and Electronic Engineering,
Nanyang Technological University
Nanyang Avenue, Singapore 639798
[†]eklchan@ntu.edu.sg,
[†]Home page: http://www.ntu.edu.sg/home/eklchan

Abstract. Image retrieval using multiple features often uses explicit weights that represent the importance of the features in their similarity metrics. In this paper, a novel retrieval method based on Bayesian Learning is presented. Instead of giving every feature a weight explicitly, the importance of a feature is regulated implicitly by learning a user's perception. Thus, the process of feature combination is adaptive and approximate to a user's perception. Experimental results demonstrate the significance of this method for improving the retrieval efficiency.

1 Introduction

Content-based image retrieval aims to find images that are similar to a user's query through extracted image features. In the early work, most research focused on retrieval by using a single feature, and the feature used is inadequate to describe the content of a general image. Hence, the retrieval performances are often unsatisfactory. To remedy the situation, retrieval using multiple features are now commonly used[4, 7, 9]. Often, weights are used in a linear combination of features. The weights are used to represent the importance of the individual features in the computation of a similarity metric. However, there is often not a linear relationship among these features in the similarity measure. In [5, 1], the rank of retrieved image is either used instead of similarity scores for combining features or used to derive weights. However, the rank is also not linearly proportional to the similarity nor to each feature. In [10], a neural network model for merging heterogeneous features is presented. This model can be used to determine nonlinear relationship between features.

When using multiple features, the key problem is how to decide the importance of individual features. After all, every user has his own subjective perception to the importance of these features. Or worse still the user's perception of the image content is more on high level semantics than low level image features. Therefore, the combination of multiple features should not be rigid but adaptive to the user. It is then essential to learn a user's perception when combining multiple features for image retrieval. By doing so, the semantics is also implicitly learned.

In this paper, a novel retrieval method based on Bayesian Learning is presented, in which Bayesian Learning is adopted to learn a user's perception. The combination of different features is regulated by the learned perception from a relevance feedback process. The probability of positive retrieval is used as the similarity metric to rank candidate images and then the top N_{out} images are output as retrieval result. Experimental results show that this method can improve the retrieval efficiency significantly.

In section 2, the system model for Bayesian Learning is presented. In section 3, the algorithm based on Bayesian Learning is introduced. Section 4 presents the results. Finally, concluding remarks are given in section 5.

2   The System Model for Bayesian Learning

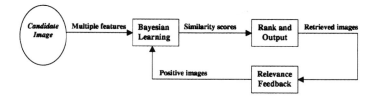

Fig. 1. The model for Bayesian Learning

The system model for Bayesian Learning is shown in Fig.1. The block of Bayesian Learning is the core of the system model. It executes the learning process and regulates the combination of multiple features. This block receives different features extracted from a candidate image and outputs the corresponding similarity scores in terms of probability. The Rank and Output block ranks candidate images according to the corresponding probabilities and output the top N_{out} images as retrieval result at each retrieval cycle. The block of Relevance Feedback [9, 1, 8, 3, 2] is used to feed a user's perception into the learning process. By Relevance Feedback, a user can submit images that he/she considers similar to the query as positive images. The connection between the two blocks of Relevance Feedback and Bayesian Learning is very important in the model because the positive images provide the successive data for learning. The block of Bayesian Learning is refreshed by learning the training data, and the user's perception reflected in the positive images is grasped. Then, the feature combination will be regulated according to the newly learned perception, and candidate images will be retrieved by a refreshed criterion. As shown in Fig.1, the whole process builds up a learning cycle. In a retrieval process, this learning cycle will continue until the retrieval process satisfactorily ends.

3   The Algorithm Based on Bayesian Learning

Let $F = \{f_i\}, (1 \leq i \leq N)$ be the set of features used in image retrieval, and f_i^q and f_i^c be the feature vectors of a query and a candidate image, respectively. Also, S represents the set of the positive images that are similar to a given query. $P(S \mid F)$ gives the probability that an image belongs to set S when multiple features $f_i (1 \leq i \leq N)$ are considered. This probability can be used as a metric to rank candidate images.

By defining a hypothesis space $H = \{S, \overline{S}\}$ and F as the observed training data, then $P(S \mid F)$ can be obtained by Bayesian Learning[6, 11, 3, 2].

$$P(S \mid F) = \frac{P(F \mid S)P(S)}{P(F)} \qquad (1)$$

To obtain the rank of candidate images, all $P(S \mid F)$ for these images are calculated and compared. However, both $P(F \mid S)$ and $P(F)$ are variables here. Yet, only $P(F \mid S)$ and $P(F \mid \overline{S})$ require learning by considering that $P(F) = P(F \mid S)P(S) + P(F \mid \overline{S})P(\overline{S})$. As for the prior probabilities of $P(S)$ and $P(\overline{S})$, it is not necessary to consider them for the reason given later.

Compared to learning $P(F \mid S)$ and $P(F \mid \overline{S})$, it is more convenient to learn their probability densities $p(F \mid S)$ and $p(F \mid \overline{S})$ in practice. In the learning algorithm, they are learned from two directions, respectively. Initially, S is a null set while $\overline{S}$ includes all of the candidate images. When some positive images are submitted, they are moved from $\overline{S}$ to S. Then, $p(F \mid S)$ and $p(F \mid \overline{S})$ will be refreshed accordingly.

Considering the rank of $P(S \mid F)$ is what a retrieval process is really concerned with, equation(1) is rewritten as

$$P(S \mid F) = \frac{1}{1 + \left[\frac{P(F|S)P(S)}{P(F|\overline{S})P(\overline{S})}\right]^{-1}} \qquad (2)$$

Because $P(S)$ and $P(\overline{S})$ are dependent on users but independent on candidate images, the ratio of $P(S)$ and $P(\overline{S})$ will not affect the rank and hence are not considered for a given query. Then the rank of $P(S \mid F)$ can be derived as

$$\begin{aligned} Rank(P(S \mid F)) &= Rank\left(\frac{P(F|S)}{P(F|\overline{S})}\right) \\ &= Rank\left(\frac{p(F|S)}{p(F|\overline{S})}\right) \end{aligned} \qquad (3)$$

Assuming that all of these $f_i (1 \leq i \leq N)$ are independent of each other for reducing the computation. Then,

$$Rank(P(S \mid F)) = Rank\left(\prod_{i=1}^{N} \frac{p(f_i \mid S)}{p(f_i \mid \overline{S})}\right) \qquad (4)$$

Since estimating $p(f_i \mid S)$ and $p(f_i \mid \overline{S})$ will bring heavy computation for large feature dimensions, a function of f_i^c, $d_i = T(f_i^c) = \| f_i^c - f_i^q \|$ is used to replace the corresponding f_i^c. Thus, only the distributions of d_i corresponding to these f_i^c from S and $\overline{S}$ need estimating.

A second assumption is that the distributions of the d_i from S and $\overline{S}$ are all normal, then equation(4) can be further simplified as

$$
\begin{aligned}
& Rank(P(S \mid F)) \\
& = Rank\left(\prod_{i=1}^{N} \frac{\sigma_{\overline{s},i}}{\sigma_{s,i}} exp(-\frac{(d_i-\mu_{s,i})^2}{2\sigma_{s,i}^2} + \frac{(d_i-\mu_{\overline{s},i})^2}{2\sigma_{\overline{s},i}^2})\right) \\
& = Rank\left(\sum_{i=1}^{N}[(\frac{d_i-\mu_{\overline{s},i}}{\sigma_{\overline{s},i}})^2 - (\frac{d_i-\mu_{s,i}}{\sigma_{s,i}})^2]\right) \\
& = Rank\left(\sum_{i=1}^{N} D(d_i)\right)
\end{aligned}
\tag{5}
$$

Note that $\mu_{s,i} = \frac{1}{T_s}\sum_{k=1}^{T_s} d_{i,k}$ and $d_{i,k}(1 \le k \le T_s)$ are the distances between the query and the T_s positive images submitted by then, while $\mu_{\overline{s},i} = \frac{1}{T_{\overline{s}}}\sum_{k=1}^{T_{\overline{s}}} d_{i,k}$ and $d_{i,k}(1 \le k \le T_{\overline{s}})$ are the distances between the query and the other $T_{\overline{s}}$ images.

From (5), it can be found that $D(.)$ plays a similar role as a weight in deciding the importance of multiple features. However, the transform is more adaptive and has a concrete base because it is derived from the user's perception. Furthermore, the more important thing is that $D(.)$ makes the rank derived identical to the user's perception. It is the ultimate goal of a retrieval process.

Let R_{f_i} be the vector whose elements are the rank values derived from feature f_i, and let R_F be the rank vector from multiple features according to the same image list. Then the distance of R_{f_i} and R_F can be shown as

$$
L_{f_i} =\| R_{f_i} - R_F \|
\tag{6}
$$

Apparently, the smaller the distance L_{f_i} for a feature is, the more powerful the feature's ability on controlling the rank R_F will be. It implies simultaneously that the feature is more important in a retrieval. Furthermore, a feature's normalized ability on controlling the rank R_F can be shown as

$$
C(f_i) = \frac{1}{N-1}\left(1 - \frac{L_{f_i}}{\sum_{i=1}^{N} L_{f_i}}\right)
\tag{7}
$$

If a user's perception can really be learned here, the function of $D(.)$ should make it true that the $C(f_i)$ for a feature f_i focused by the user should be granted a higher value than the others. Simultaneously, for the feature f_i, the corresponding retrieval efficiency should be higher than the others because it corresponds to the visual content which the user focuses on. Consequently, it can be deduced that if $E(f_i)$ is defined to represent the retrieval efficiency using f_i, then

$$
E(f_i) > E(f_j) \Longleftrightarrow C(f_i) > C(f_j) \qquad (1 \le i,j \le N, i \ne j)
\tag{8}
$$

4 Performance Evaluation

In the experiment, texture and color features are considered. The texture feature is based on Gabor Filtering of an image. For color feature, a color histogram is extracted from the RGB color space. The image database used in the experiment consists 1,400 general color images composed from $VisTex$ of MIT and Corel Stock Photos. The images are classified into 70 classes manually by several human observers for the purpose of evaluating experimental results. To illustrate the retrieval process clearly, the steps are shown below.

1. According to $f_i(1 \leq i \leq N)$, the corresponding d_i are calculated for all of the candidate images.
2. Rank the candidate images according to every type of d_i and N lists are formed. Base on the number N_{out} ($N_{out} = 10$ used here), the top $\left\lceil \frac{N_{out}}{N} \right\rceil$ images are collected from every list and output as the initial retrieval result. Duplicated images of a lower rank are ignored.
3. By relevance feedback, all positive images among N_{out} are submitted.
4. Distributions are refreshed in the following learning and for every image, its D_i's are calculated and summed.
5. A new ranking of all images is performed. Then go to step 3.

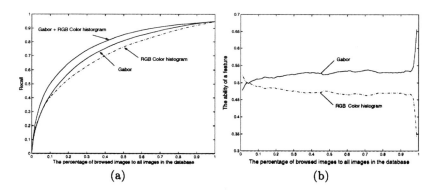

(a)   (b)

Fig. 2. (a)The retrieval efficiency   (b) The ability of a feature

Fig.2(a) gives the results for the retrieval using the combination of texture and color features. In this figure, the horizontal axis represents the percentage of browsed images over all of the images in the database, and the vertical axis represents the percentage of the retrieved positive images over all of the positive images in the database and this is known as *Recall* in image retrieval. Comparing the three curves, it can be seen that the maximum improvements on recall are 11.6% for color feature and 8.5% for texture feature, respectively. Moreover, cross-referencing Fig.2(a) and Fig.2(b), it can be found that the changes on efficiency and the feature's ability correlate. Therefore, the results support the deduction of equation (8) given in section 3. In summary, the results of experiment demonstrate the effectiveness of multiple features retrieval and prove that it is capable to learn a user's perception by Bayesian Learning.

5 Conclusion

In this paper, a novel image retrieval approach for using multiple features is presented. It adopts Bayesian Learning to learn a user's perception through relevance feedback to regulate the importance of features without using explicit weights. The combination of features in the similarity metric is adaptive and approximate to the perception of a user. Experimental results show that the presented approach is capable of learning a user's perception and hence improves the retrieval efficiency.

References

1. Tat-Seng Chua, Chun-xin Chu, and Mohan Kankanhalli, "Relevance Feedback Techniques for Image Retrieval Using Multiple Attributes", *Multimedia Computing and Systems*, IEEE International Conference, Volume 1, 1999
2. Cox, I.J., Miller, M.L., and Omohundro, S.M., Yianilos, P.N. "Pichunter: Bayesian Relevance Feedback for Image Retrieval", *Pattern Recognition*, Proceedings of the 13th International Conference, Volume: 3, 1996
3. Cox, I.J., Miller, M.L., Minka, T.P., Yianilos, P.N., "An Optimized Interaction Strategy for Bayesian Relevance Feedback", *Computer Vision and Pattern Recognition*, Proceedings of IEEE Computer Society Conference, 1998
4. W.Y. Ma, "NETRA: A Toolbox for Navigating Large Image Databases", *Ph.D. Dissertation*, Dept. of Electrical and Computer Engineering, University of California at Santa Barbara, June 1997.
5. Thomas Minka, "An image database browser that learns from user interaction", *Master's thesis*, MIT, 1996
6. Tom M. Mitchell, *Machine learning*, McGraw-Hill Companies, Inc, 1997
7. A. Pentland, R. Picard, and S. Sclaroff, "Photobook: Tools for content-based manipulation of image databases", *Int. Journal of Comp. Vision*, 18(3),1996
8. Yong Rui, Thomas S. Huang, and Sharad Mehrotra, "Content-based Image Retrieval with Relevance Feedback in Mars", *Proc. of IEEE Int. Conf. on Image Processing'97*, October 26-29, 1997 Santa Barbara, California, USA,
9. Yong Rui, Thomas S. Huang, Michael Ortega, and Sharad Mehrotra, "Relevance Feedback: A Power Tool for Interactive Content-Based Image Retrieval", *IEEE transactions on circuits and video technology*, Vol 8, No.5, Sept,1998
10. Gholamhosein Sheikholeslami, Surojit Chatterjee, and Aidong Zhang, "NeuroMerge: An Approach for Merging Heterogeneous Features in Content-based Image Retrieval Systems", *Multi-Media Database Management Systems*, Proceedings of International Workshop, 1998
11. Nuno Vasconcelos and Andrew Lippman, "A Bayesian framework for semantic content characterization", *Computer Vision and Pattern Recognition*, Santa Barbara, 1998

A Context-Based Image Retrieval Method
Using Third-Order Color Feature Relations

H.Y. Kwon[1], H.Y. Hwang[2]

[1] Dept. of Computer Science, Anyang University, Anyang-Shi, 430-714 KOREA
hykwon@aycc.anyang.ac.kr
[2] Dept. of Electronic Engineering, Hoseo University, Asan-Kun, Choongnam,
337-850 KOREA

Abstract. Each content-based image retrieval (CBIR) method using color features includes its limitations to be applied to its own application areas. We analyze that the limitations are mostly due to the adoption of first-order or second-order relations among color features from a given image as its index. In this paper, we propose a new CBIR method based on a third-order color feature relations. This new method shows robustness in retrieving geometrically transformed images and can be applied in various areas.

1 Introduction

Content-based Image Retrieval (CBIR) system retrieves relevant images based on their contents rather than their textual descriptions. Various image features such as color, texture, sketch, shape, volume, etc. are studied and used as retrieval index[1, 2]. Color features are frequently used as an index in CBIR systems. CBIR system using color features, given a query image, retrieves all the images whose color compositions are similar to that of the query image[3, 4]. They, however, are not able to represent spatial information of an image. They are weak at retrieving a translated, rotated and/or scaled image. Many efforts have been made to index the spatial information of an image. They can be classified into two classes according to the order definition and the group invariance theorem [5]. One is based on the first-order relations among color features and the other is based on the second-order relations. The theorem shows that the first-order relations among objects are variant to any transform, and the second-order ones are invariant to translation and rotation, but not to scaling. Therefore, they can retrieve translated and/or rotated images well, but not scaled ones. That is, their application areas are limited by the order relations utilized in the model[6]. We propose a new CBIR method using third-order color feature relations, which is invariant to scaling as well as translation and rotation. This extends its application into various fields.

2 CBIR Using First-Order and Second-Order Color Feature Relations

CBIR system retrieves all the images which are similar to a query image based on a predefined similarity measuring method. CBIR system using color features uses color features as an index of a given image, comparing the similarity between them. In the similarity measurement system using first-order color feature relations, an image is divided into several sub-regions[7]. Color features are then extracted from each sub-region. As color features, color histogram obtained by discretizing the image colors and counting the number of times each discrete color occurs in the image are usually utilized. Then, the similarity of two images is measured by comparing the histograms of each corresponding sub-region. This method can not retrieve an image whose objects are not in the same sub-region as that of the compared image. This results in poor retrievals of translated images.

To solve this problem, the methods using second-order color feature relations have been introduced[8, 9]. These methods assume that if two images are similar, color features extracted from a given image and the compared have the similar distance relationship in any case of translation and/or rotation of the objects in the images. Therefore, they can retrieve similar images by indexing the distance relations. For example, after a histogram is obtained from an image, three highest value histogram bins are selected and the average x, y positions of the pixels in each bin are calculated, then each distance among them are decided. Finally, they are used as an index of the image. These methods are useful for retrieving an image which has any translation and/or rotation of the objects in it. They, however, are still not able to retrieve a scaled image such as enlarged or shrunk images.

From this observation, it is noted that the previous works based on first-order or second-order color feature relations of given images have the limitation in their applications and are not proper to retrieve scaled images in which objects are enlarged or shrunk.

3 CBIR Using Third-Order Color Feature Relations

To solve these problems, we use third-order color feature relations as its retrieval index. It extracts three angles among the corresponding average x, y positions of the pixels in the three highest value histogram bins of a given image. Angle is defined as a third-order relation among three objects and is invariant to scale as well as translation and rotation of objects in the image by the group invariance theorem. The idea is described as follows. If a color histogram H is defined as a vector $(h_0, h_1, ... , h_n)$, where each element h_i represents the number of pixels of the i-th bin in a color histogram of a given image, three kinds of the similarities between two images can be measured using the following similarity measurement equation:

$$D = w_1 \cdot D_H + w_2 \cdot D_L + w_3 \cdot D_\theta \tag{1}$$

where

$$D_H = \sum_{i=0}^{n} \left| h_i - h_i' \right| + \sum_{i=0}^{n} \left(\left| \overline{x_i} - \overline{x_i'} \right| + \left| \overline{y_i} - \overline{y_i'} \right| \right)$$

$$D_L = \left| a - a' \right| + \left| b - b' \right| + \left| c - c' \right|$$

$$D_\theta = \left| \alpha - \alpha' \right| + \left| \beta - \beta' \right| + \left| \gamma - \gamma' \right|.$$

w_i are weights for each order relation, which determines the importance of each term according to its application area. $\overline{x_i}(\overline{y_i})$ are averages of x (y)-coordinate values of pixels in the i-th color histogram element(bin). a, b and c are distances between each two vertices which are determined by the average positions of the first three largest color histogram bins h_i. α, β and γ are angles among each three vertices described in the previous section. D_H, D_L and D_θ represent the similarities of first-order, second-order and third-order color feature relations in a given image respectively.

CBIR using the proposed similarity measurement in Eq. (1) can be used in any application areas such as for any translated, rotated and/or scaled images, because it includes first-order to third-order relations of color features of a given image. In addition, it performs well since each weight of order terms can be adjusted according to its application area. If we set w_1 and w_2 to zero, we can apply it to third-order application area.

4 Experiments

To evaluate the performance of the proposed method, we conducted three experiments; The first one and the second one were performed with four types of geometrically transformed pottery images and the last one with images from various domains. We used a database of 350 color images which are 256*256 in size and classified into 26 groups selected from various application domain sources. All the experiments are performed in the HIS color space, which is more similar to human visual system than RGB one. We discretize H(Hue) to 6 levels, S(Saturation) to 2 levels, and I(Intensity) to 2 levels, and made an index vector of 24 elements (bins). Experimental results are shown in Table 1, 2 and 3.

In the first experiment, the similarity using the three metric, D_H, D_L and D_θ, are demonstrated in Table 1. It shows that D_H, first-order measuring, are changed dramatically as the order of transform in the given image is increased; The order of translation and rotation transform is 2 and the order of scaling transform is 1. D_L, second-order measuring, are good for the translated image and the rotated one, which are second-order transform, but still not good enough for the scaled image, which are obtained from third-order transform. In the other hand, D_θ, third-order measuring, are good for the the scaled image as well as the other images.

Table 2 shows the retrieval results using different order relationship for four types of geometrically transformed (raw, translated, rotated and scaled) pottery images.

'O'('X') means a success(failure) in retrieving a pottery image (a member of the same group as a transformed query image). The most five similar images, which are measured by the Eq.(1), are selected as retrieval results.

Table 3 shows the retrieval success rate with 26 images (one from each group) from the whole image database. The success rate represents the percentage of the resulting images belonging to the same group as the query image.

5 Conclusions

We have proposed a new CBIR method using third-order color feature relations, which is robust to scale as well as translation and/or rotation of objects in a given image. First, we show that the previous indexing methods use first-order or second-order color feature relations, and are not adequate for retrieving an image which has enlarged or shrunk objects. Then, to solve such geometrical transform problems, we defined a third-order color feature relations with three largest color histogram components. Based on this, a geometrical transform invariant CBIR method is proposed. In addition, we have proposed an adaptation method that performs well and presented the comparative results to the previous works. The experiments show that our method based on third order relations is very efficient at retrieving scaled images as well as translated or rotated ones. The retrieving rates of the proposed method are more stable and higher than those of the previous methods based on first-order or second-order relations in case of retrieving images from various domains, too. We believe that these results are due to a superior geometrical transform invariance of third-order relations.

The proposed method, however, has some problems to be solved. First, background colors in an image affect the retrieving result. Usually, it is difficult to remove it from a given image. The other is related with normalization methods of the three metric, D_H, D_L and D_θ respectively. Currently, it depends on each application area and should be chosen case by case. Although the proposed method still has some problems, it can be applied to the multimedia data retrieval systems effectively.

References

1. Gudivada, V.: 'Content-Based Image Retrieval Systems', IEEE Computer, Sep. (1995) 18-22
2. Flickner, M.: 'Query by Image and Video Content:The QBIC System', IEEE Computer, Sep. (1995) 23-32
3. Swain, M., Ballard, D.: 'Color Indexing', International Journal of Computer Vision, 7:1, (1991) 11-32
4. Stricker, M., Orengo, M.: 'Similarity of Color Images', SPIE 95, Vol. 2420 (1995) 381-392
5. Minsky, M., Papert, S.: Perceptrons, MIT Press, Cambridge, MA. (1969)
6. Kwon, H., Kim, B., Hwang, H. and Cho, D.: 'Scale and Rotation Invariant Pattern Recognition using Complex-Log Mapping and Augmented Second Order Neural Network', IEE Electronics Letters, Vol.29, No.7 (1993) 620-621

7. Stricker, M., Dimai, A.: 'Color Indexing with Weak Spatial Constraints', SPIE 96 San Jose, Vol.2670 (1996) 1630-1639
8. Kim, J., Kim, H.: 'Content-Based Image Retrieval using Color and Spatial Information', KISS Proc., Vol.24, No.2 (1997) 483-486
9. Huang, J., Kumar,R., Mitra, M.: 'Combining Supervised Learning with Color Correlograms for Content-Based Image Retrieval', ACM Multimedia 97 Seattle, (1997) 325-334

Table 1. Three similarity measurement examples between an original image and its three typical transformed images

Measuring Methods / Transform	D_H	D_L	D_θ
Translated	83, 83	1	3
Rotated	346, 81	3	8
Rotated & scaled	15868, 277	24	10

Table 2. Retrieval result with geometrically transformed images

Retrieval Methods / Query image	1st order	2nd order	3rd order
Raw image	X O X X X	O X O O O	O O X X O
Translated	O X X X X	O O O O X	O O O O O
Rotated	X X X X X	O O X O O	O O O O O
Scaled	O X O O X	O O X X O	O O O O O

Table 3. Retrieval success rate with images from various domain

	1st order	2nd order	3rd order
Success rate (%)	38.8	53.6	55.6

Hierarchical Discriminant Regression for Incremental and Real-Time Image Classification

Wey-Shiuan Hwang and Juyang Weng

Department of Computer Science and Engineering
Michigan State University
East Lansing, MI 48824
E-mail: {hwangwey,weng,}@cse.msu.edu

Abstract. This paper presents an incremental algorithm for classification problems using hierarchical discriminant analysis for real-time learning and testing applications. Virtual labels are automatically formed by clustering in the output space. These virtual labels are used for the process of deriving discriminating features in the input space. This procedure is performed recursively in a coarse-to-fine fashion resulting in a tree, called incremental hierarchical discriminating regression (IHDR) method. Embedded in the tree is a hierarchical probability distribution model used to prune unlikely cases. A sample size dependent negative-log-likelihood (NLL) metric is used to deal with large-sample size cases, small-sample size cases, and unbalanced-sample size cases, measured among different internal nodes of the IHDR algorithm. We report the experimental results of the proposed algorithm for an OCR classification problem and an image orientation classification problem.

1 Introduction

In many document processing tasks, such as OCR and image orientation classification problems, rich information in the input image can be preserved by treating an input image as a high dimensional input vector, where each pixel corresponds to a dimension of the vector. Due to the large number of deformation variations that exist in the training samples, building a classifier corresponds to build an image information database. Therefore, the classifier must address three issues: fast retrieval, accurate performance, and the capability to incrementally update representation in the database without re-extracting features from large databases.

In this paper, we present an incremental way of constructing a decision tree that uses discriminant analysis at each internal node. Decision trees organize the data in a hierarchy so that retrieval time can be logarithmic. To acquire accurate performance, a good feature extraction method is required. The appearance approach has drawn much attention in machine vision [1]. The features derived from the linear discriminant analysis (LDA) are meant for well distinguishing different classes and thus are relatively better for the purpose of classification, provided that the samples contain sufficient information [2]. It is desirable to incorporate the incremental learning capability to a classifier. The classifier can

Fig. 1. Some sample hand-written images used in the experiment.

adapt to new training data without re-computing the statistics from the whole image database. Another advantage of incremental training is that an incremental method allows the trainer to interleave training and testing, which enables the human trainer to train the system with "weak cases", potentially reducing the database size and cost of training process.

Two problems in digital documentation analysis are used to test the newly proposed algorithm. The first one is the hand-written digits recognition problem, as shown in Fig. 1. The other problem we tested is to detect the image orientation among four possibilities. We applied our algorithms to these two applications and compared with other major algorithms.

2 The Method

Two types of clusters are incrementally updated at each node of the IHDR algorithm — y-clusters and x-clusters. The y-clusters are clusters in the output space $\mathcal{Y}$ and x-clusters are those in the input space $\mathcal{X}$. There are a maximum of q (e.g., $q = 10$) clusters of each type at each node. The q y-clusters determine the virtual class label of each arriving sample (x, y) based on its y part. Each x-cluster approximates the sample population in $\mathcal{X}$ space for the samples that belong to it. It may spawn a child node from the current node if a finer approximation is required. At each node, y in (x, y) finds the nearest y-cluster in Euclidean distance and updates (pulling) the center of the y-cluster. This y-cluster indicates which corresponding x-cluster the input (x, y) belongs to. Then, the x part of (x, y) is used to update the statistics of the x-cluster (the mean vector and the covariance matrix). These statistics of every x-cluster are used to estimate the probability for the current sample (x, y) to belong to the x-cluster, whose probability distribution is modeled as a multidimensional Gaussian at this level. In other words, each node models a region of the input space $\mathcal{X}$ using q Gaussians. Each Gaussian will be modeled by more small Gaussians in the next tree level if the current node is not a leaf node. Each x-cluster in the leaf node is linked with the corresponding y-cluster.

We define a discriminating subspace as the linear space that passes through the centers of these x-clusters. A total of q centers of the q x-clusters give $q - 1$ discriminating features which span $(q - 1)$-dimensional discriminating space. A probability-based distance called size-dependent negative-log-likelihood (SNLL) [3] is computed from x to each of the q x-clusters to determine which x-cluster should be further searched. If the probability is high enough, the sample (x, y) should further search the corresponding child (maybe more than one but with an upper bound k) recursively, until the corresponding terminal nodes are found.

The algorithm incrementally builds a regression tree from a sequence of training samples as shown in 2. Due to the space limit, we briefly give a sketch of the proposed incremental hierarchical discriminant regression algorithm in the following procedures . A more detailed description of the algorithm can be found in [4].

Procedure 1 Update-node: *Given a node N and (x, y), update the node N using (x, y) recursively. The parameters include: k which specifies the upper bound in the width of parallel tree search; δ_x the sensitivity of the IHDR tree in $\mathcal{X}$ space as a threshold to further explore a branch; and c representing if a node is on the central search path. Each returned node has a flag c. If $c = 1$, the node is a central cluster and $c = 0$ otherwise.*

1. *Find the top matched x-cluster in the following way. If $c = 0$ skip to step (2). If y is given, do (a) and (b); otherwise do (b).*
   (a) *Update the mean of the y-cluster nearest y in Euclidean distance. Incrementally update the mean and the covariance matrix of the x-cluster corresponding to the y-cluster.*
   (b) *Find the x-cluster nearest x according to the probability-based distances. The central x-cluster is this x-cluster. Update the central x-cluster if it has not been updated in (a). Mark this central x-cluster as active.*
2. *For all the x-clusters of the node N, compute the probability-based distances for x to belong to each x-cluster.*
3. *Rank the distances in increasing order.*
4. *In addition to the central x-cluster, choose peripheral x-clusters according to increasing distances until the distance is larger than δ_x or a total of k x-clusters have been chosen.*
5. *Return the chosen x-clusters as active clusters.*

Procedure 2 Update-tree: *Given the root of the tree and sample (x, y), update the tree using (x, y). If y is not given, estimate y and the corresponding confidence. The parameters include: k which specifies the upper bound in the width of parallel tree search.*

Fig. 2. An illustration of the proposed IHDR algorithm. Inside the node shown the discriminating subspace represented as images.

1. *From the root of the tree, update the node by calling* Update-node.
2. *For every active cluster received, check if it points to a child node. If it does, mark it inactive and explore the child node by calling* Update-node. *At most q^2 active x-clusters can be returned this way if each node has at most q children.*
3. *The new central x-cluster is marked as active.*
4. *Mark additional active x-clusters according to the smallest probability-based distance d, up to k total if there are that many x-clusters with $d \leq \delta_x$.*
5. *Do the above steps 2 through 4 recursively until all the resulting active x-clusters are all terminal.*
6. *Each leaf node keeps samples (or sample means) $(\hat{x}_i, \hat{y}_i)$ that belong to it. If y is not given, the output is $\hat{y}_i$ if $\hat{x}_i$ is the nearest neighbor among these samples. If y is given, do the following: If $||y - \hat{y}_i||$ is smaller than an error tolerance, (x, y) updates $(\hat{x}_i, \hat{y}_i)$ only. Otherwise, (x, y) is a new sample to keep in the leaf.*
7. *If the number of samples exceeds the number required for estimating statistics in new child, the top-matched x-cluster in the leaf node along the central path spawns a child which has q new x-clusters.*

3 The Experimental Results

We report two types of experiments for the proposed IHDR algorithm. For each experiment, we incrementally update means in input space as output label.

3.1 Recognition of hand-written digits

The data set we used for this test is the MNIST DATABASE of hand-written digits from AT&T Labs-Research [5]. The MNIST database of hand-written digits has a training set of 60,000 examples, and a test set of 10,000 examples. The digits have been size-normalized and centered in a fixed-size image.

Many methods have been tested with this training set and test set. We compared our method with others in Table 1. Since we only tested the original data

Table 1. Performance for MNIST data

Method	Test error rate (%)	Real time training	Real time testing
linear classifier (1-layer NN)	12.0	No	Yes
pairwise linear classifier	7.6	No	Yes
K-nearest-neighbors, Euclidean	5.0	Yes	No
40 PCA + quadratic classifier	3.3	No	No
1000 RBF + linear classifier	3.6	No	No
SVM deg 4 polynomial	1.1	No	No
2-layer NN, 300 hidden units	4.7	No	Yes
2-layer NN, 1000 hidden units	4.5	No	Yes
IHDR	2.66	Yes	Yes

Fig. 3. Images with different orientations

set, the comparison is only applied to the methods with original data set[1]. The result of the IHDR method gave the second best accurate, second to SVM, which is a batch method, requiring significant time for training and testing. In Table 1, we also compare the feasibility of real time training and testing among different methods. The IHDR method can be trained and tested in real time (both take about 200 ms per input) while other methods cannot do both. Fig. 2 shows the discriminating subspace of some top nodes of the automatically generated IHDR algorithm.

3.2 Detection of image orientation

The orientation of an image is possible to be at any angle. But the edge of acquired image is typically parallel to the scanner, so the orientation of the image is likely one of the four degrees: $0°, 90°, 180°$ or $270°$. The orientation detection problem is then defined as a 4-class classification problem as follows: given a scanned photograph, determine its correct orientation from among the four possible ones. Some sample images are shown in Fig. 3.

Based on the works of Vailaya and Jain [6], we process images to compute the local regional moments of the images in the LUV color space. An image is split into 10×10 blocks. 3 means and 3 variances in 3D color space on each block construct a 600-dimensional raw input space. To equally weight each input component, we further normalized the each input component so that each component is ranged from 0 to 1. We have tested our algorithms on a database of 16344 images, which consists of 7980 training samples(1995 samples per class) and 8364 test samples (2091 samples per class).

Table 2 shows the performance comparison of different 2 classifiers. Our method gave a slightly better error rate than the results reported in [6].

4 Conclusions

We proposed an incremental hierarchical discriminant regression method which clusters in both output and input spaces. To deal with high-dimensional input space in which some components are not very useful and some can be very noisy, a discriminating subspace is incrementally derived at each internal node of the

---

[1] in [5], they also reports methods using deskewed samples and augmented samples with artificially distorted versions of the original training data

Table 2. The error rates for image orientation detection

Method	TEST ERROR RATE (%)
LVQ	12.8%
IHDR	9.7%

tree. Our experimental studies with hand-written digits recognition and image orientation detection have showed that the method can achieve a reasonably good performance compared to other classifiers. Incremental building of the tree opens up the possibility of real-time interactive training where the number of training samples is too large to be stored or to be processed in a batch but the reported IHDR does not need to store all the training samples.

Acknowledgment

We would like to thank Dr. Aditya Vailaya and Dr. Yann LeCun for providing their image databases. The work is supported in part by National Science Foundation under grant No. IIS 9815191, DARPA ETO under contract No. DAAN02-98-C-4025, DARPA ITO under grant No. DABT63-99-1-0014, and research gifts from Siemens Corporate Research and Zyvex.

References

1. H. Murase and S. K. Nayar, "Visual learning and recognition of 3-D objects from appearance," *Int'l Journal of Computer Vision*, vol. 14, no. 1, pp. 5–24, January 1995.
2. D. L. Swets and J. Weng, "Using discriminant eigenfeatures for image retrieval," *IEEE Trans. Pattern Analysis and Machine Intelligence*, vol. 18, no. 8, pp. 831–836, 1996.
3. W.-S. Hwang, J. Weng, M. Fang, and J. Qian, "A fast image retrieval algorithm with automatically extracted discriminant features," in *Proc. IEEE Workshop on Content-based Access of Image and Video Libraries*, Fort Collins, Colorado, June 1999, pp. 8–15.
4. Juyang Weng and Wey-Shiuan Hwang, "An incremental method for building decision trees for high dimensional input space," Tech. Rep. MSU-CSE-00-4, Department of Computer Science and Engineering, Michigan State University, East Lansing, Michigan, March 2000.
5. Y. LeCun, L. D. Jackel, L. Bottou, A. Brunot, C. Cortes, J. S. Denker, H. Drucker, I. Guyon, U. A. Muller, E. Sackinger, P. Simard, and V. Vapnik, "Comparison of learning algorithms for handwritten digit recognition," in *International Conference on Artificial Neural Networks*, F. Fogelman and P. Gallinari, Eds., Paris, 1995, pp. 53–60, EC2 & Cie.
6. A. Vailaya, H.J. Zhang, and A. Jain, "Automatic image orientation detection," in *IEEE International Conference on Image Processing*, Kobe, Japan, October 25-28, 1999.

Distinguishing Real and Virtual Edge Intersection in Pairs of Uncalibrated Images

K.A. Al-shalfan, S.S. Ipson and J.G.B. Haigh
Department of Cybernetics, Internet and virtual Systems, University of Bradford,
Bradford, BD7 IDP, United Kingdom
E-mail: k.a.al-shalfan@bradford.ac.uk

Abstract

Precise determination of object planes in images is very important in applications of computer vision, such as pattern recognition and 3D reconstruction. The corners of a polygonal object plane, e.g. roof, wall, etc., can be determined in an image by detecting and intersecting edge straight lines bounding the plane. Any two non-parallel lines in an image intersect at an image point. If this intersection corresponds to a 3D point in the scene, it is called a real intersection, otherwise it is called a virtual intersection. An automatic system for locating image lines is likely to produce many virtual intersections. This paper presents a computational technique to discriminate between real and virtual intersections. The method is based on rectified images obtained from a pair of uncalibrated images and is illustrated with images of a real scene. The results obtained showed reliable decisions.

Keywords: intersections, image rectification, stereo matching, pattern recognition.

1. Introduction

Despite many studies in the field of boundary recognition, the question of whether the intersection of two lines in an image of a 3D scene corresponds to a real object point still merits further investigation. The technique presented here has five phases: 1) a pair of images of the scene is transformed into a pseudo stereo pair using the DRUI algorithm [1]; 2) edges are obtained using a Canny edge detector [2]; 3) straight lines are extracted from the rectified images using the Hough Transform [3] and their geometrical and photometrical properties are determined; 4) the lines in left and right rectified images are matched, and their intersections determined; 5) the decision on whether each intersection is real or virtual is taken. A flowchart for this vision system is shown in Figure 1. Each phase is discussed briefly in turn in the following sections.

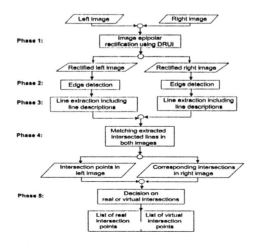

Figure 1. Flowchart of the vision system.

2. Phase 1: Image Rectification

An important stage in the 3D interpretation of two images of a scene, captured with lateral displacement between the view-points, is the production of a pair of rectified images; the depth of a point in the scene may then be related to horizontal disparity. Received methods of rectification either require some knowledge of the camera calibration [4, 5] or involve some decision-making to determine the optimal transformation [6, 7]. The DRUI algorithm provides a general and unambiguous method for the rectification of a stereo pair of images from an uncalibrated camera. The method has been applied successfully to a wide variety of images. An example is shown in Figure 2, where two 1524 by 1012 pixel images of a set of blocks have been captured with a digital camera. The fundamental matrix was determined using the eight-point algorithm [8] with 16 pairs of manually selected points. The epipolar lines corresponding to the selected points are superimposed on the images. The average root-mean-square perpendicular distance between point and corresponding epipolar line is 0.19 pixels. The details of the rectification process are described in reference [1]. The rectified images are shown in Figure 3.

Figure 2. Images of left and right views of blocks with epipolar

Figure 3. Images of left and right views of blocks after

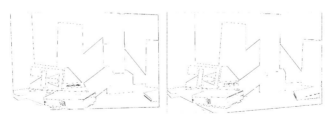

Figure 4. Results of Canny edge detection with $\sigma = 1$ in the Gaussian filtering kernel and with higher and lower threshold of 40 and 20 respectively.

3. Phase 2: Edge Detection and Thinning

It is important to use a reliable edge detection and thinning procedure, because noise tends to cause false lines. The Roberts, Prewitt, Sobel and Laplacian filters [9] together with the Canny edge detector [2] have been evaluated using the rectified images shown in Figure 3. Visual inspection of the results showed that the Canny method was the most reliable with regard to connectivity and number of extracted edges. Consequently this approach was adopted in our system for edge detection and thinning.

The performance of the Canny edge finder was investigated over a range of Gaussian smoothing functions and threshold parameters. The best results were obtained with $\sigma =$ 1 and with higher and lower thresholds [2] of 40 and 20 respectively. The resulting edge images are shown in Figure 4.

4. Phase 3: Edge Line Extraction

Many approaches have been developed to extract straight lines and determine the attributes associated with them. The most widely used is the Hough Transform (HT). The HT is used to locate collinear edge pixels, and has been shown to perform well even with noisy images [3]. In this section, extracting straight lines from images using the HT is briefly described.

The HT parameter space has angle θ ranging from 0° to 180° in steps of 1° and parameter ρ ranging from $-D$ to $+D$ in steps of 1 pixel, where D is the image diagonal. The size of the template used to define a local maximum in HT space affects the number of lines detected. If the size is too large, lines may be missed, but if it is too small then spurious lines may be generated. This is illustrated in Figure 5. A compromise size 3° × 5 pixel was chosen for the template. After creating a list of local maxima in HT space (i.e. a list of lines in the image), edge points are assigned to members of this list as follows. Each edge point is transformed into a line in HT space. If this line passes through a region of size 2° × 26 pixels centred on a local maximum, then the edge point is assigned to the image line corresponding to that maximum.

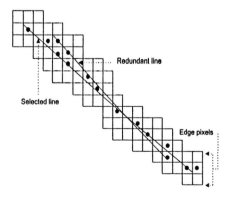

Figure 5. A simple example of redundant lines in HT space.

Once all edge points are assigned to lines, further checks are carried out. The edge points within each list are ordered and checked for line breaks. If two neighbouring pixels are found to be separated by a gap of more than 4 pixels, then the list is split into two, each containing only the pixels on one side of the gap. Any two lists of points with similar ρ and θ values are further tested. If they are found to contain two end pixels separated by a gap of less than 5 pixels, then the two lists are merged as illustrated in Figure 6. The main problem with this procedure is the difficulty in linking lines that happen to have large gaps because of occlusion.

The number of redundant line segments is further reduced by checking for overlapping lines and discarding the shorter ones if the absolute difference between their angles is less than a threshold value as shown in Figure 5. Finally a line is fitted, using the least-squares criterion, to each list of edge points. If less than 70% of the edge points are within a distance of 2 pixels from the fitted line then the line is discarded.

A line segment is defined geometrically by its end-points, from which its length, slope and intercept can be calculated. The extreme points of an extracted line do not necessarily define accurate end-points for a straight-line segment because the extracted pixels are spread around the fitted line. The estimated endpoints are therefore forced to lie on the fitted line as shown in Figure 7. The final results for straight edge lines extracted from the left and right rectified images in Figure 3 are shown in Figure 8.

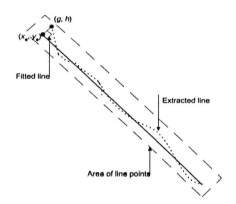

Figure 7. Line fitting and end-point determination.

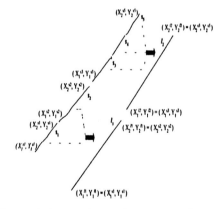

Figure 6. Separating and Merging Line

Having extracted lines from the images, additional photometric attributes of the lines are obtained as a further aid to matching in phase 5. Four photometric measures are used namely the average of intensities in strips of width 15 pixels along both sides of each lines, the average intensity gradient across the line and the sign of the intensity gradient.

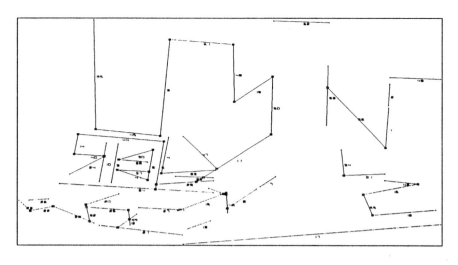

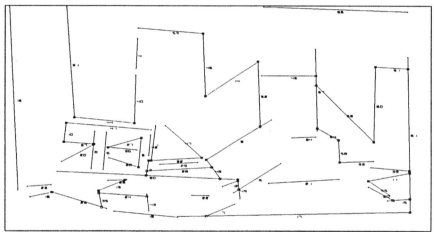

Figure 8. Straight lines extracted from rectified left (shown at top) and right (shown at bottom) images.

5. Phase 4: Matching the Straight Line Segments

Existing approaches to matching lines in pairs of images are of two types: those that match individual line segments [10, 11], and those that match groups of line segments [12]. Both approaches generally match lines on the basis of their geometrical attributes (orientation, length, etc.) but more geometrical information is available in the latter case. The authors' system falls into the latter category since it first identifies pairs of intersecting lines in left and right rectified images and then matches them.

Intersection points within each image are determined by considering each line pair in turn. First a check is made that the lines are not almost parallel and, if not, the intersection point is then found. If the intersection lies more than 4 pixels beyond the end point of either lines then it is discarded. The features used in the matching process are 1) the angle between the pair of intersecting lines; 2) the orientation of the line pair; 3) the ratio of lengths of the two lines (shorter : longer); 4) the four photometric measures specified at the end of the previous section.

An intersection formed by a pair of lines in the left image is taken to match a similar intersection in the right image if these features are the same within defined limits and the following constraints are satisfied. Spatial relationships between matching features are generally maintained and the y co-ordinates of corresponding endpoints must agree within a specified error. The results of this matching procedure, for lines in the images shown in Figure 4, are presented in Table 1. From a collection of 43 intersections in the left image and 46 in the right image, there are 26 correspondences which were matched. Visual inspection verified all matches were correct.

No.	Left Image				Right Image				Status	
	Intersecting Lines				Corresponding Intersecting Lines					
	1st. Line no.	2nd. Line no.	X	Y	1st. Line no.	2nd. Line no.	X	Y	Assigned Status	True. Status
1	1	56	1322	419	59	60	1320	392	V	V
2	3	45	511	472	40	44	461	477	V	V
3	4	33	515	307	1	32	521	308	R	V*
4	5	29	497	259	2	28	506	261	V	V
5	6	30	485	410	3	27	486	409	R	R
6	6	41	466	278	3	38	476	278	R	R
7	8	46	753	157	5	49	837	178	V	V
8	10	24	309	380	8	20	314	379	R	R
9	10	40	309	382	8	37	314	381	R	R
10	11	50	911	479	9	52	913	463	V	V
11	14	40	202	391	10	37	208	391	R	R
12	14	44	216	479	10	41	217	478	R	R
13	15	46	749	223	12	49	833	217	V	V
14	19	48	778	630	14	46	716	602	V	V
15	19	50	916	744	14	52	905	765	V	V
16	20	32	244	172	13	35	333	172	R	R
17	22	28	127	164	18	25	166	165	R	R
18	24	40	311	382	20	37	317	381	R	R
19	25	32	246	161	24	35	334	161	R	R
20	25	39	397	148	24	43	506	147	R	R
21	28	32	257	100	25	35	344	100	R	R
22	30	38	362	367	27	36	366	366	R	R
23	31	54	1173	298	33	58	1198	301	V	V
24	35	45	279	502	31	44	246	504	V	V
25	48	51	774	891	46	53	707	890	R	V*
26	53	56	1114	694	57	59	1114	652	V	V

* Incorrect Decision.

Table 1: The status of the intersections of the matched intersecting lines in the left and right images (R: Real;   V: Virtual).

6. Phase 5: Distinguishing Real and Virtual Intersection

A real intersection point should have the same vertical co-ordinate in the left and right hand rectified images. The list of intersections produced in phase 4 is checked by this criterion. Any cases showing a significant vertical discrepancy are labelled as virtual intersections. Of the remainder, there is a difficulty when one of the intersecting lines is nearly horizontal in the rectified image, since it is then impossible to determine whether the intersection is real or virtual. The remaining cases are taken to be real intersections, and the horizontal disparity may be used as an indicator of distance from the camera base line. The intersections are listed in Table 1, with indication of the true status of each, as deduced from visual analysis. The are just two cases where the assigned status is incorrect, both of which involve a nearly horizontal.

7. Discussion and Conclusion

The five-phase procedure described in this paper has been successful in identifying thirteen real intersection points in the object space from the two rectified images. At the same time eleven virtual intersections, arising from line pairs which do not intersect in object space were rejected. The thirteen real pairs can be added to the initial set of correspondences to improve the rectification procedure. There were also two incorrect assignments (number 3 and 25), where virtual intersections were assigned as real. In both of these cases one edge was nearly horizontal in the rectified images, and consequently no vertical disparity could be measured. Such cases do not interfere with the operation of the rectification procedure, but would result in spurious estimation of the apparent depth.

References

[1] K.A. Al-Shalfan, J.G.B. Haigh and S.S. Ipson, Direct algorithm for rectifying pairs of uncalibrated images, *Electr. Lett.*, 36(5), 2000, 419-420.

[2] J. A Canny, Computational Approach to Edge Detection, *IEEE Trans. Pattern. Anal. and Mach. Intel.*, PAMI-8(6), 1986, 679-698.

[3] R. O. Duda and P. E. Hart, Use of the Hough Transformation to detect lines and curves in pictures, *Commun. ACM*, 15(1), 1972, 11-15.

[4] N. Ayache and C. Hansen, Rectification of images for binocular and trinocular stereovision, *Proc. 9th Int. Conf. Pattern Recogn., IEEE*, Italy, 1988, 11-16.

[5] A. Fusiello, E. Trucco and A. Verri, Rectification with unconstrained stereo geometry, *Proc. British Machine Vision Conf. BMVC97, BMVA Press*, Essex, UK, 1998, 400-409.

[6] R. Hartley and R. Gupta, Computing matched-epipolar projections, *Proc. IEEE Comput. Soc. Conf. Comput. Vision and Pattern Recogn.*, 1993, 549-555.

[7] L. Robert, C. Zeller, O. Faugeras, and M. Hebert, Applications of non-metric vision to some visually guided robotics, *In Aloimonos, Y. (ed.) 'Visual navigation'. Lawrence Erlbaum Associates*, Mahwah, NJ, 1997, 89-134.

[8] R. I. Hartley, In defense of the eight-point algorithm, *IEEE Trans.*, PAMI-19(6), 1997, 580-593.

[9] R.C. Gonzalez and R.E. Woods, *Digital Image Processing.* (London: Addisson-Weesley, 1993).

[10] N. Ayache, *Stereovision and Sensor Fusion*, (Cambridge, MA: MIT-Press, 1990).

[11] Z. Zhang, Token tracking in a cluttered scene, *IVC*, 12(2), 1994, 110-120.

[12] C. Schmid and A. Zisserman, Automatic Line Matching across Views, *Proc. IEEE Comput. Soc. Conf. Comput. Vision and Pattern Recogn.*, CA, USA,1997, 666-671.

Stereo Correspondence Using Ga-Based Segmentation

Keechul Jung and JungHyun Han

School of Electrical and Computer Engineering
Sung Kyun Kwan University, Suwon, 440-746, Korea
{kjung, han}@ece.skku.ac.kr
http://graphics.skku.ac.kr

Abstract. This paper presents a new cooperative algorithm based on the integration of stereo matching and segmentation. Stereo correspondence is recovered from two stereo images with the help of a segmentation result. Using a genetic algorithm (GA)-based image segmentation, we can refine the depth map more effectively. Experimental results are presented to illustrate the performances of the proposed method.

1 Introduction

Recovering 3-D information from a set of several images is an active research area in computer vision. The use of a pair of stereo images as a passive approach to range sensing has been extensively studied. Stereopsis is important for object tracking and 3D shape reconstruction in the traditional computer vision, and is becoming one of the key factors for image-based modeling and rendering.

Although stereo correspondence problem has been studied for a long time, the results are not very satisfactory [1]. To overcome difficulties such as noise and occlusion effect, several integrated methods have been proposed. Anthony attempted to unify stereo and motion cues [2]. Liu and Skerjanc introduced image pyramid in the stereo and motion matching process [7]. Some difficulties in binocular stereo can be eliminated by using three or more cameras to get the input images. Ruichek tried to use a sequence of stereo pairs [4]. Resolving ambiguities in stereo matching requires additional constraints (local supports) such as continuity constraints, disparity gradient constraints, and disparity similarity functions [3]. Most of the existing approaches assume the continuity or smoothness of visible surface, and impose a smoothness constraint upon the solution. This is usually true for a single surface, but is not true for an entire scene because a scene usually consists of different surfaces between which there is a discontinuity [3].

In this paper, under the assumption that a region that with a similar depth usually has a similar color, we use a more strict constraint based on the region segmentation results. Given two stereo images, the solution for correspondence problem is in a form of a disparity map. We initialize a disparity map in a traditional manner: a disparity map is obtained by calculating the sum of the squared difference between a pair of stereo images for a particular window size. Using a GA-based segmentation image, we can refine the depth map more precisely. A mean filter is used to locally average the disparity map in the same segmentation region. Comparisons between the traditional method and the proposed method are presented.

2 GA-based Segmentation

Segmentation is a process of identifying uniform regions based on certain conditions. Since segmentation is a very highly combinatorial complex problem [5,6], many GA-based methods are proposed. In [5], we proposed a GA-based image segmentation method, which can be implemented in a massively parallel manner and can produce accurate segmentation results.

The segmentation is computed by chromosomes that evolve by a distributed genetic algorithm (DGA). Each chromosome represents a pixel and evolves independently. The chromosomes start with random solutions, and evolve iteratvely through selection and genetic operations. In DGA, these operations are performed on locally distributed subgroups of chromosomes, called a window, rather than on the whole populations. In selection, the chromosomes are updated to make new chromosomes by an elitist selection scheme. These operations are iteratively performed until the stopping criterion is satisfied. For the stopping criterion, the equilibirum is defined in [5]. The stopping criterion is reached when the euqilibrium is above the equilibrium threshold or the number of generations is more than the maximal number.

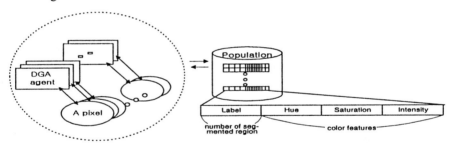

Fig. 1. The structure of GA-based segmentation [5]

In Fig. 1, the structure of chromosome is shown. A population is a set of chromosomes and represents a segmentation result. A chromosome consists of a label and a feature vector. For each chromosome k, its fitness is defined as the difference between the estimated color vector $y=\{ y_1, ..., y_p \}$ and the actual color vector $x=\{ x_1, ..., x_p \}$ at the location of the chromosome on the image. The fitness function is

$$f(k) = -\sum_{i=1}^{p} |x_i - y_i|.$$ (1)

3 Correspondence Matching

The proposed method is carried out in two steps. We initialize a disparity map in a traditional manner: a disparity map is obtained by calculating the sum of the squared difference between a pair of stereo images for a particular window size. Using the GA-based segmentation image, we can refine the depth map more effectively. In other words, the GA-based segmentation results are applied to refine the depth map at each pixel position.

3.1 Initial correspondence matching

A disparity map is obtained by calculating the sum of the squared difference (SSD) between a pair of stereo images for a particular window size, i.e.,

$$SSD(x, y) = \sum_{i=-w/2}^{w/2} \sum_{j=-w/2}^{w/2} \{I_l(x+d+i, y+j) - I_r(x+i, y+j)\}^2 , \tag{2}$$

where $SSD(x,y)$ represents the SSD of a pixel (x,y) in the left image, d is the window shift in the right image, w is the window size, and I_l and I_r are the gray-levels of the left and the right images, respectively.

The value of d that minimizes the SSD is considered to be the disparity at each pixel position (x,y). Object distance to the camera, z is related to the distance by the equation:

$$z = \frac{bf}{d} . \tag{3}$$

where b is the baseline or separation between the cameras, f is the focal length, and d is the horizontal disparity between two points.

3.2 Refinement using a segmentation-based constraint

An image segmentation result and a disparity map have been considered to be discrete; i.e., a collection of points. Let $d(i,j)=\{(i,j):1\le i \le m, 1 \le j \le n\}$ denote the $m \times n$ lattice such that the elements in d index the disparity on the image pixels. Let the segmentation result be $s(i,j)=\{(i,j):1\le i \le m, 1 \le j \le n\}$.

We use a mean filter to locally average the disparity map. We take $k \times l$ neighborhood about pixel (i,j). Let h be the refined disparity map, and n be the number of pixels which have the same segment label in the $k \times l$ neighborhood.

$$h(i, j) = \frac{1}{n}(\sum_{a=-k/2}^{k/2} \sum_{b=-l/2}^{l/2} d(a,b)u(i, j, i+a, j+b)). \tag{4}$$

$$u(i, j, k, l) = \begin{cases} 1, & if \ s(i, j) = s(k, l) \\ 0, & others \end{cases} . \tag{5}$$

We perform the Equation (4) iteratively until the stopping criterion is satisfied. We have to set the neighborhood size and stopping criterion. The values of these parameters are determined empirically.

4 Experimental Results

In this section, we briefly describe our algorithm along with a running example. In order to verify the effectiveness of the method, experiments were performed on several test images. A set of commonly used stereo images was taken as the test images: The EPI Tree Set, Ball Set, etc. (http://cmp.felk.cvut.cz/~sara/Stereo/ New/Matching/smm.html).

(a) (b)

(c) (d)

Fig. 2. Experimental result: (a) and (b) images are left and right images, respectively, (c) is the initial depth image generated by minimizing SSD, and (d) is the final depth image refined using segmentation results

In the image segmentation, it should be noted that all the DGA parameters, such as the window size and probabilities of the genetic operations, have an influence on the performance of the algorithms. The equilibrium threshold was set to 100% and the maximal number of generations was set to 500. The parameters were as follows: the window size was 5×5; the probabilities of mutation and crossover were 0.01 and 0.005, respectively. The label size was 40. DGA is simulated on a sequential machine. In the disparity refinement stage, the size of the $k×l$ neighborhood is very important for considering time complexity and performance. Too small windows contain too little information, while for large windows much time is needed. In this experiment we set the neighborhood size to 5×5. Stopping criterion for the refinement is just set to 10 times.

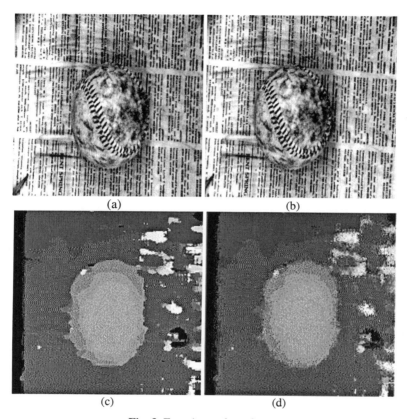

(a)   (b)

(c)   (d)

Fig. 3. Experimental result

Table 1. Processing time taken to find a disparity map for an image (256×256)

Stages			Time (sec.)
Region Segmentation	A generation	Selection	0.022
		Crossover	0.002
		Mutation	0.002
	Average time for an image (average # of generations × time for a generation)		4.940 (190 × 0.026)
Correspondence Matching	Initial stereo correspondence		1.870
	Refinery stage		3.314
Total			10.124

Figure 2 and 3 show some results produced by the new algorithm on the two classical test images. The disparity maps obtained by the proposed methods on these standard test images are compared with the traditional area-based approaches. In these figures, depth information is displayed as intensity images. The resulting disparity maps are more accurate on the borders of object and occluded regions. Table 1 shows the average time for segmentation of an image and correspondence matching process.

5 Conclusions

Experimental results in this research show that this algorithm is more robust than the traditional correspondence matching algorithm. The performance of the proposed method depends on two parts: the segmentation performance and initial stereo correspondence. If the segmentation result is not so good, the refined disparity map may be worse. We try to use relaxational scheme to refine the disparity map. Also we try to strongly integrate the segmentation stage and the stereo matching stage into a single stage. In conclusion, although the proposed method requires more time to segment and refine the depth map than the traditional method, better stereo correspondence results can be obtained.

Acknowledgement
This work was supported by the Brain Korea 21 Project.

References

1. Richard Szeliski and Ramin Zabih, An Experimental Comparison of Stereo Algorithms, *Vision Algorithms 99 Workshop*, September (1999).
2. Anthony Yuk-Kwan Ho and Ting-Chuen Pong, Cooperative Fusion of Stereo and Motion, *Pattern Recognition*, Vol. 29, No. 1, (1996) pp. 121-130.
3. Naokazu Yokoya, Takeshi Shakunaga, and Masayuki Kanbara, Passive Range Sensing Techniques: Depth from Images, *IEICE Trans. INF. & SYST.*, Vol. E82-D, No. 3, (1999) pp. 523-533.
4. Y. Ruichek and J.G. Postaire, A neural matching algorithm for 3-D reconstruction from stereo pairs of linear images, *Pattern Recognition Letters*, 17, (1996) pp. 387-398.
5. E. Y. Kim, S. H. Park, K. Jung and H. J. Kim, Genetic Algorithm-based Segmentation of Video Sequence, *IEE Electronics Letters*, Vol. 36, No. 11, (2000) pp. 946-947.
6. Suchendra M. Bhandarkar and Hui Zhang, Image Segmentation Using evolutionary Computation, *IEEE Trans. Evolutionary Computation*, 3, (1), (1999) pp. 1-21.
7. M. Yachida, Y. Kitamura, and M. Kimachi, Trinocular vision: New approach for correspondence problem, *Proc. 9th IAPR Int. Conf. On Pattern Recognition*, (1986) pp. 1041-1044.

F.

SPECIAL
SESSIONS

How Adaptive Agents in Stock Market Perform in the Presence of Random News: A Genetic Algorithm Approach

K.Y. Szeto and L.Y. Fong

Department of Physics, Hong Kong University of Science and Technology,
Clear Water Bay, Hong Kong,
phszeto@ust.hk

Abstract. The effect of random news on the performance of adaptive agents as investors in stock market is modelled by genetic algorithm and measured by their portfolio values. The agents are defined by the rules evolved from a simple genetic algorithm, based on the rate of correct prediction on past data. The effects of random news are incorporated via a model of herd effect to characterize the human nature of the investors in changing their original plan of investment when the news contradicts their prediction. The random news is generated by white noise, with equal probability of being good and bad news. Several artificial time series with different memory factors in the time correlation function are used to measure the performance of the agents after the training and testing. A universal feature that greedy and confident investors outperform others emerges from this study.

1. Introduction

In the analysis of stock market, often computer programs modelling various investment strategies are employed and statistical results on the yields of these strategies are used as a measurement for both the models and the decision process involved in the implementation of the strategies [1-4]. Usually the computer program is a given set of investment rules, extracted from historical data of the market, or rules based on fundamental analysis or news obtained from the inner circle of the trade. It is very difficult in real life to separate out the importance of technical analysis from other means of prediction, such as fundamental analysis with random news. Furthermore, the decision process of a trader with a given investment strategy may be very complex, as sudden news from fellow traders may alter the decision. Consequently, it is very difficult to combine trading strategies with the complex psychological processes taking place in the actual decision of the trader in a general model and achieve a reasonable understanding of the global behaviours of traders [3]. In order to initiate the investigation of these complex phenomena, we break the problem into several simpler problems and hope that the solution of each will shed some light on the general pattern of traders. We first modify the traditional economic models where homogeneous agents operating in isolation are used by two simple steps. The first step is to incorporate a certain level of communication among traders so that their decision processes are affected by their interactions. The second step is to relax the condition that the agents are homogeneous. There are of course many ways to introduce heterogeneous agents, but our focus is on the individuality of the agent, with personal character which entails different psychological responses to other agents. These two steps are by nature not easy to model, as human interactions and psychological responses are themselves very challenging topics. Nevertheless, we start by considering some techniques used by physicists. The first problem of incorporating interactions can be modelled by the standard technique of mean field theory, meaning that each trader will interact with the average trader of the market, who is representative of the general atmosphere of investment at the time. This will naturally incur some error as effects of fluctuation, or volatility of the stock market, may not be adequately treated. Next, we like to consider the psychological response of individual trader. We can introduce simple quantitative parameters to measure individual characteristics of the trader, so that the response to the general atmosphere of the market is activated according to these parameters. Our model includes heterogeneous agents who are represented by different rules of investment as well as different human characters. The interactions between agents are simplified into interaction with a mean field, or the general atmosphere of the market. We model the general atmosphere of the market in an ad hoc manner, in that we do not deduce it from a model of microscopic interaction between agents, but rather by a source of random news which will serve as a kind of external, uncontrollable stimulus to the market. We understand that this simple model of stock market traders lacks the generality of a realistic agent. However, the important thing to note is that refinement can be introduced later to model better the interactions, while the heterogeneity of agents can be tuned by introducing more parameters in describing their individualities. We hope that this new approach of modelling the microscopic agents is a first step towards building a more comprehensive model of the stock market and its complex patterns. Our generic trader is an optimal rule in forecasting, using a genetic algorithms framework [5-10], where the relative performance of the individual agents (chromosomes) is compared in a finite population under the Darwinian principle of the survival of the fittest. In such a model, by suitably defining a measure of fitness on the level of individual agents and group of agents, self-organized behaviour in the population during evolution emerges. Furthermore, automatic control of the diversity of the population and increase in the average fitness of the entire population are observed [8-10]. A selection of fit rule and the subsequent augmentation of individual character of the agents will follow. Their performance is measured by the net asset value of their portfolios after a given period.

2. Prediction as an Optimization Problem

In using Genetic Algorithm for forecasting [5-10], the problem can be considered as pattern recognition and the subsequent optimisation of the rate of correct prediction. Since the objective of this work is to test the effects of news on the performance of the agents, we will employ a simple Genetic Algorithm for the forecasting of the time series, and focus our attention on the performance of portfolios of the agents. We perform training and testing for a given time series, $x(t)$, with 2000 data points by first dividing it into three parts. The first 800 points form the training set for extracting rules. The next 100 points form the test set, used for evaluating the performance of the set of rules obtained after training. The last 1100 points form the news set for investigating the performance of investors with different degree of greed and different level of indifference to the random news. In the training set, we make the usual assumption that at time t, the value x(t) is a function of the value at x(t-1), x(t-2),..., x(t-k). Here k is set to 8. As to the rules of forecasting, we use the linear model of time series and assume a relation between the predicted value $\hat{x}(t)$ and its precedent: $\hat{x}(t) = \sum_{i=1}^{i=k} \beta_i x(t-i)$. The objective is to find a set of $\{\beta_i\}$ to minimize the root mean square error in $\hat{x}$ compared with the true value x. Here, we do not perform any vector quantization on the series $\{x(t)\}$, so that each x(t) is a real value. Note that these x(t) values can represent the daily rate of return of a chosen stock, with $|x(t)| \le 1$. We also assume the same condition on β_i, so that $|\beta_i| \le 1, i = 1,.., k$. Since our objective is to look at performance of agents who buy and sell the particular stock, we only care for the sign of $\hat{x}$. What this means is that for $\hat{x}$ positive, the agent predicts an increase of the value of the stock and will act according to his specific strategy of trading. If $\hat{x}$ is non-positive, then he will predict either an unchanged stock price or a decrease, and will also act according to his specific strategy. We count the guess as a correct one if the sign of the guess value is the same as the actual value at that particular time, otherwise the guess is wrong. If the actual value is zero, it is not counted. The performance index P_c that measures the fitness value of the chromosome is designed as the ratio: $P_c = N_c /(N_c + N_w)$. Here N_c is the number of correct guess and N_w is the number of wrong guess. Note that in this simple genetic algorithm, we do not worry about the absolute difference between x and $\hat{x}$, only paying attention to their signs. This feature can be refined by a more detailed classification of the quality of the prediction. Furthermore, while most investors make hard decision on buy and sell, the amount of asset involved can be a soft decision. Indeed, when we introduce the greed parameter for the agent as discussed below, the decision on the amount of asset involved in the trading of a stock can be considerably softened. For the purpose of the present work, the prediction based on signs will be sufficient to obtain general insights of the coupling between agents and news, and the effect of this coupling on the global behaviour. Finally, we should remark that agents do not predict when $\hat{x}$ is zero, corresponding to the situation of holding onto the asset. We start with a set of 100 rules (chromosomes) represented by $\{\beta_i\}$. By comparing the performance of the chromosomes, the maximum fitness value is the result found by genetic algorithm using a modification of the Monte Carlo method that consists of selection, crossover and mutation operators [5-10]. We will leave the details of the genetic algorithms in a separate paper, here we just state the results. After several thousands of generations, we observe a saturated value of P_c, and we choose the chromosome corresponding to this P_c as the generic rule of prediction. We simply make use of the adaptive nature of the different chromosomes in a Darwinian world to single out the best performing chromosome to be the prototype of agents with different human characters. We introduce two parameters to characterize different human nature of the best agent. These two parameters are the greediness "g" and level of fear "f". The final set of agents, all with the same chromosome (or rule), but with different parameters of greed g and fear f, will be used for the performance evaluation in their portfolio management in response to online news. In the news set (last 1100 data points), we assign identical initial asset to the agents. For instance, we give each rule (chromosome, portfolio manager, or agent) an initial cash amount of 10,000 USD and a number of shares =100. The value of f and g ranged from 0 to 0.96 in increment of 0.04 will be used to define a set of 25x25=625 different agents. We will then observe the net asset value of these 625 portfolios as they trade in the presence of news.

3.   News Generation

For a given past pattern, a particular agent will first make a comparison of this data with his rule and if the pattern matches his rule, then the prediction according to the rule is made. Without the news, the prediction is definite, for the agent is supposed to execute the action suggested by the rule. However, in the presence of the news, the agent will have to re-evaluate his action, reflecting the changed circumstances implied by the news. The present work treats `news' as a randomly generated time series. This can of course be made more realistic by taking some kind of average of many real series of news as the input stimulus to the agent. One can also include a more detailed model of interaction of agents so that the input stimulus to the agent is neither an artificial time series, nor an external time series of news, but an internally generated series that reflect the dynamics of interacting agents. This will be studied in a future paper. Next, we consider the interaction of an individual agent with the randomly generated time series of news. The agent has to decide whether and how his/her action should be modified in views of the news. In making these judgements, the agent must anticipate certain probability of change, which reflects the `greed' and the `fear' of the agent in his decision process. For example, when there is news that is good in conventional wisdom, the stock market price is generally expected to increase. An agent, who had originally forecasted a drop in the stock price tomorrow and planned to sell the stock at today's price by taking profit, may change his plan after the arrival of the `good' news, and halt his selling decision, or even convert selling into buying. This is a reversal of his original decision that is solely based on historical data analysis. Similarly, for an agent who originally wanted to buy the stock at today's price, as his forecast for tomorrow is a rise in stock price, may halt his buying action because `bad' news just arrives. Instead of buying today, he may sell or hold on to his cash, for fear of a crash. This kind of reversal of buying action may in reality trigger panic selling. These behaviours anticipate immediate effect of news, thereby often reverse original decision based on rational analysis on historical data through pattern matching. To incorporate these realistic features of the markets, we introduce two additional real numbers to model the market. The following features now characterize each agent. (1) An integer indicating the class of prediction. For this paper we only use two classes, 1 for increases and 0 for decreases or unchanged stock price. (2) A rule to recognize pattern in the time series. (3) A real number f to characterize the level of fear of the agent in his original decision. If f is 0.9, then the agent has 90% chance of changing his decision when news arrives that contradicts his original decision. This denotes an insecure investor who easily changes his investment strategy. If f is 0.1, then there is only 10% chance of the agent of changing his original decision, a sign of a more confident investor. Thus, f is a measure of fear. (4) A real number g to characterize the percentage of asset allocation in following a decision to buy or sell. This number can be interpreted as a measure of the greediness of the agent. If g is 0.9, it means that the agent will invest 90% of his asset in trading, a sign of a greedy gambler. On the other hand, if g is 0.1, the agent only invests 10% of his asset in trading, a sign of a prudent investor. Thus, g is a measure of greed. Algorithmically, we first choose a random number c between 0 and 1 and decide that news is good if c > 0.5, otherwise it is bad. This model of random news may not be realistic, but will serve as a benchmark test on the effect of news on the agents by saying that there is equal chance of arrival of good news and bad news. There are four scenarios for the agent with news. (1) News is good and he plans to sell. (2) News is good and he plans to buy. (3) News is bad and he plans to sell. (4) News is bad and he plans to buy. Note that there is no contradiction between the agent's original plan and the news for case (2) and (3). But in case (1), the agent may want to reverse the selling action to buying action due to the good news, anticipating a rise in stock price in the future. Also, in case (4), the agent may decide to change his decision of buying to selling today, and buying stock in the future, as the news is bad and the stock price may fall in the future. Thus, in (1) and (4), the agent will re-evaluate his decision. He will first choose a random number p. If p > f, he will maintain his prediction, otherwise he reverses his prediction from 1 to 0 or from 0 to 1. Therefore f is a measure of fear of the agent. The parameter g measures the percentage of the amount of cash used for buying stock or the shares in selling stock. Large greed parameter g implies that a big gambler, and will invest a large fraction of his asset following the rules and the news, while a small g parameter characterizes prudent investors.

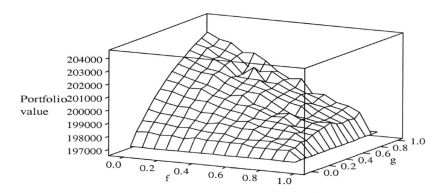

Fig.1 Final values in cash of the portfolio of the 625 agents. Initially all agents have the same value at 19900. The time series for stock is Microsoft.

4. Results

We use several sets of time series, including the real stock value of Microsoft, the long and short memory time series with controlled auto-correlation generated using the inverse whitening transformation. All these time series show similar behaviour. In

Fig.1 we show the effects of news on the performance of the agents in terms of the steady state or 'final' values of their portfolio. Empirically, we find that the net asset of the portfolio, (cash plus stock) reaches a steady value after more than 1000 responses to random news. From our numerical experiment with a ten days probation period, (we then have 110 evaluations on the news set), we observe to our surprise similar patterns to all the data sets. In Fig.1, we observe a trend of the portfolio measured in net asset value in cash to rise at large g and small f. This is an interesting universal behaviour that demands an explanation, which we leave it to a future paper. In a pool of agent that are trained by historical data, and endowed with individual characters like greed and fear in their investment exercises, the effects of news, generated randomly, show universal behaviour. This universal behaviour suggests that greedy (large g) and confident (small f) investors perform better.

References

1. Arthur W.B., " Complexity in Economic and Financial Markets", Complexity, 1, 1995.
2. Cutler, D.M., J.M. Poterba, and L.H. Summer, " What moves Stock Prices?" Journal of Portfolio Management, 4-12, 1989.
3. Palmer, R.G., W.B. Arthur, J.H. Holland, B.LeBaron, and P. Tayler, " Artificial Economic Life: A Simple Model of a Stockmarket." Physics D, 75, 264-274, 1994.
4. Friedman, D. and J. Rust. (Eds.) (1991). The Double Auction Market: Institutions, Theories, and Evidence. Proceeding Volume XIV, Santa Fe Institute Studies in the Science of Complexity. Menlo Park: Addison-Wesley Publishing.
5. Chan K.O., MPhil. Thesis, Hong Kong University of Science and Technology, Department of Physics, 1996.
6. Cheung, K.H., MPhil. Thesis, Hong Kong University of Science and Technology, Department of Physics, 1997.
7. K.Y. Szeto, K.O. Chan, K.H. Cheung; Application of genetic algorithms in stock market prediction, (Proceedings of the Fourth International Conference on Neural Networks in the Capital Markets: Progress in Neural Processing Decision Technologies for Financial Engineering, Ed. A.S. Weigend, Y. Abu-Mostafa, and A.P.N. Refenes; World Scientific), NNCM-96, 1997, p95-103.
8. K.Y. Szeto and K.H. Cheung; Multiple Time Series Prediction using Genetic Algorithms Optimizer (Proceedings of the International Symposium on Intelligent Data Engineering and Learning) Hong Kong, IDEAL'98, Oct. 1998
9. Szeto K.Y. and Luo P.X., Self-organising behaviour in genetic algorithm for the forecasting of financial time series. Proceeding of the International Conference on Forecasting Financial Markets, FFM99, 1999. CD-Rom
10. L.Y. Fong and K.Y. Szeto, Rules Extraction in Short Memory Time Series using Genetic Algorithms, accepted by European Journal of Physics, B. 2000.

Learning of Virtual Dealers in an Artificial Market: Comparison with Interview Data

Kiyoshi Izumi[1] and Kazuhiro Ueda[2]

[1] Information Science Div., ETL and PRESTO, JST,
1-1-4 Umezono, Tsukuba, Ibaraki, 305-8568, JAPAN, kiyoshi@etl.go.jp
[2] Interfaculty Initiative of Information Studies, Univ. of Tokyo,
3-8-1 Komaba, Meguro-ku, Tokyo, 153-8902, JAPAN, ueda@gould.c.u-tokyo.ac.jp

Abstract. In this study we used a new agent-based approach, an artificial market approach, to analyze the ways that dealers process the information in financial news. We compared between the simulation results with virtual dealers in our model and interview data with actual dealers. The results showed that there were similarities between the dynamics of market opinions in the artificial and actual markets.

1 Introduction

Large economic changes have recently brought to our attention the behavioral aspects of economic phenomena. And many facts shows that there is interaction of dealers' forecasts when they interpret the financial and political news related to exchange rate dynamics. Investigators examining the interaction of forecasts would find it is very useful to know how dealers interpret, classify, and use news when they forecast rates. Although some scholars have conducted fieldwork with dealers or used experimental markets with human subjects in order to investigate the way they think, it is difficult to know the thoughts of all dealers in real time.

We have therefore developed a new agent-based approach to investigating the interaction of dealers' forecasts: an artificial market approach. Artificial markets are virtual markets operating on computers. In artificial markets we can directly examine the thought processes of virtual dealers in real time and can repeatedly carry out many experiments under all market conditions.

2 Framework of the Artificial Market Approach

The artificial market approach consists of 3 steps. (1) *Fieldwork:* We gathered field data by interviewing an actual dealer and extracted some features for model construction. (2) *Construction of an artificial market:* We implemented a multi-agent model that consists of computer programs as virtual dealers, a market-clearing mechanism, and rate determination rules. (3) *Comparison with real-world data:* We compared between simulation results with the virtual dealers and interview data with actual dealers.

3 Fieldwork

We interviewed a chief dealer who engaged in exchange-rate transactions in the Tokyo foreign exchange market. The interviewee was asked to explain the rate dynamics of the two years from Jan. 1994 to Nov. 1995. We asked the dealer to do the following: (a) divide these two years into several periods according to his recognition of market situations, (b) talk about which factors he regarded as important in his rate forecasts for each period, (c) rank the factors in order of weight (importance) and explain the reason for the ranking, and (d) in case his forecast factors changed between periods, describe the reasons for the reconsideration.

Results: The following features were developed regarding the way the interviewee changed prediction methods (the weights of factors):

When the interviewee changed the prediction method, he communicated with other dealers in order to get information on which factors were regarded important, and then modified the prediction method so that it better explained recent exchange-rate dynamics. Such communication and imitation behavior are similar to genetic operations in biology. When a prediction method of a dealer is regarded as an individual in a biological framework, the communication and imitation behavior of dealers correspond to "selection" and "crossover".

When the forecast of the interviewee was quite different from the actual rate, he recognized the need to change his weights. This difference between the forecast and the actual rate can be considered to correspond to "fitness" in a biological framework.

Given the similarities between these features of interaction of dealers' forecast and genetic operations, we used a Genetic Algorithm (GA) to describe agent learning in our artificial market model.

4 Construction of an Artificial Market Model

Our artificial market model (AGEDASI TOF[1]) has 100 agents. Each agent is a virtual dealer and has dollar and yen assets. The agent changes positions in the currencies for the purpose of making profits.

Each week of the model consists of 5 steps[2]: (1) Each dealer receives 17 data items of economic and political news[3] (*Perception step*), (2) predicts the future rate using the weighted average of news data with her own weights (*Prediction step*), and (3) determines her trading strategy (to buy or sell dollars) in order to

---

[1] A GEnetic-algorithmic Double Auction Simulation in TOkyo Foreign exchange market. AGEDASI TOF is a name of Japanese dish, fried tofu. It's very delicious.

[2] The details of our model are written in preceding papers [2,3,5]

[3] The items are 1. Economic activities, 2. Price, 3. Interest rates, 4. Money supply, 5. Trade, 6. Employment, 7. Consumption, 8. Intervention, 9. Announcement, 10. Mark, 11. Oil, 12. Politics, 13. Stock, 14. Bond, 15. Short-term Trend 1 (Change in the last week), 16. Short-term Trend 2 (Change of short-term Trend 1), and 17. Long-term Trend (Change through five weeks).

maximize her utility function (*Strategy Making step*) every week. Then, (4) the equilibrium rate is determined from the supply and demand in the market (*Rate Determination step*). Finally, (5) each agent improves her weights by copying from the other successful agents using GA operators [1] (*Adaptation step*).

After the *Adaptation* Step, our model proceeds to the next week's *Perception* Step.

5 Comparison with Real-World Data

The simulation results are compared with real-world data in order to test the validity of our model. First, we conducted extrapolation simulations of the rate dynamics from Jan. 1994 to Dec. 1995. Second, the 17 data items are classified into 3 categories based on the simulation results. Finally, using this classification, dynamics of agents' prediction methods are compared with interview data.

5.1 Simulation Methods

We repeated the following procedure a hundred times in order to generate a hundred simulation paths. First, the initial population is a hundred agents whose weights are randomly generated. Second, we trained our model by using the 17 real world data streams from Jan. 1992 to Dec. 1993[4]. During this *training period*, we skipped the Rate Determination Step and used the cumulated value of differences between the forecast mean and the *actual rate* as the fitness in the Adaptation Step. Finally, for the period from Jan. 1994 to Dec. 1995 we conducted the extrapolation simulations. In this *forecast period*, our model forecasted the rates in the Rate Determination Step by using only external data. We did not use any actual rate data, and both the internal data and the fitness were calculated on the basis of the rates generated by our model. We randomly selected 20% of the simulation paths and analyzed them. In the following sections, we illustrate the results of the analysis considering one typical path. However the pattern of these results are common among the selected paths.

5.2 Classification of Data Weights

The 17 data items were, as a result of the factor analysis of dynamic patterns of their weights[5], classified into six factors. The matrix that is analyzed by factor analysis is a list of 12 weights of 100 agents every 10 week during the forecast period. Because this matrix includes the weight value in different weeks, it can represent the temporal change of weights.

The weights of Economic activities and Price data have the largest loading value of the first factor. We call the first factor the '*Price monetary factor,*

---

[4] Each weekly time series was used a hundred times, so in this training period there were about ten thousand generations.

[5] The proportion of explanation by these six factors is 67.0 %.

because these two data are used by the price monetary approach to econometrics. The second factor is related to Trade and Interest rate data, which are included in the portfolio balance approach in econometrics, so we call it the *Portfolio balance factor*. The third factor is related to Announcement and Employment data, so we call it the *Announcement factor*. The fourth factor is related to Intervention and Politics data, so we call it the *Politics factor*. The fifth factor is related to Short-term trends and Stock data, so we call it the *Short-term factor*. And the sixth factor is related to Long-term trend data, so we call it the *Long-term factor*.

We combined these 6 factors into 3 categories: the Price monetary and Portfolio balance factors are classified into an *Econometrics category*, the Announcement and Politics factors are classified into a *News category*, and the Short-term and Long-term factors are classified into a *Trend category*.

We compared this classification with real-world data gathered by questionnaires [4]. The results showed that actual dealers classified news data in the same way as the simulation results show that the model does.

5.3 Comparison with Interview Data

We held interviews with two dealers who usually engaged in yen-dollar exchange transactions in Tokyo foreign exchange market. The first dealer (X) was a chief dealer in a bank. The second dealer (Y) was an interbank dealer in the same bank. They had more than two years of experience on the trading desk. The interview methods are written in section 3. Each interviewee (the dealer X and Y) ranked the factors in order of their weights (table 1 (a) and (b)). We compared temporal changes of the rank of factors in the interview data with the dynamics of weights in the computer simulation.

Table 1. Results of interviews: The forecast factors are ranked in order of importance.

(a) Dealer X

	I Jan	II Feb-Jun	III Jul-Oct	IV Nov-Dec	V Jan	VI Feb-Apr	VII May-Jul	VIII Aug-Sep	IX Oct-Dec
	1994				1995				
Actual	→	↘	→	→	↗	↘		↗	→
Forecast	→	↘	→	↘	↗			↗	→
Factors ranking	1.Mark 2.Seasonal factor	1.Chart 2.Trade 3.Politics	1.Chart 2.Deviation 3.Politics	1.Seasonal factor	1.Seasonal factor	1.Trade 2.Politics 3.Mexico 4.Chart		1.Deviation 2.Intervention	

(b) Dealer Y

	I Jan-May	II Jun	III Jul-Dec	IV Jan-Feb	V Mar-Apr	VI May-Jul	VII Aug-Dec
	1994			1995			
Actual	↘	↘	→	↘	↘	→	↗
Forecast	↘	→	→	↘	↘	→	↗
Factors ranking	1. Trade 1. Order 3. Chart	1. Rate level	1. Order 2. Chart	1. Politics 2. Mark 2. Announcement	1. Politics 1. Order 1. Intervention	1. Chart 2. Order	1. Intervention 2. Politics

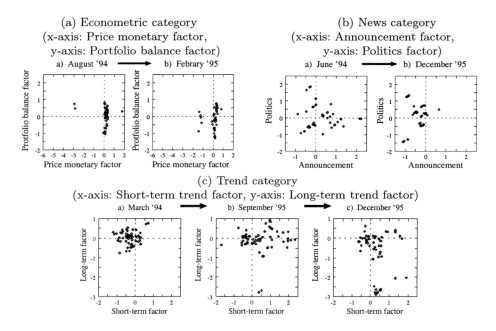

Fig. 1. Distribution of loading values of each category: Loading values of 100 agents are plotted on the planes whose axes represent factors.

Econometrics category: The distribution patterns of agents' scores of the Price monetary factor and Portfolio balance factor are illustrated in Fig.1a. The distribution patterns were stable near the origin of the coordinate axes during these 2 years, except that scores of the Portfolio balance factor slightly shift down. Thus, the simulation results showed that the influence of price monetary factor was stable but not so large, and that the agents paid attention to the portfolio balance factor in the first half of 1995.

In the interview data of the dealer X, the weight of the trade balance factor was large in the first half of 1995 (the period VI and VII in Table11). This supports the simulation results. The other econometric factors were not mentioned in the interviews. Probably it is not necessary to bother to say about them because their interpretation is so common and fixed during these two years. If so, this fact is also similar to the simulation results.

News category: The distribution patterns of agents' scores of the Announcement factor and Politics factor are illustrated in Fig.1b. The distribution patterns in 1994 and those in 1995 are clearly different. In 1994, the scores spread widely, while in 1995, they shifted to left and bottom areas. Thus, the simulation results showed that almost all the agents focused on the news category in 1995.

Both the dealer X and Y regarded the politics, intervention, and announcement factors as important during the bubble (the period VI, VII, and VIII in

Table1a and the period VI, V, and VII in Table1b). These interview data support the simulation results that market opinions about the news category converged in 1995.

Trend category: The distribution patterns of agents' scores of the Short-term factor and Long-term balance factor are illustrated in Fig.1c. At first the scores distributed in the minus are of the Short-term factor (March 1994). Then they moved to the plus area (September and December 1995). Finally, they return to the center of x axis, and shifted to the minus area of the Long-term factor (December 1995). Plus values of Short-term trend factor's weights mean that the agents tend to follow the recent chart trend. Minus values of Long-term trend factor's weights mean that the agents forecast that rates return to the previous level after large deviation. Thus, the simulation results show trend-following behavior of agents in 1995 and recursive expectation at the end of 1995.

Short-term trend factors were not explicitly mentioned in the interviews. Both of the two dealers however emphasized the importance of market sentiment (bullish or bearish) during the bubble. The market sentiment can be considered as a representation of short-term market trend. Hence, their stress on the market sentiment supports the simulation results that the trend factors magnified rate fluctuation. Both dealers regard the deviation or chart factor as important after the large deviation in 1995. This fact give agreement with the simulation results about Long-term trend factor.

6   Conclusion

In this study, we took an artificial market approach and found the categorization of factors that was similar to the actual dealers' categorization. Using this categorization, we have identified some emergent phenomena in markets such as rate bubbles [2, 3]. The overall results of this study show that the artificial market approach to modeling is effective for analyzing real-world markets.

References

1. D. Goldberg. *Genetic algorithms in search, optimization, and machine learning.* Addison-Wesley Publishing Company (1989).
2. K. Izumi and K. Ueda. Emergent phenomena in a foreign exchnage market: Analysis based on an artificial market approach. In C. Adami, R.K. Belew, H. Kitano, and C.E. Taylor, editors, *Artificial Life VI*, MIT Press (1998) 398–402.
3. K. Izumi and K. Ueda. Analysis of dealers' processing financial news based on an artificial market approach. *Journal of Computational Intelligence in Finance*, **7** (1999) 23–33.
4. K. Izumi and K. Ueda. Analysis of thought processes of virtual dealers in an artificial market. In *Proceedings of the Fifth Joint Conference on Information Science*, Association for Intelligent Machinery, Inc. (2000) 891–894.
5. K. Izumi and K. Ueda. Using an artificial market approach to analyze exchange rate scenarios. In C.-H. Chen et.al., editor, *Evolutionary Computation in Economics and Finance*. Springer Verlag (2000) (forthcoming).

Toward an Agent-Based Computational Modeling of Bargaining Strategies in Double Auction Markets with Genetic Programming

Shu-Heng Chen[1]

AI-ECON Research Center, Department of Economics
National Chengchi University, Taipei, Taiwan 11623
chchen@nccu.edu.tw

Abstract. Using genetic programming, this paper proposes an *agent-based computational modeling* of *double auction* (**DA**) *markets* in the sense that a DA market is modeled as an *evolving market* of *autonomous interacting traders* (*automated software agents*). The specific **DA** market on which our modeling is based is the Santa Fe **DA** market ([12], [13]), which in structure, is a *discrete-time* version of the Arizona *continuous-time* experimental **DA** market ([14], [15]).

1 Introduction

The purpose of this paper is to use genetic programming as a major tool to evolve the traders in an agent-based model of double auction (*DA*) market. With this modeling approach, we attempt to provide an analysis of bargaining strategies in DA markets from an evolutionary perspective. By saying that, the novelties of this paper, which helps distinguish this paper from early studies are two folds. First of all, to out best knowledge, the existing research on bargaining strategies in DA markets are not *agent-based models*. This research is, therefore, the first one. Secondly, while this research is not the first one to study the bargaining strategies from an evolutionary perspective, it is the first one to use genetic programming on this issue. We believe that genetic programming, as a methodological innovation to economics, may be powerful enough to enable us to get new insights on the form of effective trading strategies, and help us better understand the operation of the "invisible hand" in real-world markets. Furthermore, since the idea "*software agents*'" and "*automated programs*" should play an increasing important role at the era of *electronic commerce*, the agent-based model studied in this research can be a potential contribution to electronic commerce too. The rest of this section is written to justify the claimed novelties and significance.

2 Bargaining Strategies in DA Markets: Early Development

The *double auction* (**DA**) market has been the principal trading format for many types of commodities and financial instruments in organized markets around the world. The pit of the Chicago Commodities market is an example of a double auction and the New York Stock Exchange is another. In a general context, traders in these institutions face a sequence of non-trivial decision problems, such as

- how much should they bid or ask for their own *tokens*?
- how soon should they place a bid or ask?
- under what circumstance should they accept an outstanding bid or ask of some other trader?

Since [14], the experimental studies using human subjects have provided considerable empirical evidence on trading behavior of DA markets, which, to some extent, demonstrates that DA markets have remarkable efficiency properties. Nevertheless, these studies cast little light on *trading strategies* which are essentially unobservable.

Modern economic theory has attempted to explained observed trading behavior in DA markets as the rational equilibrium outcome of a well-defined game of incomplete information. The "null hypothesis" is that observed trading behavior is a realization of a Bayesian-Nash equilibrium (BNE) of this game. However, due to the inherent complexity of continuous-time games of incomplete information, it is extremely difficult to compute or even characterize these equilibria. As a result, relatively little is known theoretically about the nature of equilibrium bargaining strategies.

3   Computational Modeling of DA Markets: Zero-Intelligence "Theorem"

Recently, the computational approach, as a compliment to the analytical and the experimental ones, were also involved in the study of bargaining strategies in DA markets. Two influential early contributions in this line of research appeared in 1993. One is [7], and the other is [12]. While both addressed the nature of the bargaining strategies within the context of DA markets, the motivations behind them are quite different.

Motivated by a series of studies by Vriend Smith, [7] addressed the issue: *how much intelligence is required of an agent to achieve human-level trading performance?* Using an electronic DA market with *software agents* rather than *human subjects*, they found that the imposition of the budget constraint (that prevents zero-intelligence traders from entering into loss-making deals) is sufficient to raise the allocative efficiency of the auctions to values near 100 percent. The surprising and significant conclusion made by them is, therefore, that the traders' motivation, intelligence, or learning have little effect on the allocative efficiency, which derives instead largely from the structure of the DA markets. Thus, they claim

Adam Smith's invisible hand may be more powerful than some may have thought; it can generate *aggregate rationality* not only from individual

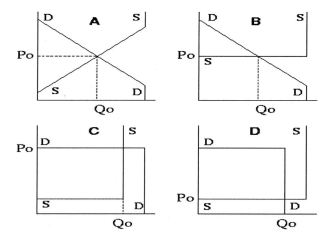

Fig. 1. Four Types of Demand and Supply Curves (Adapted from [5].)

rationality but also from *individual irrationality*." (Ibid., p.119, Italics added.).

Furthermore,

> ... the convergence of transaction price in ZI-C markets is a consequence of the market discipline; trader's attempts to maximize their profits, or even their ability to remember or learn about events of the market, are not necessary for such convergence. (Ibid, p.131)

While it sounds appealing, Gode and Sunder's strong argument on *zero intelligence* (ZI) was demonstrated to be *incorrect* by [5]. Using an analysis of the probability functions underlying DA markets populated by Gode & Sunder's ZI traders, [5] showed that the validity of *zero-intelligence "theorem"* is largely *a matter of coincidence*. Roughly speaking, only in a market whose supply and demand curves are *mirror-symmetric*, by reflection in the line of constant price at the equilibrium value P_0, over the range of quantities from zero to Q_0 (See Figure 1-(A) above), the ZI traders can trade at the theoretical equilibrium price. In more general cases, cases shown in Figure 1-(B), (C) and (D), ZI traders can easily fail. The failing of the ZI traders indicates a need for bargaining mechanisms more complex than the simple stochastic generation of bid and offer prices.

While this line of research can be further pursued, one should notice that what actually concerns traders are their own profits from trade. There is no reason why they should behave like ZI traders simply because ZI traders might collectively generate allocative efficiency. On the contrary, they may behave "*too smart for their own interests*". Consequently, models with ZI or ZI-Plus traders are unlikely to provide a good model to the understanding of human trading strategies.

4 Computational Modeling of DA Markets: SFI DA Tournaments

Leaving *collective rationality* aside, [12]'s computational study of bargaining strategies were largely motivated by *individual rationality*. Instead of asking the *minimal intelligence* required for *collective rationality*, they asked: *is the case that sophisticated strategies make individual traders better off?* Their analysis was based on the results of computerized double auction tournaments held at Santa Fe Institute beginning in March 1990. 30 programs were submitted to these tournaments. These 30 programs were written by programmers with different background knowledge (economics, computer science, cognitive science, mathematics, ...), and hence are quite heterogeneous in various dimensions (modeling strategies, complexity, adaptability, ...). For example, in complexity, they ranged from simple *rule-of-thumb* to sophisticated adaptive/learning procedures employing some of the latest ideas from the literature on *artificial intelligence* and *cognitive science*.

After conducting an extensive series of computer tournaments involving hundreds of thousands of individual DA games, the results may sounds to one's surprise: *nearly all of the top-ranked programs were based on a fixed set of intuitive rules-of-thumb*. For example, the winning program, known as Kaplan's strategy, makes no use of the prior information about the joint distribution of token values, and relies on only a few key variables such as its privately assigned token values, the current bid and ask, its number of remaining tokens, and the time remaining in the current period. Quite similar to the classical result presented by [2] in the context of *iterated prisoner's dilemma*, i.e., to be good *a strategy must be not too clever*, [12] just reconfirmed this *simplicity principle*. In [12], the effective bargaining strategies are simple in all aspects, which can be characterized as *nonadaptive, non-predictive, non-stochastic*, and *non-optimizing*.

Therefore, while Rust et al.'s auction markets were composed of traders with *heterogeneous* strategies, their results on the *simplicity* of the effective bargaining strategies, in spirit, is very similar to what Gode and Sunder found in the markets with *homogeneous* traders. Moreover, the general conclusion that *the structure of a double auction market is largely responsible for achieve high level of allocative efficiency, regardless of the intelligence, motivation, or learning of the agents in the market* is well accepted in both lines of study. However, as the reason which we shall argue below, this conclusion with the simplicity criterion is indeed *in doubt*. For convenience, we shall call this doubtful argument *the intelligence-independent property*, which should roughly capture the essence of *zero intelligence* in [7] and "rules of thumb" in [12].

5 What is Missing? Evolution

First of all, *intelligence-independent property* is clearly not true in the context of *imitation dynamics*. For an illustration, consider Kaplan's strategy. The Kaplan

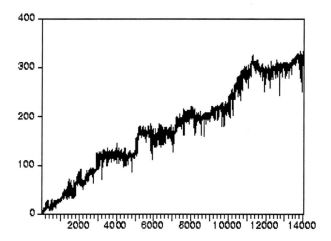

Fig. 2. Evolving Complexity of Traders' Forecasting Models (Adapted from Figure 9 in [4]).

strategy *waits in the background until the other participants have almost negotiated a trade (the bid/ask spread is small), and then jumps in and steals the deal if it is profitable.* Suppose that we allow *imitation* among traders, then we would expect growth in the relative numbers of these sorts of *background traders*. Less profitable traders should gradually exit the market due to *competitive pressure*. In the end, all traders in the market are *background traders*. However, the background traders create a negative *"information externality"* by waiting for their opponents to make the first move. If all traders do this, little information will be generated and the market would be unable to function efficiently. As a result, the *"wait in the background"* strategy would eventually be non-profitable, and hence certainly can no longer be effective. As a result, Rust et al.'s characterization of effective strategies may not able to hold in an *evolutionary* context.

In fact, the *simplicity principle* argued by [2] is recently shown to be *incorrect* by [3]. By using a larger class of strategies, they showed that the simple *Tie for Tat* strategy was beaten by a more complex strategy called *gradual* in almost all their experiments. As a conclusion, they claimed the significance of *evolution* (*adaptation*).

> Evaluation can, however, not be based only on the results of complete classes evolution, since a strategy could have a behavior well adapted to this kind of environment, and not well adapted to a completely different environment. (Ibid, p. 40)

The significance of evolution on the complexity of strategies was also shown in [4]. In their agent-based modeling of artificial stock markets, they conducted an analysis of the evolving complexity of each traders' forecasting models, and a typical result is demonstrated in Figure 2. Their results evidence that traders can evolve toward a higher degree of sophistication, while at some point in time, they can be simple as well. Therefore, it is very difficult to make much sense of the simplicity principle from a steady environment.

6 Evolving Bargaining Strategies

In literature, there are two studies which actually attempted to give an *artificial life* for bargaining strategies. One is [1], and the other is [11]. Both relied on genetic programming. Nevertheless, neither of them can be considered as a truly evolutionary model of DA markets. To see this, the market architecture of these two studies are drawn in Figure 3 and 4.

What Andrews and Prager did was to fix a trader (Seller 1 in their case) and used genetic programming to evolve the trading strategies of only that trader. In the meantime, one opponent was assigned the trading strategies *"Skeleton"*, a strategy prepared by the SFI tournament. The trading strategies of the other six opponents were randomly chosen from a selection of successful Santa Fe competitors. Therefore, what Andrews and Prager did was to see whether GP can help an individual trader to evolve very competitive strategies given their opponents' strategies. However, since other opponents are not equipped with the same opportunity to adapt, this is not a really evolutionary model of DA markets.

On the other hand, [11]'s architecture can be motivated as follows. Suppose that you are an economists, and you would like to select a pair of bargaining strategies, one for all sellers, and one for all buyers. Then you are asking how to select such pair of rules so that the allocative efficiency can be maximized (as he chose the Alpha's value as the fitness function). To solve this problem, Olsson also used genetic programming. In this application, traders are not pursuing for their own interests, but try to please the economist. Moreover, they are all shared with the same strategy at any moment in time. Hence, Olsson's model, very like the model of artificial ants, is certainly not an evolutionary model of DA markets.

In sum, while both [1] and [11] did use genetic programming to *"grow"* bargaining strategies, the style by which they used GP did not define an evolutionary model of DA markets.

7 Agent-Based Modeling of DA Markets: Trading Behavior

[6] may be considered as the first *agent-based computational model* of DA markets. Based on the WebPages of agent-based computational economics:
http://www.econ.iastate.edu/tesfatsi/ace.htm,
"Agent-based computational economics (ACE) is roughly defined by its practitioners as the computational study of economies modeled as evolving systems of autonomous interacting agents.... ACE is thus a blend of concepts and tools from evolutionary economics, cognitive science, and computer science."

Andrews and Prager (1994): Market Architecture

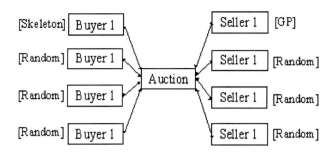

Random = Random{Kaplan, Skeleton, Anon 1,
Anon 2, Kindred, Leiweber, Gamer}

Fig. 3. The DA Market Architecture of [1]

The market architecture of [6] is depicted in Figures 5 and 6. He considered two populations of agents: 100 Buyers and 100 Sellers. Each seller has the potential to produce one unit of the commodity every period. The production costs are given by $c \in [0, 1]$ ($c = 0, 0.1$ in his experiments). The seller produces the good only if he can sell it in the same period. The buyer gain utility of $1 \geq u > c$ from consuming the good ($u = 1, 0.7$ in his cases). u and c are private information. During each period, every seller is randomly matched with a buyer and both submit a sealed bid. The buyer submits the price he is willing to pay (p_b), and the seller gives the minimum payment for which he will deliver the good (p_s). Buyers and sellers know that c and u lie in [0,1] and accordingly restrict their bids to this interval. If $p_b \geq p_s$, one unit of the good is traded at a price of

$$p_t rade = \frac{(p_b + p_s)}{2}. \tag{1}$$

Otherwise, no trade takes place. He then applied the so-called *single-population genetic algorithm* to buyers and sellers simultaneously. But, constrained by the GA, what one can observe from Dawid's model is only the evolution of bids and asks rather than the bargaining strategies by which the bids and asks are generated. Therefore, while Dawid is the first application of agent-based model to DA markets. This is really not a model suitable for the study of bargaining strategies.

8   Agent-Based Modeling of DA Markets: Trading Strategies

Given this literature development, the next step of the computational modeling of DA markets seems to be clear, and the architecture proposed in this research is briefed in Figure 7.

Olsson (1999): Market Architecture

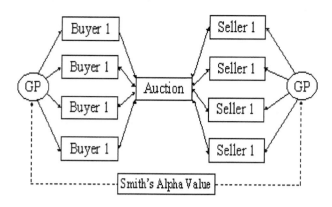

Fig. 4. The DA Market Architecture of [11]

This simple architecture shows some distinguishing features of this research. First, it is the use of *genetic programming*. But, we do not just come to say: *"Hey!. This is genetic programming. Try it! It works."* To our understanding, genetic programming can be considered a novel micro-foundation for economics. In fact, its relevance to the study of adaptive behavior in economics can be inferred from [9]. First, he gave a notion of an agent in economics.

> In general terms, we view or model an individual as a collection of *decision rules* (*rules that dictate the action to be taken in given situations*) and *a set of preferences* used to evaluate the outcomes arising from particular *situation-action* combinations. (Ibid; p.217. Italics added.)

Second, he proceeded to describe the adaptation of the agent.

> These decision rules are continuously under review and revision; *new* decision rules are tried and test against *experience*, and rules that produce desirable outcomes supplant those that do not. (Ibid; p.217. Italics added.)

Let us read these two quotations within the context of DA markets. An individual would be treated as a trader, and a decision rule is a just a *bargaining strategy*. To be specific, we consider the three strategies studied by [12] and [13], namely, the skeleton strategy, the Ringuette strategy, and the Kaplan strategy.

Dawid (1999): Market Architecture

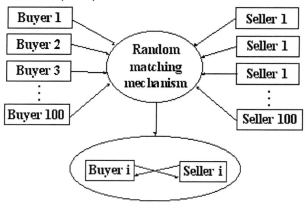

Fig. 5. The DA Market Architecture of [6]

The flowchart of there three strategies adapted from [13] is displayed in Figures 8, 9, 10.

In addition to the flow-chart representation, these three strategies can also be represented in what known as the *parse-tree* form, and are shown in Figures 11, 12, 13. In this case, what [9] meant about a *collection* of decision rules (bargaining strategies) can be concretely represented as a *collection* of *parse tress*. Then the second quotation from Lucas is about the review of these bargaining strategies (parse trees), and from this review, new bargaining strategies (parse trees) may be generated. Notice that here Lucas were not talking about just a single decision rule but a collection of decision rules. In other words, he was talking about the *evolution* of *a population of decision rules*.

Now, based on what we just described, if each decision rule can *hopefully* be written and implemented as a *computer program*, and since every computer program can be represented as a LISP parse-tree expression, then *Lucasian Adaptive Economic Agent* can be modeled as the following equivalents,

- evolving population of computer programs,
- evolving population of parse trees.

But, no matter how we may call this modeling procedure, this is exactly what *genetic programming* does, and in fact, there is no other technique known to the projector, which can accomplish this task as effective as GP. Hence, that would not be too exaggerated to claim *genetic programming as a methodological innovation to economics.*

Dawid (1999): Market Architecture

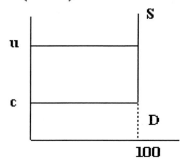

The Double Auction Market:
Demand and Supply Curve

Fig. 6. The DA Market of [6]: Demand and Supply

The second distinguishing feature is not just the use of genetic programming, but the *population genetic programming*. The weakness of using simple GP in agent-based modeling has already been well pointed out in [4]. Again, there is no reason why we can assume that traders will release their bargaining strategies to others to imitate. Therefore, to not misuse GP in the agent-based computer simulation of DA markets, it is important to use population GP.

References

1. Andrews, M. and R. Prager (1994), "Genetic Programming for the Acquisition of Double Auction Market Strategies," in K. E. Kinnear (ed.), *Advances in Genetic Programming*, Vol. 1, MIT Press. pp. 355-368.
2. Axelrod, R. (1984), *The Evolution of Cooperation*, Basic Books.
3. Beaufils, B., J.-P. Delahaye and P. Mathieu (1998), "Complete Classes of Strategies for the Classical Iterated Prisoner's Dilemma," in V. W. Porto, N. Saravanan, D. Waagen, and A. E. Eiben (eds.), *Evolutionary Programming* VII, pp. 33-42.
4. Chen, S.-H and C.-H. Yeh (2000), "Evolving Traders and the Business School with Genetic Programming: A New Architecture of the Agent-Based Artificial Stock Market," *Journal of Economic Dynamics and Control*, forthcoming.
5. Cliff, D. (1997), "Minimal-Intelligence Agents for Bargaining Behaviors in Market-Based Environments," *HP Technical Report*, HPL-97-91, 1997.
6. Dawid, H. (1999), "On the Convergence of Genetic Learning in a Double Auction Market," *Journal of Economic Dynamics and Control*, 23, pp. 1545-1567.

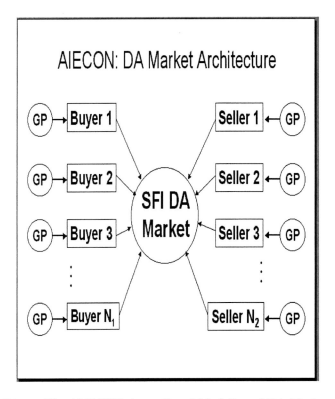

Fig. 7. The AI-ECON Agent-Based Modeling of DA Markets

7. Gode, D. K., and S. Sunders (1993), "Allocative Efficiency of Market with Zero-Intelligence Trader: Market as a Partial Substitute for Individual Rationality," *Journal of Political Economy*, Vol. 101, No. 1, pp. 119-137.

8. Lucas (1986), "Adaptive Behavior and Economic Theory", in Hogarth, R. M. and M. W. Reder (eds.), *Rational Choice: The Contrast between Economics and Psychology*, University of Chicago Press, pp. 217-242.

9. Olsson, L. (2000), "Evolution of Bargaining Strategies for Continuous Double Auction Markets Using Genetic Programming," forthcoming in *Proceedings of the First International Workshop on Computational Intelligence in Economics and Finance* (CIEF'2000).

10. Rust, J., J. Miller and R. Palmer (1993): "Behavior of Trading Automata in a Computerized Double Auction Market," in D. Friedman and J. Rust (eds.), *The Double Auction Market: Institutions, Theories, and Evidence*, Addison Wesley. Chap. 6, pp.155-198.

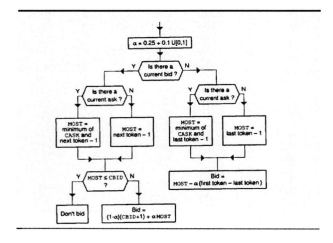

Fig. 8. The Flow Chart of the Skeleton Strategy

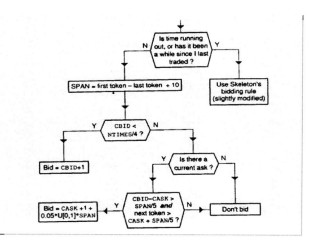

Fig. 9. The Flow Chart of the Ringuette Strategy

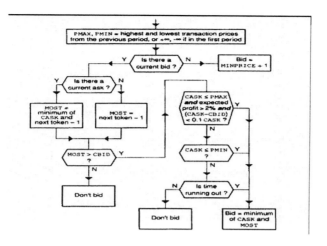

Fig. 10. The Flow Chart of the Kaplan Strategy

Skeleton's Strategy: The Tree Form

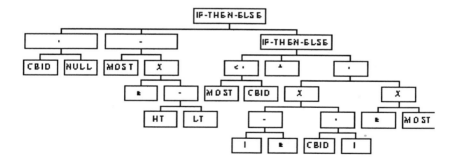

Fig. 11. The Skeleton Strategy in Parse-Tree Representation

Ringuett's Strategy: The Tree Form

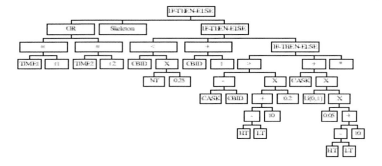

Fig. 12. The Ringuette Strategy in Parse-Tree Representation

Kaplan Strategy: The Tree Form

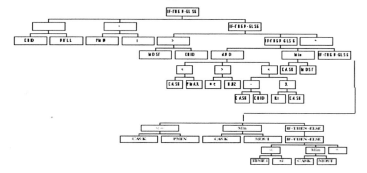

Fig. 13. The Kaplan Bargaining Strategy in Parse-Tree Representation

11. Rust, J., J. Miller, and R. Palmer (1994), "Characterizing Effective Trading Strategies: Insights from a Computerized Double Auction Market," *Journal of Economic Dynamics and Control*, Vol. 18, pp.61-96.
12. Smith, V. (1962), "An Experimental Study of Competitive Market Behavior," *Journal of Political Economy*, 70, pp. 111-137.
13. Smith, V. (1992), *Papers in Experimental Economics*, Cambridge University Press.

Combining Ordinal Financial Predictions with Genetic Programming

Edward P.K. TSANG and Jin LI

Department of Computer Science, University of Essex,
Wivenhoe Park, Colchester, Essex CO4 3SQ, United Kingdom
Email: {edward, jli}@essex.ac.uk

Abstract. Ordinal data play an important part in financial forecasting. For example, advice from expert sources may take the form of "bullish", "bearish" or "sluggish", or "buy" or "do not buy". This paper describes an application of using Genetic Programming (GP) to combine investment opinions. The aim is to combine ordinal forecast from different opinion sources in order to make better predictions. We tested our implementation, FGP (Financial Genetic Programming), on two data sets. In both cases, FGP generated more accurate rules than the individual input rules.

1 Introduction

Ordinal data could be useful in financial forecasting, as Fan et. al. [6] quite rightly pointed out. For example, forecast by experts may predict that a market is "bullish", "bearish" or "sluggish". A company's books may show "deficit" or "surplus". A share's price today may have "risen", "fallen" or "remained unchanged" from yesterday's. The question is how to make use of such data.

Let Y be a series, gathered at regular intervals of time (such as daily stock market closing data or weekly closing price). Let Y_t denote the value of Y at time t. Forecasting at time t with a horizon h means predicting the value of Y_{t+h} based on some information set I_t of other explanatory variables available at time t. The conditional mean

$$F_{t,h} = E[Y_{t+h} \mid I_t]$$

represents the best forecast of the most likely Y_{t+h} value [8]. In terms of properties of value Y, forecast could be classified into point forecast, where Y_t is a real value, or *ordinal forecasts*, where Y_t is an interval estimate. In terms of the property of I_t, forecast could be classified into *time-series forecast*, where I_t consists of nothing but Y_{t-i} where $i \geq 0$, or *combining forecast*, where I_t only includes a finite direct forecast results from different sources.

In recent years, there has been growing interest in combining forecasts; for example, see [17, 13] for combining point forecasts and [6, 3] for combining ordinal forecasts. The methodologies adopted in these researches are mainly statistical methods and operation research methods. The full potential of AI forecasting techniques such as genetic algorithms [9] has yet to be realized.

In this paper, we follow the study of Fan and his colleagues and focus on combining ordinal forecasts. We demonstrate the potential of Genetic Programming (GP) [11] in combining and improving individual predictions in two different data sets:

(i)   a small data set involving the Hong Kong Heng Seng index as reported by Fan and his colleagues [6]; and

(ii)   a larger data set involving S&P 500 index from 2 April 1963 to 25 January 1974 (2,700 trading days).

2 FGP for Combining Ordinal Forecasts

2.1 Background: Genetic Programming and Its Application to Finance

Genetic algorithm (GA) is class of optimization technique inspired by the principle of natural selection in evolution. *Genetic Programming* is a promising variant of genetic algorithms that evolves tree representations instead of strings. The basic algorithm is as follows. Candidate solutions are referred to as chromosomes and the program maintains a set of chromosomes, which is referred to as a population. Each chromosome is evaluated for its fitness according to the function that is to be optimized. Fitter strings are given more chance to be picked to become parents, which will be used to generate offspring. Offspring copy their material from both parents using various mechanisms under the name of crossover. Offspring are sometimes given a chance to make minor random changes, which are referred to as mutations. Offspring may replace existing members of the population. The hope (supported by theoretical analysis, see for example [7]) is that after enough number of iterations, better candidate solutions can be generated. GPs have been successful in many applications, including financial applications, e.g. see [1, 12, 14, 4].

FGP (Financial Genetic Programming) is a genetic programming implementation specialized for financial forecasting. It is built as a forecasting tool under the EDDIE project [16]. In this paper, we shall focus on its application in combining individual expert predictions in order to generate better predictions.

2.2 Candidate Solutions Representation

In the Hong Kong stock market example in the next section, the set of possible categories is {bullish, bearish, sluggish, uncertain}. In the S&P 500 index example in the subsequent section, the set of categories is {buy, not-buy}.

FGP searches in the space of decision trees whose nodes are functions, variables, and constants. Variables and constants take no arguments and they form the leaf nodes of the decision trees. In the applications described in this paper, both the variables (input) and the predictions (output, constants) are ordinal categories. The grammar determines the expressiveness of the rules and the size of the rule space to be searched. Functions take arguments and they form subtrees. In this paper, we take {if-then-else, and, or, not, >, <, =} as functions.

2.3 Experimental Details

Being a genetic programming system, FGP needs a suitable fitness function that measures the predictability of each decision tree. One fundamental measure of predictability is the rate of correctness (RC) – the proportion of correct predictions out of all predictions:

$$RC \equiv \text{number of correct predictions} \div \text{total number of predictions}$$

In the experiments described below, crossover rate is 90% and mutation rate is 1%. Elitism is employed by randomly picking 1% of the population, biased towards the fitter individuals, and putting them directly into the next generation. Among existed selection methods in GP, we used tournament selection with tournament size set to 4. Population size is set to 1,200. The termination condition is 40 generations or two hours, whichever reached first. Initial GDTs are limited to a depth of 5. The maximum depth of any tree is set to 17. FGP-1 was implemented in Borland C++ (version 4.5). All experiments described in this paper were run in a Pentium PC (200MHz) running Windows 95 with 64 MB RAM.

3 Application of FGP to the Hong Kong Stock Market

FGP was applied to the prediction of changes in the Heng Seng Index in the Hong Kong Stock Market. We used the data set given in the appendix of [6], which comprises 103 data cases, each of which comprises nine expert predictions for the following week and the actual market changes. Predictions by each of the 9 experts fall into four categories, which Fan et al. labeled as:
1. bullish, defined as "the index rises by over 1.3% in the next week";
2. bearish, defined as "the index falls by over 1.3% in the next week";
3. sluggish, defined as "the index is neither bullish nor bearish"; and
4. uncertain, which means the expert did not make a prediction.
The period under this study was from 25 May 1991 to 16 October 1993.

Fan et al [6] used the "leave-one-out cross-validation strategy" to assess the forecasting accuracy. This means to generate a forecasting for time t, all but the experts' predictions at time t were used to generate a combined prediction. Predictions generated this way were evaluated. For simplicity without lost of generality, we used 3-fold cross-validation to estimate FGP's forecasting performance: we partitioned the data set into three mutually exclusive subsets (the folds):
D1: 34 data cases from 25 May 1991 to 11 January 92;
D2: 35 data cases from 18 January 1992 to 5 December 1992;
D3: 34 data cases from 12 December 1992 to 16 October 1993
Each of these data sets was used as the testing data set once, whilst the remaining two sets were employed as the training data set. The mean forecasting accuracy was the overall number of correct forecasts divided by number of cases in the whole data set [10]. For each of D1, D2, D3, we ran FGP 10 times, so a total of 30 runs were used in our experiments.

FGP-1 achieved an average RC of 60.88%, 45.14% and 45.29% over D1, D2, D3, respectively. The mean RC of FGP method was 50.39%, which is comparable with (if slightly better than) the Multinomial Logic Method (MNL, 50.16%) and the Linear Programming Method (LP, 45.63%) presented in [6]. The best expert prediction input (Expert 7) achieved an RC of 43.69%. It was encouraging to see that MNL, LP and FGP can all improve the accuracy of the best expert's forecast. However, this example involves relatively small data cases and therefore one should not generalize the results without further experimentation.

4 Application of FGP to the S&P 500 Index

Encouraged by FGP's promising forecasting performance on the Heng Seng Index, we tested FGP on the S&P-500 daily index. Available to us were data from 2 April 1963 to 25 January 1974 (2700 data cases). Our goal is to see whether FGP could improve forecasting accuracy on textbook-type predictions.

Six technical rules (three different types) derived from the financial literature [2, 5, 15] are used as input to FGP-1. They were used to predict whether the following goal is achievable at any given day:

G: the index will rise by 4% or more within 63 trading days (3 months).

The six technical rules we used were as follows:
- Two Moving Average Rules (MV):
  The L-days simple moving average at time t, SMV(L, t), is defined as the average price of the last L days from time t. The rule is "if today's index price is greater than SMV(L, t), then buy; else do not buy." L = 12 and L = 50 were used.
- Two Trading Range Break Rules (TRB):
  The rule is: "buy if today's price is greater than the maximum of the prices in the previous L days; else do not buy". L = 5 and L = 50 were used.
- Two Filter Rules:
  This rule is "buy when the price rises by y percent above its minimum of the prices in the previous L days; else do not buy." Two rules, with y = 1(%) and L = 5 and L = 10 were used.

Our sole concern is whether FGP can combine technical rules in order to generate more accurate forecasting. Therefore, the quality of the individual rules is not crucial to our study.

The FGP algorithm is the same as that in the first example. In addition to the rate of correctness (RC), we added two factors to the fitness function: the rate of missing chance (RMC) and the rate of failure (RF). RMC and RF are defined as follows:

RMC ≡ # of erroneous not-buy signals ÷ total number of opportunities

RF ≡ # of erroneous buy signals ÷ total number of buy signals

Weights were given to RC, RMC and RF in the fitness function. By adjusting these weights, we can reflect the preference of investors. For example, a conservative investor may want to avoid failure and consequently put more weight on RF.

Table 1. Performance comparisons between individual rules and FGP rules

Individual rule performances			FGP rule performances		
Rules	Accuracy (RC)	ARR	Runs	Accuracy (RC)	ARR
MV (L=12)	0.4956	0.3020	FGP Rule 1	0.5400	0.3952
MV (L=50)	0.5189	0.2666	FGP Rule 2	0.5389	0.3945
TRB (L=5)	0.4733	0.3319	FGP Rule 3	0.5400	0.3952
TRB (L=50)	0.4756	0.2102	FGP Rule 4	0.5522	0.3911
Filter (L=5)	0.4944	0.3746	FGP Rule 5	0.5444	0.3964
Filter(L=10)	0.4889	0.3346	FGP Rule 6	0.5367	0.3935
			FGP Rule 7	0.5389	0.3945
			FGP Rule 8	0.5356	0.3928
			FGP Rule 9	0.5433	0.3960
			FGP Rule10	0.5300	0.4187
			Mean	0.5400	0.3968

In our experiments, RC, RMC and RF were given weights of 1, 0.2 and 0.3 respectively. 1,800 cases (02/04/1963 -- 02/07/1970) were used as training data. 900 cases (06/07/1970 -- 25/01/1974) were used as test data. We ran FGP 10 times. For each run, the best rule evolved in training was applied to the testing data. The results of FGP rules on testing data and the six individual rules were recorded in Table 1. Among the six technical rules, the MV(L=50) rule was the best individual rule for this set of data. It achieved an accuracy of 51.89%. In contrast, even the poorest FGP rule (FGP rule 10) achieved an accuracy of 53.00%. The average accuracy of FGP rules was 54.00%. So although only 10 decision trees were generated, the results were conclusive: FGP produced better forecasting consistently by combining individual decisions.

For reference, we measured the *annualised rate of return* (ARR) by the rules above using the following hypothetical trading behaviour with simplifying assumptions:

Hypothetical trading behaviour: *whenever a buy signal is generated, one unit of money is invested in a portfolio reflecting the S&P-500 index. If the index rises by 4% or more within the next 63 days, then the portfolio is sold at the index price of day t; else sell the portfolio on the 63rd day, regardless of the price.*

We ignored transaction costs and the bid-ask spread. Results in Table 1 show that rules generated by FGP achieved an ARR of 39.68% in average. In comparison, the best of the input rules (Filter rule, with L=5) achieved an ARR of 37.46%, which is lower than the poorest ARR generated by FGP in the ten runs (39.11% by rule 4).

Acknowledgements

This work is partly supported in part by the University of Essex Research Promotion Fund. Jin Li is supported by *Overseas Research Students Awards (ORS)* and University of Essex Studentship. James Butler and Tung Leng Lau contributed to earlier parts of this research.

References

1. Angeline, P. & Kinnear, K. E., (ed.), *Advances in genetic programming II*, MIT Press. 1996. Blume, L., Easley, D. & O'Hara, M., Market statistics and technical analysis: the role of volume, *Journal of finance*, 49, (1994), 153-181.
2. Brock, W., Lakonishok, J. & LeBaron, B., Simple technical trading rules and the stochastic properties of stock returns, *Journal of Finance*, 47, (1992), 1731-1764.
3. Cesa-Bianchi, N., Freund, Y., Haussler, D., Helmbold, D.P., Schapire, R.E. & Warmuth M.K., How to use expert advice, *Journal of the ACM*, Vol. 44, No. 3., (1997), 427-485.
4. Chen, S-H. & Yeh, C-H. , Speculative trades and financial regulations: simulations based on genetic programming, *Proceedings of the IEEE/IAFE 1997 Computational Intelligence for Financial Engineering (CIFEr)*, New York City, (1997), 123-129.
5. Fama, E.F. & Blume, M.E., filter rules and stock-market trading, *Journal of Business* 39(1), (1966), 226-241.
6. Fan, D.K., Lau, K-N. & Leung, P-L., Combining ordinal forecasting with an application in a financial market, *Journal of Forecasting*, Vol. 15, No.1, Wiley, January, (1996), 37-48.
7. Goldberg, D.E., *Genetic Algorithms in Search, Optimization and Machine Learning*. Addison-Wesley, 1989.
8. Granger, C.W.J., Forecasting, in Newman, P. , Milgate, M. & Eatwell, J. (ed.), *New palgrave dictionary of money and finance*, Macmillan, London, (1992), 142-143.
9. Holland, J. H., *Adaptation in natural and artificial system*, University of Michigan Press, 1975.
10. Kohavi, R., A study of cross-validation and bootstrap for accuracy estimation and model selection, *Proceedings of International Joint Conference on Artificial Intelligence* (IJCAI), (1995), 1137-1143.
11. Koza, J.R., *Genetic Programming: on the Programming of Computers by Means of Natural Selection*. Cambridge, MA: MIT Press, 1992.
12. Koza, J., Goldberg, D., Fogel, D. & Riolo, R. (ed.), *Proceedings of the First Annual Conference on Genetic programming*, MIT Press, 1996.
13. Lobo, G., Alternative methods of combining security analysts' and statistical forecasts of annual corporate earnings, *International Journal of Forecasting*, (1991), 57-63.
14. Neely, C., Weller, P. & Ditmar, R., Is technical analysis in the foreign exchange market profitable? a genetic programming approach, in Dunis, C. & Rustem, B.(ed.), *Proceedings, Forecasting Financial Markets: Advances for Exchange Rates, Interest Rates and Asset Management*, London. 1997.
15. Sweeney, R. J., Some new filter rule test: Methods and results, *Journal of Financial and Quantitative Analysis*, 23, (1988), 285-300.
16. Tsang, E.P.K, Butler, J. M. & Li, J., Eddie beats the bookies, *Journal of Software, Practice and Experience*, Wiley, Vol.28 (10), August 1998, 1033-1043.
17. Wall, K. & Correia, C., A preference-based method for forecast combination, *Journal of Forecasting*, (1989), 269-192.

Applying Independent Component Analysis to Factor Model in Finance

Siu-Ming CHA and Lai-Wan CHAN

Computer Science and Engineering Department
The Chinese University of Hong Kong, Shatin, HONG KONG
Email : {smcha,lwchan}@cse.cuhk.edu.hk
http://www.cse.cuhk.edu.hk/{~smcha,~lwchan}

Abstract. Factor model is a very useful and popular model in finance. In this paper, we show the relation between factor model and blind source separation, and we propose to use Independent Component Analysis (ICA) as a data mining tool to construct the underlying factors and hence obtain the corresponding sensitivities for the factor model.

1 Introduction

Factor model is a fundamental model in finance. Many financial theories are established based on it, for examples, Modern Portfolio Theory and Arbitrage Pricing Theory(APT). These theories assume that the returns of securities are represented as linear combinations of some factors. Modern Portfolio Theory aims at analyzing the composition of securities in the portfolio and relates the return and risk of the portfolio with the security returns and risks [20]. Factor model serves as an efficient and common model for the return generating process [21, 24, 17]. Furthermore, factor model is also the foundation of Arbitrage Pricing Theory (APT) [5, 22]. APT plays an important role in modern finance and it analyses the capital asset pricing in finance [9, 10].

Factor model relates the returns of securities to a set of factors. The factors can be system (market) factors or non-system (individual) factors. Finding the factors for the model is a challenge but not an easy task to researchers, as the factors are hidden and not necessary directly related to the fundamental factors, such as GDP, interest rate[12]. In this paper, we apply independent component analysis (ICA), a modern signal processing method, to recover the hidden factors and the corresponding sensitivities. Section 2 and 3 review the backgrounds of factor model and ICA. We apply ICA to factor model in section 4. Section 5 contains the experiment and results.

2 Factor model in finance

Multifactor model is a general form of factor model [2, 9, 21], and is the most popular model for the return generating process. The return r_i on the ith security is represented as,

$$r_i = \alpha_i + \sum_{m=1}^{k} \beta_{im} F_m + u_i \tag{1}$$

where k is the number of factors and it is a positive integer larger than zero, $F_1, F_2, ..., F_k$ are the factors affecting the returns of ith security and β_{i1}, β_{i2}, ..., β_{ik} are the corresponding sensitivities. α_i is regarded as "zero" factor that is invariant with time; u_i is a zero mean random variable of ith security. It is generally assumed that the covariance between u_i and factors F_i are zero. Also u_i and u_j for security i and j are independent if $i \neq j$.

The simplest factor model is one-factor model, i.e., $k = 1$. One-factor model with market index as the factor variable is called market model. However, factor model does not restrict the factor to be the market index. Investigators use different approaches in factor model [19, 6]. The first one assumes some known fundamental factors are the factors that influence the security and β's are evaluated accordingly. The second approach assumes the sensitivities to factors are known, and the factors are estimated from the security returns [12]. The third approach is factor analysis. This one assumes neither factor values nor the security sensitivities is known. Under factor analysis approach, principle component analysis(PCA) was the most successful method [11, 23, 25]. PCA was used to find the factors and their sensitivities[2, 8]. However it was also shown that the separated factors are not able to truly reflect the real case but only one meaningful factor, which corresponds to the market effect, is extracted. This is due to two limitations of PCA. First, the separated principal components must be orthogonal to each other. Second, PCA uses only up to second order statistics, i.e. the covariance and correlation matrix. In this paper, we apply ICA to factor model because ICA does not have those limitations PCA has. More importantly, ICA is able to reflect the underlying structures of securities[1, 18].

3 Independent Component Analysis

Blind source separation(BSS), a well-known problem, aims at recovering the sources from a set of observations. Applications include separating individual voices in cocktail party. In BSS problem, it contains two processes. They are the mixing process and demixing process. First, we observe a set of multivariate signals $x_i(t), i = 1, 2, ..., n$, that are assumed to be linearly mixed with a set of source signals. The mixing process is hidden so we can only observe the mixed signals. The task is to recover the original source signals from the observations through a demixing process. Equation 2 and 3 describe the mixing and demixing processes mathematically.

$$\text{Mixing:} \qquad x = As \qquad (2)$$

$$\text{Demixing:} \qquad y = Wx \qquad (3)$$

Each signal x_i is a t time steps series, i.e. $x_i = [x_i(1), x_i(2), ..., x_i(t)]$; x is the $[n \times t]$ observation matrix, i.e. $x = [x_1, x_2, ..., x_n]'$. In BSS problem, we assume the number of observations is equal to the number of source signals. Matrix s contains the original source signals driving the observations whereas the separated signals are stored in matrix y. They are both $[n \times t]$ matrices. A and W

are both $[n \times n]$ matrices, called mixing and demixing matrix respectively. If the separated signals are the same as the original sources, the mixing matrix is the inverse of demixing matrix, *i.e.* $A = W^{-1}$.

BSS is a difficult task because we do not have any information about the sources and the mixing process. ICA is a method tackling this problem by assuming that the sources are independent to each other[16], and finds the demixing matrix W and corresponding independent signals y from the observations x with some criteria making the separated signals as independent as possible. Various ICA algorithms have been proposed. Most of them use higher order statistics to obtain the independent components, e.g. $[13, 7, 15, 14, 3]$ and $[4]$ etc.

4 ICA and Factor model

4.1 Relationships between BSS and Factor Model

Previous works have been done on using ICA to extract components for stocks [1]. However, the independent components have never been related to the factor models. By relating the independent components to the factor model, we hope that this technique can be used in future applications of the factor model. In this section, we illustrate the application of ICA in factor model. Both of them assume the observations are under driven by a set of factors (or sources). We firstly zero mean the return as

$$r_i - E[r_i] = \sum_{m=1}^{k} \beta_{im}\{F_m - E[F_m]\} + u_i \tag{4}$$

We put $R_i = r_i - E[r_i]$ and $F'_m = F_m - E[F_m]$. Without loss of generality, we treat the noise term, u_i, as an extra factor, i.e. $u_i = \beta_{ik+1}F'_{k+1}$

$$R_i = \sum_{m=1}^{k+1} \beta_{im} F'_m \tag{5}$$

The above is a typical mixing process of observations in blind source separation problem. The factor models are under transformed to mixing matrix and factor series. After the transformation, we can apply ICA to separate the sources (or factors).

4.2 Procedures of finding factors by ICA

Here we show the procedures of finding the factors for factor model using ICA.

1. Select securities' price series as observations. We transform the security prices to returns *i.e.* $r_i(t) = (p_i(t) - p_i(t-1))/p_i(t-1)$ and making the return series zero mean *i.e.* $R_i = r_i - E[r_i]$.

2. Perform independent component separation on the return series R_i.

3. Sort the independent signals with their importance. Importance of a signal can be measured by its L_∞ [1].

4. Select the number of independent signals according to the requirements of factor model. The rest of separated signals are regarded as residuals.

5. Evaluate the sensitivities to the factors using the mixing matrix.

The separated independent signals and the corresponding sensitivities are obtained from the above procedures. Hence the factor model is constructed using the observable security movements. We will demonstrate this in the experiment.

4.3 Remarks of applying ICA to find the factors

From above, the expected return of each security, $E[r_i]$, is equal to the sum of factor means and zero factor. There is no information about zero factor given to the ICA algorithm during decomposition, because we cancelled the zero factor while subtracting the mean of each observation signal as in equation 4. As a result, we cannot separate the zero factor from the observations.[1] However we can retain the original pricing level of each security by adding its expect value $E[r_i]$ to the factor model.

5 Experiments and Results

In the experiment, we used 7 stocks, selected from the Hang Seng Index constitutes. Daily closing prices started form 2/1/1992 to 23/8/2000 were used(Figure 1).

In the experiment, we reconstruct the multifactor model of each stock using the procedures in section 4.2. Figure 2 shows the separated signals. Starting from top to bottom, the top most signals is the most important hidden factor, F_1', and so on, the last signal is named as F_7'.

We reconstruct the factor models with six hidden factors, $F_1', F_2', ..., F_6'$ where the least important factor F_7' is regarded as residual. The mixing matrix found is shown as below

$$
\begin{bmatrix}
0.0145 & -0.0119 & -0.0034 & 0.0055 & 0.0027 & 0.0138 & -0.0059 \\
0.0071 & -0.0169 & -0.0009 & 0.0067 & 0.0019 & -0.0016 & -0.0018 \\
0.0072 & -0.0137 & -0.0014 & 0.0001 & 0.0154 & 0.0031 & -0.0048 \\
0.0095 & -0.0137 & -0.0195 & 0.0016 & 0.0041 & 0.0053 & -0.0051 \\
0.0056 & -0.0180 & -0.0014 & -0.0022 & -0.0002 & 0.0122 & -0.0117 \\
0.0166 & -0.0105 & -0.0070 & 0.0035 & 0.0038 & 0.0020 & -0.0154 \\
0.0222 & -0.0158 & -0.0058 & -0.0085 & 0.0014 & 0.0037 & -0.0016
\end{bmatrix}
$$

The rows in the mixing matrix are the corresponding sensitivities to the hidden factors for the stock. To reconstruct the factor model, we take stock 1 as an example. Equations 6 and 7 show its return expressed as a 6-factor model and 3 factor model respectively.

$$R_1(t) = 0.0145 \times F_1'(t) - 0.0119 \times F_2'(t) - 0.0034 \times F_3'(t) + 0.0055 \times F_4'(t)$$

---

[1] It is also a common practice to assume the expected values of the factors are zero. In that case, the zero factor can be obtained.

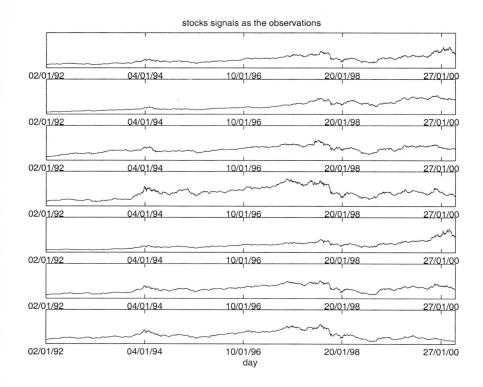

Fig. 1. Seven stocks' series in the experiment

$$+0.0027 \times F_5'(t) + 0.0138 \times F_6'(t) + u_1 \qquad (6)$$

$$where \quad u_1 = -0.0059 \times F_7'(t)$$

$$R_1(t) = 0.0145 \times F_1'(t) - 0.0119 \times F_2'(t) - 0.0034 \times F_3'(t) + v_1 \qquad (7)$$

$$where \quad v_1 = 0.0055 \times F_4'(t) + 0.0027 \times F_5'(t) + 0.0138 \times F_6'(t) - 0.0059 \times F_7'(t)$$

To express the return as in the factor model, we simply add the expected returns to R_i as $r_i = R_i + E[r_i]$.

6 Discussions and Conclusion

In this paper, we propose to apply independent component analysis (ICA) to extract the factors and the sensitivities of securities in the factor model. In some traditional applications of factor models, the returns are related to some systematic factors or macro-economic variables; for examples, unexpected changes in the rate of inflation and the rate of return on a treasury bill. On one hand, it is useful to know what the exact underlying factors are. On the other hand, the financial market nowaday is extremely complex and dynamic, especially due

factors signals separated by ICA

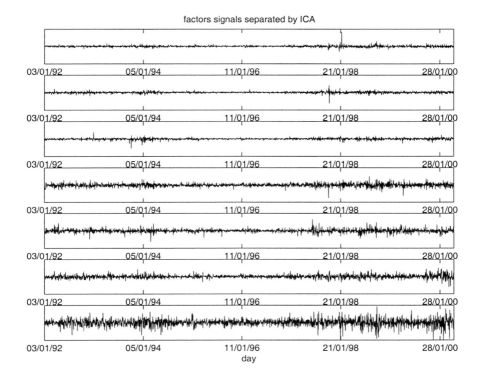

Fig. 2. The separated signals are sorted with their importance. (The y-axes of the sub-figures do not have equal scales.) The uppermost signal is regarded as the most important signal F_1' and so on.

to globalization and many newly introduced indices, such as IT index, it is not an easy task to decide which variables, among so many systematic factors and macro-economic variables, should be included in the model as factors. Our method serves as a data mining technique to automatically identify the hidden factors from historical data. Though attempts can be made to correlate the factors extracted to some known variables, it is still possible to apply these factor models in many aspects in finance. For example, we can perform risk analysis and construct portfolios which are less sensitive to the hidden factors.

Acknowledgement The authors would like to thank The Research Grants Council, HK for support.

References

1. A. Back and A. Weigend. A first application of independent component analysis to extracting structure from stock returns. *Journal of Neural Systems*, 8:473–484, 1997.

2. S. Brown. The number of factors in security returns. *The Journal of Finance*, 44(5):1247–1262, December 1989.
3. J.F. Cardoso. High-order contrasts for independent component analysis. *Neural Computation*, 11(1):157–192, 1999.
4. J.F. Cardoso and A. Souloumiac. Blind beamforming for non-gaussian signals. In *IEE Proc-F.140(6)*, pages 771–774, 1993.
5. G. Chamberlain and M. Rothschild. Arbitrage, factor structure, and mean variance analysis on large asset markets. *Econometrica*, 51(5):1281–1304, September 1983.
6. R. Chen, N.F. Roll and S. Ross. Economic forces and the stock market. *Journal of Business*, 59(3):383–403, July 1986.
7. P. Comon. Independent component analysis, a new concept ? *Signal Processing*, 36:287–314, April 1994.
8. G. Connor and R. Korajczyk. Performance measurement with the arbitrage pricing theory a new framework for analysis. *Journal of financial economics*, 15:373–394, 1986.
9. G. Connor and R. Korajczyk. A test for the number of factors in an approximate factor model. *The Journal of Finance*, 48(4):1263–1291, September 1993.
10. F. Fabozzi. *Investment Management*. Prentice Hall International, Inc, 1995.
11. G. Feeney and D. Hester. Stock market indices: A principal component analysis. *Cowles Foundation, Monograph 19*, volume 39:110–138, 1967.
12. A. Gordon, W. Sharp, and B. Jeffery. *Fundamentals of investments*. Englewood Cliffs, N.J. : Prentice Hall, second edition, 1993.
13. J. Heradult and C. Jutten. Space or time adaptive signal processing by neural network models. In *Neural Networks for Computing, Proceeding of AIP Conference*, pages 211–206, New York, 1986. American Institute of Physics.
14. A. Hyvärinen. Independent component analysis by minimization of mutual information. Technical report, Helsinki University of Technology, Laboratory of Computer and Information Science, August 1997.
15. A. Hyvärinen and E. Oja. Independent component analysis by general nonlinear hebbian-like learning rules. *Signal Processing*, 64(3):301–313, 1998.
16. A. Hyvärinen and E. Oja. Independent component analysis: algorithms and applications. *Neural Networks*, 13(4):411–430, 2000.
17. B. King. Market and industry factors in stock price behavior. *Journal of Business*, 39:139–190, 1966.
18. R. Lesch, Y. Caille, and D. Lowe. Component analysis in financial time series. In *Proceedings of the IEEE/IAFE 1999*, pages 183–190, 1999.
19. B. Manly. *Multivariate statistical methods: A primer*. Chapman and Hall, 1994.
20. H. Markowitz. Portfolio selection. *Journal of Finance*, 7(1):77–91, March 1952.
21. H. Markowitz. *Portfolio selection, efficient diversification of investment*. Blackwell Publishers Ltd, 108 Cowley Road Oxford OX4 1JF, UK, second edition, 1991.
22. S. Ross. A arbitrage theory of the capital asset pricing. *Journal of Economic Theory*, 3:343–362, 1976.
23. H. Schneeweiss and H. Mathes. Factor analysis and principal components. *Journal of multivariate analysis*, 55:105–124, 1995.
24. W. Sharp. A simplified model for portfolio selection. In *Management Science*, volume 9, pages 277–293, 1963.
25. J. Utans, W.T. Holt, and A.N. Refenes. Principal components analysis for modeling multi-currency portfolios. In *Proceedings of the Fourth International Conference on Neurals Networks in the Capital Markets, NNCM-96*, pages 359–368. World Scientific, 1997.

Web-Based Cluster Analysis System for China and Hong Kong's Stock Market

Chan Man-Chung, Li Yuen-Mei and Wong Chi-Cheong

Department of Computing
The Hong Kong Polytechnic University
Hung Hom, Kowloon, Hong Kong
csmcchan@comp.polyu.edu.hk
Tel: +852-27667280

Abstract. Data mining or knowledge discovery in database (KDD) is motivated by large amounts of computerized data and has been attracted a lot of interest in various areas. One area is to extract useful and predictive information from a huge financial data database so that investors can be more informed and makes more profitable investments. The efficiency of the information extraction has become the most concern problem when performing the extraction process. In this paper, we demonstrate how to apply conceptual clustering (hierarchical clustering algorithm), a data mining technique, on the Chinese and Hong Kong stock market's data. Conceptual hierarchical tree and cluster information table will be generated to give the concept to the clusters for further analysis in the subsequent mining process.

1 Introduction

Because of the explosive growth of many business databases, people are interested in extracting useful and predictive information from massive databases, especially from stock market database. The need for a new generation of automated and intelligent database analysis tools and techniques for Knowledge Discovery in Database has been created.

Knowledge Discovery in Database (KDD) is the overall process of discovering useful knowledge from databases including data preparation, data selection, preprocessing, transformation, mining process and evaluation of the mining results. Data Mining, which is also referred to as knowledge discovery in databases, is the process of extracting previously unknown, valid and actionable information from large databases and then using the information to make crucial business decisions.

Clustering is one of the types of data mining techniques. We examine cluster analysis on extraction of information from the financial raw data. We adopt hierarchical/Conceptual clustering technique proposed by Hu [1] to perform the clustering analysis algorithm on the Chinese and Hong Kong stock market's data to construct a hierarchical structure of the data and infer useful knowledge rules based simply on the containment relationship between different clusters.

2 Cluster Analysis

Clustering analysis is the process of grouping physical or abstract objects into classes of similar objects. It helps to construct meaningful partitioning of a large set of objects based on a 'divide and conquer' methodology, which decompose a large-scale system into smaller components to simplify design and implementation [2].

Clustering analysis is always the first step for analyzing data in KDD process. It is done to discover subsets of related objects, and to find descriptions such as D1, D2, D3, etc. that describe each of the these subsets depicted in figure 1.

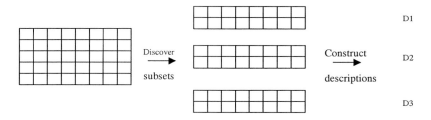

Fig. 1. Discovering clusters and descriptions in a database

During cluster analysis process, objects are grouped on the basis of similarities (associations) and distance (dissimilarities) to form the clusters. Therefore, people do not need to pre-define the number of groups to be clustered.

In this paper, conceptual clustering method proposed in [1] is adopted to develop the analysis application for financial statement data. This method is very suitable for clustering the object classes in a very large database efficiently based on similarity measure that maximizes the cohesiveness (a reciprocal of the conceptual distance) of the clusters.

In the first place, we cluster data using numerical taxonomy, then extract a characteristic feature for the cluster and finally treat each cluster as a positive sample to derive knowledge rules. The algorithm aggregates objects into different clusters first and then assigns conceptual description to object classes. Data has been pre-processed before clustering. Then the following clustering procedures undergo:

1. Calculate the common attribute values between each pair of data in database
2. Delete the cluster with common attribute values less than the pre-defined threshold value.
3. Using single-linkage method, aggregate data to form a cluster
4. If new cluster is produced, continue the process; otherwise, terminate the process
5. Form the hierarchy based on the newly formed or untouched clusters and use these clusters for the next iteration.

The following describes the steps of the single linkage nearest neighbor method:

1. If the common attribute table has more than one row, go to Step 2, otherwise terminate the process.
2. First locate the maximum common attribute value (the most nearest distance) among in the common attribute table
3. Locate two elements that has this maximum value as Ei and Ej and combine these two elements as Eij and form the new common attribute table. (i.e. Distance between the new cluster and one element Ck are computed as min[Dik, Djk].)
4. Calculate the common attribute of the new cluster
5. After forming the new attribute table, go back to step 1.

The output will be a cluster hierarchy of the data set represented in the form of Concept Hierarchical Tree [3] and cluster information table.

3   System Overview and Design

The clustering analysis system for the Chinese and Hong Kong stock Market's data is a web-based and object oriented application over the Internet. One web server and database server is able to serve multiple users simultaneously. Thus, a three-tier design is depicted:

1. User selects the appropriate criteria for cluster analysis application on client.
2. The client (web browser) sends a request with the criteria object to the server via HTTP.
3. The web server receives the HTTP request and forwards it to backend Java Servlet Program.
4. The Java Servlet program will connect to the financial statement database and perform clustering to extract useful information from the database.
5. After the clustering process, the servlet program will sent back the result object to the web server and then forward it to the client.

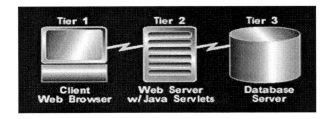

Fig. 2. Three-tier-design of the system

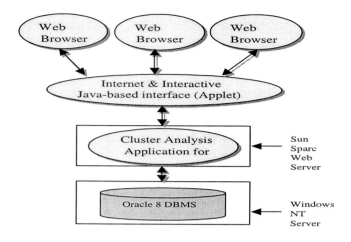

Fig. 3. Architecture of the system

4 Implementation

In the cluster analysis system, the system is implemented by three steps:

1. Select financial data (e.g. financial period, industry field, and financial Ratio fields) for clustering from the main screen of the system (see figure 4)
2. Start the clustering process.
3. View the clustering results. Two perspective results of hierarchical tree view (figure 5) and the cluster group information table (figure 6) are provided

5 Experimental Results

The following table shows the system performance according to different records sizes based on eight attributes:

Attribute no	Record Sets no	Time (sec)	Time (mins)
8	50	900	15
8	100	1800	30
8	200	2400	60
8	500	9000	150

6 Conclusion

In this paper, we adopt conceptual clustering methods, a data mining technique, to analyze the consolidated Chinese and Hong Kong Stock Market's data. We adopt the attribute-oriented concept tree ascending technique and integrate

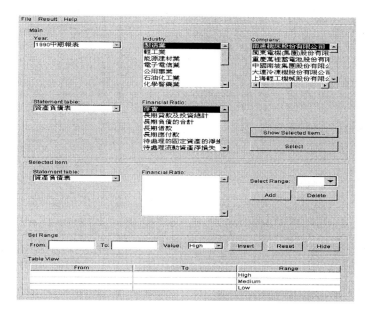

Fig. 4. Main Screen

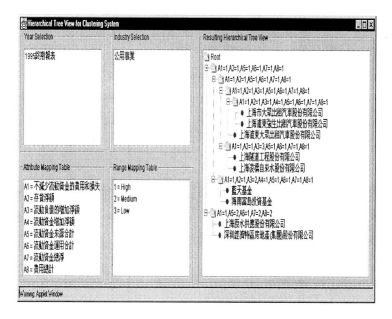

Fig. 5. Hierarchical Tree View

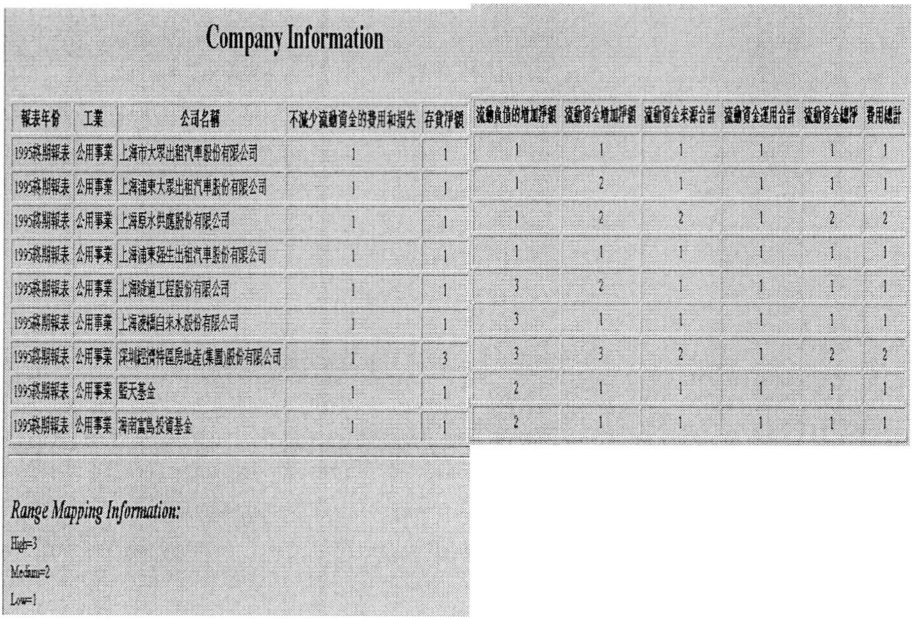

Company Information

報表年份	工業	公司名稱	不減少流動資金的費用和損失	存貨淨額	流動負債的增加淨額	流動資金增加淨額	流動資金來源合計	流動資金運用合計	流動資金總淨	費用總計
1995終期報表	公用事業	上海市大眾出租汽車股份有限公司	1	1	1	1	1	1	1	1
1995終期報表	公用事業	上海浦東大眾出租汽車股份有限公司	1	1	1	2	1	1	1	1
1995終期報表	公用事業	上海原水供應股份有限公司	1	1	1	2	2	1	2	2
1995終期報表	公用事業	上海浦東強生出租汽車股份有限公司	1	1	1	1	1	1	1	1
1995終期報表	公用事業	上海隧道工程股份有限公司	1	1	3	2	1	1	1	1
1995終期報表	公用事業	上海凌橋自來水股份有限公司	1	1	3	1	1	1	1	1
1995終期報表	公用事業	深圳經濟特區房地產(集團)股份有限公司	1	3	3	3	2	1	2	2
1995終期報表	公用事業	藍天基金	1	1	2	1	1	1	1	1
1995終期報表	公用事業	海南富島投資基金	1	1	2	1	1	1	1	1

Range Mapping Information:

High=3

Medium=2

Low=1

Fig. 6. Cluster group information

database operations with the learning process to form the concept hierarchical tree and its corresponding cluster information. The clustering result is the form of the conceptual hierarchical tree and cluster information table for investor to perform further analysis. The web-based, object-oriented and database approach's design for the financial application break through the traditional demographics problem handled by clustering methods and make the clustering process fully accessible by users through the Internet.

References

1. Hu, X.H.: Conceptual Clustering and Concept Hierarchies in Knowledge Discovery, 1993.
2. Chen, M.S.: Data Mining: An Overview from a Database Perspective, 1996.
3. Everitt B.: Cluster Analysis, Second Edition.
4. Law, Albert Y., Chan, K.H.: Financial Statement Analysis.
5. Piatesky-Shapiro, G., Frawley, W.J.: Knowledge Discovery in Databases. AAAI/MIT Press, 1991.
6. Cheng, Y., Fu, K.S.: Conceptual Clustering in Knowledge Organization, IEEE Transaction on Pattern Analysis and Machine Intelligence, Vol. 5, No. 9, pp. 592–598, 1985.
7. Holsheimer, M., Kersten, M.: A Perspective on Databases and Data Mining.

Arbitrage-Free Asset Pricing in General State Space [*]

Xiaotie Deng[1] and Shunming Zhang[23]

[1] Department of Computer Science, City University of Hong Kong, Hong Kong
[2] Department of Economics, The University of Western Ontario, London, Ontario,
Canada
[3] School of Economics and Management, Tsinghua University, Beijing 100084, China

Abstract. This paper studies asset pricing in abitrage-free financial
markets in general state space. The mathematical formulation is based
on a locally convex topological space for weakly arbitrage-free securities'
structure and a separable Banach space for strictly arbitrage-free securities' structure. We establish, for these two types of spaces, the weakly
arbitrage-free pricing theorem and the strictly arbitrage-free pricing theorem, respectively.

1 Introduction

We consider arbitrage-free asset pricing in a setting of general state spaces,
in particular, locally convex topological space for weakly arbitrage-free security
markets, and separable Banach space for strictly arbitrage-free security markets.

Arbitrage-free conditions have been an important first step in the study of
general equilibrium theorems with incomplete asset markets (Duffie & Shafer
1985; Geanakoplos 1990; Geanakoplos & Shafer 1990; Hirsch, Magill & Mas-
Colell 1990; Husseini, Lasry & Magill 1990; and Magill & Shafer, 1991). Since
the 1980s, for finite period economies, arbitrage-free pricing theory has been
applied by various authors to prove the existence of general equilibrium for
stochastic economies with incomplete financial markets (Duffie 1987, 1988, 1996;
Florenzano & Gourdel 1994; Magill & Shafer 1991; Werner 1985, 1990; and Zhang
1998). In those works, the finite number of possible states of nature and the finite-
dimensional commodity space are usually assumed in order for the proofs to be
carried out for the general equilibrium model with incomplete financial markets.

Usually Stiemke's Lemma, a strict version of Farkas-Minkowski's Lemma, is
applied to study the asset pricing theory with arbitrage-free conditions. As examples, this approach is taken in discrete-time models of dynamic asset pricing theory (Duffie 1988, 1996) and the theory of economic equilibrium with incomplete
asset markets (Geanakoplos 1990; Geanakoplos & Shafer 1990; Hirsch, Magill

---

[*] This research is supported by a CERG grant of Hong Kong RGC (CityU 1116/99E),
a SRG grant of City University of Hong Kong (7001040), and a project of Financial
Mathematics, Financial Engineering and Financial Management, which is one of
"Ninth Five-Year Plan" Major Projects of National Natural Science Foundation of
China (Grant 79790130).

& Mas-Colell 1990; Husseini, Lasry & Magill 1990; and Magill & Shafer 1991) where the commodity space is of finite dimension. Farkas-Minkowski's Lemma and Stiemke's Lemma are in essence the mathematical counter part of the asset pricing theory with arbitrage-free conditions. For the general state space model in our discussion, we obtain extensions of Farkas-Minkowski's Lemma and Stiemke's Lemma by applying Clark's separating hyperplane theorems (Clark 1993, 1994), and thus establish our main results.

Harrison & Kreps (1979) initiated the study of martingales and arbitrage in multiperiod security markets. They first introduced general theory of arbitrage in a two-period economy with uncertainty, then extended it to the models of multiperiod security markets and the models of continuous-time securities markets. Kreps (1981) studied arbitrage and equilibrium in economies with infinitely many commodities and presented an abstract analysis of "arbitrage" in economies that have infinite dimensional commodity space. Harrison & Pliska (1981) studied martingales and stochastic integrals in the theory of continuous trading. Dalang, Morton & Willinger (1990) studied equivalent martingale measures and no-arbitrage in stochastic securities market models. Back & Pliska (1991) studied the fundamental theorem of asset pricing with an infinite state space and showed some equivalent relations on arbitrage. Jacod & Sgiryaev (1998) studied local martingales and the fundamental asset pricing theorems in the discrete-time case. These papers studied fundamental theorems of asset pricing in multiperiod financial models with the help of techniques from stochastic analysis. Our work is based on separating hyperplane theorems and does not rely on assumptions made for stochastic analysis to be able to carry out in the above models.

Friction in markets has attracted attention of several works in this field recently. Chen (1995) examined the incentives and economic roles of financial innovation and at the same time studied the effectiveness of the replication-based arbitrage valuation approach in frictional economies (the friction means holding constraints). Jouini & Kallal (1995a) derived the implications of the absence of arbitrage in securities markets models where traded securities are subject to short-sales constraints and where the borrowing and lending rates differ, and showed that a securities price system is arbitrage free if and only if there exists a numeraire and an equivalent probability measure for which the normalized (by the numeraire) price processes of traded securities are supermartingales. Jouini & Kallal (1995b) derived the implications from the absence of arbitrage in dynamic securities markets with bid-ask spreads. The absence of arbitrage is equivalent to the existence of at least an equivalent probability measure that transforms some process between the bid and the ask price processes of traded securities into a martingale. Pham & Touzi (1999) addressed the problem of characterization of no arbitrage (strictly arbitrage-free) in the presence of friction in a discrete-time financial model, and extended the fundamental theorem of asset pricing under a non-degeneracy assumption. The friction is described by the transaction cost rates for purchasing and selling the securities. Deng, Li & Wang (2000) studied the computational aspect of arbitrage in frictional markets including integrality constraints. We follow the model for transaction costs from Pham & Touzi (1999), and then extend the first fundamental valuation theorems of asset pricing from frictionless security markets to frictional security markets, for general state space. Again, their stochastic analysis method requires stronger assumptions than ours. In addition, their arbitrage-free conditions are slightly different from ours based on that of Duffie (1988).

In Section 2, we first present our model in frictionless markets. Following Duffie (1988), we define the concepts of weakly arbitrage-free and strictly arbitrage-free for our model. Then, we establish the first fundamental valuation theorem of asset pricing (a necessary and sufficient condition for arbitrage-freeness) with weakly arbitrage-free security markets and strictly arbitrage-free security markets. In Section 3, we extend our work to markets with transaction costs, following the model of Pham & Touzi (1999).

2　Frictionless Security Markets

We consider a two-period model (dates 0 and 1) with uncertainty over the states of nature in the date 1. The unknown nature of the future is represented by a general set Ω of possible states of nature, one of which will be revealed as true. Here we make no assumption about the probability of these states. The J securities are given by a return "matrix" $V = (V^1, \cdots, V^J)$, where V^j denotes the number of units of account paid by security $j = 1, \cdots, J$. Let $q \in \mathcal{R}^J$ denote the vector of prices of J securities. A portfolio $\theta \in \mathcal{R}^J$ has market value $q^\top \theta$ and payoff $V\theta$.

Let T be a topological space consisting of processes in $\mathcal{R}^\Omega$, T_+ is the positive cone of T. Let T^* be the dual space composed of the continuous linear functionals on T, T_+^* the positive cone of the space T^* (the space of all positive continuous linear functionals on T) and T_{++}^* the interior of the cone T_+^* (the space of all strictly positive continuous linear functionals on T): $T_{++}^* \subseteq T_+^*$.

In this paper, we assume $V^j \in T$ for $j = 1, \cdots, J$. Then $V\theta = \sum_{j=1}^J V^j \theta^j \in T$. Our proof must adopt the following notation

$$\langle V \rangle = \{V\theta \in T \mid \theta \in \mathcal{R}^J\}$$

and $\langle V \rangle_+ = \langle V \rangle \cap T_+$.

Definition 1 *The frictionless market (q, V) is* **weakly arbitrage-free** *if any portfolio $\theta \in \mathcal{R}^J$ of securities has a positive market value $q^\top \theta \geq 0$ whenever it has a positive payoff $V\theta \in T_+$.*

Definition 2 *The frictionless market (q, V) is* **strictly arbitrage-free** *if (1) any portfolio $\theta \in \mathcal{R}^J$ of securities has a strictly positive market value $q^\top \theta > 0$ whenever it has a positive non-zero payoff $V\theta \in T_+ \setminus \{0\}$; and (2) any portfolio $\theta \in \mathcal{R}^J$ of securities has a zero market value $q^\top \theta = 0$ whenever it has a zero payoff $V\theta = 0$.*

Definition 2 implies Definition 1 obviously. We follow the definition for arbitrage opportunity as provided by Duffie (1988, 1996). An arbitrage is a portfolio $\theta \in \mathcal{R}^{\mathcal{J}}$ with either (1) $q^\top \theta \leq 0$ and $V\theta \in T_+ \setminus \{0\}$, or (2) $q^\top \theta < 0$ and $V\theta \in T_+$. That is to say, the frictionless market (q, V) admits an arbitrage opportunity if there exists an portfolio $\theta \in \mathcal{R}^{\mathcal{J}}$ of securities such that either (1) $q^\top \theta \leq 0$ and $V\theta \in T_+ \setminus \{0\}$, or (2) $q^\top \theta < 0$ and $V\theta \in T_+$. Consequently, we can define the strictly arbitrage-free (no arbitrage) frictionless market (q, V) as follows.

Definition 2′ The frictionless market (q, V) is **strictly arbitrage-free** if (1) any portfolio $\theta \in \mathcal{R}^{\mathcal{J}}$ of securities has a strictly positive market value $q^\top \theta > 0$ whenever it has a positive non-zero payoff $V\theta \in T_+ \setminus \{0\}$; and (2) any portfolio $\theta \in \mathcal{R}^{\mathcal{J}}$ of securities has a positive market value $q^\top \theta \geq 0$ whenever it has a positive payoff $V\theta \in T_+$.

Lemma 1 *Definitions 2 and 2′ are equivalent.*

An arbitrage is therefore, in effect, a portfolio offering "something for nothing". Not surprisingly, an arbitrage is naturally ruled out in reality. And this fact gives a characterization of security prices as follows: A valuation functional is a functional $v \in T_+^*$ for the weakly arbitrage-free frictionless market (q, V) with consistency $q^\top = vV$; and a functional $v \in T_{++}^*$ for the strictly arbitrage-free frictionless market (q, V) with consistency $q^\top = vV$, where $vV = (vV^1, \cdots, vV^J)$. The valuation functional is called to be a positive linear consistent valuation operator for the weakly arbitrage-free frictionless market, a strictly positive linear consistent valuation operator for the strictly arbitrage-free frictionless market, respectively.

The idea of arbitrage and the absence of arbitrage opportunities is fundamental in finance. The strict arbitrage-freeness is important in the study of general equilibrium theory with incomplete asset markets (Husseini, Lasry & Magill 1990; Werner 1990; and Magill & Shafer 1991). Theorem 2 to be presented in the following is an important step in the study of equilibrium for economies with general state spaces considered in our work. The principal mathematical tool applied here is the Separating Hyperplane Theorems of Clark (1993, 1994).

Fact 1 *(Clark 1994) Suppose M and N are non-empty disjoint convex cones in a locally convex topological vector space E. Then there exists a non-zero continuous linear functional $f : E \to \mathcal{R}$ separating N from M: $f(n) \geq 0$ for all $n \in N$ and $f(m) \leq 0$ for all $m \in M$ if and only if $\overline{M - N} \neq E$. Moreover, if $\overline{M - N} \neq E$, then for any $e \notin \overline{M - N}$ we may select f so that $f(e) > 0$.*

Fact 2 *(Clark 1993) Suppose M and N are non-empty convex cones (with vertices at the origin) in a separating Banach space E. Then there exists a non-zero continuous linear functional $f : E \to \mathcal{R}$ strictly separating N from M: $f(n) > 0$ for all $n \in N$ and $f(m) \leq 0$ for all $m \in M$ if and only if $N \cap \overline{M - N} = \emptyset$.*

Fact 1 and 2 will be used to prove Theorems 1 and 2 in Sections 3 and 4, Theorems 3 and 4 in Sections 6 and 7, respectively. We assume $E = \mathcal{R} \times \mathcal{T}$, which is a topological space, then $E_+ = \mathcal{R}_+ \times \mathcal{T}_+$ is the positive cone of E, which is a positive closed convex cone of E with its vertex at the origin. The marketed subspace

$$M = \{(-q^\top \theta, V\theta) \in E \mid \theta \in \mathcal{R}^{\mathcal{J}}\}$$

is a linear subspace of the space E.

2.1 Weakly Arbitrage-free Security Valuation Theorem

In this section, we assume that T is a locally convex topological space.

Proposition 1 *The frictionless market (q, V) is weakly arbitrage-free if and only if $M \cap E_+ = \{0\} \times \langle V \rangle_+$.*

Theorem 1 *The frictionless market (q, V) is weakly arbitrage-free if and only if there exists a positive functional $v \in T_+^*$ satisfying $q^\top = vV$.*

2.2 Strictly Arbitrage-free Security Valuation Theorem

We assume that T is a separable Banach space. We prove Proposition 2 and Theorem 2 by using Definition 2 of the strictly arbitrage-free frictionless market (q, V).

Proposition 2 *The frictionless market (q, V) is strictly arbitrage-free if and only if M and E_+ intersect precisely at $(0, 0)$, that is, $M \cap E_+ = \{(0, 0)\}$.*

Theorem 2 *The frictionless market (q, V) is strictly arbitrage-free if and only if there exists a strictly positive functional $v \in T_{++}^*$ satisfying $q^\top = vV$.*

3 Frictional Security Markets

Suppose that there are transaction costs in the trading, the coefficients $b^j \in [0, \infty)$ and $s^j \in [0, 1)$ are respectively the transaction cost rates for purchasing and selling the security j. Then the algebraic cost induced by (buying) a position $\theta^j \geq 0$ units of security j is $q^j(1+b^j)\theta^j$ and the algebraic gain induced by (selling) a position $\theta^j \leq 0$ units of security j is $q^j(1 - s^j)\theta^j$. We introduce the functions $\Phi^j : \mathcal{R} \to \mathcal{R}$ defined by

$$\Phi^j(z) = \begin{cases} q^j(1 + b^j)z, \ z \geq 0 \\ q^j(1 - s^j)z, \ z \leq 0 \end{cases}$$

and the functions $\phi^j : \mathcal{R} \to \mathcal{R}$ defined by

$$\phi^j(z) = \begin{cases} (1 + b^j)z, \ z \geq 0 \\ (1 - s^j)z, \ z \leq 0. \end{cases}$$

Then $\Phi^j(z) = q^j\phi^j(z)$.

For any integer $N = 1, 2, \cdots$, a function $\psi : \mathcal{R}^\mathcal{N} \to \mathcal{R}$ is subliner if, for any $x^1 \in \mathcal{R}^\mathcal{N}$, $x^2 \in \mathcal{R}^\mathcal{N}$, $x \in \mathcal{R}^\mathcal{N}$ and $\lambda \in \mathcal{R}_+$,

$$\psi(x^1 + x^2) \le \psi(x^1) + \psi(x^2) \qquad and \qquad \psi(\lambda x) = \lambda\psi(x).$$

The function ϕ^j is sublinear, and hence convex. Therefore the function Φ^j is also sublinear, and hence convex.

The total cost or gain induced by (trading) a portfolio $\theta \in \mathcal{R}^\mathcal{J}$ is $\sum_{j=1}^{J} \Phi^j(\theta^j) = \sum_{j=1}^{J} q^j\phi^j(\theta^j)$. We define the function $\tau : \mathcal{R}^\mathcal{J} \to \mathcal{R}$ by

$$\tau(x) = \sum_{j=1}^{J} \Phi^j(x^j) = \sum_{j=1}^{J} q^j\phi^j(x^j).$$

Then the total cost or gain induced by (trading) a portfolio $\theta \in \mathcal{R}^\mathcal{J}$ is $\tau(\theta)$. As we know, the function τ is sublinear, and hence convex.

Definition 3 *The frictional market* (q, V, b, s) *is* **weakly arbitrage-free** *if any portfolio* $\theta \in \mathcal{R}^\mathcal{J}$ *of securities has a positive total cost or gain* $\tau(\theta) \ge 0$ *whenever it has a positive payoff* $V\theta \in T_+$.

We note that Definitions 2 and 2′ are equivalent. However, in the presence of transaction costs, the correpsonding Definitions 4 and 4′ (as follows) are not. We establish Theorem 4 for Definition 4′ of the strictly arbitrage-free frictional market (q, V, b, s).

Definition 4 *The frictional market* (q, V, b, s) *is* **strictly arbitrage-free** *if (1) any portfolio* $\theta \in \mathcal{R}^\mathcal{J}$ *of securities has a strictly positive total cost or gain* $\tau(\theta) > 0$ *whenever it has a positive non-zero payoff* $V\theta \in T_+ \setminus \{0\}$; *and (2) any portfolio* $\theta \in \mathcal{R}^\mathcal{J}$ *of securities has a zero total cost or gain* $\tau(\theta) = 0$ *whenever it has a zero payoff* $V\theta = 0$.

Definition 4′ The frictional market (q, V, b, s) is **strictly arbitrage-free** if (1) any portfolio $\theta \in \mathcal{R}^\mathcal{J}$ of securities has a strictly positive total cost or gain $\tau(\theta) > 0$ whenever it has a positive non-zero payoff $V\theta \in T_+ \setminus \{0\}$; and (2) any portfolio $\theta \in \mathcal{R}^\mathcal{J}$ of securities has a positive total cost or gain $\tau(\theta) \ge 0$ whenever it has a positive payof $V\theta \in T_+$.

Definition 4 obviously implies Definition 4′. Definition 4′ does not imply Definition 4 because of the presence of friction. In the frictionless model, we define the marketed subspace

$$M = \{(-q^\top\theta, V\theta) \in E \mid \theta \in \mathcal{R}^\mathcal{J}\}$$

of the space E to prove the first fundamental theorems of asset pricing. In the frictional model, we can't consider the corresponding marketed "subspace" $\{(-\tau(\theta), V\theta) \in E \mid \theta \in \mathcal{R}^\mathcal{J}\}$. In fact, this marketed "subspace" isn't a subspace of the space E. Instead, we define the subset M' in the space E as follows

$$M' = \{(r, t) \in E \mid r \le -\tau(\theta) \text{ and } t = V\theta \text{ for } \theta \in \mathcal{R}^\mathcal{J}\}$$

Lemma 2 M' *is a closed and convex cone in the space* E.

For simplicity, we use the following notations in the subsequent sections.

$$\mathbb{1} = \begin{pmatrix} 1 \\ \vdots \\ 1 \end{pmatrix}_J \quad b = \begin{pmatrix} b^1 \\ \vdots \\ b^J \end{pmatrix} \quad and \quad s = \begin{pmatrix} s^1 \\ \vdots \\ s^J \end{pmatrix}.$$

We define the box product of two vectors $y_1 \in \mathcal{R}^N$ and $y_2 \in \mathcal{R}^N$ by

$$y_1 \,\square\, y_2 = \begin{pmatrix} y_1^1 y_2^1 \\ \vdots \\ y_1^N y_2^N \end{pmatrix}$$

3.1 Weakly Arbitrage-free Security Valuation Theorem

We assume that T is a locally convex topological space.

Proposition 3 *The frictional market* (q, V, b, s) *is weakly arbitrage-free if and only if* $M' \cap E_+ = \{0\} \times \langle V \rangle_+$.

Theorem 3 *The frictional market* (q, V, b, s) *is weakly arbitrage-free if and only if there exists a positive functional* $v \in T_+^*$ *satisfying*

$$q \,\square\, (\mathbb{1} - s) \leq vV \leq q \,\square\, (\mathbb{1} + b)$$

3.2 Strictly Arbitrage-free Security Valuation Theorem

In this section, we assume that T is a separable Banach space. We prove the following Proposition 4 and Theorem 4 for Definition 4′ of the strictly arbitrage-free frictional market (q, V, b, s).

Proposition 4 *The frictional market* (q, V, b, s) *is strictly arbitrage-free if and only if* M' *and* E_+ *intersect precisely at* $(0, 0)$, *that is,* $M' \cap E_+ = \{(0, 0)\}$.

Theorem 4 *The The frictional market* (q, V, b, s) *is strictly arbitrage-free if and only if there exists a strictly positive functional* $v \in T_{++}^*$ *satisfying*

$$q \,\square\, (\mathbb{1} - s) \leq vV \leq q \,\square\, (\mathbb{1} + b)$$

References

1. K.Back & S.R.Pliska (1991) *On the Fundamental Theorem of Asset Pricing with An Infinite State Space*. Journal of Mathematical Economics 20, 1-18
2. Z.Chen (1995) *Financial Innovation and Arbitrage Pricing in Frictional Economics*. Journal of Economic Theory 65, 117-135

3. S.A.Clark (1993) *The Valuation Problem in Arbitrage Pricing Theory.* Journal of Mathematical Economics 22, 463-478

4. S.A.Clark (1994) *Vector Space Methods in Additive Theory.* Journal of Mathematical Economics, conditionally accepted

5. R.C.Dalang, Andrew Morton & W.Willinger (1990) *Equivalent Martingale Measures and No-arbitrage in Stochastic Securities Market Models.* Stochastics and Stochastic Reports 29, 185-201

6. X.T. Deng, Z.F.Li, & S.Y.Wang (2000), *On Computation of Arbitrage for Markets with Friction.* Lecture Notes in Computer Science 1858, pp.310-319.

7. D.Duffie (1987) *Stochastic Equilibria with Incomplete Financial Markets.* Journal of Economic Theory 41, 405-416

8. D.Duffie (1988) **Security Markets: Stochastic Models**. Stanford University, California, Academic Press.

9. D.Duffie (1996) **Dynamic Asset Pricing Theory**. Princeton University, California, Academic Press.

10. D.Duffie & W.Shafer (1985) *Equilibrium in Incomplete Markets I: A Basic Model of Generic Existence.* Journal of Mathematical Economics 14, 285-300

11. M.Florenzano & P.Gourdel (1994) *T-period Economies with Incomplete Markets.* Economics Letter 44, 91-97

12. J.Geanakoplos (1990) *An Introduction to General Equilibrium with Incomplete Asset Markets.* Journal of Mathematical Economics 19, 1-38

13. J.Geanakoplos & W.Shafer (1990) *Solving Systems of Simultaneous Equations in Economics.* Journal of Mathematical Economics 19, 69-93

14. J.M.Harrison & D.M.Kreps (1979) *Martingales and Arbitrage in Multiperiod Securities Markets.* Journal of Economic Theory 20, 381-408

15. J.M.Harrison & S.R.Pliska (1981) *Martingales and Stochastic integrals in the theory of continuous trading.* Stochastic Processes and Their Applications 11, 215-260

16. M.D.Hirsch, M.J.P.Magill & A.Mas-Colell (1990) *A Geometric Approach to a Class of Equilibrium Existence Theorems.* Journal of Mathematical Economics 19, 95-106

17. S.Y.Husseini, J-M Lasry & M.J.P.Magill (1990) *Existence of Equilibrium with Incomplete Asset Markets.* Journal of Mathematical Economics 19, 39-67

18. J.Jacod & A.N.Sgiryaev (1998) *Local Martingales and the Fundamental Asset Pricing Theorems in the Discrete-time Case.* Finance and Stochastics 2, 259-273

19. E.Jouini & H.Kallal (1995) *Arbitrage in Securities Markets with Short-Sales Constraints.* Mathematical Finance 5, 197-232

20. E.Jouini & H.Kallal (1995) *Martingales and Arbitrage in Securities Markets with Transaction Costs.* Journal of Economic Theory 66, 178-197

21. D.M.Kreps (1981) *Arbitrage and Equilibrium in Economies with Infinitely Many Commodities.* Journal of Mathematical Economics 8, 15-35

22. M.Magill & W.Shafer (1991) *Incomplete Markets.* in **Handbook of Mathematical Economics** Volumn 4 Edited by W.Hildenbrand & H.Sonnenschein.

23. H.Pham & N.Touzi (1999) *The Fundamental Theorem of Asset Pricing with Cone Constraints.* Journal of Mathematical Economics 31, 265-279

24. J.Werner (1985) *Equilibrium of Economies with Incompleete Financial Markets.* Journal of Economic Theory 36, 110-119

25. J.Werner (1990) *Structrue of Financial Markets and Real Indeterminacy of Equilibrium.* Journal of Mathematical Economics 19, 217-232

26. S.M.Zhang (1998) *Existence of Stochastic Equilibrium with Incomplete Financial Markets.* Applied Mathematics – Journal of Chinese Universities 13, 77-84

A Tabu Search Based Algorithm for Clustering Categorical Data Sets

Joyce C. Wong and Michael K. Ng

Department of Mathematics, The University of Hong Kong.
E-mail: mng@maths.hku.hk

Abstract. Clustering methods partition a set of objects into clusters such that objects in the same cluster are more similar to each other than objects in different clusters according to some defined criteria. In this paper, we present an algorithm, called tabu search fuzzy k-modes, to extend the fuzzy k-means paradigm to categorical domains. Using the tabu search based technique, our algorithm can explore the solution space beyond local optimality in order to aim at finding a global optimal solution of the fuzzy clustering problem. It is found that our algorithm performs better, in terms of accuracy, than the fuzzy k-modes algorithm.

1 Introduction

Partitioning a large set of objects into homogeneous clusters is a fundamental operation in data science. A set of objects described by a number of attributes is to be classified into several clusters such that each object is allowed to belong to more than one cluster with different degrees of association. This fuzzy clustering problem can be represented as a mathematical optimization problem:

$$\min_{W, Z} F(W, Z) = \sum_{l=1}^{k} \sum_{i=1}^{n} w_{li}^{\alpha} d(\mathbf{z}_l, \mathbf{x}_i) \tag{1}$$

subject to

$$0 \le w_{li} \le 1, \quad \sum_{l=1}^{k} w_{li} = 1, \quad 0 < \sum_{i=1}^{n} w_{li} < n, \quad 1 \le l \le k, \ 1 \le i \le n, \tag{2}$$

where n is the number of objects, m is the number of attributes of each object, $k(\le n)$ is a known number of clusters, $\mathcal{X} = \{\mathbf{x}_1, \mathbf{x}_2, \cdots, \mathbf{x}_n\}$ is a set of n objects with m attributes, $Z = [\mathbf{z}_1, \mathbf{z}_2, ..., \mathbf{z}_k]$ is an m-by-k matrix containing k cluster centers, $W = [w_{li}]$ is an k-by-m matrix and $d(\mathbf{z}_l, \mathbf{x}_i)(\ge 0)$ is some dissimilarity measure between the cluster center $\mathbf{z}_l$ and the object $\mathbf{x}_i$.

The above optimization problem was first formulated by Dunn[2]. A widely known approach to this problem is the fuzzy k-means algorithm which was proposed by Ruspini [3] and Bezdek[4]. The fuzzy k-means algorithm is efficient in clustering large data sets. The fuzzy k-means algorithm is initiated by selecting a value for W, then the algorithm iterates between computing cluster centers,

Z, given W and computing W, given Z. The algorithm terminates when two successive values of W or Z are equal. It has been shown that the fuzzy k-means algorithm converges [4, 5, 10, 11]. However, the algorithm may stop at a local minimum of the optimalization problem. This is because the function $F(Z, W)$ is non-convex in general.

To obtain the global optimal solution of combinatorial optimization problems, tabu search based techniques which were introduced by Glover [6] is applied. Tabu search based techniques are concerned with imposing restrictions to guide a search process to negotiate otherwise difficult regions. The search procedures do not immediately terminate for a local optimal solution, but instead the procedures attempt to search beyond the local optimality in order to get the global optimal solution. Al-Sultan and Fedjki [1] have proposed a tabu search based algorithm for the the fuzzy clustering problem. Their proposed tabu search based algorithm has been found to outperform the fuzzy k-means algorithm considerably in their tests.

However, the fuzzy k-means algorithm only works on numeric data which limits the use in clustering where large categorical data sets are frequently encountered. To deal with categorical data sets, Huang [8], and Huang and Ng [9] suggested the fuzzy k-modes algorithm. This algorithm extends the k-means algorithm by applying a simple matching dissimilarity measure for categorical objects and using modes instead of means for clusters. The main aim of this paper is to develop tabu search based fuzzy k-modes algorithm to obtain a global solution of the fuzzy categorical data clustering problem.

The outline of the paper is as follows. In Section 2, the fuzzy k-modes algorithm is briefly reviewed. In Section 3, tabu search based techniques are introduced and the new clustering algorithm is proposed. In Section 4, the numerical results are presented to illustrate the effectiveness of our new approach.

2 Fuzzy k-Modes Algorithm

The fuzzy k-modes algorithm is modified from the k-means algorithm by using a simple matching dissimilarity measure for categorical data, and replacing the means of clusters with the modes. These modifications removes the numeric-only limitation of the k-means algorithm while maintains its efficiency in clustering categorical data sets. The simple matching dissimilarity measure between $\mathbf{z}_l$ and $\mathbf{x}_i$, for $l = 1, 2, ..., k$ and $i = 1, 2, ..., n$, is defined as:

$$d_c(\mathbf{z}_l, \mathbf{x}_i) \equiv \sum_{j=1}^{m} \delta(z_{lj}, x_{ij}) \tag{3}$$

where $\mathbf{z}_l = [z_{l1}, \cdots, z_{lm}]^T$ and $\mathbf{x}_i = [x_{i1}, \cdots, x_{im}]^T$,

$$\delta(z_{lj}, x_{ij}) = \begin{cases} 0, & \text{if } z_{lj} = x_{ij} \\ 1, & \text{if } z_{lj} \neq x_{ij} \end{cases} \tag{4}$$

Minimization of F in (1) with the simple matching dissimilarities and the constraints in (2) forms a class of constrained nonlinear optimization problems whose solution is unknown. The usual method towards optimization of F in (1) is to use partial optimization for Z and W. In this method we first fix Z and find necessary conditions on W to minimize F. Then we fix W and minimize F with respect to Z. This process is formalized in the fuzzy k-modes algorithm.

The matrices W and Z are formulated in the following way. Let Z be fixed, i.e., $\mathbf{z}_l$ $(l = 1, 2, ..., k)$ are given, we can find W by:

$$
w_{li} = \begin{cases} 1, & \text{if } \mathbf{x}_i = \mathbf{z}_l \\ 0, & \text{if } \mathbf{x}_i = \mathbf{z}_h \text{ but } h \neq l \\ 1/\sum_{h=1}^{k} \left[\frac{d_c(\mathbf{z}_l, \mathbf{x}_i)}{d_c(\mathbf{z}_h, \mathbf{x}_i)} \right]^{\frac{1}{\alpha-1}}, & \text{if } \mathbf{x}_i \neq \mathbf{z}_l \text{ and } \mathbf{x}_i \neq \mathbf{z}_h, 1 \leq h \leq k \end{cases} \tag{5}
$$

for $1 \leq l \leq k, 1 \leq i \leq n$. Let W be fixed, we can find Z by the k-modes update method. Let $\mathcal{X}$ be a set of categorical objects described by m categorical attributes $A_1, A_2, ..., A_m$. Each attribute A_j has n_j categories: $a_j^{(1)}, a_j^{(2)}, ..., a_j^{(n_j)}$ for $1 \leq j \leq m$. Let the l-th cluster center be $\mathbf{z}_l = [z_{l1}, z_{l2}, ..., z_{lm}]^T$. Then $F(W, Z)$ is minimized if and only if

$$
z_{lj} = a_j^{(r)} \quad \text{where} \quad \sum_{i, x_{ij} = a_j^{(r)}} w_{li}^{\alpha} \geq \sum_{i, x_{ij} = a_j^{(t)}} w_{li}^{\alpha}, \quad 1 \leq t \leq n_j. \tag{6}
$$

However, the fuzzy k-modes algorithm may only stop at a local optimal solution of the clustering problem. This means that the solution obtained can still be further improved. Therefore, tabu-search techniques are incorporated in order to find the global optimal solution of the optimization problem (1).

3   Tabu Search Based Categorical Data Clustering

Tabu search method is based on procedures designed to cross boundaries of feasibility or local optimality, which were usually treated as barriers, and systematically to impose and release constraints to permit exploration of otherwise forbidden regions. Tabu search is a meta-heuristic that guides a local heuristic search procedure to explore the solution space beyond local optimality. A fundamental element underlying tabu search is the use of flexible memory. A chief mechanism for exploiting memory in tabu search is to classify a subset of the moves in a neighborhood as forbidden or tabu.

Our new algorithm in Table 1 is to combine the fuzzy k-modes algorithm and the tabu search techniques in order to find the global optimal solution of the clustering problem of categorical data. In our algorithm, equation (5) is used to update the fuzzy partition matrix W. But we do not use equation (6) to update the cluster center Z. Instead Z is generated by the below method and is mapped into a value for the objective function value. This techniques has been used by Al-Sultan and Fedjki [1].

Let Z^t, Z^u, Z^b denote the trial, current and best cluster centers, and F^t, F^u, F^b denote the corresponding trial, current and best objective function values respectively. A number of trial cluster centers Z^t are to be generated through moves from the current cluster centers Z^u. As the algorithm proceeds, the best cluster centers found so far is saved in Z^b. The corresponding objective function values F^t, F^u, F^b are also operated respectively. One of the most distinctive features of tabu search is the generation of neighborhoods. Since numerical data sets have naturally ordering, the neighborhood of the center $\mathbf{z}^u$ is defined as follows:

$$N(\mathbf{z}^u) = \{\mathbf{y} = [y_1, y_2, \cdots, y_m]^T \mid y_i = \mathbf{z}_i^u + \phi d, \ i = 1, 2, \cdots, m, d = 0, -1 \text{ or } +1\}. \tag{7}$$

We note that when $\mathbf{z}^u$ is close to the solution, a small step-size ϕ can be used. The neighbors of $\mathbf{z}^u$ can be generated by picking randomly from $N(\mathbf{z}^u)$.

There are two kinds of categorical attributes, namely, ordinal and nominal. Ordinal attributes do have ordered levels, such as size and education levels. Their neighborhoods can be defined similarly as in (7) for numerical data sets. However, this approach cannot be applied to categorical data sets with nominal attributes since they do not have naturally ordering. In this paper, we propose to use the "distance" concept to make moves from the cluster center for categorical data sets. The neighborhood of $\mathbf{z}^u$ is defined as follows:

$$N(\mathbf{z}^u) = \{\mathbf{y} = [y_1, y_2, \cdots, y_m]^T \mid d_c(\mathbf{y}, \mathbf{z}^u) < d\}, \tag{8}$$

for some positive integers d. In our algorithm, we generate a set of neighbors which are of a certain distance d from the center, i.e., neighbors which have d attributes different from the center.

4 Experimental Results

The tabu search-based categorical clustering algorithm is coded in C++ programming language. The data set is the soybean disease data set [9]. We choose this data set to test these algorithms because all attributes of the data can be treated as categorical. The soybean data set has 47 records, each being described by 35 attributes. Each record is labelled as one of the 4 diseases: Diaporthe Stem Canker, Charcoal Rot, Rhizoctonia Root Rot, and Phytophthora Rot. Except for Phytophthora Rot which has 17 records, all other diseases have 10 records each. Of the 35 attributes we only selected 21 because the other 14 have only one category.

We use the fuzzy k-modes and tabu search based k-modes clustering algorithms to cluster this data set into 4 clusters. The initial modes are randomly selected k distinct records from the data set. For the fuzzy k-modes algorithm we specify $\alpha = 1.1$. We obtain the cluster memberships from W as follows. The record X_i is assigned to the lth cluster if $w_{li} = \max_{1 \le h \le k}\{w_{hi}\}$. If the maximum is not unique, then X_i is assigned to the cluster of first achieving the maximum. A clustering result is measured by the clustering accuracy r defined as $r = \frac{\sum_{l=1}^{4} a_l}{n}$ where a_l is the number of instances occurring in both cluster l and its corresponding class and n is the number of instances in the data set.

Each algorithm is run 100 times. We select values for $\gamma=0.75$, $P=0.97$, $d=3$ and $IMAX=100$ for tabu search based k-mode clustering algorithm. Moreover,

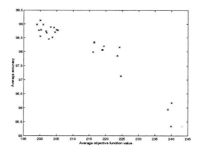

Fig. 1. Average clustering accuracy and objective function values.

the tabu list size is 100, the number of trial solutions is 50 and the probability threshold P is 0.97. It is found that the classification accuracy of the algorithm is very high. The average accuracy is about 99% and the number of runs that all records are correctly clustered into the 4 given clusters is 67. In Table 2, we compare the average accuracy of clustering and the number of runs with all correct classifications by using fuzzy k-modes and tabu search based k-modes algorithms.

Next we test different sets of parameters of tabu search based k-modes clustering algorithm. For each set of parameters, the algorithm is run 100 times. Figure 1 shows the relationship between the average clustering results and the average objective function values. We see that the average objective function values with high classification accuracy is less than those with low classification accuracy. This relationship indicates that we use the objective function values to choose a good clustering result if the original classification of data is unknown.

Finally, we report that the computational time at each step of tabu search based k-modes clustering algorithm taken increases linearly as either one of the parameters: the number of objects, the number of attributes, the size of tabu list or the number of trial solutions increases. Thus the tabu search based k-modes algorithm is efficient and effective for clustering categorical data sets.

References

1. K. S. Al-Sultan & C. A. Fedjki, A tabu search-based algorithm for the fuzzy clustering problem, *Pattern Recognition*, vol. 30, no. 12, pp. 2023–2030, 1997.
2. J. C. Dunn, A fuzzy relative of the ISODATA process and its use in detecting compact well-separated clusters, *J. Cybernet.*, 3(3), pp. 32–57, 1974.
3. E. R. Ruspini, A new approach to clustering, *Information Control*, vol. 19, pp. 22–32, 1969.
4. J. C. Bezedek, Fuzzy mathematics in pattern classification, Ph.D. Dissertation, Department of Applied Mathematics, Cornell University, Ithaca, New York, 1973.
5. J. C. Bezedek, A convergence theorem for the fuzzy ISODATA clustering algorithms, *IEEE Transactions on Pattern Analysis and Machine Intelligence*, vol. 2, pp. 1–8, 1980.
6. F. Glover & M. Laguna, *Tabu Search*, Boston: Kluwer Academic Publishers, c1997.

Tabu Search Based Categorical Clustering Algorithm:

Step 1: Initialization
Let Z^u be arbitrary centers and F^u the corresponding objective function value. Let $Z^b = Z^u$ and $F^b = F^u$. Select values for $NTLM$ (tabu list size), P (probability threshold), NH (number of trial solutions), $IMAX$ (the maximum number of iterations for each center), and γ (the iteration reducer). Let $h = 1$, $NTL = 0$ and $r = 1$. Go to Step 2.

Step 2:
Using Z^u, fix all centers and move center $\mathbf{z}_i^u$ by generating NH neighbors $\mathbf{z}_1^t, \mathbf{z}_2^t, ..., \mathbf{z}_{NH}^t$, and evaluate their corresponding objective function values $F_1^t, F_2^t, ..., F_{NH}^t$. Go to Step 3.

Step 3:
(a) Sort F_i^t, $i = 1, ..., NH$ in a nondecreasing order and denote them as $F_{[1]}^t, ..., F_{[NH]}^t$.
   Clearly $F_{[1]}^t \leq ... \leq F_{[NH]}^t$. Let $e = 1$. If $F_{[1]}^t \geq F^b$, then replace h by $h + 1$. Goto Step 3(b).
(b) If $z_{[e]}$ is not tabu or if it is tabu but $F_{[e]}^t < F^b$, then let $\mathbf{z}_r^u = \mathbf{z}_{[e]}$ and $F^u = F_{[e]}^t$ and go to step 4. Otherwise generate $u \sim U(0, 1)$ where $U(0, 1)$ is a uniform density function between 0 and 1. If $F^b < F_{[e]}^t < F^u$ and $u > P$, then let $\mathbf{z}_r^u = \mathbf{z}_{[e]}$ and $F^u = F_{[e]}^t$ and go to Step 4; otherwise, go to Step 3(c).
(c) Check for the next neighbor by letting $c = c + 1$. If $e \leq NH$, go to step 3(a). Otherwise go to step 3(d).
(d) If $h > IMAX$, then go to step 5. Otherwise select a new set of neighbors by go to step 2.

Step 4:
Insert $\mathbf{z}_r^u$ at the bottom of the tabu list. If $NTL = NTLM$, then delete the top of the tabu list; otherwise let $NTL = NTL + 1$. If $F^b > F^u$, then let $F^b = F^u$ and $Z^b = Z^u$. Go to step 3 (4).

Step 5:
If $r < k$, then let $r = r + 1$ and reset $h = 1$ and go to Step 2. Otherwise set $IMAX = \gamma(IMAX)$. If $IMAX > 1$, then let $r = 1$ and reset $h = 1$ and go to step 2; otherwise stop. (Z^b represents the best centers and F^b is the corresponding best objective function value).

Table 1. Tabu search based categorical clustering algorithm.

	average accuracy	number of runs that $r = 1$
Fuzzy k-mode	0.790	20
Tabu search based k-mode	0.991	67

Table 2. Clustering accuracy.

7. R. J. Hathaway & J. C. Bezdek, Local convergence of the fuzzy c-means algorithms, *Pattern Recognition*, vol. 19, no. 6, pp. 477–480, 1986.
8. Z. Huang, Extensions to the k-means algorithm for clustering large data sets with categorical values, *Data Mining and Knowledge Discovery*, vol. 2, no. 3, pp. 283–304, 1998.
9. Z. Huang & M. K. Ng, A fuzzy k-modes algorithm for clustering categorical data, *IEEE Transactions on Fuzzy Systems*, vol. 7, no.4, pp. 446–452, 1999.
10. S. Z. Selim & M. A. Ismail, K-means-type algorithms: a generalized convergence theorem and characterization of local optimality, *IEEE Transactions on Pattern Analysis and Machine Intelligence*, vol. 6, no. 1, pp. 81–87, 1984.
11. S. Z. Selim & M. A. Ismail, Fuzzy C-means: optimality of solutions and effective termination of the algorithm, *Pattern Recognition*, vol. 19, no. 6, pp. 651–663, 1986.

A New Methodology to Compare Clustering Algorithms

C. Robardet and F. Feschet

UMR CNRS 5823 - LASS - Bât 101 - Université Lyon 1 - 69622 Villeurbanne - France
e-mail: {robardet,feschet}@univ-lyon1.fr

Abstract In the context of unsupervised clustering, lots of different algorithms have been proposed. Most of them consist in optimizing an objective function using a search strategy. We present here a new methodology for studying and comparing the performances of the objective functions and search strategies employed.

1   Introduction

Unsupervised clustering is an important tool of data mining whose goal is to synthetize a huge amount of data by a small number of homogenous and distinct classes. Those classes form a partition of the set of objects and summarize at best the similarity between them: each cluster contains the set of objects the most similar two by two and the objects the most dissimilar belong to different classes. Those methods are useful for at least two reasons. First, they provide a summary of the dataset which is of human size and secondly they can be used as a pre-processing step to reduce the cost of subsequent treatments. On the contrary to supervised classification methods, the construction of the partition is not guided by a known class variable. This point constitutes an important difficulty since no a priori or external reference is available. The goal partition is not necessarily unique (this depends on the chosen measure) and there is no consensual external criterion for the evaluation of the quality of a solution.

Since the beginning of the sixties, a lot of different algorithms have been proposed and lead to distinct results. Three main characteristics distinguish these algorithms. First is the way they defined -in concrete terms- the similarity between object pairs. Most of algorithms use a distance on the descriptive vectors [1] (such as the Mahalanobis, the Gaussian or the Euclidean one) based on metric and separation properties of the underlying topological space $\mathbb{R}^n$. Other methods compare probabilities vectors associated to each value of the nominal variables on each class [2]. This allows for instance to search classes in which objects share the same value on most of the variables. A second characteristic of the methods is the objective function used to evaluate the relevance of a partition. This function is often a compromise between the intra-cluster similarity and the difference between clusters. Because of the combinatorial number of different partitions and overall the absence of structure between those partitions, none algorithm provides an exhaustive search and thus, it is commonly assumed that local search is preferabled. This optimization methodology constitutes the third characteristic of clustering algorithms. Those later ones are generally presented as universal methods. That is why there is not much information for the circumstances in which they can be really used. Nevertheless, several comparative studies provide results on the behavior of various algorithms on the same data set. Those studies are very useful in order to evaluate the quality of a method. But, they are not able to explain which part of the algorithm is the cause of the difference of the results. Are we sure that the objective function distinguishes well the partitions ? Which of several search strategies is the best one ? Those questions are not trivial and their answers can lead to a better understanding of the algorithms.

In this paper we propose a new methodology for studing the behavior of the objective functions of unsupervised clustering methods. This methodology is based on the construction of an order of all the partitions independently of the objective functions studied and is presented in details in the following section. Then, we present several objective functions and compare them through our protocol. The results show that this protocol is well discriminant.

2   Evaluating partitions

A way to approach the behavior of an objective function on a set of partitions, is to determine a total order on this set. The main advantage of such an approach is first to be independent of the function and second to have to contain some a priori knowledge on the subjective notion of "good" partition. However, there is no natural total order. That is why we propose the following methodology. First, we design a data set such that the goal partition is obvious and fix this partition as a reference denoted by P_0. Then we use a distance d and compare P_1 and P_2 using their respective distance towards P_0. This distance had to take into account two characteristics. In order to compare the quality of both partitions, the distance needs to consider the similarity of the clusters on the point of view of the variable description. However, this is not sufficiently discriminant especially regarding the objects in the clusters, that is why it has also to consider the similarity on the point of view of the objects.

2.1   A distance taken on the variables

We compute the L_1 distance between probabilities vectors associated to each modality of all the variables in each cluster. Let X be a finite set of objects described by p variables with m modalities each. $\mathcal{P}(X)$ is the set of all subsets of X. At each set belonging to $\mathcal{P}(X)$ a probabilistic vector of length $(p \times m)$ is associated. The following normalized distance compares two such vectors: $\forall C_k, C_{k'} \in \mathcal{P}(X)$,

$$\mu_V(C_k, C_{k'}) = \frac{1}{m \times p} \sum_{i=1}^{p} \sum_{j=1}^{m} |P(A_i = V_{ij} \mid C_k) - P(A_i = V_{ij} \mid C_{k'})|$$

with $P(A_i = V_{ij} \mid C_k)$ the conditional probability that objects in cluster C_k take the modality V_{ij} on the variable A_i.

2.2 A distance taken on the objects

For the comparison of two clusters on the point of view of the objects, we used the Marczewski and Steinhaus distance [3] proposed for the comparison of two sets. This distance is based on the symmetric difference taken on two sets (i.e. the number of objects which belong to only one of the both sets) and normalized by the cardinality of the union of the sets. In the following, $|.|$ denotes the cardinality of a set. The distance between two elements of $\mathcal{P}(X)$ is:

$$\mu_O(C_k, C_{k'}) = \begin{cases} \frac{|C_k \Delta C_{k'}|}{|C_k \cup C_{k'}|} & \text{if } |C_k \cup C_{k'}| > 0 \\ 0 & \text{otherwise} \end{cases}$$

with Δ the symmetric difference. As $C_k \Delta C_{k'} \subseteq C_k \cup C_{k'}$, this distance is normalized, taking the value 1 when $C_k \cap C_{k'} = \emptyset$ and the value 0 when $C_k = C_{k'}$.

2.3 A Hausdorff like distance between two partitions

We can compare two partitions (using a measure for evaluating the proximity between clusters) with a Hausdorff like distance [4]. This distance allows to compare all couples of partitions of a same set, even if they have different numbers of clusters. Let P_1 and P_2 be two partitions such that $P_1 = \{C_{11}, C_{12}, ..., C_{1I_1}\}$ and $P_2 = \{C_{21}, C_{22}, ..., C_{2I_2}\}$. Given a measure μ between two sets, we construct a distance between P_1 and P_2 as the following,

$$\mathcal{D}_\mu(P_1, P_2) = \frac{1}{2}\left[\max_{i \in I_1} \min_{j \in I_2} \mu(C_{1i}, C_{2j}) + \max_{j \in I_2} \min_{i \in I_1} \mu(C_{1i}, C_{2j})\right]$$

This distance is based on the principle of the worst case, that is to say for all the clusters of the first partition, we search the closest cluster of the second one, and we hold back only the worst case of those couples. We then symmetrize the result.

The both distances obtained with the comparison of clusters on the point of view of the variables and of the objects can be mixed up by the Euclidean distance thanks to common normalization,

$$\mathcal{D}_{\min-\max}(P_1, P_2) = \sqrt{\mathcal{D}^2_{\mu_O}(P_1, P_2) + \mathcal{D}^2_{\mu_V}(P_1, P_2)}$$

Let P_1 and P_2 be two partitions. We define the $\leq$ relation as,

$$P_1 \leq P_2 \iff \mathcal{D}_{\min-\max}(P_0, P_1) \leq \mathcal{D}_{\min-\max}(P_0, P_2)$$

It is obvious that two different partitions can be at the same distance to P_0 and thus be exaequo in the total order.

2.4 An improved measure

The principle of the Hausdorff like distance is very interesting, but we can suppose that its behavior would be insufficiently discriminant on the set of all partitions. Indeed, this measure takes into account only the worth *associated* couple of clusters between the both partitions. In order to overcome this drawback, we propose another distance between two partitions. This measure consists in searching for each cluster in one partition the closest cluster of another partition, not already associated to a cluster. Moreover, we associate a cost to those associations through $\mathcal{D}_{\mu_O}$ or $\mathcal{D}_{\mu_V}$. We then simply sum the values over all the associations. But, as we also want the maximum number of associations between clusters, a non association must be penalized since it corresponds to a comparison of subsets of the partitions and not the whole partitions. All of this can be express simply through the graph theory approach.

A graph G is a set of vertices V and a set of edges $E \subseteq V \times V$. The elements of V are the clusters of the partitions to be compared. Let us remark that $V = V_1 \cup V_2$, with V_1 corresponding to P_1 and V_2 corresponding to P_2 so we restrict the edges E to be of the form (v_1, v_2) with $v_1 \in V_1$ and $v_2 \in V_2$. This corresponds to a bipartite graph. This graph is complete and all the edges are weighted as previously mentioned. The problem to solve is then to find the matching of maximum cardinality and minimum weight,

$$\mathcal{C}'_\mu(P_1, P_2) = \frac{1}{\min(|\mathcal{P}_1|, |\mathcal{P}_2|)} \min \left\{ \sum_{v \in M} \mu(v) \mid M \in \max_{N \in \mathcal{C}_\mu(P_1, P_2)} |N| \right\}$$

with $\mathcal{C}_\mu(P_1, P_2)$ the set of every matching between P_1 and P_2. This distance has many advantages. It considers partitions in their whole since one association is done relatively to the others. It penalizes bad associations but weakly as in the previous distance based on worst case. Thus, we attempt to have better sensitivity on partition variations. Moreover, this approach is efficient since it has a quadratic complexity and thus is tractable even in the case of large sets [5].

2.5 The methodology

To compare several objective functions we first have to design a synthetic problem in which the goal partition is known. Then we define a subset of partitions on which the objective functions are studied. The distance between each partition and the reference defines an order. Let us remark that an ordering permits also to study the behavior of the optimization procedure through its walk on the graph of the function which associates to each partition the value of the objective function. This is currently under study.

3 Experimentation

The protocol

We compare three objective functions. The first one is used in the well known conceptual clustering algorithm COBWEB [6] and called category utility. It is a trade-off between intra-class similarity and inter-class dissimilarity of objects, where objects are described by nominal variables. It is equal to the weighted average of the Gini entropy of the variable distribution. The second function is Quinlan's gain ratio, generally used in supervised methods and, as suggested in [2], adapted to unsupervised clustering. This function is defined by the difference between the entropy of the variables conditionned by the partition and the entropy of the variables, divided by the entropy on the class variable. The third one is the Lopez de Mantaras normalized information gain, which is a slight different normalization of the Quinlan's gain ratio [7].

To evaluate the behavior of those functions, we construct synthetic datasets made of k subsets of variables and k subsets of objects resulting in a block diagonal Boolean matrix. We design two such matrices: 8 objects × 8 variables and 60 objects × 15 variables to simulate realistic datasets. It is possible to enumerate all the partitions of a set of 8 objects, but this become unpracticable for 60 objects. Consequently, on the first dataset we compute the exhaustive set of partitions, but on the second one we extract 30 000 partitions randomly. We also introduce some noise by random permutations in the dataset matrix.

Some results

On figure 1 left, we plot the distances - matching index and Hausdorff distance - as x values and Quinlan's values as y axis. As we expected, the matching

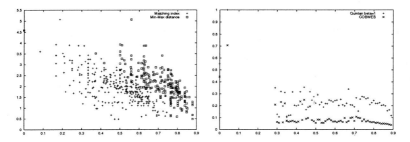

Figure1. Unnoisy case (distances in abscissa): (left) distances comparison (right) measures comparison.

index is far more discriminant than the Hausdorff like distance. Notice that we observe similar results for all the other measures and noise levels. We noticed that the worst case approach has the default to be invariant in a quite large set of partitions, being unsufficiently discriminant.We also compare the Quinlan gain ratio with the CU measure (see figure 1 on the right). It seems that the variations of CU are too small that nearly all partitions seem to be similar for the measure, except the extremal one. Following these preliminary results, Quinlan measure can be considered as a better measure than CU, however more experiments are necessary to conclude. To simulate a real case, we introduce some noise in the boolean matrix (see figure 2). Quinlan measure appears to be more noise resistant than CU. With a 5 percent noise level, it behaves like in the ideal case. When noise increases, some partitions take aberrant values (see figure 2 (left)). However, this measure remains regular when CU becomes very perturbated (see figure 2 (right)).

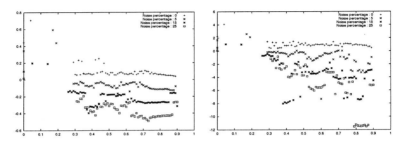

Figure2. Noise influence versus distance: (left) Quinlan gain ratio - (right) CU

4 Conclusion

We have presented a new methodology for ordering partitions to objectively compare the behavior of different quality measures used in unsupervised learning. Our methodology is independent of the studied measures, has a polynomial complexity and also permits to study the optimization procedure of various unsupervised clustering. Some works have been done in this way and will be the subject of a forthcoming article.

References

1. A. K. Jain and R. C. Dubes. *Algorithms for clustering data.* Prentice Hall, Englewood cliffs, New Jersey, 1988.
2. Doug Fisher. Iterative optimization and simplification of hierarchical clusterings. *Journal of Artificial Intelligence Research*, 4:147–180, 1996.
3. E. Marczewski and H. Steinhaus. On a certain distance of sets and the corresponding distance of functions. *Colloquium Mathematicum*, 6:319–327, 1958.
4. M. Karonski and Z. Palka. On marczewski-steinhaus type distance between hypergraphs. *Zastosowania Matematyki Applicationes Mathematicae*, 16(1):47–57, 1977.
5. J. Edmonds. Maximum matching and a polyhedron with 0-1 vertices. *Res. Nat. Bureau Standards*, 69B(1-2):125–130, 1965.
6. Douglas H. Fisher. Knowledge acquisition via incremental conceptual clustering. *Machine Learning*, 2:139–172, 1987.
7. R. López de Màntaras. A distance based attribute selection measure for decision tree induction. *Machine Learning*, 6:81–92, 1991.

Author Index

Lecture Notes in Computer Science

For information about Vols. 1–1894
please contact your bookseller or Springer-Verlag

Vol. 1928: U. Brandes, D. Wagner (Eds.), Graph-Theoretic Concepts in Computer Science. Proceedings, 2000. X, 315 pages. 2000.

Vol. 1929: R. Laurini (Ed.), Advances in Visual Information Systems. Proceedings, 2000. XII, 542 pages. 2000.

Vol. 1931: E. Horlait (Ed.), Mobile Agents for Telecommunication Applications. Proceedings, 2000. IX, 271 pages. 2000.

Vol. 1658: J. Baumann, Mobile Agents: Control Algorithms. XIX, 161 pages. 2000.

Vol. 1756: G. Ruhe, F. Bomarius (Eds.), Learning Software Organization. Proceedings, 1999. VIII, 226 pages. 2000.

Vol. 1766: M. Jazayeri, R.G.K. Loos, D.R. Musser (Eds.), Generic Programming. Proceedings, 1998. X, 269 pages. 2000.

Vol. 1791: D. Fensel, Problem-Solving Methods. XII, 153 pages. 2000. (Subseries LNAI).

Vol. 1799: K. Czarnecki, U.W. Eisenecker, Generative and Component-Based Software Engineering. Proceedings, 1999. VIII, 225 pages. 2000.

Vol. 1812: J. Wyatt, J. Demiris (Eds.), Advances in Robot Learning. Proceedings, 1999. VII, 165 pages. 2000. (Subseries LNAI).

Vol. 1932: Z.W. Raś, S. Ohsuga (Eds.), Foundations of Intelligent Systems. Proceedings, 2000. XII, 646 pages. (Subseries LNAI).

Vol. 1933: R.W. Brause, E. Hanisch (Eds.), Medical Data Analysis. Proceedings, 2000. XI, 316 pages. 2000.

Vol. 1934: J.S. White (Ed.), Envisioning Machine Translation in the Information Future. Proceedings, 2000. XV, 254 pages. 2000. (Subseries LNAI).

Vol. 1935: S.L. Delp, A.M. DiGioia, B. Jaramaz (Eds.), Medical Image Computing and Computer-Assisted Intervention – MICCAI 2000. Proceedings, 2000. XXV, 1250 pages. 2000.

Vol. 1937: R. Dieng, O. Corby (Eds.), Knowledge Engineering and Knowledge Management. Proceedings, 2000. XIII, 457 pages. 2000. (Subseries LNAI).

Vol. 1938: S. Rao, K.I. Sletta (Eds.), Next Generation Networks. Proceedings, 2000. XI, 392 pages. 2000.

Vol. 1939: A. Evans, S. Kent, B. Selic (Eds.), «UML» – The Unified Modeling Language. Proceedings, 2000. XIV, 572 pages. 2000.

Vol. 1940: M. Valero, K. Joe, M. Kitsuregawa, H. Tanaka (Eds.), High Performance Computing. Proceedings, 2000. XV, 595 pages. 2000.

Vol. 1941: A.K. Chhabra, D. Dori (Eds.), Graphics Recognition. Proceedings, 1999. XI, 346 pages. 2000.

Vol. 1942: H. Yasuda (Ed.), Active Networks. Proceedings, 2000. XI, 424 pages. 2000.

Vol. 1943: F. Koornneef, M. van der Meulen (Eds.), Computer Safety, Reliability and Security. Proceedings, 2000. X, 432 pages. 2000.

Vol. 1945: W. Grieskamp, T. Santen, B. Stoddart (Eds.), Integrated Formal Methods. Proceedings, 2000. X, 441 pages. 2000.

Vol. 1948: T. Tan, Y. Shi, W. Gao (Eds.), Advances in Multimodal Interfaces – ICMI 2000. Proceedings, 2000. XVI, 678 pages. 2000.

Vol. 1952: M.C. Monard, J. Simão Sichman (Eds.), Advances in Artificial Intelligence. Proceedings, 2000. XV, 498 pages. 2000. (Subseries LNAI).

Vol. 1953: G. Borgefors, I. Nyström, G. Sanniti di Baja (Eds.), Discrete Geometry for Computer Imagery. Proceedings, 2000. XI, 544 pages. 2000.

Vol. 1954: W.A. Hunt, Jr., S.D. Johnson (Eds.), Formal Methods in Computer-Aided Design. Proceedings, 2000. XI, 539 pages. 2000.

Vol. 1955: M. Parigot, A. Voronkov (Eds.), Logic for Programming and Automated Reasoning. Proceedings, 2000. XIII, 487 pages. 2000. (Subseries LNAI).

Vol. 1960: A. Ambler, S.B. Calo, G. Kar (Eds.), Services Management in Intelligent Networks. Proceedings, 2000. X, 259 pages. 2000.

Vol. 1961: J. He, M. Sato (Eds.), Advances in Computing Science – ASIAN 2000. Proceedings, 2000. X, 299 pages. 2000.

Vol. 1963: V. Hlaváč, K.G. Jeffery, J. Wiedermann (Eds.), SOFSEM 2000: Theory and Practice of Informatics. Proceedings, 2000. XI, 460 pages. 2000.

Vol. 1966: S. Bhalla (Ed.), Databases in Networked Information Systems. Proceedings, 2000. VIII, 247 pages. 2000.

Vol. 1967: S. Arikawa, S. Morishita (Eds.), Discovery Science. Proceedings, 2000. XII, 332 pages. 2000. (Subseries LNAI).

Vol. 1968: H. Arimura, S. Jain, A. Sharma (Eds.), Algorithmic Learning Theory. Proceedings, 2000. XI, 335 pages. 2000. (Subseries LNAI).

Vol. 1969: D.T. Lee, S.-H. Teng (Eds.), Algorithms and Computation. Proceedings, 2000. XIV, 578 pages. 2000.

Vol. 1970: M. Valero, V.K. Prasanna, S. Vajapeyam (Eds.), High Performance Computing – HiPC 2000. Proceedings, 2000. XVIII, 568 pages. 2000.

Vol. 1971: R. Buyya, M. Baker (Eds.), Grid Computing – GRID 2000. Proceedings, 2000. XIV, 229 pages. 2000.

Vol. 1972: A. Omicini, R. Tolksdorf, F. Zambonelli (Eds.), Engineering Societies in the Agents World. Proceedings, 2000. IX, 143 pages. 2000. (Subseries LNAI).

Vol. 1974: S. Kapoor, S. Prasad (Eds.), FST TCS 2000: Foundations of Software Technology and Theoretical Computer Science. Proceedings, 2000. XIII, 532 pages. 2000.

Vol. 1975: J. Pieprzyk, E. Okamoto, J. Seberry (Eds.), Information Security. Proceedings, 2000. X, 323 pages. 2000.

Vol. 1976: T. Okamoto (Ed.), Advances in Cryptology – ASIACRYPT 2000. Proceedings, 2000. XII, 630 pages. 2000.

Vol. 1977: B. Roy, E. Okamoto (Eds.), Progress in Cryptology – INDOCRYPT 2000. Proceedings, 2000. X, 295 pages. 2000.

Vol. 1983: K.S. Leung, L.-W. Chan, H. Meng (Eds.), Intelligent Data Engineering and Automated Learning – IDEAL 2000. Proceedings, 2000. XVI, 573 pages. 2000.

Vol. 1987: K.-L. Tan, M.J. Franklin, J. C.-S. Lui (Eds.), Mobile Data Management. Proceedings, 2001. XIII, 289 pages. 2001.